Religion in the Public Space

The Library of Essays on Law and Religion
Series Editors: Silvio Ferrari and Rinaldo Cristofori

Titles in the Series

Law and Religion, An Overview
Volume I
Silvio Ferrari and Rinaldo Cristofori

Freedom of Religion and Belief
Volume II
Silvio Ferrari and Rinaldo Cristofori

Religion in the Public Space
Volume III
Silvio Ferrari and Rinaldo Cristofori

Current Issues in Law and Religion
Volume IV
Silvio Ferrari and Rinaldo Cristofori

Religion in the Public Space
Volume III

Edited by

Silvio Ferrari

University of Milan, Italy

Rinaldo Cristofori

Emory University, USA and University of Milan, Italy

ASHGATE

Published by
Ashgate Publishing Limited
Wey Court East
Union Road
Farnham
Surrey GU9 7PT
England

Ashgate Publishing Company
110 Cherry Street
Suite 3-1
Burlington, VT 05401-3818
USA

www.ashgate.com

British Library Cataloguing in Publication Data
A catalogue record for this book is available from the British Library.

The Library of Congress has cataloged the printed edition as follows: 2013931874

ISBN 9781409436027

MIX
Paper from responsible sources
FSC® C013056

Printed and bound in Great Britain by
TJ International Ltd, Padstow, Cornwall.

Contents

PART III LAW, RELIGION AND THE WORKPLACE

PART IV RELIGION AND FAMILY LAW

PART V RELIGIOUS SYMBOLS IN THE PUBLIC SPACE

Acknowledgements

Ashgate would like to thank the researchers and the contributing authors who provided copies, along with the following for their permission to reprint copyright material.

Berghahn Books for the essay: David Chidester (2006), 'Religion Education and the Transformational State in South Africa', *Social Analysis*, **50**, pp. 61–83. Copyright © 2006 Berghahn Journals.

Brigham Young University Law Review for the essay: Jacques Robert (2003), 'Religious Liberty and French Secularism', *Brigham Young University Law Review*, pp. 637–60.

Cambridge University Press for the essays: Werner Menski (2012), 'Ancient and Modern Boundary Crossings between Personal Laws and Civil Law in Composite India', in J. Nichols (ed.), *Marriage and Divorce in a Multicultural Context: Reconsidering the Boundaries of Civil Law and Religion*, Cambridge: Cambridge University Press, pp. 219–52. Copyright © 2012 Cambridge University Press, reproduced with permission; Susanna Mancini and Michel Rosenfeld (2012), 'Unveiling the Limits of Tolerance: Comparing the Treatment of Majority and Minority Religious Symbols in the Public Sphere', in L. Zucca and C. Ungureanu, *Law, State and Religion in the New Europe: Debates and Dilemmas*, Cambridge: Cambridge University Press, pp. 160–91. Copyright © 2012 Cambridge University Press, reproduced with permission.

Cardozo Law Review for the essay: Frances Raday (2009), 'Secular Constitutionalism Vindicated', *Cardozo Law Review*, **30**, pp. 2769–98.

Comparative Labor Law and Policy Journal for the essay: Lorne Sossin (2008–09), 'God at Work: Religion in the Workplace and the Limits of Pluralism in Canada', *Comparative Labor Law and Policy Journal*, **30**, pp. 485–505.

Hart Publishing Limited for the essay: Lucy Vickers (2008), 'Protecting Religion at Work', in *Religious Freedom, Religious Discrimination and the Workplace*, Oxford: Hart Publishing, pp. 44–81. Copyright © 2008 Lucy Vickers.

The Hedgehog Review, University of Virginia for the essay: Charles Taylor (2010), 'The Meaning of Secularism', *The Hedgehog Review*, Fall, pp. 23–34.

Intersentia for the essay: Jane Mair (2011), 'The Place of Religion in Family Law: A Comparative Search', in Jane Mair and E. Örücü (eds), *The Place of Religion in Family Law: A Comparative Search*, Antwerp: Intersentia, pp. 359–85. Copyright © 2011 Intersentia.

Martinus Nijhoff Publishers for the essay: Jeroen Temperman (2010), 'Religion and Education', in *State–Religion Relationships and Human Rights Law: Towards a Right to*

Religiously Neutral Governance, Leiden-Boston: Martinus Nijhoff, pp. 275–305. Copyright © 2010 Koninklijke Brill NV, Leiden, The Netherlands.

Oxford University Press for the essays: Aileen McColgan (2009), 'Class Wars? Religion and (In)equality in the Workplace', *Industrial Law Journal*, **38**, pp. 1–29. Copyright © 2009 Industrial Law Society; Mark L. Movsesian (2012), 'Crosses and Culture: State-Sponsored Religious Displays in the US and Europe', *Oxford Journal of Law and Religion*, pp. 1–25. Copyright © 2012 Mark L. Movsesian.

Springer for the essay: Peter Schreiner (2006), 'The Religious, Moral and Spiritual Dimensions of Education: National, Regional and International Constitutional and Legal Frameworks', in M. de Souza, G. Durka, K. Engebretson, R. Jackson and A. McGrady (eds), *International Handbook of the Religious, Moral and Spiritual Dimensions in Education*, Dordrecht: Springer, pp. 857–68. Copyright © 2006 Springer.

Taylor & Francis for the essay: Rajeev Bhargava (2010), 'The Distinctiveness of Indian Secularism', in Aakash Singh and Silika Mohapatra (eds), *Indian Political Thought: A Reader*, London: Routledge, pp. 99–119. Copyright © 2010 Aakash Singh and Silika Mohapatra. Reproduced by permission of Taylor & Francis Books UK.

University of Detroit Mercy Law Review for the essay: Asher Maoz (2006), 'Religious Education in Israel', *University of Detroit Mercy Law Review*, **83**, pp. 679–728; 'Addendum', *Religion en la Educacion Publica* (2010), pp. 541–48.

University of Chicago Press for the essay: Mary Ann Glendon (1977), 'State, Law and Family', in *State, Law and Family: Family Law in Transition in the United States and Western Europe*, Amsterdam: North-Holland Publication Company, pp. 304–32.

Van Leer Group Foundation for the essay: S.N. Eisenstadt (2008), 'The Transformations of the Religious Dimension and the Crystallization of New Civilizational Visions and Relations', in Gabriel Motzkin and Yochi Fischer (eds), *Religion and Democracy in Contemporary Europe*, London: Alliance Publishing Trust, pp. 21–31. Copyright © 2008 Van Leer Jerusalem Institute and Network of European Foundations.

Waxmann Verlag for the essay: Jean-Paul Willaime (2007), 'Different Models for Religion and Education in Europe', in R. Jackson, S. Miedema, W. Weisse and J.-P. Willaime (eds), *Religion and Education in Europe*, Munster: Waxmann, pp. 57–66. Copyright © 2007 Waxmann Verlag GmBH.

Washington and Lee School of Law for the essay: Robin Fretwell Wilson (2007), 'The Overlooked Costs of Religious Deference', *Washington and Lee Law Review*, **64**, pp. 1363–83.

John Wiley and Sons for the essay: Jürgen Habermas (2006), 'Religion in the Public Sphere', *European Journal of Philosophy*, **14**, pp. 1–25. Copyright © 2006 Polity.

Publisher's Note

The material in this volume has been reproduced using the facsimile method. This means we can retain the original pagination to facilitate easy and correct citation of the original essays. It also explains the variety of typefaces, page layouts and numbering.

Introduction

Public and Private

Many would agree with Talal Asad that 'the terms "public" and "private" form a basic pair of categories in modern liberal society. It is central to the law, and crucial to the ways in which our liberties are protected. Our approval of other societies depends on the measure to which they reflect the categories as we do' (2003, p. 683). However, the content of these notions and their distinction has never been so controversial as in our days. First, the distinction between public and private has been criticized from many quarters as ideologically tainted, in the sense that 'the classic liberal public/private dichotomy hides lots of publics and tries to keep lots of political or public issues (e.g. structural power-asymmetries) "private", i.e. off the public/political agenda' (Bader, 2008). Second, the same distinction has been criticized as 'culture-specific'. Hanne Petersen believes that the private/public dichotomy is connected to the monotheistic way to conceive religion, 'inherited by secular state organizations and regulations. The "Atlantic-European" inspired secular normative culture introduces a division in public and private spheres, which continues a tradition of gender division and class privilege' (2012, p. 121). Others go further and identify a direct link between the public/private divide and Christianity (in particular Protestant Christianity), where religion is seen as something that primarily affects the spiritual (versus the material) side of human existence, the *forum internum* as opposed to the *forum externum*: according to Judith Butler 'we could not have the distinction between public and private were it not for the Protestant injunction to privatize religion' (2011, p. 71). In all these cases it is highlighted that the private/public distinction is culturally biased and far from being universal. Finally, others underline that it is also a crude and imprecise distinction: a sharp line neatly dividing these two dimensions of human life cannot be drawn and, whatever definition of public and private is adopted, it is impossible to remove a large grey area in which public and private overlap and mingle (see Hénaff and Strong, 2001, p. 23). These criticisms cannot be overlooked but, on the other hand, the public/private distinction is deeply ingrained in our way of understanding the social fabric and plays a positive role in building and maintaining a democratic society. 'The public/private split is normatively valuable' – Parkinson writes – because 'it creates normative room for citizens to exercise individual autonomy, and a public sphere in which conflicts between the results of those autonomous decisions can be resolved, or at least discussed' (2009, p. 75): a world where private is public and vice versa would probably be a totalitarian or a theocratic world. As underlined by Gaudreault-DesBiens and Karazivan, 'the division between the public and private spheres still matters today [...] whether we like it or not, this divide continues to inspire the state's regulatory endeavours, as well as the behaviour of many citizens' (2012, p. 94). For these reasons, a careful and prudent use of these two categories can still provide useful hints to reflect on the place to be assigned to religion and on the role it can play in either area.

Religion was never an exclusively private or public matter. In the Christian tradition (Judaism and Islam may have a different approach) faith is a personal matter that concerns the most private part of human life, the *forum internum*, the conscience. 'My kingdom is not of this world' said Jesus and, as correctly underlined by Modeér (2012), this persuasion supported the idea that state and church have distinct spheres of influence. But the evangelical dictum 'Render unto Caesar the things that are Caesar's, and unto God the things that are God's', which translates the previous principle into operative terms, was never interpreted by the church authorities in the sense that Caesar is public and God is private. The public dimension of religion was always upheld by the Christian churches and they strongly opposed the attempt to privatize religion that was pursued in particular throughout the nineteenth century: this opposition explains why such privatization was not thoroughly carried out in Europe so that, even in the most 'separatist' countries like France, religion never lost its public role (as shown by the persistence of religious chaplaincies in the army, the legal status of the Catholic places of worship, etc.).

Now the public/private divide seems to be again on the move, at least as far as religion is concerned. The privatization process has lost much of its impetus and the re-publicization of religion has become the new catch phrase in many academic circles. But this re-publicization cannot simply be a repetition of the past because something new has been happening in Europe: religion has become plural and, differently from the past, this plurality involves many followers of non-Christian religions and a growing number of Europeans who have no religion. Categories and language are inevitably more diversified and this difference has an impact also on the definition of public and private: how these two notions can be reformulated to fit this plurality is the subject of many discussions.

Defining Public Space and Public Sphere

The definition of public space and of public sphere is a particularly complex argument which has attracted the attention of urban planners, sociologists, political analysts, theologians, legal experts and economists. We should not therefore be surprised that many different notions have been proposed, even though they are not without points in common. In the first acceptation the expression 'public space' is understood as an open physical space that is accessible to a multitude of people: the square; the park; the market. This conception is widespread above all among urban planners who are engaged in building a public space that – for its characteristics – is easily accessible and pleasant to use, thus encouraging the mobility and daily interaction of citizens and opposing segregation. These features and objectives are close to those that are assigned to the public space by many sociologists for whom it is first and foremost the place of integration, where individuals can meet and establish relationships of acquaintanceship that favour social inclusion. In this perspective it is important that the public space is well designed, welcoming and easy to use so as to foster the development of the citizens' sense of belonging to an environment and to a community, increasing the social well-being and the quality of life:

> When public spaces are successful [...] they will increase opportunities to participate in communal activity. This fellowship in the open nurtures the growth of public life, which is stunted by the social isolation of ghettos and suburbs. In the parks, plazas, markets, waterfronts, and natural areas

> of our cities, people from different cultural groups can come together in a supportive context of mutual enjoyment. As these experiences are repeated, public spaces become vessels to carry positive communal meanings. (Carr *et al.*, 1992, p. 344)

Urban planners and sociologists, however, are the first to recognize that today the meaning of the public space has changed:

> We are far removed from the times when a city's central public spaces were a prime cultural and political site. In classical Rome, Renaissance Florence, or mercantile Venice, the public spaces of a city (for the minorities that counted as citizens and political actors) were key sites of cultural formation and popular political practice. What went on in them – and how they were structured – shaped civic conduct and politics in general [...]. Today, however, the sites of civic and political formation are plural and distributed. Civic practices – and public culture in general – are shaped in circuits of flow and association that are not reducible to the urban (e.g. books, magazines, television, music, national curricula, transnational associations), let alone to particular places of encounter within the city. (Amin, 2006)

This profile of associative life is at the centre of political analysts' reflections: it is no coincidence that they prefer to speak of public sphere rather than of public space. They introduce a new dimension into the debate, underlining that the public sphere is not only a physical place but more often than not it is an immaterial and metaphorical one: the mass media or internet are places where a process of communication develops around subjects and choices that interest the whole society. In other words 'the Public Sphere is a symbolic place where the various political, social, religious, cultural and intellectual discourses of people making up a society are exchanged' (Wolton, no date). A variant of this conception is proposed by some theologians, according to whom the public space is the place where the community is engaged in seeking the common good (Gorringe, 2011, p. 126).

Economists and law scholars bring to this debate a point of view that is more closely connected to practical interests. For the former the public space is 'a type of public good, a resource that individuals cannot be prevented from consuming and for which one individual's consumption does not diminish its potential consumption by others' (Neals, 2010). This does not mean that the public space does not have a measurable economic value: an attractive public space has a value in terms of tourism appeal, impact on nearby residential property values, recreation facilities and, not least, as an element of stimulus of 'community cohesion' (cf. Harnik and Welle, 2009). Finally, law scholars are reluctant to adopt a single notion of public space and they make a series of distinctions between public space, space open to the public, space visible to the public, space destined for public use and so on (cf. Bui-Xuan, 2011). Underlying these cases there is an important intuition: that the notion of public space contains different realities to which it is not opportune to apply the same rules.

At first sight this plurality of definitions can be disconcerting but a closer examination reveals that they present a point in common. All of these definitions consider that a 'good' public space and a 'good' public sphere can generate social capital as the meeting and dialogue among different people, different experiences of life, alternative conceptions of the world constitute a factor of individual and collective growth (cf. Landry, 2006, p. 245). This conviction represents the meeting point between public space and public sphere: not only the park or the square, but also the internet or the mass media play an important role in building a vital and vibrant civil society that, in turn, constitutes the premise for building a democratic state. Nevertheless there remains a difference which should not be overlooked: in speaking of the public sphere, political analysts above all highlight 'the possibility for a debate or a discourse' while – when they discuss the public space – urban planners focus on the 'physical venues of the city and the daily interactions of the citizenry'. The first conception

> can be summed up by the concept of the conversation and debate whereas the second one is best said as a question of mobility. The first one raises the important and ever pressing question of participative democracy, whereas the second one lends more attention to the idea of individual liberties, notably under the form of a 'right to the city'. (Tonnelat, 2010, p. 2)

It is therefore opportune to re-examine the point of view of the legal scholars and develop their intuition, according to which it is necessary to differentiate between different types of public space and to avoid applying the same rules to each of them (see Bader, 2012). The square, the TV talk show and the courtroom are three public spaces but their different characteristics and functions require a diversified legal discipline. This is also true for the rules regarding the manifestation of religious convictions in these spaces.

Religion in the Public Domain

Religion – more exactly, Christianity – has always been present in the Western public domain (including in this expression both the public space and the public sphere), as clearly indicated by the traces it left in the art and literature of the European and American countries. For many centuries Christianity dominated the public life. However, since the end of the eighteenth century the idea that the appropriate place of religion was more in the private than in the public domain started gaining ground among the European cultural élites. It paved the way to the conviction that, to be truly neutral and impartial towards different religious (and non-religious) life conceptions, the public domain must be secular. Decisions affecting politics, law and economics are to be based on reason, not on the faith of the one or the other citizen. While the private choices of each person may be taken only on the basis of religious motivations, public choices – and the whole decision-making process from which they arise – have to be based on rational principles, the only ones that can be shared by people professing different (or no) religions.[1] In this perspective the need to keep religion out of the public domain is justified by the fact that every religion teaches a particular conception of life, potentially conflicting with the conceptions upheld by other religions. To prevent the danger of a clash and to ensure the equal treatment of all religions, it is essential to ground the public space on a principle that is universal and neutral and therefore capable of being accepted by all people regardless of their religion: this principle is human reason. The universality of reason prevails on the particularity of religions and justifies their exclusion from the public domain, which must be designed and constructed exclusively in secular terms.[2]

---

1 Craig Calhoun underlines that 'the emerging theory of a reasoned public sphere was partly a response to religiously informed conflicts' (2011, p. 120) and this explains why the emergence of the public sphere and the public decline of religion have been frequently seen as interdependent processes (see Mayer and Moors, 2006, p. 4).

2 For an overview of this debate see the essays collected in Hosen and Mohr (2011).

To understand the origins of this construction of the public domain as a secular arena it is necessary to go back to what happened in the Old Continent in the sixteenth and seventeenth centuries. After the Lutheran Reformation, large regions of Europe were plagued by wars of religion that set Catholics and Protestants against each other for over a century. Wars of religion were a novelty in Europe and they could not find a suitable place in the theoretical framework in which war had been considered up to then. The Protestant Reformation had shattered the common religious horizon of the Medieval period, when most Western Europeans believed in the same God and recognized the same religious authority, the Pope. Wars of religion were fought by each opponent in the name of a different God and the Pope was no longer a *super partes* referee but had become the head of one of the conflicting parties. Therefore these wars could not be ended by appealing to the judgement of the Pope, which had been possible (at least in principle) during the Middle Ages. A new way out had to be found to put an end to wars that seemed endless. Two solutions were found for this problem: one short-term and political in nature, the other long-term and philosophically oriented. The first consisted of the application of the principle 'cuius regio, eius et religio' which, through the forced emigration of religious minorities, led to the creation of religiously homogeneous confessional states: although it cost considerable 'religious cleansing', it had the merit of putting an end to civil wars. The second solution was found by Grotius and was expressed with the famous saying 'etsi Deus non daretur'. The problem Grotius had to solve was a religiously motivated conflict: if a peaceful society had to be rebuilt, the starting point could no longer be religion, which had to be confined to one's private life. A new starting point was required and it was found in a natural law integrally founded on God's rationality and therefore fully accessible to man's reason. In other words, to make peaceful coexistence possible between Catholics and Protestants, Anglicans and Puritans, politics, the law, the economy and the other areas of public life had to be secularized, placing them under the exclusive control of reason and philosophy and freeing them from the control of religion and theology: that is, they had to be conceived and regulated 'etsi Deus non daretur'. The centre of gravity of religion is shifted from the public to the private life and at the same time the centre of gravity of public law moved from divine law to natural law based on reason. Alberico Gentili's 'silete theologi in munere alieno' – the admonition addressed to theologians to keep silent in matters which concern others – finds in Grotius' 'etsi Deus non daretur' its most convincing justification.[3]

It took almost two centuries to transfer Grotius' intuition from the world of philosophical speculation to that of political action, but in the end this principle inspired the (never completed) secularization of the public institutions that took place in much of Europe during the nineteenth century.

Grotius' solution granted the religious peace of Europe for a long time. However, in the last two decades of the past century the division between private and public domains became more and more contested mainly because of the immigration into Europe of people who are not familiar with this distinction and do not think that religion should be confined to the first field. As a consequence the assumption that religion is a private matter which should not influence public choices started being questioned and a new demand emerged to recognize the public role of religion. But how is it possible to do so without endangering the secular state

3 On the relations between Grotius and Gentili see Simmonds (1959).

and its core characteristic, the separation of religion and politics? This is precisely the theme discussed in the contributions republished in this volume.

The Secular State and the Public Domain

The first group of contributions, entitled 'Secularism, Pluralism and Multiple Modernities', brings together different proposals for regulating the public domain within the secular state. The terms of the question are identified in the essay by S.N. Eisenstadt (Chapter 3). This author notes that the 'resurgence of religion' has triggered 'the attempt to radically decouple modernity from Westernization; to take away from the West – from the original Western Enlightenment and even Romantic programmes – the monopoly of modernity and to define it in their own terms or vision'. This analysis leads Eisenstadt to speak of 'multiple modernities' that coexist in different parts of the world and among which increasing tensions emerge.

From this evaluation there derive two different interpretations of the Western secular state and its capacities to govern the current religious diversity through a new regulation of the public domain. The first is proposed by Rajeev Bhargava (Chapter 6) and it leaves little room for optimism:

> Western states need to improve the understanding of their own secular practices just as Western secularism needs a better theoretical self-understanding. Rather than get stuck on a model they developed at a particular time in their history, they would do well to learn from the original Indian variant. (p. 126)

This variant, according to Bhargava, guarantees the fundamental values of the secular state (prevention of religious conflicts, freedom of opinion within religious organizations, equality of citizens, freedom to change religion) by means of a model that differs from the Western one on two fundamental points: on the one hand it recognizes the rights of the religious communities in the public domain and on the other it permits the state to intervene in their internal organization when this is necessary for the good of the whole society. These two principles that distinguish Indian secularism, however, are so distant from the model of secularism prevailing in Europe and in the Americas that one may legitimately wonder whether Bhargava's proposal can be accommodated without repudiating the very roots of Western modernity.

A different interpretation is provided by the other contributions collected in this first part, all of which start from the premise that it is possible to transform the Western secular state and its notion of public domain from within. Frances Raday (Chapter 4) thinks that 'secularism is essential to human rights' (p. 82) and underlines 'the benefits of secular constitutionalism for democratic regimes' (p. 53), particularly when contrasted with the non-secular alternatives of religious diversity, pluralism or theo-democracy. For this reason it is necessary to develop the secular constitutionalism that provides 'an infrastructure of rights which deny the hegemony of religion' and 'a forum, conceptual and jurisdictional, for challenging religious dictates' (p. 82). Jürgen Habermas (Chapter 1) introduces a distinction between political and institutional levels of the public sphere. The liberal state cannot

> expect of *all* citizens that they also justify their political statements independently of their religious convictions or world views. This strict demand can only be laid at the door of politicians, who within

> state institutions are subject to the obligation to remain neutral in the face of competing world views. (pp. 10–11, emphasis in original)

It would instead be erroneous to extend 'this principle from the institutional level and apply it to statements put forward by organizations and citizens in the political public sphere' (p. 11). In this sphere, which is that of civil society, it is of fundamental importance for a liberal state to safeguard the plurality of the conceptions and life experiences: in Habermas's conception, then, the principles of the 'secular constitutionalism' invoked by Raday are applied to the space of the institutions but not to the broader space of public life. Finally, Charles Taylor (Chapter 2) criticizes the 'fetishization' (p. 34) of the principle of secularism and the conviction that the solution to the problems of contemporary society can be found in 'timeless principles [...] found in reason alone, or in some outlook which is itself free from religion, purely *laïque*' (p. 30). Taylor identifies three values that should guide the action of the state:

> no one must be forced in the domain of religion, or basic belief [...]; there must be equality between people of different faiths or basic beliefs [...]; all spiritual families must be heard, included in the ongoing process of determining what the society is about (its political identity) and how it is going to realize these goals (the exact regime of rights and privileges). (p. 29)

Authentically secular states have 'to be conceived not primarily as bulwarks against religion but as good faith attempts to secure' these three goals, shaping their 'institutional arrangements, not to remain true to hallowed tradition, but to maximize the basic goals of liberty and equality between basic beliefs' (p. 39). Such an objective and such a strategy seem to set Taylor on a collision course with Raday's 'secular constitutionalism'.

The other parts of the volume examine the place and the role of religion recognized in some particular settings of the public domain. The first of these is school and, more generally, the education process. Increasing religious diversity has severely challenged models of teaching centred on the transmission of a single religious tradition and it has opened up discussion on the best strategies for providing students with adequate knowledge for becoming citizens of a religiously plural world. The supply of several religious teachings for students to choose from, the teaching of the science and history of religions, the inclusion of notions of religion within courses of history and literature are some of the hypotheses that have been put forward. The second group of contributions regards the workplace. In this setting the debate has focused on the principle of non-discrimination. Is it opportune to include religion in the system of protection against discrimination for reasons of the gender, race or political convictions of the worker? And above all, is it opportune to make the employer responsible for an obligation of reasonable accommodation of the religious practices of his workers? The family is the third theme to be dealt with in this part of the volume. For a long time the family was considered the private space *par excellence* but today, above all since the legal recognition of same-sex marriages in some Western countries, this is perhaps the 'hottest' subject of public debate. Family law has gone through a long process of secularization, as described in the contribution by Mary Ann Glendon (Chapter 15). Today the problems of arranged marriages, honour killings, repudiation and polygamy – which seemed to belong to an increasingly distant past – have revealed how strong the ties of cultural and religious traditions still remain. The controversies over the recognition of personal legal statuses based on religion and therefore the application of a family law that is different depending on the religion of the spouses should be seen in this context. But whether to go down this road is a matter for discussion, as it might deprive the weaker parties of the protection offered by the laws of the state. Nor are the limits clear within which such a choice should be contained. Finally, two contributions are dedicated to the theme of religious symbols in the public space: the Islamic veil of French students, the crucifix displayed in the classrooms of Italian schools, the minarets prohibited by law in Switzerland, the burqa banned from the streets of Belgium are just some of the examples of the tensions that, in the last twenty years, have developed around this theme.

The introduction of the first volume of this collection of reprints states that the definition and role of religion in the public space constitutes the 'new frontier' of studies on law and religion. These examples are sufficient to indicate how this task is important, complex and at the same time indispensable for building a legal system that is able to manage the new visibility and diversity of religions in contemporary society.

SILVIO FERRARI

References

Amin, Ash (2006), *Collective Culture and Urban Public Space*, at: http://www.publicspace.org/es/texto-biblioteca/eng/b003-collective-culture-and-urban-public-space (accessed 30 November 2012).

Asad, Talal (2003), 'Boundaries and Rights in Islamic Law: Introduction (Part II: Islamic Law: Boundaries and Rights)', *Social Research*, **70**, p. 683–86.

Bader, Veit (2008), *Eurospheres? Fragmented and Stratified or Integrated and Fair? A Conceptual and Pre-Theoretical Mapping Exercise*, Eurospheres Working Papers Series, no. 9, at: http://dare.uva.nl/document/115557 (accessed 30 November 2012).

Bader, Veit (2012), 'The "Public–Private" Divide on Drift: What, if Any, Is Its Importance for Analysing Limits of Associational Religious Freedoms?', in Silvio Ferrari and Sabrina Pastorelli (eds), *Religion in Public Spaces: A European Perspective*, Farnham: Ashgate, pp. 47–70.

Bui-Xuan, Olivia (2011), 'L'espace public: L'émergence d'une nouvelle catégorie juridique?', *Droits et libertés*, May–June, pp. 551–59.

Butler, Judith (2011), 'Is Judaism Zionism?', in Eduardo Mendieta and Jonathan Vanantwerpen (eds), *The Power of Religion in the Public Sphere*, New York: Columbia University Press, pp. 70–91.

Calhoun, Craig (2011), 'Afterword: Religion's Many Powers', in Eduardo Mendieta and Jonathan Vanantwerpen (eds), *The Power of Religion in the Public Sphere*, New York: Columbia University Press, pp. 118–34.

Carr, Stephen, Francis, Mark, Rivlin, Leanne G. and Stone, Andrew M. (1992), *Public Space*, Cambridge: Cambridge University Press.

Gaudrealt-DesBiens, Jean-François and Karazivan, Noura (2012), 'The "Public" and "Private" in the Common Law and Civil Law Traditions and the Regulation of Religion', in Silvio Ferrari and Sabrina Pastorelli (eds), *Religion in Public Spaces: A European Perspective*, Farnham: Ashgate, pp. 93–118.

Gorringe, T.J. (2011), *The Common Good and the Global Emergency*, Cambridge: Cambridge University Press.

Harnik, Peter and Welle, Ben (2009), *Measuring the Economic Value of a City Park System*, The Trust for Public Land, at: http://cloud.tpl.org/pubs/ccpe-econvalueparks-rpt.pdf (accessed 30 November 2012).

Hénaff, M. and Strong, T.B. (eds) (2001), *Public Space and Democracy*, Minneapolis: University of Minnesota Press.

Hosen, N. and Mohr, R. (2011), *Law and Religion in Public Life*, Abingdon: Routledge.
Landry, Charles (2006), *The Art of City-Making*, Abingdon: Routledge.
Mayer, Birgit and Moors, Annalies (2006), *Religion, Media, and the Public Sphere*, Bloomington: Indiana University Press.
Modéer, Kjell Å. (2012), 'Public and Private, a Moving Border: A Legal-Historical Perspective', in Silvio Ferrari and Sabrina Pastorelli (eds), *Religion in Public Spaces: A European Perspective*, Farnham: Ashgate, pp. 25–34.
Neals, Zachary (2010), *Seeking Common Ground: Three Perspectives on Public Space*, Proceedings of the Institution of Civil Engineers, udp900031.3d, 15 January, at: https://www.msu.edu/~zpneal/publications/neal-seekingcommon.pdf (accessed 30 November 2012).
Parkinson, John (2009), 'Holistic Democracy and Public Space', in Mark Kingwell and Patrick Turmel (eds), *Rites of Way: The Politics and Poetics of Public Space*, Waterloo: Wilfrid Laurier University Press, pp. 71–84.
Petersen, Hanne (2012), 'Contested Normative Cultures: Gendered Perspectives on Religions and the Public/Private Divide', in Silvio Ferrari and Sabrina Pastorelli (eds), *Religion in Public Spaces: A European Perspective*, Farnham: Ashgate, pp. 119–38.
Simmonds, Kenneth R. (1959), 'Hugo Grotius and Alberico Gentili', *Jahrbuch für Internationales Recht*, **8**, pp. 85–100.
Tonnelat, Stéphane (2010), 'The Sociology of Urban Public Spaces', in Hongyang Wang, Michel Savy and Guofang Zhai (eds), *Territorial Evolution and Planning Solution: Experiences from China and France*, Paris: Atlantis Press, at: http://www.academia.edu/313641/The_Sociology_of_Urban_Public_Spaces (accessed 30 November 2012).
Wolton, Patrick *Espace public*, at: http://www.wolton.cnrs.fr/spip.php?article 67 (accessed 30 November 2012).

Part I
Secularism, Pluralism and Multiple Modernities

[1]

Religion in the Public Sphere

Jürgen Habermas

1

Religious traditions and communities of faith have gained a new, hitherto unexpected political importance since the epochmaking change of 1989–90.[1] Needless to say, what initially spring to mind are the variants of religious fundamentalism that we face not only in the Middle East, but also in Africa, Southeast Asia, and in the Indian subcontinent. They often lock into national and ethnic conflicts, and today also form the seedbed for the decentralized form of terrorism that operates globally and is directed against the perceived insults and injuries caused by a superior Western civilization. There are other symptoms, too.

For example, in Iran the protest against a corrupt regime set in place and supported by the West has given rise to a veritable rule of priests that serves other movements as a model to follow. In several Muslim countries, and in Israel as well, religious family law is either an alternative or a substitute for secular civil law. And in Afghanistan (and soon in Iraq), the application of a more or less liberal constitution must be limited by its compatibility with the Sharia. Likewise, religious conflicts are squeezing their way into the international arena. The hopes associated with the political agenda of *multiple modernities* are fueled by the cultural self-confidence of those world religions that to this very day unmistakably shape the physiognomy of the major civilizations. And on the Western side of the fence, the perception of international relations has changed in light of the fears of a 'clash of civilizations'—'the axis of evil' is merely one prominent example of this. Even Western intellectuals, to date self-critical in this regard, are starting to go on the offensive in their response to the image of Occidentalism that the others have of the West.[2]

Fundamentalism in other corners of the earth can be construed, among other things, in terms of the long-term impact of violent colonization and failures in decolonization. Under unfavorable circumstances, capitalist modernization penetrating these societies from the outside then triggers social uncertainty and cultural upheavals. On this reading, religious movements process the radical changes in social structure and cultural dissynchronies, which under conditions of an accelerated or failing modernization the individual may experience as a sense of being uprooted. What is more surprising is the political revitalization of religion at the heart of the United States, where the dynamism of modernization unfolds most successfully. Certainly, in Europe ever since the days of the French Revolution we have been aware of the power of a religious form of traditionalism that saw itself as counter-revolutionary. However, this evocation of religion as the power of tradition implicitly revealed the nagging doubt that the vitality of that which is already reflexively passed down *as* tradition may have been broken. By contrast, the political awakening of an ongoing strong religious consciousness in the United States has apparently not been affected by such doubts.

There is statistical evidence of a wave of secularization in almost all European countries since the end of World War II—going hand in hand with social modernization. By contrast, for the United States all data show that the comparatively large proportion of the population made up of devout and religiously active citizens has remained constant over the last six decades.[3] More importantly: the religious Right is not traditionalist. Precisely because it unleashes a spontaneous energy for revivalism, it causes paralyzing irritation among its secular opponents.

The movements for religious renewal at the heart of Western civilization are strengthening, at the *cultural* level, the *political* division of the West that was prompted by the Iraq War.[4] The divisive issues include, among others, the abolition of the death penalty; more or less liberal regulations on abortion; setting homosexual partnerships on a par with heterosexual marriages; an unconditional rejection of torture; and in general the prioritization of rights over collective goods, e.g., national security. The European states appear to keep moving forward alone on that path which, ever since the two constitutional revolutions of the late 18th century, they had trodden side by side with the United States. The significance of religions used for political ends has meanwhile grown the world over. Against this background, the split within the West is rather perceived as if Europe were isolating itself from the rest of the world. Seen in terms of world history, Max Weber's 'Occidental Rationalism' now appears to be the actual deviation.

From this revisionist viewpoint, religious traditions appear to continue with undiminished strength, washing away or at least leveling the thresholds hitherto assumed to pertain between 'traditional' and 'modern' societies. In this way, the Occident's own image of modernity seems, as in a psychological experiment, to undergo a switchover: the normal model for the future of all other cultures suddenly becomes a special-case scenario. Even if this suggestive Gestalt-switch does not quite bear up to sociological scrutiny and if the contrasting evidence can be brought into line with more conventional explanations of secularization,[5] there is no doubting the evidence itself and above all the symptomatic fact of divisive political moods crystallizing around it.

Two days after the last Presidential elections, an essay appeared, written by a historian, and entitled 'The Day the Enlightenment Went Out'. He asked the alarmist question: 'Can a people that believes more fervently in the Virgin Birth than in evolution still be called an Enlightened nation? America, the first real democracy in history, was a product of the Enlightenment values ... Though the founders differed on many things, they shared these values of what then was modernity ... Respect for evidence seems not to pertain any more, when a poll taken just before the election showed that 75% of Mr. Bush's supporters believe Iraq either worked closely with Al Qaeda or was directly involved in the attacks of 9/11'.[6]

Irrespective of how one evaluates the facts, the election analyses confirm that the cultural division of the West runs right through the American nation itself: conflicting value orientations—God, gays and guns—have manifestly covered over more tangibly contrasting interests. Be that as it may, President Bush has a coalition of primarily religiously motivated voters to thank for his victory.[7] This shift in power indicates a mental shift in civil society that also forms the background to the academic debates on the political role of religion in the state and the public sphere.

Once again, the battle is over the substance of the first sentence of the First Amendment: 'Congress shall make no law respecting an establishment of religion, or prohibiting the free exercise thereof'. The United States was the political pacemaker en route to establishing a freedom of religion that rested on the reciprocal respect of the religious freedom of the others.[8] The marvelous Article 16 of the Bill of Rights penned in Virginia in 1776 is the first document of freedom of religion guaranteed as a basic right that democratic citizens accord *each other* across the divides between the different religious communities. Unlike in France, the introduction of the freedom of religion in the United States of America did not signify the victory of laicism over an authority that had at best shown religious minorities tolerance in line with imposed standards of its own. Here, the secularization of state powers did not serve primarily the negative purpose of protecting citizens against the compulsion to adopt a faith against their own will. It was instead designed to guarantee the settlers who had turned their backs on Old Europe the positive liberty to continue to exercise their respective religion without hindrance. For this reason, in the present American debate on the political role of religion all sides have been able to claim their loyalty to the constitution. We shall see to what extent this claim is valid.

In what follows I shall address the debate that has arisen in the wake of John Rawls' political theory, in particular his concept of the 'public use of reason'. How does the constitutional separation of state and church influence the role which religious traditions, communities and organizations are allowed to play in civil society and the political public sphere, above all in the political opinion and will formation of citizens themselves? Where should the dividing line be in the opinion of the revisionists? Are the opponents who are currently out on the warpath against the liberal standard version of an ethics of citizenship actually only championing the pro-religious meaning of a secular state held to be neutral, versus a *narrow secularist* notion of a pluralist society? Or are they more or less inconspicuously changing the liberal agenda from the bottom up—and thus already arguing from the background of a *different* self-understanding of Modernity?

I would like first of all to bring to mind the liberal premises of the constitutional state and the consequences which John Rawls's conception of the public use of reason has on the ethics of citizenship (2). I shall then go on to treat the most important objections to this rather restrictive idea of the political role of religion (3). Through a critical discussion of revisionist proposals that do touch on the foundations of the liberal self-understanding I shall develop a conception of my own (4). However, secular and religious citizens can only fulfill the normative expectations of the liberal role of citizens if they likewise fulfill certain cognitive conditions and ascribe to the respective opposite the corresponding epistemic attitudes. I shall explain what this means by discussing the change in the form of religious consciousness which was a response to the challenges of Modernity(5). By contrast, the secular awareness that one is living in a post-secular society takes the shape of post-metaphysical thought at the philosophical level (6). In both regards, the liberal state faces the problem that religious and secular citizens can only acquire these attitudes through complementary learning processes, while it remains a moot point whether these are 'learning processes' at all, and ones which the state cannot influence by its own means of law and politics anyway (7).

2

The self-understanding of the constitutional state has developed within the framework of a contractualist tradition that relies on 'natural' reason, in other words solely on public arguments to which supposedly *all* persons have *equal access*. The assumption of a common human reason forms the basis of justification for a secular state that no longer depends on religious legitimation. And this in turn makes the separation of state and church possible at the institutional level in the first place. The historical backdrop against which the liberal conception emerged were the religious wars and confessional disputes in early Modern times. The constitutional state responded first by the secularization and then by the democratization of political power. This genealogy also forms the background to John Rawls's *Political Liberalism*.[9]

The constitutional freedom of religion is the appropriate political answer to the challenges of religious pluralism. In this way, the potential for conflict at the level of citizens' social interaction can be restrained, while at the cognitive level deep-reaching conflicts may well continue to exist between the existentially relevant convictions of believers, believers of other denominations, and non-believers. Yet the secular character of the state is a necessary though not a sufficient condition for guaranteeing equal religious freedom for everybody. It is not enough to rely on the condescending benevolence of a secularized authority that comes to tolerate minorities hitherto discriminated against. The parties themselves must reach agreement on the always contested delimitations between a positive liberty to practice a religion of one's own and the negative liberty to remain spared from the religious practices of the others. If the principle of tolerance is to be above any suspicion of oppressive features, then compelling reasons must be found for the definition of what can just about be tolerated and what cannot, reasons that all sides can equally accept.[10] Fair arrangements can only be found if the parties involved learn to take the perspectives of the others. The procedure that fits this purpose best is the deliberative mode of democratic will formation. In the secular state, government has to be placed on a non-religious footing anyway. The liberal constitution must flesh out the loss of legitimation caused by a secularization that deprives the state of deriving its authority from God. From the practice of constitution-making, there emerge those basic rights that free and equal citizens must accord one another if they wish to regulate their co-existence reasonably on their own and by means of positive law.[11] The democratic procedure is able to generate legitimation by virtue of two components—first the equal political participation of all citizens, which guarantees that the addresses of the laws can also understand themselves as the authors of these laws;—and second the epistemic dimension of a deliberation that grounds the presumption of rationally acceptable outcomes.[12]

These two legitimacy components explain the kind of political virtues the liberal state must expect from its citizens. It is precisely the conditions for the successful participation in the shared practice of democratic self-determination that define the ethics of citizenship: For all their ongoing dissent on questions of world views and religious doctrines, citizens are meant to respect one another as free and equal members of their political community. And on this basis of civic solidarity when it comes to contentious political issues they are expected to look for a way to reach a rationally motivated agreement—they owe one another good reasons. Rawls speaks in this context of the 'duty of civility' and 'the public use of reason': 'The ideal of citizenship imposes a moral, not a legal, duty—the duty of civility—to be able to explain to one another on those fundamental questions how the principles and policies they advocate and vote for can be supported by the values of public reason. This duty also involves a willingness to listen to others and a fairmindedness in deciding when accommodations to their views should reasonably be made'.[13]

Only with the legal frame for a self-governing association of free and equal citizens does the point of reference arise for the use of public reason which requires citizens to justify their political statements and attitudes before one another in light of a (reasonable interpretation)[14] of valid constitutional principles. Rawls refers here to 'values of public reason' or elsewhere to the 'premises we accept and think others could reasonably accept'.[15] In a secular state only those political decisions are taken to be legitimate as can be impartially justified in the light of generally accessible reasons, in other words equally justified vis-à-vis religious and non-religious citizens, and citizens of different confessions. A rule that cannot be justified in an impartial manner is illegitimate as it reflects the fact that one party *forces* its will on another. Citizens of a democratic society are obliged to provide reasons for one another, as only thus can political power shed its repressive character. This consideration explains the controversial 'proviso' for the use of non-public reasons.

The principle of separation of state and church obliges politicians and officials within political institutions to formulate and justify laws, court rulings, decrees and measures only in a language which is equally accessible to all citizens.[16] Yet the proviso to which citizens, political parties and their candidates, social organizations, churches and other religious associations are subject is not quite so strict in the political public sphere. Rawls writes: 'The first is that reasonable comprehensive doctrines, religious or non-religious, may be introduced in public political discussion at any time, *provided that in due course proper political reasons—and not reasons given solely by comprehensive doctrines—are presented that are sufficient to support whatever the comprehensive doctrines are said to support*'.[17] This means that political reasons may not simply be put forward as a pretext, but must 'count' irrespective of the religious context in which they are embedded.[18]

In the liberal view, the state guarantees citizens freedom of religion only on the condition that religious communities, each from the perspective of its own doctrinal tradition, accept not only the separation of church and state, but also the restrictive definition of the public use of reason. Rawls insists on this requirement even when confronted by the objection, which he himself raises: 'How is it possible . . . for those of faith . . . to endorse a constitutional regime even when their comprehensive doctrines may not prosper under it, and indeed may decline?'[19]

Rawls's concept of public reason has met with resolute critics. The objections were leveled not at his liberal premises per se, but against an overly narrow, supposedly secularist definition of the political role of religion in the liberal frame. This is not to play down the fact that eventually the dissent also touches the real substance of the liberal state. What interests me (here) is what line gets drawn to claims that reach beyond a liberal constitution. Arguments for a more generously dimensioned political role for religion that are incompatible with the secular nature of the state should not be confused with justifiable objections to a secularist understanding of democracy and the rule of law.

The principle of separation of church and state demands that the institution of the state operate with strict impartiality vis-à-vis religious communities; parliaments, courts, and the administration must not violate the prescription not to privilege one side at the cost of another. But this principle is to be distinguished from the laicist demand that the state should defer from adopting any political stance which would support or constrain religion per se, even if this affects all religious communities equally. That would amount to an overly narrow interpretation of the separation of state and church.[20] At the same time, the rejection of secularism must not succumb to leaving the door wide open for revisions that would undermine the principle itself. The toleration of religious justifications within the legislative process is, as we shall see, a case in point. That said, Rawls's liberal position has tended to direct his critics' attention less to the impartiality of state institutions than to the ethics of citizenship.

3

Rawls's opponents cite historical examples of the favorable political influence that churches and religious movements have actually had on the assertion of democracy and human rights. Martin Luther King and the US Civil Rights Movement illustrate the successful struggle for a broader inclusion of minorities and marginal groups in the political process. In this context, the religious roots to the motivations of most social and socialist movements in both the United States and European countries are highly impressive.[21] There are obvious historical examples to the contrary, namely for the authoritarian or repressive role of churches and fundamentalist movements; however, in well-established constitutional states, churches and religious communities generally perform functions that are not unimportant for stabilizing and advancing a liberal political culture. This is especially true of the form of civil religion that has developed in American society.[22]

Paul J. Weithmann makes use of these sociological findings for a normative analysis of the ethics of democratic citizenship. He describes churches and religious communities as actors in civil society who fulfill functional imperatives for the reproduction of American democracy. They provide arguments for public debates on crucial morally-loaded issues and handle tasks of political socialization by informing their members and encouraging them to take part in the political process. The churches' commitment to civil society would, however, wither away, so the argument goes, if each time they had to distinguish between religious and political values in keeping with the yardstick set by Rawls' 'proviso'—in other words if they were obliged to find an equivalent in a universally accessible language for every religious statement they pronounce. Therefore, if only for functional reasons, the liberal state must refrain from obliging churches and religious communities to comply to such standards of self-censorship. And it must then eschew all the more imposing a similar limitation on its citizens.[23]

That is, of course, not the central objection to Rawls's theory. Irrespective of how the interests are weighted in the relationship between the state and religious organizations, a state cannot encumber its citizens, whom it guarantees freedom of religious expression, with duties that are incompatible with pursuing a devout life—it cannot expect something impossible of them. This objection bears closer scrutiny.

Robert Audi clothes the duty of civility postulated by Rawls in a special 'principle of secular justifications' when he writes: 'One has a prima facie obligation not to advocate or support any law or public policy . . . unless one has, and is willing to offer, adequate secular reasons for this advocacy or support'.[24] Audi adds to the principle a requirement that goes even further, namely the demand that the secular reasons must be strong enough to direct the citizen's own behavior, for example when voting in elections, quite independent of simultaneous religious motivations.[25] With regard to a moral judgment on any individual citizen, the link between the actual motivation for his actions and those reasons he gives in public may be relevant. But a gap between reason and action is of no consequence from the perspective of what is necessary for maintaining the democratic system as a whole, namely in terms of the contribution citizens must make to maintain a liberal political culture. At the end of the day only manifest reasons can, and only those do have an impact on the political system as actually affect the formation of majorities and their decisions within political bodies.

As regards the political consequences, all and only those issues, statements, and reasons 'count' that find their way into the impersonal flow of public communication and contribute to the cognitive motivation of *any* decision (backed and implemented by state power)—be it directly in support of the decisions of voters or indirectly in support of the decisions taken by party leaders, members of parliament or by persons holding office (such as judges, ministers or staff attached to the administration). This is why I shall disregard Audi's additional requirement for motivation and his distinction between publicly expressed reasons and those motivating behavior in the polling booth.[26] What is of material import for the standard version of political liberalism is simply the requirement of 'secular justifications': Given that in the liberal state only secular reasons count, citizens who adhere to a faith are obliged to establish a kind of 'balance' between their religious and their secular convictions—in Audi's words a theo-ethical equilibrium.[27]

This demand is countered by the objection that many religious citizens would not be able to undertake such an artificial division within their own minds without jeopardizing their existence as pious persons. This objection is to be distinguished from the empirical observation that many citizens who take a stance on political issues from a religious viewpoint, do not have enough knowledge or imagination to find secular justifications for them that are independent of their authentic beliefs. This fact is compelling enough given that any 'ought' implies a 'can'. Yet we can go one step further. There is a normative resonance to the central objection, as it relates to the integral role that religion plays in the life of a person of faith, in other words to religion's 'seat' in everyday life. A devout person pursues her daily rounds by *drawing* on belief. Put differently, true belief is not only a doctrine, believed content, but a source of energy that the person who has a faith taps performatively and thus nurtures his or her entire life.[28]

This totalizing trait of a mode of believing that infuses the very pores of daily life runs counter, the objection goes, to any flimsy switchover of religiously rooted political convictions onto *a different* cognitive basis: 'It belongs to the religious convictions of a good many religious people in our society that *they ought to base* their decisions concerning fundamental issues of justice *on* their religious convictions. They do not view it as an option whether or not to do it. It is their conviction that they ought to strive for wholeness, integrity, integration in their lives: that they ought to allow the Word of God, the teachings of the Torah, the command and example of Jesus, or whatever, to shape their existence as a whole, including, then, their social and political existence. Their religion is not, for them, about *something other* than their social and political existence'.[29] Their religiously grounded concept of justice tells them what is politically correct or incorrect, meaning that they are incapable of discerning 'any "pull" from any secular reasons'.[30]

If we accept this to my mind compelling objection, then the liberal state, which expressly protects such forms of life in terms of a basic right, cannot at the same time expect of *all* citizens that they also justify their political statements independently of their religious convictions or world views. This strict demand can only be laid at the door of politicians, who within state institutions are subject to the obligation to remain neutral in the face of competing world views; in other words it can only be made of anyone who holds a public office or is a candidate for such.[31]

The institutional precondition for guaranteeing equal freedom of religion for all is that the state remains neutral towards competing world views. The consensus on constitutional principles, which all citizens must mutually assume their fellow citizens share, pertains also to the principle of the separation of church and state. However, in light of the afore-mentioned objection it would be to over-generalize secularization if we were to extend this principle from the institutional level and apply it to statements put forward by organizations and citizens in the political public sphere. We cannot derive from the secular character of the state a direct obligation for all citizens personally to supplement their public statements of religious convictions by equivalents in a generally accessible language. And certainly the normative expectation that all religious citizens when casting their vote should *in the final instance* let themselves be guided by secular considerations is to ignore the realities of a devout life, an existence led *in light of* belief. This proposition has however been countered by pointing to the actual situation of religious citizens in the secular milieus of a modern society.[32]

The conflict between a person's own religious convictions and secularly justified policies or bills can only arise by virtue of the fact that the religious citizen should also have accepted the constitution of the secular state for good reasons. He no longer lives as a member of a religiously homogeneous population within a religiously legitimated state. And therefore certainties of faith are always already networked with fallible beliefs of a secular nature; they have long since lost—in the form of 'unmoved' but not 'unmovable' movers—their purported immunity to the impositions of modern reflexivity.[33] In the differentiated architecture of modern societies, the religious certainties are in fact exposed to an increasing pressure for reflection. This epistemological objection meets in turn a counterargument: By dint of their possibly even rationally defended reference to the dogmatic authority of an inviolable core of infallible revelatory truths, religiously rooted existential convictions evade that kind of *unreserved* discursive deliberation to which other ethical orientations and world views, i.e., secular 'concepts of the good' expose themselves.[34]

4

The liberal state must not transform the requisite *institutional* separation of religion and politics into an undue *mental* and *psychological* burden for those of its citizens who follow a faith. It must of course expect of them that they recognize the principle that political authority is exercised with neutrality towards competing world views. Every citizen must know and accept that only secular reasons count beyond the institutional threshold that divides the informal public sphere from parliaments, courts, ministries and administrations. But all that is required here is the epistemic ability to consider one's own faith reflexively from the outside and to relate it to secular views. Religious citizens can well recognize this 'institutional translation proviso' without having to split their identity into a public and a private part the moment they participate in public discourses. They should therefore be allowed to express and justify their convictions in a religious language if they cannot find secular 'translations' for them.

This need by no means estrange 'mono-glot' citizens from the political process, because they do take a position with political intent even if they field religious reasons. Even if the religious language is the only one they can speak in public, and if religiously justified opinions are the only ones they can or wish to put into political controversies, they nevertheless understand themselves as members of a civitas terrena, which empowers them to be the authors of laws to which as its addressees they are subject. Given that they may only express themselves in a religious idiom under the condition that they recognize the institutional translation proviso, they can, trusting that their fellow citizens will cooperate for accomplishing a translation, grasp themselves as participants in the legislative process, although only secular reasons count therein.

The permissibility of non-translated religious utterances in the political public sphere can be normatively justified not only in view of the fact that we must not *expect* Rawls's proviso to apply to those of the faithful who cannot abstain from the political use of 'private' reasons without endangering their religious mode of life. For functional reasons, we should not over-hastily reduce the polyphonic complexity of public voices, either. For the liberal state has an interest in unleashing religious voices in the political public sphere, and in the political participation of religious organizations as well. It must not discourage religious persons and communities from also expressing themselves politically *as such*, for it cannot know whether secular society would not otherwise cut itself off from key resources for the creation of meaning and identity. Secular citizens or those of other religious persuasions can under certain circumstances learn something from religious contributions; this is, for example, the case if they recognize in the normative truth content of a religious utterance hidden intuitions of their own.

Religious traditions have a special power to articulate moral intuitions, especially with regard to vulnerable forms of communal life. In the event of the corresponding political debates, this potential makes religious speech a serious candidate to transporting possible truth contents, which can then be translated from the vocabulary of a particular religious community into a generally accessible language. However, the institutional thresholds between the 'wild life' of the political public sphere and the formal proceedings within political bodies are also a filter that from the Babel of voices in the informal flows of public communication allows only secular contributions to pass through. In parliament, for example, the standing rules of procedure of the house must empower the house leader to have religious statements or justifications expunged from the minutes. The truth content of religious contributions can only enter into the institutionalized practice of deliberation and decision-making if the necessary translation already occurs in the pre-parliamentarian domain, i.e., in the political public sphere itself.

This requirement of translation must be conceived as a cooperative task in which the non-religious citizens must likewise participate, if their religious fellow citizens are not to be encumbered with an asymmetrical burden. Whereas citizens of faith may make public contributions in their own religious language only subject to the proviso that these get translated, the secular citizens must open their minds to the possible truth content of those presentations and enter into dialogues from which religious reasons then might well emerge in the transformed guise of generally accessible arguments.[35] Citizens of a democratic community owe one another good reasons for their political statements and attitudes. Even if the religious contributions are not subjected to self-censorship, they depend on cooperative acts of translation. For without a successful translation there is no prospect of the substantive content of religious voices being taken up in the agendas and negotiations within political bodies and in the broader political process. By contrast, Nicholas Wolterstorff and Paul Weithman wish to jettison even this proviso. In so doing, contrary to their own claim to remain in line with the premises of the liberal argument, they violate the principle that the state shall remain neutral in the face of competing world views.

In Weithman's opinion citizens have the right to justify public political statements in the context of a comprehensive world view or a religious doctrine. In the process they are supposed to meet two conditions. First, they must be convinced that their government is justified in carrying out the laws or policies they support with religious arguments. Second, they must be willing to declare why they believe this. This milder version of the proviso[36] amounts to the demand that a universalization test be undertaken from a first-person perspective. In this way, Weithman wishes to have citizens make their judgment from the viewpoint of a conception of justice even if they conceive 'justice' in terms of a religion or another substantive world view. Citizens are to consider, if only from the respective perspective of their own doctrine, what would be equally good for everyone. However, the Golden Rule is not the Categorical Imperative; it does not oblige each person among all the people involved to *reciprocally* assume the perspective of everybody else.[37] For with this method each person's own perspective on the world forms the insurmountable horizon of her deliberations on justice: 'The person who argues in public for a measure must be prepared to say what she thinks would justify the government in enacting it, *but the justification she is prepared to offer may depend on claims, including religious claims, which proponents of the standard approach would deem inaccessible*'.[38]

Since no institutional filter is envisaged between the state and the public domain, this version does not exclude the possibility that policies and legal programs will be implemented solely on the basis of the religious or confessional beliefs of a ruling majority. This is the conclusion explicitly drawn by Nicholas Wolterstorff, who does not wish to subject the political use of religious reasons to any restraints whatsoever. At any rate, he allows for a political legislature making use of religious arguments.[39] If one thus opens the parliaments to the battle on religious beliefs, governmental authority can evidently become the agent of a religious majority that asserts its will and thus violates the democratic procedure.

What is illegitimate is of course not the majority vote, assuming it has been correctly carried out, but the violation of the other core component of the procedure, namely the discursive nature of the deliberations preceding the vote. What is illegitimate is the violation of the neutrality principle according to which all enforceable political decisions *must be formulated* in a language that is equally accessible to all citizens, and it *must be possible to justify them* in this language as well. Majority rule turns into repression if the majority deploys religious arguments in the process of political opinion and will formation and refuses to offer those publicly accessible justifications which the losing minority, be it secular or of a different faith, is able to follow and to evaluate in the light of shared standards. The democratic procedure has the power to generate legitimacy precisely because it both includes all participants and has a deliberative character; for the justified presumption of rational outcomes in the long run can solely be based on this.

Wolterstorff pre-empts this argument by rejecting the whole idea of a reasonable background consensus on constitutional essentials. In the liberal view, political power only loses its inherent violence by virtue of a legal domestication which accords to agreed upon principles.[40] Wolterstorff raises empirical objections here to counter this conception. He ridicules the idealizing presuppositions, inscribed in the very practices of the constitutional state, as some 'Quaker meeting ideal' (though the Quaker principle of unanimity is untypical of the democratic process). He maintains that the argument between different conceptions of justice grounded in competing religions or world views can never be solved by the common presupposition of an however formal background consensus. Although he wishes to retain the majority principle from the liberal consensus, Wolterstorff imagines that majority resolutions in an ideologically divided society can at best yield reluctant adaptations to a kind of *modus vivendi*. A defeated minority will feel like saying: 'I do not agree, I *acquiesce*—unless I find the decision truly appalling'.[41]

It is unclear why under this premise the political community should not at any time be in danger simply of disintegrating into religious struggle. Certainly, the usual empiricist reading of liberal democracy has always construed majority decisions as the temporary subjection of a minority to the actual power of a numerically prevailing party. But this utilitarian theory explains the acceptance of the voting procedure by the willingness of rational choosers to compromise; it reckons with parties who concur in their preference for the largest possible share of basic goods such as money, security or leisure time. The parties can conclude compromises because all of them aspire to the *same* categories of divisible goods. Yet precisely this condition is not met as soon as the conflicts no longer flare up over the share in the same kind of material goods, but on competing values and mutually exclusive 'goods of salvation'. The conflict on existential values between communities of faith cannot be solved by compromise. They can be contained, however, by losing any political edge against the background of a presupposed consensus on constitutional principles.

5

Conflicts between world views and religious doctrines that lay claim to explaining man's position in the world as a whole cannot be laid to rest at the cognitive level. As soon as these cognitive dissonances penetrate as far as the foundations for a normative integration of citizens, the political community disintegrates into irreconcilable segments so that it can only survive on the basis of an unsteady *modus vivendi*. In the absence of the uniting bond of a civic solidarity, which cannot be legally enforced, citizens do not perceive themselves as free and equal participants in the shared practices of democratic opinion and will formation wherein they *owe one another reasons* for their political statements and attitudes. This reciprocity of expectations among citizens is what distinguishes a community integrated by constitutional values from a community segmented along the dividing lines of competing world views. The latter frees religious and secular citizens in their dealings with one another from any reciprocal obligation to justify themselves in political debate *before one another*. In such a community the dissonant background beliefs and sub-cultural bonds out-trump the supposed constitutional consensus and the expected civic solidarity; in the case of conflicts that cut deep, citizens need not adapt to or face *one another* as second persons.

The assumption of forgoing reciprocity and of mutual indifference seems to be justified by the fact that the liberal standard version is intrinsically self-contradictory if it equally imputes to all citizens a political ethos which in fact distributes cognitive burdens unequally between secular and religious citizens. The translation requirement for religious reasons and the subsequent institutional precedence of secular reasons demand of the religious citizens an effort to learn and adapt that secular citizens are spared having to make. This would concur at any rate with the empirical observation that even within the Churches a certain resentment has persisted for so long toward the secular state. The duty to 'make public use of reason' can only be discharged under certain cognitive preconditions. Yet required epistemic attitudes are the expression of a given mentality and cannot, like motives, be made the substance of normative expectations and political appeals. Every 'ought' presupposes a 'can'. The normative expectations of an ethics of citizenship have absolutely no impact unless a required change in mentality has been forthcoming first; indeed, they then serve only to kindle resentment on the part of those who feel misunderstood and their capacities over-taxed.

However, in Western culture we do indeed observe a change in the form of religious consciousness since the Reformation and Enlightenment. The sociologists have described this 'modernization of religious consciousness' as a response to the challenge religious traditions have been facing in view of the fact of pluralism, the emergence of modern science, and the spread of both positive law and profane morality. In these three respects, traditional communities of faith must process cognitive dissonances that do not arise for secular citizens, or arise for them only if they adhere to doctrines that are anchored in a similarly dogmatic way:

> Religious citizens must develop an epistemic attitude toward other religions and world views that they encounter within a universe of discourse hitherto occupied only by their own religion. They succeed to the degree that they self-reflectively relate their religious beliefs to the statements of competing doctrines of salvation in such a way that they do not endanger their own exclusive claim to truth.
>
> Moreover, religious citizens must develop an epistemic stance toward the independence of secular from sacred knowledge and the institutionalized monopoly of modern scientific experts. They can only succeed if from their religious viewpoint they conceive the relationship of dogmatic and secular beliefs in such a way that the autonomous progress in secular knowledge cannot come to contradict their faith.
>
> Finally, religious citizens must develop an epistemic stance toward the priority that secular reasons enjoy in the political arena. This can succeed only to the extent that they convincingly connect the egalitarian individualism and universalism of modern law and morality with the premises of their comprehensive doctrines.

This arduous work of hermeneutic self-reflection must be undertaken from within religious traditions. In our culture, it has essentially been performed by theology, from the Catholic side also by a philosophy of religions that proceeds apologetically in explicating the reasonableness of a faith.[42] Yet in the final instance it is the faith and practice of the religious community that decides whether a dogmatic processing of the cognitive challenges of modernity has been 'successful' or not; only then will the true believer accept it as the result of a 'learning process'. We may describe the new epistemic attitudes as 'acquired by learning' only if they arise from a reconstruction of sacred truths that did indeed convince people of faith in the light of modern living conditions for which no alternatives any longer exist. If those attitudes were merely the contingent result of drill and forced adaptation, then the question, how those cognitive preconditions for imputing a liberal ethics of citizenship are met, has to be answered *à la* Foucault—namely in the wake of the kind of 'discursive power' that asserts itself in the purported transparency of enlightened knowledge. Of course, this answer would contradict the normative self-understanding of the constitutional state. Such a response contradicts, of course, the normative self-understanding of any constitutional state.

Within this liberal framework, what interests me is the unanswered question whether the revised concept of citizenship that I have proposed in fact imposes an asymmetrical burden on religious traditions and religious communities after all. Historically speaking, religious citizens had to learn to adopt epistemic attitudes toward their secular environment, attitudes that enlightened secular citizens enjoy anyway, since they are not exposed to similar cognitive dissonances in the first place. However, secular citizens are likewise not spared a cognitive burden, because a secularist attitude does not suffice for the expected cooperation with fellow citizens who are religious. This cognitive act of adaptation needs to be distinguished from the political virtue of mere tolerance. What is at stake is not some respectful feel for the possible existential significance of religion for some other person. What we must also expect of the secular citizens is moreover a self-reflective transcending of a secularist self-understanding of Modernity.

As long as secular citizens are convinced that religious traditions and religious communities are to a certain extent archaic relics of pre-modern societies that continue to exist in the present, they will understand freedom of religion as the cultural version of the conservation of a species in danger of becoming extinct. From their viewpoint, religion no longer has any intrinsic justification to exist. And the principle of the separation of state and church can for them only have the laicist meaning of sparing indifference. In the secularist reading, we can envisage that, in the long run, religious views will inevitably melt under the sun of scientific criticism and that religious communities will not be able to withstand the pressures of some unstoppable cultural and social modernization. Citizens who adopt such an epistemic stance toward religion can obviously no longer be expected to take religious contributions to contentious political issues seriously and even to help to assess them for a substance that can possibly be expressed in a secular language and justified by secular arguments.

Under the normative premises of the constitutional state, the admission of religious statements to the political public sphere only makes sense if all citizens can be expected not to deny from the outset any possible cognitive substance to these contributions—while at the same time respecting the precedence of secular reasons and the institutional translation requirement. This is what the religious citizens assume anyway. Yet on the part of the secular citizens such an attitude presupposes a mentality that is anything but a matter of course in the secularized societies of the West. Instead, the insight by secular citizens that they live in a post-secular society that is *epistemically adjusted* to the continued existence of religious communities first requires a change in mentality that is no less cognitively exacting than the adaptation of religious awareness to the challenges of an ever more secularized environment. In line with this changed yardstick, the secular citizens must grasp their conflict with religious opinions as a *reasonably expected disagreement*.

In the absence of this cognitive precondition, a public use of reason cannot be imputed to citizens, at least not in the sense that secular citizens should be willing to enter and engage in a discussion of the content of religious contributions with the intention of translating, if there is such a content, morally convincing intuitions and reasons into a generally accessible language.[43] An epistemic mindset is presupposed here that would originate from a self-critical assessment of the limits of secular reason.[44] However, this cognitive precondition indicates that the version of an ethics of citizenship I have proposed may only be expected from all citizens equally if both, religious as well as secular citizens, already have undergone complementary learning processes.

6

The ostensibly critical overcoming of what to my mind is a narrow secularist consciousness is itself an essentially contested issue—at least to the same extent as the demythologizing response to the cognitive challenges of Modernity. While we already observe the 'modernization of religious consciousness' with hindsight and consider it the subject matter of theology, the naturalist background of secularism is still the object of an ongoing and open-ended philosophical debate. The secular awareness that we live in a post-secular world is reflected philosophically in the form of post-metaphysical thought. This mode of thought is not exhausted by an emphasis on the finiteness of reason, or by the combination of fallibilist and anti-skeptical attitudes that has characterized modern science since Kant and Peirce. The secular counterpart to religious modernization is an agnostic, but non-reductionist philosophical position. It refrains on the one hand from passing judgment on religious truths while insisting (in a non-polemical fashion) on drawing a strict line between faith and knowledge. It rejects, on the other, a scientistically limited conception of reason and the exclusion of religious doctrines from the genealogy of reason.

Post-metaphysical thought admittedly refrains from passing ontological statements on the constitution of the whole of beings; but this does not mean reducing our knowledge to the sum total of statements that at each time represents the respective 'state of science'. Scientism often tempts one to blur the borderline between proper scientific knowledge, which gains relevance with regard to how man interprets himself and his position in nature as a whole, on the one hand, and a naturalist world view synthetically derived from this, on the other.[45] This radical form of naturalism devalues all categories of statements that cannot be reduced to controlled observations, nomological propositions or causal explanations; in other words moral, legal and evaluative judgments are no less excluded than are religious ones. As the renewed discussion on freedom and determinism shows, advances in biogenetics, brain research and robotics provide stimuli for a kind of naturalizing of the human mind that casts into question our practical self-understanding as responsibly acting persons and encourages a call for revisions to criminal law.[46] A naturalistic self-objectification of persons that penetrates everyday life is incompatible with any idea of political integration that imputes to all citizens the presupposition of a normative background consensus.

One promising route to a multi-dimensional concept of reason that is no longer exclusively fixated on its reference to the objective world but becomes self-critically aware of its boundaries is to reconstruct the history of its own genesis. In this respect post-metaphysical thought does not restrict itself to the heritage of Western metaphysics. At the same time, it also makes sure of its internal relationship to those world religions whose origins, like the origins of Classical Greek philosophy, date back to the middle of the first millennium before Christ—in other words to what Jaspers termed the 'Axis Age'. The religions which have their roots in this period achieved the cognitive leap from mythical narratives to a logos that differentiates between essence and appearance in a very similar way as did Greek philosophy. And in the course of the 'Hellenization of Christianity', philosophy in turn took on board and assimilated many religious motifs and concepts, specifically those from the history of salvation.[47]

The complex web of inheritance cannot be understood solely along the line of a history of Being, as Heidegger claimed.[48] Greek concepts such as 'autonomy' and 'individuality' or Roman concepts such as 'emancipation' and 'solidarity' have long since been shot through with meanings of a Judeo-Christian origin.[49] Philosophy has recurrently found in its encounters with religious traditions, and they include Muslim traditions as well, that it receives innovative stimulation if it succeeds in liberating the cognitive substance from its dogmatic encapsulation in the melting pot of rational discourse. Kant and Hegel are the best examples of this. And further evidence provides the encounter of prominent philosophers of the 20th century with a religious writer such as Kierkegaard, who thinks in a post-metaphysical, but not a post-Christian vein.

Some religious traditions would appear, even if they at times take the stage as the opaque Other of reason, to have remained present in a more vital manner than has metaphysics. It would not be reasonable to reject out of hand the idea that the world religions—as the only remaining element of the distant cultures of the Old Empires—assert a place for themselves in the differentiated architecture of Modernity because their cognitive substance has not yet waned. We cannot at any rate exclude the thought that they still bear a semantic potential that unleashes an inspiring energy for *all of* society as soon as they release their profane truth content.

In short, post-metaphysical thought is prepared to learn from religion, but remains agnostic in the process. It insists on the difference between the certainties of faith, on the one hand, and validity claims that can be publicly criticized, on the other; but it refrains from the rationalist presumption that it can itself decide what part of the religious doctrines is rational and what part irrational. The contents which reason appropriates through translation must not be lost for faith. However, an apology of faith with philosophical means is not the task of philosophy proper. At best, philosophy *circles* the opaque core of religious experience when reflecting on the intrinsic meaning of faith. This core must remain so abysmally alien to discursive thought as does the core of aesthetic experience, which can likewise only be circled but not penetrated by philosophical reflection.

Post-metaphysical thought's ambivalent attitude to religion corresponds to the epistemic attitude which secular citizens must adopt, if they are to be prepared to learn something from the contributions to public debates made by their religious counterparts, something that can also be expressed in a generally accessible language. The philosophical appropriation of the genealogy of reason appears to play that role for a self-reflection of secularism as the reconstruction work of theology plays for the self-reflection of religious faith. The required work of philosophical reconstruction goes to show that the ethics of democratic citizenship assumes secular citizens exhibit a mentality that is no less demanding than the corresponding mentality of their religious counterparts. This is why the cognitive burdens that both sides have to shoulder in order to acquiring the appropriate epistemic attitudes are by no means asymmetrically distributed.

The fact that the 'public use of reason' (in the interpretation I have given of it) depends on cognitive preconditions which require learning processes has interesting, but ambiguous consequences. It reminds us firstly that that the democratic constitutional state, such as relies on a deliberative form of politics, is an epistemically discerning form of government that is, as it were, truth-sensitive. A 'post-truth democracy', such as the *New York Times* saw on the horizon during the last Presidential elections, would no longer be a democracy. Moreover, the requirement of complex mentalities draws our attention to an improbable functional imperative that the liberal state can hardly meet by employing its own means. The polarization of world views in a community that splits into fundamentalist and secular camps, shows, for example, that an insufficient number of citizens matches up to the yardstick of the public use of reason and thereby endanger political integration. Such mentalities are pre-political in origin, however. They change incrementally and unforeseeably in response to changed conditions of life. A long-term process of this kind gets at best accelerated in the medium of public discourses among the citizens themselves. Yet is this a cumulative cognitive process at all, one that we may describe as a learning process in the first place?

7

A third consequence is most disquieting of all. So far, we have assumed that citizens of a constitutional state can acquire the functionally requisite mentalities by embarking on 'complementary learning processes'. The following consideration shows that this assumption is not unproblematic: From what perspective may we claim that the fragmentation of a political community, if it is caused by a collision of fundamentalist and secularist camps, can be traced back to 'learning deficits'? Let us bring to mind here the change in perspective which we have made when moving from a normative explanation of an ethics of citizenship to an epistemological investigation of the cognitive preconditions for the rational expectation that citizens are able to meet the corresponding obligations. A change in epistemic attitudes must occur for the religious consciousness to become reflective and the secularist consciousness to transcend its limitations. But it is only from the viewpoint of a specific, normatively charged self-understanding of Modernity that we can qualify these mentality changes as complementary 'learning processes'.

Now, this view can of course be defended in the framework of an evolutionary social theory. Quite apart from the controversial position which such theories have within their own academic discipline, from the viewpoint of normative political theory we may at no point impose on citizens our expectation that they describe themselves in terms, for example, of a theory of religious evolution, or even rate themselves as cognitively 'backward'. Only the participants and their religious organizations can resolve the question of whether a 'modernized' faith is still the 'true' faith. And whether or not, on the other side, a scientistically justified form of secularism will not in the end win out against a more comprehensive concept of reason conceived in terms of some post-metaphysical thought is, for the time being, a moot point even among philosophers themselves. However, if political theory must leave it unanswered whether the functionally requisite mentalities can at all be acquired through learning process, then political theorists must accept that a normatively justified concept such as 'the public use of reason' may for good reasons remain 'essentially contested' among citizens themselves. For the liberal state is allowed to confront its citizens only with duties which the latter can perceive as reasonable expectations; this will be the case only if the necessary epistemic attitudes are in turn acquired from insight, i.e. through 'learning'.

We must not be misled into drawing the wrong conclusions from this self-limitation of political theory. As philosophers and as citizens, we can well be convinced that a strong reading of the liberal and republican foundations of the constitutional state should *and can* be successfully defended both intra muros and in the political arena. However, this discourse on whether a liberal constitution and an ethics of democratic citizenship is correct and we have the right understanding of it inevitably leads us into a terrain where the normative arguments no longer suffice. The controversy also extends to the epistemological question of the relationship between faith and knowledge, which itself touches on key elements of Modernity's background understanding of itself. Interestingly enough both the philosophical and the theological efforts to define the relationship between faith and knowledge generate far-reaching questions as to the genealogy of Modernity.

Let us return to Rawls's question: 'How is it possible for those of faith, as well as the nonreligious, to endorse a secular regime even when their comprehensive doctrines may not prosper under it, and indeed may decline?'[50] In the final analysis, the question cannot be answered just by reference to the normative explanations of political theory. Let us take the example of 'radical orthodoxy',[51] an approach that takes up the intentions and fundamental ideas of the political theology of a Carl Schmitt and develops them with the tools of deconstruction. If theologians of this ilk deny Modernity any intrinsic right[52] with the intention to once again give a nominalistically uprooted Modern world ontological anchors in the 'reality of God', then the debate has to be conducted on the respective opponent's playing field. In other words, theological propositions can only be countered by theological arguments, and historical or epistemological propositions by historical and epistemological arguments.[53]

The same applies to the opposite side. Rawls's question is leveled equally at both the religious and the secular sides. A differentiated debate on fundamental philosophical issues is most certainly necessary if a naturalist world view overdraws the account of scientific knowledge in the proper sense. There can be no deriving the public demand that religious communities must now at long last cast aside the traditional statements on the existence of God and or an eternal after-life from recent neurological insights into the dependence of all mental operations on brain processes, not that is until we have clarified, from the philosophical point of view, the pragmatic meaning such Biblical statements assume in the context of the doctrine and practice of religious communities.[54] The question as to how from this angle science relates to religious doctrine again touches on the genealogy of Modernity's self-understanding. Is modern science a practice that is completely understandable in its own terms, establishing the measure of all truths and falsehoods? Or should modern science rather be construed as resulting from a history of reason that includes the world religions?

Rawls developed his 'Theory of Justice' into 'Political Liberalism' because he increasingly recognized the immeasurable relevance of the 'fact of pluralism'. He did posterity a great service in thinking at an early date about the political role of religion. Yet precisely these phenomena should have made a supposedly 'free-standing' political theory aware of the limits of normative arguments. After all, whether the liberal response to religious pluralism can be accepted by the citizens themselves as the single right answer depends not least on whether secular and religious citizens, each from their own respective angle, are prepared to embark on an interpretation of the relationship of faith and knowledge that first enables them to behave in a self-reflexive manner toward each other in the political public sphere.[55]

Jürgen Habermas
Johann-Wolfgang-Goethe Universität
Grüneburgplatz 1
D 60629 Frankfurt/M
Germany

Translated by Jeremy Gaines
First published in English as chapter 5 of *Between Naturalism and Religion* (Cambridge: Polity Press, 2006). Originally published in *Zurischen Naturalismus und Religion* (Frankfurt: Suhrkamp Verlag, 2005).

NOTES

1 Cf. Berger (ed.) 1999.
2 Cf. Buruma and Margalit 2004.
3 Cf Norris and Inglehart 2004: Ch.4.
4 Cf. Habermas 2004.
5 Norris and Inglehart 2004: Ch. 10 defend the classical hypothesis that secularization wins out to the extent that along with improved economic and social conditions for life it also spreads the feeling of 'existential security'. Alongside the demographic assumption

that fertility rates in developed societies are falling, this hypothesis initially explains why secularization today has all in all only seized root in the 'West'. The United States forms an exception, mainly because of two facts. First of all a rather blunt kind of capitalism has effects which are less cushioned by a welfare state and thus exposes the population on average to a higher degree of existential uncertainty. And second the comparatively high rate of immigration from traditional societies where the fertility rates are correspondingly high explains the stability of the relatively large proportion of religious citizens.

[6] Wills 2004.

[7] Goodstein and Yardley 2004. Bush was voted for by 60% of the Spanish-speaking voters, by 67% of the white Protestants, and by 78% of the Evangelical or Born-Again Christians. Even among the Catholics, who previously tended to vote Democrat, Bush turned the traditional majorities around. The fact that the Catholic bishops took sides is astonishing, for all the concurrence on the question of abortion, if we bear in mind that unlike the Church the administration defends the death penalty and put the lives of tens of thousands of US soldiers and Iraqi civilians at risk for a war of aggression that violated international law for which it could only cite dubious reasons.

[8] On this 'concept of respect' see the wide-ranging historical and yet systematically convincing study in Forst 2003.

[9] Rawls 1971: §§ 33f.

[10] On the concept of tolerance as reciprocal respect see Forst 2003.

[11] See Habermas 1996: Ch. 3.

[12] See Rawls 1997: 769: 'Ideally citizens are to think of themselves as if they were legislators and ask themselves what statutes, supported by what reasons satisfying the principle of reciprocity, they would think it most reasonable to enact.'

[13] Rawls 1993: 217.

[14] Rawls speaks of a 'family of liberal conceptions of justice' to which the use of public reason can refer when interpreting constitutional principles; see Rawls 1997: 773f.

[15] Rawls 1997: 786.

[16] For a specification of the demand for reasons in a 'generally accessible' language see Forst 1994: 199–209.

[17] Rawls 1997: 783f. (my italics). This amounts to a revision of the more narrowly formulated principle in Rawls 1994: p. 224f. Rawls confines the proviso to key issues relating to 'constitutional essentials'; I consider this reservation unrealistic with regard to modern legal systems in which basic rights in both, legislation and adjudication apply immediately to specific statutes so that almost all controversial legal issues can be redefined such as to become issues of principle.

[18] Rawls 1997: 777: 'They are not puppets manipulated from behind the scenes by comprehensive doctrines'.

[19] Rawls 1997: 781. I shall return to this objection later.

[20] See the debate between Robert Audi and Nicholas Wolterstorff in Audi and Wolterstorff 1997: 3f., 76f. and 167f.

[21] Cf. Birnbaum 2002.

[22] See the influential study by Bellah, Madsen, Sullivan, Swidler and Tipton 1985.On Bellah's decisive publications in this field see the festschrift: Madson, Sullivan, Swindler and Tipton (eds.) 2003.

[23] On this empirical argument see Weithman 2002: 91: 'I argued that churches contribute to democracy in the United States by fostering realized democratic citizenship. They encourage their members to accept democratic values as the basis for important political decisions and to accept democratic institutions as legitimate. The means by which

they make their contributions, including their own interventions in civic argument and public political debate, affect the political arguments their members may be inclined to use, the basis on which they vote, and the specification of their citizenship with which they identify. They may encourage their members to think of themselves as bound by antecedently given moral norms with which political outcomes must be consistent. The realization of citizenship by those who are legally entitled to take part in political decision-making is an enormous achievement for a liberal democracy, one in which the institutions of civil society play a crucial role'.

24 Audi and Wolterstorff 1997: 25

25 Audi and Wolterstorff 1997: 29

26 This distinction also prompts Paul Weithman to differentiate the argument in line with his modified proviso; see Weithman 2002: 3.

27 Meanwhile, Robert Audi has introduced a counterpart to the principle of secular justification: 'In liberal democracies, religious citizens have a prima facie obligation not to advocate or support any law or public policy that restricts human conduct, unless they have, and are willing to offer, adequately religiously acceptable reasons for this advocacy or support' (Audi 2005: 217). This principle of religious justification is evidently meant to impose an act of critical self-scrutiny on citizens who are informed in their thinking by religious reasons.

28 On the Augustinian distinction of *fides quae creditur* and *fides qua creditur* see R. Bultmann 1984: 185 ff.

29 Wolterstorff in Audi and Wolterstorff 1997: 105.

30 Weithmann 2002: 157.

31 This brings us to the interesting question of the extent to which during an election campaign candidates may confess or indicate that they are religious persons. The principle of separation of church and state certainly extends to the platform, the manifesto, or the 'line', which political parties and their candidates promise to realize. Seen normatively, electoral decisions that boil down to a question of personality instead of programmatic issues are problematic anyway. And it is all the more problematic if the voters take their cue from candidates' religious self-presentations. See on this point the ideas elaborated by Weithman 2002: 117–20: 'It would be good to have principles saying what role religion can play when candidates are assessed for what we might call their "expressive value"—their fittingness to express the values of their constituencies....What is most important to remember about these cases, however, is that elections should not be decided nor votes cast entirely or primarily on the basis of various candidates' expressive value'.

32 Schmidt 2001.

33 Schmidt bases his objection on Gaus 1966.

34 Incidentally, this special status prohibits an assimilation of religious convictions to ethical conceptions, as proposed by Forst (1994: 152–61) who, from the perspective of normative political theory, gives the difference between religious and secular reasons a backseat to the precedence of procedural over substantive criteria of justification. Only from competing religious beliefs do we know a fortiori that a justified consensus cannot be reached. In his latest book Forst (2002: 644–47) recognizes the special status of this category of beliefs.

35 Habermas 2003: 256ff.

36 Weithman 2002: 3: 'Citizens of a liberal democracy may offer arguments in public political debate which depend on reasons drawn from their comprehensive moral views, including their religious views, without making them good by appeal to other arguments—provided they believe that their government would be justified in adopting

the measures they favor and are prepared to indicate what they think would justify the adoption of the measures'.

37 Habermas 1991.

38 Weithman 2002: 121 (my italics).

39 Audi and Wolterstorff 1997: 117f.

40 Rawls 1994: 137: 'Our exercise of political power is fully proper only when it is exercised in accordance with a constitution the essentials of which all citizens as free and equal may reasonably be expected to endorse in the light of principles and ideals acceptable to their common human reason'.

41 Wolterstorff 1997: 160.

42 I have my correspondence with Thomas M. Schmidt to thank for the characterization of a philosophy of religion that is not pursued from the agnostic side: it aims at religion's self-enlightenment, but does not speak, like theology, 'in the name of' religious revelation, nor just as 'its observer'. See also Lutz-Bachmann 2000. On the Protestant side, Friedrich Schleiermacher played an exemplary role. He carefully distinguished between the role of the theologian and that of the apologetic philosopher of religion (who did not rely on the Aquinian tradition but instead on Kant's transcendental idealism) and combined both in his own person. See the introduction to his explication of the Christian doctrine in Schleiermacher 1830–1: §§ 1–10.

43 In this sense, Forst (1994: 158) likewise speaks of 'translation' when he demands that 'a person must be able to make a (gradual) *translation* [his emphasis] of his/her arguments into reasons that are acceptable on the basis of the values and principles of public reason'. However, he considers translation not as a joint venture in the search for truth, in which secular citizens should take part even if the other side restricts itself to religious statements. Forst formulates the demand the way Rawls and Audi do, as a civic duty for the religious person, too. Incidentally, the purely procedural definition of the act of translation with a view to a 'unrestricted reciprocal justification' does not do justice to the semantic problem of transposing the contents of religious speech into a post-religious and post-metaphysical form of representation. As a result, the difference between ethical and religious discourse gets lost. See, for example, Arens 1982,who interprets Biblical metaphors as innovative speech acts.

44 In his masterful study of the history of the notion of tolerance, Rainer Forst termed Pierre Bayle the 'greatest thinker on tolerance' because Bayle provides in exemplary fashion such a reflexive self-limitation of reason in relation to religion. On Bayle see Forst 2003: § 18 as well as §§ 29 and 33 on the systematic argument.

45 Wolterstorff draws our attention to an all too often blurred distinction between secular reasons, that are meant to count, and secular world views, that like all comprehensive doctrines are not meant to count. See Audi and Wolterstorff 1997: 105: 'Much if not most of the time we will be able to spot religious reasons from a mile away… Typically, however, comprehensive secular perspectives will go undetected'.

46 Geyer (ed.) 2004; Pauen 2004.

47 Lutz-Bachmann 1992.

48 See the sketches to a history of Being in Heidegger 1989.

49 See the interesting discussions in Brunkhorst 2002: 40–78.

50 See footnote 19.

51 Milbank 1990; Milbank, Pickstock, and Ward (eds.) 1999.

52 On the opposite position see the early work of Hans Blumenberg (1985).

53 Schmidt 2005.

54 See the final comment by W. Detel in his marvelously informed article Detel 2004.

[55] My thanks go to Rainer Forst and Thomas M. Schmidt for their insightful comments, both of whom have already published several instructive works on this theme. I am also grateful to Melissa Yates for useful references and stimulating discussions.

REFERENCES

Arens, E. (1982), *Kommunikative Handlungen*. Düsseldorf: Patmos Verlag.

Audi, R. and Wolterstorff, N. (1997), *Religion in the Public Sphere*. New York: Rowman and Littlefield.

Audi, R. (2005), 'Moral Foundations of Liberal Democracy, Secular Reasons, and Liberal Neutrality Toward the Good', *Notre Dame Journal of Law, Ethics, & Public Policy*, 19: 197–218.

Bellah, R., Madsen, R., Sullivan, W. M., Swidler, A. and Tipton, S. M. (1985). *Habits of the Heart*. Berkeley. First published in English as chapter 5 of *Between Naturalism and Religion* (Cambridge: Polity Press, 2006). Originally published in Zurischen Naturalismus and Religion (Frankfurt: Suhrkamp Verlag, 2005): University of California Press.

Berger, P. L. (ed.) (1999), *The Desecularization of the World*. Washington, DC: Ethics and Public Policy Center.

Birnbaum, N. (2002), *After Progress*. Oxford: Oxford University Press.

Blumenberg, H. (1985), *Legitimacy of the Modern Age*, tr. Wallace R. M. Cambridge, MA: MIT Press.

Brunkhorst, H. (2002), *Solidarität*. Frankfurt/Main: Suhrkamp.

Bultmann, R. (1984). *Theologische Enzyklopädie*, Annex 3: *Wahrheit und Gewissheit*. Tübingen: Mohr Siebeck.

Buruma, I. and Margalit, A. (2004), *Occidentalism. The West in the Eyes of its Enemies*. Harmondsworth: Penguin.

Detel, W. (2004), 'Forschungen über Hirn und Geist', *Deutsche Zeitschrift für Philosophie*, 6: 891–920.

Forst, R. (1994), *Kontexte der Gerechtigkeit*. Frankfurt/Main: Suhrkamp.

—— (2003), *Toleranz im Konflikt*. Frankfurt/Main: Suhrkamp.

Gaus, G. F. (1966), *Justificatory Liberalism*. New York: Oxford University Press.

Geyer, C. (ed.) (2004), *Hirnforschung und Willensfreiheit*. Frankfurt/Main: Suhrkamp.

Goodstein, L. and Yardley, W. (2004). 'President Bush Benefits from Efforts to Build a Coalition of Religious Voters', *New York Times*, Nov. 5, 2004, A 19.

Habermas, J. (1996), *Between Facts and Norms*, tr. Rehg William. Cambridge, MA: MIT.

—— (1991), 'Vom pragmatischen, ethischen und moralischen Gebrauch der praktischen Vernunft, Abschnitt IV', in his *Erläuterungen zur Diskursethik*. Frankfurt/Main: Suhrkamp, 112–5.

—— (2003), 'Glauben und Wissen, in his *Zeitdiagnosen*. Frankfurt/Main: Suhrkamp, 249–263.

—— (2004), *Der gespaltene Westen*. Frankfurt/Main: Suhrkamp.

Heidegger, M. (1989), *Beiträge zur Philosophie (Vom Ereignis)*. Frankfurt/Main: Klostermann.

Lutz-Bachmann, M. (1992), 'Hellenisierung des Christentums?', in C. Colpe, L. Honnefelder and M. Lutz-Bachmann (eds.), *Spätantike und Christentum*. Berlin: Wiley, pp. 77–98.

—— (2002), 'Religion-Philosophie-Religionsphilosophie', in M. Jung, M. Moxter and T. M. Schmit (eds.), *Religionsphilosophie*. Würzburg: Echter, 19–26.

Madson, R., Sullivan, W. M., Swindler, A. and Tipton, S. M. (eds.), *Meaning and Modernity: Religion, Polity, and Self*. Berkeley, CA: University of California Press.
Milbank, J. (1990), *Theology and Social Theory: Beyond Secular Reason*. Oxford: Oxford University Press.
Milbank, J., Pickstock, C and Ward, G. (eds.) (1999), *Radical Orthodoxy*. London and New York: Routledge.
Norris, P. and Inglehart, R. (2004), *Sacred and Secular, Religion and Politics Worldwide*. Cambridge: Cambridge University Press.
Pauen, M. (2004), *Illusion Freiheit?* Frankfurt/Main: Fischer Verlag.
Rawls, J. (1971), *A Theory of Justice*. Cambridge, Mass: Harvard University Press.
—— (1993), *Political Liberalism*. New York: Columbia University Press.
—— (1997), 'The Idea of Public Reason Revisited', *The University of Chicago Law Review*, 64: 765–807.
Schleiermacher, F. (1830–1). *Der christliche Glaube*; reprinted Berlin: De Gruyter, 1999.
Schmidt, T. M. (2001), 'Glaubensüberzeugungen und säkulare Grunde', *Zeitschrift für Evangelische Ethik*, 4: 248–61.
—— (2005), 'Postsäkulare Theologie des Rechts. Eine Kritik der radikalen Orthodoxie', in M. Frühauf and W. Löser (eds.), *Biblische Aufklärung—die Entdeckung einer Tradition*. Frankfurt/Main: Knecht, 91–108.
Weithman, P. J. (2002), *Religion and the Obligations of Citizenship*. Cambridge: Cambridge University Press.
Wills, G. (2004). 'The Day the Enlightenment Went Out', *New York Times*, Nov. 4/2004, A 31.

[2]

The Meaning of Secularism[1]

Charles Taylor

1

It is generally agreed that modern democracies have to be "secular." There is perhaps a problem, a certain ethnocentricity, involved in this term. But even in the Western context the term is not limpid and may in fact be misleading. What in fact does it mean? There are at least two models of what constitutes a secular regime. Both involve some kind of separation of church and state. The state can't be officially linked to some religious confession, except in a vestigial and largely symbolic sense, as in England or Scandinavia. But secularism requires more than this. The pluralism of society requires that there be some kind of neutrality, or "principled distance," to use Rajeev Bhargava's term.[2]

If we examine it further, secularism involves in fact a complex requirement. There is more than one good sought here. We can single out three, which we can classify in the categories of the French Revolution trinity: liberty, equality, fraternity. First, no one must be forced in the domain of religion, or basic belief. This is what is often defined as religious liberty, including of course, the freedom not to believe. This is what is also described as the "free exercise" of religion, in the terms of the U.S. First Amendment. Second, there must be equality between people of different faiths or basic beliefs; no religious outlook or (religious or areligious) *Weltanschauung* can enjoy a privileged status, let alone be adopted as the official view of the state. Third, all spiritual families must be heard, included in the ongoing process of determining what the society is about (its political identity) and how it is going to realize these goals (the exact regime of rights and privileges). This (stretching the point a little) is what corresponds to "fraternity."

These goals can, of course, conflict; sometimes we have to balance the goods involved. Moreover, we might add a fourth goal: that we try as much as possible to maintain relations of harmony and comity between the supporters of different religions and *Weltanschauungen*. (Maybe this is what really deserves to be called "fraternity," but

Charles Taylor is Professor Emeritus of Philosophy at McGill University. His most recent books are *Modern Social Imaginaries* and *A Secular Age*.

A "Marianne" bust, the symbol of the French Republic, is displayed in the town hall council room in Nice, November 18, 2009. The bust of Marianne represents former French actress Brigitte Bardot and the slogan reads "French Republic, Liberty, Equality, Fraternity."

I am still attached to the neatness of the above schema, with only the three traditional goods.)

Sometimes the claim seems to be made, on behalf of one or another definition of secularism, that it can resolve the question of how to realize these goals in the domain of timeless principles, and that no further input or negotiation is required to define them for our society now. The basis for these principles can be found in reason alone, or in some outlook which is itself free from religion, purely *laïque*. Jacobins are on this wavelength, as was the early John Rawls.

The problem with this is that there is no such set of timeless principles that can be determined, at least in the detail they must be for a given political system, by pure reason alone, and situations differ very much and require different kinds of concrete realization of agreed general principles, so that some degree of working out is necessary in each situation. It follows that dictating the principles from some supposedly higher authority above the fray violates the good of fraternity, that is, the idea that all spiritual families must be heard. It deprives certain spiritual families of a voice in this working out. And, therefore, this leaves us very often with difficult conflicts and dilemmas between our basic goals.

The issues concerning secularism have evolved in different Western societies in recent decades because the faiths represented in those societies have changed. We need to alter the way in which we proceed when the range of religions or basic philosophies expands: for example, the arrival of substantive communities of Muslims in contemporary Europe and the U.S. and the recent legislation in France against wearing the *hijab* in schools. Normally, this kind of thing needs to be negotiated. Of course, sometimes this is not possible; certain basic laws have to be observed. But the general principle is that religious groups must be seen as much as interlocutors and as little as menace as the situation allows.

These groups also evolve if they're in a process of redefinition of this kind in a democratic, liberal context. José Casanova has pointed out how American Catholicism was originally targeted in the nineteenth century as inassimilable to democratic mores, in ways very analogous to the suspicions that nag people over Islam today. The subsequent history has shown how American Catholicism evolved, and in the process changed world Catholicism in significant ways. There is no reason written into the essence of things why a similar evolution cannot take place in Muslim communities.[3] If this doesn't happen, it will in all likelihood be because of prejudice and bad management.

Indeed, the point of state neutrality is precisely to avoid favoring or disfavoring not just religious positions, but any basic position, religious or nonreligious. We can't favor Christianity over Islam, but also we can't favor religion over against nonbelief in religion, or vice versa.

One of our basic difficulties in dealing with these problems is that we have the wrong model, which has a continuing hold on our minds. We think that secularism (or *laïcité*) has to do with the relation of the state and religion, whereas in fact it has to do with the (correct) response of the democratic state to diversity. If we look at the three goals above, they have in common that they are concerned with protecting people in their belonging and/or practice of whatever outlook they choose or find themselves in; treating people equally whatever their option; and giving them all a hearing. There is no reason to single out religious (as against nonreligious), "secular" (in another widely used sense), or atheist viewpoints. Indeed, the point of state neutrality is precisely to avoid favoring or disfavoring not just religious positions, but any basic position, religious or nonreligious. We can't favor Christianity over Islam, but also we can't favor religion over against nonbelief in religion, or vice versa.

The late-Rawlsian formulation for a secular state cleaves very strongly to certain political principles: human rights, equality, the rule of law, democracy. These are the very basis of the state, which must support them. But this political ethic can be and is shared by people of very different basic outlooks (what Rawls calls "comprehensive views of the good"). A Kantian will justify the rights to life and freedom by pointing to the dignity of rational agency; a Utilitarian will speak of the necessity to treat beings who can experience joy and suffering in such a way as to maximize the first and minimize the second; and a Christian will speak of humans as made in the image of God. They concur on the principles, but differ on the deeper reasons for holding to this ethic. The state must uphold the ethic, but must refrain from favoring any of the deeper reasons.

2

The idea that secularism makes a special case of religion arises from the history of its coming to be in the West (as does, indeed, the name). To put it briefly, there are two important founding contexts for this kind of regime, the U.S. and France. In the U.S. case, the whole range of comprehensive views, or deeper reasons, were in the original case variants of (Protestant) Christianity, stretching to a smattering of Deists. Subsequent history has widened the palette of views beyond Christianity, and then beyond religion. But in the original case, the positions between which the state was to be neutral were all religious. Hence the First Amendment: Congress shall pass no law establishing religion or impeding the free exercise thereof.

The word "secularism" didn't appear in the early decades of American public life, but this was the sign that a basic problem had not yet been faced. Because the First Amendment concerned the separation of church and state, it opened the possibility of giving a place to religion that no one would accept today. Thus in the 1830s, a judge of the Supreme Court could argue that while the First Amendment forbade the identification of the federal government with any church, since all the churches were Christian (and in effect Protestant), one could invoke the principles of Christianity in interpreting the law. For Judge Joseph Story, the goal of the First Amendment was "to exclude all rivalry among Christian sects," but nevertheless "Christianity ought to receive encouragement from the state." Christianity was essential to the state because the belief in "a future state of rewards and punishments" is "indispensable to the administration of justice." What is more, "it is impossible for those who believe in the truth of Christianity, as a divine revelation, to doubt, that it is a special duty of government to foster, and encourage it among the citizens."[4]

This primacy of Christianity was upheld even later in the nineteenth century. As late as 1890, 37 of the 42 existing states recognized the authority of God in the preambles or texts of their constitutions. A unanimous judgment of the Supreme Court of 1892 declared that if one wanted to describe "American life as expressed by its laws, its business, its customs and its society, we find everywhere a clear recognition of the same truth...that this is a Christian nation."[5] In the latter part of the century, resistance began to build to this conception, but a National Reform Association (NRA) was founded in 1863 with the following goal:

> The object of this Society shall be to maintain existing Christian features in the American Government...to secure such an amendment to the Constitution of the United States as will declare the nation's allegiance to Jesus Christ and its acceptance of the moral laws of the Christian religion, and so indicate that this is a Christian nation, and place all the Christian laws, institutions and usages of our government on an undeniable legal basis in the fundamental law of the land.[6]

After 1870, the battle was joined between the supporters of this narrow view, on one hand, and those who wanted a real opening to all other religions and also to nonreligion. The latter included not only Jews, but also Catholics who (rightly) saw the "Christianity" of the NRA as excluding them. It was in this battle that the word "secular" first appeared on the American scene as a key term, and very often in its polemical sense of non- or antireligious.[7]

In the French case, *laïcité* came about in a struggle *against* a powerful church. The strong temptation was for the state itself to stand on a moral basis independent from religion. Marcel Gauchet shows how Charles Renouvier laid the grounds for the outlook of the Third Republic radicals in their battle against the church. The state has to be "*moral et enseignant*" [moral and instructive]. It has "*charge d'âmes aussi bien que toute Église ou communauté, mais à titre plus universel*" [responsibility for souls as well as the whole church and community, but with a more universal scope]. Morality is the key criterion. In order not to be under the church, the state must have "*une morale indépendante de toute religion*" [a morality independent of all religion] and enjoy a "*suprématie morale*" [moral supremacy] in relation to all religions. The basis of this morality is liberty. In order to hold its own before religion, the morality underlying the state has to be based on more than just utility or feeling; it needs a real "*théologie rationnelle*" [rational theology] like that of Kant.[8] The wisdom of Jules Ferry, and later of Aristide Briand and Jean Jaurez, saved France at the time of the Separation (1905) from such a lopsided regime, but the notion stuck that *laïcité* was all about controlling and managing religion.

> *If we... look at the kinds of societies in which we are now living in the West, the first feature that strikes us is the wide diversity, not only of religious views, but also of those which involve no religion, not to speak of those which are unclassifiable in this dichotomy.*

If we move, however, beyond such originating contexts and look at the kinds of societies in which we are now living in the West, the first feature that strikes us is the wide diversity, not only of religious views, but also of those which involve no religion, not to speak of those which are unclassifiable in this dichotomy. The goals of liberty, equality, and fraternity require that we treat all of these even-handedly.

3

This fixation on religion is complex, and it is bound up with two other features we often find in the debates on secularism: the first is the tendency to define secularism or *laïcité* in terms of some institutional arrangement, rather than starting from the goals I proposed above. And so you hear mantra-type formulae, like "the separation of church and state," or the necessity of removing religion from public space ("*les espaces de la République*" [the spaces of the Republic] as in the recent French debate). The second follows from the first, or may easily seem to. If the whole matter is defined by one institutional formula, then one must just determine which arrangement of things best meets this formula, and there is no need to think further. One cannot find oneself in a dilemma, as will easily happen if one is pursuing more than one goal, because here there is just one master formula.

Muslim women wearing Islamic headscarves demonstrate in the streets of Marseille to protest against a looming ban on headscarves in French state schools, January 17, 2004. The French government planned to submit to parliament a draft law banning religious symbols such as Islamic headscarves, Jewish skullcaps, and large Christian crosses from state schools. The banner reads "Equality, Fraternity."

Hence one often hears these mantras employed as argument-stoppers, the ultimate decisive response which annuls all objections. In the U.S., people invoke the "Wall of Separation" as the ultimate criterion, and hyper-Republicans in France cite *laïcité* as the final word. (Of course, if one consulted the First Amendment of the U.S. Constitution, one would find two goals mentioned, the rejection of establishment and the assurance of "free exercise." It is not inconceivable that these could conflict.)

This kind of move amounts, from the standpoint I am adopting here, to a fetishization of the favored institutional arrangements, whereas one should start from the goals and derive the concrete arrangements from these. It is not that some separation of church and state, some mutual autonomy of governing and religious institutions, will not be an inescapable feature of any secularist regime, and the same goes for the neutrality of the public institutions. These are both indispensable, but what these requirements mean in practice ought to be determined by how we can maximize our three (or four) basic goals.

Take for example the wearing of the *hijab* by Muslim women in public schools, which has been a hot issue in a number of Western democracies. In France, pupils in public schools were famously forbidden the headscarf, seen as a "*signe religieux ostentatoire*" [an ostentatious religious sign] according to the notorious Loi Stasi of 2004. In certain German states, pupils can wear it, but not teachers. In the UK and other countries, there is no general interdict, but the individual schools can decide.

What are the reasons for this variation? Plainly in all these cases, legislators and administrators were trying to balance two goals. One was the maintenance of neutrality in public institutions seen (rightly) as an essential entailment of equality between all basic beliefs. The other was ensuring the maximum possible religious liberty, or in its most general form, liberty of conscience. The goal of equality seems to push us towards permitting the *hijab* anywhere. But various arguments were made to override this in the French and German cases. For the Germans, what was disturbing was that someone in authority in a public institution should be religiously marked, as it were. In the French case, an attempt was made to cast doubt on the proposition that wearing the *hijab* was a free act. There were dark suggestions that the girls were being forced by their families, or by their male peers, to adopt this dress code. That argument was frequently used, however dubious it might appear in the light of the sociological research carried out among the pupils themselves, but the Stasi Commission largely ignored it.

For the people to be sovereign, they need to form an entity and have a personality.

The other main argument was that wearing the headscarf in school was less an act of piety than a statement of hostility against the Republic and its essential institution of *laïcité*. This was the meaning behind the introduction of the concept of "*signe ostentatoire*" [ostentatious sign]. A smaller discrete sign would be no problem argued the Stasi Commission, but these attention-grabbing features of dress were meant to make a highly controversial statement. It was in vain that Muslim women protested that "*le foulard n'est pas un signe*" ["the headscarf is not a sign"].

On one level, these different national answers to the same question reflect different takes on how to balance the two main goals of a secular regime. But on another level, the dilemma and its resolution remain hidden under the illusion that there is only one principle here, say, *laïcité* and its corollary of the neutrality of public institutions or spaces, that it's just a matter of applying an essential feature of our republican regime, and that there is no need or place for choice or the weighing of different aims.

Perhaps the most pernicious feature of this fetishization is that it tends to hide from view the real dilemmas that we encounter in this realm, and that leap into view once we recognize the plurality of principles at stake.

4

This fetishization reflects a deep feature of life in modern democracies. We can see why as soon as we ponder what is involved in self-government, what is implied in the basic mode of legitimation of states that are founded on popular sovereignty. For the people to be sovereign, they need to form an entity and have a personality.

The revolutions that ushered in regimes of popular sovereignty transferred the ruling power from a king onto a "nation," or a "people." In the process, they invented a new kind of collective agency. These terms existed before, but the thing they now indicated, this new kind of agency, was something unprecedented, at least in the immediate context of early modern Europe. Thus the notion "people" could certainly be applied to the ensemble of subjects of the kingdom, or to the nonelite strata of society, but prior to the turnover, it hadn't indicated an entity that could decide and act together, to whom one could attribute a will.

But for people to act together, in other words, to deliberate in order to form a common will on which they will act, requires a high degree of common commitment, a sense of common identification. A society of this kind presupposes trust, the basic trust that members and constituent groups have to have, the confidence that they are really part of the process, that they will be listened to and their views taken account of by the others. Without this mutual commitment, this trust will be fatally eroded.

And so we have in the modern age a new kind of collective agency. It is one with which its members identify, typically as the realization/bulwark of their freedom and/or the locus of their national/cultural expression (or most often, some combination of the two). Of course, in premodern societies, too, people often "identified" with the regime, sacred kings, or hierarchical orders; they were often willing subjects. But in the democratic age, we identify as free agents. That is why the notion of popular will plays a crucial role in the legitimating idea.

This means that the modern democratic state has generally accepted common purposes, or reference points, the features whereby it can lay claim to being the bulwark of freedom and locus of expression of its citizens. Whether or not these claims are actually founded, the state must be so imagined by its citizens if it is to be legitimate.

Democracy obliges us to show much more solidarity and much more commitment to one another in our joint political project than was demanded by the hierarchical and authoritarian societies of yesteryear.

So questions can arise for the modern state for which there are no analogues in most premodern forms: what/whom is this state for? whose freedom? whose expression? These questions seem to make no sense applied to, say, the Austrian or Turkish Empires—unless one answered the "whom for?" question by referring to the Habsburg or Ottoman dynasties, and this would hardly give you their legitimating ideas.

This is the sense in which a modern state has what I want to call a political identity, defined as the generally accepted answer to the "what/whom for?" question. This is distinct from the identities of its members, that is, from the reference points, many and varied, that define for each of them what is important in their lives. There better be some overlap, of course, if these members are to feel strongly identified with the state, but the identities of individuals and constituent groups will generally be richer and more complex, and often quite different from each other.[9]

In other words, a modern democratic state demands a "people" with a strong collective identity. Democracy obliges us to show much more solidarity and much more commitment to one another in our joint political project than was demanded by the hierarchical and authoritarian societies of yesteryear. In the good old days of the Austro-Hungarian Empire, the Polish peasant in Galicia could be altogether oblivious of the

Hungarian country squire, the bourgeois of Prague, or the Viennese worker, without this in the slightest threatening the stability of the state. On the contrary, this condition of things only becomes untenable when ideas about popular government start to circulate. This is the moment when subgroups that will not, or cannot, be bound together, start to demand their own states. This is the era of nationalism, of the break up of empires.

I have been discussing the political necessity of a strong common identity for modern democratic states in terms of the requirement of forming a people, a deliberative unit. But this is also evident in a number of other ways. Thinkers in the civic humanist tradition, from Aristotle to Arendt, have noted that free societies require a higher level of commitment and participation than despotic or authoritarian ones. Citizens have to do for themselves, as it were, what otherwise the rulers do for them. But this will only happen if these citizens feel a strong bond of identification with their political community, and hence with those who share with them in this.

...contemporary democracies as they progressively diversify will have to undergo redefinitions of their historical identities, which may be far-reaching and painful.

From another angle again, because these societies require strong commitment to do the common work, and because a situation in which some carry the burdens of participation and others just enjoy the benefits would be intolerable, free societies require a high level of mutual trust. In other words, they are extremely vulnerable to mistrust on the part of some citizens in relation to others, that the latter are not really assuming their commitments—for example, that others are not paying their taxes, or are cheating on welfare, or are benefitting as employers from a good labor market without assuming any of the social costs. This kind of mistrust creates extreme tension and threatens to unravel the whole skein of the mores of commitment that democratic societies need to operate. A continuing and constantly renewed mutual commitment is an essential basis for taking the measures needed to renew this trust.

The relation between nation and state is often considered from a unilateral point of view, as if it were always the nation that sought to provide itself with a state, but there is also the opposite process. In order to remain viable, states sometimes seek to create a feeling of common belonging. This is an important theme in the history of Canada, for example. To form a state, in the democratic era, a society is forced to undertake the difficult and never to be completed task of defining its collective identity.

Thus what I have been calling political identity is extremely important in modern democratic states. And this identity is usually defined partly in terms of certain basic principles (democracy, human rights, equality), and partly in terms of their historical, or linguistic, or religious traditions. It is understandable that features of this identity can take on a quasi-sacred status, for to alter or undermine them can seem to threaten the very basis of unity without which a democratic state cannot function.

It is in this context that certain historical institutional arrangements can appear as untouchable. They may appear as an essential part of the basic principles of the regime, but they will also come to be seen as a key component of its historic identity. This is what one sees with *laïcité* as invoked by many French *républicains*. The irony is that in the face of a modern politics of (multicultural) identity, they invoke this principle as a crucial feature of (French) identity. This is unfortunate, but very understandable. It is one illustration of a general truth: that contemporary democracies as they progressively diversify will have to undergo redefinitions of their historical identities, which may be far-reaching and painful.

5

We should see this in the context of the modern understanding of political society. The crucial move that we see in the modern West from the seventeenth century, the move that takes us out of the cosmic religious conceptions of order, establishes a new "bottom-up" view of society, as existing for the protection and mutual benefit of its (equal) members. There is a strong normative view attached to this new conception, which I have called the "modern moral order."[10] It enshrines basically three principles: 1) the rights and liberties of the members, 2) the equality among them (which has of course been variously interpreted, and has mutated towards more radical conceptions over time), and 3) the principle that rule is based on consent (which has also been defended in more and less radical forms).

These basic norms have been worked out in a host of different philosophical anthropologies, and according to very different concepts of human sociability. It very soon transcended the atomism that narrowed the vision of its early formulators, like Locke and Hobbes. But the basic norms remain and are more or less inseparable from modern liberal democracies.

The rejection of cosmic-religious embedding thus was accomplished by a new conception of "the political," a new basic norm, which, as Claude Lefort suggests, involved its own representation of political authority, but one in which the central spot remained paradoxically empty. If the notion of sovereignty is retained, no one person or group can be identified with it.

Democratic societies are organized not necessarily around a "civil religion," as Jean-Jacques Rousseau claimed, but certainly around a strong "philosophy of civility," enshrining the three norms, which in contemporary societies are often expressed as 1) human rights, 2) equality and nondiscrimination, and 3) democracy.

But in certain cases, there can be a civil religion: a religious view incorporating and justifying the philosophy of civility. This was arguably so for the young American republic. It was adopting a form that was clearly part of God's providential plan for mankind ("We hold these truths to be self-evident, that all men are created equal..."). Or it can alternatively be part of a non- or even antireligious ideology, as with the First French Republic. One can even argue that all-englobing views of this kind seem more "natural" to many of our contemporaries. After all, the principles of our civil philosophy seem to call for deeper grounding. If it's very important that we agree on the principles, then surely things are much more stable if we also accept a common grounding. Or so it may appear, and the centuries-long tradition of political life seems to testify for this idea.

For indeed the overlapping consensus between different founding views on a common philosophy of civility is something quite new in history, and relatively untried. It is consequently hazardous. And besides, we often suspect that those with different basic views can't really subscribe to these principles, not the way we do (because, as "we" know, "atheists can't have principles," or as another "we" knows, "religions are all against liberty and /or equality").

The problem is that a really diverse democracy can't revert to a civil religion, or antireligion, however comforting this might be, without betraying its own principles.

The problem is that a really diverse democracy can't revert to a civil religion, or antireligion, however comforting this might be, without betraying its own principles. We are condemned to live in an overlapping consensus.

6

We have seen how this strongly motivated move to fetishize our historical arrangements can prevent us from seeing our secular regime in a more fruitful light, which foregrounds the basic goals we are seeking, and which allows us to recognize and reason about the dilemmas which we face. But this connects to the other main cause of confusion I cited above, our fixation on religion as the problem. In fact, we have moved in many Western countries from an original phase in which secularism was a hard-won achievement warding off some form of religious domination, to a phase of such widespread diversity of basic beliefs, religious and areligious, that only clear focus on the need to balance freedom of conscience and equality of respect can allow us to take the measure of the situation. Otherwise we risk needlessly limiting the religious freedom of immigrant minorities, on the strength of our historic institutional arrangements, while sending a message to these same minorities that they by no means enjoy equal status with the long-established mainstream.

This whole matter deserves much further consideration, more than I can give it here, but I am convinced that this further examination would lend even more credibility to the revisionary ideal I am proposing here, which amounts to this: what deserve to be called "secularist" regimes in contemporary democracy have to be conceived not primarily as bulwarks against religion but as good faith attempts to secure the three (or four) basic goals I outlined above. And this means that they attempt to shape their institutional arrangements, not to remain true to hallowed tradition, but to maximize the basic goals of liberty and equality between basic beliefs.

Endnotes

1 This essay is adapted from Charles Taylor, "The Polysemy of the Secular," *Social Research* 76.4 (Winter 2009): 1,143–1,166; and Charles Taylor, "Foreword. What is Secularism?," *Secularism, Religion and Multicultural Citizenship*, ed. Geoffrey Brahm Levey and Tariq Modood (Cambridge: Cambridge University Press, 2009) xi–xxii.

2 Rajeev Bhargava, "What is Secularism for?," *Secularism and its Critics*, ed. Rajeev Bhargava (Delhi: Oxford University Press, 1998) 486–520 (see especially 493–4 and 520 for "principled distance"); and Rajeev Bhargava, "The Distinctiveness of Indian Secularism," *The Future of Secularism*, ed, T. N. Srinavasan (Delhi: Oxford University Press 2007) 20–58, especially 39–41.

3 See, for example, José Casanova, "Immigration and the New Religious Pluralism: A European Union-United States Comparison," *Secularism, Religion and Multicultural Citizenship*, ed. Geoffrey Brahm Levey and Tariq Modood (Cambridge: Cambridge University Press, 2009) 139–63.

4 Andrew Koppelman, "Rawls and Habermas," private communication.

5 *Church of the Holy Trinity v. United States*, 143 U.S. 457 at 471 (1892).

6 See Article II at <http://candst.tripod.com/nra.htm>.

7 Christian Smith, *The Secular Revolution* (Berkeley: University of California Press, 2003). See also Tisa J. Wenger, "The God-in-the-Constitution Controversy: American Secularisms in Historical Perspective," *Comparative Secularisms in a Global Age*, ed. Linell E. Cady and Elizabeth Shakman Hurd (New York: Palgrave Macmillan, 2010).

8 Marcel Gauchet, *La Religion dans la Démocratie* (Paris: Gallimard 1998) 47–50.

9 I have discussed this relation in "*Les Sources de l'Identité Moderne*," *Les Frontières de l'Identité: Modernité et Postmodernisme au Québec*, ed. Mikhaël Elbaz, Andrée Fortin, and Guy Laforest (Sainte-Foy: Presses de l'Université Laval, 1996) 347–64.

10 See Charles Taylor, *Modern Social Imaginaries* (Durham: Duke, 2004).

[3]

The transformations of the religious dimension and the crystallization of new civilizational visions and relations

S N EISENSTADT

I

A far-reaching resurgence or reconstruction of religions is taking place in the contemporary world. This resurgence is manifest in many ways, including the rise of new religious (especially fundamentalist and communal-national) movements; the crystallization of new diasporas with strong religious identities; profound transformations within the major religions; and the growing importance of religious components in the constitution of contemporary public arenas and in the constitution of collective identities. All these developments have far-reaching implications for the place of religion in the contemporary era, calling into question a basic assumption of public discourse which assumed the weakening and 'privatization' of religions as concomitant with modernization.[1]

Indeed, in the early stages of the crystallization of the post-World War II social and political scene, it seemed as if several aspects of the development of religious organizations and behaviour in modern societies had become predominant, attesting indeed to the continual secularization of modern societies. The most important of these aspects were: first, the growing specialization of the religious sphere in the modern world and its differentiation from other institutional arenas – the religious sphere having become just one institutional and semantic sphere, among many others; second, the weakening or loss of the predominant place of religion in the modern world-view as compared to earlier periods; and third, the growing deritualization both of the central public sphere and of many components of private life, and the weakening of official religious institutions.

Yet, in fact, the picture was much more complex and became even more so during the last quarter of the 20th century. All these developments did not necessarily mean the disappearance of strong transcendental orientations from the cultural and political panorama. Rather, there developed a multiplicity of orientations to the transcendental realm, as well as a very important shift in the focus of the transcendental and utopian orientations predominant in these societies from the constitution of modern centres to more heterogeneous or dispersed arenas, often in various 'multicultural' and 'post-modern' directions.

Nor did religion disappear from the public arenas of their respective societies or from the constitution of collective identities. In fact, religion started to re-enter these arenas – very forcibly. Indeed, one of the most important aspects of the contemporary scene was that of religions, which, relegated or confined in the classical model of the nation-state and revolutionary state to private or secondary public spheres, re-entered the major political and cultural arenas and the central frameworks of collective identities of many societies.

Indeed, one of the most important developments in the constitution of the political arenas and collective identities on the contemporary scene, attendant on the weakening or transformation of the nation and revolutionary states, has been the 'resurgence' of the religious national-ethnic components – their move as it were into the constitution of collective identities and into the centres of national and international political activities.

This resurgence of religion does not involve a simple return of some traditional forms of religion, but rather a far-reaching reconstitution of the religious components which transcends the vision of the 'classical' cultural and political programme of modernity, as well as far-reaching civilizational transformation. This new religious constellation that crystallized during the last two decades of the 20th century was characterized by the paradoxical combination of, first, growing multiplication and privatization of religious orientations and sensibilities; the concomitant enhancement of possibilities of choice, for individuals and groups, between such visions, with utopian orientations becoming focused on the search for some creativity or authenticity within multiple dispersed social settings, connected with a growing trend to much more diversified, 'multicultural' orientations. Second, these new religious constellations were characterized by the weakening of institutionalized religion and of the major official religious institutions and organizations and by the decline in their membership. Third, it was characterized by the resurgence of religious sensibilities and their transformation and transposition into the centres of national and international political activity, and in the constitution of collective identities. Religious identity and practices, which in the classical model of the nation-state were relegated or confined in theory (although much less so in practice) to private or secondary spheres, have been transposed into the public political and cultural arenas, in some cases acquiring central roles in the contemporary national and international public arenas.

These changes in the religious arena were closely connected with far-reaching developments within all the major religions, in all of which the relations between different dimensions or components of religion – the cosmological-transcendental, the institutional-organizational, the structure of religious authority and that of the individual religious sensibility and orientations – have been radically reformulated, as were also their relations to the major political formations, social arenas and the constitution of collective identities. Concomitantly, there developed within most religions a growing emphasis on their inherent authentic universalisms as being independent of or distinct from (even if interwoven with) the universalistic orientations of the cultural programmes of modernity, as promulgated above all in the programme of the Enlightenment and as embodied in the nation- or revolutionary state.

II

One of the most important changes in the contemporary global scene has been the development of transnational, mostly, but not exclusively, religious and/or ethnic virtual associations, communities and networks, among which diasporic communities and networks are most important. The most significant among such diasporic communities and networks are the Muslim one, or ones, especially in Europe and in the USA. Also – though with significant differences – there are the Chinese and possibly Indian and Korean diasporas in East Asia, in the USA and in Europe, as well as Jewish communities, especially in Europe. It is true that diasporic communities such as 'overseas' Chinese or Indian ones have existed for long periods of history – as did, of course, transnational or trans-imperial religions such as the Catholic, 'Orthodox' Christian and Buddhist ones, not to mention the Jewish religious ones. But in the contemporary scene, under the impact of extensive migratory movements accompanying the processes of globalization, a large number of such diasporic networks, communities and organizations – many of them new – have developed. These have also brought about a far-reaching transformation in the constitution of religious communities and their participation in public spheres and in the constitution of collective identities.

In most of these communities orientations to some 'home base' developed, but basically they all went beyond them. There developed within them a strong tendency to deny various local traditions in favour of the new universalistic translocal identities promulgated by them, carried above all by numerous translocal networks. These networks, without the mediation of the 'home' centres or indeed of any single territorial centre or regulative principle, directly connected similar 'ideological' religions and ethnic communities, and entailed new patterns of participation and new decentralized patterns of authority and accountability.[2]

Concomitantly, a resurgence of trans-state religious organizations and encounters occurred, accompanied by a far-reaching shift in the relations and confrontations between religious groups and institutions and the major political and cultural secular institutions.

These developments were closely related to growing contestations between different religious organizations, movements and leaders about the proper interpretation of their basic principles and of their relation to the modern world and about the loci of authority within them.

All these new trans-world communities and networks constituted not only a new organizational or structural element on the contemporary scene, but also important foci for the reconstitution of collective identities and of new civilizational visions and contours. It was these new virtual communities and networks that produced such a fertile ground for processes within the changing intercivilizational scene, above all for highly extensive and intensified 'reactions' to the processes of globalization. Chief amongst these was the reaction to the claims of different major centres of globalization, a reaction that gave rise to multiple and paradoxical 'global' anti-globalization movements and demands. These demands challenge some of the basic premises of the tendency towards global hegemony and attempt to create alternative patterns of modernity and of globalization.[3]

III

Within all these settings new movements appeared, making powerful demands for greater cultural autonomy for the newly emerging local, regional and transnational cultural spaces and conceptions of collective identity. The common denominator of many of these demands has been that they do not see themselves as bound by the strong homogenizing cultural premises of the classical model of the nation and revolutionary state, especially by the places allotted to the religious dimension in the public spheres. These movements make far-reaching claims to redefine citizenship and the rights and entitlements connected with it; to construct new public spaces and to reconstitute the symbols of collective identity promulgated in their respective states. It is not that these movements or sectors do not want to be 'domiciled' in their respective countries. Indeed, part of their struggle is precisely to become domiciled, but on new terms that are far removed from classical models of assimilation. They aim to be recognized in domestic public spheres, and not to be confined only to the private sphere, as culturally distinct groups in the constitution of civil society in relation to the state.

Indeed, even in the period of the presumed hegemony of the pristine model of the modern state, there existed (though often in subdued and subterranean ways) a much greater variety and heterogeneity of collective identities than was presumed in the homogenizing models of the nation-state. Religious (as well as 'cultural' and linguistic) identities and cultural space did not disappear – although they were of course stronger in those societies such as England, where multifaceted patterns of collective identity prevailed, than in societies such as France and the Scandinavian countries with their strong secular homogenizing premises. In other societies, such as imperial Germany, such identities could become foci of political dispute. Moreover, contrary to many implicit liberal assumptions, citizenship was never 'culture-blind' or culturally neutral. Citizenship usually entailed participation in a distinct community or 'nation' and acceptance of at least some of its ways of life and collective identities.

Nevertheless, however strong these identities and ways of life may have been, in the heyday of the nation- and revolutionary states, most of them (with the partial exception of religious identities, especially the Catholic ones and to a lesser extent the Jewish) were effectively marginalized and kept apart from the central public domain or arena. They were relegated to the private domain and at most accepted semi-publicly and in a very limited way. They did not form major components of the central cultural and political programme as it was promulgated by the central socializing agencies of the nation or revolutionary state, such as the educational system, the army and the various mass media (newspapers and popular books, and later radio and television). Above all, these identities did not form the central pivot of the membership that formally defined the nation-state, namely citizenship, and of the various entitlements that depended on it. Similarly, in this period the ideological, cultural and institutional relations between various immigrant communities and their mother countries were, to a very large extent, mediated by the images of the new nation-state and by its model of citizenship that was supposedly based on universalistic homogeneous criteria.

The situation with respect to the place of religion in the constitution of collective identities has indeed greatly changed in the contemporary era. The demands of new movements and new settings went far beyond the 'original' premises of the nation- and revolutionary state. These demands called for far-reaching changes in the constitution of collective identities and of political arenas and activities. They entailed the transposition of most of these hitherto 'subdued' identities – albeit, of course, in a highly reconstructed way – into the centres of their respective societies and into international arenas. Here they would contest the hegemony of the older homogenizing programmes of modernity and claim their own autonomous places in the central symbolic and institutional spaces of their respective societies, whether in educational programmes, in public communications or in the media. Very often they also made far-reaching claims with respect to the redefinition of citizenship and of the rights and entitlements connected with it, all of which indeed went far beyond the classical models of the nation- and revolutionary states.[4]

All these developments gave rise to strong tendencies to redefine boundaries of collectivities and to devise new ways of combining 'local', transnational or trans-state orientations, global and cosmopolitan. In many of these movements, as well as among many of the new diasporas or new minorities, the local and the transnational orientations, often combined in universalistic themes, were frequently brought together in new ways. Thus while many of these new collective identities emphasized local or particularistic themes rather than the homogenizing universalistic premises of the nation- and revolutionary states, at the same time many of them also promulgated broader transnational or trans-state identities. These were often couched in universalistic terms rooted in the great religions – Islam, Buddhism, even various branches of Christianity – and reconstructed in modern ways, or in new broader visions of Europe. At the same time, far-reaching changes took place in relations between overall, historical grand narratives of modernity and social visions that were more localized, either in space or in time.

IV

These changes in the place of religious movements and revolutionary states and their far-reaching civilizational implications developed in a specific historical context. The most important characteristic of this was the combination of, first, changes in the international systems and shifts of hegemonies within them; second, development of new processes of globalization; third, processes of internal ideological changes in western societies; and fourth, far-reaching processes of democratization and growing demands of various social sectors for access to the centres of their respective societies, as well as to international arenas.[5]

The most important changes in the international arena were, first, the continual weakening and ultimately the disintegration of the 'Westfalian' international order; second, the disappearance of the bipolar order of the Cold War; third, continuous shifts in the relative hegemonic standing of different centres of modernity, moving from Europe and the US to East Asia, then back to the US, and then (possibly) back to China and India; fourth, simultaneous growth in competition and conflict between such centres about their presumed hegemonic standing; fifth, the simultaneous intensification of the conflicts between different social sectors and societies about their place in the international order; and sixth, the increasing destabilization of many state structures, above all but not exclusively in the different peripheral societies. All of these factors contributed greatly to the development of 'New World Disorder'.[6]

New actors became prominent on the international scene – first of all, the various international agencies of the UN, then the agencies of the European Union and a plethora of new legal institutions such as the International Court of Justice. At the same time, these developed multiple new international regulatory arenas and networks – juridical, legal, economic, as well as a multitude of new international NGOs, associations and movements – among which an important role was played by religious, national and transnational associations, which acted beyond the scope of any single nation-state and even beyond the more formal international agencies. All these agencies focused on the constitution of new institutional spaces; on access to international agencies and arenas; and on influencing their policies and those of the various states. Many of these agencies and actors often competed with one another for the right to shape the new rules of the game in international arenas. Moreover, they espoused new premises of legitimation, above all those of human rights couched in different and distinct religious persuasions, such as Christian, Islamic or Buddhist, which transcend any national boundaries. In the name of these they called the different states to accountability. These developments have been presented by some of the actors promulgating them as constituting arenas of new international civil society, which transcends existing political boundaries. While the power of all these agencies was limited and the implementation of their recommendations depended to a large extent on the agreement of and cooperation between the respective states, particularly but not solely the stronger or hegemonic ones; and while many of the older actors, especially the states, continued to play a very important role in the international arenas – and some of them, indeed, as Michael Mann has shown,[7] increased their power – the new actors became very important.

V

These changes in the international arenas were closely interwoven with processes of contemporary globalization. The most distinctive characteristic of these processes in comparison with the 'earlier' processes of globalization have not been confined to the extent of the global flow of various, especially economic, resources. Indeed, such flows of economic resources that developed in this period were not necessarily greater in comparison to some periods in the late 19th and early 20th centuries. Rather, the specific characteristics of contemporary globalization have been the predominance of new forms of international capitalism, which have displaced other, older ones based to a large extent on 'Fordist' assumptions; a shift from industries to service, financial and professional sectors; worldwide processes of migration; continual movements of hitherto non-hegemonic, secondary or peripheral societies and social sectors into the centres of their respective national and international systems, often bypassing existing national institutions as well as trans-state ones; continual growth in the discrepancies and inequalities between various central and peripheral sectors within and between societies. Of special importance in this context has been the combination of discrepancies between, on the one hand, those social sectors which were incorporated into the hegemonic financial and 'high tech' economic frameworks and, on the other hand, those which were left out and became dislocated sectors, which saw a decline in their standards of living and suffered acute feelings of dislocation and dispossession. Most visible among such dislocated or dispossessed groups were not necessarily – and certainly not only – those from the lowest economic echelons: poor peasants or the urban lumpenproletariat, important though they were in these situations. Rather, most prominent among such dispossessed sectors were, first, groups from the middle or lower echelons of more traditional sectors, hitherto embedded in relatively stable (if not very affluent) social, economic and cultural frameworks or niches, which were transposed into generally lower, insecure sectors of the new global economies; and second, various highly mobile, 'modern', educated groups – professionals, graduates of modern universities and the like, who were denied autonomous access to or participation in the new political centres – very much in contradiction to their own premises.

Of special importance in this context was the fact that many of the inequalities, discrepancies and dislocations that developed as a consequence of these processes of globalization, both within states and between them, coalesced with religious, ethnic or cultural divisions and with that continually growing mutual impingement throughout the world of social sectors of 'peripheral' societies and sectors on different centres of globalization.

All these developments were perhaps most clearly visible in the various new diasporas and virtual communities and networks. It was indeed within these communities and networks that there developed extensive and intensified highly transformed 'reactions' to the processes of globalization, especially to the hegemonic claims of the different, often competing, centres of globalization, attesting, to follow Arjun Appadurai's felicitous expression, to 'the power of small numbers',[8] and constituting one of the most volatile and highly inflammatory components on the global scene; as well as an important factor in the transformation of intercivilizational relations in the contemporary scene, often promulgating visions of clashes of civilizations.

VI

These various anti-global movements became closely interwoven with the new ones which, as we have seen, developed from about the mid-1960s. This process occurred first in the west – for example, the famous movements of 1968 and the various postmodern, post-materialist ones such as the women's ecological and anti-globalization movements; and then expanded throughout the rest of the world, where orientations and themes of protest and the revolutionary imaginaires became radically transformed. These transformations have often been presented or perceived as the harbingers of far-reaching changes in the contemporary cultural and institutional scene and possibly also as indications of the exhaustion of the entire programme of modernity.

The basic orientations of the earlier, 'classical' social movements had focused above all on the constitution and possible transformations of the socio-political centre, of the centres of the nation or state, or of the boundaries of major macro-collectivities. In contrast to this, the new movements of protest were oriented to what one scholar has defined as the extension of the systemic range of social life and participation, manifest in demands for growing participation in work, diverse communal orientations, citizen movements, and the like. In Habermas's words,[9] these movements moved from focusing on problems of distribution to emphasis on the 'grammar of life'. One central aspect of these movements was the growing emphasis, especially among sectors dispossessed by processes of globalization, on the politics of identity and on the constitution of new religious, ethnic and local collectivities promulgating narrow exclusivist, particularist themes, often formulated in highly aggressive terms.[10]

VII

All the new multiple changes analysed, especially those resulting from the re-entry of religion into both the national and the international public spheres, culminated in the crystallization of new intercivilizational orientations and relations.

In most historical cases of globalization, intercivilizational, 'anti-globalization' or anti-hegemonic tendencies combined with an ambivalent attitude to the cosmopolitan centres of globalization. So it was in the Hellenistic, Roman, Chinese Confucian and Hinduistic cases, in the case of 'classical' Islam, and in early modern cases. Yet on the contemporary scene such tendencies have been transformed. First, they have become widespread throughout the world, especially by means of the media. Second, they have entailed a continual reconstitution, in a new global context, of collective identities and oppositions between them. Third, they have become highly politicized, interwoven with fierce oppositions between them and the hegemonic conflict between political and ideological terms. Fourth, they have given rise to new intercivilizational orientations. The central focus of these orientations has been the attempt to radically decouple modernity from westernization; to take away from the west – from the original western Enlightenment and even Romantic programmes – the monopoly of modernity; and then to appropriate modernity and to define it in their own terms or visions. They have espoused new civilizational visions – highly reformulated images and symbols of civilizational and religious identity, very often formulated in terms of the universalistic premises of their respective religions or civilizations and grounded in their respective Axial religions. It was in terms of such visions that they attempted to transform the global scene.

A central component of this discourse was a highly ambivalent attitude to the west, above all to the US, its predominance and its hegemony. This attitude was most fully manifest in this period in powerful anti-American movements that burgeoned throughout the world, including many European countries.

These developments signalled far-reaching changes from the earlier reformist and traditional religious movements that had developed throughout non-western societies from the 19th century onwards. Within the recent anti-global movements, confrontation with the west has not taken the form of a quest to become incorporated in the modern hegemonic civilization on its terms, but rather to appropriate for themselves the new international global scene and modernity and to define them in terms of their own traditions.

These visions become fraught with increasing contestations, very often couched in civilizational terms which may endow them with highly ideological absolutizing dimensions, in many societies, in local and global scenes and arenas alike. These contestations take place between, on the one hand, the original western conceptions of modernity as embodied in the modern nation-state or revolutionary state and promulgated by the different centres of western hegemony; and, on the other hand, the newly emerging local, regional and above all transnational civilizational ones. At the same time, however, the vistas grounded in these traditions have been continually reconstituted under the impact of 'modern' programmes. Indeed, these discourses and the discussions around them resemble in many ways the discourse of modernity as it developed from its very beginning in the centres of modernity in Europe, including far-reaching criticisms of the predominant Enlightenment programme of modernity which has developed in the framework of this discourse. Thus, for instance, many of the criticisms of the Enlightenment project made by Qutub, possibly the most eminent fundamentalist theologian, are in many ways very similar and often also related to the major religious and 'secular' critics of the Enlightenment from its very beginning: from de Maistre and the romantics; to the many populists (Slavophiles and the like) in central and eastern Europe, especially in Russia; to those who have in general emphasized, in Charles Taylor's words,[11] the expressivist dimension of human experience; and then, of course, to Nietzsche and Heidegger.

Such attempts at the reformulation of civilizational premises have been taking place not only in these movements, but also in new institutional formations such as the European Union and in various local and regional frameworks. The process is also to be seen in the diverse attempts by the different 'peripheries' – as, for instance, in the discourse on Asian values – to contest the western, especially American, hegemony, and to forge their own constitutive modernities.

The debates and confrontations in which these movements and actors engage and oppose each other may be formulated in 'civilizational' terms, but these very terms – indeed, the very term 'civilization' as construed in such a discourse – are already couched in the language of modernity, in totalistic, essentialistic and absolutizing terms derived from the basic premises of the discourse of modernity (even if it can often draw on older religious traditions). When such clashes and oppositions are combined with political, military or economic struggles and conflicts, they can indeed become very violent. In contrast to the symmetric wars between nation-states in the framework of the Westfalian order, they may give rise to what H Münkler[12] has defined as non-symmetric wars, which have become a continual component of the international order. Of special importance have been the multiplication, extension and intensification of aggressive terrorist movements and intercivilizational conflicts and encounters, which have become a seemingly permanent component of the new international intercivilizational scene.

[1] Juergensmeyer, Mark (ed), 2003. *Global Religions*, New York: Oxford University Press.

[2] Hannerz, U, 1999. *Cultural Complexity: Studies in the social organization of meaning*, New York: Columbia University Press; Hannerz, U, 1996. *Transnational Connections: Culture, people, places*, London and New York: Routledge.

[3] See, for instance, Kiely, Ray, 2005. *The Clash of Globalizations: Neo-liberalism, the Third Way and anti-globalization*, Leiden/Boston: Brill.

[4] Eisenstadt, S N, 2006. 'The outcomes of revolutions: the variability of revolutionary symbolism in modern societies – preliminary indications', in Eisenstadt, *The Great Revolutions and the Civilizations of Modernity*, Leiden/ Boston: Brill, pp 159–84.

[5] Eisenstadt, S N, 2006. 'The new setting: changes in the modes of the models of the nation and revolutionary state', in Eisenstadt, op cit (previous note), pp 185–220.

[6] Jowitt, Ken, 1993. *New World Disorder: The Leninist extinction*, Berkeley: University of California Press.

[7] Mann, Michael, 1997. 'Has globalization ended the rise and rise of the nation state?', in *Review of International Political Economy* 4 (3), 472–96.

[8] Appadurai, Arjun, 2006. *Fear of Small Numbers: An essay on the geography of anger*, Durham: Duke University Press.

[9] Habermas, J, 1981. 'New social movements', in *Telos* 49 (Fall), 33.

[10] See note 5 above.

[11] Taylor, Charles, 2004. *Modern Social Imaginaries (Public Planet)*, Durham: Duke University Press.

[12] Münkler, H, 2003. *Über den Krieg: Stationen der Kriegsgeschichte in Spiegel ihrer theoretischen Reflexion*, Weilerwist: Velbrück.

[4]

SECULAR CONSTITUTIONALISM VINDICATED

*Frances Raday**

In discussing whether constitutionalism must necessarily be secular, it should first be made clear that the topic of constitutional secularism is not about belief. In addressing this theme and arguing in favor of secularism, I am not engaging in the deconstruction of religious belief which has been prominent in recent literature, such as Richard Dawkins in *The God Delusion*[1] or of Sam Harris in *The End of Faith*.[2] I am not decrying the dangers of belief in God or in gods or in "teapots orbiting the earth." On the contrary, religious belief and its manifestation are guaranteed in the context of international human rights and secular constitutions. Secular constitutionalism guarantees a neutral public space for equal participation by those of religious belief and non-belief alike, and private space for matters, including religious matters, in which the state may not enter. What I aim to discuss in this paper is the benefits of secular constitutionalism for democratic regimes when contrasted with the alternatives and the alternatives are the non-secular: religious diversity, pluralism or theo-democracy. On this analysis, followed with examples of constitutional adjudication of the clash between each of the monotheisms and human rights, I argue that secular constitutionalism is essential to human rights.

SECULARISM AND SECULAR HUMAN RIGHTS

Secular constitutionalism is a system not an ideological monolith. Secularism unadorned is the relegation of the eschatological ideology of religions to the private sphere, divorced from political power. The secular state bases the regulation of society on political decision-making made in accordance with prevailing norms of the times. In democracies, this decision-making is made by the elected

---

* Director, Concord Research Center for Integration of International Law in Israel, College of Management—Academic Studies; University College London, Honorary Professor; University of Copenhagen, Honorary Doctor; Hebrew University, Elias Lieberman Chair for Labour Law (Emeritus).

[1] RICHARD DAWKINS, THE GOD DELUSION (2006).

[2] SAM HARRIS, THE END OF FAITH: RELIGION, TERROR, AND THE FUTURE OF REASON (2004).

representatives of the majority. It is a system which allows pluralism of thought and conscience to thrive. It is a system which allows individuals and groups to express themselves freely, not coerced by a prevailing creed. Under secular democracies, this may be achieved either by guaranteeing non-interventionist neutralism or of permitting promotion of religion in accordance with constitutional principles. Where the State adopts a policy of non-interventionist neutralism toward all the various forms of ethical ideology, religious or ethical belief remains a private matter and there is theoretically no problem in ensuring equal treatment. In such a situation the State needs only to ensure absolute non-intervention in the realm of private conscience and equal treatment for members of society; different beliefs or non-beliefs naturally follow. The solution of separation of State and religion has been intended to achieve this kind of egalitarianism on a conceptual level.[3] However, where religious or other forms of ethical expression are perceived as requiring public expression, and where the State adopts a promotionalist and not a non-interventionist stance, the problem of securing equal treatment for the various forms of religious belief, for non-belief and for secular conviction becomes crucial and problematic.

The value content of secular regimes is not in secularism as such but in secular human rights. Although human rights are not a sine qua non of secularism they are the child of secularism. Human rights doctrine is a product of the shift from a religious to a secular state at the time of the Enlightenment in 18th century Europe. The religious paradigm was replaced by secularism, communitarianism by individualism and status by contract. As historian Yehoshua Arieli writes, the modern concept of human rights is the product of secularism:

> The secular character of the normative system embodied in human rights doctrine is essential to its comprehension. All its premises, values, concepts and purposes relate to the homocentric world and to ways of thought freed from the transcendentalist premises and from the jurisdiction of religious authority. And so, the development of the doctrine of human rights is inseverably connected to the process

[3] Eric Mack, *Liberalism, Neutralism and Rights*, *in* RELIGION, MORALITY, AND THE LAW 46 (J. Ronald Pennock & John W. Chapman eds., 1988). Although, as I will show below, it must be admitted that non-interventionist neutralism cannot be complete in a welfare state since there is inevitably support for humanist activities of one kind or another. In North America, where separation of church and state has been the constitutional precept, there are signs that—alongside the ideological conviction that promotionism is in essence inegalitarian—the inegalitarianism of non-promotionism is also beginning to be recognized. Irwin Cotler comments, "a more restrictive definition [of religion] is called for under the establishment clause, lest all 'humane government' programs be deemed constitutionally suspect." Irwin Cotler, *Freedom of Conscience and Religion*, *in* YOUR CLIENTS AND THE CHARTER, LIBERTY AND EQUALITY 165, 174 (Gérald A. Beaudouin ed., 1988); *see* Norman L. Cantor, *Religion and State in Israel and the United States*, 8 TEL AVIV UNIV. STUDIES IN L. 185, 197-200 (1988).

of secularisation of Western society.[4]

Human rights developed as legal rights in the 20th century in international and in constitutional law. They represented a breakthrough from the religious past. In secular human rights regimes, individuals within a community were entitled to autonomous moral judgment; this entailed freedom of religion, conscience and expression. All citizens were entitled to equal opportunity to participate in social, political and economic institutions; this right to equal participation came to be extended over time to different racial and religious groups, to women and homosexuals.

CHALLENGES TO SECULARISM AND TO SECULAR HUMAN RIGHTS

The concept of human rights is currently challenged by traditionalist religious ideologies. These ideologies threaten the paradigm which lies at the heart of human rights. There is a confrontational stance opposing human rights on the part of orthodox religious institutions in most regions of the world, manifested in attacks on the political and civil rights of women, homosexuals, Dalits, heretics or non-believers. These orthodox religious institutions reject the norms of equality, freedom of conscience and freedom of expression where these infringe on religious sensibilities. Deference to religious values in negation of human rights in constitutional democracies has, in some cases, secured the exclusion of rights to equality, freedom of conscience and expression and freedom of religion from full constitutional recognition;[5] in others, it has resulted in legal policies which violate these rights.[6] Constitutional deference to religious norms or sensitivities is on a spectrum, which ranges from religious pluralism to theo-democracy.

Secularism is under attack not only by religious observers but also by academic and liberal commentators. During the present symposium, Michel Rosenfeld and Pavel Kloczowski, each from the perspective of their own discipline, called to abandon the secular monolith and adopt regimes of religious diversity and pluralism. In recent literature, Charles Taylor and Paul Horowitz critique the impact of the secular, liberal state on religious subgroups.[7] Arguing for a more supportive and

[4] Yehoshua Arieli, *The Theory of Human Rights, its Origin and its Impact on Modern Society*, *in* MISHPAT VE-HISTORYAH 25 (Daniel Gutwein & Menachem Mautner eds., 1999).

[5] The prime example is Israel, which in concession to the religious lobby omitted these human rights from the Basic Law: Human Dignity and Liberty, 1992, S.H. 1391.

[6] Constitutional case law in various countries has focused on these violations. *See* Frances Raday, *Traditionalist Religious and Cultural Challengers—International and Constitutional Human Rights Responses*, 41 ISR. L. REV. 596 (2008).

[7] CHARLES TAYLOR, PHILOSOPHICAL ARGUMENTS 249 (1995); Paul Horowitz, *The Sources*

accommodating approach toward religious belief and practices, they claim that liberalism is not value-neutral, it is a "fighting creed": "At the very least, liberalism's focus on the autonomous individual, and on the maximization of individual concepts of the good, tends to give it in practice an emphasis on freedom over tradition, will over obligation, and individual over community."[8] John Gray, in *Black Mass*, compares the attempt to impose secular Utopias on the world by force with the crusades of religion and observes: "The hope of Utopia spilt blood on a scale that traditional creeds cannot match."[9] In proof, he draws on the travesties of human rights in 20th century eschatological ideologies: National Socialism, Communism, Stalinism and Maoism. In conclusion, he concludes: "It is time the diversity of religions was accepted and the attempt to build a secular monolith abandoned. . . . It embodies a type of toleration whose goal is not truth but peace."[10] David Kennedy suggests that "Assessing—or celebrating—humanist governance requires that we focus on humanism as a political project. Not humanism against power, talking to power, advising power, restraining power, but humanism as power." Kennedy also critiques human rights idealism as "idolatry."[11] Almond, Appleby and Sivan consider that religious fundamentalism has been a reaction against "aggressive secularization," which they identify in the success of modernization, secularization and the scientific revolution;[12] they argue:

> The strongest counter to the 'strong religion' of the fundamentalists would be economic reforms that promote economic growth and greater equality of income distribution, as well as political reform that extends the process of self-determination well beyond its current narrow circle of governing elites. . . . Given the opportunity to integrate into the polity, the disillusioned Islamists might opt for peaceful activism.[13]

Two major critical themes emerge from these attacks on secular human rights: first, the thesis of symmetry between religious and secular values as eschatological ideologies, which represents secularism as another competitor on the ideological map rather than a neutral facilitator of differing ideologies (Taylor and Horowitz); and second,

and Limits of Freedom of Religion in a Liberal Democracy: Section 2(a) and Beyond, 54 U. TORONTO FAC. L. REV. 1, 14 (1996).

8 Horowitz, *supra* note 7, at 14; Taylor, *supra* note 7, at 249.

9 JOHN GRAY, BLACK MASS: APOCALYPTIC RELIGION AND THE DEATH OF UTOPIA 209 (2008).

10 *Id.* at 208.

11 David Kennedy, Apogee and Epitaph: Celebrating the 60th Anniversary of the Universal Declaration of Human Rights, Keynote Address at the Minerva Biennial Conference on Human Rights at the University of Tel Aviv (Dec. 9, 2008).

12 GABRIEL A. ALMOND, R. SCOTT APPLEBY & EMMANUEL SIVAN, STRONG RELIGION: THE RISE OF FUNDAMENTALISMS AROUND THE WORLD 20, 224 (2003).

13 *Id.* at 241.

the claim that there is a threat to peace resulting from secular intolerance, either directly as a result of secularism's utopian wars (John Grey), or reflexively, as a result of the religious fundamentalist violence which secularism incites (Almond, Appleby and Sivan). It seems that none of these themes can ultimately justify the abandonment of secular human rights in favor of the religious alternatives.

The claim of symmetry between religious and liberal values does not justify—as suggested by the protagonists of this approach—accommodation and support for religious values even where they clash with human rights. In the case of an irresolvable clash of values between the secular-liberal and the religious, the outcome of symmetry would, logically and at the most, lead to stalemate and not deference to religious values. Nor would it lead to restriction of the reach of secular constitutionalism, which provides a facilitative framework for pluralism of belief and non-belief. Furthermore, there are good grounds for rejecting the symmetry thesis. There is no symmetry between religious and liberal human rights values. The idea that there is a secular monolith is misplaced. Inverting Taylor's and Horowitz's critique of liberalism, you find the values of tradition over freedom, obligation over will, and community over individual. While liberal values leave space for the religious individual and, to a considerable extent, the religious community, religious values do not recognize the entitlement of the liberal individual or community. There is no symmetry between the normative dominance of liberal values (freedom, will, individual) and the normative dominance of religious values (tradition, obligation, community) because the latter does not even acknowledge the private space of the dissident, the heretic, or the silenced voice within its own jurisdiction.[14] These values are primarily tools for the perpetuation of existing power hierarchies. The claim for symmetry is, therefore, based on tolerance of inequality and lack of liberty for those deprived of a voice by, or within, the religious community.

There is a flaw, as well, in the reasoning that calls for the autonomy of communities within a constitutional democracy, where that autonomy denies or reduces the right of some of its members or of non-members to equality and liberty, since the basis for the community's claim to autonomy vis-à-vis the constitutional regime rests on these very norms of equality and liberty.[15] Autonomy demands by minority communities have been organized in a useful typology by Jacob Levy.

[14] *See* Yossi Nehushtan, Religious Conscientious Exemptions (2008) (Ph.D. Philosophy thesis, University of Oxford) (arguing that there should be no constitutional exemptions based on tolerance for religions which are in essence intolerant).

[15] ALISON DUNDES RENTELN, INTERNATIONAL HUMAN RIGHTS: UNIVERSALISM VERSUS RELATIVISM 62-65, 163 (1990); MELVILLE J. HERSKOVITS, CULTURAL RELATIVISM: PERSPECTIVES IN CULTURAL PLURALISM 11-34 (1972).

Under that typology, Levy describes various minority claims for external rules limiting the freedom of non-members and for internal rules limiting the freedom of members, all in order to protect an endangered culture or cultural practice.[16] However, were such rules used to defeat equality claims, they would use the value of liberty to defeat liberty and of equality to defeat equality. They would allow deference to an inegalitarian cultural or religious hegemony over the right to equality and freedom of conscience.[17] Hence, the premise to be derived from an analysis of the divide between traditionalist culture and religion versus equality and human rights is that, in constitutional societies, equality and liberty should be the governing norms—the Grundnorm on which the whole system rests—including the right to enjoy one's culture and religion. Constitutional democracy cannot tolerate enclaves of illiberalism whose inhabitants are deprived of access to human rights guarantees of equality and liberty.

The call for demoting secular human rights because they are intolerant and are a threat to peace is presented as an empirical observation. The empirical argument is made that it is secularism, not religion, which has wrought disaster in the 20th century. This assertion is arguable. Although the devastation and slaughter of the 20th century wars and revolutions were not waged in the name of religion; they were not waged against religion or in the name of secularism either. These ravages of humanity were certainly not committed in the name of secular human rights. On the contrary, critique of the worst excesses of these regimes is enhanced by application of secular human rights premises, and it was in revulsion against them that the International Declaration of Human Rights was promulgated.[18]

---

16 Jacob T. Levy establishes a useful typology for the rights claims of subgroups, identifying a range of claims, such as immunity from unfairly burdensome laws; assistance; self-government; external rules limiting freedom of non-members; internal rules limiting the freedom of members; recognition and enforcement of autonomous legal practices; guaranteed representation in government bodies; and symbolic claims. Jacob T. Levy, *Classifying Cultural Rights*, *in* ETHNICITY AND GROUP RIGHTS 22, 39 (Ian Shapiro & Will Kymlicka eds., 2000).

17 Martha Nussbaum has documented the widespread existence of dissent among women in traditionalist cultures or religious communities in her outstanding work on women and culture. The presence of such dissent is also palpable in the shadow reports of NGOs from the countries reporting to the Committee on the Elimination of Discrimination against Women, which present the claims of women who seek to have the equality principles of the convention applied in full. This dissent requires the application of human rights standards to orthodox religions and traditionalist cultures in order that full expression be given to the human rights of the group as it really is and not as it is hegemonically represented in the voice of its traditionalist leadership. MARTHA CRAVEN NUSSBAUM, WOMEN AND HUMAN DEVELOPMENT: THE CAPABILITIES APPROACH 229-30 (2000).

18 By contrast, the Crusades, the Christian religious wars of the Middle Ages, and Islamic Jihad have all been waged in the name of religion and in order to further the goal of domination by a certain religion. Dostoevsky said, "without religion, anything will be permitted" but it might be countered "with religion, anything will be permitted." Malene Busk, Remarks at the International Conference in Gothenburg, Sweden: Why is Secularism Essential? (Mar. 7, 2009).

The peace motive in the proposal to restrict secularism because it incites fundamentalist religious responses, put differently, condones surrender to the power of the religious. This is abundantly clear in Pakistan's surrender of the Swat Valley to the Taliban. This motif is, however, applicable beyond the sphere of fundamentalist violence. It recurs where religious institutions acquire political power through manipulation of coalition politics, such as that by the religious parties in Israeli parliamentary democracy, and where they promote welfare dependence and totalitarian politics backed with violence, such as the domination of Hamas in the Palestinian territories. In this peace motive there is a disguised normative preference. There is a compromise for peace in exchange for the human rights of those who are oppressed by religious hegemony. This involves the compromise of the constitutional human rights values of equality and liberty.

The justification of this compromise in the theoretical literature is based, additionally, on arguments of diversity and pluralism, or of communitarianism and shared belonging. The literature justifies the need to respect the autonomy of the religious hegemony as though it were a legitimate choice for constitutional democracy. The impact of a choice of religious pluralism on human rights is ignored or marginalized in the anti-secularist literature. This is illustrated by the fact that the words gender, women, feminism, freedom of conscience or speech, homosexuality, patriarchy, apostasy, and heresy are usually not even to be found in the index. Occasionally, in this literature, the sacrifice of human rights is made explicit. Norman Solomon, who proposes that where religious demands conflict with universal human rights, "solutions can be approached in a pragmatic fashion accepting compromise," also observes:

> [W]hereas anti-slavery consensus is strong enough for us to demand the abolition of slavery in any society that still endorses it on religious or other grounds [in the Bible the New Testament condoned slavery], there may not in practice be a strong enough consensus for a parallel demand to be made for the equalisation of women's status.[19]

Indeed, amongst those human rights to be sacrificed on the altar of religion, women's rights are foremost. It is, then, at women's expense and that of homosexuals and non-believers that the peace and tolerance of religious diversity or pluralism is to be purchased.

---

[19] DOES GOD BELIEVE IN HUMAN RIGHTS? ESSAYS ON RELIGION AND HUMAN RIGHTS 101 (Nazila Ghanea, Alan Stephens & Raphael Walden eds., 2007).

HUMAN RIGHTS COSTS OF DEFERRING TO RELIGION

There are current manifestations of the dissonance between orthodox religions and human rights standards in most regions of the world. The revival in the public sphere of Catholicism and Russian Orthodoxy in the ex-Soviet states, of orthodox Judaism in Israel, of radical Islam in Asia and in immigrant communities in Europe has put religion on the constitutional agenda. This revival resonates with no small measure of nostalgia for, in the words of Adam Seligman in this symposium, "trust, empathy and mercy."[20] Indeed the magnetic pull of religion has been documented by sociologists who explain that religions offer social solidarity, psychological comfort, ways of coping with the unknown and death; they are inculcated by ritual, repetition, music and fear of transcendental as well as temporal punishment. However, whatever the benefits of these attributes of religion in the private sphere and in personal belief, it is doubtful that they can in any way justify deference to religion in the constitutional framework. Religion is not only a philosophical or psychological system operative at the level of thought, expression and choice, which are to be protected as human rights. In the case of the monotheisms, religions are socio-political institutions that operate as normative systems. As such, institutionalised religions are in confrontation with human rights, and deference to religion means surrender of human rights.

The fundamental tenets of monotheistic religions are at odds with the basis of human rights doctrine. Human rights doctrine is human-centric; it is based on the autonomy and responsibility of the individual (individualism) and systemic-rational principles (rationalism).[21] The doctrine takes as its premise the authority of the State (secularism)[22] and, as its goal, the prevention of abuse of the State's power over the individual. Monotheistic religion, in contrast, is based on the subjection of the individual and the community to the will of God and on a transcendental morality. The confrontation between monotheistic religion and modern human rights is clearly evidenced in the gap between the concept of religious duty and human right;[23] in the clash between the religious prohibition of apostasy or heresy and freedom of

[20] Adam B. Seligman, *Living Together Differently*, 30 CARDOZO L. REV. 2881 (2009).

[21] Talcott Parsons, *On the Concept of Influence*, 27 PUB. OPINION Q. 37 (1963). There is a rich literature on such hermeneutical efforts. *See, e.g.*, Abdullahi Ahmed An-Na'im, *Human Rights in the Muslim World: Socio-Political Conditions and Scriptural Imperatives*, 3 HARV. HUM. RTS. J. 13 (1990).

[22] *See* Arieli, *supra* note 4, at 44.

[23] Robert Cover, *Obligation: A Jewish Jurisprudence of the Social Order*, 5 J.L. & RELIGION 65 (1987).

speech, conscience, and religion;[24] and, in the patriarchal, religious opposition to women's right to equality and to homosexuals' right to be homosexual. Within some divisions of monotheism as a whole, there has been a movement to reform and to close the gap with human rights doctrine, e.g., in Protestantism and Reform Judaism. There are also interpretations of Catholicism[25] and Islam,[26] issued by individual religious leaders, which are more consonant with a human rights approach. However, this hermeneutical endeavor is far from complete, in the best of cases, and is demonstratively absent in those cases where the religious community is asserting a defense against human rights claims.[27]

The idea that religions provide empathy, and that it is this empathy which is lacking from the human rights project, is misplaced. It is human rights, rather than religion, which provides empathy. It is true that the shared starting point of religion and human rights is considered to be in the monotheistic concept of *bezelem*, imago dei, which is considered to be the source of the right to human dignity. However, although *bezelem* acknowledged the common core of spiritual humanity in all human beings, it did not confer entitlement to equal treatment in religious or social institutions. Human rights created an entirely new concept of equal treatment to those who are other or different. They recognized the right of the other to experience the world in a way of equal value as oneself, insofar as the experiencing is regulated by political and legal organization. Religions have not been empathetic to the other. Based on a chain of authority leading to God, there is a clear mandate for authoritarianism in societal institutions.

Thus, patriarchy is a core message of the monotheistic religions. Rita Gross writes:

> [I]n Christianity and Judaism . . . continued reflection and experiences led us to the realization that we were excluded from ritual and leadership because of certain theological concepts, especially the image of the deity as exclusively male. It became clear that if patriarchal control of ritual was eliminated, the patriarchal naming of God would closely follow, which could lead to even more experimentation with praxis in other areas.[28]

The monotheistic religions are hierarchical and patriarchal by definition. Carol Christ, for instance, claims that the Bible's core

---

24 Haim H. Cohn, *The Law of Religious Dissidents: A Comparative Historical Survey*, 34 ISR. L. REV. 39 (2000).

25 POPE JOHN PAUL II, LETTER TO WOMEN (1995).

26 MARTHA CRAVEN NUSSBAUM, SEX AND SOCIAL JUSTICE 86 (1999). There is a rich literature on such hermeneutical efforts. *See, e.g.*, An-Na'im, *supra* note 21, at 13.

27 Raimundo Pannikar, *Is the Notion of Human Rights a Western Concept?*, 120 DIOGENES 75 (1982).

28 RITA M. GROSS, FEMINISM & RELIGION: AN INTRODUCTION 200 (1996).

message is one of intolerance and that its core symbolism makes male domination appear normal and legitimate, a mirroring on earth of male authority on high.[29] The hierarchically gendered family is the primary social unit in this system of male dominance, with men ruling over women in the home. Religious abhorrence of homosexuality is an inevitable emanation of this need to establish men as natural rulers, as opposed to those who are ruled. What religion offered to those who were not identified with the male hegemony of the monotheisms was compassion or charity, not empathy.

This discussion of religious patriarchy cannot be schematically separated from cultural practices. Indeed, the religious values discussed above are a part of human culture. However, religious norms form the hard core of culture, with a holy text, official interpreters, judgment and transcendental punishment. Religion interacts with traditionalist cultures. Although authoritarian and patriarchal cultural practices may not be directly mandated in the documentary sources of religion, there appears to be a correlation between certain violent cultural practices and the religious environments in which they thrive. A definitive correlation would require careful research, but an example of the symbiosis between the two may be found in the policy of the Islamic Republic of Iran to expand the culture of chastity, impose stricter veiling requirements, and to provide for imprisonment of up to twelve months and flogging of up to seventy-four lashes for offences relating to the dress code.[30] An extreme example is in the Taliban's prohibition of girls' education on pain of death. Violent traditional practices, defended in the name of traditionalist culture, that impinge on human rights are thus frequently protected under the wings of one religion or another. Such practices include: a preference for sons, leading to female infanticide (Islam and Hindu); female genital mutilation (Islam); a husband's right to obedience and power to discipline or commit acts of violence against his wife (Islam); marital rape (Islam and Christianity); family honor killings by the shamed father or brothers of a girl who has been sexually violated, whether with consent or by rape (Islam); stoning of adulterous women (Islam); compulsory dress codes for women, the violation of which results in violent punishment (Islam); prohibition of women's participation in religious ritual, enforced by violence (Judaism); and persecution of homosexuals (Judaism, Christianity and Islam). Thus, religion may condone violence in the enforcement of its patriarchal regime.

---

[29] CAROL P. CHRIST, LAUGHTER OF APHRODITE: REFLECTIONS ON A JOURNEY TO THE GODDESS 59-60 (1987); *see also It's Too Broken to Be Fixed: The Feminist Case Against Theological Transformation of Traditional Religions*, *in* GROSS, *supra* note 28, at 140-46.

[30] The Secretary-General, *Situation of Human Rights in the Islamic Republic of Iran*, delivered to the General Assembly, U.N. Doc. A/52/472 (Oct. 15, 1997).

SECULAR CONSTITUTIONALISM IN ACTION

It is secular constitutionalism which can provide a forum for women, homosexuals, Dalits, heretics and non-believers to assert their rights to equality and freedom of conscience in the face of repression by the hegemony of religious normative institutions. International treaty regulation establishes a hierarchy in which the rights to equality and to freedom of expression or conscience take precedence over the right to manifest one's religion or to enjoy one's culture. The clash between culture and religion, on the one hand, and human rights, on the other, is expressly regulated in two international conventions: ICCPR[31] and CEDAW.[32] Of the two, CEDAW provides a more specific hierarchy of rights. At the constitutional level, no express hierarchy has been articulated such as that found in international treaties. There may be some indication of a hierarchy of rights in that the right to equality is one of the few rights declared in absolute terms in some of the constitutions of Western democracies.[33] On this basis, the potential for establishing such a hierarchy of rights seems to be conceivable. Furthermore, even without the express determination of the primacy of equality and freedom of conscience over the right to manifestation of religion or enjoyment of culture, there is a mode of interpretation which regards the right to religious expression as private and not extending to the exercise of power or rights over others. By this interpretation, the secular constitutional realm will occupy the public space, guaranteeing pluralistic equality and with it a space for the manifestation of religion in a way that does not violate human rights.

It is in the courts that the constitutional struggle between traditionalist religious or cultural values and human rights has been waged. I have analyzed a sample of cases in which the cultural defense and the right to religious freedom have been raised in opposition to women's and homosexuals' claims to gender equality in constitutional courts. Traditionalist religions and cultures are bastions of patriarchal authority with regards to a wide range of issues in both the public and the private or domestic sphere, and there is a considerable body of constitutional case law concerning the clash with women's and homosexuals' human rights. My purpose was to compare the rhetoric and the outcome of the judgments in order to extrapolate some

31 International Covenant on Civil and Political Rights, Dec. 19, 1966, 999 U.N.T.S. 171, 173.

32 Convention on the Elimination of All Forms of Discrimination against Women, Dec. 18, 1979, 1249 U.N.T.S. 13.

33 ALEC STONE SWEET, GOVERNING WITH JUDGES: CONSTITUTIONAL POLITICS IN EUROPE 97 (2000).

empirical data as to the readiness of constitutional courts to apply rights in the hierarchical fashion required by the international treaties.

A. *Polygamy, Adultery, Obedience and Divorce*

The monotheistic religions all have regulatory norms on marriage, which share the theme of patriarchy in a hierarchical gendered family. There are significant differences in the specific marital laws of each religion, but the patriarchal asymmetry in power between husbands and wives is evident in all. Multicultural relativists, of the feminist and non-feminist variety, have argued that some of the specific rules are not necessarily repressive for women. And there has been a considerable amount of literature extolling the virtues of polygamy as benefiting women because multiple wives may share the burdens of family, or because it is a matter of free choice. However, polygamy seen in the comparative religious context is an ode to patriarchy. Polygamy in early Judaism (abandoned in the 6th century and prohibited in the 11th century) and in Islam, is neither symmetrical nor mutual as between men and women. Free choice is not accorded to existing wives when a new wife is brought in by the husband. The recognition of polygamy entails a different approach to adultery by men or by women, and in Islam women's adultery is penalized by stoning. In Jewish law, even after the prohibition of polygamy, women's adultery is punished by heavier penalties than those imposed on men, such as *mamzerut* of the children born of the adulterous union and prohibition of her marriage with her adulterous partner even after divorce. Asymmetrical divorce rules are clear evidence of patriarchy: in Judaism, the husband has absolute patriarchal power to refuse to divorce his wife and no authority other than that of the husband can release her from the chains of marriage; and in Islam, men have the patriarchal power to unilaterally divorce their wives by merely announcing "talak." Christian marriage vows retain an asymmetrical duty of obedience for the woman and a degrading ethos of chastity for real women, personified in the Virginity of the Holy Mother.

The approach of constitutional courts to marital status issues has varied as between jurisdictions. The United States Supreme Court has upheld women's right to equality in marital status, in the context reviewing statutory prohibitions on Mormon polygamy. In a series of cases, starting in 1879, the United States Supreme Court held that the free exercise clause did not protect polygamy from criminal sanction. The decisions related to the Mormons, a minority sect of Christianity, which is the religion of the majority. In *Reynolds*, the United States Supreme Court upheld a prohibition on the Mormon practice of polygamy.[34] In 1980, in *Davis v. Beason*, Justice Field said: "Bigamy and polygamy are crimes by the laws of all civilized and Christian countries. . . . They tend to destroy the purity of the marriage relation, to disturb the peace of families, to degrade women, and to debase man."[35] As a constitutional matter, the Court held that, "[w]hile legislation for the establishment of a religion is forbidden, and its free exercise permitted, it does not follow that everything which may be so called can be tolerated. Crime is not the less odious because sanctioned by what any particular sect may designate as 'religion.'"[36] In 1946, in *Cleveland*, the majority opinion, delivered by Justice Douglas, held that the transportation of women across state lines for the purpose of polygamous cohabitation was "an immoral purpose" under the statutory language of the Mann Act and, hence, a criminal offence.[37] Citing *Reynolds*, the Court ruled: "it has long been held that the fact that polygamy is supported by a religious creed affords no defense in a prosecution for bigamy."[38] In his dissent, Justice Murphy introduced a note of doubt. He wrote:

> It is not my purpose to defend the practice of polygamy or to claim that it is morally the equivalent of monogamy. But it is essential to understand what it is as well as what it is not. . . . Historically its use has far exceeded any other form. It was quite common among ancient civilizations and was referred to many times by the writers of the Old Testament; even today it is to be found frequently among certain pagan and non-Christian peoples of the world. We must recognize, then, that polygyny, like other forms of marriage, is basically a cultural institution rooted deeply in the religious beliefs and social mores of those societies in which it appears. . . . There is thus no basis in fact for including polygyny within the phrase 'any other immoral purpose' [along with prostitution and debauchery].[39]

In India, the Supreme Court refused to strike down the Muslim practice of polygamy for the large and politically active Muslim minority but refused to extend the right to polygamy to Hindu men who had converted to Islam. In 1995, in *Sarla Mudgal*, the Indian Supreme Court decided, in the case of a man who was married in a monogamous Hindu marriage, under the Hindu Marriage Act, and who converted to Islam, only to remarry without dissolving the first marriage, that the second marriage was prohibited.[40] The Court refused to recognize the second marriage as a polygamous marriage under the Muslim law. The

34 Reynolds v. United States, 98 U.S. 145 (1878).
35 Davis v. Beason, 133 U.S. 333, 341 (1890).
36 *Id.* at 345.
37 Cleveland v. United States, 329 U.S. 14 (1946).
38 *Id.* at 20.
39 *Id.* at 25-27.
40 Sarla Mudgal v. Union of India, (1995) 3 S.C.C. 635.

Court, pointing out that polygamy had been held injurious to public morals in the United States, said: "in the Indian Republic, there was to be only one Nation—the Indian Nation—and no community could claim to remain a separate entity on the basis of religion."[41] In 1997, the Indian Supreme Court handed down a more ambivalent decision on polygamy. In *Ahmedabad Women Action Group*, the Court dismissed constitutional challenges by a women's NGO to the Muslim practices of polygamy and triple talaq (a form of summary unilateral divorce by the husband) and to provisions of the Hindu Succession Act that discriminated against women.[42] The Court used very different rhetoric from that used only two years earlier: "a uniform law, though highly desirable, may be counter-productive to the unity and integrity of the nation" and "polygamy is recognised as a valid institution when a Muslim male marries more than one wife."[43]

The Israeli Supreme Court has rigidly refrained from interfering in statutory provisions which empower the courts of the religious communities to determine the marital status of members of the three communities in Israel—Jewish, Muslim and Christian—even where the Court has acknowledged their violation of women's human rights. The acquiescence of the Court is in the context of a powerful Orthodox Jewish political lobby which succeeds in keeping the religious legislation in place. In 1971, in *Boronovski*, Israel's High Court of Justice rejected a woman's claim to cancel the rabbinical license, issued in accordance with Jewish law, allowing her husband to remarry without her agreement to give him a ghet (divorce).[44] The woman petitioner had claimed discrimination on grounds of gender, since women are not symmetrically entitled to a similar rabbinical license in case of refusal of a ghet by their husbands. The majority decision rejected the petitioner's claim and, although expressly recognizing the injustice to women and expressing regret, refused to find unjustifiable discrimination. In a minority opinion accepting the claim, Justice Haim Cohen concluded that there were no differences between men and women that could justify the difference in treatment.[45] In 1997, in *Rephaeli*, a woman petitioned to overturn the refusal of the Grand Rabbinical Court to oblige her husband—separated from her for more

---

[41] *Id.* at 650; *see also* K. N. Chandrasekharan Pillai, *Women and Criminal Procedure*, *in* ENGENDERING LAW: ESSAYS IN HONOUR OF LOTIKA SAKAR 139-60 (Amita Dhanda & Archana Parashar eds., 1999).

[42] Ahmedabad Women Action Group v. Union of India, (1997) 3 S.C.C. 573.

[43] *Id.* at 577.

[44] HCJ (En Banc) 10/69 Boronovski v. Chief Rabbinate, [1971] IsrSC 25(1) 7.

[45] *Id.* at 18. It is interesting to note that the Court's validation of the legislation results in a situation of greater equality, on the issue of men's multiple marriages, for Muslim and Christian than for Jewish women.

than six years—to give her a divorce.[46] The High Court of Justice ruled unanimously to dismiss, holding that it could not intervene in the Grand Rabbinical Court's decision. Although concurring in the judgment, Justice Cheshin remarked that, under Jewish law, the situation of a slave was preferable to that of a wife since even a slave would have been released after seven years of bondage.[47]

In 2007, the Canadian Supreme Court upheld the enforceability of a Jewish husband's agreement, which had been made in made in the course of proceedings for a civil divorce, to appear before the rabbinical authorities to obtain a Jewish divorce, or ghet, immediately upon the granting of the divorce.[48] A wife cannot obtain a ghet unless her husband agrees to give it. Without one, she remains his wife and is unable to remarry under Jewish law. In this case, despite the wife's repeated requests, in breach of the agreement, the husband consistently refused to provide a ghet for 15 years, and the wife sued for damages. The husband argued that his agreement to give a ghet was not valid under Quebec law and that he was protected by his right to freedom of religion from having to pay damages for its breach. The Supreme Court held the agreement enforceable. In its judgment, the Court took note of the gender discrimination the religious barriers to remarriage may represent and held that enforcement of agreements to release the wife harmonizes with Canada's approach to equality rights, to divorce and remarriage and to religious freedom.

B. *Purchase, Matrimonial Property and Maintenance*

Underlying patriarchal religious matrimonial regimes there is a property rationale. In the Jewish marriage ceremony the woman is purchased. Judaism, Islam and some branches of Christianity impose a patriarchal division of property, according to which full property rights are vested in the husband or sons, and women are compensated either with reduced property rights or with compensation for loss of income or property on divorce.

In both India and Israel, the Supreme Courts have recognized women's right to equality in the division of matrimonial property where the division is being determined by religious authorities. In both countries the civil law provisions have introduced egalitarian matrimonial property and maintenance laws but, in both, there are religious sub-systems which apply religious law to these issues—in

---

46 HCJ 1371/96 Rephaeli v. Rephaeli, [1997] IsrSC 51(1) 198.

47 *Id.* at 213. Nevertheless, despite this powerful rhetoric, Justice Cheshin, like the other judges, did not find a way to intervene.

48 Bruker v. Marcovitz, [2007] 3 S.C.R. 607, 2007 S.C.C. 54.

India, Muslim and Christian minority sub-systems, and in Israel the Jewish Orthodox minority in a Jewish majority.

In India, with its Hindu majority, the clash between religion and women's right to equality has been examined in relation to the two minority religions (Islam and Christianity). For Hindu women, India follows a system in which personal status laws are determined by the law of the religion of the parties involved but are applied in civil courts. Many of the problems of inequality in Hindu family law were removed by the Hindu Marriage Act.[49]

In the 1985 *Shah Bano Begum* case, the Indian Supreme Court confirmed a maintenance award for a divorced Muslim woman, allegedly contrary to Shari'a law.[50] The Court was composed of five Hindu judges and the case was decided unanimously. On the question of the religious claims underlying opposition to the maintenance award, Chief Justice Chandrachud was, on the one hand, scathing about the inequality wrought by the Muslim personal code:

> Undoubtedly the Muslim husband enjoys the privilege of being able to discard his wife whenever he chooses to do so, for reasons good, bad or indifferent. Indeed, for no reason at all. But is the only price of that privilege the dole of pittance during the period of iddat? And is the law so ruthless in its inequality that, no matter how much the husband pays for the maintenance of his divorced wife during the period of iddat, the mere fact that he has paid something, no matter how little, absolves him forever from the duty of paying adequately so as to enable her to keep her body and soul together?[51]

The Court also found Islamic authority in verses 241 and 242 of the Qur'an for the proposition that there is an obligation to pay maintenance to divorced wives who are unable to maintain themselves.[52] The ratio of the case was, however, based on the Code of Criminal Procedure, under which a maintenance obligation may be imposed on a person who neglects or refuses to pay maintenance to a wife who is unable to maintain herself. In the aftermath of *Shah Bano*, the statutory Muslim Personal Law Board campaigned to reverse the ruling. It succeeded on

---

[49] The Hindu Marriage Act, No. 25 of 1955; India Code (1955).

[50] Ahmed Khan v. Shah Bano Begum, (1985) 2 S.C.C. 556.

[51] *Id.* at 559.

[52] *Cf.* Abu Bakar Siddique v. S.M.A. Bakkar, 38 D.L.R. (AD) (1986). In Bangladesh, in 1986, the High Court ruled on a petition by a mother to retain custody of her son after the age of seven. The Court held that although the principles of Islamic law allowed the woman to be guardian of a male child only until the age of seven, a deviation from this rule would be possible where the child's welfare required it. According to the judge, there was no authoritative ruling on this issue in the Qur'an or the Sunnah, and hence he was within the principles of Islamic law in awarding custody to the mother in this unusual case, where the child was afflicted with a rare disease and the mother, a doctor, was able to take care of his treatment. In that case, the Court was ruling on a Muslim issue in a Muslim state and the decision does not appear to have been opposed by public opinion.

all fronts. The ruling Congress Party introduced legislation to reverse the judgment, and the petitioner waived all her rights under the Supreme Court judgment.[53]

In 1986, in *Mary Roy*, the Indian Supreme Court considered the constitutionality of the unequal inheritance provisions in the Christian Succession Act of 1916.[54] The petitioner, a Christian woman and resident of Kerala, claimed that the act infringed women's right to equality in that it provided for a lower inheritance share for women. The Supreme Court avoided the issue of constitutionality, holding that the Indian Succession Act of 1925, which grants equal inheritance rights to men and women, governed Christians in Kerala. According to Martha Nussbaum, the Synod of Christian Churches has supported opposition by the Christian community to the *Mary Roy* decision and has financed the drafting of wills to disinherit female heirs.[55]

In Israel, the *Bavli* case, in 1994, involved the division of matrimonial property.[56] Jurisdiction for determining the division of matrimonial property is sometimes under the rabbinical courts and sometimes the civil courts: jurisdiction is vested in the rabbinical courts either where both partners to the marriage agree to it or where one of the partners (usually the husband) has reached the rabbinical court with a request for a divorce and a request to include adjudication of the property issues, before the other partner has brought action in a civil court. Different regimes regarding the division of matrimonial property are applied in the two jurisdictions; in the rabbinical courts, the Jewish law regime of property separation is applied, and, in the civil courts, there is both a judicial and statutory presumption of community property, which is to be divided equally between the spouses on dissolution of the marriage. In the case in hand, the rabbinical courts had jurisdiction and refused to divide the matrimonial property equally. The divorced wife's petition to the High Court of Justice was accepted and the case returned to the rabbinical courts. Justice Barak, the president of the High Court, rejected the claim that the Jewish law regime of separate matrimonial property could not be considered discriminatory as it applied to men and women equally, holding that the social facts showed women are disadvantaged where a separate property

[53] Amendments to the code of criminal procedure have strengthened women's right to maintenance in divorces. *See* Code of Criminal Procedure, 1973, No. 2 of 1974; INDIA CODE CRIM. PROC. (1974), § 125.

[54] Mary Roy v. State of Kerala, A.I.R., 1986 S.C. 1011.

[55] NUSSBAUM, *supra* note 26, at 98; *see also* Marc Galanter & Jayanth Krishnan, *Personal Law and Human Rights in India and Israel*, 34 ISR. L. REV. 101 (2000). According to Galanter and Krishnan, the rejection of the decision by the Christian minority group demonstrates concern about losing their identity if they do not keep the established personal law.

[56] HCJ 1000/92 Bavli v. High Rabbinical Court, [1994] IsrSC 48(2) 221.

regime is applied.[57] Following this decision, there were vociferous protests from Orthodox Jewish groups, and it is common knowledge that the rabbinical courts do not apply the ruling by the High Court of Justice.

Thus, in both countries the judicial rulings have failed to effect comprehensive social change. In India, Moslem riots against the judicial rulings led to a legislative override. In Israel, the rabbinical courts, exercising exclusive jurisdiction over divorce in Israel, do not implement the women's right to equality in divorce proceedings.

C. *Control of Women's Reproductive Role*

Prohibition of abortion is ostensibly based on a contest between the rights of the woman and the rights of the child and, hence, not a matter of control of women's reproductive role. The right to life regards the prohibition as necessitated for protection of the "unborn child," based on the categorization of the fetus as a person from the moment of conception. However, deconstruction of the arguments presented in support of the right to life reveal clearly that the issue is one of control over women's reproductive role and denial of their autonomous moral agency. The idea that life begins at conception—and hence the fetus has equal rights to be balanced against those of the mother—is predicated not as claimed by some commentators[58] as a religious view as to when life begins, but one particular Christian religious view, accepted by most, though not all, branches of Christianity and not at all stages in the history of those branches which do prohibit abortion. It is not fully accepted by Judaism or Islam. The Christian prohibition of abortion is in a context which restricts women's autonomy independently of the existence of a fetus. The prohibition extends to prohibition of contraception. While this apparently affects men as it does women, it prejudices women's autonomy far more than it does that of men, who do not become pregnant or bear the child. Additionally, the restriction of women's autonomy has been presented, in Kennedy's plurality opinion in the United States Supreme Court's decision in *Carhart*, as protection of pregnant women as mothers, described by Reva Siegel as the "woman-protective rationale" which is not connected with the fetus' right to life.

Women's rights are violated by restriction of their right to decide whether to continue with a pregnancy or have an abortion: women's personhood, autonomy and individual dignity, their right to privacy,

[57] *Id.* at 234.

[58] Judith Resnik, *Courts and Democracy: The Production and Reproduction of Constitutional Conflict*, *in* THE COURTS AND SOCIAL POLICY IN THE UNITED STATES (2008).

equality, health and welfare are infringed. Furthermore, women's rights as citizens to freedom of conscience and freedom from religious coercion, irrespective of membership in the Christian faith or community which prohibits abortion, is violated. Beyond all of these, in numerous tragic cases, women's right to life is sacrificed. The WHO estimates that induced abortion, performed in an adverse social and legal climate under unsafe conditions, results in approximately 70,000 deaths each year.[59]

The Supreme Courts of the US, Canada, Germany, Columbia and Mexico have made rulings on this issue.

In 1973, in *Roe v. Wade*,[60] the United States Supreme Court, by a seven to two majority, struck a blow for women's autonomy. The Court ruled that because the fetus is not yet viable outside of the mother's womb, the woman has a right to decide during the first trimester whether to abort the pregnancy. This decision was followed by persistent state legislative attempts to limit women's autonomy in deciding on abortion, by requiring parental consent, spousal consent, doctors' right to refuse, funding restrictions and restrictions on certain kinds of abortion procedures. In 1992, in *Casey*,[61] the Court held by five to four, that before fetal viability, a woman has a right to terminate her pregnancy and a state law is unconstitutional if it imposes on the woman's decision an "undue burden." Justice Kennedy, writing for the majority, commented:

> [T]he liberty of the women is at stake in a sense unique to the human condition and so unique to the law. . . . Her suffering is too intimate and personal for the State to insist, without more, upon its own vision of the woman's role, however dominant that vision has been in the course of our history and culture. The destiny of the woman must be shaped to a large extent on her own conception of her spiritual imperatives and her place in society.[62]

Justice O'Connor found it necessary to point out that spousal notification is an undue burden: "Women do not lose their constitutionally protected liberty when they marry."[63] In 2000, in *Stenberg* again a five to four majority struck down legislative attempts to restrict women's autonomy in deciding whether to have an abortion: the majority struck down Nebraska Partial Birth Abortion statute as unconstitutional because it lacks the requisite exception "for the

---

59 *See* WORLD HEALTH ORG., SAFE ABORTION: TECHNICAL AND POLICY GUIDANCE FOR HEALTH SYSTEMS 7 (2003), *available at* http://whqlibdoc.who.int/publications/2003/9241590343.pdf.

60 Roe v. Wade, 410 U.S. 113 (1973).

61 Planned Parenthood v. Casey, 505 U.S. 833 (1992).

62 *Id.* at 852.

63 *Id.* at 898.

preservation of the . . . health of the mother."[64] However, Justice Kennedy switched positions, voting to uphold the partial birth abortion statute on the grounds that "moral principles having their foundation in the intrinsic value of human life including the life of the unborn."[65] Jeffrey Toobin comments that "Kennedy's hymn to autonomy in 1992 turned into a paean to the life of the unborn in 2000."[66] In 2007, in *Gonzales v. Carhart*,[67] Justice Kennedy's dissent in *Stenberg* became the majority opinion, with Justice Alito replacing Justice O'Connor, and a five to four majority upheld the Partial Birth Abortion Act as constitutional, even without a women's health exception: "While we find no reliable data to measure the phenomenon, it seems unexceptionable to conclude some women come to regret their choice to abort the infant life they once created and sustained."[68] Justice Ginsburg, in dissent, considered the majority decision "alarming."[69]

The German Constitutional Court[70] held in 1975, just two years after *Roe v. Wade*, that the unborn have a right to life guaranteed by the constitution, that abortion is "an act of killing," and that the fetus deserves legal protection throughout its development. In the required balancing,

> both constitutional values are to be viewed in their relationship to human dignity, the center of the value system of the constitution. . . . A decision oriented to Article 1, Paragraph 1, of the Basic Law must come down in favor of the precedence of the protection of life for the child [in the womb] over the right of the pregnant woman to self-determination. Regarding many opportunities for development of personality, she can be adversely affected through pregnancy, birth and the education of her children. On the other hand, the unborn life is destroyed through the interruption of pregnancy. According to the principle of the balance which preserves most of competing constitutionally protected positions in view of the fundamental idea of Article 19, Paragraph 2, of the Basic Law, precedence must be given to the protection of the life of the child about to be born. This precedence exists as a matter of principle for the entire duration of pregnancy and may not be placed in question for any particular time.[71]

In the early 1990s, the German legislature (Bundestag) introduced

---

64 Stenberg v. Carhart, 530 U.S. 914, 930 (2000).

65 *Id.* at 979.

66 JEFFREY TOOBIN, THE NINE: INSIDE THE SECRET WORLD OF THE SUPREME COURT 328 (2007).

67 Gonzales v. Carhart, 550 U.S. 124 (2007).

68 *Id.* at 159.

69 *Id.* at 170.

70 39 Entscheidungen des Bundesvfassungsgerichts [BverfGE] [Federal Constitutional Court] 1975, 1 (F.R.G.).

71 *Id.*

a system where a woman having an abortion during the first three months of her pregnancy does not face legal sanctions if she undergoes mandatory counseling which has as one of its goals to present the case that the developing fetus is an independent human life, and obeys a 72 hour waiting period between counseling and the abortion. Later abortions are not punishable if medical reasons, such as possible harm to the woman from continued pregnancy, or a severely deformed fetus, indicate so.

In 1988, the Supreme Court of Canada decision in *R. v. Morgentaler*, declared the entire section restricting women's right to have an abortion to be of no force or effect because it was held to violate section 7 of the Canadian Charter of Rights and Freedoms, which provides that: "Everyone has the right to life, liberty, and the security of the person and the right not to be deprived thereof except in accordance with the principles of fundamental justice."[72]

The majority of the Court held that "the structure—system regulating access to therapeutic abortions—is manifestly unfair. It contains so many potential barriers to its own operation that the [exception] it creates will in many circumstances be practically unavailable to women who would *prima facie* qualify."[73] As such, the provision was held to violate the principles of fundamental justice and was struck down, leaving Canada with a legislative vacuum to this day. Justice Wilson wrote:

> The right to 'liberty' contained in s. 7 guarantees to every individual a degree of personal autonomy over important decisions intimately affecting his or her private life. Liberty in a free and democratic society does not require the state to approve such decisions but it does require the state to respect them. . . . 'Freedom of conscience and religion' should be broadly construed to extend to conscientiously-held beliefs, whether grounded in religion or in a secular morality and the terms 'conscience' and 'religion' should not be treated as tautologous if capable of independent, although related, meaning. The state here is endorsing one conscientiously-held view at the expense of another. It is denying freedom of conscience to some, treating them as means to an end, depriving them of their 'essential humanity'.[74]

There is a legislative proposal, which passed a second reading in 2008, to create a double offense in which injury to a pregnant woman would be regarded as a separate offense against the fetus; in this Bill the word "fetus" is replaced by "unborn child," and "pregnant woman" by "mother."[75] Opponents argue that the whole thing is just a pretext to

72 R. v. Morgentaler, [1988] 1 S.C.R. 30, 50.
73 *Id.* at 72-73.
74 *Id.* at 36-37.
75 Unborn Victims of Crime Act, Bill C-484, 39th Parliament, 2d Sess. (Can. 2007)

legislate a concept that will facilitate Charter challenges to abortion rights.

D. *Modesty and Restrictive Dress Codes*

Restrictive dress and behavioral codes to preserve women's modesty exist in all three monotheistic religions. The insistence on the covering of hair for married women in Judaism and Islam or the covering of their hair in church for Christian women are all related to modesty. The most severe remaining strictures are in ultra-orthodox Judaism, in which a very small community still requires women to shave their heads on marriage and in the Islamic world, where many millions of women are forced, by custom and sometimes by law, to wear covering ranging from the headscarf (*hijab*) to the *chador*, *niqab* and, in the most extreme cases, to the *burqa*. The Islamic feminist argument made in favor of the veil is that it protects women from sexual harassment. However, it seems scarcely feminist to argue that a woman's way to protection against sexual harassment is by restricting her own freedom of movement rather than restricting the male's freedom to harass. It is further claimed that in the West, Muslim immigrants wear the veil as a form of ideological and ethnic identity symbol. Although there are undoubtedly a significant number of Muslim women who express these views, it is clear from the comparative religious context that religious rules on modesty for women are not merely neutral cultural manifestations, but are connected to repression of women's sexuality and their subjection to male power in the family. Indeed the veil has been described by an Iranian women's movement as "the ideological banner of Iran's sexual apartheid and misogynist values."[76]

Two contrary trends regarding women's human rights as religious women have been brought before constitutional courts. There are those women who regard themselves as religious feminists who, rejecting the patriarchal norms of their religions, have demanded full and equal religious personhood. This includes Lutheran and Protestant women who have sought admission to the priesthood, and it includes Orthodox Jewish women who have sought equality in the rituals of worship, as practiced in the public arena. In the only constitutional case brought on this issue, the Israeli Supreme Court ultimately refused the women's claim to equality in ritual. In a different trend, there are Muslim women

(sponsored by Conservative MP Ken Epp, a strong Mennonite Christian).

76 AZAR MAJEDI, WOMEN'S RIGHTS VS POLITICAL ISLAM: A SERIES OF POLITICAL WRITINGS ABOUT THE DEVASTATING EFFECTS OF POLITICAL ISLAM ON WOMEN'S SITUATION AND THE STRUGGLE OF WOMEN AGAINST IT (2007).

who are asserting the right to conform to evidently patriarchal religious norms and express this through the demand to wear various forms of the Muslim head scarf in public and private institutions. These claims have produced a mass of constitutional and labor court decisions in Europe, where the Muslims are minority communities and in Turkey, where traditionalist religious Muslims are regarded as a minority in a secular constitutional state. The overall trend seems to be to recognize adult religious women's right to wear the veil, except where there are dress codes to which all members of an institution must adhere. However, the Courts have been more circumspect as regards the wearing of Muslim female apparel in educational institutions, regarding this as contrary either to state secularism or to gender equality.

In a series of three decisions between 1994 to 2004, Israel's High Court of Justice rejected the petition of the Women of the Wall (WOW) to pray at the Kotel (the Western Wall of the second Temple and a central national, cultural, and religious site for Jews) in a group (*tefila*), wearing prayer shawls (*tallit*) and reading aloud from the Torah Scroll (*Torah*), a manner of prayer customary for men, but not for women, and a subject of much controversy among Orthodox Jewish authorities.[77] The women's prayer in this manner—the three Ts—had been greeted with violent opposition from other Orthodox worshippers and prohibited by the secular authorities. The objections raised against the women's mode of prayer included the biblical restriction on women's wearing men's apparel and the Talmudic restriction on women raising their voices in song or prayer, which is considered seductive provocation.

In the first of its decisions, the Court recommended that the government find a way to enforce the WOW's right to freedom of worship while minimizing the injury to the sensitivities of worshippers.[78] In the second decision, the Court, composed of two women justices and one man, directed the government to implement the WOW's prayer rights at the Kotel within six months.[79] Orthodox Jewish political parties immediately presented a bill to convert the area in front of the Kotel into a religious shrine exclusively for Orthodox religious practice with a penalty of seven years' imprisonment for any person violating the current Orthodox custom of prayer. The attorney general requested a further hearing, and the president of the Supreme Court appointed an expanded panel of nine justices to reconsider the

[77] HCJ 257/89 Anat Hoffman v. Commissioner of the Western Wall, [1994] IsrSC 48(2) 265.

[78] *Id.* at 356.

[79] HCJ 3358/95 Anat Hoffman v. Director General of Prime Minister's Office, [2000] IsrSC 54(2) 345. The author acted as counsel for the WOW. For a full discussion, see Frances Raday, *Claiming Equal Religious Personhood: Women of the Wall's Constitutional Saga*, *in* RELIGION IN THE PUBLIC SPHERE: A COMPARATIVE ANALYSIS OF GERMAN, ISRAELI, AMERICAN AND INTERNATIONAL LAW 255-98 (Winfried Brugger & Michael Mousa Karayanni eds., 2007).

issue. The Court held, by a majority of nine to two, that the members of WOW were entitled to pray in their manner at the Kotel; however, it also decided, by a majority of five to four, that, in order to prevent injury to the sensitivities of other worshippers, the government should make arrangements for a suitable prayer area for WOW at an adjacent site known as Robinson's Arch—an alternative to which the WOW were totally opposed—and only if the government failed to do so within a year would the WOW have the right to pray at the Kotel.[80] The government constructed a prayer area at Robinson's Arch at which the WOW do not pray.

There has been a series of cases, in Europe and in Turkey, on the wearing of Muslim head scarves—the hijab—in educational institutions or workplaces. The most rigid dress code has been the burqa (head-to-toe covering, with a veiled window for seeing through) or the veil (head-to-toe covering with an open slit for the eyes) and, in less extreme forms, the hijab (headscarf tied under the chin). In constitutional democracies, the issue is represented as a clash between the right of the women themselves to exercise freedom of religion and expression, on one hand, and the right to gender equality or to the freedom to express secular values, on the other.

In 1989, the Constitutional Court in Turkey held unconstitutional a bylaw of the Institutions of Higher Education that, as an exception to the requirement of "modern clothing" in universities, allowed the neck and hair to be veiled by a head scarf because of religious belief.[81] The Court held that the bylaw undermined the secular character of the state, was inconsistent with the law requiring civil servants to have their heads unveiled, and was invalid. This decision thus obliged the universities to ban the wearing of Muslim head scarves. In 2008, the Islamic AKP—the ruling party in Turkey—reversed the ban. The French courts have wavered on the issue of Muslim head scarves. In 1989, the Conseil d'Etat ruled that "the ostentatious wearing" of head scarves at state schools violated a law prohibiting proselytisation in the schools.[82] This decision was followed by unfavorable media attention to the wearing of the hijab; and in 1994, the Ministry of Education issued a directive prohibiting the wearing of "ostentatious political and religious symbols" in state schools.[83] In 1995, however, the Conseil d'Etat held that the

80 HCJ 4128/00 Director General of Prime Minister's Office v. Anat Hoffman, [2003] IsrSC 57(3) 289.

81 Constitutional Court of Turkey, Decision 1989/652.

82 Lionel Jospin, Circulaire relative au port d'insignes religieux à l'école se referent à l'avis du Conseil d'Etat, Journal Officiel de la Republique [J.O.] [Official Gazette of France], Dec. 15, 1989, p. 15577.

83 U.S. DEP'T OF STATE, REPORT ON FRANCE HUMAN RIGHTS PRACTICES, 1995 (1996), *available at* http://dosfan.lib.uic.edu/ERC/democracy/1995_hrp_report/95hrp_report_eur/France.html.

simple wearing of a Muslim head scarf does not provide grounds for exclusion from school.[84] This was settled by the legislature in 2004 in a law which upheld secularity of French state schools and prohibited the wearing of conspicuous religious symbols by students or teachers.

In 1999, in Switzerland, the Geneva Conseil d'Etat dismissed a teacher's challenge to a ban imposed by the Educational Department on Muslim teachers wearing headscarves in the public, secular education system. That judgment was upheld by the federal court, which, noting that the applicant's job made her a representative of the state, held that the head scarf constituted a strong vestimental sign of belief in a particular religion and that the restriction imposed by the education authorities was accordingly necessary to preserve both the principle of neutrality between different faiths and that of equality between the sexes within the school.[85] In 2003, Germany's Federal Constitutional Court ruled that Muslims could wear their veils while teaching but at the same time encouraged new laws to ban religious symbols.[86] Subsequently, eight of sixteen German states passed school laws that banned headscarves, saying they were an affront to Christian values.

The House of Lords adopted a contextualized approach in the *Denbigh High School* case in 2006.[87] It rejected a Muslim student's petition to be allowed to wear a jilbab to a school which had made provision for tunics and trousers acceptable to the local Muslim community. The opinion in the Court was divided between those judges who held that the school's refusal to allow Shabina Begum to wear a jilbab at school did not interfere with her article 9 right under the European Convention of Human Rights to manifest her religion and those who restricted themselves to holding that, even if it did, the school's decision was objectively justified. The majority of the judges thought it proper that schools should be called upon to explain and justify their decisions, as did the Denbigh High School in the specific context. Baroness Hale of Richmond was the only one of the judges to analyze the equality implications of the wearing of the veil. She wrote:

> [S]trict dress codes may be imposed upon women, not for their own sake but to serve the ends of others. Hence they may be denied equal freedom to choose for themselves. They may also be denied equal treatment. A dress code which requires women to conceal all but their face and hands, while leaving men much freer to decide what

---

84 *Id.*

85 Dahlab v. Switzerland, App. No. 42393/98, 2001-V Eur. Ct. H.R. 447.

86 Kopftuch-Urteil [Headscarf Decision], Entscheidungen des Bundesverfassungsgerichts [BVerfGE] [Federal Constitutional Court] 108, 282, Sept. 24, 2003, 2 BvR 1436/02, NJW 2003, 3111 (F.R.G.).

87 R (on the application of Begum) v. Denbigh High School Govenors [2006] UKHL 15, [2007] A.C. 100 (U.K.).

> they will wear, does not treat them equally.[88]

She went on to explain that while adult women may choose the veil, schools are different. "Their task is to educate the young from all the many and diverse families and communities in this country in accordance with the national curriculum. Their task is to help all of their pupils achieve their full potential."[89] In deciding how far to go in accommodating religious requirements within its dress code, such a school has to accommodate some complex considerations. These are helpfully explained by Professor Frances Raday in an earlier article:

> [G]enuine individual consent to a discriminatory practice or dissent from it may not be feasible where these girls are not yet adult. The question is whether patriarchal family control should be allowed to result in girls being socialized according to the implications of veiling while still attending public educational institutions. . . . A mandatory policy that rejects veiling in state educational institutions may provide a crucial opportunity for girls to choose the feminist freedom of state education over the patriarchal dominance of their families. Also, for the families, such a policy may send a clear message that the benefits of state education are tied to the obligation to respect women's and girls' rights to equality and freedom. . . . On the other hand, a prohibition of veiling risks violating the liberal principle of respect for individual autonomy and cultural diversity for parents as well as students. It may also result in traditionalist families not sending their children to the state educational institutions. In this educational context, implementation of the right to equality is a complex matter, and the determination of the way it should be achieved depends upon the balance between these two conflicting policy priorities in a specific social environment.[90]

It seems to me that that was exactly what this school was trying to do when it devised the school uniform policy to suit the social conditions in that school, in that town, and at that time.

The workplace issue arose in Denmark in 2000, in the context of a Muslim girl's demand to wear the Muslim head scarf at work. In August 2000 the Danish High Court held that, because the workplace did not have a general dress code, it could not forbid the girl to wear the head scarf.[91] Kirsten Ketscher comments: "Regrettably the question of the girl's rights in relation to the non-discrimination principle of women was not raised. Therefore the outcome of the case was that a religion was being protected not a woman!"[92] In a later case, in 2005, the

88 *Id.* at 133.

89 *Id.* at 134.

90 Frances Raday, *Culture, Religion, and Gender*, 1 INT'L J. CONST. L. 663, 709 (2003).

91 Eastern High Court, Aug. 10, 2000, Ugeskrift for Retsvaesen U2000.2350Ø (Den.).

92 Kirsten Ketscher, Lecture at the Hebrew University of Jerusalem: Women's Fundamental Rights and the Freedom of Religion (2000) (on file with author); *see also* Kirsten Ketscher, *Etnisk Liegebehandling, religionsfrihed og ligestilling mellem kvinder og maend – set i lyset af*

Supreme Court of Denmark held that employers may prohibit Muslim headscarves if it is in the framework of a general dress code that is part of the company's external presentation and is enforced consistently towards all employees in similar positions.[93] In 2003, the German Federal Labor Court held that a department store was not entitled to dismiss an employee who worked at the cosmetics counter because she insisted on wearing a headscarf.[94]

E. *Homosexuality*

Religious abhorrence for homosexuality continues into the 21st century. Pope Benedict was accused of stoking homophobia in December 2008 after a speech, in which he declared that saving humanity from homosexuality was just as important as saving the rainforest from destruction. He said that humanity needed to listen to the "language of creation" to understand the intended roles of man and woman and behavior beyond traditional heterosexual relations was a "destruction of God's work." In Islam, the legal punishment for sodomy has varied among juristic schools: some prescribe capital punishment while others prescribe a milder discretionary punishment. Homosexuality is a crime and forbidden in most Islamic countries.

In the United Kingdom, the United States and Ireland, the approach of constitutional courts towards homosexuality was initially based on acceptance of religious abhorrence and criminal prohibition. From the time of the infamous trial of Oscar Wilde and up until 1980s, the courts did not insist on the right of homosexual partners to privacy, equality and human dignity. It was only some considerable time after the European Court of Human Rights had taken a clear stand on this human rights issue in 1981, in *Dudgeon v. United Kingdom*,[95] that constitutional systems followed suit. These developments, regarding the human rights of homosexuals, place the transition from religious edict to human rights pluralism in sharp focus and indicate the central part played by international human rights law in the process.

Despite the holding in the *Dudgeon* case, in 1983, the Supreme Court of Ireland upheld the prohibition of homosexual conduct.[96] The Court based its decision explicitly on the Christian character of the State and Justice O'Higgins wrote:

Føtex-sagen, U2005B.235.

93 22/2004 Højesteret [Supreme Court of Denmark], Dec. 18, 2003, Ugeskrift for Retsvaesen U2005.1265H (Den.).

94 Bundesarbeitsgericht [BAG] [Federal Labor Court] Oct. 10, 2002, 2 AZR 472/01, NJW 2003, 1685 (F.R.G.).

95 Dudgeon v. United Kingdom, 4 Eur. Ct. H.R. 149 (1982) .

96 David Norris v. Attorney General, [1984] I.R. 36 (Ir.).

> From the earliest days, organised religion regarded homosexual conduct, such as sodomy and associated acts, with deep revulsion as being contrary to the order of nature, a perversion of the biological functions of the sexual organs and an affront to both society and God. With the advent of Christianity this view found clear expression in the teachings of St Paul.[97]

The Court held that the decision of the European Court of Human Rights, which had decided in the *Dudgeon* case that the Irish legislation violated article 8 of the European Convention of Human Rights, was not binding law in Ireland. In 1986, the United States Supreme Court similarly held in *Bowers*[98] that homosexuality was contrary to public morals and thus upheld criminal prohibitions of consensual sexual intercourse between adults of the same sex.

It took twelve years after *Dudgeon* before homosexuality was decriminalized in both Ireland and the United States. In Ireland, homosexuality was formally decriminalized in 1993. In 2003, in *Lawrence v. Texas*,[99] the United States Supreme Court overruled *Bowers*, with Justice Kennedy writing for the majority:

> The statutes do seek to control a personal relationship that, whether or not entitled to formal recognition in the law, is within the liberty of persons to choose without being punished as criminals. . . . [The nation] has been shaped by religious beliefs, conceptions of right and acceptable behavior, and respect for the traditional family.[100]

The Court relied in part on the fact that laws prescribing this sort of conduct are invalid under the European Convention of Human Rights. In 1998, the Constitutional Court of South Africa, acting on the Equality Clause of South Africa's 1996 constitution—the first constitution ever to include sexual orientation in its anti-discrimination provisions—unanimously overturned "sodomy laws" in the country.[101] In a sweeping decision, it held that laws criminalizing consensual homosexual conduct violated not only privacy protections but the principles of equality and dignity as well. In eloquent language, both the majority opinion and a concurring opinion affirmed that respecting gay and lesbian equality and dignity was a key aspect of overcoming South Africa's repressive past.

---

97 *Id.*

98 Bowers v. Hardwick, 478 U.S. 186 (1986).

99 Lawrence v. Texas, 539 U.S. 558 (2003).

100 *Id.* at 567-71.

101 *Nat'l Coal. for Gay & Lesbian Equal. v. Minister of Justice*, 1998 (12) BCLR 1517 (CC) at 28 (S. Afr.).

F. *Freedom of Expression*

Freedom of expression also remains a constitutional issue. The opposition of religions to freedom of expression is not new. The Christian church has continued its tradition of banning heresy, from Galileo and Darwin to Voltaire and Thomas Hobbes, into the current era: the banning of Darwinism from school syllabuses and the banning of public advertising of family planning services. In the United States, following on the famous 1925 *Scopes* trial,[102] named in popular tradition the *Monkey Trial*, the issue of Darwinism remains moot. In 1987 a constitutional challenge was brought against a Louisiana law, which prohibited the teaching of the theory of evolution in the public schools unless that instruction was accompanied by the teaching of creation science, a Biblical belief. Schools were not forced to teach creation science. However, if either topic was to be addressed, evolution or creation, teachers were obligated to discuss the other as well. The Supreme Court held that the law violated the Establishment Clause. Writing for the majority, Justice Brennan found that Louisiana's law was not enacted to further a clear secular purpose as requiring schools to teach creation science alongside evolution does not advance academic freedom, the primary effect of the law was to advance the viewpoint that a "supernatural being created humankind," a doctrine central to the dogmas of certain religious denominations, and the law significantly entangled the interests of church and state by seeking "the symbolic and financial support of government to achieve a religious purpose."[103] This decision was followed by a Christian campaign for the teaching of intelligent design, and in 2005, a group of parents of high school students challenged a public school district requirement for teachers to present intelligent design in biology classes as an alternative "explanation of the origin of life." In *Kitzmiller v. Dover Area School District*,[104] the U.S. District Court for the Middle District of Pennsylvania ruled that intelligent design is not science, that it "cannot uncouple itself from its creationist, and thus religious, antecedents"; therefore, the school district's promotion of it violated the Establishment Clause.[105]

The Islamic *fatwahs* issued against Salman Rushdie and Hirsi Ali are well-known examples of current Islamic totalitarianism. Thus, in November 2008, the Organization of the Islamic Conference, whose members account for 57 of the U.N.'s 192 member states, won United

---

102 Scopes v. State, 278 S.W. 57 (Tenn. 1925).

103 Edwards v. Aguillard, 482 U.S. 578, 591, 591 (1987).

104 Kitzmiller v. Dover Area Sch. Dist., 400 F. Supp. 2d 707 (M.D. Pa. 2005).

105 *Id.* at 765.

Nations backing for an anti-blasphemy measure: the U.N. General Assembly passed a nonbinding resolution that condemned "defamation of religion." The resolution links religious defamation to incitement to violence, which would severely limit a broad range of peaceful speech and expression. This resolution was included in the agenda for the Durban II Anti-Racism Conference but was later withdrawn after threats by the European Union to join the United States, Italy, Israel and Canada in boycotting the conference.

CONCLUSION

Secular constitutionalism is essential to human rights. Secular constitutionalism, in its endorsement of freedom of conscience, of expression and of religion, provides true pluralism for individual and community choice. Secular constitutionalism has recognized and insisted upon the full and equal constitutional personhood of each human being, without discrimination on grounds of race, sex, religion or sexual preference. On this conceptual basis, the tension between religious norms and the human rights of the religious and non-religious other has been tested in constitutional courts. The outcome of those cases is not the determining factor in establishing that secularism is essential to human rights. It is the fact that constitutions provide an infrastructure of rights which deny the hegemony of religion and provide a forum, conceptual and jurisdictional, for challenging religious dictates which is so essential to the human rights era. Current academic endorsements of pluralistic religious autonomy, or of a preferred status for religious ideologies in constitutional democracies, relegate the human rights of women, homosexuals and dissenters to obscurity.

[5]

Religious Liberty and French Secularism*

*Jacques Robert***

I. Religious Liberty

The democratic state that endeavors to respect the opinions of all its constituents must extend its protection to all religious groups if religious freedom is to be considered more than a particular, subordinate aspect of the freedom to form one's own opinion. These two freedoms seem to merge into one, but, at the same time, religious freedom both falls within and extends beyond the bounds of the freedom of opinion.

Religious liberty is first and foremost an individual liberty because it represents an individual's ability to give, or not to give, intellectual attachment to a religion—to choose the religion freely or to refuse it. But it is also a collective liberty in that, not exhausting itself in faith or belief, it necessarily gives birth to a practice whose free exercise must be guaranteed. Free exercise of religion must be assured in order to guarantee complete religious liberty. This proposition presupposes that every religious movement must be the master of its own activities, possessing the right to organize itself freely. This free organization inevitably poses the delicate problem of relations between religions—or churches—and the state.

II. Church-State Relations

It is necessary to point out that the relations between churches and the state are not necessarily indicative of the general level of religious freedom in France. It is enough to say that such relations

---

* This article is a slightly modified excerpt from JACQUES ROBERT, ENJEUX DU SIÈCLE: NOS LIBERTÉS [STAKES OF THE CENTURY: OUR LIBERTIES] 120–43 (2002). Professor Robert presented this material at the Ninth Annual International Law and Religion Symposium held at Brigham Young University on October 6–9, 2002. This article was translated from French to English by the Brigham Young University Law Review.

** Professor Jacques Robert is the Honorary President of l'Université Panthéon-Assas, and a former member of the French Conseil Constitutionnel.

can be on equal footing with religious liberty—at least as much as any other specific relations.

France, for its part, has experimented throughout its history with nearly all of the existing formulas for church-state relations. If France has finally opted for what is termed a secular stance, it is because France found, at the beginning of the twentieth century, that the secular stance conforms more than any other to France's inclinations and ideals. This secular approach is not the only one to be practiced among democratic states; indeed, the secular approach is rare. Other approaches are perfectly conceivable and have been adopted by many states.

Even in a democratic state, it is possible that a sort of fusion exists between the "temporal" and the "spiritual," or at the very least a union between them that can manifest itself in various forms: a state religion, recognized churches, and incorporation of the church into the state.

Even if Europe alone is considered, one notices an extraordinary complexity in relationships between church and state. Although all European countries demonstrate a profound Christian influence, no juridical system is comparable to another. One finds in Europe a mixture of state-church systems (for example, the systems of England, Denmark, Greece, Sweden, and Finland); systems of separation (such as the systems of Holland, Ireland, and France); and systems using formulas that combine basic separation and cooperation (such as the systems of Germany, Belgium, Austria, Spain, Italy, and Portugal). However, profound influences are diverse, and not always in the way that one would think. For example, religious influence is stronger in Ireland (in spite of its system of separation) than in Sweden (which maintains a state-church system).[1] The church-state connections are weaker in Catholic Europe than in Protestant or Orthodox Europe.[2]

From a legal perspective—especially in terms of sources of law—the fundamental principles that govern the relations between political power and religions are widely dispersed. They can be found in national constitutions, in European texts (European Convention

1. *See* JACQUES ROBERT, LA LIBERTÉ RELIGIEUSE ET LE RÉGIME DES CULTES 109 (1977).

2. *See id.*

on Human Rights[3]), in the laws of each state, in each country's historically observed practices, in concordats formed with the Roman Catholic Church, in international law, in various conventions passed with particular religious confessions (for example, in Spain or Italy), and in informal accords. Also, note that the varied nature of the state's recognition of denominations implicitly permits a distinction between the more represented denominations (and presumably the better established or more serious denominations) and certain others. Unfortunately, this distinction is often left to the arbitrary discretion of political decision makers.

Certain groups also form under the auspices of a statute of public or private law; others form under common law or *sui generis*—the formulas vary. Radical separation is rare but is more frequent when it finds itself blended with the idea of a positive neutrality, or unofficial cooperation.

The cultural role of churches is marked, especially in education, with every modality of adaptation imaginable. Further, financing of churches by the government is rarely direct; it is usually masked by the cover of secret payments, public or discrete subsidies, tax exemptions, or payment through the maintenance of historic monuments. Secularization itself remains limited. In Holland, for example, the distinctive secularization of Dutch society does not keep a great number of social institutions or political parties from being organized on a religious basis.

These varied religious forms are not, in and of themselves, incompatible with the recognition of general religious tolerance. For a state to choose a privileged church or religion does not necessarily signify that others are disadvantaged, much less persecuted. It has simply become evident to France that a regime of total separation—by no means hostile to, but rather largely tolerant of religion—was the approach that conformed most with a modern democratic state.

III. French Secularity

The substance of the notion of secularity is found entirely within two articles of the French Law of 1905:

3. *See* European Convention for the Protection of Human Rights and Fundamental Freedoms, Apr. 11, 1950, art. 10-1, Europ. T.S. No. 5.

Article 1: The Republic ensures the liberty of conscience. It guarantees the free exercise of religion, under restrictions prescribed by the interest in public order.

Article 2: The Republic does not recognize, remunerate, or subsidize any religious denomination.[4]

IV. The Neutrality of the State

The fact that the French Republic no longer recognizes any religion does not signify that the state fails to appreciate the existence of religions, churches, or religious movements. This fact simply means that the state has definitively abandoned the system of "recognized religions." The state wished to erase all distinction between the old recognized religions—the Catholic Church, the two principal Protestant churches, Judaism—and the others. By removing the distinction of recognized religions, the state put all religions on the same level politically.

This policy of nonrecognition should not be understood to signify that the state does not wish to maintain good relations with religious groups. Nonrecognition is not an attitude of hostility or of suspicion. It simply implies that the existence of religion, contrary to concordative solutions, ceases to be a public affair. The inescapable consequence of this is that the state can no longer finance or subsidize a religion.

V. Separation

At first, the implications of removing public funding for religious public services were notable: the disappearance of the Ministry of the Religious Budget and an end to favored treatment for religious ministers, particularly the naming of ecclesiastical dignitaries. Indeed, once a church fails to accomplish a mission of public service, a "public" religious organization ceases to exist and, therefore, the church or organization no longer has a right to be viewed as "institutional" by public authorities. The corollary of this end to public service by organized religions is that all churches are left with

4. *See* Law of Dec. 9, 1905, arts. 1–2, J.O., Dec. 11, 1905, p. 7205 [hereinafter Law of 1905].

total liberty to organize themselves and to interpret their internal rules.

The jurisprudence of French tribunals—judicial and administrative—bears witness to their wisdom in not meddling in religious rules, in a law which is not their own.[5] The courts do not take jurisdiction unless a threat to public order exists.

VI. FINANCIAL "COEXISTENCE"

From a financial point of view, the law of separation only prohibits the inscription of credits intended to subsidize, permanently and regularly, service by churches. One can therefore conclude that the Law of 1905 allows for:

- The possibility of state subsidies for activities that have a general character despite taking place in a religious setting: charities, hospitals, nurseries, general charitable activities, etc.
- Direct administration by public collectives of certain religious services (religious instruction in public establishments such as high schools, junior high schools, hospitals, asylums, prisons, etc.) if the organization is deemed indispensable to insure for everyone the free exercise of religion.
- The payment of religious ministers when they render services to the general public (national religious ceremonies, media events, etc.).

On the other hand, tribunals exercise a certain oversight function over "disguised subsidies"; even so, their jurisprudence often appears indulgent.[6] The institutional separation of the churches from the state, which was sought in 1905, implies that the state does not disadvantage religions but ceases to recognize, to pay, and to subsidize them; such a separation comes with the obligation to be "religiously neutral."

5. *See* Conseil d'État, Feb. 8, 1908, Abbé Deliard, Rec. P. 128; C. Cass., Feb. 6, 1912, S. Jur. I, 1912, 137; Conseil d'État, Feb. 16, 1923, Presbyterian Association of the Reformed Church, Rec. P. 115; Conseil d'État, Jan. 25, 1943, Reformed Church of Marseille, Rec. P. 116; T.G.I., Paris, Oct. 29, 1976, *SOVEVOCA and the Consistorial Israelite Assembly of Paris*, JCP 1977, No. 18664 (note by Jean Carbonnier); Cass. 1e civ., Oct. 17, 1978, Abbe Coache v. Abbe Bellgo, D. 1979, at 120, 1979 Bull. Civ. I, No. 308.

6. *See* Conseil d'État, Nov. 28, 1913, Commune de Chambon, Rec. P. 774; Conseil d'État, May 16, 1919, Commune de Montjoie, Rec. P. 429.

VII. NEGATIVITY AND POSITIVITY

This religious neutrality is, however, simultaneously negative and positive.[7] It is negative because the state that allows for all the diverse manifestations of thought, that does not reject any ideology but welcomes them all, would not know how to choose one it would officially champion and promote. Of course, the state might have secret preferences, but it must keep from publicizing these preferences, from supporting or giving priority to those who share these preferences, and from attempting to impose these preferences on other groups through pressure.

Two texts are worth invoking here:

- Article 10 of the Declaration of the Rights of Man and the Citizen, which establishes that no one should be harassed about his or her opinions, including religious opinions.[8]
- Article 2 of the Constitution of 4 October 1958 under the terms of which France is a "secular" state that "assures equality before the law for all citizens without distinction based on origin, race or religion."[9]

These two texts create a perfect connection between the notion of negative neutrality that presupposes the discretion of the state and that of positive neutrality that implies the engagement of the state to guarantee to each person in his or her daily experience the free exercise of his or her religion. This puts at the disposition of all, if the situation requires, the means to observe their religions' rules. From this exigency, several statutes have evolved in France, including the Statute of Chaplaincies, the regulation of the animal-slaughtering methods and slaughterhouse conditions, the recognition of conscientious objectors, and the de facto rearrangement of certain school schedules.[10]

7. *See* Jean Rivero, *La notion juridique de laïcité*, D. 1949 CHRONIQUE 137; J.B. Trotabas, *La notion de laïcité dans le droit de l'Eglise catholique et de l'Etat républicain*, Paris L.G.D.J. 19670, at 223; J. Coulombel, *Le droit privé francais devant le fait religieux depuis la separation de l'Eglise et de l'Etat*, 1956 REVUE TRIM. DE DROIT CIVIL 7.

8. *See* Jacques Robert & Henri Oberdorff, *Libertés fondamentales et Droits de l'homme*, *in* TEXTES FRANCAIS ET INTERNATIONAUX (5th ed. 2002).

9. *See id.*

10. *See* JACQUES ROBERT & JEAN DUFFAR, DROITS DE L'HOMME ET LIBERTÉS FONDAMENTALES 298 (7th ed. 1999).

Thus, it is formally demonstrated that the "neutrality"—positive or negative—of the state cannot proceed without respect for liberty of conscience.

VIII. LIBERTY OF CONSCIENCE

The nonreligious nature of the state places citizens on equal moral footing with respect to the state. This equality is rigorous because the state does not claim to profess any particular faith in the name of the nation. Therefore, no room exists for categorization of second-class citizens on the basis of religious convictions. The will of the state to avoid knowledge of citizens' spirituality is, from this fact, a guarantee of liberty for the diverse religious confessions.[11]

The "indifferent" state has no need to ask itself what counts as a religion because, in principle, it neither professes nor knows one. The principle of religious liberty precludes the operation of any type of distinction between religions, whether the religion is practiced by a "cult"[12] or by a traditional church. One finds in this preclusion the principal applications of religious freedom that are the principles of equality and nondiscrimination between religions. Further, the principle of nondiscrimination itself induces a positive attitude on the part of the state; the state must protect minority religions in the very name of religious freedom. The affirmation that the state guarantees liberty of conscience signifies not only that the state is itself obligated to respect this liberty, but also that it will take responsibility for preventing violations of this liberty by its citizens and others.[13]

The principle of liberty of conscience is also under the sanction of French penal law. The Law of 1905 created the crime of harming liberty of conscience. Article 31 of this law provides for the

11. *See* L. De Naurois, *Aux confins du droit prive et du droit public*, 1962 REVUE TRIM. DE DROIT CIVIL 242.

12. Editor's note: Professor Robert employs the French term *secte* here. The translation of the French word *secte* into English is problematic because in French, *secte* has almost as many negative connotations as does our English word "cult." However, despite these negative connotations the word *secte* remains theoretically slightly neutral. Thus, there is a distinction in French between a *secte* and a *secte dangereuse*. The most accurate way to translate *secte* would probably be "rather unknown and probably dangerous religious movement." For practical reasons, we have chosen to translate most instances of *secte* as "cult." Where the author employs the term *secte* as a neutral term to refer to a new religious movement, it has been translated as "sect." Also note that the French word *culte* has no negative connotation at all, and is best translated simply as "religion."

13. *See* Naurois, *supra* note 11.

punishment of those who utilize violent acts or threats against an individual (creating either fear of job loss or causing injury to the individual's person, family, or wealth) to force that individual to participate, or to refrain from participating, in a religion.[14]

In a larger context, respect for freedom of conscience is affirmed by the recognition of the illicit character of all attitudes that show an attempt to discriminate on the basis of expressed or supposed beliefs and to cause one to fear, in any manner, because of these religiously held opinions.[15] This interdiction of all attitudes that are hostile to any religion is imposed on all: on individuals, on churches, and on the state itself.

Neutral and secular, the state would not be able to practice the slightest discrimination with regard to any religious movement nor favor any particular propaganda that could harm a religion, insofar as each movement respects the restrictions prescribed by the state according to its interest in public order.

IX. Public Order and Religious Liberty

French texts have often—and perhaps abusively—linked public order and religious liberty. One remembers the ambiguous and restrictive formulation of Article 10 of the Declaration of the Rights of Man: "No one shall be harassed on account of his or her opinions, including religious views, provided their manifestation does not disturb the public order established by law."[16] One must also remember that even though the first French Constitution[17] considers the liberty conferred upon all people to exercise their religious beliefs to be a "natural and civil right," its first article, consecrated to "fundamental provisions guaranteed by the Constitution," defines the limits of that liberty. That article specifies that liberty only consists of the power to act in a manner that does not endanger public safety or

14. *See* Law of 1905, *supra* note 4, art. 31.

15. *See* Conseil d'État, July 9, 1943, Ferrand C.D. 1944, at 150 (Corbinnier note); Conseil d'État, April 28, 1938, Demoiselle Weiss R.D.P. 1938, at 553; Conseil d'État, Dec. 8, 1948, Demoiselle Pasteau R.D.P. 1949, at 73; C. Cass. July 19, 1898, D.P. I 424; Trib. civ. Seine, Mar. 3, 1933, S. Jur. II 1934, 2, 67; Trib. civ. Seine June 18, 1945, Gaz. Pal. 1945, 2, 38; CA Amiens, March 3, 1975, Guy Ferchault v. Marcell Bascot, épouse Ferchault, D.1975, at 706 (note by Géraldy). See also for all these points: Jacques Robert, *La liberté religieuse et le régime des cultes*, *in* PUF Collection SUP 109 (1977).

16. Declaration of the Rights of Man and of the Citizen, art. 10 (Fr.) (approved by the National Assembly of France on Aug. 26, 1789).

17. La Constitution (1791).

individual rights. Thus the law, and the law alone, is always authorized to penalize the authors of those acts that would prove harmful to society because of their threat to public safety or their erosion of others' rights.

X. The Islamic Scarf

Reference to public order is found in the Law of 1905,[18] and it recently reappeared in an opinion from the Conseil d'Etat dated November 27, 1989.[19] That opinion discussed whether the wearing of religious badges or religious identifiers in French public schools is compatible with the principle of secularism in the public service of education.

Following a review of the internal and international texts upon which this principle is founded, the Conseil d'Etat clearly indicated that allowing students to wear such identifiers is merely an aspect of the general principle of secularism and neutrality of the state. The Conseil d'Etat found that these principles require the state to respect the students' liberty of conscience, meaning that the state should abolish all discrimination by public schools based on their students' religious convictions or beliefs.

The religious freedom thus recognized for these students secures for them the right to express and to manifest their religious beliefs within scholarly establishments, in the spirit of pluralism and respect for the rights of others. However, this recognition does not grant students free rein to flaunt symbols of religious adherence that by their nature, by the conditions under which they would be worn individually or collectively, or by their ostentatious or aggressive character would constitute an act of pressure, provocation, proselytism, or propaganda. Such flaunting would bring harm to the dignity and liberty of the students and other members of the educational community and would compromise the students' security and well-being, disturbing the teaching process and the teachers themselves. In the end, such flaunting would disturb the

18. *See* Law of 1905, *supra* note 4, art. 1.

19. Opinion from the Conseil d'Etat dated November 27, 1989. The Conseil d'Etat has two roles. The first is as a judicial body that resolves litigation between individuals and the state. The second is as an advising body that provides non-binding opinions and advice to the executive branch. Often when a difficult legal question arises for the French government, the government turns to the Conseil d'Etat as a first step in finding a solution.

public order and the normal functioning of the public teaching establishment.[20]

Since this opinion, the Conseil d'Etat has been obliged to clarify its position. The council overturned a school's internal regulation stipulating that "wearing any distinctive sign, clothing or otherwise, of a religious, political or philosophical order is strictly forbidden."[21] Such a regulation, by the generality of its terms, effectively created a general and absolute prohibition that completely ignored the students' recognized freedom of expression in the context of the principles of neutrality and secularism in public education. Given this result, the decisions to exclude several young girls from junior high on the sole basis of this general prohibition must be overturned. Indeed, for those decisions to have been correctly made, the schools would have needed to establish that, under the circumstances, the wearing of this type of Islamic scarf constituted by its very nature "an act of pressure, provocation, proselytism or propaganda, or [that disturbs] the public order and the normal functioning of the teaching process."[22]

At first, the issue of the Islamic scarf only seemed to bother the conscience of other students. In the end, however, it might also disturb the conscience of the instructors. Certain instructors had already indicated that they were not far from refusing to teach students whose clothing negated, for the teachers, the very values that a republican school should represent. But such an attitude was intolerable. The principle of secularism requires the total absence of discrimination between students on the basis of their religion. The faculty must not be authorized to make any kind of distinction between students based on religious attire.

In summary, the state—secular, neutral, respectful of all opinions and beliefs, guarantor of freedom of religion and worship, and propagandist for no faith or ideology—cannot oppose religious movements that prosper in its territory using as its reason only the policy of protecting the public order. Further, all religious movements that respect the public order must have their religious practices protected equally. If not, history has given a privileged

20. *See* Avis, No. 34893, *Assemblée générale plénière*, 1990 A.J.D.A. 3945 (note by P.P.C.); R.F.D.A., 1990, at 1–9 (note by Jean Rivero).

21. *See* Conseil d'État, Nov. 2, 1992, Kherovara & Kachour, N. Balo and Mme. Kizic.

22. Conseil d'État, Nov. 2, 1992, Les Petites Affiches, May 24, 1993, No. 62 (see note by Gilles Lebreton, *Port de signes religieux et laicité de l'enseignement public*).

position to certain religions, favored only because they have been around longer and have been accepted with less reticence because society is more accustomed to having them in France.

Many today point out that the landscape has completely transformed into an environment of religious liberty confronted with a proliferation of movements whose dynamism and originality are simultaneously fascinating and worrisome. Identifying and characterizing these movements is difficult. Moreover, faithful members of much older religions are becoming more numerous in France, and they are also pressing for a de facto "official" status, which is recognized for others.[23]

XI. The Sectarian Phenomenon

French society is unfamiliar with the proliferation of religious denominations and the multiplicity of churches that are familiar to Anglo-Saxon societies. For us, the notion of a *secte* has a pejorative connotation that some great democracies of our day reject.[24] In France, a juridical theory of *secte* has been painstakingly elaborated after many years and through a constant flow of often passionate debates. This theory distinguishes *sectes* from religions; thus, the theory does not provide *sectes* with the same protection provided to religions by international texts.

Therefore, it is necessary to define the determinative criteria of a *secte* with precision. Many criteria have been successively advanced by modern sociology and, taken together, will identify a *secte*. However, these criteria, heretofore advanced by sociology, have been somewhat abandoned in our day.

23. Even though France is a secular state that does not officially recognize any religion, in effect there remains a de facto regime of "recognized religions" consisting of the Catholic Church, the Reformed Church, the Lutheran Church, and the Jewish religion. These are the only churches to maintain official relations with the state. Other religions exist, of course, but they are simply "tolerated" and do not enjoy "official status." Their lack of status is undoubtedly because they do not have a representative structure that is capable of ready dialogue with the state.

24. *See supra* note 12.

XII. Establishing Criteria

A. Number of Adherents

The first criterion of a *secte* is that it has a small number of adherents. One here could easily bring up the contradiction that arises by retaining such a criterion in an era where respect of minorities is proclaimed as a national and international moral principle. However, by simply stepping inside the very notion of religion, one cannot help but notice that it is the religions (whose character as a religion is not or is no longer contested) that choose, by theological exigence, to be religions for those who profess membership, rather than simply religions for the masses. Based simply on the facts, one must expect many setbacks when attempting to use quantitative criteria. A community, numerically weak in a country, is often no more than a particular branch of a much larger group dispersed among different countries.

B. Eccentricity

A second criterion of a *secte* is eccentricity. If a *secte* must be defined with reference to rationality, one cannot differentiate between religion and *secte* because the nature of a religious faith is, at least in certain respects, irrational and mystic.

C. Newness

Another criterion of a *secte* is newness. Newness is probably the criterion that has the greatest impact. This is true because the age of a religious movement is easy to verify, but also perhaps because time is a familiar dimension in the law. A *secte* is essentially a "newly-born" religion.[25] The phenomena so frequently analyzed in religious studies, such as dissidence, schism, heresy, and reform, attest to the possibility of newly-formed confessions, created in a single moment. To forbid all creativity in theological research is, above all, to deny

25. This idea of newness is determined with respect to the religion's emergence in France. This is the only criterion that concerns French law, which does not consider itself competent to judge or regulate all the new religious movements that begin in other countries. French authorities only begin tracking a religious movement when it appears in France for the first time.

one of the most essential forms of liberty of conscience and to diminish the religious experience.

D. External Origin

Objection to newness is sometimes transposed from history into geography and becomes a type of objection to anything of external origin; but this is an inadmissible objection. In fact, it would be more valid against an established religion and, taken to its logical extreme, against Christianity as a whole. In law, this argument against anything of external origin is condemned by the principle of free communication, which today is inscribed in Article 10-1 of the European Convention for the Protection of Human Rights and Fundamental Freedoms.[26] This convention recognizes the right of every person to receive or to communicate ideas without regard to national borders.[27] Thus, the notion of a *secte* is difficult to define.[28]

XIII. THE NOTION OF RELIGION

One could say that religion is defined by two elements: one objective and the other subjective. The objective element is given by the existence of a community. A community is more than a simple aggregation of individuals; it is a coherent group, a moral being. Religion is a collective phenomenon; it is not necessarily a mass phenomenon. There are churches that consider themselves national churches; others recognize their own minority status or micro-minority status. French positive law has wisely refused to integrate confessional statistics into its standards. Article 19 of the Law of 1905 is significant.[29] It does not give the slightest consideration to the makeup of a particular sectarian organization, whether it has a greater or smaller number of adherents that profess to be members.

The subjective element defining religion is faith or religious belief. Faith has its center in the individual conscience. Nevertheless, faith is not a solitary conscience, but a reciprocity of consciences that

26. European Convention for the Protection of Human Rights and Fundamental Freedoms, Apr. 11, 1950, art. 10-1, Europ. T.S. No. 5.

27. *See id.*

28. Incidentally, is it not the same with religion? Do we know today with exactness what really constitutes a religion? *See* Jacques Robert, *Accepter la foi*, LE MONDE DES DÉBATS, Feb 1994, at 9; *see also* Robert & Duffar, *supra* note 9, at 298.

29. *See* Law of 1905, *supra* note 4, art. 19.

engenders religion. Because of this fact, these two elements—community and faith—are mutually dependent. One must have faith to give meaning to a group, but it requires a group, restrained as it might be, to bring faith to an expression which law cannot accomplish.

It is from a common faith, a spiritual communion, or a community of beliefs that a group draws its coherence. However, religious belief is equally difficult to define. One may be tempted to define religious belief with reference to the behaviors that manifest it: practices, observances, rights, liturgies, and sacraments. These behaviors often have an originality that signals the presence of a religion. Even so, this argument is not necessarily decisive. After all, municipalities were the first to organize civil baptism, and the *Cour d'assises* has its own ritual. Gestures alone are empty forms; only the belief that animates them can give them a religious significance.

One must return then to what is at the heart of the question: the object of the belief. Not every conviction is a faith. Neither a political party nor a school of philosophy constitutes a religion. The essence of religion is the call to a divinity, or at least to a supernatural power, transcendence, the absolute, or the sacred. The individual formulas vary.

Nevertheless, not all cases are equally litigious. There can exist, for example, an indecisive zone between the invocation of the supernatural, which is religion, and metaphysical speculation, which is no more than philosophy. Belief in a god, however, gives the general impression of a religion without requiring some sort of external representation of that god.

XIV. Everyone Must Respect The Law

In the final analysis, no religious movement is above the law. Each church, association, or *secte* is responsible for its acts. French law will not leave unpunished the condemnable actions of all those who come to illegitimately proselytize and who thus contravene—voluntarily or not—the law's mandates. By contravening the law, these people situate themselves in the outer margins of society.

Penal infractions are numerous and strictly defined: fraud, abuse of trust, violence and assault, illegal confinement, lack of assistance to a person in danger, extreme breaches of fundamental social mores, organizing prostitution, illegal practice of medicine, abduction and brainwashing of a minor, etc.

Aside from criminal prosecution, the administration could either nullify an organization that was founded for an illicit purpose, that acts with illicit objectives, or that acts contrary to the law or to fundamental social mores. The administration could also pronounce a dissolution of the organization based on the ordinance of October 2, 1943, which allows the dissolution of groups and associations "having an activity contrary to the liberty of conscience and the liberty of worship."[30] The administration could also invoke the text, modified in 1972, of the Law of January 10, 1936, which deals with combat groups and private militia.[31]

With regard to old as well as new religions, the state will not tolerate the slightest affront to order or law.

XV. Preventive Action

It is noteworthy that, in the area of private prevention, none are prohibited (especially not families) from warning their children or those close to them—those who are most vulnerable—against all temptations and social perils. Parents have always had complete latitude to protect their children from dangerous associations, perverse seductions, and harmful contagions. It remains true that the notion of public order can lead to different interpretations.

XVI. Against All "Moral Religious Orders"

Today, public and social order is no longer confused with moral and religious order; the secular state, since 1905, respects and protects all religious denominations. However, it must not be forgotten that Judeo-Christian thought has forged the Western mentality and that we are more familiar with certain denominations than with others that may shock us by their exterior aspect, their esotericism, or their ostensible attachment to beliefs and rituals that are foreign to our culture. Cults are not the only groups that need be worried. The awakening of certain ancient religions and the expansion of their practice may also pose problems. From this point forward, a danger exists that discrimination will arise between old

30. Ordinance of Oct. 2, 1943, J.O., Aug. 10, 1944, p. 32.

31. See the Law of January 10, 1936, J.O., Jan. 12, 1936, p. 522, regarding militant groups and private militias. *See also* CODE PÉNAL arts. 431-13–431-20 (Fr.) (amended by Ordinance No. 2000-916 of Sept. 19, 2000, J.O., Sept. 22, 2000, p. 14877), *noted in* Robert & Oberdorff, *supra* note 7, at 676.

and new religions since all do not exercise the same influence on the national culture and all do not have the same place in our common heritage.

If public law cannot ignore such "specific religious characteristics," the recognition of a difference between religions will in no case lead to state sponsored discrimination between them. The protective equality of secularity must not be wiped out in the name of differentiation.

XVII. WHAT ABOUT PUBLIC OPINION?

Two major currents underlie public opinion. On the one hand, some—admitting that Max Weber's classic analyses distinguishing churches from cults are completely outdated—believe that the evolution of science and faith has led to a sort of "deregularization" of all beliefs and to transfers and migrations heavy with amalgamations and derivatives. On the other hand, some continue to believe that to avoid abuses by certain misguided groups, it is better to put in place a systematic and nondiscriminatory general policy for all groups that appear to be cults. This goal may seem praiseworthy, but it brings us back to the problem of definitions that is so difficult to resolve.

Even so, a permanent tension currently exists between the temptation of ideological denunciation and the legal neutrality of the state.

XVIII. THE FRENCH LEGISLATIVE APPROACH

The fluctuations and frequent changes in the French legislative approach with regard to cults perfectly reflect the ambiguity of this redoubtable dilemma. Early in the process, numerous initiatives were launched that attempted to block new cults, or at least to keep them under surveillance to prevent them from branching further. In November 1998, the Prime Minister replaced the "l'Observatoire international des sects", created in 1996 to analyze the development of cults (International Cult Surveillance Center), with a "Mission interministérielle de lutte contre les sectes" ("MILS") (Inter-Ministerial Mission for the Fight Against Cults). The MILS was established with a goal of creating a more operational tool to analyze cults and to improve the methods of fighting against them.

Similarly, one of the laws of December 18, 1998, regarding scholastic obligations, allowed the state to verify through accreditation officers the substance of the instruction provided in the setting of "private structures." In June 1999, a parliamentary investigative commission presided over by Jacques Guyard submitted a report on "cults and money" that offered thirty propositions for countering the influence of cults in all domains where cults—an arbitrary and strongly-contested list of cults had earlier been prepared—were at work. And finally, in December 1999, the Senate Commission on Laws adopted a proposition by Nicolas About aimed at dissolving "malicious groups."

All these initiatives clearly show that the phenomenon of cults is considered suspect and that plans are being made to protect society from these cults.

The clear excess of certain positions against cults and the impossibility—legal as well as political—of implementing the proposed anticult methods currently show that authorities are somewhat powerless to deal with this problem. Some groups are lobbying for an approach that would classify repeat criminal offenders and all groups that constitute "a threat to public order or a great danger to mankind"[32] within the statutory category of "combat groups and armed militias." This statutory category was created by the law of January 10, 1936.

The Ministry of the Interior carefully clarified in a flyer dated December 20, 1999, that "the designation as part of the cult movement that is given to a group by the various parliamentary reports should not be considered enough alone to impute any kind of threat to public order by that group."[33] It thus appears that the very idea of general legislation applicable to all cults has been definitively pushed aside. However, it was not ruled out that a fight against cults should begin based on existing legislation and the related case law concerning tax-related and scholastic obligations.

Another report, officially submitted on February 7, 2000, by the president of the MILS in Matignon, revived the idea of an emphasis on repressive legislation against cults. The report seemed to reserve these new methods for only those cults considered dangerous—

32. *See supra* note 31.
33. *See supra* note 31.

groups considered to be totalitarian organizations that employ manipulative methods.

However, in May 2001, the senate adopted a "law tending to reinforce the prevention and repression of groups of a cultic nature."[34] This text was the result of a long negotiation between the two assemblies, the government, and the MILS. The first version of the text, adopted by the senate at its first reading on December 16, 1999, had been largely modified on June 22, 2000, when it went before l'Assemblée Nationale. The deputies had introduced into the text, at the request of Madame Catherine Picard, the creation of a specific crime of "mental manipulation." This change had evoked numerous hostile reactions and Madame Elisabeth Guigou, then Keeper of the Seals, requested further study on this point in association with the Commission nationale consultative des droits de l'homme ("CNCDH"), (National Consulting Commission on the Rights of Man). Because this commission esteemed the creation of such a crime inadvisable, the text was modified to only punish the crime of fraudulent abuse of ignorance or weakness. Thus the text, which is still in force today, only accounts for the case where a person is psychologically or physically subject to another as a result of serious or repeated pressure or techniques calculated to alter that person's judgment or to lead that minor or that person to an act or omission that is seriously detrimental to that person.

Representatives of large religions are asking themselves today who will judge the detrimental character of that act or omission. Of necessity, it will be the judge. And the judgment will be subject to recent trends, to variations over time, and to external pressures. Even judges are currently asking themselves just how far one can go in applying such a text.

It is also noteworthy that this text envisions the possibility of judicial dissolution of cultic groups when a group has repeatedly engaged in such prohibited conduct as attempted murder, torture, rape and sexual aggression, or the illegal practice of medicine or pharmacy. What else is there, then, for the fight against cults, besides an arsenal of repressive laws? The state would be better off developing preventive methods and perhaps spending more time considering the true roots of the evil.

---

34. This text is not the current law but was only part of the draft before its presentation to the National Assembly.

The National Assembly unanimously approved a law on June 12, 2001, that essentially adopts two provisions that were discussed at length. One has, in a way, dressed up the old notion—dating back to the Napoleonic Code—of fraudulent abuse of a state of ignorance or weakness. This language signifies that although any church leader, guru, or mage is free to deliver any message she wishes to deliver, she will still be subject to the law if she imperils the physical, moral, or material security of those who decide to follow her or if she derives a profit from her followers. Moreover, this text gives associations that attempt to fight cults the right to file a civil action against them. Certain organizations, associations, or groups who energetically combat the new religious movements could thus possibly step into the shoes of abused or victimized former adepts to seek convictions and reparations. This right promises considerable conflict with pro-*secte* groups formed by these movements who openly express desires to be present in the legal domain.

Thus, it remains that by extending criminal liability to new categories of crimes, by developing criminal liability for legal entities, and by creating the possibility of dissolution if the implicated legal entity or its leaders were convicted of any one of the infractions listed in the new text, the law of June 12, 2001, constitutes a new instrument in the struggle against cults. Additionally, it should be conceded that each analysis will have to be subject to very delicate handling and will require a necessarily subjective application.

How does one define—as noted above—and, even more important, how does one manage to circumscribe this complex and fluid notion of "a subjective state"? As for the necessity that the act or omission be seriously detrimental, this requirement leads one to an analysis in which it is difficult to remain objective. After all, certain rules or practices, respected through the ages by well-known religious congregations, such as fasting, poverty, chastity, obedience, and becoming part of a monastic order, could one day also be considered seriously detrimental to the individual. And, it does not make good legal sense to label a group as a "cult" solely by the nature of the crime that one suspects it will one day commit.

XIX. French Muslims

The problem of Islam in France is evidently completely different from the problem of cults. The questions it poses, however, are nonetheless delicate. Today, Islam is numerically the second largest religion in France. However, given this fact, Islam does not occupy as prominent a place in French social life as one might expect.

That the presence of so many Muslims in France is a recent phenomenon explains why there are comparatively few Islamic churches in France. Indeed, such an underrepresentation would seem all the more clear if the French system of jurisprudence was somehow linked to religious symbols and sounds; the ringing of church bells, Presbyterian attributions, and processions far outnumber such sights as minarets and such sounds as the muezzin's call to prayer.

One thus witnesses a great discrepancy between law and reality. As has been demonstrated, the legal equality between religions is total and may be considered a constitutional principle drawn from secularism. However, the Law of 1905 actually only recognizes churches, or Christian institutions, and it is terribly complex and difficult to make Islamic communities fit the church mold. Moreover, the Law of 1905 was limited to the management of then-existing issues, namely, the allocation of goods formerly belonging to public religious establishments between the various new religious associations. The law did not look to the future and did not foresee the possibility that new religious groups, absent from France in 1905, would later entrench themselves in France. For Islam, therefore, France is neither a land of heritage nor of sufficient infrastructure. It was in this context that the *imams* came to be. To make its voice heard in the future, Islam needs to have access to religious broadcasting and quality radio stations to present a positive image of itself and its rich diversities.

Where liberty is concerned, all religions are, of course, on an equal plane. Some, however, are more equal than others because they benefit from available legal advantages. These are the old recognized religions. These groups have solid structures that are accustomed to interfacing with the state. Additionally, as discussed above, the issues of property rights and allocation of goods are settled. In contrast, nothing similar has been contemplated to build up the religions that were not present in France in 1905. A number of solutions are being proposed today. Local collectives are being encouraged to construct mosques, to guarantee loans for their construction, or to consent to sell or lease land under favorable terms. But Islam today should be allowed to count on something beyond its own internal and foreign resources.

Will increased foreign influence be the price we pay for the absence of any public subsidies and for the weakness of indirect aid (training and education) for Muslims? It is urgent that we begin to carefully innovate these ideas without damaging the Law of 1905 and the principle of secularism. It is absolutely necessary that the state have representative Muslim structures in place to negotiate with directly.

The fluctuation of Paris Mosque, which seemed for a long time to be controlled by Algeria, led Pierre Joxe to create the Conseil de réflexion sur l'Islam de France ("CORIF"), (Council for Reflection on French Islam) in 1990. This council consisted of persons from different origins who were designated *intuitu personae*. The objective was twofold: first, to create a harmonizing organization that would advise public authorities on concrete problems regarding the exercise of the Muslim religion; and second, to encourage the creation of a representative structure for Islam in France. CORIF helped to advance many useful causes, such as the creation of religious plazas in cemeteries, the authorization of Muslim high priests, the construction of mosques, and the recognition of religious holidays. However, the absence of a truly representative Islamic structure is being felt more and more. Its absence grates on national and local public authorities who would like to permit Muslims to have a legitimate place in French society—to occupy the entire domain legally and permissibly in order to foster an integration respectful of beliefs and religious identities. The French government recently introduced some interesting initiatives to better structure French Islam and to replace CORIF with organizations more representative of the diversity of French Islam.

XX. Official Representatives of Churches

All other major religions have a type of structure that can act as its official representative. The Catholic Church of France has a veritable government of shared responsibility: the Conference of Bishops of France meets each year and its president is the only person authorized to speak for all the French bishops.

For its part, the Protestant Federation of France is an association under the Law of 1901 that groups several religious associations under the Law of 1905. Four principal churches make up this group: the Reformed Church of France, the Reformed Church of Alsace-Lorraine, the Church of the Confession of Augsburg of Alsace-

Lorraine, and the Lutheran Church. One must also add to this list the Independent Reformed Evangelic Church, the Federation of Baptist Churches, the Evangelical Mission, and others. Some confessions remain independent, however, like the Federation of Evangelical Churches, the Darbists, and the Adventists.

As for the Christian Orthodox churches, they are grouped in an Orthodox Episcopal Confederation, but each church retains its autonomy (which is the same for the Armenians and the Coptics). All churches of Eastern tradition have collaborated to create a religious broadcast on public channels, entitled "Chrétiens orientaux" (Eastern Christians), in an attempt to strengthen the group and increase the religion's influence.

The Central Israelite Consistory of France and Algeria designates the Grand Rabbi of France but has differing tendencies (orthodox and liberal) in its core beliefs. Further, there are other Jewish movements that defend, on a secularist plane, the material and moral interests of the Jewish community. Most are grouped in the Conseil représentatif des organisations juives de France ("CRJF") (Representative Council of Jewish Organizations of France) that sometimes comes into conflict in its relationship with the Consistory. Finally, there is the Fondation du judaisme français (French Foundation of Judaism) that follows principally the religion of the Shoah, allying itself to the World Jewish Congress.

XXI. Adopting an Official Muslim Representation

The organizational structure of Islam in France is still up for debate. Evidence shows that a hierarchical structure such as that of the Catholic Church does not correspond to the Muslim religion—a religion that has never created a church and does not have a true clergy. And a corresponding structure must continue to be sought in other countries; after all, the French Catholic Church has been aptly criticized for being too papal and not Gallican enough. It would definitely be worthwhile today to begin planning for the establishment of a confederation grouping—for example, either ideologically or regionally—of the different Islamic religious associations.

In November 1999, Jean Pierre Chevenement launched a broad-based discussion on Islam that supported the notion of a national representative body elected by regional representatives chosen by leaders of the mosques.[35] But no agreement was reached on the possible presence of independent entities. Even so, the deliberations on Islam have led to progress. This success gives hope that there is light at the end of the long tunnel France has been traveling. However, every time the proponents of a system of Muslim representation seem to come to a basic agreement on a process—however complicated—for the designation of future delegates to a central body, the date and details of implementation are again placed in doubt or postponed.

XXII. The Power of Signs

All religions use symbols as landmarks and measure time with their own holidays and historical calendar. Thus, their history takes root in their tradition and defines a self-perpetuating destiny. Therefore, for the state to designate an official holiday or to determine a celebration date is never a neutral process.

The French calendar is above all Christian, and even "Western-Gregorian" in that it is not even followed by Eastern-Orthodox Christians or Armenians. With the exception of the French national holidays (January 1, May 1, July 14, November 11, and May 8), all other holidays are Christian (Ascension, Easter, Passover, Christmas) and even Roman Catholic (August 15). Other large religions—often forgotten (Judaism, Islam, etc.)—also have their own holidays, and these holidays are numerous. But the state does not officially recognize these holidays. France permits them, of course; occasionally we mark the date. And in some cases, these holidays are accommodated—Friday for the Muslims, Saturday for the Jews. We also accommodate dietary restrictions and arrange for Kosher food and its equivalents. But is this a worthy solution? Why are there such differences for the different religions?

It is clear that we have not been able to truly get out of our rut—so convenient to maintain—of recognized religions. These are the religions with which we are familiar and with whom we have been dealing for a long time. And what if, without our having noticed, these traditional religions were to be today completely discredited, rejected, and replaced? Were this to happen, non-traditional

35. This is currently not law, but only a proposal floated by Jean Pierre Chevenement.

spirituality would have senselessly given way to the dominant monotheistic traditions that have forged the Judeo-Christian or Islamic civilizations. Given that the great religious traditions and ideologies have been shown dramatically incapable of stopping the tragedies and massacres of history, how is it that the very word "religion" has not become suspect?

Now, in an attempt to see a little more clearly into the morass of churches and dispersed religions, efforts are currently underway to try to categorize them—divide them into categories of good and bad. Lists have been prepared, and these lists denounce "dangerous cults,"[36] based on uncertain criteria and unverified rumors. But among these sects and the major traditional religions that are supposed to be so steady and above suspicion, what is the status of all of the religious movements—new or old—that are not found in any list? These religions should enjoy the same official recognition as that of the traditional religions to which we are accustomed. If the state refuses to treat these religions equally simply because too few exist, this argument should also apply to all religious associations—and isn't it impossible to number the various associations that could exist? And yet many of them do benefit from advantages, aid, and special consideration.

Further, as to the dangerous nature ascribed to and condemned in certain sects, some of our major religions are not totally innocent in this regard. Indeed, fanaticism has often reigned. Let us not reawaken the witch hunts and the Inquisition. And let us remember that, in spite of the recent decline in religious practice and the crisis involving the priesthood vocations, man has never had so great a need to reconnect to transcendental values.[37]

Andre Malraux predicted long ago that our new century would be religious, or would not be at all.

36. The term in French is "sectes nocives."

37. *See* JACQUES ROBERT, ENJEUX DU SIÈCLE: NOS LIBERTÉS [STAKES OF THE CENTURY: OUR LIBERTIES] 292 (2002).

[6]

The distinctiveness of Indian secularism

Rajeev Bhargava

Though the election of a Congress-led coalition has opened up new opportunities for secular space, only someone with a blinkered vision would assert that the growth of militant Hindu nationalism has been stalled and deny that secularism in India continues to be in crisis. However, an ambiguity lying at the very heart of this claim has not altogether been dispelled: is the crisis due primarily to external factors as when a good thing is undermined by forces always inimical to it, when it falls into incapable or wrong hands, when it is practised badly? Or, is it rather that the blemished practice is itself an effect of a deeper conceptual flaw, a bad case of a wrong footed ideal? Madan, Nandy and Chatterjee have all argued that the external threat to secularism is only a symptom of a deeper internal crisis. Secularism in their view has long faced an internal threat in the sense that the conceptual and normative structure of secularism is itself terribly flawed. In different ways, each argues that secularism is linked to a flawed modernization, to a mistaken view of rationality, to an impractical demand that religion be eliminated from public life, to an insufficient appreciation of the importance of communities in the life of people and a wholly exaggerated sense of the positive character of the modern state. In what follows, I try to argue against this view. I do not dispute their claims about modernity, rationality and the importance of religion and community. But I do disagree on their understanding of secularism and with their view that it is necessarily tied to a flawed modernist project. In particular, I contend that these critics fail to see that India developed a distinctively Indian and differently modern variant of secularism. Ideals are rarely if ever and never simply transplanted from one cultural context to another. They invariably adapt, sometimes so creatively to suit their new habitat that they seem unrecognizable. This is exactly what happened to secularism in India. Indian critics of secularism neither fully grasp the general conceptual structure of secularism nor properly understand its distinctive Indian variant. Indian secularism did not erect a strict wall of separation, but proposed instead a 'principled distance' between religion and state. Moreover, by balancing the claims of individuals and religious communities, it never intended a bludgeoning privatization of religion. It also embodies a model of contextual moral reasoning. All these features that combine to form what I call contextual secularism remain screened off from the understanding of these critics.

Though I do not agree with these critics that secularism is conceptually flawed, I do agree that it faces an internal threat. However, I have a different understanding of the nature of this threat. Isaiah Berlin has reminded us that the history of ideas is replete with great liberating ideas slowly turning into suffocating straightjackets. One reason for this is that we forget that they need continual interpretation: no idea can flourish without its defenders finding better and better ways of articulating and formulating them. An idea faces an internal threat when its supporters, out of akrasia, willful or unwitting neglect, ignorance, confusion or delusion cease to care for it, or when its own proponents mistakenly turn against it. I have no reason to doubt secularism is threatened by forces fiercely opposed to it. But my focus in this chapter is on the internal threats to secularism. The principal contention of my chapter is that one such internal threat is the failure of secularists to properly defend it largely because they see it as a mere replication of one of the Western variant rather than as embodying an alternative modern ideal with real trans-cultural potential.

Three preliminary points

I cannot proceed further without making three preliminary points. The term 'distinctive' in the title of the chapter may lead someone to expect that I will unravel something startlingly uncommon about Indian secularism. If I believed so, I would have used the term 'unique'. I have not. This is because of my belief that, by now, the elementary formal constituents of secularism are the same throughout the world. Broadly speaking, secularism, anywhere in the world, means a separation of organized religion from organized political power inspired by a specific set of values. Just as without separation there is no secularism, just so a value-less separation does not add up to secularism. In this sense, secularism is a universal normative doctrine. But it does not follow that these elements are interpreted or related to each other in any one particular way or that there is a single ideal way in which they should be interpreted or related to one another. Many ways exist of interpreting these elements as do different ways of relating them. Each conception of secularism may unpack the metaphor of separation differently or select different elements from the stock of values that give separation its point. It may also place different weights on the same values. So when I talk about the distinctiveness of Indian secularism, I do not imply that it has a unique conceptual structure. I only mean that embedded in it is a specific and interestingly different way of interpreting and relating the basic constituents of secularism. Indeed this is why the distinctive character of Indian secularism does not make it non-universalizable. Indian secularism has trans-cultural potential.

My *second* point concerns a mistake not uncommon among those who write and think about contemporary secularism. They unwittingly assume that it is a doctrine with a fixed content. It is also believed to be timeless, as if it has always existed in the same form. But all living doctrines evolve and therefore have a history. Secularism too has a history made at one time largely by Europeans, then a little later by North Americans and much later by non-Western countries. Non-Western societies inherited from their Western counterparts specific versions of secularism but they did not always preserve them in the form in which they were received. They often added something of enduring value to them and, therefore, developed the idea further. Western theorists of secularism do not always recognize this non-Western contribution. It may have once been adequate for Western scholars to focus exclusively on that part of the history of secularism which was made in and by the West. But today it would be a gross mistake to identify Western variants of secularism with the entire doctrine, if the part was viewed as the whole. For a rich, complex and complete understanding of secularism, one must examine how the secular idea has developed over time trans-nationally.

There are other reasons why we must attend to the histories of secularism. The current crisis of secularism must compel one to ask why we need it at all. After all, one rarely mourns the loss of a useless thing. But it breaks one's heart to see a valuable thing decay. In such transitional moments, when a thing is born, is dying or in crisis, evaluative judgments become especially urgent and it is crucial to get them right. However, when a thing is in good health, when it is working well and effectively, such judgments appear to be redundant. In these periods of the stability and well-being of an entity, we bother little about its value and purpose. As it is taken for granted, its purpose, as Charles Taylor has reminded us, frequently recedes into the background. Over time, its underlying point may even be forgotten. This may happen with material things as well as with institutions, ideas and doctrines. Now, something like this appears to have happened also to secularism. When it was working well, no one took the trouble to foreground its purpose, taking it for granted and eventually forgetting it. This forgetting was not troublesome or threatening as long as the secularism remained challenged. But when increasingly questioned, this forgetfulness becomes a terrible handicap. To reduce a rich and complex idea to a dead and monotonously repeated formula is bad enough but to know that an ideal is valuable and yet not know what precisely its value consists in is worse. The only option in such situations is to bring the idea back to life, to remember and retrieve its value-content.

But why must this be done with the help of a historical account? I believe this necessity arises because at some remote point in the past, say at the time of its birth, the idea had to prove its worth to its potential beneficiaries. To make place for itself in a climate of fierce competition it had to marshal all forms of argumentative resources. It could not have survived without being explicit about its normative structure. In short, it could not be in the state of inarticulacy in which it currently happens to be. This is why its retrieval from the background involves going back in time. We can no longer do without its history.

It is not a coincidence that the external threat to Indian secularism has intensified precisely at a time of its degeneration into a meaningless formula (Perhaps the real crisis of Indian secularism began when the real meaning of secularism was forgotten and ritualistically, the word 'secular' was introduced in the Indian constitution) or when it is viewed purely as a procedural doctrine that mechanically separates religion from the state and is foolishly innocent of its ties with substantive values. Critics of secularism are quick to point out its links with all kinds of things they dislike: the nation state, instrumental rationality, the hegemony of science, mindless industrialization and realist state-craft. But both its critics and its defenders appear to have forgotton its constitutive relation with substantive values. Undoubtedly, because of a history that it shares with the West, Indian secularism is at least partly Western. But this Western history can also be told as a history of important values. The distancing of religion from the state became necessary, both in India and the West, to protect individual citizens from their own oppressive religiously sanctioned social customs. Hence the connection of secularism with individualistically conceived liberty and equality. Unfortunately, Indian critics of secularism have developed an amnesia about these values. They also seem not to recall that 'separation' in the early constitutional history of India was never understood to mean the blanket exclusion of religion from the state.

Thus, it is important that we go back in time and retrieve the complex purposes underlying it, to examine how Indian secularism was originally conceived and identify the distinctiveness of Indian secularism. However, this is not always easy. To answer why brings me to my *third* point. In India, everything has begun to be seen in terms of an irritatingly dichotomous grid that divides the social world into two groups, the

Western modern and the indigenous traditional. Those who accept this grid are ineluctably inducted into a certain pattern of thinking. If secularism is modern, they believe, then it must be Western. The whole of Western secularism is then identified with one's preferred variant, usually that which is currently dominant. For example, the currently dominant Western stereotype has it that secularism entails a strict separation of religion and the state for the sake of religious liberty and individual autonomy. This stereotype is uncritically also accepted in India by its defenders as well as its opponents. Thus those who defend secularism in India proclaim unstinting support for this Western stereotype. Similarly, secularism is opposed in India because critics have good reason to be unhappy with this Western stereotype. Since they also accept the view that to be Indian, a thing or an idea must be rooted wholly in home-grown traditions uncontaminated by the West, they seek to replace secularism by ideas of toleration available within indigenous religious traditions. Much of the debate on secularism in India has been framed by this interpretative framework. But I wonder how useful it is to hold on to it, for it misses out on the simple point that something can be at once Indian and modern, that something that started out as Western can over time be transformed, and in responding to specific Indian problems and by being nurtured in an Indian context, can become distinctively Indian; different from both its Western counterpart and from anything found within indigenous traditions. Unless those who defend secularism grasp this point, they will continue to defend a version that has little validity in the Indian context. Since they are seen to support a doctrine that can be legitimately criticized, the popular legitimacy of every version of secularism is bound to be eroded in the long run. Critics of secularism too fail to realize that a persistent attack on the very idea of secularism has grave practical consequence. In a context in which secularism is anyhow under threat from Hindu extremists, the mistaken occlusion of the distinctiveness of Indian secularism only ends up granting intellectual legitimacy to the larger political attack on the secular idea.

In these preliminary remarks, I hope to have drawn attention to the importance of grasping that Indian secularism provides an alternative to mainstream, Western conceptions. In what follows I must try to demonstrate this to be so. I argue that Indian secularism is distinguished from other versions because of the full-blooded self-recognition of its multi-value character. It is also distinctive because it rejects the claim that separation must mean strict exclusion or neutrality and espouses what I call principled distance. In my view, this particular feature of Indian secularism is unique to it.

The conceptual structure of secularism

Theocracy, establishment, multiple establishment

To identity the conceptual structure of secularism, it is best to begin with some ideal-typical distinctions, the first of which is between a state that establishes religion and a theocratic state. A theocratic state is governed by divine laws directly administered by a priestly order claiming a divine commission. The Islamic republic of Iran run by Ayatullahs is an obvious example. On the other hand, a state that establishes religion grants it official, legal recognition. Here, religion benefits from a formal alliance with government. The sacerdotal order does not govern a state where religion is established.

Establishment of religion takes two forms. On the classical European view, it means that 'a *single* Church or religion enjoys formal, legal, official monopolistic privilege through a union with the government of the state' (Levy 1997: 7). The phrase 'establishment' has been used for centuries to describe the established Protestant Churches of England, Scotland and Germany, and the Catholic Churches in Italy and Spain. Thus, if, in preference to all other religions, the state recognizes a particular religion as the official religion, compels individuals to congregate for only one religion, punishes them for failing to profess a particular set of religious beliefs, levies taxes in support of one particular religion or makes instruction in one religion mandatory in educational institutions or in the media, then it is known as the establishment of religion. Where a particular religion is established, equality among religions is non-existent, and while members of the established religion may enjoy a modicum of religious liberty, those belonging to religions that have not been established are unlikely to enjoy any liberty. If the number of such persons is large, then such a multi-religious society may be wrecked by inter-religious wars. If the number is small, then religious minorities may not only fail to enjoy full religious liberty but may not even be tolerated. They are likely to face persistent religious persecution.

This classical European view of establishment is to be distinguished from one where the state respects more than one religion, recognizes and perhaps nurtures all religions without preferring one over the other. This might be termed 'multiple establishment' or 'establishment without a name' (Levy 1997: 12). Such a state may levy a religious tax on everyone and yet grant the freedom to remit the tax money to a Church or religious organization of their choice. It may financially aid schools run by religious institutions but on a non-discriminatory basis. It may punish people for disavowing or disrespecting religion, though not compel them to profess the beliefs of a particular religion. A state that respects multiple establishment treats all religion non-preferentially. It gives liberty to each group to conduct its religious affairs but is indifferent to the freedom of members within the group. The state of New York in the middle of the 17th century that allowed every Church of the Protestant faith to be established furnishes perhaps the earliest example of 'multiple establishment'. The colonies of Massachusetts, Connecticut and New Hampshire show a similar pattern (Levy 1997: 11). Related examples abound in India, for example the 14th century Vijayanagar kingdom that granted official recognition to the Shaivites, the Vaishnavites and perhaps even the Jains. Arguably, the British empire gave de facto legitimacy to multiple establishments.

States with multiple establishments are better than states with singular establishments. For example, such states are likely to be relatively peaceful. Members of each religious group are likely to tolerate one another. There may even be inter-religious equality; the state may treat all religions equally and grant each religious group considerable autonomy in its own affairs. But states with multiple establishments have their limitations. For a start, they may persecute atheists. Second, they are indifferent to the liberty of individuals within each religious group. Even the slightest internal dissent may not be tolerated. Third, they may not allow an individual to exit his religious community and embrace another religion or remain unattached to any religion whatsoever. Fourth, such states give recognition to particular religious identities but fail to recognize what may be called non-particularized identities, i.e. identities that simultaneously refer to several particular identities or transcend all of them. Fifth, such states are unconcerned with the non-religious liberties of individuals or groups. Finally, such states are entirely indifferent to citizenship rights.

A secular state is to be distinguished not only from theocracy but also from a state where religion is established. A non-theocratic state is not automatically secular because it is entirely consistent for a state not to be run by priests inspired by 'divine laws', but to have a formal alliance with one or more religions. A secular state on the other hand refuses to establish religion or has disestablished it. Therefore, it follows what can be called the principle of non-establishment. The non-establishment of religion means that the state is separated not merely from one but from all religions (I shall call it feature-a). No religious community in such a state can say that the state belongs to it. A secular state is not anti-religious but exists and survives only when religion is no longer hegemonic. It admits a more general equality between believers and unbelievers. It allows freedom for all religions but also freedom from religion itself. Thus, in a secular state, a formal or legal union between state and religion is impermissible. Official status is not given to religion. Persons are as free to disavow religion as they are to profess one. No one is compelled to pay tax for religious purposes or to receive religious instruction. No automatic grants to religious institutions are available.

Values of a secular state

This brings me to more explicitly articulate the connection of a secular state with several important and substantive values. The first of these is peace or rather the prevention of a society from its regression into barbarism, not an uncommon tendency where there exist two or more incompatible visions of the good life. The second is toleration, i.e. the state does not persecute anyone on grounds of religion. I may here mention an auxiliary point. We must eschew the tendency within Western modernist discourse to conceive of civil strife as a result purely of a clash of interests. The development of secularism in the West and elsewhere cannot be properly understood without fully comprehending the fear of cruelty and disorder that marks the conflict of ultimate ideals. This is equally true of the American and the French experience as it is of India. Consider the United States. One might say that the first amendment, the pivot of American secularism is a product of the widespread feeling of vulnerability experienced in different religious denomination such as the Anglicans, the Presbyterians and the Quakers, each dominant in one particular area but vulnerable in others and each viewing the other as fanatical, or at least as extremely odd (McConnell 1993: 497–510).

Third, a secular state is constitutively tied to the value of religious liberty that has three dimensions. The first refers to the liberty of members of any one religious group (feature-b). It is a brute fact that in most religious communities, one or two interpretations of its core beliefs and practices come to dominate. Given this dominance, it is important that every individual or sect within the group be given the right to criticize, revise or challenge these dominant interpretations. The second aspect of this important liberty in a secular state (feature-c) is that it is granted non-preferentially to all members of every religious community. It is entirely possible that non-preferential treatment by the state of groups that accord religious liberty to its members is also found in states respecting multiple establishment. But religious liberty is not part of the core principles of multiple establishment. However, it is a constitutive feature of the secular state. The third dimension of religious liberty (feature-d), unthinkable in states with multiple establishment, is that individuals are free not only to criticize the religion into which they are born, but at the very extreme, to reject it and further, given ideal conditions of deliberation, to freely embrace another religion or to remain without one.

Religious liberty, when understood broadly, is one important value of a secular state. To understand another crucial ingredient, it is necessary to grasp the point that liberty and equality in the religious sphere are all of a piece with liberty and equality in other spheres. It is not a coincidence that the disestablishment clause in the first amendment to the American constitution institutes not only religious freedom but also the more general freedom of speech, of peaceful assembly and political dissent. It is entirely possible that a state respecting multiple establishment permits *religious* liberty and equality but forbids other forms of freedom and equality. For instance, a person may challenge the authority of the religious head of his own denomination but not be free to challenge the authority of the state. This is impossible in a secular state which is committed to a more general freedom and equality. Thus, the second value to which a secular state is constitutively linked is the equality of free citizenship.

The value of equal citizenship has two dimensions, one active, the other passive. It is a feature of democratic polities that these two roles of citizens coincide and therefore a democratic government must be continuously justifiable from both points of views (Beitz 1989: Chapter 5). To be a passive citizen is to be entitled to physical security, a minimum of material well-being and a sphere of one's own in which others ought not to interfere. Although a part of this idea of passive citizenship goes back to ancient Rome, the radical emphasis on material well-being and on privacy is a result of a profound trans-valuation of values that has taken place under conditions of modernity (Taylor 1989). This lies at the root of the idea of the right to life, liberty, material welfare and perhaps, education – crucial elements if ordinary people are to lead their ordinary life with dignity. Any citizen of the state must be entitled to these benefits. This is partly an extension of the point implicit in the defence of religious liberty but in part it adds something substantial of its own. The benefits of citizenship – resources that enable a dignified ordinary life – must be available to everyone and there is no room here for discrimination on grounds of religion (feature-e). This equal treatment is entailed by equal (passive) citizenship. State agencies and the entire system of law must not work in favour of one religious group. If the state works to protect the security and well-being of some individuals or groups but fails to secure these meagre but important benefits to others then the principle of equal (passive) citizenship is violated. Likewise, since citizenship is conditional upon education, no one must be denied admission to educational institutions, solely on grounds of religion (feature-f).

The active dimension of citizenship involves the recognition of citizens as equal participants in the public domain. Such active citizenship rights can be denied in two ways. Either when they are brutally excluded from the political domain (they are politically dead) (Beitz 1989: 109), or when their recognition in the public domain betrays the social acceptance of a belief in the intrinsic superiority of one group as when there is communally weighed voting or efforts to dilute the votes of religious minorities through the use of gerrymandering techniques (Beitz 1989: 110). Groups singled out as less worthy are demeaned and insulted, encouraged to feel that patterns of disrespect existing in society at large enjoy official sanction. In contrast to this, equality of citizenship to which secularism is tied conveys a community wide acknowledgement of equal respect for everyone in the political domain (feature-g).

A simple comparison between different types of state-religion political orders shows that at least in multi-religious society and relative to theocracies and states with established religion, a secular state gives maximum liberty and equality, conceived individualistically or non-individualistically to all its citizens.

Indian secularism

The state in the Indian constitution appears to possess all the features (feature-a to-g) of a secular state. Feature-a is specified in Article 27 which rules out the public funding of religion and Article 28(1) under which 'no religious instruction is to be provided in any educational institution wholly maintained out of state funds'.

Articles 25, 27 and 28 guarantee religious liberty and meet the conditions specified by features-b, c and d. Under Article 25(1), 'all persons are equally entitled to freedom of conscience and the right freely to profess, practice and propagate religion' (feature-b and -c). The phrase 'freedom of conscience' is meant to cover the liberty of persons without a religion (feature-d). Under Article 27, 'no person is compelled to pay any taxes, the proceeds of which are specifically appropriated in payment of expenses for the promotion or maintenance of any particular religion or religious denomination.' Finally, under Article 28(3), 'no person attending any educational institution ... shall be required to take part in any religious instruction or to attend any religious worship that may be conducted in such institution'.

Equality of citizenship is guaranteed by Articles 14, 15(1) and 29(2) of the Indian constitution. Article 15(1) states that the state shall not discriminate against any citizen on grounds only of religion, race, caste, sex, place of birth or any of them (feature-e). Article 29(2) declares that no citizen shall be denied admission into any educational institution maintained by the state on grounds only of religion, race etc. (feature-f). Article 16(1) and (2) of Indian constitution affirm an equal opportunity for all citizens in matters relating to employment or appointment of any office under the state. It further affirms that no citizen, on grounds of religion or race be eligible for or discriminate against in respect of any employment or office under the state. The clause on universal franchise as well as Article 325 that declares a general electoral roll for all constituencies and states that no one shall be ineligible for inclusion in this roll or claim to be included in it on grounds only of religion, etc. embody the value of equal active citizenship. Thus feature-g is specified in the Articles on equality of active citizenship.

The implications of accepting that the state in the Indian constitution is meant to possess features-a to -g are not always spelt out. First, the constitution rules out theocracy and the establishment of religion. The term 'secular state' is usually contrasted simply with theocracy. This is misleading, if not false, because the absence of theocracy is compatible with the establishment of religion. The secular credentials of the state cannot be derived from the mere absence of theocracy.[2] Second, the Indian state is not meant to be merely tolerant (in the sense specified above). Indian secularism must not be confused with a generally professed Hindu tolerance. It is frequently claimed that Indians have a natural, traditional affinity with secularism. In view of our traditional obsession with subtle and not so subtle hierarchies, this claim must be taken with a pinch of salt if not pepper. Of course, this should not detract from the important point that tolerance, even within a hierarchical framework, forms an important background condition for the development of modern secularism. Elements of this important background condition can certainly be found within India. Third, the secularism of the Indian constitution is neither a simple-minded single-value idea nor over-inflated and hyper-substantive. Rather, it is a complex, multi-value doctrine.

A further point to note concerns the precise form of secularism to be found in the constitution. Broadly, secularism is taken to be the view that religion must be separated from the state for the sake of extensive religious liberty and equality of citizenship. This view can be differently interpreted. For Donald Smith, the secular state involves three distinct but interrelated relations concerning the state, religion and the individual (Smith 1963: 3–8). The first relation concerns individuals and their religion, from which the state is excluded. Individuals are thereby free to decide the merits of the respective claims of different religions without any coercive interference by the state – the libertarian ingredient in secularism. The second concerns the relation between individuals and the state, from which religion is excluded. Thus, the rights and duties of citizens are not affected by the religious beliefs held by individuals – the egalitarian component in secularism. Finally, for Smith, the integrity of both these relations is dependent on the third relation, between the state and different religions. Here he argues that secularism entails the mutual exclusion of state and religion. Just as political power is outside the scope of religion's legitimate objectives, just so it is not the function of the state to promote, regulate, direct or interfere in religion. This interpretation is in line with the dominant American interpretation of secularism as erecting 'a wall of separation' between religion and state. On the classical American view of disestablishment, there can be no support for religion even on a non-preferential basis. Even partial aid to educational institutions run by religious organizations will constitute some form of establishment. Moreover, a state that disestablishes all religions is one that has no power to interfere in the affairs of religious institutions. For better or for worse, the state is powerless to bring about changes in religion. So, for Smith, secularism means the strict exclusion of religion from the state for the sake of the religious liberty and equal citizenship of individuals. This is also the dominant understanding of Western secularism.

Departures from mainstream Western secularism

Does Indian secularism erect a similar 'wall of separation' for the sake of individualistically construed values? Is it a Western idea on Indian soil? Articles 15, 16, 25, 29(2) and 325 support this interpretation. Though there is no direct reference to disestablishment, Articles 27 and 28(1) imply strict separation. By giving the President of the Republic the option of not taking an oath in the name of God, Article 60 confirms the strictly neutral character of the Indian constitution. From the discussion so far, it appears that the state in India is constitutionally bound to follow Smith's model of Western secularism. However, further examination of the constitution reveals this impression to be mistaken. To begin with, Article 30(1) recognizes the rights of religious minorities and therefore, unlike other Articles applicable to citizens qua individuals, it is a community-based right. Indeed, another community-specific right granting political representation to religious minorities was almost granted and was removed from the constitution only at the last minute. Second, Article 30(2) commits the state to give aid to educational institutions established and administered by religious communities. Also permitted is religious instruction in educational institutions that are partly funded by the state. These are significant departures from the 'wall of separation' view of the secular state. Even more significant are Articles 17 and 25(2) that require the state to intervene in religious affairs. Article 25(2)(b) states that 'nothing in Article 25 (1) prevents the state from making a law providing for social welfare and reform or the throwing open of Hindu religious institutions of a public character to all classes and sections of Hindus.' Article 17 is an uninhibited, robust attack on the caste system, arguably the central feature of Hinduism, by abolishing untouchability and by making the enforcement of any disability arising out of it an offence punishable by law. Both appear to take away the individual freedom of religion granted under Section 1 of Article 25 and to contravene Article 26.

These features of the Indian constitution depart from the stereotypical Western model in two ways. First, unlike the strict separation view that renders the state powerless in religious matters, they enjoin the state to interfere in religion. Second, more importantly, by giving powers to the state in the affairs of one religion, they necessitate a departure from strict neutrality or equidistance. This power of interference may be interpreted to undermine or promote Hinduism. Either way it appears to strike a powerful blow to the idea of non-preferential treatment.

In short, some Articles in the Indian constitution support an individualist interpretation and others a non-individualist one. Some conceive separation as exclusion, others as non-preferential treatment and, finally, some depart altogether from separation understood as exclusion or neutrality. At the end of the day, a confusing, somewhat contradictory picture on secularism emerges from a reading of the constitution. Critics could hardly fail to notice this and for many of them, Articles 17, 25(2) and 30 (1 and 2) comprise the secularity of the Indian state. For Donald Smith, any intervention in Hinduism – for example the legal ban on the prohibition of Dalit entry into temples or any protection of the rights of communities – seriously compromises secularism. For others, like Chatterjee, the presence of these features in the Indian constitution shows why the Indian state cannot be really secular. The Indian constitution does not give an unambiguous criteria for maintaining the secularity of the state and, quite simply, given Indian conditions, it could never have.

By accepting community-based rights for religious minorities and endorsing state-intervention in religion, did the constitution depart from secular principles? I do not think it did. Rather, it developed its own modern variant. This distinctiveness of the Indian secularism can be understood only when the cultural background and social context in India is properly grasped. At least four such features of this socio-cultural context call for attention. First, there exists the mind boggling diversity of religious communities in India. Such diversity may coexist harmoniously but it invariably generates conflicts, the most intractable of which, I believe, are deep conflicts over values. Second, within Hinduism in particular and in South Asian religions more generally, a greater emphasis is placed on practice rather than belief. A person's religious identity and affiliation are defined more by what she or he does with and in relation to others, than by the content of beliefs individually held by them. Since practices are intrinsically social, any significance placed on them brings about a concomitant valorization of communities. Together, these two features entail inter-community conflicts which are further exacerbated if fuelled by competing conceptions of democracy and nationalism. Third, many religiously sanctioned social practices are oppressive by virtue of their illiberal and inegalitarian character, and deny a life of dignity and self-respect. Therefore, from a liberal and egalitarian standpoint, they desperately need to be reformed. Such practices frequently have a life of their own, independent of consciously held beliefs, and possess a causal efficacy that remains unaffected by the presence of conscious beliefs. Furthermore, a tendency to fortify and insulate themselves from reflective critique makes them resistant to easy change and reform. It follows that an institution vested with enormous social power is needed to transform their character. Fourth, in Hinduism, the absence of an organized institution such as the Church has meant that the impetus for effective reform cannot come exclusively from within. Reform within Hinduism can hardly be initiated without help from powerful external institutions such as the state.

In such a context, India needed a coherent set of intellectual resources to tackle inter-religious conflict, and to struggle against oppressive communities not by disaggregating them into a collection of individuals or by de-recognizing them (and therefore, not by privatizing religion) but by somehow making them more liberal and egalitarian. A political movement for a united, liberal, democratic India had to struggle against hierarchical and communal conceptions of community but without abandoning a reasonable communitarianism. Besides, the state had an important contribution to make in the transformation of these communities; for this reason, a perennial dilemma was imposed on it. The state in India walked a tight rope between the requirement of religious liberty that frequently entails non-interference in the affairs of religious communities, and the demand for equality and justice which necessitates intervention in religiously sanctioned social customs. Secularism in India simply had to be different from the Western liberal model that does not recognize communities, and dictates strict separation between religious and political institutions.

If we abandon the view, such as Donald Smith's, that political secularism entails a unique set of state policies valid under all conditions which provide the yardstick by which the secularity of any state is to be judged, then we can better understand why despite 'deviation' from the ideal, the state in India continues to embody a model of *secularism.*[3] This can be shown even if we stick to Smith's working definition of secularism as consisting of three relations. Smith's first relation embodies the principle of religious liberty construed individualistically, i.e., pertaining to the religious beliefs of individuals. However, it is possible to make a non-individualistic construal of religious liberty by speaking not of the beliefs of individual but rather of the practices of groups. Here religious liberty would mean distancing the state from the practices of religious groups. The first principle of secularism can then be seen to also grant the right to a religious community to its own practices. Smith's second relation embodies the value of equal citizenship. But this entails – and I cannot substantiate my claim – that we tolerate the attempt of radically differing groups to determine the nature and direction of society as they best see it. In this view, then, the public presence of the religious practices of groups is guaranteed and entailed by the recognition of community-differentiated citizenship rights. Smith's version of secularism entails a charter of uniform rights. But it is clear that the commitment of secularism to equal citizenship can dictate community-based rights and therefore differentiated citizenship. In principle, this could easily accommodate a reasonable demand for community-specific political rights. In India, for reasons outlined above, it meant community-specific social rights, such as the right to administer and maintain educational institutions. Smith's third principle pertains to non-establishment and therefore to a strict separation of religion from state, under which religion and the state both have the freedom to develop without interfering with each other. Separation, however, need not mean strict non-interference, mutual exclusion or equidistance, as in Smith's view. Instead, it could be a policy of principled distance, which entails a flexible approach on the question of intervention or abstention, combining both, dependent on the context, nature or current state of relevant religions. This theoretical interpretation of separation sits much better with its own best practice but perhaps also with the practice of other Western secular states, something that is never properly recognized by Western theories of secularism. But what is this idea of principled distance?

Principled distance

Principled distance is one particular way of unpacking the metaphor of separation. In conventional Western secularism, separation of state and religion means either mutual exclusion or neutrality. Let me elaborate. Clearly, the demand for separation comes in the wake of some undesirable pre-existing unity, in this case, a complete intermeshing of religion and state. Against the view that religion and state possess an identical overall agenda, a common, indistinguishable project, the separationists argue for a parting of ways. This much is uncontroversial. But from here, a bifurcation occurs. One avenue leads to total exclusion; separation here means the meticulous refusal of any contact whatsoever between religion and the state. The two must keep off one another. This stand-offishness may be robust or mild. When robust, it generates mutual hostility. For example, the secular state, on this view, must be anti-religious. This anti-religiosity may be interventionist or non-interventionist. In its interventionist form the state actively discourages religion. In its non-interventionist incarnation it typifies a hysterical brahminical attitude: Religion is untouchable, so any contact with it contaminates secularist purity. Secularism here becomes a doctrine of political taboo; it prohibits contact with certain kinds of activities. The milder variety of exclusion of religion from politics proposes that religious and political institutions live as indifferent strangers to each other. At best, this mutual incomprehension leads to some perplexity. But no further curiosity is possible. The second view on separation does not demand total exclusion. Some contact is possible but also some distance. But the terms of engagement and disengagement are antecedently fixed. This is central to the notion of strict neutrality. Those who interpret separation as neutrality demand that a secular state be neutral with respect to all religions. It may help or hinder all religions to an equal degree. If it intervenes in one religion, it must also do so in others.

Principled distance must be distinguished from both strict mutual and equally strict neutrality. This complex notion builds upon two ideas, at least one of which derives from a distinction explicitly drawn by the American philosopher, Ronald Dworkin between equal treatment and treating everyone as an equal (Dworkin 1978: 125). The principle of equal treatment, in the relevant political sense, requires that the state treat all its citizens equally in relevant respect, for example in the distribution of a resource of opportunity. The principle of treating people as equals entails that every person is treated with equal concern and respect. This second principle may sometimes require equal treatment, say equal distribution of resources but it may also occasionally dictate unequal treatment. Treating people as equals is entirely consistent with differential treatment. This idea is the second ingredient in what I have called principled distance. To say that a state keeps principled distance from religion is to claim that it intervenes or refrains from interfering in religion, depending entirely upon whether or not some values are protected or advanced. Moreover, it is to admit that a state may interfere in one religion more than in others, depending once again on the historical and social condition of all relevant religions. For the promotion of a particular value constitutive of secularism, some religion, relative to other religions, may require more interference from the state. For example, suppose that the value to be advanced is social equality. This requires in part undermining caste hierarchies. If this is the aim of the state, then it may be required of the state that it interferes in caste-ridden Hinduism much more than say Islam or Christianity. However, if a diversity-driven religious liberty is the value to be advanced by the state, then it may have to intervene in Christianity and Islam more than in Hinduism. If this is so, the state can neither strictly exclude considerations emanating from religion nor keep strict neutrality with respect to religion. It cannot antecedently decide that it will always refrain from interfering in religions or that it will interfere in each equally. Indeed, it may not relate to every religion in society in exactly the same way or intervene in each religion to the same degree or in the same manner. To want to do so would be plainly absurd. All it must ensure is that the relationship between the state and religions is guided by non-sectarian motives consistent with the values and principles mentioned above.

Consider those laws that interfere with Hinduism. The relevant consideration in their evaluation is not whether they immediately encompass all groups but whether or not they are just and consistent with the values undergirding secularism. Three reasons exist for why all social groups need not be covered by these laws. First, they may be relevant only to Hindus. Take the abolition of child marriage and devadasi dedication or the introduction of the right to divorce. Here, before deciding whether it was necessary to enact a special provision for Hindus, the legislature took into account their social customs and beliefs. Similar laws for Muslims were simply redundant. Second, laws in liberal democracies require legitimacy; the consent of at least the representatives of communities is vital. If consent has indeed been obtained from the representatives of only one community, it is sometimes prudent to enact community-specific laws. It is wise to apply the general principle in stages, rather than not have it at all. Finally, 'it is perfectly within the competence of the legislature to take account of the degree of evil which is prevalent under various circumstances and the legislature is not bound to legislate for all evils at the same time. Therefore, an act passed by the legislature cannot be attacked merely because it tackles only some of the evils in society and does not tackle other evils of the same or worse kind which may be prevalent.' Thus, if the legislature acting on these considerations, wanted to enact a special provision in regard to, say, bigamous marriages among Hindus, it cannot be said that the legislature was discriminating against Hindus only on the ground of religion (AIR 1952). The Indian courts have frequently followed this line of reasoning. They have defended a policy if they found that its purpose is the eradication of a social evil traceable to religious practices, even if the policy was targetted at specific communities. It has argued that so long as the state has taken gradual steps towards social welfare and reform and has not introduced distinctions or classifications that are unreasonable or oppressive, equality before law is not breached. A state interfering in one religion more than in others does not automatically depart from secularism. Indian secularism rejects the assumption that one size fits all. Thus, secularism requires principled distance, not exclusion or equidistance.

Contextual secularism

A context-sensitive secularism, one based on the idea of principled distance, is what I have elsewhere called contextual secularism. Contextual secularism is contextual not only because it captures the idea that the precise form and content of secularism will vary from context to context and from place to place but also that it embodies a certain model of contextual moral reasoning. This it must do because of its character as a multi-value doctrine. Let me explain this point by introducing a distinction between types of situations and types of moral doctrines. Some conflict-ridden human situations are such that their morally defensible resolution is dictated by single-value doctrines, i.e., those which give priority to a value held to be supreme. For example, bodily integrity may be viewed as such an important value that nothing can justify its violation. I may be prevented from torturing someone no matter what my reasons for doing so: neither self-interest nor pursuit of truth can justify it. Other human situations are different because they genuinely involve a value conflict and the resolution of this conflict cannot be read off the values themselves. Single-value doctrines do not suffice here because they always dictate a unique outcome antecedently favourable to the protection of one value. In these situations multi-value doctrines are more appropriate. They take on board these conflicts and admit that no general a priori procedure can antecedently arbitrate between competing value claims. Rather, whether a value will outweigh others or which, if at all, will override others will be decided entirely by the context. Frequently, such situations necessitate a trade-off or compromise albeit one that is morally defensible.

By explicitly accepting that secularism is a multi-value doctrine, we recognize that its constitutive values do not always sit easily with one another. On the contrary, they are frequently in conflict. Some degree of internal discord and therefore a fair amount of instability is an integral part of secularism. For this reason, it forever requires fresh interpretations, contextual judgments and attempts at reconciliation and compromise. No general a priori rule of resolving these conflicts exist; no easy lexical order, no pre-existing hierarchy among values or laws that enables us to decide that, no matter what the context, a particular value must override everything else. Everything then is a matter of situational thinking and contextual reasoning. Whether one value overrides or is reconciled with another cannot be decided before hand. Each time the matter presents itself differently and will be differently resolved. If this is true, then the practice of secularism requires a different model of moral reasoning than the one that straight-jackets our moral understanding in the form of well delineated, explicitly stated rules (Taylor 1994: 16–43). This contextual secularism recognizes that the conflict between individual rights and group rights or between claims of equality and liberty or between claims of liberty and the satisfaction of basic needs cannot always be adjudicated by a recourse to some general and abstract principle. Rather they can only be settled case by case and may require a fine balancing of competing claims. The eventual outcome may not be wholly satisfactory to either but will still be reasonably satisfactory to both. Multi-value doctrines such as secularism encourage accommodation – not the giving up of one value for the sake of another but rather their reconciliation and possible harmonization, i.e., to make each work without changing the basic content of apparently incompatible concepts and values.

This accommodation may be accomplished in a number of ways. First, by placing values at different levels (see Austin 1962). Second, by seeing them as belonging not to water-tight compartments but as sufficiently separate so that an attempt is made to make a value work within its own sphere without frontally conflicting with another value operating in a different sphere. This endeavour to make concepts, view-points and values work simultaneously does not amount to a morally objectionable compromise. This is so because nothing of importance is being given up for the sake of a less significant thing, one without value or even with negative value. Rather, what is pursued is a mutually agreed middle way that combines elements from two or more equally valuable entities. The roots of such attempts at reconciliation and accommodation lie in a lack of dogmatism, in a willingness to experiment, to think at different levels and in separate spheres and in a readiness to take decisions on a provisional basis. It captures a way of thinking characterized by the following dictum: 'why look at things in terms of this or that, why not try to have both this and that.' In this way of thinking, it is recognized that though we may currently be unable to secure the best of both values and therefore be forced to settle for a watered-down version of each, we must continue to have an abiding commitment to search for a transcendence of this second best condition. Such contextual reasoning was not atypical of the deliberations of the Constituent Assembly in which great value was placed on arriving at decisions by consensus. Yet, the procedure of majority vote was not given up altogether. On issues that everyone judged to be less significant, a majoritarian procedure was adopted. It is by virtue of this kind of reasoning that the Indian constitution appears at once federal and unitary, and why it favours both individual and group-specific rights. It is frequently argued against Indian secularism that it is contradictory because it tries to bring together individual and community rights, and that articles in the Indian Constitution such as 25 and 26(b) that have a bearing on the secular nature of the Indian state are deeply conflictual and at best ambiguous. This is to misrecognize a virtue as a vice. In my view, this attempt to bring together seemingly incompatible values is a great strength of Indian secularism. Secularism in India is not understood to be a mechanical doctrine with a uniform, technical application. Therefore, the demand that the relevant articles in the Indian constitution give us unambiguous criteria for evaluating separation or the complaint that the best of Indian secularists have an inconsistent understanding of the relationship between state and religion remains wide off the target and altogether fails to grasp the conceptual structure of secularism in India. If secularism embodies contextual reasoning, it must be understood that this is not private-moral reasoning applied to politics but rather public-political reasoning infused with a moral character.

Back to preliminaries

This is an appropriate point at which to briefly elaborate two points I made at the very beginning. First, that it is inadequate if not mistaken to focus on current formulations of Western secularism. To grasp the rich and complicated structure of secularism, it is extremely important to examine the history of the secular ideal. An idea begins to have a life much before its clear formulation and before human beings bring it to self-consciousness. Often what is taken to be the birth of an idea is partly a discovery, a re-articulation of older ideas and only in part an invention. And, as Hegel reminded us, we grasp this point only when that idea achieves a distinct and clear self-consciousness. This is certainly true of secularism. The complex set of values that coalesce around what later came to be called secularism began to live much earlier. For example, in a religiously diverse society, organized political power simply had to maintain some distance from the dominant religious group for the sake of stability and peace. The same motivation lay behind a partial acceptance and therefore the toleration of the less dominant religious groups and the half-hearted recognition of particular religious identities. States that promoted peace and toleration can certainly not be called secular but there is no doubt that they are historically connected to modern secular states and can be said to constitute the latter's pre-history. At best they may be seen to embody a local, customary or traditional secularism.

This traditional secularism is found in different societies and cultures. This is why the development of modern secularism cannot be understood as growing out of the relationship between the Church and the state. The Church-state model is one variant of traditional secularism. The presence in background cultural conditions of other variants such as the religious strife model is equally conducive to the growth of modern secularism. I have elsewhere written in detail about these two models (see Bhargava 1997, 1998). Suffice here to say that it is sufficient for the Church-state model to be operating within a non-pluralist Christian society. However, a religious strife model necessarily operates within a society in which there exist diverse and radically differing religions or religious denominations. The Church-state model is operative in societies in which separation is an internal feature of the dominant religion. The religious strife model of secularism, on the other hand, develops even if separation within some religions is not internally permissible but purely out of the contextual necessity in a situation of contending religions. In short, in the first model, the state wrenches away from one religion whereas in the other model, it must distance itself from all religions at once. And, as I mentioned, this distancing is dictated by the vulnerabilities experienced by every single religious group. Each one fears persecution from the other as well as the disorder resulting from religious conflict.

Secular states really began to exist when, apart from securing peace and toleration, they protected the religious liberties of individuals, in particular by providing secure conditions in which individuals could lead a decent life even when they dissented from the orthodoxy or orthopraxy of their own respective religions. Secularism advanced further when many aspects of an individual's well-being began to be regulated not simply by a regime of toleration but rather by a formal and legal regime of rights, so that it became possible for individuals to make formal claims of entitlement against each other or against the state: to the protection of their life, or to a private sphere in which they were free to do what they want and were secure that any interference by the state in the life or private world of the individual could proceed only according to due process of law. Thus, a secular state comes into its own when it does not discriminate on grounds of religion in the distribution of passive citizenship rights.

It would be wrong however to identify secularism simply with the view for which the state must be separated from organized religion for the sake of peace, toleration, religious liberty and equality of passive citizenship rights. For over time at least two values have gradually become integral to the secular idea. First, that a state must not discriminate on grounds of religion in the distribution of active citizenship rights. For example, a state must not debar members of minority religious groups from standing for public office. Second, in keeping with the spirit of inter-religious equality as well as equality of citizenship, a fully secular state extends rights to minority religious groups qua groups. In short, it grants community-based rights to religious minorities.

One can now see that over time the secular idea has both transcended already existing values and/or added to them. For example, after the advent of nationalism and democracy, the value of treating everyone as equal and therefore not discriminating in the distribution of active citizenship rights was added to existing conceptions of secularism. Similarly, there is a sense in which a regime of rights better articulates the point behind toleration. A rights-based secularism supersedes toleration because it incorporates all values served by toleration and adds something more and valuable to it. Yet, it would be wrong to think that a secular state has no need at all for a regime of toleration. The regime of rights to which it is attached cannot reach every social space and in such not-so-easily approachable spaces, the ones not covered by legal rights, there still remains a need for decent relations governed by the value of toleration.

This brings me to the second point. Western theories of secularism have tended to see it as a single-value doctrine. For them, the state is to be separated from organized religion for the sake of the fullest possible liberties of individuals including their religious liberty. More recently, this separation is seen to serve individual autonomy. However, a history of the secular idea shows secularism to be a multi-value doctrine, as tied to several important values. The Indian variant of secularism more explicitly recognizes it to be a multi-value doctrine. Furthermore, Western theories of secularism, quite in contrast to the internally variegated practice of Western states, have tended to unpack the metaphor of separation to mean either exclusion or neutrality. To my mind, this has been a very limiting interpretation of what is meant by separation.

Thus, a proper study of Indian secularism shows not only that it shares a past with the West but also that it has its own distinctive past. Indian and Western secularisms have their own distinctive pre-histories as well as a common history. But apart from and beyond these histories, the Indian version has taken forward the idea of secularism because, from the very beginning, by virtue of an integral link with nationalism and democracy, it has had to be explicitly tied to citizenship rights, including to the rights of religious minorities. By doing so, it has never tried to completely annul particular religious identities. To discover its own rich and complex structure, Western secularism can either look backward, to its own past or else look sideways, at Indian secularism that mirrors not only the past of secularism, but in a way, also its future. Doing so will certainly benefit the secularisms of many Western societies. For example, French secularism needs to look beyond its own conceptions of laicite in order to take into account its own multi-cultural and multi-religious reality. It cannot continue to take refuge in claims of exceptionalism (Baubérot 1998: 94–136). In theory, the early French model of laicite introduced a strict separation between church and state. However, strict separation was not interpreted as mutual exclusion or neutrality but rather as one-sided exclusion. In another words, while religion was excluded from the affairs of the state, the state had the power to intervene in religion in order to control and subordinate it. The social sentiment of anti-clericism was frequently made into state policy. By 1905, however, this one-sided exclusion gave way to mutual exclusion. Anti-clericism declined. Indeed, mutual exclusion gave way to neutrality which in some aspects permitted contact with and recognition to religion as much as in other aspects it disallowed it. In 'normal' periods, when Islamic identity was not unusually assertive, this policy of neutrality was useful in handling the demands of France's Muslim population. However, the moment some controversial issues such as the wearing of the head scarf entered public life, the French state fell back sometimes on the idea of mutual exclusion and at other times on one-sided exclusion. Either way neutrality gave way to strict separation between church and state. Likewise, the more accommodative flirtation with multiple values was set aside in favour of a commitment to equal citizenship rights, even when it conflicted with the value of religious freedom of Muslims. The controlling authority of the state over religion was re-asserted. The idea that a religious group may have some limited right to express itself in public spaces such as schools was decisively abandoned. In short, the moment a deeper religious diversity began to question the theoretical model of laicite, its more accommodating interpretation, one that would have made it resemble the Indian model, was quickly abandoned. To my mind, this is unfortunate. It is myopic not to let the idea of laicite theoretically grow, particularly in response to the needs of a changing, now increasingly multi-religious society. Clearly, the French can benefit from the lessons implicit in the Indian conception of secularism. I feel that a good hard look at Indian secularism could also change the self-understanding of American liberal secularism.

Ironically, this need to attend to the distinctiveness of Indian secularism is as pressing in India as it is in the West. Several critics of Indian secularism have identified it with one or the other Western versions and have ignored its special character. This has been a source of gross misinterpretation and several problems. For example, it is frequently argued that secularism is purely a Christian, Western doctrine and therefore, cannot adapt itself easily to the cultural conditions of India, infused as they are by religions that grew in the soil of the sub-continent. This necessary link between secularism and Christianity is exaggerated, if not mistaken. It is true that traditional secularism is derived almost wholly from Christianity. The idea that to achieve religious integrity, peace or toleration, the state must be strictly separated from religion is part of Christianity and its internal history. But as I have argued, the mutual exclusion of religion and the state is not the defining feature of secularism. The idea of separation can be interpreted differently. Nor are religious integrity, peace and toleration uniquely Christian values. Most non-Christian civilizations have given significant space to each. Therefore, none of them are exclusively Christian. It follows that, even though it is in Christian writings that we find the clearest and most systematic articulation of this doctrine, even traditional secularism is not exclusively Christian. More importantly, traditional secularism must not be confused with its modern counterpart. Traditional secularism is a sufficient but not necessary part of the background condition of modern secularism. Modern secularism may be helped by the presence of traditional secularism but it can also be nourished by other traditions of peace and toleration.

All right, one might say, secularism is not just a Christian doctrine, but is it not Western? I have argued above that the answer to this question is both yes and no. Up to a point, it is certainly Western. More specifically, as a clearly articulated doctrine, it has distinct Western origins. Although elements that constitute secularism assume different cultural forms and are found in several civilizations, one cannot deny that the idea of the secular first achieved self-consciousness and was properly theorized in the West. One might then say that the middle history of secularism is almost entirely dominated by Western societies. However, the same cannot be said of its later history. Nationalism and democracy arrived in the West after the settlement of religious conflicts, in primarily religiously homogenous societies. The absence of deep religious diversity and conflict meant that issues of citizenship could be addressed almost entirely disregarding religious context; the important issue of community specific rights to religious groups could be wholly ignored. This could not be done in India. Both national and democratic agendas in India had to face issues raised by deep religious difference and diversity. In India, nationalism had to choose between the religious and the secular. Similarly, the distribution of active citizenship rights could not be conceived or accomplished by ignoring religion. It could be done either by actively disregarding religion or by developing a complex attitude to it. It also had to balance claims of individual autonomy with those of community obligations. In addressing these complex issues, the very idea of the secular was taken further than had been evolved in the West. In the course of doing so, it also began to embody a form of contextual moral reasoning with which the notion of principled distance is associated. This distinguishes it from other variants of modern secularism that are grounded in more abstract, theoreticist and context-insensitive conceptions of rationality. There is nothing particularly Western about these ideas. On the contrary, most conceptions of Western secularisms have taken little note of them and therefore are struggling to deal with post-colonial religious diversity of their societies. The later history of secularism is more Indian than Western.[4]

It may still be argued that the Indianness of Indian secularism is derived entirely from its strong link with home-grown traditions and that therefore India had worked out its own conception of secularism that is neither Christian nor Western. For example, secularism for many means 'sarva dharma sambhava': (a) religious coexistence or (b) inter-religious tolerance or finally (c) equal respect for all religions. Each of these interpretations of 'sarva dharma sambhava' point to a crucial ingredient of secularism but not only fails to capture its full richness and complexity but entirely ignores its relationship with extremely significant, internally constitutive values of secularism. I take religious co-existence to be equivalent to peace but to identify the secular state with a state that maintains peace between religions, that allows different religions to co-exist does little justice to the rich history and conceptual structure of secularism as a multi-value doctrine. Much the same is true of the interpretation of Indian secularism as inter-religious toleration. There are many good reasons why these two ideals should not be conflated but I shall mention only one. The mainstream idea of toleration is that it enjoins us to refrain from interfering in the affairs of others, even when one has the power to do so and additionally, even when one finds the beliefs and practices of others morally repugnant. In this sense, toleration is entirely consistent with a total refusal to respect the religion of others. It is also compatible with gross inequality and hierarchy. One may tolerate the religion of another person even as one treats him as inferior. Secularism, on the other hand, is grounded in notions of equality – equal concern and respect – and therefore goes far beyond the notion of inter-religious tolerance.

It is equally inappropriate to identify secularism with equal respect for all religions. Now it must be conceded that there is something valuable in this interpretation and something Indian about this idea. The internal plurality of Hinduism has the potential for a space where equal respect can indeed be accorded to all religions. Besides, a respect for other religions is entirely consistent with the development of their critique and the identification of local faults within them. Respecting other religions as equals does not entail their blind acceptance or endorsement. Indeed, it is precisely because respect is consistent with difference and critique that the idea of equal respect for all religions is closely linked with the proposal for an inter-faith dialogue. Yet, even an important ingredient of secularism cannot become the whole of it. Indeed, to equate the two is to do gross injustice to secularism. This equation implies that one ignores the non-religious part of human existence that all modern states must confront and which are also an integral part of modern secularism. Let me take an example. The idea of equal respect for all religions is entirely consistent with the equal unavailability of active citizenship rights to all members of society. It is also consistent with a total indifference to the freedom of individuals within each religious group. A fruitful dialogue on equal footing is entirely possible between religious groups that sanction gender and caste-related injustices or remain indifferent to them. But sensitivity to such issues is the hallmark of modern secularism. If so, it would be a terrible mistake to identify secularism with equal respect for all religions or modern Indian secularism with 'sarva dharma sambhava'. As political attitude and practice, 'Sarva dharma sambhava' is more in tune with states that establish multiple religions than it does with states that are secular.

I have argued that it is wrong to identify Indian secularism with Western secularism or with notions of inter-religious tolerance. No doubt, Indian secularism has some relationship with both but it is not one of identity. At the heart of such identification is a failure to notice that we developed a version of secularism that was at once modern and Indian. Those who identify Indian secularism entirely with home-grown traditional conceptions are able to grasp the pre-history of Indian secularism (even though they do not see it as such, as pre-history), but they entirely bypass its connection with a larger common trans-national history as well as with its later history towards which Indians contributed significantly. On the other hand, those who identify the Indian variant with Western conceptions fail to notice both the pre-history and the later history of secularism. As I mentioned above, like Western theorists, they focus only on the middle history of secularism, one developed almost exclusively by Western societies. This limited vision is shared by both advocates and opponents of secularism. For example, Indian critics of Indian secularism claim that it has privatized religion. Nothing could be further from the truth. Indian religion has a public presence that is ratified by the Indian constitution. The constitution gives official recognition to religious communities to maintain their own educational institutions. Such institutions foster particular religious identities and are sometimes even funded by the state. There could not be a more suitable illustration of the point that far from privatizing religion, the Indian constitution continues to support its publicization.

I have focused in this chapter on internal threats to secularism. I have argued that a continuous failure to recognize the distinctiveness of Indian secularism strengthens this threat. I believe this problem afflicts the self-understanding of secularism in both India and several Western countries. Western states need to improve the understanding of their own secular practices just as Western secularism needs a better theoretical self-understanding. Rather than get stuck on a model they developed at a particular time in their history, they would do well to learn from the original Indian variant. Equally, both the self-proclaimed supporters of secularism and some of its misguided opponents could learn from examining the original Indian variant. Indeed it is my conviction that many critics of Indian secularism will embrace it once they better understand its nature and point.

Notes

1 This article was originally published in T. N. Srinivasan (ed.) *The Future of Secularism* (New Delhi: Oxford University Press, 2006).

2 Partha Chatterjee's piece on secularism exemplifies this error. Thus he mistakenly concludes that since the Hindu right does not want the laws of the state to be in conformity with the general spirit of the Dharmasastra, it is at peace with the institutional procedures of modern

Western secularism (see Chatterjee 1998: 345–79). Arguably, the Hindu Right may wish the de facto, somewhat disguised establishment of its own variant of Hinduism.

3 For an interesting critique of Smith's interpretation of Indian secularism as derived from the American model with an 'extra dose of separation', see Galanter (1998: 234–67).

4 And by implication, the history of secularism must include the history of other non-western societies that have sought to install and maintain secular states.

References

AIR (1952) Bom.84, *The State of Bombay vs. Narasu Appa.*

Austin, Granville (1962) *The Indian Constitution: Cornerstone of a Nation*, New Delhi: Oxford University Press.

Baubérot, Jean (1998) The two thresholds of laicization, in Rajeev Bhargava (ed.) *Secularism and its Critics,* New Delhi: Oxford University Press.

Beitz, Charles R. (1989) *Political Equality*, Princeton NJ: Princeton University Press.

Bhargava, Rajeev (1997) Review of T. N. Madan's *Modern Myths, Locked Minds*, *Book Review*, 21(8), August, pp. 11–13.

—— (1998) 'What is secularism for?', in Rajeev Bhargava, (ed.) *Secularism and its Critics*, New Delhi: Oxford University Press.

Chatterjee, Partha (1998) 'Secularism and tolerance', in Rajeev Bhargava, (ed.) *Secularism and its Critics*, New Delhi: Oxford University Press.

Dworkin, Ronald (1978) 'Liberalism', in Stuart Hampshire (ed.) *Public and Private Morality*, Cambridge: Cambridge University Press.

Galanter, Marc (1998) 'Secularism, east and west', in Rajeev Bhargava, (ed.) *Secularism and its Critics*, New Delhi: Oxford University Press.

Levy, Leonard W. (1994) *The Establishment Clause*, Chapel Hill: The University of North Carolina Press.

McConnell, Michael (1993) 'Taking religious freedom seriously', in Terry East Land (ed.) *Religious Liberty in the Supreme Court,* Michigan and Cambridge: William B. Eerdamans Publishing Company.

Smith, Donald (1963) *India as a Secular State*, Bombay: Oxford University Press.

Taylor, Charles (1989) *Sources of the Self*, Cambridge: Cambridge University Press.

—— (1994) 'Justice after virtue' in John Horton and Susan Mendus (ed.) *After MacIntyre*, Cambridge: Polity Press.

Part II
Law, Religion and Education

[7]

RELIGION & EDUCATION

Jeroen Temperman

It is hard to ignore the tension that exists between the liberty of parents or legal guardians "to ensure the religious and moral education of their children in conformity with their own convictions"[1] on the one hand, and children's autonomous right to freedom of religion or belief on the other.[2] The recognition of parental rights in this context can be considered rather unique in so far as it provides a third party with rights vis-à-vis the individual. In other words, it provides a third party with a right to interfere with someone's (the child's) freedom or at least to temporarily exercise it on the latter's behalf. With the entry into force of the *Convention on the Rights of the Child*, the paradigm has arguably shifted from prior and decisive parental rights to an autonomous children's right to freedom of religion or belief (with parental rights being accessory).[3] The Children's Rights Convention has sought to constructively deal with the tension at stake: it recognizes children's right to freedom of religion or belief whilst urging state parties at the same time:

> ...to respect the rights and duties of the parents and, when applicable, legal guardians, to provide direction to the child in the exercise of his or her right [to freedom of religion or belief] *in a manner consistent with the evolving capacities of the child.*[4]

---

[1] Art. 18, para. (4), of the ICCPR. This provision was ultimately added after extensive debates in the drafting committees. Originally proposed by Greece (A/C.3/L.875) and therefore often referred to as the "Greek Amendment" in the *travaux préparatoires*. For opposition, see, *e.g.*, A/C.3/SR.1025 (1960), para. 57 (USSR). See also art. 26, para. (3), of the UDHR; art. 14, para. (2), of Convention on the Rights of the Child, G.A. res. 44/25, annex, 44 U.N. GAOR Supp. (No. 49) at 167, U.N. Doc. A/44/49, of 20 November 1989 (entered into force: 2 September 1990) [hereinafter: CRC]; art. 13, para. (3), of ICESCR; and art. 5, paras. (1) and (2), of the UN Religious Tolerance Declaration (1981).

[2] Art. 14, para. (1), of CRC states: "States Parties shall respect the right of the child to freedom of thought, conscience and religion." For a recent, comprehensive study of children's right to freedom of religion or belief as a right recognized by international law, see SYLVIE LANGLAUDE, THE RIGHT OF THE CHILD TO RELIGIOUS FREEDOM IN INTERNATIONAL LAW (Leiden: Martinus Nijhoff Publishers, 2007).

[3] Cf. EVA BREMS, ARTICLE 14: THE RIGHTS TO FREEDOM OF THOUGHT, CONSCIENCE AND RELIGION (A COMMENTARY ON THE UNITED NATIONS CONVENTION ON THE RIGHTS OF THE CHILD) (Leiden/Boston: Martinus Nijhoff Publishers, 2006), p. 25. In this context it is worth emphasizing that the children's right to freedom of religion of belief as incorporated into CRC is of a later date and the CRC could be considered the *lex specialis* in this context.

[4] Art. 14, para. (2), of CRC (emphasis added); for a study on this parameter and its legal relevance, see G. LANSDOWN, THE EVOLVING CAPACITIES OF THE CHILD (Florence: UNICEF Innocenti Research Centre, 2005).

It would indeed appear to be essential to take account of the evolving capacities of the child if we want the 'best interest of the child' to be our guiding principle.[5] Parental guidance, in the words of Brems, "has to recede as the child's capacities evolve".[6] Taking that conception as the point of departure, this Chapter examines the state's role in guaranteeing children's rights (to education, freedom of religion or belief and equality), as well as parental rights, in the context of its obligation to provide education. As soon as it is clear what an educational system that takes sufficient account of these rights looks like, it will be possible to further scrutinize the position and role of teachers within such a system.

10.2 Access to Appropriate Education

The state has to respect the child's right to education which implies, *inter alia*, making available free primary education to all.[7] The following overview is intended to outline the relevant religious freedoms and equality norms and the various human rights violations that are discernable in this context.

10.2.1 *Prohibition of Compulsory Religious Upbringing*

A child's upbringing and its education obviously touch upon each other in many ways. In that respect, it may be noted as a preliminary observation that a legal requirement that would force parents to raise their children as a member of a particular religion would constitute an infringement of both parental and children's rights. Such a coercive measure, naturally, would annihilate parents' liberty to decide (in a manner consistent with the evolving capacities of the child) on the religious and moral education of their children in conformity with their own convictions. It would be wrong, in this context, to solely associate this position with the more stringent Islamic states[8] as the Norwegian Constitution provides:

> The Evangelical-Lutheran religion shall remain the official religion of the State. *The inhabitants professing it are bound to bring up their children in the same.*[9]

---

[5] See art. 3 and 18, para. (1), of CRC on the 'best interests of the child' notion. See also art. 5 of the UN Religious Tolerance Declaration (1981).

[6] Brems, *supra* note 3, p. 26.

[7] Art. 13 of ICESCR.

[8] *E.g.* art. 9 of the Basic Law of Saudi Arabia (1992) stipulates: "The family is the kernel of Saudi society, and its members shall be brought up on the basis of the Islamic faith, and loyalty and obedience to God, His Messenger, and to [its] guardians..."; art. 21 of the Const. of Qatar (2003) states: "The family is the basis of the society. A Qatari family is founded on religion...".

[9] Art. 2, para. (2), of the Const. of Norway (1814) (emphasis added).

There is clearly no place for such a coercive norm in a liberal democracy as it makes (*de jure*, at least) a travesty of religious freedom.[10] Most religious people will want to teach their children the essence of their beliefs, but it is certainly not for the state to command that they in fact do so. Moreover, it is certainly not unimaginable that liberal (nominal) church members would wish for their children to make up their own mind when the time is right. Under human rights law they are most definitely entitled to make that decision. In the latter respect, Slovenian constitutional provisions stand out positively in so far they have due regard for the child's evolving capacities and best interests:

> Parents have the right to provide their children with a religious and moral upbringing in accordance with their beliefs. The religious and moral guidance given to children must be appropriate to their age and maturity, and be consistent with their free conscience and religious and other beliefs or convictions.[11]

10.2.2 *Prohibition of Compulsory Religious Education*

Compulsory religious education is contrary to international human rights law.[12] In the view of the Human Rights Committee solely "public school instruction in subjects such as the general history of religions and ethics [which] is given in a *neutral and objective way*" is compatible with the norms on freedom of religion or belief.[13] Consequently, "public education that includes instruction in a particular religion or belief is inconsistent with article 18.4 [of the ICCPR: parental liberties]".[14] Having said that, the Human Rights Committee does sanction religious instruction in public schools if adequate provision is made for opt-out clauses, thus accommodating the wishes of parents or legal guardians who do not want their child to attend religion classes.[15]

---

[10] The Human Rights Committee has repeatedly condemned Norway's state practice: A/55/40 vol. I (2000) 22 at para. 78; and A/49/40 vol. I (1994) 21 at para. 93.

[11] Art. 41, para. (3), of the CONST. OF SLOVENIA (1991).

[12] *E.g.* CRC/C/150 (2005) 149 at paras. 694 and 695 (Costa Rica): "the Committee is concerned at the fact that classes on Catholicism are part of the curriculum, which is discriminatory for non-Catholic children…The Committee recommends that the State party devise a curriculum that will ensure that the child's freedom of religion can be fully realized in the educational system without any discrimination"; and CRC/C/62 (1997) 25 at paras. 150 and 171 (Myanmar); see also ICESCR Committee, E/1994/23 (1993) 32 at para. 126 (Iran).

[13] Human Rights Committee, General Comment No. 22, para. 6 (emphasis added; particularly referring to art. 18, para. (4), of the ICCPR).

[14] *Ibid.*

[15] *Ibid.* The Committee on Economic, Social and Cultural Rights is roughly of the same view as it has postulated that "public school instruction in subjects such as the general history of religions and ethics *if it is given in an unbiased and objective way*, respectful of the freedoms of opinion, conscience and expression" is permitted and "public education that includes instruction in a particular religion or belief" is in principle inconsistent with human rights law "unless provision is made for non-discriminatory exemptions or alternatives that would accommodate the wishes of parents and guardians". See Committee on Economic, Social and Cultural Rights,

The state thus can be said to fulfil its human rights obligations if it either designs an educational system (a public school curriculum) which is sufficiently neutral or non-religious in itself or, in case it does allow religious education in public schools, if it grants adequate opt-out rights. The Human Rights Committee applied these principles to the case of *Leirvåg v. Norway*.[16] The case revolved around a new mandatory religious subject that the Norwegian government had introduced (in August 1997) in the Norwegian school system entitled "Christian Knowledge and Religious and Ethical Education" (CKREE), replacing the previous Christianity subject and the life stance subject.[17] This was challenged by humanist parents who felt that the subject was not neutral enough and that the available opt-out clauses were insufficient. The Human Rights Committee concluded that the teaching of CKREE cannot be said to meet the requirement of being delivered in a neutral and objective way. It reached this conclusion, firstly, in light of the fact that the object clause of the Education Act in question prescribed that the object of primary and lower secondary education shall be "in agreement and cooperation with the home, to help to give pupils a Christian and moral upbringing".[18] And, secondly, because of the fact that some of the *travaux préparatoires* of the Act made it clear that the subject gives priority to tenets of Christianity over other religions and philosophies of life.[19] In line with the Human Rights Committee's reading of the international norms on freedom of religion or belief in this context, this new course could still be saved if it could be concluded that Norway had sufficiently guaranteed exemption rights that would accommodate the wishes of parents or guardians. However, the Human Rights Committee noted that only a partial exemption scheme was in place and that the way in which this scheme was implemented in practice left the rights of the applicants unprotected.[20] In this context the Human Rights Committee considered that:

> ...the present system of partial exemption imposes a considerable burden on persons in the position of the authors, insofar as it requires them to acquaint themselves with those aspects of the subject which are clearly of a religious nature, as well as with other aspects, with a view to determining which of the other aspects they may feel a need to seek – and justify – exemption from. Nor would it be implausible to expect that such persons would be deterred from exercising that right, insofar as a regime of partial exemption could create problems

General Comment No. 13: The Right to Education (Art. 13), E/C.12/1999/10, of 8 December 1999 (emphasis added), basing its considerations on art. 13 of ICESCR. It will be contended *infra*, however, that such opt-out clauses in practice often prove to be highly problematic.

16 Human Rights Committee, *Leirvåg v. Norway*, Communication No. 1155/2003, Views of 3 November 2004.

17 It must be noted that the Committee on the Rights of the Child had raised objections with regard to the previous situation: CRC/C/15/Add.23 (1994), para. 9.

18 *Leirvåg v. Norway, supra* note 16, para. 14.3.

19 *Idem.*

20 *Ibid.*, para. 14.4.

> for children which are different from those that may be present in a total exemption scheme. Indeed as the experience of the authors demonstrates, the system of exemptions does not currently protect the liberty of parents to ensure that the religious and moral education of their children is in conformity with their own convictions. In this respect, the Committee notes that the CKREE subject combines education on religious knowledge with practising a particular religious belief, e.g. learning by heart of prayers, singing religious hymns or attendance at religious services...While it is true that in these cases parents may claim exemption from these activities by ticking a box on a form, the CKREE scheme does not ensure that education of religious knowledge and religious practice are separated in a way that makes the exemption scheme practicable.[21]

The Committee furthermore highlighted the problem of 'loyalty conflicts' that can be experienced by children in this context.[22] The latter point reveals a more fundamental concern about religious education in the curriculum of public schools: though opt-out clauses may remedy the compulsion element, such safeguards cannot prevent possible ostracization of those children that avail of these exemption schemes (something that has also been observed by the Committee on the Rights of the Child with respect to Italy).[23] The Human Rights Committee also explicitly objected to the requirement to give reasons for exempting children from lessons focusing on imparting religious knowledge, as this practice creates even further obstacles for parents who seek to ensure that their children are not exposed to religious ideas.[24] The Committee on the Rights of the Child has expanded the state duties in the present context as it has determined that the state is under an obligation to ensure that parents are actually aware of the fact that religious instruction is not compulsory.[25]

It follows from the above considerations that any constitutional provision along the lines of 'the teaching of religion *x* shall be compulsory for pupils' is fundamentally contrary to parental and children's rights.[26] Saudi Arabia, for instance, has constitutionally stipulated that education must aim at "instilling the Islamic faith in the younger generation".[27] Maldives' educational system is framed so as to "inculcate obedience to Islam" and "instil love for Islam".[28] The combined focus of protecting youth "against perversions" and providing

---

21 *Ibid.*, para. 14.6.

22 *Ibid.*, para. 14.7.

23 CRC/C/15/Add.198 (2003), para. 29 (Italy): "children, especially in elementary schools, may suffer from marginalization if they abstain from religious instruction, which is mainly covering Catholic religion."

24 *Leirvåg v. Norway, supra* note 16, para. 14.7.

25 CRC/C/15/Add.198 (2003), paras. 29–30 (Italy).

26 *E.g.* art. 24, para. (10), of the Transitional Federal Charter of the Somali Republic (2004) provides: "Teaching of Islam shall be compulsory for pupils in both Public and Private Schools".

27 Art. 13 of the Basic Law of Saudi Arabia (1992).

28 Art. 36, para. (c), of the Const. of Maldives (2008).

them with religious knowledge as the main objective of state education (as in Yemen) will also fail the above human right test.[29] Compulsory state education that is aimed at the development of the "religious consciousness" (Greece)[30] of pupils or state education that is organized to endow "members of the younger generation...with religious...learning" (Liechtenstein)[31] may similarly be deemed contrary to the religious rights of parents and the religious and educational rights of children. The Constitution of Malta provides that "[r]eligious teaching of the Roman Catholic Apostolic Faith shall be provided in all State schools as part of compulsory education".[32] This is in keeping with Malta's policy of delegating the teaching of "which principles are right and which are wrong" to authorities of the Roman Catholic Apostolic Church.[33] The Slovak Republic, though officially secular, has included a (Christian) religious subject in the public school curriculum.[34] Turkey, an otherwise strictly secular state, has made religious instruction (with a profound emphasis on Sunni Islam) a compulsory part of the curricula of primary and secondary schools.[35] It can be argued, at the same time, that state-run compulsory instruction—or indoctrination—in secular ideologies such as the North Korean *Juche* ideology is similarly at odds with the prohibition of coercion.[36]

10.2.3 *Access to Non-Denominational Education*

State duties in the area of education consist of obligations to refrain from interferences but also, importantly, of obligations to proactively guarantee availability and access. Thus, the state must respect the right of parents not to avail of the schools established by the public authorities and their right to opt for private educational institutions (i.e. denominational schools) so as to ensure the religious and moral education of their children in conformity with

[29] Art. 53 of the CONST. OF YEMEN (1990).
[30] Art. 16, para. (2), of the CONST. OF GREECE (2001).
[31] Art. 15 of the CONST. OF LIECHTENSTEIN (1921).
[32] Art. 2, para. (3), of the CONST. OF MALTA (1964).
[33] Art. 2, para. (2), of the CONST. OF MALTA (1964).
[34] As per the Concordat between the Slovak Republic and the Holy See about Catholic Upbringing and Education of March 2004. Art. II(4) provides: "The Catholic religion is taught as one of the compulsory eligible subject matters in primary schools and in secondary schools..." Officially, an ethics subject may be taught as an alternative; it should be acknowledged, however, that the Catholic ecclesiastical authorities, as per the Concordat, seem to be very influential in the field of education.
[35] Art. 24 of the CONST. OF TURKEY (1982).
[36] DPRK's constitutional provision on public education stipulates that: "the State shall put the principles of socialist education into practice and raise the new generation to be steadfast revolutionaries who will fight for society and the people, to be people of a new communist type who are knowledgeable, morally sound and physically healthy" (art. 43 of the CONST. OF DPRK OF 1972). See also art. 39 of the CONST. OF CUBA (1976) which requires that state education is based on the "ideology of Marx".

their own convictions.[37] Furthermore, public school education, it goes without saying, should be open to all children regardless of their parents' religious affiliation.[38] The standards on the right to education further imply that the state is under a positive obligation to ensure that sufficient public schools with appropriate curricula are available at all times. This means that a predominantly religious society cannot completely contract out the issue of education to private religious institutions. In this respect, the Human Rights Committee very recently reproached Ireland, observing that:

> ...the vast majority of Ireland's primary schools are privately run denominational schools that have adopted a religious integrated curriculum thus depriving many parents and children who so wish to have access to secular primary education... The State party should increase its efforts to ensure that non-denominational primary education is widely available in all regions of the State party, in view of the increasingly diverse and multi-ethnic composition of the population of the State party.[39]

If the state fails in its positive duty to provide for non-denominational education, be it by actively contracting out this issue to religious organizations or by maintaining historical church prerogatives (effectively allowing primary school education to be monopolized by religion), various educational and religious rights are inevitably infringed.[40] Ireland's Equality Act makes the situation for children of non-religious parents worse as it allows denominational schools (which are nearly all Catholic) to refuse admission of pupils who do not adhere to the denomination concerned, on the grounds of the preservation of the 'religious ethos' of the school.[41] Such a system fosters serious human rights violations: (i) given the lack of secular state-run schools and the possibility that children of non-religious parents are turned away by denominational schools, no appropriate form of education might be available at all to children of non-religious parents; (ii) secular parents who prefer religious education over no education at all might feel compelled to obtain the necessary religious affiliation (e.g. by means of conversion or baptism of their children) so as to be able to enrol their children.[42]

---

[37] As long as these schools conform to such minimum educational standards laid down by the state. *E.g.* art. 13, paras. (3) and (4), of ICESCR; art. 5, para. (1)(b), of the UNESCO Convention against Discrimination in Education of 14 December 1960; also implied by art. 5, para. (2) of the UN Religious Tolerance Declaration (1981).

[38] See also Carolyn Evans, *Religious Education in Public Schools: An International Human Rights Perspective*, 8(3) Human Rights Law Review 449 (2008), p. 451.

[39] CCPR/C/IRL/CO/3 (2008), para. 2.

[40] See Alison Mawhinney, *Submission to the Human Rights Committee with Respect to the Third Periodic Report of Ireland* [NGO Information], March 2008; this shadow report is a response to CCPR/C/IRL/3, paras. 409–411.

[41] Art. 7, para. (3)(c), of the Equal Status Act, No. 8/2000, of 2000.

[42] Both problems are reported in the mentioned shadow report, *supra* note 40, pp. 2 and 4; similar concerns have been raised by CERD Committee: A/60/18 (2005), 30 at para. 142.

The state is also under an obligation to ensure that public schools are not only public schools on paper and that, if teaching in religion takes place, non-discriminatory exemptions (opt-out clauses) and/or alternative non-religious classes (e.g. ethics classes) are offered. The Committee on the Rights of the Child criticized Polish state practice in this respect, observing that:

> ...despite regulations guaranteeing that parents can choose for their children to attend ethics classes instead of religion classes in public schools, in practice few schools offer ethics courses to allow for such a choice and students require parental consent to attend ethics courses.[43]

The state is arguably also under an obligation to ensure that public schools uphold their public (non-denominational) character so that all who wish to attend may do so without obstacles or scruples. For instance, as Russo points out in relation to Republika Šrpska, if religious symbols are present in public schools all over the state, children of non-believers or of persons belonging to minority religions may not have access to adequate state education.[44] Very recently, the European Court of Human Rights (in a Chamber judgement) considered in relation to the Italian public educational system that the display of Catholic symbols in classrooms amounts to an illegitimate restriction of the right of parents to educate their children in conformity with their convictions and of the right of children to believe or not to believe.[45] This essentially means that, under the European Convention system, states must observe confessional neutrality in the context of public education (moreover, the judgement seems to indicate that the same arguments may apply to all premises used by public authorities).

Some treaty monitoring bodies have criticized the *laissez-faire* attitude towards education for other, perhaps even more fundamental reasons. It has been observed that whenever the state fails in its positive duty to provide for sufficient non-denominational schools, or if it is satisfied with a situation wherein the different religions organize education in accordance with their tenets, it may be actively contributing to religious segregation. The Committee on Economic, Social and Cultural Rights, for instance, assessing the educational system in Northern Ireland, observed that it:

> ...is heavily segregated, with most Protestants attending Protestant schools and most Catholics attending Catholic schools and only approximately 2 per cent of the school population attending integrated schools. The current government

[43] CRC/C/15/Add.194 (2002), para. 32.

[44] Charles J. Russo, *Religion and Education in Bosnia: Integration Not Segregation?*, 3 Brigham Young University Law Review (2000), p. 945, on the fact that Christian Orthodox religious symbols are present in most public schools.

[45] ECtHR, *Lautsi v. Italy*, Application No. 30814/06, Judgement of 3 November 2009, determining a violation of art. 2 of Protocol No. 1 (right to education) examined jointly with Article 9 (freedom of thought, conscience and religion) of the European Convention. See Protocol No.1 to the ECHR, ETS No. 009, of 20 March 1952 (entry into force: 18 May 1954).

> policy, which appears to consist of a willingness to consider the conversion of existing Protestant or Catholic schools into integrated schools if it is the wish of the majority in a given school, is ineffective and likely to preserve the status quo.[46]

It is thus clear that a far more pro-active policy on making appropriate education accessible to all is called for.

Granting religious ethos exemptions to denominational schools in states that provide sufficient secular public education does not need to be too problematic (albeit perhaps fundamentally objectionable). Be that as it may, the above example of Ireland shows that the opposite situation needs to be firmly criticized: if the state fails in its obligation to provide sufficient non-denominational public education it is clear that the policy of granting religious ethos exemptions aggravates the lack of access to education. Besides Ireland, the UK[47] and New Zealand[48] expressly sanction religious discrimination by denominational schools in their enrolment policies.

10.2.4 *Further Access Issues: State Schools & Secular Dress Codes*

The question of dress codes has become a contentious issue that can in practice affect access to education. Banning the wearing of religious symbols or clothing in state schools may affect access to those for whom wearing such items is religiously compulsory.[49] Wearing clothes or displaying symbols is indisputably covered by freedom of religion or belief.[50] It must be reiterated, however, that the freedom to manifest a religion is not absolute. The question thus is whether in the educational context interests can be advanced that warrant interference with this freedom.

Unlike the European Court of Human Rights, which has sanctioned such bans in the interest of preserving secularism and the rights and freedoms of others,[51] the UN treaty monitoring bodies have not yet fully come to terms

---

[46] E/1998/22 (1997) 56 at para. 301 (UK); reiterated in 2002: E/2003/22 (2002) 39 at paras. 226 and 245 (UK).

[47] Art. 59 of the Equality Act of 2006, Law c.3/2006.

[48] Art. 58 of the [New Zealand] Human Rights Act of 1993.

[49] The issue of religious attire clearly cuts across a broad range of fundamental rights, freedoms and principles as well as state interests that all need to be considered in this debate (*e.g.* the right to freedom of religion or belief in both its positive and negative forms, elimination of religious discrimination, elimination of racial discrimination, elimination of gender discrimination, access to employment, access to education, children's rights, teachers' rights, etc.). For a comprehensive account, see Dominic McGoldrick, Human Rights and Religion: The Islamic Headscarf Debate in Europe (Portland: Hart Publishing, 2006), particularly Chapter 9 (for a human rights approach).

[50] Art. 6, para. (c), of the UN Religious Tolerance Declaration (1981); Human Rights Committee, General Comment No. 22, para. 4.

[51] ECtHR, *Leyla Şahin v. Turkey*, Application No. 44774/98, Judgement of 10 November 2005, para. 116. However, as dissenting Judge Tulkens rightly pointed out, it cannot, *in abstracto*, be taken for granted that wearing a headscarf, in the capacity of a student, in university

with this type of prohibition.[52] It could be argued though that the major concerns the latter bodies have identified so far lean towards a disapproval of such state practice. The Human Rights Committee, in *Hudoyberganova v. Uzbekistan*,[53] concluded that the suspension of a female Muslim student by a language institute for wearing a headscarf constituted a violation of her right to freedom of religion or belief.[54] However, it must be borne in mind that the Committee came to this decision mainly because Uzbekistan had not advanced any particular ground for limiting this student's religious rights.[55] This would suggest that the outcome of similar cases before the Committee could be different in the future if the state could convincingly argue that recognized grounds for limitations are at stake and if the state would substantiate the necessity of upholding those grounds at the expense of the freedom to manifest a religion. Committee member Wedgwood (who deemed the facts of the case, as presented by the different parties, too obscure to rule on it) considered that:

> ...a state may be allowed to restrict forms of dress that directly interfere with effective pedagogy, and the covering of a student's face would present a different set of facts.[56]

---

buildings per se contravenes the principle of secularism or is aimed at calling the principle of secularism into question (see Dissenting Opinion Judge Tulkens, para. 7). The *Şahin* line of reasoning was confirmed by the European Court in: *Dogru v. France*, Application No. 27058/05, Judgement of 4 December 2008. More recently (and arguably in an attempt to prevent a further accumulation of similar cases against France), the European Court, based on these earlier judgements, has started to declare all such cases against France that revolve around the expulsion of pupils from schools for wearing conspicuous symbols of religious affiliation, inadmissible (*e.g.*, *Aktas v. France*, Application No. 43563/08, Judgement of 17 July 2009; *Bayrak v. France*, Application No. 14308/08, Judgement of 17 July 2009; *Gamaleddyn v. France*, Application No. 18527/08, Judgement of 17 July 2009; *Ghazal v. France*, Application No. 29134/08, Judgement of 17 July 2009; *J. Singh v. France*, Application No. 25463/08, Judgement of 17 July 2009; *R. Singh v. France*, Application No. 27561/08, Judgement of 17 July 2009).

52 In addition to the cases dealt with and observations made by the treaty bodies in the following overview, attention may be drawn to a headscarf case before the CEDAW Committee: *Rahime Kayhan v. Turkey*, Communication No. 8/2005, Decision of 27 January 2006, which was declared inadmissible for failure to exhaust domestic remedies.

53 Human Rights Committee, *Raihon Hudoyberganova v. Uzbekistan*, Communication No. 931/2000, U.N. Doc. CCPR/C/82/D/931/2000 (2004), Views of 05 November 2004.

54 The duty for Muslim women to wear a headscarf is said to follow from the Qur'an, *e.g.* sura 24:31 (THE HOLY QUR'AN, transl. Abdullah Yusuf Ali): "And say to the believing women that they should lower their gaze and guard their modesty; that they should not display their beauty and ornaments except what (must ordinarily) appear thereof; that they should draw their veils over their bosoms and not display their beauty except to their husbands, their fathers, their husband's fathers, their sons, their husbands' sons, their brothers or their brothers' sons, or their sisters' sons, or their women, or the slaves whom their right hands possess, or male servants free of physical needs, or small children who have no sense of the shame of sex; and that they should not strike their feet in order to draw attention to their hidden ornaments. And O ye Believers! Turn ye all together towards Allah, that ye may attain Bliss."

55 *Raihon Hudoyberganova v. Uzbekistan, supra* note 53, para. 6.2.

56 *Ibid.*, Individual opinion by Committee member Ms. Ruth Wedgwood.

The pedagogy argument (including the issue of identification of students during examinations) particularly pertains to religious attire that covers the face (such as the *niqāb*) or the face and parts of the body (such as the *burqa*).

The recently adopted French Law on Secularity and Conspicuous Religious Symbols in Public Schools has been scrutinized by various treaty bodies and though no outright condemnation can be discerned, the concerns that have been raised lean towards a disapproval of this state practice.[57] The Committee on the Rights of the Child, for instance, noted that:

> ...the [French] Constitution provides for freedom of religion and...the law of 1905 on the separation of church and State prohibits discrimination on the basis of faith. The Committee equally recognizes the importance the State party accords to secular public schools. However, in the light of articles 14 and 29 of the Convention [CRC], the Committee is concerned by the alleged rise in discrimination, including that based on religion. The Committee is also concerned that the new legislation...on wearing religious symbols and clothing in public schools may be counterproductive, by neglecting the principle of the best interests of the child and the right of the child to access to education, and not achieve the expected results.[58]

The CRC Committee, short of condemning the law in absolute terms, clearly challenges the necessity of this interference with religious rights.[59] As France is under a clear human rights obligation to guarantee that children are not excluded from the school system or marginalized, the Committee suggests that France should "consider alternative means" (e.g. mediation) of ensuring the secular character of public schools.[60] It further argues that the "dress code of schools may be better addressed within the public schools themselves, encouraging participation of children."[61] Also the Committee on the Elimination of Racial Discrimination is concerned that the ban might have a discriminatory impact and may affect the universality of the right to education in France.[62] The Special Rapporteur on freedom of religion or belief, during her fact-finding mission in France, confirmed the negative human rights implications of the ban on religious symbols and clothing in public schools. She observed that "[a]lthough the scope of the new law applies equally to all

---

[57] *Loi en application du principe de laïcité, le port de signes ou de tenues manifestant une appartenance religieuse dans les écoles, collèges et lycées publics*, Law No. 2004-228, of 15 March 2004.

[58] CRC/C/140 (2004) 124 at para. 604; see also CRC/C/15/Add.240 (2004).

[59] Similarly, CRC/C/118 (2002) 68 at paras. 285 and 286 (Tunisia): "The Committee is concerned about information brought to its attention which indicates that the exercise of the right to freedom of religion may not always be fully guaranteed, particularly with regard to regulations prohibiting the wearing of a headscarf by girls in schools...The Committee recommends that the State party take all necessary measures to ensure the full implementation of the right to freedom of thought, conscience and religion."

[60] CRC/C/140 (2004), para. 605.

[61] *Idem.*

[62] A/60/18 (2005) 26 at para. 112.

religious symbols, its application disproportionately affects young Muslim women wearing the headscarf".[63] Many other negative developments were observed which are worth quoting in some detail:

> ...47 children have been expelled from schools, including three Sikh pupils who had refused to remove their under-turban. French tribunals have usually upheld these expulsions...It is however difficult to assess the number of pupils who have chosen not to abandon their religious signs. In addition to dismissals, some have removed themselves from the school system by abstaining from registering with a school...A large number of...women told the Special Rapporteur about the difficulties they had endured because they had freely chosen to wear the headscarf. Many had been intimidated or humiliated for expressing their personal opinion on the question. Even in cases where young girls were obliged to wear headscarves by their families, the law is said to have provoked particularly painful situations within the families. Some girls who did not wear the headscarf before the law have decided to wear it when they leave the school as a form of protest. Some informed the Special Rapporteur that they felt torn between loyalty to their religious community and their commitment to women's rights...The adoption of the law is also said to have radicalized a fraction of the Muslim youth...Another religious minority that has been seriously affected by the adoption of the law is the Sikh community. Their members reported to the Special Rapporteur that displaying religious symbols was an essential part of their faith. They described the painful experiences they endured when their children had to cut their hair, as a result of the rigid application of the law by some educational institutions...The law also appears to have sent the wrong message to a certain portion of the population which has come to believe that the wearing of religious symbols per se, and in particular headscarves, is generally unlawful. As a result of the new law, a portion of the population has come to associate the headscarf solely with gender inequality and oppression. The Special Rapporteur was informed about instances where women were refused access to shops or were insulted in the street because they wore the headscarf. For the same reasons, some women were dismissed from their employment, while others found it difficult to find employment.[64]

Short of condemning the ban in absolute terms, the concerns raised by the Special Rapporteur reveal that she has serious misgivings about the state practice concerned.

An issue that seems to be under-emphasized in both in the European Court's approach as well as in the considerations of the UN treaty monitoring bodies is the distinction between teacher vs. pupil.[65] Krishnaswami, in his seminal study published in 1960, already argued that though the preservation of the non-denominational character of a school is a legitimate concern, "it is desirable that persons whose faith prescribes such apparel should not be

---

[63] E/CN.4/2006/5/Add.4, para. 63.

[64] *Ibid.*, paras. 61–67. This study concerns 2005 data.

[65] Judge Tulkens in her Dissenting Opinion to the case of *Leyla Şahin v. Turkey (supra* note 51) notes the legal relevance of this distinction (para. 7 *et seq.*).

unreasonably prevented from wearing it."[66] It can certainly be acknowledged that the preservation of the non-denominational character of public schools is a legitimate state interest as it touches upon the state obligation to protect "the rights and freedoms of others" (a legitimate ground for limiting manifestations of religion). The key question thus is which acts do and which acts do not affect the neutral character of public schools. Do religious manifestations by pupils necessarily have a bearing on the non-denominational character of public schools and do religious manifestations by pupils necessarily affect the fundamental rights and freedoms of others?

Though certainly entering the 'public realm', public school pupils do not represent the state in any way whatsoever as they simply make use, in a private capacity, of a service that is provided by the state (to that it can be added that freedom of religion or belief is in principle protected "in public or private"[67]). As to public school teachers who have voluntarily taken up posts in a neutral environment, one could advance arguments based on the teacher's position as role-model and deduce from this position a need to maintain a sense of neutrality. It would be hard to establish such a duty of impartiality for pupils. The argument that tolerating the wearing by pupils of religious clothing in the class room might negatively affect the right to freedom of religion or belief of others is, *in abstracto*, too vague or theoretical a risk to function as a ground for limitation. Certainly, the freedom to manifest a religion or belief is subject to the protection of the rights and freedoms of others. However, as Judge Tulkens notes in her dissenting opinion in *Leyla Şahin v. Turkey* (in which the European Court sanctioned a ban on headscarves in Turkish university buildings), the application of this ground for limitation can only be deemed necessary in a democratic society if it can be established, *in concreto*, that a person, by means of wearing a religious symbol or piece of clothing, undermined or was liable to undermine the convictions of others (for instance, if it can be established that a headscarf is worn as a means to exert pressure or to proselytise young children, etc.).[68] Similarly, if public order arguments are advanced to legitimize interferences with the right to display religious symbols or wear distinctive clothes, it must, on a case-by-case basis, be established that the latter religious manifestations actually undermine or jeopardize public order.

Finally, it should be pointed out that the UN Special Rapporteur on freedom of religion or belief has developed general criteria in order to evaluate, from a human rights perspective, restrictions and prohibitions on wearing religious symbols (consisting of "aggravating indicators" that identify legislative and

---

[66] Arcot Krishnaswami, *Study of Discrimination in the Matter of Religious Rights and Practices* (U.N. Doc. E/CN.4/Sub.2/200/Rev.1, 1960), p. 33.

[67] Art. 18, para. (1), of the ICCPR.

[68] Dissenting Opinion Judge Tulkens appended to the case of *Leyla Şahin v. Turkey* (*supra* note 51), para. 8.

administrative actions which typically are incompatible with international human rights law and "neutral indicators" that identify policies that in themselves do not contravene these standards).[69] These indicators provide a well-balanced set of legal benchmarks.

10.2.5 *The Problem with Opt-Out Provisions*

It was indicated before that the Human Rights Committee has argued that religious instruction in public schools could be sanctioned if adequate provision is made for non-discriminatory exemptions or alternatives that would accommodate the wishes of parents or legal guardians. However, the Committee has at the same time indicated in its case law that the actual application of exemption schemes proves highly problematic. Many human rights related problems surrounding the issue of opt-out clauses can be discerned.

First of all, opt-out clauses are, naturally, not adequate remedies if the subject of religion is too closely integrated into the curriculum. For instance, in its reply to the issues raised by the Human Rights Committee, Ireland pointed out that an exemption scheme is in place for the withdrawal of pupils from religious instruction.[70] However, since all schools that receive state funding ('national schools') are obliged to teach an 'integrated curriculum' whereby religion is integrated with other subjects so as to ensure that a religious spirit informs the whole work of the school,[71] it is clear that the provision of opt-out clauses in Ireland is purely symbolic. As Mawhinney argues, a "child cannot be opted out of unscheduled and potentially continuous religious teaching which is woven into the very fabric of daily education."[72] It is clear that if the state fails to provide sufficient exemption schemes in this context, serious human rights violations are inevitable: people are forced to sacrifice either their religious freedoms or the right to education.

Furthermore, as no one may be forced to reveal one's religion or belief,[73] opt-out schemes may not require parents or children to outline their precise objections to attending the religion classes that are part of the curriculum. The Human Rights Committee reprimanded Greece for precisely this reason, as Greek public school students can opt-out of compulsory instructional classes in the Christian Orthodox religion only after declaring their religion.[74] Requirements that fall short of disclosure of one's religious affiliation may

---

[69] E/CN.4/2006/5, paras. 36–60 (Ch. III: "Religious Symbols"), particularly para. 55.

[70] CCPR/C/IRL/Q/3/Add.1 (2008), paras. 136–137.

[71] Cf. Alison Mawhinney, *Freedom of Religion in the Irish Primary School System: a Failure to Protect Human Rights*, 27(3) Legal Studies 379 (2009). See the [Irish] Education Act, Law No. 51/1998, of 1998, in particular art. 9, para. (d), which stipulates that schools must "promote the...spiritual...development of students".

[72] Mawhinney, *supra* note 40, p. 3.

[73] Human Rights Committee, General Comment No. 22, para. 3.

[74] A/60/40 vol. I (2005) 60 at para. 90(14).

nonetheless be problematic from a human rights perspective. For instance, a condition to give reasonable grounds for obtaining the exemption carries with it the risk that parents might feel compelled to disclose intimate aspects of their own religious and philosophical convictions.[75]

Exemption schemes must be non-discriminatory. People of all religions and religious denominations must be in a position to avail of the existing opt-out provisions. If a subject that is a compulsory part of the curriculum of a public school is intended to instruct pupils solely or predominantly in the tenets of the dominant religion, children of parents belonging (nominally) to that religion must be in a position to be exempted from this subject. What counts, after all, is not one's religious affiliation, but whether religious instruction is desired or objected to.[76]

A contentious issue arises when parents and child disagree about the desired form of education. For instance, the parents want the child to take religious classes but the child does not or, vice versa, the parents want the child to be exempted from religion classes but the child actually wants to be enrolled. The Committee on the Rights of the Child has expressed its concern that in Poland "students require parental consent to attend ethics courses".[77] As the CRC Committee explicitly reiterated the notion of "the child's evolving capacities" in the same context,[78] it could be deduced that from a certain age on the child's autonomous right to freedom of religion or belief prevails in case of a conflict with the parents' wishes. The same could be argued with respect to disagreements over the larger educational enrolment choice between denominational and non-denominational education. The CRC Committee has not determined the precise age from when the child is empowered to make such decisions. From the fact that the CRC Committee requires, under the state reporting procedure,[79] information on the legal age for choosing a religion or attending religious school teaching in conjunction with the Committee's emphasis on the evolving capacities of the child, one could deduce that autonomous children's rights must be granted to children some years before maturity.[80] In view

[75] Both the Human Rights Committee as well as the European Court of Human Rights have considered the Norwegian exemption scheme for this reason contrary to religious rights. See Human Rights Committee, *Leirvåg v. Norway, supra* note 16, para. 14.7; and European Court of Human Rights, *Folgerø and Others v. Norway*, Application No. 15472/02, Judgement of 29 June 2007, particularly para. 98.

[76] This argument is based on a case before the European Court of Human Rights: *Hasan and Eylem Zengin v. Turkey*, Application No. 1448/04, Judgement of 9 October 2007. Turkish educational law provided for the possibility of exemption only to two categories of pupils of Turkish nationality, namely those whose parents belong to Christianity or the Jewish faith; children of Muslim parents, consequently, could not opt-out these classes.

[77] CRC/C/15/Add.194 (2002), para. 32.

[78] *Ibid.*, para. 33.

[79] Committee on the Rights of the Child, *General Guidelines for Periodic Reports* (CRC/C/58, 1996), para. 24.

[80] Cf. Brems, *supra* note 3, p. 30; she notes that some states have adopted legal provisions in that respect. *E.g.*, Germany has stipulated that children can make these choices autonomously

of this, setting the age of acquiring fully autonomous rights at the age of 20 years (e.g. Nauru)[81] surely amounts to an interference with religious rights. If we take the Children's Rights Convention's notion of the "evolving capacities of the child" seriously, we must conclude that parental rights and powers diminish as the child gets older. Indeed, as Brems argues, it is the state's duty:

> ...to guard the limits of parental direction in matters of religion and conscience, and if necessary to *offer protection to children against infringement of their freedom of thought, conscience and religion by their parents.*[82]

In conclusion, considering the range of serious human rights related problems that emerge within the context of applying opt-out provisions one may very well wonder whether opt-out provisions in practice can actually ever *fully* protect the religious rights of parents and children and the educational rights of children. It is submitted that exemption schemes must meet the following minimum conditions: (i) religious instruction must be limited to a specific subject (and not inextricably interwoven with the educational system); (ii) exemptions must be open to everyone; and (iii) people, both parents and children, must be informed about the availability of these schemes. Carolyn Evans argues, moreover, that exemption schemes "work best when they can be for a whole subject and when a meaningful alternative class is available to substitute for the one that is being missed."[83] Even if all these conditions are met, the fact remains that opt-out clauses in the reality of every day school life may have a negative (stigmatizing) impact on those children that are exempted from certain classes.[84] If the latter concern holds true and cannot be remedied, we may have to reconsider the tenability of religious instruction in public schools. The issue of potential marginalization, in other words, provides a firm case against doctrinal religious instruction in public

---

from age 14: Religious Education Act, RGBl S. 939, of 15 July 1921; while the Swiss Civil Code sets this age at 16 years.

[81] Art. 11, para. (3), of the CONST. OF NAURU (1968). Antigua and Barbuda, Belize, Dominica, Fiji, Grenada, Saint Kitts and Nevis, Saint Lucia, Saint Vincent and the Grenadines and Singapore set the age rather high as well (thus not taking seriously the evolving capacities of the child), namely at 18 years. See art. 11 of the CONST. OF ANTIGUA AND BARBUDA (1981); art. 11 of the CONST. OF BELIZE (1981); art. 9 of the CONST. OF DOMINICA (1978); art. 35 of the CONST. OF THE FIJI ISLANDS (1998); art. 9 of the CONST. OF GRENADA (1973); art. 11 of the CONST. OF SAINT KITTS AND NEVIS (1983); art. 9 of the CONST. OF SAINT LUCIA (1978); art. 9 of the CONST. OF SAINT VINCENT AND THE GRENADINES (1979); art. 16 of the CONST. OF SINGAPORE (1963).

[82] Brems, *supra* note 3, p. 29.

[83] C. Evans, *supra* note 38, p. 469.

[84] Cf. Alison Mawhinney, *The Opt-Out Clause: Imperfect Protection for the Right to Freedom of Religion in Schools*, 2(2) EDUCATIONAL LAW JOURNAL 102 (2006); pp. 109–113. Russo, *supra* note 44, p. 945, argues something similar in relation to Bosnia and Herzegovina: "In theory, religious education classes in public schools in BiH are optional. The reality is that in some cantons and municipalities, children who do not choose to attend these classes are subject to pressure and discrimination from peers and teachers."

schools per se, something that does not prejudice the possibility of neutral education *about* religions (see the conclusion to this Chapter).

10.2.6 *No State Duty to Provide Religious Education*

The right to freedom of religion or belief and the right to education taken in conjunction do not constitute a state duty to provide religious education.[85] Quite the contrary, as we have seen before, the state is forbidden to pursue policies that do not respect parents' religious and philosophical convictions or the child's right to freedom of religion or belief. Any type of compulsory religious education in public schools would inevitably interfere with some children's right to freedom of religion or belief and with parental rights in this context.[86] In view of these considerations and the conclusions reached in the previous sub-section, it is submitted that under human rights law the state may stipulate that all state-administered educational activity will be strictly "non-denominational" (e.g. Portugal),[87] "non-religious" (e.g. Mali),[88] "neutral" (e.g. Gabon),[89] "secular" (e.g. Azerbaijan, Belarus, Burkina Faso, France, Mexico, Moldova, Nicaragua, New Zealand),[90] or of an otherwise non-religious nature (e.g. Cape Verde, India, Japan, Mozambique and the USA).[91] It must be observed that a non-denominational public school criterion does not, strictly speaking, rule out a neutral subject *about* religion. Some Constitutions or laws speak of a 'separation between religion and education' (e.g. Tajikistan,

---

[85] Cf. Brems, *supra* note 3, p. 26. Also the *travaux préparatoires* pertaining to art. 14 CRC reveal that states did not wish to commit to such a duty.

[86] Cf. Brems, *ibid*, p. 26–27.

[87] Art. 43, paras. (2) and (3), of the Const. of Portugal (1976); see also art. 4 of the Law on Religious Freedom, No. 16/2001, of 21 June 2001. In practice, however, and as per the 2004 Concordat with the Holy See, public schools may teach a course on Catholicism. See particularly the clauses (art. 19) of the Concordat between Portugal and the Holy See of 18 May 2004 on the role of Catholicism in the public school curriculum and the dominance if not monopoly of the Catholic ecclesiastical authorities in the field of teaching of religious subjects.

[88] Art. 18 of the Const. of Mali (1992).

[89] Art. 1, para. (19), of the Const. of Gabon (1991).

[90] Art. 18, para. (3), of the Const. of Azerbaijan (1995); art. 9 of the Law of the Republic of Belarus on Religious Freedom and Religious Organizations, Law No. 137-3, of 31 October 2002; art. 27 of the Const. of Burkina Faso (1991); [French] Law Concerning the Separation of the Churches and the State of 1905 (see also the preamble to the former (1946) Constitution, which contained the principle of secular education as its 11th principle: "secular education ... is a duty of the State"); art. 3 of the Const. of Mexico (1917); art. 35, para. (8), of the Const. of Moldova (1994); art. 124 of the Const. of Nicaragua (1986); New Zealand Education Act of 1964.

[91] Art. 49, paras. (4) and (5) Const. of Cape Verde (1992): "The State shall not program education and culture in conformity with any philosophical, aesthetical, political, ideological or religious directives...Public education shall not be religious"; art. 28, para. (1), of the Const. of India (1950): "No religious instruction shall be provided in any educational institution wholly maintained out of State funds"; art. 20 of the Const. of Japan (1946): "The State and its organs shall refrain from religious education"; art. 113 of the Const. of Mozambique (1990): "Public education shall not pertain to any religion"; USA: as per Supreme Court jurisprudence on the First Amendment.

Turkmenistan, Ukraine and Uzbekistan).[92] This, presumably, does rule out any subject on religion, including neutral ones.[93]

The state, however, may not prohibit educational activity outside these state schools and must allow religion-oriented education as an alternative so as to guarantee that parents are in a position to ensure the religious and moral education of their children in conformity with their own convictions. In other words, an absolute ban on religious education (i.e. in both public as well as private educational institutions) would constitute a human rights violation (e.g. Ethiopia).[94] It is precisely because there is under human rights law in principle no room for religious instruction in public schools and consequently no state duty to provide religious instruction, that the right to give and receive denominational education elsewhere (outside the realm of the state educational system) must be ensured. Many states constitutionally guarantee that right.[95] Education given in such (private) institutions must, however, conform to minimum standards laid down by the State.[96]

---

[92] Art. 6 of the Law of the Republic of Tajikistan on Religion and Religious Organizations of 1994 (amended 1997 and 1999); art. 11 of the Const. of Turkmenistan (1992); art. 35 of the Const. of Ukraine (1996); art. of the [Uzbek] Law on Freedom of Conscience and Religious Organizations of 1 May 1998.

[93] In the conclusion of this Chapter a state duty to include a neutral subject on religions into the curriculum is developed. These forms of state practice would clearly run counter to such a duty.

[94] Art. 90, para. (2), of the Const. of Ethiopia (1995): "Education shall be provided in a manner that is free from any religious influence"; which provision in practice is interpreted to mean that religion courses may not be taught in public or in private educational institutions.

[95] *E.g.* art 11, para. (2), of the Const. of Botswana (1966); art. 27 of the Const. of Burkina Faso (1991); art. 23 of the Fundamental Law of Equatorial Guinea (1991); art. 78, para. (2), of the Const. of Kenya (1969); art. 13, para. (2), of the Const. of Lesotho (1993); art. 22 of Const. of Senegal (2001); art. 30 of the Const. of Togo (1992); art. 19, para. (3), of the Const. of Zimbabwe (1979); art. 35, para. (3), and art. 39, para. (2), of the Const. of the Fiji Islands (1998); art. 22, para. (3), of the Const. of the Bahamas (1973); art. 11, para. (3), of the Const. of Belize (1981); art. 93 of the [Canadian] Constitution Act (1867) and art. 29 of the [Canadian] Constitution Act (1982) (Schedule to the Canada Act); art. 9, para. (3), of the Const. of Dominica (1978); art. 21, para. (4), of the Const. of Jamaica (1962); art. 9, para. (3), of the Const. of Saint Lucia (1978); art. 9, para. (3), of the Const. of Saint Vincent and the Grenadines (1979); art. 19, para. (3), of the Const. of Barbados (1996); art. 14 of the Const. of Mauritius (1968); art. 21, para. (7), of the Const. of Seychelles (1993); art. 24, para. (3), of the Const. of Sierra Leone (1991); sec. XXVIII(iii) of the Const. of Uganda (1995); art. 19, para. (3), of the Const. of Zambia (1991); art. 45, para. (4), of the Const. of East Timor (2002); art. 11, paras. (2) and (3), of the Const. of Kiribati (1979); art. 2, para. (3), of the Const. of the Marshall Islands (1979); art. 12, para. (2), of the Const. of Samoa (1960); art. 16, para. (2), of the Const. of Singapore (1963); art. 11, para. (2), of the Const. of Solomon Islands (1978); art. 22, para. (3), of the Const. of Tuvalu (1986); art. 28 of the Const. of Šrpska (1992); art. 41 of the Const. of Croatia (1990); art. 23 of the Const. of the Netherlands (1983); art. 53, para. (3), of the Const. of Poland (1997); art. 43 of the Const. of Serbia (2006); art. 15, para. (3), of the Const. of Switzerland (1999); art. 68 of the Const. of Colombia (1991); art. 9, para. (3), of the Const. of Grenada (1973); art. 11, para. (3), of the Const. of Saint Kitts and Nevis (1983); and art. 1, para. (19), of the Const. of Gabon (1991).

[96] See art. 13, paras. (3) and (4), of the ICESCR.

The state is under no obligation to fund these special (private) denominational schools: if sufficient public education is made available and if the state allows parents to send their children to alternative schools, the state has discharged its duties flowing from the international standards on the right to education.[97] The argument that funding public education, but not religious education, amounts to discrimination between secularists and religious people can be dismissed: public education, ideal-typically, is offered to everyone and is not designed for the purposes of educating children of secular parents solely or designed so as to instil secular principles into youths. This is not to say that the topics covered—e.g. biology, history or sexual education classes—or the teaching methods employed—e.g. mixed gymnastics classes—could not be objectionable to religious parents. The latter does not render the exclusive funding of public education discriminatory. True, religion as a subject might not be covered in public schools or religion might be taught in a neutral fashion ('teaching about religions'); however, public education cannot be said on that account to be designed to actively promote secularism as an ideology.

Having said that, under human rights law the state is in principle free to fund denominational schools.[98] If it does so, it must make this funding available without discrimination. In *Waldman v. Canada* the Human Rights Committee considered that Canada's differential treatment of Roman Catholic religious schools (which are publicly funded as a distinct part of the public education system; something that is constitutionally protected) and other types of religious schools (which are private by legal necessity; in the present case it concerned a private Jewish school) was at odds with the non-discrimination principle.[99]

[97] Human Rights Committee, *Arieh Hollis Waldman v. Canada*, Communication No. 694/1996, U.N. Doc. CCPR/C/67/D/694/1996, Views of 5 November 1999, para. 10.6: "the Committee observes that the Covenant does not oblige States parties to fund schools which are established on a religious basis".

[98] Some states constitutionally guarantee a right for private, denominational schools to receive funding. *E.g.* art. 14 of the Const. of Benin (1990) "private schools may benefit from state subsidies under conditions determined by law"; art. 20, para. (3), of the Const. of Zimbabwe (1979); art. 35, para. (3), and art. 39, para. (2), of the Const. of the Fiji Islands (1998); art. 22, para. (3), of the Const. of the Bahamas (1973); art. 9, para. (3), of the Const. of Dominica (1978); art. 73 of the Const. of Guatemala (1985); art. 21, para. (4), of the Const. of Jamaica (1962); art. 9, para. (3), of the Const. of Saint Lucia (1978); art. 9, para. (3), of the Const. of Saint Vincent and the Grenadines (1979); art. 19, para. (3), of the Const. of Barbados (1996); art. 24 of the Const. of Belgium (1994); art. 23, para. (7), of the Const. of the Netherlands (1983); art. 24, para. (3), of the Const. of Swaziland (2005); art. 35, para. (3), of the Const. of the Fiji Islands (1998); art. 2, para. (3), of the Const. of the Marshall Islands (1979); art. 213 of the Const. of Brazil (1988).

[99] *Arieh Hollis Waldman v. Canada*, *supra* note 97, para. 10.6. Interestingly, a similar case was declared inadmissible by the Human Rights Committee a day earlier as the applicants did not seek publicly funded religious schools for their children, but on the contrary, sought the removal of the public funding to Roman Catholic schools. The Committee reasoned that if this were to happen, the applicants' personal situation in respect of funding for religious education would not be improved. As the applicants, in the eyes of the Human Rights

10.2.7 *Neutral and Objective Public School Education About Religions*

Religious instruction in the public educational system is not compatible with human rights law unless sufficient provision is made for non-discriminatory exemptions or alternatives that would accommodate the wishes of parents. In line with these benchmarks, the Human Rights Committee has considered that compulsory public school instruction in subjects such as the general history of religions and ethics, if given in a neutral and objective way, is permissible and does not, as such, affect the liberty of parents to ensure the religious and moral education of their children in conformity with their own convictions (the state may offer exemption rights also in the context of neutral education about religions, though such is, strictly speaking, not necessary). This was first established in *Hartikainen v. Finland* (1981).[100]

The question that emerges is: what does neutral and objective public school education about religions entail? It is at least clear what would not qualify as neutral and objective education about religions:[101] (i) any form of religious instruction in which religious claims are made and presented as truths and/or which aims at making the pupils (better) members of the religion involved; or (ii) any form of anti-religious education, i.e. education that renders all religious belief superstition, or active propagation of atheism.[102] It would appear that the most important criterion in this context is that the manner in which the subject is taught reflects a profound commitment to the freedom of religion or belief of all pupils. It is clear in that respect that much care should be taken that religious claims are indeed presented as religious claims and not as absolute truths. Consistently instructing pupils in a specific religion would

Committee, had consequently not sufficiently substantiated how the public funding given to the Roman Catholic schools at present causes them any disadvantage or affects them adversely, the Committee deemed they could not claim to be victims of a human rights violation; see Human Rights Committee, *Grant Tadman et al v. Canada*, Communication No. 816/1998, U.N. Doc. CCPR/C/67/D/816/1998, Views of 4 November 1999. Thus, it would appear that the nature of the complaint was decisive in generating so different an outcome compared to the (otherwise very similar) *Waldman v. Canada* case.

[100] Human Rights Committee, *Erkki Hartikainen v. Finland*, Communication No. 40/1978, U.N. Doc. CCPR/C/OP/1 at 74 (1984), Views of 9 April 1981; the gist of this decision was later incorporated into: Human Rights Committee, General Comment No. 22. This case dealt specifically with an *alternative subject* on the history of religions and ethics that was offered and made compulsory to those children whose parents or legal guardians objected to religious instruction (i.e. those children that availed of the available exemption scheme). It may be added at this point that the Human Rights Committee in the meantime has explained that also a *regular subject* on the history of religions and ethics (provided that it is taught in a neutral and objective way) is permitted as part of the curriculum of public schools. See Human Rights Committee, General Comment No. 22, para. 6.

[101] Cf. C. Evans, *supra* note 38, p. 463. Evans' model (*ibid.*, p 461) consists of 6 approaches to dealing with religion in the educational framework; she categorises these objectionable forms as "religious or ideological instruction".

[102] *E.g.* art. 39 of the Const. of Cuba (1976) requires that state education is based on the "ideology of Marx".

clearly be at odds with the requirements of neutrality and objectivity; however, giving more attention to certain religions (for instance, the three largest present in a country) than to others is not necessarily a sign that the norms of neutrality or objectivity are transgressed as long as the focus on any specific religion is not disproportionate. Care should also be taken to include sufficient emphasis on non-religious beliefs (humanism, agnosticism, atheism, etc.). Inaccurate and prejudicial materials need to be avoided at all costs and negative stereotypes about certain religions which are based on such inaccurate information should certainly not be reinforced.[103] As one authoritative study sums it up:

> Preparation of curricula, textbooks and educational materials for teaching about religions and beliefs should take into account religious and non-religious views in a way that is inclusive, fair, and respectful...Curricula should be developed in accordance with recognized professional standards in order to ensure a balanced approach to study about religions and beliefs. Development and implementation of curricula should also include open and fair procedures that give all interested parties appropriate opportunities to offer comments and advice... Curricula focusing on teaching about religions and beliefs should give attention to key historical and contemporary developments pertaining to religion and belief, and reflect global and local issues. They should be sensitive to different local manifestations of religious and secular plurality found in schools and the communities they serve. Such sensitivities will help address the concerns of students, parents and other stakeholders in education.[104]

It is submitted that compliance with those benchmarks would indeed be a first decisive step towards ensuring the neutral and objective nature of a religion subject taught at public schools.

10.3 Teachers, Education & Human Rights Law

We have seen how parental guidance rights and children's autonomous right to freedom of religion or belief have a major impact on how the educational system of a state must be framed. It is not surprising therefore that human rights law will also have a bearing on the providers of education. Focusing on fundamental rights of teachers but also on their professional duties, this section will scrutinize the concrete ramifications of human rights law on the position of teachers.

10.3.1 *Employing Teachers*

As to the issue of hiring policies regarding teachers, it is necessary to distinguish between public schools and denominational (private) schools.

[103] Seventh key guiding principle of the OSCE Office for Democratic Institutions and Human Rights (ODIHR), *Toledo Guiding Principles on Teaching About Religions and Beliefs in Public Schools* (Warsaw: OSCE/ODIRH, 2007) [hereinafter also: "Toledo Guidelines"], p. 17.

[104] *Ibid.*, 7th–10th key guiding principles, p. 17.

296 *Religion & Education*

(i) *Public Schools: No Religious Discrimination*

It will be clear that religious affiliation (or the lack of it) may not be posed as an occupational requirement for public school teachers or staff.[105] No one may be disqualified by reason of his or her religious opinions or his or her observing of or omitting to observe religious duties or practices from being a teacher or any other type of employee at a public school.[106] It is submitted, furthermore, that religious affiliation cannot be posed as an occupational requirement for teaching a neutral subject *about* religions (rather than 'religious instruction') at public schools. It would appear, after all, that for this type of position it is essential to possess "knowledge, attitude and skills to teach religions and beliefs in a fair and balanced way".[107] As the most important skills and qualities that need to be considered in this regard relate to professional expertise and specifically to a commitment to the right to freedom of religion or belief of pupils, an individual's personal set of beliefs of lack thereof cannot be sufficient reason to hire or exclude that person from the teaching position.[108]

As has been outlined already, religious instruction within public schools is compatible with human rights law if sufficient provision is made for non-discriminatory exemptions or alternatives that would accommodate the wishes of parents. A very limited religious occupational requirement provision could thus be acceptable solely covering these positions.[109] This does not mean, however, that the state has no obligations in this regard or that all arrangements as to hiring appropriate persons to teach the religion subjects suffice. The Human Rights Committee has, for instance, condemned Costa Rican legislation[110] which confers on the National Episcopal Conference the power to select the providers of such religious instruction, something that effectively means that non-Catholics are barred from teaching religion in the

---

105 See *infra* for one exception in this regard.

106 Some states have specific legal provisions in place to guarantee this; *e.g.* art. 59, para. (2), of the UK School Standards and Framework Act 1998 (c. 31).

107 *Toledo Guidelines, supra* note 103, p. 16 (6th key guiding principle).

108 *Ibid.*, p. 59 (Section D: "Who Should Teach about Religions and Beliefs?").

109 Notwithstanding the arguments of a more fundamental nature that were made regarding religious subjects taught at public schools and the related concern that opt-out mechanisms often appear not to be sufficient to remedy all human rights issues that emerge in this context (see section 10.2.5, *supra*). If we were to conclude, on the basis of those concerns, that religious instruction at public schools is no longer tenable, the present discussion on the possibility of allowing for a genuine occupational requirement scheme regarding the position of religion teachers, naturally, loses its significance.

110 *Ley de Carrera Docente* [Teacher's Career Law], Law No. 4565, of 4 May 1970. The Portuguese system, based on the 2004 Concordat with the Holy See, could be criticized for the same reasons. See particularly the clauses (art. 19) of the Concordat between Portugal and the Holy See of 18 May 2004 on the role of Catholicism in the public school curriculum and the dominance if not monopoly of the Catholic ecclesiastical authorities in the field of teaching of religious subjects.

public school curricula.[111] In other words, even if in a specific public school class there would be a higher demand to receive instruction in Protestantism, this class is unlikely to get a Protestant teacher to teach the religion subject as religious education teachers in public schools must be certified by the Catholic Bishops' Conference.

(ii) *Denominational Schools: Genuine Occupational Requirement Exemptions*

It stands to reason that denominational schools may pose religion as an occupational requirement in their policy regarding the hiring of teachers insofar as religious instruction forms an essential aspect of the position and religious affiliation, therefore, constitutes a genuine and determining occupational requirement.[112] In order to facilitate this, general religious occupational requirements exemption schemes may be declared applicable to functions within denominational schools. Some states have concrete legal exemptions in place regarding teaching positions (e.g. Greece, Malta, Netherlands, New Zealand and the UK).[113] It is clear that the state in this context is to strike a balance between the non-discrimination principle (equal rights of candidate employees), on the one hand, and the need to facilitate and foster the liberty of individuals and private legal entities to establish and direct educational institutions outside the state educational system on the other. As long as an appropriate public school system is in place (creating teaching positions for people of all religious or non-religious affiliations), these exemption schemes do not need to be too problematic from a human rights perspective.

It is submitted that exemptions from the non-discrimination principle may not extend to positions for which religious affiliation is not a genuine and determining requirement (cleaning personal, canteen personnel, receptionists, etc). Requiring religious affiliation as a condition for obtaining non-teaching positions would amount to discrimination on the ground of religion or belief as there are no reasonable and objective criteria discernible that

[111] A/49/40 vol. I (1994), paras. 158 and 162 (interestingly, the Human Rights Committee seems to deviate here from *Delgado Páez v. Colombia*, see subsequent footnote, para. 5.7, in which it had sanctioned Colombia's state practice to allow the Church authorities to select religion teachers).

[112] See Human Rights Committee, *William Eduardo Delgado Páez v. Colombia*, Communication No. 195/1985, U.N. Doc. CCPR/C/39/D/195/1985, Views of 12 July 1990, para. 5.7.

[113] Artt. 58 and 60 of the UK School Standards and Framework Act 1998 (c. 31); art. 16 of Greek Law 1771/1988; art. 5, para. (2)(c), of the [Dutch] General Law on Equal Treatment of 2 March 1994; art. 28 of the Human Rights Act of New Zealand, Act No. 82/1993 (amended through 3 December 2007) (in conjunction with sec. 65 of the Private Schools Conditional Integration Act 1975); art. 45 of the Const. of Malta (1964). See Chapter 9, section 9.5.1, *supra*, for a discussion on religious occupational requirements in general and on concrete state practice in this regard.

would merit making distinctions in this context. Moreover, in the event that religion is not integrated into the overall curriculum and religious subjects and non-religious subjects are taught separately, it will be difficult, under human rights law, to justify a religious occupational requirement for teachers of other subjects than the religion subject—even in the context of a denominational school. It is reiterated that the interest of upholding a 'religious ethos' does not justify forms of discrimination on any ground under human rights law ('religious ethos exemption' schemes have been criticized in Chapter 9).[114]

10.3.2 *Position and Role of Teachers*

As to the issue of the position and role of teachers, it is again necessary to distinguish between public schools and denominational (private) schools.

(i) *Public School Teachers & Religion*

Though under human rights law religious instruction in public schools can be sanctioned if appropriate opt-out provisions are in place, it is clear at the same time that public school teachers themselves cannot be required to give religious instruction.[115] Teachers at a public school may not receive any less remuneration or be deprived of, or disqualified from, any promotion or other advantage by reason of the fact that he or she does or does not give religious education or by reason of his or her religious opinions or of his or her observing of or omitting to observe religious duties or practices.[116] That being said, it is submitted that in the interest of the child's right to freedom of religion or belief appropriate steps may be taken against public school teachers who are hired to *neutrally* teach about religion but are found to contravene the norms of neutrality and objectivity (be it because too confessional an approach is taken or because the person reveals anti-religious sentiments). As instruction in a particular religion or belief within public schools is in principle inconsistent with the ICCPR, such neutrality requirements can easily be extended to all teaching positions: public school teachers may not abuse their position so as to instil religious or atheist views in pupils. This is not to say, however, that religion may never be made the subject of discussion in classes other than the religion subject (e.g. in history classes, etc.). It is submitted that the right to freedom of religion of belief and parental guidance rights do not embody any

---

[114] See Chapter 9, section 9.5.1, *supra*.

[115] Some states have laws in place to guarantee this; *e.g.* art. 59, para. (3), of the UK School Standards and Framework Act 1998 (c. 31): "No teacher at the school shall be required to give religious education"; art. 7 of the Basic Law for the Federal Republic of Germany (1949): "No teacher may be obliged against his will to give religious instruction".

[116] Some states have laws in place to guarantee this; *e.g.* art. 59, para. (4), of the UK School Standards and Framework Act 1998 (c. 31).

right to be kept ignorant about religion or secular philosophies in the course of one's public school education.[117]

(ii) *Public Schools & Religious Dress*

A very topical and contentious debate revolves around the question of to what extent public school teachers may convey religious messages or propagate their religious affiliation in non-verbal ways in front of pupils, i.e. by means of displaying religious symbols or wearing religious clothing. The interests that are to be balanced in this context are the right to freedom of religion or belief of the teacher and the right to freedom of religion or belief of pupils, including the right to be free from religious coercion. In that regard it may be reiterated that the freedom to manifest a religion or belief covers both private as well as public acts of religious observance and that the freedom to manifest a religion is not absolute. Unlike the regional European Court of Human Rights (see below), the international (UN) human rights bodies have not yet resolved this issue in a resolute manner. In general, following the UN Special Rapporteur's recommendations on the matter, it can be said that:

> ...contentious situations should be evaluated on a case-by-case basis, e.g. by weighing the right of a teacher to manifest his or her religion against the need to protect pupils by preserving religious harmony according to the circumstances of a given case.[118]

The Committee on the Rights of the Child has declared itself (somewhat) against religious dress prohibitions aimed at public school teachers. Scrutinizing Germany's state practice, the CRC Committee expressed its concern at draft-laws:

> ...aiming at banning schoolteachers from wearing headscarves in public schools, as *this does not contribute to the child's understanding of the right to freedom of religion and to the development of an attitude of tolerance*...The Committee recommends that the State party take educational and other measures aimed at children, parents and others to develop a culture of understanding and tolerance, particularly in the area of freedom of religion, conscience and thought by, inter alia, avoiding measures which single out a particular religious group.[119]

The CRC Committee makes a fair point here, particularly considering the fact that the Children's Rights Convention explicitly states that the state parties agree that the education of the child be directed to the development of respect for human rights and fundamental freedoms.[120] Fostering such respect for

[117] This argument is based on considerations expressed by the European Court of Human Rights in the *Folgerø and Others v. Norway* case, *supra* note 75, para. 89.

[118] E/CN.4/2006/5, para. 51.

[119] CRC/C/137 (2004) 51 at paras. 281 and 282 (emphasis added).

[120] Art. 29, para. (1)(b), of CRC.

fundamental rights including respect for everyone's right to freedom of religion or belief requires a level of religious tolerance; something to which a child's education should also contribute.[121] Banning public expressions of religions may not be most conducive to that cause.

On the other hand, a meaningful distinction can be made between pupils and teachers in this context. The former do not represent the state in any why whatsoever while public school teachers carry out a public service and thus can be considered to represent the state.[122] Particularly in the public domain the state needs to guard against infringements of the freedom from religion principle, to prevent all forms of religious coercion and above all to avoid all forms of religious indoctrination. The latter point seems to have been a relevant factor in the eyes of the European Court of Human Rights in *Dahlab v. Switzerland*. The case revolved around a Swiss primary school teacher who was (pursuant to the Swiss Public Education Act which contains norms on the non-denominational nature of the Swiss educational system) instructed by the educational authorities to stop wearing a headscarf whilst discharging of her professional duties. The European Court reasoned that:

> ...it is very difficult to assess the impact that a powerful external symbol such as the wearing of a headscarf may have on the freedom of conscience and religion of very young children. The applicant's pupils were aged between four and eight, an age at which children wonder about many things and are also more easily influenced than older pupils. In those circumstances, it cannot be denied outright that the *wearing of a headscarf might have some kind of proselytising effect*, seeing that it appears to be imposed on women by a precept which is laid down in the Koran and which, as the Federal Court noted, is hard to square with the principle of gender equality. It therefore appears difficult to reconcile the wearing of an Islamic headscarf with the message of tolerance, respect for others and, above all, equality and non-discrimination that all teachers in a democratic society must convey to their pupils. Accordingly, weighing the right of a teacher to manifest her religion against the need to protect pupils by preserving religious harmony, the Court considers that, in the circumstances of the case and having regard, above all, to the tender age of the children for whom the applicant was responsible *as a representative of the State*, the Geneva authorities did not exceed their margin of appreciation and that the measure they took was therefore not unreasonable.[123]

It appears that for the European Court two factors are decisive: the impressionable nature of children as well as the fact that primary school teachers are state representatives and in that capacity need to abide by the state's

[121] Art. 29, paras. (1)(d), of CRC.

[122] The latter holds true, *de facto*, regardless of the question of how the position of teachers is precisely dealt with at the municipal level, i.e. whether they are considered civil servants or not.

[123] ECtHR, *Dahlab v. Switzerland*, Application No. 42393/98, ECtHR Judgement of 15 February 2001 (emphasis added).

self-addressed rules on neutrality. *In abstracto* this would appear to be a sound reasoning. Protection of the rights of others is a recognized ground for limiting the freedom to manifest a religion. However, the European Court's reasoning contained little in the way of substantiation of how, in this case, the rights of others (the pupils) were undermined. It actually follows from the facts of the case that during the period of this teacher's employment the school had not received a single complaint from parents. In that respect it is hard to see how the argument that the wearing of a headscarf "might have some kind of proselytising effect" could in itself amount to a pressing social need to interfere with someone's freedom of religion or belief.[124] In this particular case the interference could only be based on the argument that primary school teachers are state representatives and that state neutrality needs to be upheld. If the preservation of notions of state neutrality (or secularism) is indeed among the decisive factors for the European Court of Human Rights (being an 'public order' issue and, more indirectly, a matter of protecting 'the rights and freedoms of others'), then it must be noted that the European Court failed to make an appropriate distinction between teachers and pupils in cases that concern the wearing of religious clothing or the display of religious symbols in public schools.[125]

In conclusion, states are well-advised to follow the recommendation of the UN Special Rapporteur on freedom of religion or belief to evaluate contentious situations on a case-by-case basis by weighing the right of a teacher to manifest his or her religion against the need to protect the fundamental rights and freedoms of pupils.[126] The key question in this debate seems to be: what contributes most to the child's right to freedom of religion or belief and to the development of an attitude of tolerance. States certainly have an interest in upholding the neutrality of the state and thus must be in a position to take appropriate action if in a concrete case it is established that a teacher's manifestation of a religion or belief in the classroom actually harms or jeopardizes the fundamental rights of pupils. The possibility of such state interferences need to be provided by laws on religious symbolism in the public realm that are sufficiently neutral and not needlessly rigid. The message which pupils are likely to get from blanket bans (i.e. regulations in which there is no room for taking account of the particulars of the case) or from specific bans on Islamic headscarves, is one of intolerance against religions or one of intolerance against Muslims specifically.[127]

---

[124] See also Dissenting Opinion Judge Tulkens (in *Leyla Şahin v. Turkey, supra* note 51), para. 5.

[125] Compare *Dahlab v. Switzerland (supra* note 123) and *Leyla Şahin v. Turkey (supra* note 51).

[126] E/CN.4/2006/5, para. 51.

[127] Cf. Paul M. Taylor, Freedom of Religion: UN and European Human Rights Law and Practice (Cambridge: Cambridge University Press, 2005), p. 172 (on the Dahlab case specifically).

(iii) *Denominational School Teachers*

Needless to say that the position and role of teachers in denominational schools is fundamentally different: they are generally expected if not required to instruct pupils in the tenets of the religious denomination in question. The only question that remains to be answered is to what extent teachers in religious schools are free in how they give effect to the denominational character of the school. May a school take steps against a teacher who deviates from religious orthodoxy or from the school's specific religious standpoints or religious mission statement? This issue was put before the Human Rights Committee in *Delgado Páez v. Colombia*. William Eduardo Delgado Páez was appointed and functioned as a teacher of religion and ethics at a secondary school in Leticia, Colombia. However, being an advocate of 'liberation theology', his views on how these religion classes should be run differed from the views of the local ecclesiastical and educational authorities. At some point he was informed that he could no longer teach religion classes and ultimately the incident and subsequent discontent resulted in Mr. Delgado's resignation.[128] The Human Rights Committee concluded that the requirements posed by the ecclesiastical and educational authorities to teach the Catholic religion in its traditional form did not violate Mr. Delgado's right to freedom of expression or freedom of religion or belief.[129] From this case the rule may be deduced that anyone who voluntarily becomes an employee of a denominational school may, to a reasonable extent, be required to abide by this organization's ethos.[130]

10.4 Conclusion: An Emerging State Duty to Provide Neutral Education about Religions?

This Chapter focused on children's, parental and teachers' rights (and duties), in the light of the state's overall obligation to provide for appropriate education. It has been emphasized that any form of compulsory religious education is contrary to international human rights law. A religious subject may be

[128] *Delgado Páez v. Colombia, supra* note 112; see paras. 2.1–2.10 for the particulars of the case.

[129] *Ibid.* paras. 5.7–5.9. The Committee did ultimately establish a violation of art. 25, para. (c), of the ICCPR as it considered that the constant harassment and the threats against his person (in respect of which the state party had failed to provide protection) made the author's continuation in public service teaching impossible (para. 5.9) (something that clearly was specific to this case).

[130] Some states have laws in place to guarantee this. *E.g.* art. 60, para. (5)(b), of the UK School Standards and Framework Act 1998 (c. 31), which deals with schools with a religious character and provides that "regard may be had, in connection with the termination of the employment of any teacher at the school, to any conduct on his part which is incompatible with the precepts, or with the upholding of the tenets, of the religion or religious denomination so specified".

taught in public schools if adequate opt-out clauses are provided for. Case law and state practice, however, show that the application of exemptions in this field often proves highly problematic. The inoperable nature of the opt-out clauses in the reality of every day school life and the potentially stigmatizing impact on the child are obstacles that cannot be easily dismissed or remedied.

The state is under no duty to provide religious instruction. In this Chapter we have seen that human rights law provides convincing arguments to keep religious instruction out of the public school curriculum. Teaching *about* religions in a neutral and objective way in public schools, on the other hand, is perfectly compatible with international human rights law. Compulsory public school instruction in subjects such as the general history of religions and ethics, if given in a neutral and objective way, is permissible and does as such not affect the liberty of parents to ensure the religious and moral education of their children in conformity with their own convictions. The question that emerges is whether, from a human rights perspective, a case could be made for a state *duty* to include neutral education about religions into the public school curriculum? Voices to that effect can increasingly be heard.

Carolyn Evans argues that "'plural religious education' is the approach to religion in public schools that best complies with international human rights standards."[131] She describes this type of education as follows:

> ...students learn about the basic practices, beliefs, rituals etc of a variety of religions. They are presented with information about these religious traditions but are not taught that any of them are (un)true. The instruction may also extent to philosophies and beliefs of a non-religious nature.[132]

Evans' account is focused on the question of how children can be given the tools to understand the role of religion in society and in the world in a way that they are protected from religious indoctrination. She concludes that neutral education about religions compares favourably to all types of religious instruction but also to forms of strict educational secularism in which there is no place for religion at all in the class room.[133] The *Toledo Guiding Principles on Teaching About Religions and Beliefs in Public Schools*, a study recently issued by the OSCE Office for Democratic Institutions and Human Rights (ODIHR), can be seen as a strong plea for the inclusion of neutral subjects about religions and beliefs into the curriculum of public schools in a way that respects children's rights.[134] In what follows some of the arguments in support of this idea will be outlined.

First of all, one could wonder with some justification whether strict educational secularism is feasible as such a curriculum, in the words of Evans,

---

131 C. Evans, *supra* note 38, p. 449.
132 *Ibid.* p. 461.
133 *Idem.*
134 *Toledo Guidelines*, *supra* note 103.

"would be unable to properly examine causes of many European wars, to explore the meaning of great works of art, music and literature, or engage with current debates..."[135] In other words, as religions and beliefs will inevitably be touched upon in the curriculum, public school officials would be well-advised to reflect on this issue and develop an informed approach to dealing with the issue of religion in a way that would enable the school to do justice to children's and parental rights. The message pupils could get from obstinately avoiding religious issues at all costs could be that religion and religious persons are to be avoided at all costs.

Second, international human rights law contains explicit requirements related to the content of children's education.[136] States parties to the Children's Rights Convention have agreed that the education of the child shall be directed to the "development of respect for human rights and fundamental freedoms" and to the "preparation of the child for responsible life in a free society, in the spirit of understanding, peace, tolerance, equality of sexes, and friendship among all peoples, ethnic, national and religious groups and persons of indigenous origin".[137] The state duty to promote religious tolerance also flows from the UN Religious Tolerance Declaration (1981). The latter document argues that "it is essential to promote understanding, tolerance and respect in matters relating to freedom of religion and belief" and, more concretely, that children shall be "brought up in a spirit of understanding, tolerance, friendship among peoples, peace and universal brotherhood, respect for freedom of religion or belief of others".[138] One could argue that these state duties include a positive obligation for the state to design an educational system in which pupils are taught the idea of religious tolerance and respect for freedom of religion or belief of others.[139] It could also be contended that these notions—religious tolerance and respect for freedom of religion or belief of others—require a basic level of understanding of religious beliefs. If children do not receive any neutral education on the issue of religious beliefs they are likely to base their knowledge solely or chiefly on insights conveyed by close relatives or the media. These portrayals of, and insights on, (certain) religions may not always be accurate or conducive to tolerance. Thus, neutral education about religions and beliefs based on sound scholarship and taught in an inclusive, fair and respectful manner could offer a welcome if not necessary counterbalance.

---

[135] C. Evans, *supra* note 38, p. 461, fn 39. The *Toledo Guidelines, supra* note 103, p. 19, make a similar point: "Much history, literature and culture is unintelligible without knowledge of religions and beliefs. Therefore study about religions and beliefs is an essential part of a well-rounded education. Learning about religions and beliefs forms part of one's own stock of education, broadens one's horizon and deepens one's insight into the complexities of both past and present."

[136] See also C. Evans, *supra* note 38, p. 454–455.

[137] Art. 29, paras. (1)(b) and (d), of CRC.

[138] Preamble and art. 5, para. (3), of the UN Religious Tolerance Declaration (1981).

[139] Cf. the *Toledo Guidelines, supra* note 103, p. 19.

As we are dealing with public school education on the subject of religion that is given in a neutral and objective way, this subject may be made compulsory to all pupils[140]—and in light of the above considerations it perhaps ought to be made compulsory. Inevitably there will be parents who do not want their children to receive such pluralist religious education, even if—or possibly because—it is taught in a neutral fashion. Here the question is to what extent these parents should be accommodated by making provision for opt-out clauses: which norm is to prevail if the child's right to education is to be balanced with parental rights? It is submitted that precisely because the paramount value of religious tolerance is at stake, and because of the existence of clear state duties to promote that value, that children's educational rights should triumph in this balancing act. As children have a right to education that is directed to preparing them for a responsible life in a free and tolerant society in which human rights are respected, it could be argued that "[t]oo significant a system of exclusions may end up denying the child an education that fulfils...the aims of developing respect for civilisations other than his or her own and for human rights more generally."[141]

Finally, states that aim at incorporating a neutral subject about religions and beliefs into the curriculum of public schools are well-advised to follow the guidelines issued by the OSCE/ODIHR on this subject as in these benchmarks a commitment to religious freedom and other human rights is thoroughly integrated into curriculum building endeavours.[142]

---

140 Human Rights Committee, General Comment No. 22, para. 6.
141 C. Evans, *supra* note 38, p.455.
142 *Toledo Guidelines*, *supra* note 103.

[8]

THE RELIGIOUS, MORAL AND SPIRITUAL DIMENSIONS OF EDUCATION: NATIONAL, REGIONAL AND INTERNATIONAL CONSTITUTIONAL AND LEGAL FRAMEWORKS

Peter Schreiner

Comenius-Institute, Protestant Centre for Research and Development in Education

Introduction

The important role which education, in partnership with the family, the public school system, religious communities, and the other institutions of society, can and should play in the religious, moral and spiritual development of children and young adults hardly needs emphasising. Whereas international constitutional and legal frameworks provide a kind of general framework in a protective and regulatory sense, especially concerning individual rights and the freedom of religion and belief, each national constitutional and legal framework shapes the education system more precisely and concretely. The right to education is mentioned in several international declarations and treaties as well as the right of parents or legal guardians to decide about the education, and especially the form of religious education, their child should receive. Often while education is compulsory, schooling itself is not, at least in several Western European countries. The interplay between the family, the religious communities, and non-religious belief organisations and the public school system varies according to the value placed upon various layers in the individual country context. Parental rights concerning school education are protected by international human rights conventions. Parents have also the right – as well as religious and other organisations – to establish private schools as an alternative to public schools. However the general right to found private schools under a specific ethos are dealt with differently in different countries. In general one can say that the place of religion in the public forum is contested especially concerning schooling. Nonetheless in many countries it is a fact that the school system in general has deep connections with religion at least in the past.

Thus existing models of education and schooling exhibit a great variety of approaches based on different conceptions of the role of the school concerning the religious, moral and spiritual dimension of education. Where they are part of the general concept of education these dimensions provide a vital underpinning of all aspects of school life, not only in the teaching of concrete curriculum subjects such as religious education, ethics, philosophy or citizenship education, but also in the underlying philosophy of education, in ancillary activities, in the school ethos and in the relationship between the different stakeholders.

International Frameworks

The Universal Declaration of Human Rights (United Nations)

The *Universal Declaration of Human Rights*, adopted by the United Nations in 1948, is the seminal document for all other human rights documents. The declaration is not an international treaty; it has no legally binding character for participating States. Rather it is a catalogue of rights containing rights of freedom and protection as well as rights of participation concerning politics, the economy, social issues and culture.

The Universal Declaration begins by affirming that human beings, 'born free and equal in dignity and rights', are entitled to human rights 'without distinction of any kind, such as race, colour, sex, language, religion, political or other opinion, national or social origin, property, birth or other status.' Among the rights guaranteed by the Universal Declaration is the right to freedom of religion:

> 'Everyone has the right to freedom of thought, conscience and religion; this right includes freedom to change his religion or belief, and freedom, either alone or in community with others and in public or private, to manifest his religion or belief in teaching, practice worship and observance' (Art. 18).

The Universal Declaration also states that parents have the right 'to ensure the religious and moral education of their children in conformity with their own convictions.' Concerning education generally the Universal Declaration of Human Rights states in Article 26 that:

1. Everyone has the right to education. Education shall be free, at least in the elementary and fundamental stages. Elementary education shall be compulsory. Technical and professional education shall be made generally available and higher education shall be equally accessible to all on the basis of merit.
2. Education shall be directed to the full development of the human personality and to the strengthening of respect for human rights and fundamental freedoms. It shall promote understanding, tolerance and friendship among all nations, racial or religious groups, and shall further the activities of the United Nations for the maintenance of peace.
3. Parents have a prior right to choose the kind of education that shall be given to their children.

Based on the Universal Declaration a number of conventions have been subsequently adopted that have a high legal status – mostly in form of an international committee, an obligation on the part of signatory States to provide regular reports and other mechanisms of monitoring the practice of the agreement. These conventions can be seen as efforts to differentiate and concretise the human right of education by emphasising the basic values of the Universal Declaration concerning 'the right to education', the aim of 'the full development of the human personality' and parental rights. Frequently they also promote and defend religious freedom and belief. The most important agreements are:

- The ***Convention Against Discrimination in Education***, adopted by the General Conference of the UN Educational, Scientific and Cultural Organisation (UNESCO) in 1960. This convention embodies functions similar to those of the 1958 convention in regard to access to education.
- The ***International Covenant on Civil and Political Rights (1966) and the Optional Protocol***. This document underlines 'the right (of the individual) to freedom of thought, conscience and religion (...) to adopt a religion or belief of his (or her) choice, and freedom, either individually or in community with others and in public or private, to manifest his religion or belief in worship, observance, practice and teaching' (...) (Art. 18).
- The ***International Covenant on Economic, Social and Cultural Rights (1966)***.This document recognises the liberty of parents 'to choose for their children schools, other than those established by the public authorities, which conform to such minimum educational standards as may be laid down or approved by the State and to ensure the religious and moral education of their children in conformity with their own convictions' (Art. 13).
- The ***Declaration on the Elimination of all Forms of Intolerance and of Discrimination based on Religion or Belief (1981)*** This Declaration is entirely dedicated to freedom of religion or belief. The text underlines the protection of the child 'from any form of discrimination on the grounds of religion and belief'. It underlines that the child 'shall be brought up in the spirit of understanding, tolerance, friendship among peoples, peace and universal brotherhood, respect for freedom of religion or belief of others, and in full consciousness that his energy and talents should be devoted to the service of his fellow men' (Art. 5,3). It also underlines the right 'to education, regarding religion or belief, in accordance with the wishes of his parents' (Art. 5,2).

In the above documents, freedom of religion is widely recognised as a fundamental human right. It is commonly described as including two aspects: first, the realm of a person's internal beliefs (*forum internum*), and secondly an external realm, where beliefs are manifested in many forms, such as teaching (*forum externum*). International human rights doctrines usually describe the first aspect as being 'absolute', being an area in which governments are prohibited from interfering in any way. In the external realm, however, human rights instruments provide that under certain specified and narrow circumstances governments may limit external manifestations of religion or belief.

The Convention on the Rights of the Child (United Nations)

Adopted by the General Assembly of the UN in 1989, the *Convention on the Rights of the Child* is regarded the most universally accepted human rights instrument in history. It has been ratified by every country in the world except two and therefore uniquely places children centre-stage in the quest for the universal application of human rights. By ratifying this instrument, national governments have committed themselves to protecting and ensuring children's rights and they have agreed to hold themselves accountable for this commitment before the international community.

The formation of the 1989 convention has a long history. The first legal step was taken in 1924 when the League of Nations endorsed the first **Declaration of the Rights of the Child**. In 1948 the General Assembly of the newly formed United Nations adopted a second **Declaration of the Rights of the Child**, a brief, seven-point statement that built on the 1924 Declaration. 'By the present Declaration of the Rights of the Child (...) men and women of all nations, recognising that Mankind owes to the child the best that it has to give, declare and accept it as their duty to meet its obligation in all it respects.' It is interesting to note that the Geneva declaration includes the right of being enabled to develop 'spiritually.' The 1948 Declaration was almost followed immediately by the decision to draft a still more detailed Declaration, resulting just over a decade later in a third **Declaration of the Rights of the Child** by the General Assembly in 1959 (www.unicef.org).

It was only in 1989 that the standards concerning children were brought together in a single legal instrument spelling out in an unequivocal manner the rights to which every child is entitled, regardless of where born, or to whom, and regardless of sex, religion, or social origin. The body of rights enumerated in the Convention is the rights of all children everywhere. Every right spelled out in the final 1989 Convention is inherent to the human dignity and harmonious development of every child. The Convention protects children's rights by setting standards in health care, education and legal, civil and social services. These standards are benchmarks against which progress can be assessed. States that are party to the Convention are obliged to develop and undertake all actions and policies in the light of the best interests of the child.

The 1989 convention emphasises that:

> 'Education shall aim at developing the child's personality, talents and mental and physical abilities to the fullest extent. Education shall prepare the child for an active adult ,life in a free society and foster respect for the child's parents, his or her own cultural identity, language and values, and for the cultural background and values of others.'

It is this stated aim of education of developing the child 'to the fullest extend' that can be linked directly to the religious, moral, and spiritual dimensions of Education.

Tensions can arise between the public educational aim of promoting tolerance and mutual understanding and the rights of the parents to have the last say in the religious and moral education of their children. The Convention has inspired a process of national implementation in all regions of the world (examples at www.unicef.org). The challenge presented can be seen in the fact that three-quarters of the world's entire population of children are not in school despite education being recognised as a right of every child.

Education for Tolerance

In 1994 the *UN Commission on Human Rights* encouraged the Special Rapporteur on Freedom of Religion or Belief to examine the role of education in the promotion of tolerance of different religious views and traditions. The Special Rapporteur conducted a survey concerning how the curricula for religious education at primary and secondary school levels contribute to the protection of human rights in general, to the protection of freedom of religion or belief, and to a climate of tolerance and non-discrimination in particular (Hera & Martinez de Codes, 2002, p. 35–116). On the basis of these findings an international consultative conference in Madrid in November 2001 focused on the role of schooling in relation to the promotion of tolerance, non-discrimination and freedom of religion or belief. The final Madrid document includes recommendations at the national and international levels. The importance of securing the parents and children's rights and the right to freedom of religion and belief in relation to school education was underlined (Hera & Martinez de Codes, 2002, p. 443–452). While these recommendations do not have a legal status they support initiatives that can influence legal frameworks on national level.

Regional Frameworks

Increasingly international bodies are taking over legislative and political competencies previously vested solely in national States (a good example is the development of the European Union) and their legal frameworks have to be implemented at regional and local level. The above international agreements often set the parameters for regional and national constitutional and legal frameworks.

In 1950 the Members of the Council of Europe agreed the ***European Convention for the Protection of Human Rights and Fundamental Freedoms***. This recognises the right of parents to ensure such education and teaching in conformity with their own religious and philosophical convictions. To this was added a number of protocols. ***Protocol No. 1 to the European Convention for the Protection of Human Rights and Fundamental Freedoms*** (1952) underlines that 'no person shall be denied the right to education' (Art.2).

The right to education is also confirmed in the ***Charter of the Fundamental Rights of the European Union*** (2000) that may eventually form part of a European Constitution. In the draft text the already mentioned rights are combined with 'the freedom to found educational establishments with due respect to democratic principles (...) in accordance with the national laws governing the exercise of such freedom and right' (Art. 14, 3).

In summarising the international and regional legal frameworks one can identify four core areas that serve as guidelines for the national level:

1. The right of parents to decide about the provision of the religious education of their children.
2. The public educational aim of promoting tolerance and non-discrimination.
3. The right of the child to education and to the development of its personality to its fullest extent.
4. The right of various groups, including religious bodies, to establish private schools in addition to the public school system.

The aim of developing the child's personality to its 'fullest extent' includes the religious, moral and spiritual dimensions of education along with those other skills and competencies that enable 'an active life in a free society'.

National Frameworks

National laws must be applied so as to benefit all citizens in accordance with international obligations. Under international law human rights, such as the right to education, may be restricted by Governments by means of, *inter alia*, reservations, declarations of interpretation or specific limitation clauses. Such limitations are only justified if they are prescribed by law and if they serve the purposes of public safety, order, health, morals, or the protection of the rights and freedoms of others (Nowak & Vospernick, 2001, p. 57).

Where education is mentioned in most existing legal frameworks the focus is on the right to education according to the international legislation, the general aim of public schooling and, frequently, on the question of religious education. While national Constitutional frameworks often include general remarks about education, national educational legislation deal more specifically with the objectives and underlying values of education. The precise legal framework at national level depends upon a number of interrelated factors, e.g. the relation between State and religious institutions, the religious demographic landscape, the structure of the education system and the value and perspective of religion in the society. Such factors have also to be situated within an historical context.

Europe

For Europe the current status of national legal frameworks has to be seen against the background of historical developments such as the Reformation (1517–1648), the French revolution (1787–1799), and the political frictions resulting from World War II. In Western Europe generally these historical experiences laid the ground for the 'religiously neutral State' as the dominant model based upon the notion of human dignity and the specification of human rights. The general European trend is one of the increasing secularisation of society and of an education system that was formerly under the control of the (established State) churches. In the Constitutions of Western European countries freedom of religion and of belief and non-discrimination are guaranteed for all citizens as well as the right to education.

Europe of course does not provide a uniform picture. The significance of religion in society and especially its relevance for national identity differs in Europe. Ireland and Poland are examples of countries where religion still has a central place in society and where a close link between religion and culture exists. This is mirrored in the constitutions of these countries, e.g. in Poland, 'God as the source of truth, justice, goodness and beauty' is mentioned as well as the fact that the Polish culture is 'rooted in the Christian heritage of the Nation and in universal human values'. Other countries can be seen as highly secularised (like Sweden or the Netherlands), and in others a negative image of religion exists e.g. in some central and eastern European countries.

Across Europe there are different solutions to the religious, spiritual and moral dimensions in education. These usually focus on the provision of religious education in 'State' or 'public' schools and on the establishment of private schools. Legal rights for the establishment of private schools exist in most European countries though the size of the private sector varies widely. According to comparative studies (Mackinnon et al., 1997, p. 263), the highest percentage of pupils in private schools can be found in the Netherlands (75%), in Belgium (61%), Spain (31%) and in France (20%). Private schools are based on a specific school ethos, or characteristic spirit, that cares for the religious, spiritual and moral development of the pupils. In such a decentralised school system the right of the parents concerning education is afforded a high value.

Different models exist across Europe concerning the legal basis for religious education. These can be classified as the denominational or confessional approach, the religious studies approach and the prohibition of religious education in public schools approach.

Austria is an example of a *denominational approach* based on legally underpinned cooperation between the State and religious communities. The constitution or school law guarantees the religious communities the right to establish religious education in public schools. Religious education (RE) is taught under the supervision of the State and in general accordance to the national education policy. This approach is considered an expression of the balance between State neutrality and the individual right to freedom of religion. The State does not influence the content of Religious Education as a subject, but remains neutral concerning religions and belief.

The German constitution (from 1949) includes the following provisions:

a) The entire education system is under the supervision of the State.
b) The persons entitled to bring up a child have the right to decide whether they shall receive religious instruction.

c) Religious instruction forms part of the ordinary curriculum in State and municipal schools, excepting secular schools.
d) Without prejudice to the State's right of supervision, religious instruction is given in accordance with the tenets of the religious communities.
e) No teacher may be obliged against his will to give religious instruction (Art. 7).

Where RE is denominationally oriented (e.g. in the south of Europe, partly in Switzerland, Austria, Belgium, Germany, central and eastern Europe) different kinds of religious education, or alternative subjects like ethics or philosophy, are offered on an equal basis. In Austria, Belgium and partly in Germany denominational religious education is not limited to Catholic or Protestant teaching but it includes also Orthodox, Jewish, Muslim, Buddhist and other forms of religious education (Robbers, 2005).

The second European model, the *religious studies approach* (for example to be found in England, Denmark, Sweden, Norway, Scotland), does not include the direct participation of religious communities, at least not in a continuous manner, nor do pupils have a general right to opt out, although in some countries this option is given to members of certain religious minorities. The general aim of this approach is to examine religious knowledge and understanding within the context of the diversity of human experience. The neutrality of the State and the right of religious freedom are also guaranteed in this approach, however this occurs in a different way than with denominational religious education. The religious studies approach is carried out under the sole authority of the State. Instruction is not to be neutral in respect to values but must be neutral in respect to worldviews including religion, a demand that reflects the religious neutrality of the State. From this perspective, such neutrality guarantees that the religious education provided is equally acceptable to all denominations and religions.

Taking England and Wales as an example for the religious studies approach, the Education Reform Act (1988) sets education within the context of the spiritual, moral, cultural, mental and physical development of pupils and of society. These dimensions underpin the curriculum and the ethos of the school. They apply not only to Religious Education and collective worship but also to every area of the curriculum and to all aspects of school life. While the Cowper-Temple Clause of the Elementary Education Act of 1870 confirms the non-confessional character of religious education ('No religious catechism or religious formulary which is distinctive of any particular denomination shall be taught in school') the Education Act (1988) confirms the multi-religious character of RE: 'Any Agreed Syllabus (...) shall reflect the fact that the religious traditions in Great Britain are in the main Christian whilst taking account of teaching and practices of the other principal religions represented in Great Britain' (Education Reform Act, 1988, chapter 40, Section 8:3). In other (former) State church systems in Europe (especially Denmark, Sweden and Norway) a development has taken place from a confessional approach to religious education as a multi-religious study approach for all pupils that provides Christian knowledge and religious and ethical education.

France represents a unique model of a strict separation of State and church (laïcité), where the State is exclusively responsible for the public school system and no religious or spiritual education exists as an independent subject in school. The public authorities' approach to issues of religion is named *laïcité* [roughly translated as 'secularism']. The concept implies the existence of the public world and the religious world as two independent worlds, radically separate from each other and wholly ignorant of one another. Religious issues are seen as private matters for individuals and families which lie beyond the bounds of public life and thus do not concern the State. The term *laïcité* appears in positive law in the 1946 French Constitution, the preamble of which stipulates that the provision of free and secular public education at all levels is a duty of the State. Article 2 of the 1958 French Constitution declares, 'France is an indivisible, secular, democratic, and social Republic.' Section 2 of the law of 28 March 1882 requires State primary schools to leave free 'one day a week apart from Sunday, so that parents, if they so wish, may give their children religious instruction.' This is confirmed and safeguarded by section 1 of the 'Debré' Law of 31 December 1959 that provides that 'The State shall take all appropriate measures to assure freedom of worship and religious instruction for children in public education.' This has allowed the establishment in France of a robust private school sector that today includes 16% of all pupils. 90% of these institutions are Catholic based, the other 10% are Protestant, Jewish and, occasionally, non-confessional. Such private schools are fully acknowledged by the State according to the Debré Law (1959). Slovenia and Albania are other countries in which no religious education is allowed in public schools.

The United States of America

In the U.S.A. the Religious Liberty Clauses of the First Amendment to the United States Constitution state, 'Congress shall make no law respecting an establishment of religion, or prohibiting the free exercise thereof...' The 'no establishment' and 'free exercise' clauses of the First Amendment provide the constitutional basis for what Thomas Jefferson described as 'a wall of separation between Church & State.' These clauses set the ethical, legal, and pedagogical contexts for any discussion of religious education in the USA. The guarantee of individual freedom is prior to State power. Educational sovereignty rests mainly with the individual States. On this basis no religious education is allowed in a public school. However a special characteristic of the US American school system is the coexistence of private and public schools. At the beginning of American history there was no such clear distinction between public and private schools. Religious content (referring mainly to the faith convictions and moral principles of the Protestant traditions) was part of the curriculum and also shaped the ethos of the school. Subsequently, with the Public Education Movement during the 19th century and the founding of an extensive public school system based on State funds, Religious Education in schools became a political issue. Parallel to the increasing success of the Public Education Movement the constitutional principle of denationalisation of religion was interpreted in a way that 'sectarian' Religious Education was banned from public schools. During the 20th century there were a number of court judgements that banned all religious expressions from teaching. Today there is a new debate in the USA questioning if such a strict exclusion of a consideration of religion from the public school system is adequate to a situation of globalised and pluralised societies (Osmer & Schweitzer, 2003).

Latin America

Latin America is a diverse region consisting mainly of culturally Roman Catholic countries. Over the past century there have been three significant developments, the spread of the ecumenical spirit within the Catholic Church itself, a dramatic increase in the numbers of, and militancy of, Evangelical and Pentecostal Churches, and the adoption of new or amended constitutions which include guarantees of freedom of religion and which have limited, or ended, the privileged legal status of Roman Catholicism in the region (Sigmund, 2001).

The educational systems and the overall culture of Latin America have moved from the (sometimes contested) dominance of a single religion (Catholicism) to the acceptance and even promotion of religious diversity. 'While much of Latin America had been under military rule from the mid 1960s to the late 1980s, the return of civilian rule provided an opportunity to revise or replace earlier constitutions, including provision on religion' (Sigmund, 2001, p. 56). For a long time instruction in Catholicism had been an integral part of the public school in some of the more Catholic countries such as Columbia and Argentina. In recent years it has been offered on a voluntary basis. Provision has been made in some countries to offer also education in other faith traditions. Also in many countries Catholic schools have largely come to endorse and promote religious freedom and good ecumenical relations. In those cases in which a civic education programme is offered in public schools, the constitutional and legal provisions favouring religious freedom are described and supported. Many Latin American countries also offer voluntary religious education in public schools.

Asia

In many Asian countries the prevailing religious traditions have been used in varying degrees as vehicles for promoting national unity. Indonesia, one of the largest Islamic countries of the world, is known for its unique, interfaith conception of national identity known as the *Pancasila* ideology. According to the Pancasila principles, Indonesian identity is bound together by the five beliefs in 'the One and Only God, just and civilised humanity, the unity of Indonesia, democracy guided by the inner wisdom of deliberations amongst representatives, and the realisation of socials justice for all the people of Indonesia' (see the preamble to the Indonesian constitution). 'Enhancement of 'faith and piety' and of 'morals and noble character' are stated as general aims of school education which should apply to all subjects, together with the recognition of 'local religion and culture' as well as 'the dynamic of global development' (Leirvik, 2002, p. 40). According to the new Bill of Education of 2002, Pancasila education will now be integrated in a revised subject of Civic Education that will also include the study of human rights. A kind of religious education or religiously informed communal education has been encouraged in the State schools of many countries. Efforts have been made to bring together traditional and modern teachings and practices.

Africa

The education systems throughout Africa have been continued into modern era from the colonial times. Pre-colonial education responded to the needs of the community and of the environment. It was integrated with the indigenous situation and highlighted the values, needs and aspirations of pre-colonial society. Subsequently colonial education was designed to make objects of most Africans and has largely succeeded in programming them into conformity to the logic of the colonial system (Fanon, 1986).

The task of post-colonial education is seen as being to 'Africanise' the education system, 'decolonising the mind' (Ngugi wa Thiong'o, 1994), and developing an integrated type of modern education that serves the needs of African society. This started with the achievement of independence from the 1960s. At the start of that decade, sub-Saharan Africa's primary school gross enrolment ratio (all enrolled primary students, including those under- or over-aged, as a percentage of the primary school age-group) was just 39 per cent. That was far behind Asia's ratio of 67 per cent and Latin America's 73 per cent. By virtually any standard, education in sub-Saharan Africa lags far behind most other developing regions. One obvious reason is that the continent is the world's poorest. Without large and growing economies, governments have a very limited tax base to finance public school systems, while the majority of African families cannot afford the high fees charged by private schools.

Some African countries have taken steps to try to reverse the declines of the previous decades. Overall, public spending on education has increased markedly. This has been facilitated by a revival of economic growth in a number of countries, and by a somewhat greater attention paid by economic policy officials to safeguarding education budgets. As a result, in sub-Saharan Africa, primary school enrolment has increased from 54 per cent in 1990 to 60 per cent in 1998. Benin, Gambia, Guinea, Mali, Mauritania, Senegal, Swaziland, Togo and Uganda have all registered notable improvements in primary school enrolments, some with striking advances in girls' enrolment.

Some of the most innovative work in terms of cooperative curriculum development has been undertaken in post-apartheid South Africa, particularly in the area of educational research and in the formulation of proposals for new curricula aiming at advancing mutual understanding and respect while reducing prejudice, based on a multi-religious models (Chidester, 2001, 2002). This is reflected in the Revised

National Curriculum Statements (2002): 'Religious Education contributes to the wider framework of education by developing in every learner the knowledge, values, attitudes and skills necessary for diverse religions to co-exist in a multi-religious society' (Chidester, 2002, p. 55).

References

Chidester, D. (2001). Multiple voices: Challenges Posed for Religious Education in South Africa. In International Association for Religious Freedom (Ed.), *Religious Education in Schools: Ideas and Experiences from around the World* (pp. 26–31). Oxford.

Chidester, D. (2002). Religion education in South Africa—Teaching and learning about religion, religions, and religious diversity. In L. Larsen & I. T. Plesner (Eds.), *Teaching for tolerance and freedom of religion or belief* (pp. 55–68). Oslo.

Fanon, F. (1986). *Black skins, white masks*. London: Pluto Press.

Hera de la, Alberto Martinez de Codes, and Rosa, M. (2002). *La libertad religiosa en la educación escolar: Conferencia international consultativa de Naciones Unidas (Madrid 23–25 Noviembro, 2001)*. Madrid.

International Association for Religious Freedom (IARF) (Ed.) (2001). *Religious Education in Schools: Ideas and Experiences from around the World*. Oxford.

Larsen, L., & Plesner, I. T. (2002). *Teaching for tolerance and freedom of religion or belief*. Report from the preparatory seminar held in Oslo December 7–9, 2002.

Leirvik, O. (2002). Religious education, communal identity and national politics in the Muslim world. In L. Larsen & Plesner, I.T. (Eds.), *Teaching for tolerance and freedom of religion or belief* (pp. 37–45). Oslo.

Mackinnon, D., et al. (1997). *Education in Western Europe: Facts & figures*. London: Hodder & Stockton.

Martinez de Cordes Rosa, M., & Rossell, J. (Eds.) (2001). *Religious freedom, tolerance and non-discrimination in education*. Cáceres.

Ministry of Foreign Affairs (The Netherlands). (2001). *Seminar on Freedom of Religion or Belief in the OSCE Region: Challenges to Law and Practice*. The Hague.

Nowak, M., & Vospernik, T. (2001). Permissible restrictions on Freedom of Religion or Belief. In Ministry of Foreign Affairs (the Netherlands), *Seminar on Freedom of Religion or Belief in the OSCE Region: Challenges to Law and Practice* (pp. 54–77). The Hague.

Ngugi wa Thiong'o. (1994). *Decolonising the mind*. Harare: Zimbabwe Publishing House.

Osmer, R. R., & Schweitzer, F. (2003). *Religious Education between Modernization and Globalization: New Perspectives on the United States and Germany*. Grand Rapids: Michigan.

Robbers, G. (2005). State and Church in the European Union. 2nd edition. Baden-Baden.

Sigmund, P. (2001). Education and Religious Freedom in Latin America. In International Association for Religious Freedon (Ed.), *Religious Education in Schools: Ideas and Experiences from around the World*. (pp. 54–58). Oxford.

Encyclopaedia Britannica. (1979). *Religious education* (Vol. 15, pp. 640–647).

[9]

Different Models for Religion and Education in Europe[1]

Jean-Paul Willaime

The relationship between school and religion, like that between state and church, is a matter of national sovereignty in each European country and the EU does not have any uniform approach towards teaching religion in public schools. Yet, as we will see, though the breadth of the different national solutions is great, there is a degree of European integration in this field, as in many others. Be it for social or legal reasons, we discern an effective convergence in the way European countries attempt to meet the challenges facing public education in secularised, pluralistic societies.

In the first part, we will develop certain general questions on teaching about religion in Europe. In the second part we will then present the three principal approaches we can see in order to, in the third, explore the directions that different national policies are currently taking. This will allow us, in conclusion, to state whether, and to what degree, we can identify European convergences beyond the historical diversity of individual nations.

General Observations

1) School instruction about religious faith is a strong indicator of the way church-state and school-religion relations are constructed inside a given national framework. Thus, in countries where national identity is strongly tied to a particular confession (such as Lutheranism in Denmark, Orthodoxy in Greece, or Catholicism in Italy) there are notable effects on the way school education is understood. We note especially that, in some countries, the very definition of the goals of school education encompasses the religious dimension. For example:

The Greek constitution, which was framed 'in the name of the Holy Trinity, consubstantial and indivisible' and which, in article 3.1., indicates that 'the dominant religion in Greece is that of the Eastern Orthodox Church of Christ', closely associates the development of the religious consciousness of students with that of their national consciousness:

1 We allow ourselves to revisit the work issued by an international colloquium which we organised in the context of the Institut Européen en Sciences des Religions in October 2004: Des maîtres et des dieux. Ecoles et religions en Europe (sous la direction de Jean-Paul Willaime avec la collaboration de Séverine Mathieu), Paris, Belin, 2005. See also: Gerhard Robbers (Ed.), State and Church in the European Union, Second Edition, Baden-Baden, Nomos Verlag, 2005. (the presentation of each of the 25 EU countries contains information regarding religious instruction in schools), Peter Schreiner, Religious Education in Europe: A Collection of Basic Information about RE in European Countries, Münster, Comenius Institut/Intereuropean Commission on Church and School, 2000 and Jean-Paul Willaime: Europe et religions. Les enjeux du XXIe siècle, Paris, Fayard, 2004, 'Cultures, religions, laïcités. Divergences et convergences des modèles nationaux', in 'Faire' des Européens ? L'Europe dans l'enseignement de l'histoire, de la géographie et de l'éducation civique (Alain Bergounioux, Pascal Cauchy, Jean-François Sirinelli, Laurent Wirth dir.), Paris, Delagrave, 2006, p.69-82.

> 'Instruction constitutes a fundamental mission of the state. Its purpose is the moral, cultural, professional and physical education of the Hellenes as well as the development of their national and religious consciousness and their formation into free and responsible citizens' (Article 16.2.).

In *Great Britain*, the Education Act of 1988 sets out that the overall curriculum of public school education is to promote 'the spiritual, moral, cultural, mental and physical development of students in school and society'. The fact of adding 'spiritual development' to the list of general educational goals cannot fail to stress the proximity of school and religious faith.

In Germany, the goals of public education in several Länder are defined in connection with religion. Thus, in the Land of Hessen, the educational mission of the public school is defined as embedded in 'the Christian and Humanist tradition' while, in Baden-Wurttemberg, it is stated that instruction is to take place 'in responsibility before God and Christian love'.

Regarding Italy, the Concordat of 1984 states in article 9.2.:

> 'The Italian Republic, recognising the value of religious culture and taking into account the fact that the principles of Catholicism are part of the historical patrimony of the Italian people, continues to ensure within the school system the instruction in the Catholic religion in non-university public schools of all levels and types'.

Though the role and prerogatives of the state in matters of school education are strongly emphasised everywhere, in some countries, such as Ireland, the constitution particularly stresses the importance of parents' rights in this field:

> 'The state recognises that the primary and natural educator of the child is the family and promises to respect the inalienable right and duty of parents to ensure, within their means, the religious and moral, intellectual, physical and social education of their children.
>
> 2. The parents are free to ensure that education, be it privately, be it through private schools or through schools recognised or established by the state'.

Though the central government invariably exercises some responsibility in educational matters, in many countries regional or local authorities play an important role. Thus in *Germany*, though education is placed 'under the supervision of the federal government' (article 7.1. of the Grundgesetz, the constitutional law), it is the responsibility of the Länder. This is also evidently the case in Switzerland, where every canton constitutes a separate state within the Helvetic Confederation. Religious instruction in those countries needs to be studied at the regional level.

Finally it needs to be stated that the distinction between public and private schools does not necessarily mirror that between lay and religious schools. Europe has public confessional and interconfessional schools as well as private secular ones. In some countries, such as Belgium with its extensive network of Catholic schools, the contribution of religious schools to public education is vitally important. Article 2 of the first additional protocol of the European Declaration of Human Rights forbids, among other things, all state monopolies on education, stating:

> 'Nobody may be refused the right to education. The state, in the exercise of the functions it assumes in the domain of education and instruction, shall respect the rights of parents to ensure an education and instruction conforming to their religious and philosophical convictions'.

However, it places no financial obligations towards private education on the state. The scope of this study is limited to religious instruction at non-confessional public schools.

2) However great the diversity of state-church and school-religion relations in the various European countries may be, and however many national approaches to the treatment of religion in education they may have, they are all confronted with similar challenges. Secularisation, and the increase in the number of people declaring themselves 'of no religion' (see the European Studies of Moral Values), the lack of religious acculturation among school students and their loss of contact with religious life, the existence of strong Muslim minorities in some countries, an overall religious pluralisation manifest in European societies through the presence of all sorts of religious groups and networks, worries about sectarian splinter groups of various kinds, the current interrelationship of religion and politics in various international conflicts, Antisemitism and Islamophobia, and the question of limits to religious expression in the educational context are issues facing European societies. They are seeking to address them by rethinking how schools approach, treat and teach religion. Faced with these challenges, not only was the necessity to understand and live with and beyond our respective differences stressed, but also and above all, with increasing strength, the need to give much more importance to the study of religions in the school curriculum. Though there has not always been a Europeanization of responses, there is a Europeanization of the challenges facing each national approach to religion in school education.

3) There is also a European consensus about the need to strengthen the role of religious knowledge in public school education. In Recommendation 1720, adopted on 4 October 2005, the Parliamentary Assembly of the Council of Europe declared:

> '6. Education is essential to combat ignorance, stereotyping, and incomprehension of religions. Governments must also do more to guarantee freedom of conscience and religious expression, to encourage religious instruction, to promote dialogue with and between religions, and to further the cultural and social expression of religions'.

> '7. The school is an important element in the education and the formation of the critical faculties of future citizens, and also in intercultural dialogue. It shall lay the foundation of tolerant conduct based on respect for the dignity of every human being. It shall teach its students the history and philosophy of all major religions in a measured and objective fashion, respecting the values of the European Convention of Human Rights, and it shall fight fanaticism, effectively. It is essential to understand the history of political conflicts on the name of religion'.

> '8, The understanding of religion is an integral part of understanding the history of humanity and its civilisations. It is entirely different from belief in one particular religion or its practice. Even the countries in which one confession largely predominates must teach the origins of all religions rather than privilege one or promote proselytising'.

Thus in spite of a high degree of difference which shows no sign of disappearing, there is a broad consensus in Europe on the need for instruction on religions in public schools.

4) Regarding the question of school instruction on religion, the situation in France differs markedly from that in other European countries. In practically all those countries, including those which joined the EU in 2004, there exist courses dedicated to the study of a religion or religious matters in general, managed by teachers having received special training for the purpose. These courses, be they confessional or non-confessional, form an especially designated school subject (religious education, Religionsunterricht ...). By

opting to introduce the study of religious matters across existing school subjects without introducing either a specific new subject or a specifically trained teaching body, France represents an original solution in Europe. Though, through its laical and interdisciplinary approach to religious education, France distinguishes itself strongly from those countries that developed a confessional system of religious instruction (Alsace-Lorraine excepted), it is meanwhile no longer alone in this. By now, numerous courses of religious education have evolved, as we shall see, towards non-confessional approaches integrating the plurality of religions, even giving equal treatment to atheist Humanism. In the matter of non-confessional religious education, France is thus not isolated in Europe, yet that non-confessional, interdisciplinary instruction has been conceived differently there.

Three Situations Existing in Europe

When it comes to religious education in schools, European countries can be grouped into the following three categories: 1) *no religious instruction in schools*; 2) *confessional religious instruction*; 3) *non-confessional religious education.* In each of these categories, though, there are differences between the various national systems. The first category is unique to France. Although the situation in some other countries, such as Hungary, comes close, they cannot be included in the same group (in Hungary, confessional religious instruction can effectively be given in school hours, even if the instructors are not part of the school faculty). For the situation in France, we refer to the presentation given by Mireille Estivalèzes. It is, then, through a variety of confessional and non-confessional courses that religious education is given in schools throughout the rest of Europe.

In the essay collection 'Des maîtres et des dieux. Ecoles et religions en Europe', the Italian jurist Silvio Ferrari summarises the characteristics of confessional religious education in Europe thus:[2]

> 'Religious instruction is organised and controlled by religious communities which are charged with the training and selection of educators, the drafting of curricula, and the approval of materials (Austria, Belgium, Cyprus, Spain, Greece, Malta, Poland, Portugal, Czech Republic). In some countries (e.g. Hungary, Italy, Latvia, Lithuania, Germany, Finland), state and religious communities cooperate in the abovementioned tasks. In these systems, religious instructors require a certification by the religious communities (this is the case in Austria, Belgium, Germany, Spain, Greece, Hungary, Italy, Latvia, Lithuania, Luxembourg, Malta, Poland, Portugal, the Czech Republic and Slovakia). Most frequently, religious instruction is an optional or elective school subject. Where it is obligatory, students have the right to receive dispensation (Germany, Austria, Cyprus, Finland, Greece, Malta, Slovakia). Confessional religious instruction is subject in organisational and economic respects to the state (which remunerates instructors and provides localities and school time). The problem is that this state organisation is selective and that only certain religions may be taught. Thus, the question of the selection criteria poses itself' (2005, p. 36).

2 We follow the incisive analysis undertaken by Silvio Ferrari in Des maîtres et des dieux. Ecoles et religions en Europe (sous la direction de Jean-Paul Willaime avec la collaboration de Séverine Mathieu), Paris, Belin, 2005, p. 31–39): 'L'enseignement des religions en Europe: un aperçu juridique'. Subsequent references to this essay will be by page number only for simplicity.

Under these systems, each country must determine which religions may be taught in schools. Most use both historical and statistical criteria to enable them to make this decision (Spain now recognises the Catholic, Protestant, Jewish and Muslim faiths owing to their historical importance). It is thus not surprising at all to see that the main problems arising from this structure to stem from the handling of minority religions and that recently established faiths need to be taken into account. Silvio Ferrari points out that where such systems are established, we have also found the willingness to listen to other religions (such as in Italy, in Spain or Portugal), yet this quickly comes up against the practical limits of the system (set by the small number of students, their diffusion, the effective training and choice of teachers etc.). In bi-confessional countries (such as Switzerland or Germany) we can see the tendency towards a Protestant-Catholic ecumenicalisation of religious courses. Finally, confessional religious instruction itself increasingly includes, among its core elements, the study of religion in general and knowledge of other religions, even though these are still filtered through a teacher trained in a particular religious tradition. However, although of necessity some degree of confessionality continues to exist, in practice, it plays very little part in the actual coursework. We must not forget that teachers of religion are, in effect, obliged to take account of the wishes of their students who might desert them if the course does not come up to their expectations. Thus, participant pressure equally works towards ~~a~~ secularisation, with many sessions transforming into general discussions of the existential questions that interest young people today.

The third category is represented by non-confessional religious education. We meet this particularly in Northern European Protestant countries. There, religious education used to be confessional, though under the direction of the state, not the church (in a system of close alignment of Lutheran national churches to the state according to the 'Volkskiche' model). Yet, as Silvio Ferrari explains, 'secularisation has slowly transformed this confessional instruction into a non-confessional one. Thus in Sweden, religious education, originally having been instruction in the Protestant faith, was changed into 'instruction in Christianity' (1919), the 'study of Christianity' (1962), the 'study of religion' (1969) and finally into 'education on the questions of life and existence' (1980). Sweden thus offers a very characteristic example of an originally confessional curriculum secularising from within'. We can observe a similar development in the Swiss cantons such as Zurich and Lucerne and in the German Land of Hamburg, where a 'religious education for everyone' (Religionsunterricht für alle) is developing. In England and Wales, a confessional 'religious instruction' has morphed into non-confessional 'multifaith religious education' with programmes including elements of the principal religious traditions present in the country: many syllabuses include Christianity in its various forms together with Judaism, Islam, Hinduism, Buddhism and Sikhism, and may also include other traditions. Since the implementation of the 1988 Education Reform Act, it has been a requirement that religious education in state-funded community schools should be both pluralistic and non-confessional. Various pedagogical approaches have been developed as a consequence. For example, a pedagogical approach developed by Robert Jackson,[3]

3 Aside from his contribution to Des maîtres et des dieux 'L'évolution vers un enseignement religieux multiconfessionnel en Grande-Bretagne' (2005, p. 101–111), we refer to his works: Re-

uses the findings of cultural anthropology and develops a deontology respectful of the conscience of all students, while preparing them for citizenship in a pluralist society.

According to Silvio Ferrari (2005, p. 35), the characteristics on non-confessional religious education in Europe are the following:

> 'Religious education is organised and controlled by the state which is charged with the training selection and remuneration of instructors, the definition of curricula and the approval of materials (possibly, as is the case in the United Kingdom, in consultation with the religious communities). In these countries, educators do not require a certification by the religious communities. Religious instruction is obligatory, but dispensation is possible. No alternative courses are provided... The non-confessional character of the courses does not preclude particular emphasis being placed on Christianity (as is the case in Denmark or the United Kingdom)' (Ferrari, 2005, p. 35).

Across the Channel the Education Act of 1988 specifies that *religious education* 'must reflect the fact that the religious traditions of Great Britain are principally Christian while including in its curriculum the practice of the other great religions represented in the country'. In Denmark, a similar adherence to Christian dominance can be observed, though the subject, especially in higher secondary education, is largely open to religious pluralism.

The Direction of Current Developments

The diversity present in Europe is no obstacle to notable developments. Thus we have already noted a process of deconfessionalisation and secularisation in religious education in some countries characterised by traditions of confessionalism. Throughout, three main lines of development are noticeable:

1.) **A growing integration of religious education, be it confessional or not, with the overall educational goals of the school and its specific mission**. In most countries, religious instruction is required to contribute to the education of students towards responsible citizenship in pluralist societies. In *Belgium* we see the confessional religious instruction curriculum espouse the same ideals of emancipation and autonomy as the secular ethics curriculum, both coming together, at least in their stated intentions, to promote a shared ideal of citizenship. Thus we read the following text in a brochure published by the Francophone Community in Belgium titled *Les cours de morale et de religion. Des lieux d'éducation*:[4]

> 'Whether it is in religious experience, the memory of a people, or secular culture, human existence is always confronted by the same fundamental questions. Birth, life, and death invariably pose the same great metaphysical problems. Social inequalities, the refusal of democratic rights, and crimes against humanity impose new demands on justice. The progress of technology, medicine, surgery, and genetics poses new ethical questions.

---

ligious education: an interpretative approach (London, Hodder and Stoughton, 1997) and Rethinking Religious Education and Plurality: Issues in Diversity and Pedagogy (London, Routledge Falmer, 2004).

4 At the end of this brochure, six contact addresses are given for: Non-Confessional Morality, Catholic Religion, Israelite Religion, Protestant Religion, Islamic Religion and Orthodox Religion.

There are values that every one of us, in all our difference, may call upon, ideals that we continue to uphold to unite us in common action:

- The dynamic of liberation, understood as the liberation of thought, where unfreedom produces a reduction, impoverishment, oppression and negation of the human.
- The indefatigable quest for peace, fraternity, justice, friendship and love
- The development of democratic engagement to develop dialogue and tolerance in the spirit of mutual respect and understanding of differences
- An education towards citizenship, understanding of and for human rights and fundamental liberties.

The school needs to center on the human being. Ethical and religious instruction is a subject of education which, while respecting all their different convictions, favour integration into a pluralist society. Within a coherent educational action plan, they allow us to fight indifference, fanaticism, dogmatism, intolerance, violence, negativism, and other dehumanising evils of our time'.

The Council of Europe, through its Commission of Human Rights, is particularly sensitive to that aspect. Concluding a seminar dedicated to 'Human rights, culture, and religion: Convergence or Divergence? Dogma, norms and education' organised by the Commission (Louvain-le-Neuve 9-10 December 2002), the participants declared:

'The religions, playing an important role in the education of young people, must in their instructions in equal measure teach the value of human rights, promoting knowledge and respect. In order to ensure the highest possible quality in an educational subject as important as it is sensitive, the participants believe that it is time to set up a dedicated place of learning where a methodology for the integration of human rights in religious education and the integration of religious matters into education in general can be developed'.

2.) **The second great tendency is an increased openness, in different degrees, to the religious and philosophical plurality of European societies**. This is particularly evident in the initiatives in many European countries to either organise a Muslim religious education, where religion is part of the school curriculum, or to better take account of the Muslim faith in the overall school curriculum. As we have outlined earlier, the most important example here is the British development of multifaith religious education and the internal secularisation of religious instruction courses in general which it represents. The fact that it is becoming ever more difficult not to approach religious faith in all its diversity in the school environment requires a socio-historical objectivity towards religion that, in some ways, mirrors the pluridisciplinary and laical approach taken in France.

In Europe, there are two approaches towards a non-confessional religious education which can be categorised respectively as secular and laical. The first, which is increasingly unfolding in Great Britain (especially in England and Wales and in Scotland, which has its own education system), develops an approach towards religion along non-confessional lines, adopting a position derived from the Humanities and viewing religion as a regular dimension of the human experience to be understood through empathy, but also, in England and Wales, encouraging the idea that students might learn form religions whilst studying them in an impartial way. From this perspective, non-religious options (atheist conceptions of the world and Secular Humanist philosophy) are on an equal footing with religious ones; they do not constitute an encompassing system for everyone, but rather philosophical systems that take their place at the same level as, not above, religions. The second approach, developed in France, privileges an approach towards religion through its works, its cultural traces, and its inclusion in the different school subjects while refusing to take specific account of religion in its own dimension through a dedicated subject (though the approach through various disciplines does not in itself preclude this). In this case, the school opens itself to the religious dimension of history and culture without constituting religions and secular philosophies as subjects in their own right. In all other countries, meanwhile, for all the differences in modality and internal development, we are looking at the model of a dedicated school subject. Behind the difference between the secular and laical approach lie layers of singular historical experiences with the interrelationship of politics and religion which, in turn, have contributed to shaping the different relations between political and scholastic culture on the one hand and religion on the other. Secular approaches can progress as well as laical ones, just as laical approaches are capable of gradually converging with secular ones.

Where confessional religious instruction exists, we have seen the insertion of such courses into scholastic culture forcing them to subscribe to the goals of school education in democratic and pluralist societies. Religion in school – and it does not matter here which religion this is – comprises those religious expressions compatible with human rights and a democratic ordering of society. Thus in Turkey, the laical state now believes that the establishment of Islamic instruction in its schools will form the best defence against radical Islamism. An ambitious and far-reaching plan – its successful realisation is hardly as clear-cut as this – it must especially not lose sight of the fact that human rights are also women's rights. However, insofar as the integration of religious instruction into the general school curriculum renders it, so to speak, 'reasonable', how far is this so? While all issues are not yet resolved, its exclusion from general education leaves the subject to its own internal logic, and the maintenance of confessional courses in schools which are difficult to justify. Passing through the filter of a historical approach and free critical examination, do not secular and laical approaches both contribute much more to understand religious and philosophical stances and to education in human rights and democratic citizenship?

3.) **Finally, the third great characteristic of current developments is the fact that they raise tensions and engender conflicts.** National systems grown from historical roots have found themselves buffeted by sociological developments, and the necessary adjustments are not always made without conflict peacefully. They activate or reactivate fissures on issues like the place of religion in society, especially the question of the place of Islam. Two countries are especially significant in this respect: Spain and Russia. In Spain, the privileged status of Catholic religious instruction in public schools (e.g. the grade received being taken into account for promotion into higher grades) is under attack from the left who, aside from criticising the difficulties it causes in offering equivalent courses for religious minorities, intend to replace it with a course of non-confessional religious studies. As in other countries, the establishment of Muslim religious instruction in public schools is beset with difficulties. In Russia, the partisans of a curriculum dedicated to 'the foundations of Orthodox culture' are supported by the Russian Orthodox Church in their opposition to the introduction of a course of comparative religious history. The state authorities are carefully equivocating between these two positions which have re-opened a debate on the nature of national identity. In Germany, the reintroduction of confessional religious instruction in the Eastern Länder following reunification has also produced conflicts (e.g. the controversy in Brandenburg around the course on 'life education, ethics, science and religion' proposed as an alternative to confessional religious instruction). The question poses itself how alternative courses for students not following this or that confession can be organised. Be they called Ethics, Non-confessional Morals, Values – even the naming of such courses is not without its own problems (not least in that subject names implicitly express a conception of the relationship between a course of morals and one of religion, either as alternatives or as closely associated subjects).

Conclusion: European Convergence or Divergence?

According to Silvio Ferrari, 'there does not appear to be today in Europe a significant demand for the abolition of religious instruction in schools in those countries where it is given, either on a confessional or non-confessional basis ...' (2005, p. 38). This view is confirmed by recent developments in former Communist Bloc countries where, in the course of their various paths towards democracy, the role and place of religion is being redefined by establishing (mostly confessional) religion curricula in state schools. However, that does not stop Silvio Ferrari from arguing that confessional religious instruction in school, deeply anchored in the legal tradition of European countries, requires reform. As Ferrari remarks:

> '...the school as an institution at the service of different demands made upon it by civil society', is in dire need of reform if it is to withstand the exigencies of pluralist societies and conform to European rules seeking to enforce non-discrimination of all individuals regardless of their religious belief or non-belief. 'It is especially necessary to render it entirely non-obligatory, to take account of more religions, and to see to it that state support is given on a more equal basis; According to the situation in different countries, it may be placed within or outside of school hours, be paid for by the state or not. Only if these conditions are respected can confessional religious instruction survive to play a positive role in a situation increasingly characterised by religious pluralism', the Italian jurist concludes (2005, p. 39).

The first convergence we can observe in Europe is an internal development within the confessional courses of religious instruction themselves. They continue to exist, but develop under a double constraint: a *sociological* one, in that the religious and philosophical pluralisation of European societies obliges them to include ever more alternative religions and non-religious positions into their curricula, and a *legal* one, through the importance of the principle of non-discrimination on religious or philosophical grounds (as well as others such as gender or race) in international law, especially in the European Convention of Human Rights. Although the confessional religious instruction courses do evolve, they remain dominant on the European scene. Many former East Bloc countries introduced them to their school systems in the 1990s (Poland, Latvia, Lithuania etc.) whereas few, like Estonia, privilege a non-confessional religious education or, like Slovenia, forbid all confessional instruction in their schools. However, such confessional instruction can also evolve into a non-confessional model, as seen in Sweden, Switzerland, and especially England and Wales. This gradual development or more sudden reverse towards a non-confessional curriculum may just as well be coming about through the convergence of the contents of confessional and non-confessional religious education. Yet one essential question remains: that of the relationship between academic and religious authorities. Do the former teach religious education independently, or do the latter in some fashion or other exert control over it? This question is an important indicator of the degree of secularisation in religious education.

The other great European convergence is the development of non-confessional religious education through the establishment of secular and multi-disciplinary approaches to religious faith. This development is encouraged by European authorities and mirrors, in some ways, the French experience, although it takes place within the context of an established subject. There is, in our view, nowhere that European integration is felt more strongly than in this development where non-confessional approaches meet the legal and sociological changes we see in Europe. As the educational challenges of European societies are increasingly formulated in terms of 'How can we live together with our differences' (be they cultural, religious etc.), having the ability to discuss all religions with all students increasingly appears to be a pedagogical and civic necessity in pluralist and secular societies.

References

Estivalèzes, M. (2005) L'enseignement religieux en France. Un état des lieux de la situation contemporaine, in: J.-P. Willaime, (Ed.) & S. Mathieu *Des maîtres et des dieux. Ecoles et religions en Europe* (Paris, Belin) 223–235.

Ferrari, S. (2005) L'enseignement des religions en Europe: un aperçu juridique, in: J.-P. Willaime, (Ed.) & S. Mathieu *Des maîtres et des dieux. Ecoles et religions en Europe* (Paris, Belin) 31–39.

Jackson, R. (1997) *Religious education: an interpretive approach* (London, Hodder and Stoughton).

Jackson, R. (2004) *Rethinking Religious Education and Plurality: Issues in Diversity and Pedagogy* (London, Routledge Falmer).

Jackson, R. (2005) L'évolution vers un enseignement religieux multiconfessionnel en Grande-Bretagne in: J.-P. Willaime, (Ed.) & S. Mathieu *Des maîtres et des dieux. Ecoles et religions en Europe* (Paris, Belin) 101–111.

Robbers, G. (Ed.) (2005) *State and Church in the European Union* (second edition) (Baden-Baden, Nomos Verlag).

Schreiner, P. (2000) *Religious Education in Europe: A Collection of Basic Information about Religious Education in European Countries* (Münster, Comenius Institut/Intereuropean Commission on Church and School).

Willaime J.-P. (2004) *Europe et religions. Les enjeux du XXIe siècle* (Paris, Fayard).

Willaime, J.-P. (Ed.) & Mathieu S. (2005) *Des maîtres et des dieux. Ecoles et religions en Europe* (Paris, Belin).

Willaime J.-P. (2006) Cultures, religions, laïcités. Divergences et convergences des modèles nationaux, in: A. Bergounioux, P. Cauchy, J.-F. Sirinelli, L. Wirth (Eds.) *'Faire' des Européens? L'Europe dans l'enseignement de l'histoire, de la géographie et de l'éducation civique* (Paris, Delagrave) 69–82.

[10]

Religion Education and the Transformational State in South Africa

David Chidester

Abstract: In 2003, after more than 10 years of policy debate and public controversy, the South African minister of education announced a new policy for religion and education that distinguished between religious interests, which are best served by religious communities, and educational objectives for teaching and learning about religion, religions, and religious diversity that should be served by the curriculum of public schools. This article locates South Africa's new policy for religion and education in relation to attempts to redefine the role of the state in the transition from apartheid to democracy. The policy emerged within a new constitutional framework, which ensured freedom for religious expression and freedom from religious discrimination, but also within the context of state initiatives to affirm cultural diversity and mobilize unifying resources for social transformation. Accordingly, this article examines South Africa's policy for religion and public education as an index for understanding post-apartheid efforts in redefining the state as a constitutional, cultural, and transformative state.

Keywords: culture, diversity, education, human rights, religion, South Africa, state, transformation

Since 1994, when the country emerged from the oppressive, racist era of apartheid to become a unified and democratic nation, South Africa has tested the potential (and limits) of religion in nation building. Adopting a 'cooperative model' for relations between religion and state, the new constitutional order has not created a 'wall of separation', cordoning off privatized religion from the public sphere. Rather, in keeping with the national motto, "Diverse people unite," the post-apartheid state, under the government of the African National

Congress (ANC), has tried to draw upon the resources of the many religions of the country in the national interest. For example, during a busy weekend in September 2003 that was spent visiting religious communities, including the Jewish Board of Deputies, a new Hindu organization, and the Zionist Christian Church, South African President Thabo Mbeki observed: "Given our divided history, religious organizations have an important role to play in the reconstruction and development of our country, especially in the welfare and civil society sectors" (Anonymous 2003).

While seeking to mobilize all the religious constituencies of the country, the post-apartheid state has also implemented a new policy for teaching and learning about religion, which Minister of Education Naledi Pandor identified in 2005 as "an exciting and distinctively South African response to an educational challenge faced by our society." In contradistinction to the policy of the old regime, which had established "Christian National Education," not only in religious education, but also throughout the entire curriculum, the new democratic government sought to redress such religious privileging and discrimination (Kallaway 2002). Basically, the policy distinguished between religious and educational aims, finding that religious instruction and nurture are the province of the family, home, and religious community, while teaching and learning about religion, religions, and religious diversity are important aspects of the school curriculum. A new subject, Religion Education, was designed to achieve specifically educational, rather than religious, goals, while contributing to nation building. As Minister Pandor (2005) explained: "Our educational policy recognizes the difference between religious, theological, or confessional interests, and the educational objectives of Religion Education. While respecting religious interests and valuing religious contributions to our country, the policy charts a course for our schools to make their own, distinctive contribution to teaching and learning about religion in ways that will celebrate our diversity and affirm our national unity" (see Department of Education 2003; Jeenah 2005). Certainly, these engagements with religion—harnessing the potential of religious communities, limiting discrimination on the basis of religion, and expanding the scope of mutual human recognition and understanding in the midst of religious difference—were difficult and problematic, but they grew out of a willingness to take religion seriously as a significant feature of public life.

In return, a variety of religious actors took the new policy for religion and education very seriously, resulting in vigorous controversies and polemics. Christian protectionists, protecting the privilege of the Dutch Reformed Church in the educational policy of the old regime, wanted to preserve the religious character of religious education. Christian Reconstructionists, calling themselves Concerned Christians, but informed by right-wing Christian organizations in the United States, wanted to advance the kingdom of God through religious education. Many other religious voices were heard during this public debate about religion in public education (see Chidester 2002, 2003a). There were expressions of support for the policy from religious leaders, including the National Forum of Religious Leaders, whose chair, Ashwin Trickamjee, observed: "Initially there was some resistance in certain quarters but it's not the case now. The policy is part of a way forward" (Govender 2003). Such expressions of support, however, were drowned out in the media by the volume of organized opposition to the new policy orchestrated by Concerned Christians. Dominating discussion in mainstream media, these Christian voices were further extended through church services and mass rallies, as well as publications in print and on the Internet.

Religious opponents of the new policy warned that removing Christian instruction and Christian worship from public schools would deprive children of divine protection (Atkins 2003), and that asking children to learn about other religions, especially about South Africa's indigenous religious heritage, would expose them to demonic possession (Horn 2003: 62). Although these religious concerns featured prominently in Christian objections to the new policy, what was most remarkable about the controversy was the ways in which Christian opponents asserted expertise in the interpretation of South African constitutional law. In any legal dispute, it has been said, only the lawyers win, but in this public debate about educational policy for religion in South African schools, everyone became a lawyer. Although Christian lawyers certainly had religious objections, which they often articulated, they persistently attacked the government's new policy on the grounds that it violated specific provisions of the Constitution. At this point, without assessing the merits of any of the legal arguments advanced, framers of the South African Constitution, most of whom are still among us, might draw some satisfaction from this fact that all disputants at least agreed to take recourse to the same text—not the Bible, but the Constitution of the Republic of South Africa.

The Constitution, formally adopted in 1996, was the product of a negotiated revolution. Replacing the old apartheid regime's parliamentary supremacy with the supremacy of the rule of law, the new South Africa could be defined, first and foremost, as a constitutional state. In the first instance, therefore, the role of religion in public education had to be clarified in terms of the provisions, but also in the light of the values, enshrined in the Constitution. Provisions for freedom of religion and freedom from discrimination on the basis of religion were supplemented in the Constitution by clauses ensuring the promotion and protection of the rights of linguistic, cultural, and religious communities. At the same time, the text of the Constitution was premised on basic values. Constitutional values, which were essentially devoted to establishing a culture of human rights, were potentially in tension with collective rights asserted by any cultural community. This tension between the commitment to a human-rights culture and the commitment to promote and protect cultural rights, which is implicit in the Constitution, has required the South African state to be both a constitutional and a cultural state. While protecting the cultural integrity of the many, under the auspices of a national commitment to diversity, the state has also engaged in unifying cultural projects.

South Africa's new policy for religion in public education must be located at the intersection of human-rights principles and human-rights culture, between what has been called "rights talk" and "culture talk" (Mamdani 2000). But a third feature of the policy—its engagement with the long, difficult, and contested process of transformation from apartheid oppression to democratic dispensation—is equally crucial. While taking actions to enshrine individual rights and protect collective rights, the South African Constitution embodied a vision for the progressive realization of human potentiality and the progressive transformation of South African society.

Against this background, I want to position South Africa's new policy for religion and education in relation to the state—the constitutional state, the cultural state, and the transformational state. A modern state, as Max Weber (1958: 78) taught us, is the organized exercise of legitimated violence over a territory. All of these features of the state—coercive power, compelling legitimacy, and territorial sovereignty—have lately been called into question. In recent social and cultural analyses of the state, power has been disaggregated into multi-sited processes of governmentality (Foucault 1991), institutionalized functions (Mitchell 2002), and everyday practices (Herzfeld 1992). Legitimacy has been recast as fluid and unstable circulations of imagination (Anderson 1991; Hanson and Stepputat 2001) and even magic (Taussig 1997). Sovereignty has been rendered a social construction (Bierstecker and Weber 1996), critiqued as "organized hypocrisy" (Krasner 1999), reconstructed as spatial (Ferguson and Gupta 2002), and deconstructed as "spectral" (Butler 2004: 61).

In theory and practice, these challenges to the modern state have carried specific force in South Africa. During the anti-apartheid struggle, the legitimacy of the apartheid state was vigorously challenged by liberation movements, international organizations, and religious bodies (Borer 1998). After the democratic elections of 1994, with legitimacy ostensibly underwritten by popular mandate, the post-apartheid state was faced with the challenge of sovereignty (Vale 2003). Becoming a nation just when nations were supposedly going out of style, as national sovereignty was allegedly being swept away by global market forces, the new South Africa was faced with crucial dilemmas of nation building and social cohesion (see Chidester, Dexter, and James 2003). The new democratic government was also confronted with the risk of being captured by the state. In education, for example, the new government's Ministry of Education inherited all of the bureaucratic structures and racist inequities established by the apartheid state. Faced with the monumental task of creating a unified educational system out of this fractured legacy, even the most radical, revolutionary educationalists from the liberation movements soon found themselves "seeing like a state" (Scott 1998).

In my discussion of religion, education, and the South African state, I will be adopting a state-centered perspective on policy while concentrating on official discourse and public debate. Certainly, there are limits to this approach, but I want to highlight the ways in which policy debates about religion in schools figured into the process of imagining a new South Africa. As more than a public-relations exercise in building a new nation as an imagined community, policy for religion and public education engaged the state. It was about nation building, but it was also about state making. As I will argue, these religion and education debates focused public attention on South Africa's new Constitution, the state's commitment to promote and protect diversity, and the new government's promise to advance redress and equity. In other words, these controversies were about defining the constitutional, cultural, and transformational state.

Under the influence of globalizing conditions, we have been led to accept the "myth of the powerless state" (Weiss 1997). But we might also hold out hope for the emergence of the 'transformational state', one that is not essentially or exclusively defined by global market forces (see, for example, Bhaduri 2000). Since 1994, the fate of the new South Africa has been poised between the myth of powerlessness under globalizing conditions and the imperative to transform a racist state into a transformational state. South Africa's new policy for religion and education, I hope to show, is situated in this dilemma, raising the question of the efficacy of the state in advancing human rights, engaging cultural diversity, and progressively transforming society.

The Constitutional State

The Constitution of the previous, apartheid regime explicitly identified South Africa as a "Christian country," which was said to uphold freedom of religion, but was also bound to obey the will of Almighty God. Accordingly, religion was drawn into reinforcing racist legislation and segregation on the basis of racial, ethnic, cultural, linguistic, and religious signs of difference. During the constitutional negotiations of the 1990s, the role of religion was intensely contested, with almost as much attention devoted to the text's symbolic invocation of God as to its substantive provisions for freedom of religious exercise and freedom from religious discrimination. While God was finally included in the preamble—in large part thanks to the fact that the ANC's anthem was the hymn, "Nkosi Sikel' iAfrika" (God Bless Africa)—negotiators worked out a compromise that sought to balance basic human rights with the varied interests of linguistic, cultural, and religious communities (Republic of South Africa 1996a). Section 15 ensured individual freedom of religion and belief, guaranteeing that "[e]veryone has the right to freedom of conscience, religion, thought, belief and opinion." Section 31 ensured collective rights of cultural, religious, and linguistic communities (or an individual's right to freedom of association, depending upon interpretation) by specifying that "[p]ersons belonging to a cultural, religious or linguistic community may not be denied the right, with other members of that community (a) to enjoy their culture, practice their religion and use their language; and (b) to form, join and maintain cultural, religious and linguistic associations and other organs of civil society." These liberty rights, however, were also balanced with equality rights, as Section 9 prohibited unfair discrimination on many grounds, including religion, giving force to the most basic constitutional values of human dignity and equality (see du Plessis 1996, 2001; van der Vyver 2001).

A significant compromise with the Christian nationalism of the previous regime was embedded in the clauses ensuring freedom of religion, belief, and opinion in Section 15. Following the assertion of basic belief rights, this section proceeded to address religious practice: "Religious observances may be conducted at state or state-aided institutions, provided that (a) those observances follow rules made by the appropriate public authorities; (b) they are conducted on an equitable basis; and (c) attendance at them is free and voluntary." From the perspective of ANC negotiators, this inclusion of religious practices in state institutions was not an "establishment" of religion but an engagement with religion by a secular state that was neither religious nor anti-religious (see Sachs 1993). Nevertheless, these constitutional provisions, in particular, provide ample grounds for disputation in response to the new policy for religion and education.

In a democratic and religiously diverse South Africa, the previous regime's system of religious education, with its indoctrination of Christian children and denigration of adherents of other religions, certainly could not be sustained. But what were the alternatives? Preparing for the democratic transition as early as 1992, the National Education Policy Investigation (NEPI) considered the options. In its report on curriculum, NEPI insisted that a democratic South Africa had to abandon the previous system of religious education in which particular religious principles were explicitly taught in Christian religious instruction and implicitly taught throughout the entire curriculum in the name of Christian National Education. As NEPI found, such an agenda for religious education, instruction, or indoctrination established religious discrimination and religious coercion in education.

Recognizing the need for change, NEPI considered three options. First was eliminating religion entirely from the school curriculum. However, NEPI concluded that neglecting such a principal feature of South African life would not do justice to the importance of religious diversity in the nation's history and society. Second was establishing parallel programs in religious instruction, developed by different religious groups. But such a parallel model, entrenching a kind of 'religious apartheid', would still embody religious discrimination and coercion, since all students would be required to study a single-tradition religious education program devoted to particular religious interests. Third was introducing a program of multi-religion education that would teach students *about* religion rather than engaging in the teaching, confession, propagation, or promotion *of* religion. Guided by clear educational objectives, teaching and learning about different religions in public education held out the hope of social benefits such as increased tolerance and understanding of diversity (National Education Coordinating Committee 1992: 74–75; see Chidester et al. 1994). Following the publication of these NEPI findings, debates about religion and public education generally revolved around the question of whether or not a compromise could be worked out that accommodated both the second and third options, mixing separate programs of religious instruction, which serve religious interests in the promotion of a state-sanctioned, implicitly supported set of religions, with teaching and learning about religion, religions, and religious diversity.

In 1998, the minister of education, Sibusiso Bengu (see Weisse 1998), appointed an advisory committee for religious education. At the beginning of four weeks of deliberations, the committee started by reviewing the Constitution; it ended in deadlock. As Janet Stonier (1998), a member of the committee, recalls, the composition of the committee, with a predominance of committed Christians, made it impossible to arrive at a common understanding of religious education, whether it was about educating learners to be religious or educating learners about religion and religions. As a compromise, or contradiction, the centerpiece of this ministerial committee's report was the proposal that local schools should be allowed to choose from a menu of options: teaching learners to be religious, teaching learners about religions, or a combination of both (Department of Education 1999: 5; see Steyn 1999).

Shortly after the publication of this report on religious education, a new minister of education, Kader Asmal, took office. Minister Asmal was committed to addressing the issue of religion and education within the framework of international human rights and constitutional values. Convening a new advisory committee, he insisted that any new policy had to be based on human-rights principles of freedom of religious and other convictions and freedom from religious and other forms of discrimination. As one of the architects and negotiators of the South African constitutional settlement, Asmal was ultimately committed to advancing the values enshrined in the Constitution—"human dignity, equality, and freedom" (Republic of South Africa 1996a). Educational policy, he insisted, had to flow from those essential constitutional values.

Applying constitutional principles and values, this new advisory committee found that the proposed mixture—the teaching *of* religion and the teaching *about* religion—was an educational contradiction rather than a viable compromise. Certainly, it was inconsistent with an international human-rights framework, which has increasingly positioned teaching and learning about religion in the service of the educational mandate, embedded in the Universal Declaration of Human Rights (Art. 26, par. 2), to "promote understanding, tolerance and friendship among all nations, racial or religious groups" (see Andrássy 1995). Under the auspices of the United Nations High Commissioner for Human Rights, the consultative conference on religion in school education that was convened in Madrid during November 2001 found that teaching about religion, rather than religious teaching, held the potential for achieving these goals. By definition, according to Abdelfattah Amor, UN Special Rapporteur on Freedom of Religion or Belief, "Religious Education should be conceived as a tool to transmit knowledge and values pertaining to all religious trends, in an inclusive way, so that individuals realize their being part of the same community and learn to create their own identity in harmony with identities different from their own. As such, religious education radically differs from catechism or theology, defined as the formal study of the nature of God and of the foundations of religious belief, and contributes to the wider framework of education as defined in international standards" (Amor 2001; see Hera and Martínez de Codes 2002). Minister Asmal sought to bring educational policy for religion and education into line with such a human-rights agenda that was international in scope but also embodied in the South African Constitution.

Informed by these principles, and convinced that policy must also be animated by values, Minister Asmal convened an expert panel to identify basic values in South African education, such as equity, tolerance, multi-lingualism, openness, accountability, and social honor (Asmal and James 2002b: 185). In its publication, the *Manifesto on Values, Education, and Democracy*, the Department of Education (2001) first announced its policy of Religion Education. In the revised national curriculum, which was open for public scrutiny and debate, the Department of Education (2002a, 2002b) published the primary educational objective of Religion Education, within a constitutional and human-rights framework: "The learner should be able to demonstrate an active commitment to constitutional rights and social responsibilities and show sensitivity to diverse cultures and belief systems."

Public controversy ensued, raising important issues, not only about educational policy, but also about the spirit of the nation. Clearly, Minister Asmal had resolved the earlier dilemma—teaching of, teaching about—in favor of a policy committed to teaching about religion, religions, and religious diversity in ways that were thoroughly educational but also promised to realize certain social benefits by reducing prejudice, advancing toleration, and expanding respect for difference in a shared society. Of course, this is a lot to expect from education, but it is hard to see how anyone would object to these goals. Yet objections were vigorously registered. Although religious objections were heard, the prevailing strategy of opponents of the new policy was to cite and interpret the provisions of the Constitution. Before assessing the merits of contending interpretations, therefore, we must acknowledge that this public debate about religion and education represented a kind of victory for the Constitution. Within a very short period of time, less than 10 years, the provisions and protections of the new Constitution provided the framework for adjudicating religious interests within a secular state.

Frequently, Christian opponents of the new policy insisted that Minister Asmal had misinterpreted the Constitution. This argument entailed a wonderful irony, because, according to ANC legend, the first draft of what would eventually become the South African Constitution was written by Asmal himself, at his kitchen table in Dublin, with Albie Sachs, who would later become a justice of South Africa's Constitutional Court, while they were in exile during the late 1980s. In basing their arguments on the Constitution, therefore, opponents only reinforced Minister Asmal's contention that policy should be informed by constitutional principles and flow from essential constitutional values.

Constitutional principles, inscribed in specific provisions, posed one kind of problem of interpretation. As noted, Section 15, which ensures freedom of religion and belief, had made provision for religious observances that might include religious instruction, serving specifically religious interests, aims, and objectives, in South African schools. Limiting conditions, however, which were specified in the same section, were open to interpretation.

First, religious activities in schools were to be permitted and protected as long as they "follow rules made by the appropriate public authorities." In this conflict of constitutional interpretation, the minister of education determined that the national Department of Education, guided by constitutional principles and values, was the appropriate public authority. Exercising its authority over public schools, the national department advanced a policy in which religious instruction was the responsibility of the family, home, and religious community, while teaching and learning about religion was the responsibility of the public school. Contesting this interpretation, Christian opponents of the policy, such as the Christian Lawyers Association, argued that the minister of education was not, in fact, the appropriate public authority to determine policy for religion. Local school governing bodies, composed of parents, teachers, and administrators, should be free to determine the religious ethos, observances, and instruction in their schools. Significantly, those who argued this point accepted the way in which the new policy located the religious in the home and the educational in the school. But they tried to leverage this distinction by arguing that parents, responsible for the religious life of their homes, were also key members of school governing bodies that should be able to determine the religious life of local schools (McCafferty 2003).

Second, religious activities in schools were allowed so long as they were "conducted on an equitable basis." The question of equity was much disputed. If a policy of multiple single-faith religious instruction were to be adopted, how could it be carried out equitably? Some religious communities, such as Jews, Muslims, Hindus, Bahai's, and Rastafaris, might find themselves unfairly disadvantaged, while other religious constituencies, whether the old guard of the Dutch Reformed Church or the new evangelical formations of Concerned Christians, might be unfairly privileged in local schools. In the process of providing for single-faith religious instruction, the state inevitably would become entangled in discriminating not only among different religions but also among competing constructions of a single religion. Opponents of the new policy, however, argued that the Constitution did not prevent religious discrimination; it only prevented "unfair" religious discrimination. Preventing a blind person from being a bus driver, as one Christian lawyer argued, might be discrimination, but it could not be considered "unfair" discrimination. Likewise, he argued, the state could engage in religious discrimination, providing separate programs in religious instruction for Christians, Muslims, Jews, Hindus, and others (Atkins 2003). Even academic analysis, reflected in international journals, repeated this allegation that separate religious instruction was "equitable," even if it entrenched religious apartheid in schools, but teaching and learning about religion and religions was not. According to Dickinson and van Vollenhoven (2002: 16): "The change from the Bengo [*sic*] to the Asmal policy seems basically to be one from an equitable religious education that may be offered from the point of view of a particular religion, to a comparative study of different religions."

Third, religious activities were permitted in schools as long as they were "free and voluntary." Opponents of the new policy, trying to retain Christian instruction and worship in the schools, often proposed a "conscience clause," arguing that teachers or pupils could be exempted from these exercises, thereby fulfilling the condition that participation must be free and voluntary. Wrestling with this question, the US Supreme Court, in *Abington Township School District v. Schempp*, 374 US 203 (1963), found that having to exercise such a "conscience clause" already places children in the "path of compulsion" and therefore is not an obvious solution to creating an environment that is "free and voluntary" (see Chidester 1988: 265–268). The new government's policy for religion and education in South Africa argued along these lines, but tried to carry the argument further in advancing a policy based on human dignity, equality, and freedom. If a pupil has to invoke a "conscience clause," then that pupil's freedom of conscience, belief, or religion has already been violated. The best policy, therefore, would create an educational environment that did not advance potentially divisive religious interests. Instead, freely and voluntarily, everyone could participate in learning about religion and religions in South Africa and the world.

In the vigorous public debate over the new policy, for all of its heat, some illumination was gained by the fact that even those who rejected the policy accepted the Constitution. Legal arguments, in the process, were often inflected by specific religious commitments. With respect to proper authority, for example, Christian opponents of the new policy could argue, on legal grounds, that the South African Schools Act of 1996 had vested authority in school governing bodies and therefore in parents, who should have the right to determine the religious ethos of public schools, while also observing, religiously, that God had ordained that parents should have authority over their children. At the same time, while demanding, on religious grounds, certain kinds of Christian instruction in schools, they could invoke the constitutional principle of equity to allow for the extension of similar privileges to other religions (as long as they could ensure that Christian religious education would teach about other religions from a Christian perspective) (Malherbe 2003; see also Malherbe 2000, 2002). Although certain aspects of the debate bore traces of influence from right-wing Christians in the United States, such as the recurring argument that the "humanistic" approach to teaching and learning about religions was itself a religion, the application of this argument to the Constitution, proposing that the imposition of this secular religion violated the provision that religious observances must be free and voluntary, suggested that the South African Constitution was actually winning in these debates.

The Cultural State

As noted, the new South African constitutional order was born out of the compromise, or contradiction, implicit in advancing a unified democratic culture of human rights while promising the promotion and protection of a diversity of cultural rights. Distilled into a national motto, "Unity in diversity," this arrangement remains a dilemma. On the one hand, the new constitutional order is dedicated to creating a shared, common culture, a human-rights culture, with a statutory commission, the South African Human Rights Commission, explicitly charged by the Constitution with the responsibility of promoting a "culture of human rights" (Sections 184, 234). In its interpretations of the Constitution, the Constitutional Court has used the language of culture, referring, for example, to "the development of a democratic culture" (2002 5 SA 401 (CC) par. 24) or the need to develop a "culture of respect for human life and dignity" (2002 4 SA 613 (CC) par. 6) (Constitutional Court 2006). On the other hand, the new constitutional order, committed to protecting and promoting the integrity of cultural communities, finds the diversity of "cultural life" worthy of affirmation (Sections 30, 31). Accordingly, the Constitution established a body, the Commission for the Promotion and Protection of the Rights of Linguistic, Cultural, and Religious Communities. As one of six statutory commissions, including the Truth and Reconciliation Commission, mandated by the Constitution, this commission for attending to collective, cultural rights was the last to be formed. It was not until 2002 that it was passed into law (Republic of South Africa 2002), to be composed the following year. In the interim, the South African government was engaged in cultural work, with an emphasis on unifying a divided society.

The new policy for religion and education was formulated in this context as an initiative of the cultural state. Essentially, the policy was a cultural project about culture, seeking to create an attitude of informed respect for the many religious cultures of South Africa. As part of the Department of Education's major cultural project, the Values in Education Initiative, attention to religion was framed by reflection on values. Although Minister of Education Asmal aggressively drove this campaign for identifying, clarifying, and actualizing basic values in South African education, this attention to values went back to the presidency of Nelson Mandela, who in 1997 initiated the campaign for advancing a "Culture of Learning, Teaching, and Service." In these efforts, the South African state intervened directly in the arena of culture, creating culture—a learning culture, a democratic culture, and a human-rights culture—while seeking to draw support from people of all the many cultures of the country.

Affirming unity in diversity, the cultural state has had to deal with difficult questions of linguistic, cultural, and religious diversity in many areas of South African public life. For example, in public broadcasting, a particular kind of Christian privilege, especially enjoyed by the Dutch Reformed Church, was replaced by a new policy premised on equity. Here equity was interpreted as 'parity of esteem', in which all religious communities were in principle granted equal respect but differential allocations of broadcasting time based on calculations, subject to adjustment, of the country's religious demography. Although all religions were held in equal esteem, not all received equal time on television and radio after 70 percent of religious broadcasting had been allocated to programming for the Christian majority. Independent enterprises, such as international Christian television or local Muslim radio, entered the field of religious broadcasting to complicate this formula (Hackett 2006; Haron 2002). But the South African Broadcasting Corporation worked out a policy—parity of esteem, access by demography—for allocating time and space for religion in the media.

This formula, it should be noted, was not adopted in the policy for religion in education. Here the state was not interested in using schools as media for broadcasting religious programming. Instead, the state's policy distinguished between the time and space of the school, removing religious programming from the time schedule of the daily curriculum, but allowing schools to make space available, after hours, for religious activity. Although critics might find inconsistency in these policies for media and schools, they were formulated, with considerable deliberation and public participation, in different arenas of public life. The dissimilar outcomes of these deliberations are not necessarily contradictory. In public broadcasting, adherents of the majority religion might warrant receiving greater time and space to address the religious interests of the majority. In public education, however, on educational grounds, adherents of the majority religion might need greater exposure to the beliefs and practices of other religions in order to develop understanding and respect for religious diversity.

As a constitutional state, but also as a cultural state, the new South Africa has had to contend with such dilemmas in every arena of public life. In it cultural interventions, the state has deployed powerful unifying metaphors, such as the 'Rainbow Nation' or the 'African Renaissance', in the interests of creating a unifying South African culture. As a cultural project, the African Renaissance is particularly significant, both for its potential and for its problems in providing a stable symbolic underpinning for the cultural state.

In South Africa, the African Renaissance is premised on a basic cultural value, *ubuntu*, which has been rendered as meaning anything from individual integrity, or humanness, to collective solidarity, since humans *are* human only in and through their relations with other humans. This value or virtue of *ubuntu* is firmly enshrined in the South African Constitution. In seeking to identify and clarify basic values in education, the Department of Education's *Manifesto on Values in Education* also ascribed to *ubuntu*. In our commodifying era, the fact that *ubuntu* has been exploited by any number of entrepreneurial or commercial ventures should not necessarily discount its relevance in referencing a basic human value. However, invoking *ubuntu*, advocates of the African Renaissance, including South African President Mbeki, have often discounted the small-scale, village-based, and religious contexts in which such a notion of humanness might have traditionally made sense. Accordingly, adherents of indigenous African religion, such as Nokuzola Mndende (1998, 1999), have argued that African religion, which was forced underground during the apartheid era, still suffers unfair discrimination in the new South Africa.

Christian opponents of the new educational policy have objected to the inclusion of indigenous African religion. For example, Irmhild H. Horn, professor of primary school education at the University of South Africa, argued in a South African academic journal (2003: 52), the *Journal for Christian Scholarship*, that African traditional religion (ATR), like contemporary postmodernism, is a threat to Bible-based Christianity. "Contemporary Africa," she noted, "is seeking to revive and reinstate its traditional primal worldview." Drawing on recent Christian polemics against indigenous African religion (Gehman 1990; Nyirango 1997; Turaki 1999), Professor Horn (2003: 64) provided a profile of ATR as a world-view based on animism, fetishism, and collectivism. "Both ATR and postmodernism," she asserted, "regard humans as primarily social beings." Horn accused this collectivist world-view of cultivating a "spiritual openness," whether based on primal religion or the postmodern "denial of truth," that runs contrary to the biblically informed spiritual discernment that is required of Christians. Objecting to the revival of indigenous religion among Africans, Horn (ibid.: 60) also complains: "Many Westerners, like many black Africans, are seeking to revitalize primal beliefs. The Internet, television, films, books and games are primary vehicles for promoting primal beliefs and practices." The inclusion of ATR in Religion Education, she insisted, was symptomatic of both African religious revival and New Age spirituality.

Professor Horn supplemented her religious objections with reflection on pedagogical method. In South African educational reforms of the 1990s, the entire curriculum had adopted the theory and methods of 'outcomes-based education' (OBE). In principle, OBE promised a student-centered, lively, engaging, and participatory approach to teaching and learning (Coetzer 2001). Horn (2003: 62–63) worried that such an application, with its emphasis on participation, would expose students to dangerous contact with spirits. "The OBE-approach favours experience and active participation," she noted. "It is therefore quite conceivable that children will, for example, participate in dances that induce spirit possession." Students ran the risk, she warned, not only of learning about an indigenous African world-view, but of participating in spiritual practices based on magic and ultimately on Satanism, because magic, she observed, "always has Satan as its source."

Clearly, Horn had strong religious objections to the new policy for teaching and learning about religion, religions, and religious diversity in South African schools. As a professor of education, she could not be expected to help prepare teachers for the challenges of the new curriculum. Although she objected to the inclusion of indigenous African religion, Horn also attacked other religions, having achieved some notoriety in the popular press in 2001 by claiming that Hindu meditation practices "encourage psychological escapism and ultimately schizophrenia" (Naidu 2001). In her article in the *Journal for Christian Scholarship*, Horn (2003) was most concerned with the consideration of ATR in Religion Education. She sought to counter its "animistic" world-view by advocating the teaching of "Intelligent Design" by a supreme God, although "Satan is prince of this world," and to counter its "collectivism" by advocating the theocratic Christian Reconstruction of Rousas John Rushdoony as the best formula for religion and society. All of these religious concerns, however, were orchestrated against the use of education—and especially Religion Education—in the nation-building projects of a new South Africa. "In the name of unity and nation-building," Horn concluded, "our young are being influenced to accept unbiblical ideas and practices, even those that are expressly forbidden in the Bible" (ibid.: 65).

In seeking to advance a human-rights culture, the South African state was engaged in a range of cultural work. The challenge of giving substance to the motto, "Diverse people unite," required difficult negotiations between adherents of differing linguistic, cultural, and religious interests and advocates of national unity. For the most part, these cultural negotiations, like the constitutional negotiations, produced workable compromises. In the case of the new policy for religion in public education, as Ashwin Trikamjee observed on behalf of the National Religious Leaders Forum, South Africa had found a "way forward"

(Naidu 2001). An ethos of tolerance was an important part of this human-rights culture, fulfilling the mandate of the Universal Declaration of Human Rights that education should advance civil toleration, mutual understanding, and even friendship among religions, even though Christian educators, such as Professor Horn, might contest this understanding of toleration. "There will always be a chasm between religions," Trikamjee maintained. "Tolerance is about agreeing to differ" (Naidu 2001; see Gouws and du Plessis 2000).

The cultural politics of the new South Africa, however, was not only about creating an environment of civil toleration in which people could live together despite their differences. The new Constitution had also mandated a politics and poetics of transformation—a politics based on the progressive realization of socio-economic rights and a poetics of memory and imagination, remembering the inequities of the past, redressing them in the present, and ensuring that they would never happen in the future. The Constitution's preamble, announcing a solemn undertaking to "[h]eal the divisions of the past and establish a society based on democratic values, social justice and fundamental human rights" (Republic of South Africa 1996a), introduced the new South Africa to the world as a transformational state.

The Transformational State

According to Constitutional Court Justice Kate O'Regan, the South African Constitution is not a description of South African society. "On the contrary," she observed (2002: 165), "it is a Constitution that compels transformation. The Constitution recognizes that for its vision to be attained, the deep patterns of inequality that scar our society, and that are the legacies of apartheid and colonialism, need to be addressed urgently. Nowhere are these scars more marked or more painful than in the education sector."

As part of the Values in Education Initiative, the new policy for religion in public education was one of many strategies, including anti-racist education, anti-sexist education, and revitalizing teaching and learning about history, within a coordinated educational agenda for transformation. The entire educational system, of course, was undergoing dramatic change, moving from a racially segregated, fragmented system to a unified national department setting policy for nine new provincial departments. As one compromise of the negotiated settlement of the 1990s, considerable autonomy had been devolved to provinces for the management of education. In the new arrangement, the national minister of education had direct responsibility for higher education but was limited to providing policy guidelines and perhaps moral leadership in exercising authority over schools. As minister of education from 1999 to 2003, Kader Asmal took the role of moral engagement seriously, seeing educational policy as a crucial arena for advancing the transformational values of the Constitution, and insisting that schools must "reflect a South African identity in their culture, ethos, sport and teaching philosophy and practice" (Pretorius 2000: 2). Minister Asmal understood South African "identity," in the first instance, as derived from the Constitution, but also as drawn from the country's rich diversity. As a strategy for teaching diversity and fostering unity, Religion Education was introduced by his department as a subject that would "teach students about a world of religious diversity, and, at the same time, encourage them to think in terms of a new national unity in South Africa." Here was a transformational strategy for "affirming and celebrating unity in diversity" (Department of Education 2001: 45).

Embedded in this educational transformation, the new policy for religion in education also intersected with a variety of transformational initiatives in public education. On the one hand, the state engaged in public ethics, seeking to instill (or revive) moral values in its citizens. South Africa's National Crime Prevention Strategy of 1996 included educational proposals, a School Education Programme, which would focus on "values," and a Public Education Programme for the "creation of strong community values and low tolerance for criminal behaviour" (Republic of South Africa 1996b). While President Nelson Mandela (2003: 165) emphasized the theme of "moral regeneration," calling on South Africans to "firm up the moral fibre of our nation," in October 1998 the ANC convened a "Moral Summit," bringing together political and religious leaders to plan a campaign for public morality. Under the presidency of Thabo Mbeki, this campaign was eventually formalized as the Moral Regeneration Movement (MRM), which was launched in April 2002. This effort in public moral education maintained a dual focus in attending to the moral values of citizens, which had been part of the crime-prevention strategy, and insisting on the moral integrity of leaders in business, politics, and government. Seeking support from the leadership of all religious communities, the MRM also stressed the "moral" value of national unity by insisting that "moral regeneration must aim at fostering greater religious tolerance and co-operation for moral renewal" (Rauch 2005).

In counterpoint to this movement for public morality, the South African government undertook a new initiative in public ritual that was anchored in a new sacred site, Freedom Park. As a Presidential Legacy Project, with a mandate to memorialize the struggle for liberation, Freedom Park features a shrine, Isivivane, for the spirits of all the heroes and heroines who have sacrificed their lives for freedom. Adjacent to the Voortrekker Monument, the monumental shrine to white Afrikaner nationalism, this new ceremonial complex represented a ritualized bridge from the cultural nationalism of the old regime to the cultural nationalism of the new government. Other design features of Freedom Park—a Wall of Remembrance, a museum of 3.6 billion years of South African history, and a Pan-African archive—were being positioned to do significant symbolic, cultural, and religious work. Although the site was planned for completion in 2009, by 2005 it was already actively involved in public ritual. As a heritage site for pilgrimage, drawing visitors into its architecture of memory, which was explicitly defined as a "sacred place," Freedom Park was also a missionary project, going out to perform new purification rituals—cleansing, healing, and symbolic reparations ceremonies—in every province within South Africa and even in some neighboring countries that had been frontline states in the struggle against apartheid (Freedom Park 2005).

Public morality, public ritual—these initiatives of the transformational state were addressed to the spirit of the nation, as if nineteenth-century historian Ernest Renan (1990) had been right in defining a nation as "a soul, a spiritual principle." While trying to transform the material conditions of the African majority, who had suffered under the racist exclusions and extractions of apartheid, the new South African government, initially through a policy known as the Reconstruction and Development Programme (RDP), embarked on a range of essentially spiritual projects in advancing what President Mandela (2003: 170) called the "RDP of the soul." Under the presidency of Mbeki, this spiritual work has generally been carried out in the name of an African Renaissance. But his presidential legacy project, Freedom Park, could be seen as the spiritual heir to South Africa's Truth and Reconciliation Commission, which its chair, Archbishop Desmond Tutu (1995), proclaimed as not merely a legal mechanism for adjudicating amnesty, but also a public ritual, a "corporate nationwide process of healing through contrition, confession and forgiveness."

Mandated by the Constitution, these transformational initiatives of healing divisions and creating unity informed a variety of public projects, including policy in public education. As we have seen, opponents of the new policy for religion objected on both religious and political grounds, opposing what they regarded as "state interference" with religious freedom (Snyman 2003) and state manipulation of religion for national "unity and nation-building" (Horn 2003: 65). During the debate about policy for religion in public education, transformation was intensely contested. In terms of the new curriculum, the controversy seems to have been exaggerated, since very little time was actually allocated to this new subject—Religion Education—dedicated to teaching and learning about religion, religions, and religious diversity but also to advancing transformational goals of unity, based on mutual understanding in the midst of religious diversity. In Grades R (reception age) to 9, the learning area of Life Orientation, which included four outcomes—Health Promotion, Social Development, Personal Development, and Physical Development and Movement—was allocated 8 percent of the teaching time out of the total curriculum. As one of four outcomes in Life Orientation, Social Development could be expected to account for 2 percent of teaching time. As one in four assessment standards within Social Development, the new and contested subject, Religion Education, ended up accounting for perhaps 0.5 percent of the overall curriculum. Although these calculations cannot be applied mechanically, we can only conclude that Religion Education, the focus of so much controversy, actually comprised only a very small part of the general curriculum in South African schools.

Conclusions

So, in the end—if we have reached the end, with the adoption of a new policy in 2003 and the implementation of a new curriculum in 2006—has all of this controversy been over almost nothing? Was it merely a distraction? Linda Chisholm (2003: 1), who chaired the national curricular review committee, has suggested that the policy regarding religion education galvanized conservative objections, thereby deflecting attention from broader changes in the curriculum. However, as I have suggested, debates about the policy for religion in public education raised the national question by focusing attention on both religious freedom and educational transformation. Guaranteed by the Constitution, freedom of religion has not been tested very extensively by the Constitutional Court. Specific cases have dealt with the constitutionality of banning alcohol sales on Sunday (upheld) and allowing cannabis use for Rastafari (denied). A Christian school was denied its claim to be exercising a religious right to exact corporal punishment on children, because this practice contravened the right to human dignity and the right to security of the person, while a Muslim mosque was denied the right to broadcast the call to prayer by loudspeakers, based on the sanctity of contract, because it had previously signed an agreement that it would not (du Plessis 2000). Although the new policy has not been challenged in the Constitutional Court, we have seen that even the most ardent religious opponents base their opposition, and therefore their definition of religious freedom, on the new South African Constitution.

Certainly, other constructions of religious freedom have entered the debate. For example, Pieter Coertzen (2002: 190), professor of church history and church polity at the University of Stellenbosch, invoked the authority of the unanimous Declaration of the Reformed Ecumenical Synod of 1949 for an understanding of "freedom of religion and the task of the state in a plural society," insisting that "it is the task of the state to guarantee for the church to be able to preach the Gospel; to serve God with a free conscience according to his Word; and to resist and prevent any anti-Christian power which would threaten the church in the exercise of its holy ministrations." Accordingly, Professor Coertzen found that the new policy was a violation of religious freedom, because the church's "religious education of its members either by office bearers of the church itself or by school teachers approved by the church is certainly part of these holy ministrations of the church" (ibid.: 194). However, as noted, most Christian opposition to the new policy maneuvered within the terrain established by the Constitution for a secular state, which might very well cooperate with religion but is not bound to advance the "holy ministrations" of any religion.

Controversy over the new policy, therefore, reaffirmed the constitutional state. But it also raised questions about education, even about pedagogy. While the most vocal opponents of the new policy insisted that teaching and learning about religions should not be included in the curriculum, usually for religious reasons, some argued on pedagogical grounds that it simply cannot be done: teachers cannot teach it, and students cannot learn it. Nevertheless, researchers in South Africa have found that teachers in fact can teach about religion, religions, and religious diversity (Ferguson and Roux 2003a, 2003b), and students can learn together in multi-religious classrooms (Matsaung 2003). Although considerable work remained to be done, especially with respect to teacher training, an enormous amount of educational groundwork had gone into responding to the challenge of Religion Education. Furthermore, educators in the academic study of religion had succeeded in motivating the introduction in 2006 of a new examinable subject, Religion Studies, for the higher grades 10–12 (Department of Education 2005).

These educational innovations within South Africa bore traces of a distinctive local history, from colonialism through apartheid, but they also resembled developments elsewhere in Africa—for example, in Zambia (Carmody 2003), Malawi (Jarhall 2001), and Zimbabwe (Ndlovu 2004)—in moving from a 'religious' to an 'educational' understanding of religious education, in the process creating curricula that are designed for diversity but also seek out indigenous African grounds for establishing national unity. Religious diversity, of course, can mean very different things in different places, registering, for example, as civil accommodation in the United States of the 1950s (Herberg 1955) or as a clash of cultures at the beginning of the twenty-first century (Huntington 1996). The tension, creative or conflictual, between religious diversity and national unity is inflected differently all over the world, especially in negotiating the meaning—as well as the rights and responsibilities—of citizenship (Chidester 2003b). Creating consultative mechanisms for dealing with diversity, such as the National Religious Leaders Forum or the Commission for the Promotion and Protection of the Rights of Linguistic, Cultural, and Religious Rights, the South African state has also engaged in transformative projects for memory and memorialization, for values and moral renewal, for effecting spiritual healing of the past and advancing an African Renaissance for the future.

All of these initiatives, as we have seen, are mandated by the South African Constitution. However, while the supremacy of the Constitution, as the rule of law, became established in South Africa within a remarkably short period of time, the cultural and transformational politics of the country have persisted in exposing the tensions between the many and the one, between the old and the new, in an emerging nation. Should these strains be considered creative tensions or crippling contradictions? Critics of the new policy, especially critics linked with transnational conservative Christian organizations, have attacked what they see as a globalizing, homogenizing force exercised by the South African state, whether that force be disguised as a liberal 'secular humanism' or as a syncretistic 'interfaith religion'. Essentially, these religious critics have argued that the state has exceeded its sovereignty by interfering with religion. At the same time, social and cultural critics who argue that the South African state has sold out its sovereignty to a globalizing neo-liberal economic agenda might see the new policy for religion and education, along with state initiatives for moral regeneration and ritualized solidarity, as providing ideological support for the advent of millennial capitalism (Comaroff and Comaroff 2001). The policy's grounding in universal human rights and civil toleration, it might be argued, have made it congruent with the demands for global homogeneity in the "religion of the market" (see Chidester 2005: 131–149).

These critiques, from the Right and the Left, strangely mirror each other in discerning that global forces have had an impact on national policy. Certainly, globalizing conditions have affected policy, but South African educators have been struggling primarily to work out a distinctive strategy of redress and equity. In religion education, redress has required creating space for teaching and learning about religious forms of life that had been denied and excluded by the Christian educational policy of the apartheid regime. Equity has required creating space for teaching and learning about religious identity and difference in ways that are consistent with the inclusive citizenship of a new democratic state. As I have recounted, arriving at a new policy for religion and education has been a slow and contested process, extending from the ANC's national policy investigations at the beginning of the 1990s, through cycles of controversy, to parliamentary promulgation in 2003. Implementation of the policy, which has involved formulating qualification frameworks, designing curricula, and developing textbooks and teaching materials, has proceeded more quickly, but many challenges remain, especially the challenge of enabling teachers to respond confidently and creatively to the new policy. Ultimately, in religion education, as in other curricular innovations, the promises of the constitutional, cultural, and transformational state will be worked out in detail, day by day, in the classroom.

David Chidester is Professor of Religious Studies, Head of the Department of Religious Studies, and Director of the Institute for Comparative Religion in Southern Africa at the University of Cape Town. He has also served as Special Advisor to the Minister of Education and Visiting Fellow with the Human Sciences Research Council in South Africa. He is the author or editor over 20 books in North American studies, South African studies, and comparative religion, including *Salvation and Suicide: Jim Jones, the Peoples Temple, and Jonestown* (1988; rev. ed. 2003), *Savage Systems: Colonialism and Comparative Religion in Southern Africa* (1996), *Christianity: A Global History* (2000), *Nelson Mandela: In His Own Words* (2004), and *Authentic Fakes: Religion and American Popular Culture* (2005). Chidester received the American Academy of Religion's Award for Excellence in Religious Studies in 1990 and 1997 and the Alan J. Pifer Award for Social Research in 2005.

References

Amor, Abdelfattah. 2001. *The Role of Religious Education in the Pursuit of Tolerance and Non-Discrimination*. Geneva: United Nations, Office of the High Commissioner for Human Rights. http://www.unhchr.ch/html/menu2/7/b/cfedu-basicdoc.htm (accessed 20 January 2006).

Anderson, Benedict. 1991. *Imagined Communities: Reflections on the Origins and Spread of Nationalism*. London: Verso.

Andrássy, György. 1995. "Religious Education and State Schools." *History of European Ideas* 20, nos. 4–6: 739–744.

Anonymous. 2003. "Religions 'Rebuilding SA' Mbeki." *Bua News*, 9 September.

Asmal, Kader, and Wilmot James, eds. 2002a. *Spirit of the Nation: Reflections on South Africa's Educational Ethos*. Pretoria: Human Sciences Research Council.

______. 2002b. "Education and Democracy in South Africa." Pp. 174–189 in Asmal and James 2002a.

Atkins, Michael John. 2003. "Submission on Policy: Religion in Education." *Christian Lawyers Association*. http://www.cla.org.za/index.php? = 25 (accessed 23 December 2005).
Bhaduri, Amit. 2000. "Reflections on the Economic Role of the Transformational State." In *On the Border of Economic Theory and History*. New York: Oxford University Press.
Bierstecker, Thomas J., and Cynthia Weber, eds. 1996. *State Sovereignty as Social Construct*. Cambridge: Cambridge University Press.
Borer, Tristan Anne. 1998. *Challenging the State: Churches as Political Actors in South Africa, 1980–1994*. Notre Dame: University of Notre Dame Press.
Butler, Judith. 2004. *Precarious Life: The Powers of Mourning and Violence*. London: Verso.
Carmody, Brendan. 2003. "Religious Education and Pluralism in Zambia." *Religious Education* 98, no. 2: 139–154.
Chidester, David. 1988. *Patterns of Power: Religion and Politics in American Culture*. Englewood Cliffs, NJ: Prentice-Hall.
______. 2002. "Religion Education: Learning about Religion, Religions, and Religions Diversity." Pp. 91–102 in Asmal and James 2002a.
______. 2003a. "Religion Education in South Africa: Teaching and Learning about Religion, Religions, and Religious Diversity." *British Journal of Religious Education* 25, no. 4: 261–278.
______. 2003b. "Global Citizenship, Cultural Citizenship, and World Religions in Religion Education." Pp. 31–50 in *International Perspectives on Citizenship, Education, and Religious Diversity*, ed. Robert Jackson. London: Routledge.
______. 2005. *Authentic Fakes: Religion and American Popular Culture*. Berkeley: University of California Press.
Chidester, David, Phillip Dexter, and Wilmot James, eds. 2003. *What Holds Us Together: Social Cohesion in South Africa*. Cape Town: HSRC Press.
Chidester, David, Gordon Mitchell, Isabel Apawo Phiri, and A. Rashied Omar. 1994. *Religion in Public Education: Options for a New South Africa*. Cape Town: UCT Press.
Chisholm, Linda. 2003. "The Politics of Curriculum Review and Revision in South Africa." *Human Sciences Research Council*. http://www.hsrc.ac.za/research/output/outputDocuments/2285_Chisholm_PoliticsofCurriculumReview.pdf (accessed 10 June 2006).
Coertzen, Pieter. 2002. "Freedom of Religion and Religious Education in a Pluralistic Society." *Dutch Reformed Theological Journal/Nederduitse Gereformeerde Teologiese Tydsrkif* 43, nos. 1–2: 185–196.
Coetzer, I. A. 2001. "A Survey and Appraisal of Outcomes-Based Education (OBE) in South Africa." *Educare* 30, nos. 1–2: 73–93.
Comaroff, Jean, and John Comaroff. 2001. "Millennial Capitalism: First Thoughts on a Second Coming." Pp. 1–56 in *Millennial Capitalism and the Culture of Neoliberalism*, ed. Jean Comaroff and John Comaroff. Durham, NC: Duke University Press.
Constitutional Court. 2006. "Constitutional Court of South Africa's Website." http://www.constitutionalcourt.org.za/site/home.htm (accessed 19 January 2006).
Department of Education (of South Africa). 1999. *Religion in Curriculum 2005: Report of the Ministerial Committee on Religious Education*. Pretoria: Department of Education.
______. 2001. "Introducing Religion Education into Schools." Pp. 43–45 in *Manifesto on Values, Education, and Democracy*. Pretoria: Department of Education.
______. 2002a. *Revised National Curriculum Statement Grades R–9*. http://education.pwv.gov.za/DoE_Sites/Curriculum/Final%20curriculum/policy/English/life%20orientation%2015-5-02.pdf (accessed 7 July 2005).
______. 2002b. *National Curriculum Statement Grades 10–12, Life Orientation*. http://education.pwv.gov.za/DoE_Sites/FET_Folder/FET_schools/ncs/default.htm (accessed 7 July 2005).
______. 2003. *National Policy on Religion and Education*, 12 September. http://www.info.gov.za/gazette/notices/2003/25459.pdf (accessed 18 January 2006).
______. 2005. *National Curriculum Statement—Religion Studies*. http://www.education.gov.za/mainActivities.asp?src = rdoc&xsrc = FET%20In%20Schools (accessed 17 January 2006).
Dickinson, Greg, and Willem van Vollenhoven. 2002. "Religion in Public Schools: Comparative Images of Canada and South Africa." *Perspectives in Education* 20, no. 3: 1–19.

du Plessis, Lourens M. 1996. "Religious Human Rights in South Africa." In *Religious Human Rights in Global Perspective: Legal Perspectives*, ed. Johan D. van der Vyver and John Witte, Jr. The Hague: Martinus Nijhoff.

______. 2000. "Doing Damage to Religious Freedom: Discussion of the High Court Decision of *Christian Education South Africa v. Minister of Education of the Government of the Republic of South Africa 1999*. BCLR 951 (SE)." *Stellenbosch Law Review* 2: 295–305.

______. 2001. "Freedom *of* or Freedom *from* Religion? An Overview of Issues Pertinent to the Constitutional Protection of Religious Rights and Freedom in 'the New South Africa.'" *Brigham Young University Law Review* 4: 439–466.

Ferguson, James, and Akhil Gupta. 2002. "Spatializing States: Toward an Ethonography of Neoliberal Governmentality." *American Ethnologist* 29: 981–1002.

Ferguson, René, and Cornelia Roux. 2003a. "Teacher Participation in Facilitating Beliefs and Values in Life Orientation Programmes: Reflections on a Research Project." *South African Journal of Education* 23, no. 4: 272–275.

______. 2003b. "Mediation in the Context of Teaching and Learning about Religions in Tertiary Education." *South African Journal of Education* 23, no. 4: 292–296.

Foucault, Michel. 1991. "Governmentality." Pp. 87–104 in *The Foucault Effect: Studies in Governmentality*, ed. Graham Burchell, Colin Gordon, and Peter Miller. Chicago: University of Chicago Press.

Freedom Park. 2005. "The Freedom Park Heals and Reconciles the South African Nation." http://www.freedompark.co.za/index.php (accessed 20 January 2006).

Gehman, Richard J. 1990. *African Traditional Religion in Biblical Perspective*. Kijabe, Kenya: Kesho.

Gouws, Amanda, and Laurens M. du Plessis. 2000. "The Relationship between Political Tolerance and Religion: The Case of South Africa." *Emory International Law Review* 14, no. 2: 657–698.

Govender, Peroshni. 2003. "New Religious Education Aims to Expose Children to All the Major Faiths." *Cape Times*, 9 September.

Hackett, Rosalind I. J. 2006. "Mediated Religion in South Africa: Balancing Airtime and Rights Claims." Pp. 166–187 in *Religion, Media, and the Public Sphere*, ed. Birgit Meyer and Annelies Moors. Bloomington: Indiana University Press.

Hanson, Thomas, and Finn Stepputat, eds. 2001. *States of Imagination: Ethnographic Explorations of the Postcolonial* State. Durham, NC: Duke University Press.

Haron, Muhammed. 2002. "The South African Muslim Making (Air)Waves during the Period of Transformation." *Journal for the Study of Religion* 15, no. 2: 111–144.

Hera, Alberto de la, and Rosa María Martínez de Codes, eds. 2002. *La libertad religiosa en la educación escolar: Conferencia internacional consultiva de naciones unidas, Madrid, 23–25 Noviembre 2001*. Madrid: Ministry of Justice.

Herberg, Will. 1955. *Protestant, Catholic, Jew*. Garden City, NY: Doubleday.

Herzfeld, Michael. 1992. *The Social Production of Indifference: Exploring the Roots of Western Bureaucracy*. Oxford: Berg.

Horn, Irmhild H. 2003. "African Traditional Religion, Western Religious Shifts and Contemporary Education." *Journal for Christian Scholarship/Tydskrif vir Christelike Wetenskap* 39, nos. 3–4: 51–66.

Huntington, Samuel. 1996. *The Clash of Civilizations and the Remaking of World Order*. New York: Simon & Schuster.

Jarhall, Jessica Olausson. 2001. *A Look at Changes in Primary Religious Education in Malawi from a Swedish Perspective*. Linköping Studies in Religion and Religious Education, No. 3, Linköping University Electronic Press. http://www.ep.liu.se/ea/rel/2001/003/rel003-contents.pdf (accessed 8 January 2006).

Jeenah, Na'eem. 2005. *Religion and Schools*. Ed. Brian Ramadiro and Salim Vally. Johannesburg: Education Rights Project. http://naeemjeenah.shams.za.org/religion-schools.pdf (accessed 10 January 2006).

Kallaway, Peter, ed. 2002. *The History of Education under Apartheid, 1948–1994*. Cape Town: Maskew Miller Longman.

Krasner, Stephen. 1999. *Sovereignty: Organized Hypocrisy.* Princeton, NJ: Princeton University Press.
Malherbe, Rassie. 2000. "A Fresh Start I: Education Rights in South Africa." *European Journal for Education Law and Policy* 4: 49–55.
______. 2002. "The Constitutionality of Government Policy Relating to the Conduct of Religious Observances in Public Schools." *Journal of South African Law/Tydskrif vir die Suid-Afrikaanse Reg* 3: 391–418.
______. 2003. "Comments on Policy on Religion in Education: Draft 20 June 2003." *United Christian Action.* http://www.christianaction.org.za/media_egroups/uca_2003-07-04.htm (accessed 10 January 2006).
Mamdani, Mahmood, ed. 2000. *Beyond Rights Talk and Culture Talk: Comparative Essays on the Politics of Rights and Culture.* Cape Town: David Philip.
Mandela, Nelson. 2003. *Nelson Mandela: In His Own Words.* Ed. Kader Asmal, David Chidester, and Wilmot James. New York: Little, Brown.
Matsaung, Lesiba E. 2003. "The Teaching of Religious Education in Multi-Religious Classes: Is It a Problem to Students?" *Educational Research* 45, no. 1: 79–82.
McCafferty, Rob. 2003. "Religion Education is the Responsibility of the Family." *Christian Action for Reformation and Revival Magazine* 3. http://www.christianaction.org.za/articles_ca/2003-3-Religion_Education.htm (accessed 18 January 2006).
Mitchell, Timothy. 2002. *Rule of Experts: Egypt, Techno-politics, Modernity.* Berkeley: University of California Press.
Mndende, Nokuzola. 1998. "From Underground Praxis to Recognized Religion: Challenges Facing African Religions." *Journal for the Study of Religion* 11, no. 2: 115–124.
______. 1999. "From Racial Oppression to Religious Oppression: African Religion in the New South Africa." Pp. 143–156 in Walsh and Kaufmann 1999.
Naidu, Buddy. 2001. "Hindus labeled Heathens: University of SA Lecturer Claims Yoga Could Cause Mental Derangement." *Sunday Times*, 1 July. http://www.suntimes.co.za/2001/07/01/news/durban/ndbn02.htm (accessed 15 January 2006).
National Education Coordinating Committee. 1992. *Curriculum: Report of the National Education Policy Investigation Curriculum Research Group.* Cape Town: Oxford University Press.
Ndlovu, Lovemore. 2004. "Religious Education in Zimbabwe Secondary Schools: The Quest for a Multi-Faith Approach." PhD diss., University of South Africa.
Nyirongo, Lenard. 1997. *The Gods of Africa or the God of the Bible? The Snares of African Traditional Religion in Biblical Perspective.* Potchefstroom: University of Potchefstroom.
O'Regan, Kate. 2002. "Equality: Constitutional Imperatives." Pp. 164–168 in Asmal and James 2002a.
Pandor, Naledi. 2005. "Address by the Minister of Education, Naledi Pandor, MP, at the World Halaal Council AGM, Civic Centre, Cape Town, 13 September 2005." http://www.info.gov.za/speeches/2005/05091616151001.htm (accessed 26 October 2005).
Pretorius, C. 2000. "Asmal Plans a Lesson for the Rainbow Classroom." *Sunday Times*, 9 January.
Rauch, Janine. 2005. *Crime Prevention and Morality: The Campaign for Moral Regeneration in South Africa*, Institute for Security Studies Monograph no. 114. http://www.iss.org.za/pubs/Monographs/No114/Contents.htm (accessed 16 January 2006).
Renan, Ernest. 1990. "What Is a Nation?" Pp. 8–22 in *Nation and Narration*, ed. Homi Bhabha. London: Routledge.
Republic of South Africa. 1996a. *Constitution of the Republic of South Africa*, Act no. 108 of 1996. http://www.polity.org.za/html/govdocs/constitution/saconst.html?rebookmark=1 (accessed 15 January 2006).
______. 1996b. *National Crime Prevention Strategy*, 22 May 1996. http://www.info.gov.za/otherdocs/1996/crime1.htm (accessed 15 January 2006).
______. 2002. *Commission for the Promotion and Protection of the Rights of Cultural, Religious and Linguistic Communities*, Act no. 19, 30 July. http://www.polity.org.za/pdf/CommissionForThePromotion.pdf (accessed 15 January 2006).

Sachs, Albie. 1993. *Religion, Education, and Constitutional Law*. Cape Town: Institute for Comparative Religion in Southern Africa.
Scott, James. 1998. *Seeing Like a State: How Certain Schemes to Improve the Human Condition Have Failed*. New Haven, CT: Yale University Press.
Snyman, A. H. 2003. "The Draft Policy on Religion in Education: A Clear Example of State Interference." *Journal for Christian Scholarship* 39, nos. 3–4: 43–55.
Steyn, H. Christina. 1999. "The Role of Multi-Religious Education in the Transformation of South African Society." Pp. 131–142 in Walsh and Kaufmann 1999.
Stonier, Janet. 1998. "A New Direction for Religious Education in South Africa? The Proposed New Religious Education Policy." *Journal for the Study of Religion* 11, no. 1: 93–115.
Taussig, Michael. 1997. *The Magic of the State*. London: Routledge.
Turaki, Yusuf. 1999. *Christianity and African Gods: A Method in Theology*. Potchefstroom, South Africa: Potchefstroom University.
Tutu, Desmond. 1995. "Archbishop Desmond Tutu's Address to the First Gathering of the Truth and Reconciliation Commission." http://www.doj.gov.za/trc/pr/1995/p951216a.htm (accessed 19 January 2006).
Vale, Peter. 2003. *Security and Politics in South Africa: The Regional Dimension*. Boulder: Lynne Rienner.
van der Vyver, Johan D. 2001. "Constitutional Perspective of Church-State Relations in South Africa." *Brigham Young University Law Review* 4: 635–673.
Walsh, Thomas G., and Frank Kaufmann, eds. 1999. *Religion and Social Transformation in Southern Africa*. St. Paul, MN: Paragon House.
Weber, Max. 1958. *From Max Weber: Essays in Sociology*. Ed. and trans. H. H. Gerth and C. Wright Mills. New York: Basic Books.
Weiss, Linda. 1997. *The Myth of the Powerless State*. Cambridge: Polity Press.
Weisse, Wolfram. 1998. "Interview with Minister Sibusiso Bengu: Africanisation—Religion—Education." *Journal for the Study of Religion* 11, no. 2: 208–215.

[11]

Religious Education in Israel

ASHER MAOZ*

A WORD OF INTRODUCTION

A stranger that would examine the system of education in Israel, especially religious education, might describe it in one word – chaos. He would not be far from the truth. The area of religious education in the State of Israel is one of the most complex issues, possibly without comparison to other modern countries. The reason for this complexity is complex in itself. It has religious, national, historical and economical backgrounds and above all political grounds that account for it.

The value of education in Jewish tradition is without comparison. Jewish communities were the first to introduce compulsory education for which the organized institutions, not less than the parents, were responsible. The rift within Jewish society, starting with the Renaissance and Enlightenment and continuing with Zionism, circled to a large extent around the issue of education. Segments of the Jewish people that were attracted by the Enlightenment Movement changed the curriculum at school. So did the segments that followed Zionism. The Orthodox circles, feeling threatened by these new trends, closed themselves off from the outer world and clung to the traditional teachings. They, moreover, kept their children from being influenced by the outside world.

When massive immigration to Palestine started, these distinct groups brought with them their convictions, way of life and system of education. Even after the State of Israel was established they kept their old ways. This was possible since self-sufficient autonomous Jewish communities existed in the Diaspora for many years.

The newly born State embarked on a melting pot policy but soon realized it was futile. Then there was another issue. Even before the establishment of the State, the Zionist leadership needed the cooperation, or at least the non-disturbance, of the Orthodox segments. The Zionist leaders, fighting for Jewish statehood, were willing to reward the Orthodox groups by respecting their educational autonomy. This continued after the establishment of the State of Israel when religious political parties were constant partners to the coalition governments. This resulted not only in

---

* Associate Professor, Tel-Aviv University Faculty of Law. Amnon de-Hartog read a former version of the article and made valuable suggestions. Dan Gibton and Yael Kafri supplied helpful information. Moran Yahav and Lydia Mandelbaum rendered excellent research assistance. I am indebted to all of them.

the non-enforcement of State education on ultra-Orthodox children but even by supporting their "non-official" education networks. These arrangements - which were not based on law and were even contrary to law - grew out of control. It is, moreover, hard to get precise figures of this support, as it is difficult to even receive agreed upon numbers of students attending these schools.

The State established several commissions to try and introduce some order in this chaos, to no avail. As this article is going to press a new effort to organize the education network is taking place.

RELIGIOUSLY ORIENTED PRIMARY SECONDARY AND HIGH SCHOOL EDUCATION

1. Historical background

The State of Israel recognizes the status of religious schools at all levels, from kindergarten to high school, as well as institutions for the training of school and kindergarten teachers.[1] The education system includes both religious and non-religious state schools as well as private schools.[2] To better understand the Israeli education system some historical background might be helpful.[3] Through the British Mandate over Palestine most Jewish schools were affiliated with political parties and belonged to three streams: the General Stream connected to the centrist parties, mainly the General Zionist party, that encompassed fifty-two percent of the pupils in 1948; the Labor Stream operated by the workers union, *Ha'Histadrut ha'Kelalit shel ha'Ovdim ha'Ivriyyim be'Eretz Yisrael* [The General Federation of Jewish Labor in Palestine] (27.3%); and the Mizrahi Stream, affiliated with the religious-Zionist parties *Mizrahi* [an acronym for *merkaz ruhani* (spiritual center)], and *Hapoel Hamizrahi* [Spiritual Center Worker] (22.5%). All three streams were financed by the World Zionist Organization. Alongside these streams religious ultra-Orthodox non-Zionist schools operated. All three streams, or trends, as termed by statutory law, were recognized by the State of Israel upon its establishment

1. *See* State Education Law, 5713-1953, 7 LSI 113 (1952-53) (Isr.). There were several amendments to the statute. A Hebrew consolidated version is available at: http://www.education.gov.il/zchuyot/chukim4.htm.

2. *See generally* Asher Maoz, *Religious Human Rights in the State of Israel*, *in* JOHN WITTE, JR., RELIGIOUS HUMAN RIGHTS IN GLOBAL PERSPECTIVE: LEGAL PERSPECTIVES 349, 373-76 (Johan D. Van Der Vyver & John Witte, Jr. eds., Martinus Nijhoff Pub. 1996), *reprinted in* JASON ARONSON, HUMAN RIGHTS IN JUDAISM: CULTURAL, RELIGIOUS, AND POLITICAL PERSPECTIVES 113, 144-49 (Michael J. Broyde & John Witte, Jr. eds., 1998); Stephen Goldstein, *The Teaching of Religion in Government Funded Schools in Israel*, 26 ISRAEL L. REV. 36 (1992); Stephen Goldstein, *Multiculturalism, Parental Choice and Traditional Values: A Comment on Religious Education in Israel*, *in* CHILDREN'S RIGHTS AND TRADITIONAL VALUES 118 (Gillian Douglas & Leslie Sebba eds., Ashgate 1998).

3. *See* ZVI ZAMERET, ACROSS A NARROW BRIDGE: SHAPING THE EDUCATION SYSTEM DURING THE MASSIVE IMMIGRATION (Ben-Gurion Research Centre, Sede Boker 1997) (Isr.).

together with a stream connected to the *Agudat Yisrael* [Union of Israel] ultra-Orthodox party, as well as the Arab educational system, as schools that fulfil the requirement of compulsory education and were fully funded by the State.[4] The recognition of the *Agudat Yisrael* stream was a result of a commitment given to that party, before the establishment of the state, known as "the *status quo* agreement,"[5] to respect the autonomy of its educational system. Alongside a stream of "Religious - Labor System," that was part of the Labor Stream operated.[6]

However, the streams were not allowed to operate in immigrant camps. There a system of uniform education was established to further the policy of a "melting pot" that would result in modernizing the newcomers, most of them from oriental countries (known as *Sephardic* [Spanish] Jews) and assisting them in becoming an integral part of Israeli society. Soon accusations were raised that these schools enforced secular education on the students, most of whom came from religious backgrounds and infringed their freedom of religion. The pressure of religious circle, both from Israel and from the United States, led to the establishment of a governmental commission of inquiry headed by Gad Frumkin, a former judge of the Mandatory Supreme Court.[7] The commission found that though not a result of governmental policy of anti-religious coercion, the uniform education resulted in harsh infringement of the religious freedom of the new immigrants. As the supreme authority for administering the State's business, the government bore collective responsibility for this situation. The Frumkin report led to the forced resignation of the Minister of

---

4. Compulsory Education Law, 5709-1949, 3 LSI 125 (1948-49) (Isr.).

5. *See* Menachem Fridman, *The Chronicle of the Status Quo: Religion and State in Israel*, *in* TRANSITION FROM "YISHUV" TO STATE 1947-1949: CONTINUALITY AND CHANGE (Varda Filobsky ed., Univ. of Haifa, Herzal Institute for the Research in Zionism 1990) (Isr.). For an English translation of the *status quo* agreement, see THE DILEMMA OF RELIGION AND POLITICS 151 (Susan H. Rolef ed., Semana Pub. Co. 1986). Actually, this was not an agreement, but rather a letter sent on behalf of the Jewish Agency executive to the *World Agudat Yisrael Union.*

6. On this stream, see Zvi Zameret, *The Religious – Labor System – The History of an Unsuccessful Attempt at Building a Bridge between Secular and Religious Jews*, *in* RESHAFIM: HISTORICAL, PHILOSOPHICAL AND SOCIOLOGICAL ASPECTS OF EDUCATION 121 (Arye Kasher & Rina Shapira eds., Tel-Aviv Univ. 1991).

7. On the Frumkin Commission, see ZVI ZAMERET, THE MELTING POT IN ISRAEL: THE COMMISSION OF INQUIRY CONCERNING EDUCATION IN THE IMMIGRANT CAMPS DURING THE EARLY YEARS OF THE STATE (State Univ. of New York Press 2002); Eliezer Don-Yihya, *The Struggle over the Education in the Immigrants' Camps and its Manifestations in the Public Arena* 18-19, *in* NIV HA'MIDRASHIYA 198 (1985-86), *available at* http://www.daat.ac.il/daat/kitveyet/niv/donyihye-1.htm (Isr.); Dov Levitan, *First State Investigation Commission: The Education in the Immigrants' Camps* 20-21, *in* NIV HA'MIDRASHIYA 290 (1987-88), *available at* http://www.daat.ac.il/daat/kitveyet/niv/levitan-1.htm (Isr.). The Commission also investigated accusations made regarding pressure to abandon the religious way of life of Yemenite youth educated in special educational camps and found them groundless.

Education. Combined with future developments regarding religious education it also led to the fall of the government, dissolvent of the *Knesset* and to early elections.

The accusations investigated by the Frumkin Commission regarding secular education enforcement in the immigrants' camps were not isolated. Alongside the episode of education in the immigrants' camps, religious education was denied to new immigrants who were absorbed in cooperative agriculture settlements dominated by the Labor Party. The new immigrants were forced to attend the Labor Stream educational institutions in dire contradiction of Compulsory Education Law.[8] Even prior to the establishment of the State of Israel, a scandal known as "The Teheran Children Affair" broke out. In 1943, 1,228 Jewish children, most of them orphans who had fled from Poland to the Soviet Union at the outbreak of war in 1939, arrived in Palestine via Iran. Seven-hundred and nineteen of them were placed in various institutions of *Aliyath Ha'noar* [Youth Immigration],[9] many of them secular. This caused an outcry from religious circles, which led to the establishment of a commission of clarification, that found no ground for the sharp criticism launched against the Jewish Agency,[10] yet declared that most of the teachers in the institutions were indifferent or even hostile to the childrens' religious needs.[11]

A year after the submission of the Frumkin Commission report another investigating commission found that accusations of anti-religious coercion of Yemenite children in immigration camps were unfounded, yet their religious needs were not looked after. Moreover, the submission of the Frumkin Commission report did not put an end to accusations regarding anti-religious coercion in education in immigrants' camps and in transit settlements [*ma'abara* in Hebrew].[12]

The second *Knesset* enacted the State Education Law designated to bring about the abolishment of the various educational streams.[13] Originally the proposed legislation attempted to establish a single Jewish educational system to be based on "the values of Jewish culture and scientific achievement, love of the homeland and loyalty to the State of

8. *See* Zvi Zameret, *The Integration of Yemenites in Israeli Schools*, ISRAEL STUD., Fall 2001, at 1.

9. An organization founded in 1933 to rescue Jewish youth from Nazi Germany which later became a Department of the Jewish Agency. On the history of Aliyath Ha'noar, see NORMAN BENTWICH, JEWISH YOUTH COMES HOME: THE STORY OF THE YOUTH ALIYA 1933-1943 (Victor Gollancz 1944).

10. Note the sharp title of a book published then by Jacob Rosenheim, a leader of Agudat Yisrael: THE TEHERAN CHILDREN ACCUSE: ORIGINAL DOCUMENT AND FULL STORY OF THE SEIZURE AND NON RELIGIOUS EDUCATION OF REFUGEE CHILDREN BY THE JEWISH AGENCY IN PALESTINE (Jacob Rosenheim 1944) (Hebrew, Yiddish, and English).

11. *See* TOMER BEN-ZION, RED, WHITE AND THE SMELL OF ORANGES (The Zionist Library 1972) (Isr.).

12. *See* ZAMERET, *supra* note 7, at 101-22.

13. *See supra* note 1.

Israel and the Jewish People."[14] Yet, due to religious opposition, the draft legislation has been changed to enable religious state schools alongside the general state schools.

2. *State Education Law*

2.1 Israeli Educational System

The system of education in Israel consisted originally of kindergarten until the age of six; primary (or elementary) school for grades one to eight; and four years of high-school. This structure has been adopted during the British mandate in Palestine following the Central Europe model. In 1968 the Knesset adopted a reform under which primary school lasts for six years followed by an intermediate division (secondary or junior high school) and (senior) high school.[15] As of today most schools have adopted the reform though its advantages are still debatable and suggestions for deviation from it were made along the years.[16] Compulsory education covers nine years of school, namely primary and secondary schools. Save for a couple of exceptions, there are no State high schools. Instead, they are usually run by local councils or are private.

2.2 Jewish Studies in State School

Judaic texts, such as the Bible, as well as Jewish history and Jewish holidays, are taught in all schools, including those that are not religious, though the Bible is being taught from a critical view and not as a divine book.[17] This is natural considering that those texts constitute part of Jewish culture and history beyond their religious manifestations.[18] Indeed, State Education Law outlines the objects of state education, *inter alia*, as

---

14. *See* State Education Law Bill, 1953, HH, 242, § 2.

15. *See* RONIA BRITBART & MICHAL TAVIVIAN-MIZRAHI, CHANGES IN THE EDUCATIONAL SYSTEM STRUCTURE IN ISRAEL AND PROPOSALS FOR CHANGES MADE ALONG THE YEARS – BACKGROUND DOCUMENT (Knesset 2003) (Isr.), *available at* http://www.knesset.gov.il/mmm/data/docs/m00742.doc.

16. *See e.g.*, Shimshon Shoshani, *Nothing Can Stand Up to Necessity*, *in* 16 OFAKIM HADASHIM (New Horizons 2004), *available at* http://ofakim.org.il/zope/home/he/1101583653/1104935041?curr_issue=1101583653 (Isr.). *See also infra* note 203.

17. *See* Walter Ackerman, *Making Jews: An Enduring Challenge in Israeli Education*, ISRAEL STUD., Fall 1997. For the objective of teaching the Bible in State schools, see JOSEPH GOLDSMIT, OF THE FOUNDATIONS OF STATE RELIGIOUS EDUCATION 64-65 (Ministry of Education 1976). Compare this with the objective of teaching the Bible in Religious State schools. *Id.* at 65-66. For a comparison between teaching *Mishna* and *Talmud* in State schools and in Religious State schools, see YEHUDA SHWARTZ, TEACHING ORAL LAW: TEACHING MISHNA AND TALMUD IN ISRAELI EDUCATION IN VIEW OF THE CURRICULA AND THE DIDACTIC LITERATURE (Hebrew Univ., 2002).

18. *See* Asher Maoz, *State and Religion in Israel*, *in* INTERNATIONAL PERSPECTIVES OF CHURCH AND STATE 239 (Menachem Mor ed., 1993).

educating the students to respect their heritage, their cultural identity and their language.[19] The Law specifically provides that these objects include "teaching the Torah of Israel, the history of the Jewish people, Israel's heritage and Jewish tradition."[20] A few years after the introduction of the state education system a special Center for the Fostering of Jewish Consciousness was formed in the Ministry of Education to enhance the knowledge of Jewish tradition in the State schools, including prayers and practices of traditional Jewish life.[21] The center operated for some ten years and the overall appreciation was that the program was not very successful, due to, *inter alia*, a rejection by teachers and parents of what they regarded as an attempt to introduce religious education into the State schools. In the 1980s, a Division for Strengthening Jewish Education had been established in the Ministry of Education. The programs developed by the Division included exposing high school students to Jewish teachings on the problems confronting modern man; teaching Jewish holidays in primary school; teachings school students about the Bar Mitzvah and providing seminars on Judaism for teachers. Two aspects signified these curricula. First, they were optional and encouraged school-based curricula. Second, the individual schools were free to invite outside organizations and institutions to teach Judaism. Indeed, schools invited religious instructors, mainly from the *Habad* (*Lubavitch*) Hassidic group to teach Judaism.

In addition to formal study programs, informal educational techniques have also been used in order to guide youngsters toward a sense of themselves as Jews. One day, as well as longer seminars, conducted away from school and by staff who were not regular school teachers, used practices adapted from group work theory and encountered group experiences in moving participants toward an exploration of the self and the others. Beyond the classroom, activities have also been incorporated on a much grander scale in the teaching of the Holocaust.

In 1991 the minister of education appointed a commission headed by the Rector of Haifa University, Professor Aliza Shinhar, to examine the status of Jewish studies in State schools and offer recommendations regarding approaches and goals, curricula and other initiatives capable of advancing Jewish education in Israel. The Commission submitted its report three years later, entitled "A Nation and the World – Jewish Culture in a

---

19. State Education Law, 5713-1954, 7 LSI 113, § 2(1) (1952-53) (Isr.), *as amended by* Statutes Education Law, 2000, S.H. 122.

20. *Id.* § 2(4).

21. *See* Government of Israel, DEEPENING JEWISH CONSCIOUSNESS (1959) (Isr.). For an evaluation of the Center's activity, see ADRIAN TOMA & YESHAYAHU GUTTMANN, EVALUATION OF THE ACTIVITY OF CENTER FOR THE FOSTERING OF JEWISH CONSCIOUSNESS (Sold Institute 1973); Zvi Zameret, *An Attempt that Failed – Zalman Aran and the Jewish Consciousness*, *in* VALUES AND EDUCATING TO VALUES – ISSUES IN TEACHERS' ADVANCED STUDIES 345 (Ministry of Education & Hebrew Univ. 1999).

Changing World."[22] The Commission viewed Judaism as "a national and pluralistic culture in a continuous state of development."[23] This culture contains "national-religious" motifs, including "personal and social moral values derived from the Jewish tradition, from the Zionist ethos, and from generally human ideologies and moral theories."[24]

The Commission explicitly did not address its recommendations to the "national-religious or the independent ultra-Orthodox trends, which are defined by their nexus to a cultural system with an integrated view and respond to a clear spiritual and civic authority."[25]

The Commission decried the "continuing decline in the prestige of Jewish studies in State school education," and determined that "we should strive to teach the subjects of Judaism in a way that emphasizes their humanistic character, imparts culture and values, and provides tools for constructing an outlook."[26] It proposed the placement of Jewish studies in the broader framework of the humanities. The Commission called for the development of curricula and other materials that encourage dialogue and critical inquiry and emphasized the importance of an interdisciplinary approach. It advocated knowledge of the history of the Jewish people and culture as an essential element in the development of the identity and the shaping of the spiritual and ethical world of Israeli youth.[27]

The Government endorsed the Shinhar report and the Ministry of Education set up a special headquarters to implement its recommendations, together with the recommendations of a steering commission nominated by the Minister "for the purpose of developing a comprehensive programme for inculcating in the students a citizenship that will serve as a common ethical and behavioral foundation for all citizens of the State."[28] The Commission, headed by Professor Mordechai Kremnitzer, submitted its report, entitled "Being Citizens" in 1996.[29] The Ministry explained the common enterprise of the two reports as a result of the fact that "the common starting point of both is the existence of the State of Israel as a

22. A NATION AND THE WORLD – JEWISH CULTURE IN A CHANGING WORLD (Ministry of Education and Culture 1994) (Isr.) (translation by author), *available at* http://cms.education.gov.il/EducationCMS/Units/Mazkirut_Pedagogit/Mate/Dochot/AmOlam.htm.

23. *Id.* at 4.

24. *Id.* at 5.

25. *Id.* at 11.

26. *Id.* at 10.

27. *Id.* at 12.

28. BEING CITIZENS 5 (Ministry of Education and Culture 1996) (Isr.) (translation by author), *available at* http://cms.education.gov.il/EducationCMS/Units/Mazkirut_Pedagogit/Mate/OdotHamate/OdotMate.htm. For an English concise version, see http://cms.education.gov.il/EducationCMS/Units/Owl/English/Pedagogic/Being/.

29. *Id.*

Jewish and democratic state."[30] It should be emphasized that while the Shinhar report relates to State schools only, the Kremnitzer report applies to all schools in Israel.

However, the implementation depends to a large extent on the personality of the Minister of Education at the time. Thus, while the Shinhar Commission was established during the term of a National-Religious Party minister, the report was handed to his successor from the secular left-wing Meretz party. The latter attempted to break Orthodox monopoly in religious education and enabled Conservative and Reform streams in Judaism to join in implementing the Shinhar recommendations. Dozens of private non-profit organizations have been established to promote a Jewish pluralistic education in State schools even before the Commissions report was submitted, and more energetically afterward. Some of the organizations were secular, viewing Judaism as culture; others belonged to progressive religious movements. Schools, however, terminated their contacts with these organizations following the decision of the Ministry of Education, now headed by a minister from the right-wing *Likud* [unity] party, to stop engaging external contractors.[31] Instead the Ministry encouraged the recruitment of female graduates from State religious schools to teach Judaic studies in general State schools in lieu of military service. Some secular, reform and conservative organizations petitioned against this decision; however the Supreme Court ruled that the ministry may change its policy of contracting external organizations. Yet the Court disqualified the criteria for funding Torah and Jewish culture lessons in non formal education that clearly discriminated against these organizations.[32]

Professor Shinhar herself vigorously attacked the Ministry's policy of "encouraging National Service girls (religious girls from schools of the state-religious stream) to teach diverse Judaic subjects; [of] supporting Orthodox educational societies [and] withholding the transfer of funds to Jewish education in the pluralistic spirit – and obligating junior high school students to memorize Jewish concepts that are not taught in a manner espousing dialogue and criticism."[33] Professor Shinhar emphasized that by

30. Ministry of Education, http://cms.education.gov.il/EducationCMS/Units/MazkirutPedagogit/Mate/Dochot/DohBeEzrah.htm (translation by author). For the implementation of both reports, see Ministry of Education, Culture and Sport, *The Development of Education*, § 8-9 (National Report of Israel Submitted to the 45th Session of the International Conference on Education 1996), *available at* http://www.ibe.unesco.org/countries/countryDossier/natrep96/israel96.pdf.

For Israel as a Jewish and democratic state, *see* Asher Maoz, *The Values of a Jewish and Democratic State*, 26 IYHR 289 (1996).

31. HCJ 1447/03 Panim for Jewish Renaissance in Israel v. Minister of Education [2004] IsrSC 59(3) 942.

32. *Id.*

33. Aliza Shinhar, *A Nation without a World*, 30 OFAKIM HADASHIM [New Horizons] (2006) (translation by author), *available at*

doing so the Ministry frustrated the Commission's recommendation to resort to "the pluralistic-liberal approach in teaching Judaic studies in the general State school" and engage "teachers whose viewpoint and lifestyle are acceptable upon the versified secular public, according to the varied communities served by the schools."[34]

The attempts to implement the Shinhar recommendations are continuing and substantial resources have been allocated towards that end. However, the recommendations and their implementation are a subject for ongoing controversy. In this regard it is important to point out the fact that the Commission itself found it hard to reach common recommendations and commission members took reservations from substantial parts thereof.

At the beginning of 2007 the Minister of Education, herself a secular person, appointed a Public Committee for Bible Education. She did so "in view of the growing gap between schoolchildren and the Bible's world and language and the growing polarization between the religious and secular in Israeli society."[35] The committee consists of thirty-nine public figures, headed by former Supreme Court Deputy President Justice Mishael Cheshin. The committee's goal has been described as turning the study of the Bible to a more central focus in the educational system. It should "lead [to] a change in the student's capture of the Bible through intellectual and experimental study."[36] The committee recommended the institution of a discussion of Bible stories and subjects in the morning roll-call in each school. The recommendation, which would take effect in the upcoming school year and can be implemented at the discretion of a school's principal, applies to all schools in the State and State religious school systems. The enhanced studies program planned by the committee includes trips around the country in the footsteps of Bible stories, musical, literary and artistic competitions on Biblical themes, after-school events, and a Bible studies corner in each elementary school.

In launching the committee's activities, Education Minister Professor Yuli Tamir stated: "'The beauty of the Bible is reflected in the values and moral dilemmas it raises.'... 'I believe that dealing with moral issues can help develop students' moral judgment'" and mold their image as tomorrow's citizens.[37] The Ministry's Director General declared that "the

---

http://ofakim.org.il/zope/home/he/1138194787/1147600179?curr_issue=1138194787. English synopsis: http://ofakim.org.il/zope/home/en/1138194787/1147600179_en.

34. *Id.*

35. *See* The Public Committee for Bible Education is being launched, The Ministry's spokesperson's announcement, Jan. 9, 2007 (Isr.) (translation by author), *available at* http://209.85.135.104/search?q=cache:0o4ld_9qU1kJ:cms.education.gov.il/EducationCMS/PortalOvdeyHoraa/Taarich/LimodTanach.htm.

36. *Id.*

37. Haviv Rettig, *New committee to bolster Bible study in schools*, JERUSALEM POST, Jan. 10, 2007, *available at*

Bible is the constitutive book of the Jewish people that planted in it eternal life. It is our duty to bequest the Jewish heritage to the young generation. I am certain that the Public Committee will offer practical means to return the Bible to the center of our cultural life."[38]

2.3 State Religious Education

The Religious State schools formally constitute an amalgamation of the former recognized religious streams. However, in practice they are a continuation of the *Mizrahi* stream schools; this is so since the *Agudat Yisrael* schools did not join the State schools and the Religious - Labor System faded away upon the abolition of the educational streams. Even the teachers and inspectors of that *Mizrahi* stream continued to work for the new religious State schools.

Religious education is defined, in the State Education Law, as "State education, yet its institutions are religious according to their way of life, their curricula, their teachers and inspectors."[39] A Religious State education institution is defined as "an official education institution in which state religious education is being provided and which educate to a life of *Torah* and *mitzvoth* [religious commandments] according to the religious tradition and in the spirit of religious Zionism."[40] These institutions may enrich their curricula "to include *Torah* and Talmudic studies and will direct to a religious way of life, including religious observance and a religious atmosphere within the institution."[41]

A separate Council of Religious State Education, has been established by law, comprising of fifteen members, six of them recommended by the Minister of Religious Affairs,[42] and three recommended by the Organization of Religious Teachers.[43] The Minister of Education must consult with the Council before exercising any of his or her powers relating to the State Religious Education. This includes the appointment of the Director of the Division of Religious Education in the Ministry and the appointment of inspectors, school headmasters and teachers for the

http://www.jpost.com/servlet/Satellite?pagename=JPost%2FJPArticle%2FShowFull&cid=1167467697826.

38. Moran Zelikovitz, *Recommendation: School will start with a Bible roll-call*, YNET, Jan. 9, 2007 (Isr.) (translation by author), *available at* http://www.ynet.co.il/articles/0,7340,L-3350317,00.html.

39. State Education Law, 5713-1953, 7 LSI 113, § 1 (1952-53) (Isr.).

40. *Id.*

41. *Id. See also* MATTITYAHU DAGAN ET AL., GUIDELINES FOR STATE-RELIGIOUS EDUCATION POLICY (Ministry of Education Culture and Sports, Religious Education Administration 3d ed. 1996).

42. The Ministry of Religious Affairs was abolished since and this authority has been transferred to the Prime Minister.

43. State Education Law, 5713-1953, 7 LSI 113, § 13 (1952-53) (Isr.).

religious schools.[44] Various powers entrusted to the Pedagogical Secretariat at the Ministry have been allocated to the Director with regard to religious schools. Regulations promulgated by the Minister categorically state that "[t]he supreme pedagogical authority regarding the religious nature of the said educational institutes shall be entrusted to the Director of the Division of Religious Education."[45] In each district an inspector of State Religious Education must be appointed to supervise these schools rather than the general inspector.[46] The Division for Religious Education has, moreover, been elevated to an autonomous Administration for Religious Education.

The Law provides for the religious way of life of the educators. It states that the Council "may, on religious grounds only, disqualify a person for appointment or further service as a principal, inspector or teacher at a religious State-educational institution."[47] The Labor Court ruled, however, that the council may not fire a teacher who leads a religious life merely because he is married to a secular spouse or that his children do not attend religious schools.[48] No restrictions relating to secular background or lifestyle apply to students and their families, save for the schools right to insist on the students not infringing, in their appearance and conduct, the religious way of life within school. Indeed, a substantial portion of the student body of the schools comes from non-religious homes.[49]

The Religious State education struggles with the need to combine State Zionist education with religious education. It experienced in recent

44. *Id.* § 15.

45. State Education Regulations (Inspection Procedure), 1957, KT 5717, 116, § 6(b), *amended by* 1980, KT 5740, 1487, *and* 1992, KT 1152.

46. *Id.* § 10(a).

47. State Education Law, 5713-1954, 7 LSI 113 (1952-53) (Isr.) (translation by author), *available at* http://www.edu-negev.gov.il/matefet/koch/k6.doc.

48. LC (Nazareth) 1693/98 Rosenbaum v. The Ministry of Education [1999] Tak-Labor 99(1) 253; *available at* http://www.lawandreligion.org.il/topics/17edu_religion/17psak_deen/17pd2.doc.

49. A survey conducted in State-Religious schools in Tel-Aviv, several years ago revealed that as many as one quarter of the student body come from non-religious families. JOSEPH GALANZ, THE OTHER CHILD IN CLASS: STUDENTS FROM A NON-RELIGIOUS HOME IN A RELIGIOUS SCHOOL 80 (Bar Ilan Univ. 1981) (Isr.). At the same time, in another study, the author suggests that non-religious parents be requested to cooperate in respecting religious values at home and in observing religious precepts that are maintained at school. JOSEPH GALANZ, STUDENTS FROM A NON-RELIGIOUS HOME AT A RELIGIOUS SCHOOL (COMPARATIVE STUDY) (Ministry of Education and Culture & The Religious Education 1988) (Isr.). It has been further suggested that "since it is impossible to insulate completely the religious nature of a school from the religious nature of its student body, the preservation of a given school's religious way of life may justify restricting the number of non-religious students in the school." Goldstein, *supra* note 2, at 133 n.7.

years a withdrawal of students to ultra-Orthodox institutions[50] and came

---

50. Between 1995 and 2000 the percentage of the students in religious State primary schools dropped from 26.50% to 20%. The percentage of students in ultra-Orthodox schools rose to 19.20% by the year 2000; *see* SHIRA BEN SASOON-FORSTENBERG, THE CORE OF EDUCATION – FROM SECTARIANISM TO STATEHOOD? (Knesset 2002) (Isr.), *available at* http://www.knesset.gov.il/mmm/doc.asp?doc=m00276&type=pdf. A survey of the student body of the school year 2004 to 2005 reveals that out of a total of 573,937 students in the Israeli Hebrew primary education system, 318,821 (55.5%) were enrolled in State schools; 104,455 (18.2%) in Religious-State schools and 150,661 (26.2%) in ultra-Orthodox schools. *See* ETTI WEISBLAI, DATA ON THE NUMBER OF STUDENTS IN HEBREW ELEMENTARY EDUCATION ACCORDING TO THE TYPE OF INSPECTION AND LEGAL STATUS (Knesset 2005) (Isr.), *available at* http://www.knesset.gov.il/mmm/doc.asp?doc=m01375&type=pdf. A report submitted by the Ministry of Education to UNESCO reveals that between the years 1989-1990 and 2002-2003 the percentage of students enrolled in religious recognized and exempt primary schools raised from 11.9% to 23.6% out of the total number of students in Hebrew primary education. At the same time the proportion of students in State-religious schools dropped from 20.5% to 18.8%. In State education the percentage dropped from 67.6% to 57.6%. The same tendency occurred in secondary education as well, where the recognized non-official and exempt student body rose from 3.8% to 10% (State education dropped from 78.6% to 72.2% while State-religious schools maintained their stability and even raised from 17.6% to 17.8%).

The figures of the rise in the ultra-Orthodox student body in various sources may be somewhat misleading. This is a result of the fact that until the school year 1998-1999 the figures of enrollment in ultra-Orthodox schools, as published by the Central Bureau of Statistics, included only recognized ultra-Orthodox schools. Since that year they include also exempt institutions. Hence, while the percentage of students in ultra-Orthodox primary schools rose from 6.6% in the year 1959-1960 to 7.6% in the year 1989-1990, it rose to 20.4% in the year 1999-2000. However, even after the inclusion of the exempt schools the figure kept growing to 25.1% in the year 2005-2006. At the same time the ratio of students in religious state schools dropped from 26.5% in 1959-1960 to 19.2% in 1999-2000 and then to 18.8% in 2005-2006. State education enrollment dropped from 66.9% in 1959-1960 to 60.4% in 1999-2000 and then to 55.3% in 2005-2006. The figures of enrollment in ultra-Orthodox high schools seem even more impressive. They rose from 3.7% in 1969-1970 to 14.8% in 1999-2000 and to 19.9% in 2005-2006. Religious State high school enrollment dropped from 21.9% in 1969-1970 to 17.2% in 1999-2000 to 16.7% in 2005-2006. State high school enrollment dropped from 74.4% in 1969-1970 to 68% in 1999-2000 to 63.4% in 2005-2006; Central Bureau of Statistics, *Statistical Abstract of Israel 2006 No. 57*, at 39.1 (2006), *available at* http://www1.cbs.gov.il/reader/shnatonenew_site.htm.

When reviewing the statistics in kindergartens one may venture to predict that the proportion of ultra-Orthodox students might even rise. In 2002-2003, 27.7% of kindergarten kids were enrolled in ultra-Orthodox institutions while only 52.0% were enrolled in State education. At the same time 20.3% were enrolled in State-religious education. *See Document Submitted to the Forth-Seventh Session of the International Conference on Education*, DEVELOPMENT OF EDUCATION: FACTS AND FIGURES 73-75 (Ministry of Education, Culture and Sport 2004), *available at* http://www.ibe.unesco.org/International/ICE47/English/Natreps/reports/israel_part_2.pdf.

It is doubtful, however, whether the proportion in pre-primary education will fully perpetuate itself in primary and higher education. This is so because, unlike State schools – including State-religious institutions – the ultra-Orthodox institutions are usually long-day institutions and provide bussing as well as hot meals for their students. This factor might be of major importance to young age children, especially for those who come from poor neighborhoods. It is, moreover, hard to compare among these numbers as the various surveys might have related to different classifications of the ultra-Orthodox schools. *See* under pressure from parents to enrich their religious curricula and introduce a more Orthodox atmosphere in school. This led to the establishment of networks within state religious education that put more emphasis on religious studies. The leading network is Noam-Zviya that separates between boys and girls. These networks joined large networks of high-school *yeshivas* [institutions of Talmudic studies] for boys, most of them boarding schools and colleges for girls, the Zviya network. Some secondary schools are attached to high-school *yeshivas*. The proportion of these networks within State religious education is in a constant rise. Thus, by the year 2002, forty schools out of 407 primary schools were affiliated with the Noam network. In secondary and high schools the proportion of high-school *Yeshivas* and girl colleges rose to fifty percent.[51] Critics of these schools point to the fact that they tend to be elitist and frustrate one of the main targets of the educational reform of 1968, to enhance integration of various socio-economic sectors. This is so both because of the high standard of study and the substantial participation of parents in funding studies beyond those financed by the state. Another phenomenon of secondary State Religious schools is the high percentage of schools that introduce different levels of studies within the school.[52] Researchers have pointed out that the difficulties of State Religious schools in introducing integration stems from the fact that while a successful integrative class must consist of at least sixty percent of the students coming from established families, seventy-three percent of the students in State Religious schools are "special care" students coming from lower socio-economic homes.[53]

---

infra Part 2.5. Moreover, over the years there were changes in the educational structure and the division between elementary and higher education. However, the drop in the student population of the Religious-State schools continued while the student body of the ultra-Orthodox schools grew parallelly. Finally, the figures were presented by various departments within the Ministry and doubts have been raised as to their accuracy. *See* SHLOMO SWIRSKI, ETTI KONUR & YARON YECHESKEL, GOVERNMENT ALLOCATIONS TO ULTRA-ORTHODOX (HAREDI) SECTOR IN ISRAEL (Adva Center 1998), *available at* http://www.adva.org/UserFiles/File/Government%20Allocations%20to%20the%20ultra%20ortodox.pdf.

51. Records of Meeting 481 of the Education, Culture, and Sports Committee of the Knesset, June 12, 2002, at 5 (Isr.), *available at* http://www.knesset.gov.il/protocols/data/html/chinuch/2002-06-12-02.html [hereinafter Records].

52. While merely 7% of State schools have separate classes according to the students' standards, it rises to 26% in State Religious secondary schools. *See* State Comptroller, *Annual Report No. 43*, 277 (1992), *available at* http://www.mevaker.gov.il/serve/contentTree.asp?bookid=164&id=57&contentid=&parentcid=undefined&sw=1024&hw=698.

53. *See* CHAIM LAGZIEL, EDUCATION POLICY AT A CROSSROAD BETWEEN CHANGE AND CONTINUITY- EDUCATION IN ISRAEL DURING THE LAST DECADE (Institute for the Research of Education Systems 1993).

In the early 1950's, primary schools, run by the *Chabad* (*Lubavitch*) Hassidic community were recognized as "a non-stream stream."[54] After the State Education Law passed they were included as an independent network in the Religious State education stream. By the year 2002 the Chabad network comprised ten percent of the primary religious-State schools.[55] They include over 10,000 students.[56] The willingness of this ultra-Orthodox Hassidic sect to join State education that emphasizes the Zionist nature of its religious education seems remarkable. Although, *Lubavitch* Hassidism are unique among the ultra-Orthodox Hassidic sects, in its nationalistic aspects and its involvement in Israeli society, its submitting to "education . . . according to the religious tradition and in the spirit of religious Zionism"[57] seems far reaching. Not less far reaching is the State's readiness to recognize a particular stream within religious-national education, thus reverting in a way to pre-statehood educational streams system. One cannot overlook, moreover, the fact that by joining State education the *Lubavitch* educational network became fully financed by the State. It should be, moreover, emphasized that unlike other Hassidic educational networks, *Lubavitch* primary schools cater to a large extent to students who come from outside of this sect. In a biography of the founder of the Chabad network, it is revealed that this was part of a strategic plan: Not merely to receive state funding but also to enlist students from non-religious backgrounds that might be deterred from joining independent religious schools.[58]

Several Knesset Members submitted a bill proposing the amendment of the State Education Law establishing a third stream of State education – the Judaic-Pluralistic Stream similar to the Religious State Education stream. This stream was designed to emphasize "the importance of tolerance and co-existence among religious, secular and conservative people as well as persons of other Jewish identities."[59] The bill was not accepted.[60]

54. *See* Menachem Cohen, *The Rabbi and the Network: The Rabbi: The Network is "a non-stream stream"*, HA'CHINUCH [The Education – The educational site of Chabad schools], Mar. 9, 2006 (Isr.), *available at* http://www.reshet.org.il/chinuch/arc1.asp?aid=412&catid=2.

55. Records, *supra* note 51.

56. *See* Reshet Chabad, *Religious Public Schools, Israel, available at* http://www.reshet.org.il/en/html/ourstory.asp.

57. *See supra* text accompanying note 39.

58. MENACHEM B-E ZIGELBOIM, DAVID MY SERVANT: TAILS FROM THE LIFE OF RABBI DAVID CHANZIN (Eshel Library 2004).

59. Draft bill amending the State Education Law (Recognition of Institutions for Jewish-Pluralistic Education), 5764 (P/1821) (2004) (translation by author) (Isr.), *available at* http://www.knesset.gov.il/privatelaw/data/16/1821.rtf.

60. An identical bill has been submitted a year later and defeated as well: Draft bill amending the State Education Law P/3160 (Isr.), *available at* http://www.knesset.gov.il/privatelaw/data/16/3160.rtf.

2.4 Arab, Druze and Circassian State Schools

Arab State schools operate in Arab towns and villages and in city quarters with large Arab populations.[61] The same goes for Druze[62] and Circassian[63] villages. Students belonging to these ethnic groups may choose to attend these schools or a general ("Jewish" or "Arab") school where available.

The Arab schools are part of the general State schools and are not regarded as religious schools. State Education Law does not classify them as separate schools; however, the Law provides for a curriculum, in non-Jewish schools, that will fit "their special conditions."[64] The Law provides for the Minister of Education to promulgate regulations for the adaptation of the provisions of the Law to the needs of those students.[65] In practice the curriculum is adapted to the religion of the student body, whether Muslim or Christian. Schools operating in Druze villages adapt their curriculum to that population. The same goes for Circassian villages. There exists, moreover, a separate Division for Arab education at the Ministry of Education. The Regulations of State Education (Consultative Council for Arab Education), 5756-1996[66] established a Consultative Council for Arab Education, to advise the Minister on matters concerning Arab education. The regulations charged the council with the formulation of an educational and pedagogical policy that would ensure the equal status of Arab citizens, taking into account their linguistic and cultural individuality and their heritage. The council is entrusted further with the task of paving a policy for the development of curricula "that will express the needs and culture of the Arab population."[67] However, the regulations

---

61. For a discussion about the Arabs in Israel see ORI STENDEL, THE ARABS IN ISRAEL (Arie Yisrael trans., Sussex Academic Press 1997).

62. The Druze are a distinct religious community residing mainly in Lebanon, Israel, Syria, Turkey and Jordan. Small communities of expatriates also live in other parts of the world, including the United States, Canada, Latin America, Australia, and Europe. There are some 90,000 Druze living in Israel, mainly in villages in the Galilee. In five of them they constitute the entire population. The origin of the Druze is debatable; however, they are regarded as stemming from the *Isma'alia*, an extreme sect of *Sh'ite* Muslims. Yet, they are not Muslims. The tenets of their faith are kept secret even within the community. They do not accept converts nor do they recognize converting out. For further information about the Druze in Israel, see ORI STENDEL, THE MINORITIES IN ISRAEL : TRENDS IN THE DEVELOPMENT OF THE ARAB AND DRUZE COMMUNITIES (Israel Economist 1974).

63. The Circassians are Sunni Muslims of the *Hanafi* School, yet they maintain a distinct ethnic identity and share neither the Arab origin nor the cultural background of the larger Islamic community. They are of Caucasian origin and arrived in the Middle East towards the end of the 19th century. In Israel there are some 4,000 Circassians. Most of them live in two villages in the Galilee. For more about the Circassians in Israel, see DAVID WASSERSTEIN, THE DRUZES CAND CIRCASSIANS OF ISRAEL (Anglo-Israel Ass'n 1976).

64. State Education Law, 5713-1953, 7 LSI 113, § 4 (1952-53) (Isr.).

65. *Id.* § 34(4).

66. Regulations of State Education, 1996, KT 5756, 1407.

67. *Id.* § 5(1).

do not provide that the Minister must consult with the council before making decisions and he is not bound by its recommendations.

The main language of instruction in these schools is Arabic, and Arab culture is being taught.[68] The use of Arabic represents a characteristic of cultural autonomy, the language being related to cultural, historical, and religious attributes of the Arab minority in Israel.[69]

In the year 2000, the State Education Law was amended and it decreed that among the objectives of education was the learning of "the language, culture, history, heritage, and unique tradition of the Arab population and of other population groups in Israel, and recognition of the equal rights of all citizens of Israel."[70] It was also stated that the objective of State education was "to educate people to love others, their nation, and their country, to be loyal citizens of the State of Israel, to respect their parents and family, their heritage, their cultural identity, and their language."[71] Yet, Arab politicians and educators are not content with these provisions. They argue that the content of the studies has been dictated to a large extent by the Ministry and does not include sufficient Arab studies. They demand, moreover, full autonomy for Arab education. This is so in spite of the fact that in recent years the autonomy of the Arab school widened. Thus since 1989 the Division for Arab Education is headed by an Arab educator and Arab education has been decentralized as to enable the administration of the schools on a district level. Moreover, the teaching of Arab culture and the belonging to the Arab nation and the Palestinian nation has also increased since the seventies.[72] A bill aimed to create a separate Arab State stream, similar to the Religious State stream has been submitted to the Knesset, yet has not been accepted.[73]

---

68. *See* Suzie Navot, *Language Rights in Israel*, *in* ISRAELI REPORTS TO THE XV INTERNATIONAL CONGRESS OF COMPARATIVE LAW 43 (Alfred M. Rabello ed., Harry Sacher Institute for Legislative Research and Comparative Law 1999).

69. HCJ 4112/99 Adalah v. City of Tel Aviv-Jaffa [2002] IsrSC 56(5) 393, 418. Nevertheless, the Court criticized the degree of national-cultural autonomy granted to the Arab education system. *See* MAJID AL-HAJ, EDUCATION, EMPOWERMENT AND CONTROL: THE CASE OF THE ARABS IN ISRAEL (State Univ. of New York Press 1998).

70. State Education Law, 5713-1953, 7 LSI 113, § 2(11) (1952-53) (Isr.).

71. *Id.* § 2(1).

72. For the development of Arab education, see Chaled Abu-Asaba, *The Arab Education Network: Developments and Contemporary Reality*, *in* ARAB SOCIETY IN ISRAEL (1): POPULATION, SOCIETY, ECONOMICS (Aziz Chidar ed., Van Lir Institute 2005). *See also* Ruth Gavison and Tali Bebelfor, *Background Material for a Discussion on Collective Rights of Minorities* (Presented to the Constitutional Committee of the Knesset 2005) (Isr.), *available at*
http://www.huka.gov.il/wiki/material/data/H13-09-2005_8-54-06_miutim.doc.

73. *See* Draft bill amending the State Education Law, 5766 (P/339/17) (2006) (amending law on Arab education); *available at*
http://www.knesset.gov.il/privatelaw/data/17/339.rtf. Five identical Bill Proposals have been defeated by the 14th (P/1666, P/2453), 15th (P/4228, P/52), and 16th Knesset (P/977).

Recently some bi-national and bi-lingual schools have been established.

2.5 State Schools With Reinforced Jewish Studies

There are provisions in the State Education Law that though not designed solely for religious education, may serve to further it. Section 4 imposes on the Minister of Education the task of establishing a curriculum for all State schools. Section 5 charges the Minister with establishing a "supplementary programme" to the prescribed curriculum of every official educational institution encompassing one quarter of the total curriculum. In a Religious State-educational institution this must be "one of the special programmes designed for such school."[74] Section 6 enables the Minister to establish a unique programme, if so requested by the parents of the students in a certain educational institution. Additionally, the Law allows the parents of three-quarters of the students in a class to demand the Minister to establish a special curriculum beyond the prescribed curriculum.[75] Parents may also request the Minister's approval for an additional curriculum above the prescribed teaching hours to be financed by the parents or by the local council.[76]

Under this aegis, parents joined to create schools with an enhanced program of Jewish studies, yet not Orthodox oriented. These schools, the first of which was founded in 1976, known under the name "Tali" [a Hebrew acronym for "reinforcement of Jewish studies"], operate with the sponsorship of the Schechter Institute for Jewish Studies, which provides pedagogical and educational support with a Conservative orientation.[77] In the early 1990s, the Ministry of Education adopted the Tali network in an effort to encourage Jewish education within non-religious State schools. A special inspector charged with the task of supervising the network was appointed within the Ministry. Moreover, State resources were made available to Tali, which became a semi official stream within the State

See also raft bill amending the State Education Law, 5764 (P/2680) (2004) (amending laws to include Arab heritage, *available at* http://www.knesset.gov.il/privatelaw/data/16/2680.rtf. A Druze educational network petitioned the High Court of Justice demanding that it be recognized as an official institution. The petition has been rejected since the network insisted on its independence and rejected the Ministry's inspection. HCJ 2828/02 Al-arfan v. Minister of Education [2004] IsrSC 2004(2) 232.

74. State Education Law, 5713-1953, 7 LSI 113, § 5 (1952-53) (Isr.).

75. State Education Regulations (Supplementary program), 1953, KT 5713, 102, § § 6, 2.

76. State Education Law, 5713-1953, 7 LSI 113, § 8 (1952-53) (Isr.).

77. On the Tali education, see Eitan Chikli, *Tali Education: The Development and Realization of an Educational Concept in the Context of Changing Realities* (Doctoral Thesis, The Jewish Theology Seminary 2004) (Isr.); HARVEY MEIROVICH, THE SHAPING OF MASORTI JUDAISM IN ISRAEL (Argov Center 1999) (Isr.); Lee Levine, *The Tali Schools*, 7 STUD. IN JEWISH EDUC. 259 (1995). On the Schechter Institute for Jewish Studies, see § 2.5.

schools. At present, some seventy schools are part of the Tali network. In most cases the entire school belongs to the system; in other cases only individual classes. In addition, over one-hundred kindergartens belong to the network. The population of the Tali network totals some 30,000 students. Most of the schools were not founded as Tali schools. Rather, existing State schools joined the chain at the initiative of the principals and parents.

The program defines its mission as "providing Jewish, Zionist, and democratic education in an open atmosphere and in the spirit of the time, with the cooperation of parents and educators. The education aspires to form a broad-minded personality, whose outlook contains layers of both the Jewish and general culture."[78] The curriculum includes prayers, welcoming the Sabbath, the weekly Torah portion, holidays, and sources of the Jewish tradition as well as both Jewish and universal values.[79] Some thirty schools also include daily prayers in their curriculum. Thus, the Supreme Court declared as follows, "[t]rue, from the formal-organizational aspect, the Tali schools are state education schools. They do not belong to the religious state education. Yet, on the substantial level they are very similar to the religious state schools."[80]

In the 1980's, the Movement for Progressive Judaism, which is part of the World Reform Movement, joined the Tali network in opening a school in Jerusalem. However, the cooperation between the two movements came to an end when, according to Tali Foundation director, it became obvious that the Reform movement attempted to take a lead of the Tali network alongside the Tali Educational Fund.[81] According to the Reform Movement the source of this tension was the fact that, unlike Tali schools in general, the schools run by that movement comprise of students from families who belong to the movement and are an integral part of the local community. In recent years the cooperation between the Tali network and the Reform Movement resumed. At present there are three primary schools and one high-school that belong to the movement and are operated as Tali schools. On top of that, the Reform Movement runs a network of some fifty kindergartens that are part of its communities. Some of them are municipal kindergartens that operate under the pedagogical responsibility of the movement. A primary municipal state school that belongs to the movement is now under construction in Tel-Aviv. On top of that, the movement operates a program of educational involvement in some forty

78. From a memo of the General Director of the Ministry of Education and Culture, May 1, 2003.

79. *See* http://www.tali.org.il.

80. HCJ 8186/03 Tali Education Fund v. The Ministry of Education [2004] IsrSC 59(3) 873, 889 (ordering the Ministry to allocate additional funding to the Tali schools that introduced daily prayers as part of their curricula, though unlike Religious State-schools they are not imposed by the Ministry).

81. *See* Chikli, *supra* note 77, at 147-65.

state schools. The movement runs also an MA program in Jewish education in conjunction with the religious (Orthodox) Bar-Ilan University. Some of the sixty graduates of the program teach at those schools.[82]

There are other State schools that do not belong to the official religious stream but reinforce Judaic studies. Thus, there are joint schools for religious and secular students, founded originally in mixed communities. Some five years ago the Meitarim network was set up to spread the gospel of religious-secular education across the country. Approximately twenty institutions joined the chain and it totals close to 3,000 students from kindergartens to high schools. The student body comes from all range of society, such as former religious families, secular families and children born to parents of mixed marriages.[83] The revival of the interest of seculars in Judaic studies may be attributed to a recent trend of viewing Judaism as a culture rather than merely a religion. While in the past non-religious people regarded Judaic sources as entirely religious in nature thus showing little interest in them, the recent approach is to view them as part of Jewish national identity.[84] This trend led to the establishment of various secular institutions that study Judaism from a secular point of view.

2.6 Recognized Non-official Schools and Non-recognized Schools[85]

Alongside the State schools, operate schools that are recognized by the State yet are "non-official." These are "[an] educational institution which the Minister by declaration published in Reshumot [Official Gazette], has declared to be a recognized educational institution."[86] Under this provision various types of "non-official" schools have been established. These include agriculture settlements, mainly kibbutzim, as well as specialized schools[87] or schools that wish to preserve utmost autonomy. Some schools

---

82. *See The Israel Movement for Progressive Judaism Education Department 2006 Summary* (Isr.).

83. *See* Ilan Shahar, *More Secular Parents Look to Schools to Provide Missing Jewish Education*, HA'ARETZ, July 21, 2004.

84. *Cf.* Asher Maoz, *The Place of Jewish Law in the State of Israel*, 40 HAPRAKLIT 53 (1991-92) (Isr.).

85. *See* Leslie Sebba and Varda Shiffer, *Tradition and Rights to Education: The Case of the Ultra-Orthodox Community in Israel*, *in* CHILDREN'S RIGHTS AND TRADITIONAL VALUES, *supra* note 2, at 160.

86. Compulsory Education Law, 5709-1949, 3 LSI 125, § 1 (1948-49) (Isr.). Section 11 of the State Education Law empowered the minister to promulgate in regulations the procedure and conditions for such declaration, which the minister did in State Education Law (Recognized Institutions) Regulations, 1953, KT 5713, 399; *See* HCJ 8437/99 Network of Lubbavitch Kindergartens in the Holy Land v. Minister of Education [2000] IsrSC 54(3) 69.

87. As an illustration, the International American School in Israel is organized as a recognized school. It caters to children of diplomats, U.N. representatives, representatives of overseas institutions as well as foreign businesspersons. However, a substantial portion

have been privately organized prior to the enactment of the State Law Education and did not wish to join the State education system. However, most of the recognized schools are religious schools, both Jewish and Christian. The latter include schools that are operated by the Greek-Catholic Malachite Church, the Latin Patriarch, and the Anglican Church. Muslim and Druze students also study in these schools, and at times they form a substantial portion of the student body.[88] There are even church schools where most of the student body does not belong to that church. Nevertheless, while the percentage of Christian students who attend private schools reaches forty-two percent of all students in the Christian population, only fifteen percent of Druze students and one percent of Muslim students attend these schools. There is also a Druze network of recognized schools.[89]

Most of the recognized religious Jewish schools are ultra-Orthodox. There are at least fifteen variants of these schools' networks, belonging to various Hassidic communities as well as to "opponent" communities.[90] The main networks are the Independent Education Network and the *Sephardic* Centre of Fountain of Religious Education in Israel, known as "The Fountain of Religious Education" [*"Mayan Ha'hinuch Ha'torani"* in Hebrew]. The first network is the former *Agudat Yisrael* network that was an official stream under Compulsory Education Law, yet declined to integrate into the Religious-State Education. The latter was founded in 1984, by the Sephardic religious new political party, "*Sephardi* Keepers of the Torah" ["*Hitahdut Sephardim Shomrei Torah*"], known as *Shas*. While the Independent Education Network caters exclusively to the ultra-Orthodox population, the Fountain of Religious Education includes students from various backgrounds, most of them of non-Orthodox, but rather traditional or even non-religious background. The Independent Education Network established in the late nineties a network for students that come from non-religious families called *Shuva* [repent]. This network caters, to a large extent, to Russian immigrants. There is a strict sexual division among the students in these networks. Such division exists also in many Religious-State education schools, as well as in the *Chabad* network. The educational system of male students within the Independent Education Network is divided into four age groups: *Talmudei Torah* [verb. Torah Studies] for ages five to thirteen; *Yeshiva* [verb. session, sitting] divided

of its student body population consists of Israeli children. The school adopted the International American Curriculum for English Speaking Students.

88. Moreover, there are church schools where most of the student body does not belong to that church.

89. HCJ 2828/02 Al-arfan v. Minister of Education [2004] TakSC 2004(2) 232. The total number of students enrolled in Christian primary schools during the school year 2005-2006 was 22,632 out of a total of 137,192 in all primary recognized schools; *see* Ministry of Education, *Budget Proposal for the Budget Year 2007 No. 11*, at 11 (Oct. 2006).

90. *See* ZAMERET, *supra* note 7, at 142 ("Opponent" communities oppose Hasidism. They are also known as Lithuanians).

between a "Small *Yeshiva*" [*Yeshiva ketana*] for ages thirteen to sixteen and "High - *Yeshiva*" [*Yeshiva gevoha*] from the age of seventeen. Girls are educated in a separate network.

The number of students in the ultra-Orthodox schools has increased significantly, from 5,000 (five percent of primary school age population) upon the establishment of the State of Israel to about 200,000 (12.7 percent) at the turn of the century,[91] and the numbers keep growing. At the same time the proportional numbers of students, both in State Education schools and in Religious-State Education schools, dropped substantially.[92] A special division was set in the Ministry of Education, which is administratively in charge of these schools – The Division of Recognized Non-official Education.

A further category includes schools that are neither State nor recognized schools, but which the Minister of Education has decreed that parents and children attending them are exempt from the obligation "to ensure that such child or adolescent attends a recognized educational institute."[93] Though the students and their parents are those who are exempt from the duty to attend State or recognized schools, in jargon the schools themselves are known as "non-recognized" or "exempt" institutions. These institutions belong to ultra-Orthodox Judaism and are run like old fashion education as prevailed in the Diaspora.[94]

A religious community may run schools belonging to various classifications. Thus, the *Chabad* community has an education network belonging to the Religious-State schools alongside with *Talmudei Torah* which are recognized institutions. Likewise, the Noam network runs both schools that are part of the Religious-State schools and others that are recognized schools. Originally these schools have been organized as recognized institutions in order to enable them to establish exclusive schools. Once established as such they endeavor to join the Religious-State

91. *Id.*

92. *See* VARDA SHIFFER, THE HAREDI EDUCATION SYSTEM: ALLOCATION, REGULATION AND CONTROL (Floresheimer Institute for Policy Studies 1998) (Isr.). *See also supra* note 49. A former minister of education predicted that if this trend continues ultra-Orthodox education will account for one-third of elementary school population by the year 2020. Amnon Rubinstein, *The Secular Hourglass*, HA'ARETZ, May 8, 1998.

93. Compulsory Education Law, 5709-1949, 3 LSI 125, § 5(a) (1948-49) (Isr.).

94. *Id.* § 5. Section 5 of the Law refers to "educational institutions"; however, this provision is practically being applied to ultra-Orthodox schools. In a case that came before the Supreme Court, the Ministry of Education ordered the closure of a primary school that was opened in an exclusive settlement in contravention of the Ministry's provision to register the children to the regional school. In an attempt to frustrate the order, some of the parents approached the Minister of Education requesting to apply to their children the provision of § 5. Upon the Minister's refusal they petitioned the Supreme Court. The Court dismissed the petition in a short opinion stating that "Section 5 does not apply to this case. This section is not aimed to circumvent the requirements of the Compulsory Education Law. It rather applies to anomalous exceptional cases." HCJ 4901/98 Carmei Yosef v. The minister of Education [1998] IsrSC 98 (3)705.

schools and enjoy full financial support by the State. A further example is the Reform Movement primary school that is being established at the Leo Beck high-school Haifa campus. In this case the movement finds itself obliged to operate the school as a recognized institution due to the fact that the Haifa municipality rejected the movement's request to operate it as a municipal State school.

The autonomy of private schools, especially religious schools, and the extent of State supervision that may be exercised over them, varies. Generally speaking, the autonomy of exempt institutions is much wider than that of recognized schools. However, even among the latter institutions there exist substantial differences. First, a distinction must be drawn between schools that operate under the Education Ordinance enacted by the British Mandatory government in 1933,[95] which remained valid in the State of Israel,[96] and other schools. Secondly, a distinction should be drawn between Religious Communities' schools and others. Church schools in Israel operate under the rules of the Education Ordinance. The right to operate those schools had been recognized by the Palestine Mandate, granted by the League of Nations to Britain, which provides: "The right of each community to maintain its own schools for the education of its own members in its own language, while conforming to such educational requirements of a general nature as the Administration may impose, shall not be denied or impaired."[97]

The Ordinance recognizes as community schools "any school of which the proprietor is a community . . . organized under the Religious Communities (Organization) Ordinance[98] or exercising jurisdiction in accordance with . . . the Palestine Order in Council."[99] The Ordinance granted broad autonomy to these schools. Among others, the Ministry of Education is not entitled "to demand any change in the curriculum or internal administration of the school"[100] and its supervision is limited to preserving public order and proper management."[101]

95. 1 Laws of Palestine 623.

96. A revised version of the Ordinance was published in LSI (N.V.) 31, 15.8.1978 (Isr.).

97. Terms of the British Mandate for Palestine confirmed by the Council of the League of Nations on July 24, 1922; League of Nations Official Journal, August 1922, at 1007-12; Terms of League of Nations Mandates, 2-7, art. 15, U.N. Doc. A/70 (Oct. 1946).

98. 2 Laws of Palestine 1292. It was under this ordinance that the organization of religious communities was made possible.

99. 3 Laws of Palestine 2569. This legislation, which was regarded as supreme law in Palestine, recognized various religious communities and granted their courts jurisdiction in matters of personal status. *See* Asher Maoz, *Matrimonio E. Divorzio Nel Dirrito Israeliano*, 2 DAIMON 222 (2002). *See also* State Education Ordinance, in LSI (N.V.) 31, § 1, 15.8.1978 (Isr.).

100. *Id.* § 6(b).

101. *Id.* § 6(c).

The Ordinance and the Regulations made under it "give clear expression to the intention of the Government to refrain from all interference in the conduct and management of private schools [conducted by foreign religious and charitable organizations] which is not absolutely necessary for the maintenance of order and good Government."[102]

According to State Education Law the Minister of Education may regulate the basic curriculum of recognized schools, as well as their administration and inspection. The minister issued the State Education (Recognized Institutions) Regulations, 5714-1953.[103] According to these regulations, no institution will be recognized, unless it fulfills "the basic curriculum," which "will consist [of] seventy-five percent of the total curriculum hours in an official education institution."[104] However, "the basic curriculum" is defined as "the number of hours according to the subjects that are compulsory on each educational institute."[105] There are no provisions as to the content of this curriculum, save for the fact that an institution wishing to be granted recognition, must submit "a curriculum, including extra-curricular activities."[106] There are no provisions that the curriculum is subject to the approval of the minister. The result was that these schools enjoyed vast independence in calculating their educational system.[107] In 1969, the Knesset enacted the Inspection of Schools Law.[108] The Law introduced an important innovation in the subjection of schools to State control. Section 28, entitled "Inspection of schools," provides as follows:

> (a) The Minister of Education and Culture may issue to the holder of a license directions which, in the opinion of the Minister, are necessary in order to ensure that the education provided at the school is based on the principles set out in section 2 of the State Education Law 5713-1953.[109]

---

102. *See* Report by His Majesty's Government in the United Kingdom of Great Britain and Northern Ireland to the Council of the League of Nations on the Administration of Palestine and Trans-Jordan for the year 1932, *available at* http://domino.un.org/unispal.nsf/d80185e9f0c69a7b85256cbf005afeac/73f844e0122d67720 52565d80053b611!OpenDocument.

103. State Education Regulation, 1953, KT 5714, 104.

104. *Id.* § 3(c).

105. *Id.* § 1.

106. *Id.* § 2(6).

107. Sebba and Shiffer suggest, however, that the Minister indeed imposed on the non-recognized schools the "*adoption of the basic curriculum.*" Sebba & Shiffer, *supra* note 85, at 166-67 [emphasis in the original]. They, moreover, submit that the expression "basic curriculum" in § 11 of the Law, "refer to the 'basic curriculum' that constitutes the compulsory element in the teaching curriculum which the Minister has to determine for official schools . . . unless it was anticipated that he would provide for a *different* basic curriculum for unofficial schools." *Id.*

108. Inspection of Schools Law, 5729-1969, 23 LSI 180 (1968-69) (Isr.).

109. *Id.* § 28(a).

(b) The curriculum, textbooks, references books, teaching aids and teaching achievements of the school shall be subjected to the inspection of the Minister of Education and Culture and shall conform to the general directions obtaining in the type of school.

However, attention must be called to the fact that the subjection of schools to the principles of State education is not automatic and depends upon directives issued by the Minister.

The law applies, according to its definition, to "any school in which more than ten students study or are being educated systematically."[110] Section 36 originally provided that the Law will apply to existing schools six months after its publication, unless the Minister postponed this date. This provision has been repealed, however, and its existing version empowers the Minister to gradually apply the Law to existing schools after consulting the Education and Culture Committee of the Knesset.[111] Indeed, the Minister issued several orders, the latest from 1977, providing for a wide application thereof. The Law does not apply, however, to *yeshivas*, as well as seminaries for the training of clergies. Nor does it apply to religious studies in high-school *yeshivas*.[112] In the same vain it does not apply to institutions of higher education.[113]

Another important statute regarding the administration of, *inter alia*, recognized non-official schools, as well as exempt institutions, is the Student Rights Law, 5761-2000.[114] This Law was enacted in order to comply with the U.N. Convention on the Rights of the Child[115] of which Israel is a signatory.[116] The Law prohibits an educational institution from discriminating against a student, or a potential student, on the basis of ethnic affiliation, socio-economic background or political views.[117] This provision applies both to the admittance and expulsion of students and to their treatment in school.[118] The provision expressly does not apply to exempt schools;[119] However, this provision has been introduced in the

110. *Id.* § 2(a).

111. *Id.* § 36, *amended by* Inspection of Schools Law, 5729-1970, 24 LSI 157 (1969-70) (Isr.).

112. *Id.* § 2(a)(4).

113. *Id.* § 2(a)(2).

114. Student Rights Law, 2000, S.H. 42.

115. Convention on the Rights of the Child, G.A. Res. 44/25, U.N. Doc. A/RES/44/49 (Nov. 20, 1989), *available at* http://www.unhchr.ch/html/menu3/b/k2crc.htm.

116. *See* U.N. Convention on the Rights of the Child, KA 31, 279. A commission appointed by the Minister of Justice recommended alterations in the Student Rights Law in order to make it more compatible with the provisions of the convention and apply them to all the students in the education system; *see The Commission for the Examination of Basic Principles in the area of the Child Rights and the Law and their Application in Legislation: Report of the sub-Commission on Education* (Feb. 2003) (Isr.).

117. Student Rights Law, 2000, S.H. 42, § 5.

118. *Id.* § 5(a)(1).

119. *See id.* § 16.

Inspection of Schools Law,[120] and as such applies also to them. Several provisions, referring to the procedure of expelling students from school and to the establishment of student councils do not apply to non-official schools unless the Minister has otherwise ordered.[121]

Another relevant statute is the Prohibition of Discrimination in Supplies, Services and Entrance into Entertainment Areas and Public Venues Law, 5761-2000.[122] Section 3 of the statute prohibits a supplier of public services from discriminating, *inter alia*, on grounds of race, religion, nationality and origin. According to section 2, public service includes services in the area of education. In the explanatory notes to the statute bill[123] it was made clear that the law also applies to the private sector when engaging in public services. In a case involving a claim of discrimination in admittance to school, the court stated: "A refusal to register a student to a school due to his or her ethnic origin, when registration is open to other ethnic groups … constitutes a discrimination in the supply of a public service."[124]

The question of the autonomy of private schools, especially of religious schools, and the extent of the supervision that can be exercise over them, has come before the courts on several occasions.

In the *Jabareen* case,[125] the issue was the refusal of the St. Joseph high school, owned by the Greek-Catholic Malachite community, to enroll a female Muslim student unless she agreed to attend school bare headed and to participate in co-gender physical education activities wearing a gym suit. The school is managed by the Church and has educated the community's priests in the past. Over the years it has opened its gates to students of other communities, and at present, most of the students do not belong to the Greek-Catholic community; in fact, a third are Muslim.

The Israeli legislator refrained from applying the Inspection of Schools Law, which as we have seen entitles the Minister of Education to issue directives to the owner of the school so as to ensure that the education provided at the school is based on the principles of State Education Law. The Ministry of Education pursued a stated policy of "broad discretion and freedom of choice for schools, consistent with the special needs of each community served by the school," especially "for private schools serving a

120. *See* Inspection of Schools Law, 5729-1969, 23 LSI 180, § 32(a1) (1968-69) (Isr.), *as amended by* the Student Rights Law, 2000, S.H. 402.

121. Inspection of Schools Law, 5729-1969, 23 LSI 180, § 16(a) (1968-69) (Isr.).

122. Prohibition of Discrimination in Supplies, Services and Entrance into Entertainment Areas and Public Venues Law, 2000, S.H. 58.

123. Prohibition of Discrimination in Supplies, Services and Entrance into Entertainment Areas and Public Venues Law, 2000, HH, 370.

124. CC (Kefar Sabba) 5244/02 Nathan v. Ministry of Education [2006] Tak-Magistrate 2006(3) 14118, § 73.

125. HCJ 4298/93 Jabareen v. Minister of Education [1994] IsrSC 48(5) 199.

recognized religious community in Israel."[126] In the *Jabareen* case, the Supreme Court indicated that had it been a State school, the student would have been entitled to cover her head, because "it is right to grant every student the freedom to express in her dress the principles of her religion. Rules regarding the uniformity of dress should not prevail over the student's freedom of religion."[127] But the situation was different in the case of a private school belonging to a religious community, which is by definition entitled to reject students who are not part of the community. In this case,

> the requirement for uniform dress and conduct reflects educational considerations related to the character and essence of the school as an institution of that religious community. The uniform dress and conduct serve as a common denominator that allows all students — Christians of the Greek-Catholic community and Christians of other communities, as well as non-Christians — to lead a common life within the school, based on religious and ethnic pluralism. Violation of the uniform dress code and conduct will harm the character and the unique feature of the school, which will harm the unique character and the (moderate) religious spirit that is prevalent in the school.[128]

The Court made it clear, however, that "the educational autonomy of a 'community school' is not absolute," and that if the school's decision had not been substantively just, and "if these reasons had been based on uniformity as an independent value, [we] would have been ready to rule that the freedom of religion of the appellant outweighs them."[129]

These issues were discussed extensively in a Jerusalem District Court ruling.[130] The case involved an ultra-Orthodox school (*Talmud Torah*), an "exempt institution" with a student body from Hassidic families, which refused to admit students of the *Lubavitch* Hassidic community. The school offered two justifications for its refusal. First, the students and their parents believed that the Lubavitch Rabbi was the Messiah, "which is contrary to the fundamental faith of the Hassidic group."[131] Second, the language of instruction of the *Talmud Torah* was Yiddish, not Hebrew, a

126. Quotation from the Ministry's response to the petition. *Id.* at 202.

127. *Id.* at 203 (Barak, D.P.). It is submitted that this statement must be read subject to the right of Religious-State schools to maintain a religious way of life. Indeed, one of the Justices referred, in an obiter, to a pupil in such school refusing to cover his head. He stated that he was not convinced that "in a conflict between freedom of expression of the pupil and the educational framework within which he studied, he would prevail, in spite of the education for tolerance and pluralism." *Id.* at 204-05 (Goldberg, J.).

128. *Id.* at 204 (Barak, D.P).

129. Administrative Petition (Jerusalem) 1320/03 Alkeslasi v. City of Betar Illit [2004] Tak-District 2004 (2) 6351.

130. *Id.* § 20.

131. *Id.* § 3.

language that the said students did not master.[132] Nevertheless, the local council offered to admit the students within the framework of a *Lubavitch* track operating in the very same school, but this offer was rejected by the parents.

In a comprehensive ruling, the Court discussed the status of private schools that operate as exempt institutions, and the extent of state oversight exercised over these schools.

> The existence of private schools alongside the official ones is one of identifying marks of participatory democracy. This type of regime encourages community action and makes it possible for the community to manage its affairs as it best understands, among others by operating educational institutions. Private schools relate to the need to ensure the continued existence of various streams within a multi-cultural society, thereby also promoting the personal autonomy of individuals as expressed in their ability to exercise control over their education. The attempt to dictate the content and method of education is liable to create opposition by causing injury to this autonomy. Imposing a uniform educational policy may harm the special needs of various communities and their desire to preserve their unique culture and identity. It can be said that a complete rejection of private schools is liable to harm human dignity and in certain circumstances even the fabric of democratic life. In addition, such rejection injures the right of the minority to organize as a community where such right is recognized.[133]

This is especially true "when a community with unique characteristics, including religious ones, exists."[134]

At the same time, the Court pointed out that,

> it is necessary to examine not only the contribution of a unique education system to the preservation of the tradition and culture of a minority group, but also the abilities that its graduates bring to the labor market and the opportunities open to them for creative involvement with society at large. It follows that a solution is needed that prevents the involuntary disintegration of minority groups but at the same time protects their members and affords them sufficient mobility to migrate toward the majority if they so desire.[135]

Consequently, it is necessary "to ensure equality. Equality must exist both in the conditions of the community vis-à-vis general public and vis-à-vis

132. *Id.*
133. *Id.* § 10.
134. *Id.* § 12.
135. *Id.* § 15.

other communities, and in the terms under which it is possible to join the community."[136] Nevertheless, "it is necessary to safeguard a minimal level and compliance with borderline requirements of openness, equality, and variety."[137] The Court ruled that the respondent school, as part of a separate community education system, was exempt from the uniform curriculum of the Ministry of Education so that it may promote the cultural values of the community," but the institution is subject to the basic kernel of social values" and is not immune from State supervision.[138] The Court ruled that the Ministry of Education must verify that the institution complies with the said minimal conditions before recognizing it as an "exempt institution" and must supervise their implementation. The Court added that "the level of supervision does not depend on the values of the supervised entities. Supervision and its extent are determined by the values that society is interested in promoting."[139] These values also apply to schools whose budget the state does not contribute, "the more so to an exempt institution that is financially supported by the State."[140] The Court charged the school in question to establish clear rules; to be supervised by the Ministry of Education, which would prevent discrimination in student admissions. In this regard, the Court ruled that students who seek to be admitted to an "exempt institution" and who can overcome the "language barrier and are willing to accept the school's customs and rules cannot be rejected on the ground of their parents' world view."[141]

This decision seemed far-reaching in Israeli reality where there was no actual supervision over "exempt institution" except for safety and sanitary conditions. Although the Ministry of Education dispatched a supervisor to submit a pedagogical evaluation and to approve the curriculum, in practice the Ministry did not exercise any substantial supervision over "exempt institutions."

This decision was followed in a further case, involving ultra-Orthodox high-schools for girls. The schools were accused of exercising a discriminatory policy by applying a quota in admitting candidates of oriental origin. Referring to these schools, that were recognized non-official institutions, the Court said:

> These institutions enjoy wide pedagogical autonomy which is a manifestation of the democratic regime. This regime encourages the opportunity of communities to preserve their distinctive framework, *inter alia*, by operating separate education institutions. The need to preserve the distinctive character of the

136. *Id.* § 17.
137. *Id.* § 21.
138. *Id.* § 20.
139. *Id.* § 26.
140. *Id.* §§ 26-27.
141. *Id.* § 27.

> various communities does not surpasses however the need for public authority supervision when basic rights of utmost importance are at stake. The principle of equality, that negates discrimination, must be highly guarded even within the closed and unique framework of the community particularly within the non-official education institutions... In balancing between the preservation of the autonomy of the education institutions and the preservation of equality and the dignity of the child, priority should be accorded to the basic values.[142]

Following the Court's ruling the Ministry of Education issued directives to all recognized non-official schools ordering them to adopt "an equal, clear and measurable procedure, which will facilitate control and inspection by the Ministry." The criteria to be applied in the registration and admittance of students must be "professional, equal and clear."[143]

In further rulings the courts intervened in cases of expulsion of students from recognized non-official schools without granting them fair hearing and without providing them alternative schooling. The courts did so in spite of the fact that the relevant provisions of the Student Rights Law do not apply to them. The courts did so since the expulsions did not conform to the Circular of the Director General of the Ministry of Education. The courts stated that this circular was binding upon the schools under section 28 of the Inspection of Schools Law, authorizing the Minister to issue orders in order to affect schools' conformity with the objectives of State Education Law.[144] The Court applied the circular also to church schools, which are not subject to the Inspection of Schools Law. It found the authority to issue such directives in section 6(c) of the Education Ordinance enabling the Minister to exercise inspection over the school "as necessary for the preservation of public order and proper management."[145] The Court distinguished this case from the *Jabareen* decision asserting that

142. Administrative Petition (Jerusalem) 241/06 The Association for Civil Rights in Israel v. Ministry of Education [2006] Tak-District 2006 (2) 2143.

143. *See Instructions for the admittance and registration of students by schools that are supervised by the Department of Recognized Non-Official Education* (May 7, 2006) (Isr.), *available at* http://cms.education.gov.il/EducationCMS/Units/Owl/Hebrew/Nehalim/Naalim/Hanchayot Lerishum.htm. Based on these directives, the court rejected the Association for Civil Rights petition to apply contempt of court proceedings against the Ministry for not complying with the courts ruling; Court decision from Oct. 20, 2006 (unpublished). *See also* Yuval Vergen, *Procedures for Admitting Students into the Haredi recognized non-official education* (Knesset Oct. 22, 2006) (Isr.), *available at* http://www.knesset.gov.il/mmm/data/docs/m01660.doc.

144. *See* Administrative Petition (Jerusalem) 7267/03 Abu-Zayad v. "El Farid" School [2003] Padaor 708(4) 03. *See also* HCJ 4363/00 Committee of Poriya Ilit v. Minister of Education [2004] IsrSC 56(4) 203.

145. Civil Application (Nazareth) 1090/05 Anonymous v St. Joseph School, [2005] Tak-District 2005 (2) 365, 368.

the expulsion of students is not included within the inner administration of the church school that is submitted to the school's autonomy.[146]

A mirror case of the *Jabareen* decision has been tried recently by the Jerusalem Magistrate Court.[147] A Jewish ultra-Orthodox recognized primary school cancelled the admittance of an applicant on the ground that her mother did not dress modestly enough, especially so when appearing in school where her three other children were already enrolled. When admitted to school parents of applicants were made to sign a document. In the document they made several commitments: that they run their home according to *Halakhic* requirements; that the father steadily studies Torah; that the mother always covers her hair and follows *Halakhic* rules of modest dressing and that the children do not watch television without the parents supervision. The parents moreover agree that should their declaration prove false the school may expel the child. The Court approved the school's privilege "to set standards and requirements for admittance of students in order to carry out the objectives of the Law and maintain the distinction and character of the institution."[148] The court ruled, however, that the set standards and requirements must be reasonable and should not infringe basic rights set out in the Student Rights Law. Moreover, "they should be qualitative in the sense that they must ensure the goal of Compulsory Education Law, *i.e.* – to enable the creation of a unique educational frame that corresponds to the needs of various populations."[149] The Court added that "in view of the special status that the law bestows upon the recognized non-official institution, in view of its goal and the unique benefits provided by law, when fixing the standards for admittance the institution must ensure that they represent the substantial educational goals for which the institution operates."[150] The court refrained from ruling upon the school's criteria, since in any case they were obscure and the steps taken by the school were disproportionate.[151] The court found that by rejecting the student, while her brothers were enrolled in the same school, and by doing so at a late stage, the school infringed the dignity of both the student and parents and ordered the school to pay them compensation.[152]

In another case[153] a child was rejected by an ultra-Orthodox school due to the fact that "her mother did not conform with the modesty standards as specified in the school's spiritual rules." The Ministry of Education

146. *Id.*

147. Petty Claims (Jerusalem) 2873/06 Bernstein v. Baror [2006] Tak-Magistrate 2006(4) 20621.

148. *Id.* at 15.

149. *Id.*

150. *Id.* at 16.

151. *Id.* at 19.

152. *Id.* The plaintiffs did not ask that their daughter be reinstituted.

153. Administrative Petition (Tel-Aviv) 2176/06 M.Y. (Minor) v. Ministry of Education, [2006] Tak-District 2006(4) 8156.

declared that there was "no defect in the admission requirements of the spiritual rules, including the issue of modesty of the parents." This was so "due to the special nature of the *Haredi* population and the need for full conformity between the school values and behavior and the students home." The Ministry added that the school, which is a recognized non-official institute, must be given autonomy "to choose its students in consideration with their reliability and behavior, in accordance with the rules that will express the school's spirit."[154]

Ultra-Orthodox schools go much further in intervening in the lifestyle of their student body's families. Their educational system is supervised by the Rabbinical Committee on Education. Two years ago the Rabbinical Communications Committee ruled that one may only use an approved "kosher" cellular telephones that block access to Internet and erotic phone calls. Recently, the Rabbinical Committee on Education issued, a decree, supported by Rabbi Yosef Shalom Elyashiv, who is regarded as the leading contemporary Halakhic authority. In the decree the committee declared that "parents who use non-approved cellular phones remove themselves from the Haredi community that united to root out the disease." The committee ordered the schools to demand parents to sign a declaration that they do not use non-approved cellular phones as a condition for admitting their children to school.[155]

2.7 State Funding and School Curriculum

State schools are fully funded by the State and local authorities.[156] Recognized schools, on the other hand, are not automatically entitled to State funding.[157] The logic behind this distinction has been explained by the Supreme Court as follows:

154. The court refrained from examining the schools spiritual rules, since they were not challenged by the petitioners. In the same vain, the Ministry backed a decision by a *Haredi* school to expel a female senior student after her boyfriend proposed to her via a poster he hanged opposite the school gate. "In these schools," explained the Ministry's inspector, "contacts with a male means crossing a clear red line, and is an issue that cannot be ignored"; Yuli Haromentchko, *"Karin will you marry me?" said the poster at the entrance to a Haredi high-school in Tel-Aviv – and Karin was expelled from school,* HA'ARETZ (Isr.), *available at* http://www.haaretz.co.il/hasite/pages/ShArtPE.jhtml?itemNo=551782&contrassID=2&subContrassID=21&sbSubContrassID=0. *See also* CC (Kefar Sabba) 5244/02 Nathan v. Ministry of Education [2006] Tak-Magistrate 2006(3) 14118, § 73 (where a child was rejected by a national religious school due to the fact that "her mother did not conform to the school's spiritual rules regarding the required modesty standards").

155. *See* YATED NE'EMAN, Feb. 2, 2007 (Isr.), *available at* http://www.yated.com/.

156. *See* Compulsory Education Law, 5709-1949, 3 LSI 125, § 6 (1948-49) (Isr.).

157. The only exception is the Minister's authority to provide, by order, that a child who cannot pursue his studies in an official school will study in another institution and his schooling be funded by the State.

> Whoever wishes his child to study [in a private recognized school] accepts upon him willingly the burden of financing that is not imposed on students in the official education. This rule stems from the fact that studying in this school is a result of free choice, and there is no duty incumbent upon the public authority to bare the cost of studying there.[158]

However, under provisions of the Law, the Minister of Education may fix regulations, the State's participation in the budget of non-official schools, "if the Minister so decides and to the extent that he will decide."[159] From the very first days, the State supported recognized non-official schools, including church schools, though the scope of supported institutions, as well as the amount of support varied over the years. "Exempt" schools managed to receive State funding as well.[160]

As with State funding in general, the allocation of support for education institutes was made on an administrative level. It lacked any clear criteria and was a result of political pressure.[161] The Supreme Court ruled, however, that the State cannot spend money without clear statutory authorization.[162] This ruling led to a change in practice, under which State funding of private schools was provided for by the Annual Budget laws. This practice brought about no improvement in ensuring equality in the allocation of funds. The budget laws used to state individually the funds allocated for each and every institution without any clear and equal criteria. As a matter of fact, the amount allocated to a specific institution often reflected the political power of a Haredi party or a Haredi Member of the Knesset with whom the institution was affiliated.[163] Further criticism led to an amendment of the Budgetary Principles Law.[164] The Law, as amended, mandates "equitable tests for the disbursement of the amount allocated in

158. *See* HCJ 4363/00 Committee of Poriya Ilit v. Minister of Education [2004] IsrSC 56(4) 203, 217.

159. *See* State Education Law, 5713-1953, 7 LSI 113, § 11 (1952-53) (Isr.).

160. Extreme ultra-Orthodox schools are also exempt institutions, yet they decline to accept State funding as they do not recognize the legitimacy of the State of Israel; this is so since they regard the establishment of a Jewish state without awaiting Messiah a revolt against God. Such are the institutions of the *Eda Haredit* [the *Haredi* community] or *Naturei Karta* [Guardians of the City].

161. For a comprehensive analysis of State finances see Amnon De Hartog, *State Support for Public Institutions – The Emergence of Special Allocations*, 29 MISHPATIM 75-107 (1998) (Isr.). *See also* AMNON RUBINSHTEIN & BARAK MEDINA, 1 THE CONSTITUTIONAL LAW OF THE STATE OF ISRAEL: BASIC PRINCIPLES 289-96 (Schocken 6th ed. 2005) (Isr.).

162. *See* HCJ 59/88 Tzaban v. Finance Minister [1989] IsrSC 42(4) 705.

163. *Cf.* HCJ 166/84 Yeshivat Tomchei Temimim v. The State of Israel [1984] IsrSC 38(2) 273.

164. Budgetary Principles Law, 5745-1985, 39 LSI 61 (1984-85) (Isr.), *as amended by* 1992, S.H. 34.

the budget for the support of public institutions."[165] The Law defines a "public institution" as including "an entity that is not one of the State's institutions operated for an educational purpose."[166]

Nevertheless, the Law did not eliminate the discrimination among the institutions. This is so because it does not provide for equal funding of all the institutions, but rather for equal funding within the same kind of public institutions.[167] The Law does not prohibit the creation of several categories of education institutions that would be funded according to different criteria. Moreover, religious institutions, including schools, were funded by other governmental sources - such as the Ministry of Religious affairs - on top of the funding by the Ministry of Education. The Ministry of Social Affairs also funded boarding schools for children at risk, including a high proportion of ultra-Orthodox institutions.[168] In 2003, the Attorney General provided that educational institutions may not received funding from the Ministry of Religious affairs as well, as this would mean double funding. The funds for supporting religious schools – secondary schools, girls' colleges, high-school *yeshivas* and small *yeshivas* – were therefore transferred to the Ministry of Education.

A ministerial committee established the criteria for funding reinforced Judaic studies in State schools, Religious-State schools and ultra-Orthodox schools. The funds were divided into two tracks. The first track (amounting to 85m NIS in the year 2005) was to support Religious-State in schools preparation of students for expanded matriculation exams in Judaic subjects. The second track was supporting reinforced classic Judaic studies. The funding under this heading was allocated as follows: 62m NIS to ultra-Orthodox schools and merely 7.8m NIS (5.2 percent of the total budget) to State schools. A coalition of Jewish organizations whose aim is to advance the renaissance of pluralistic Judaism challenged these criteria arguing that they discriminate against State schools. The Supreme Court

---

165. *Id.* § 3A(e).

166. *Id.* § 3A(a).

167. It is doubtful, moreover, whether the old defective system has completely vanished. As late as 1998 it has been noted that "[a] close examination of the figures leads to the conclusion that the increases and decreases in State allocations over the years result not from changes in the financial needs of ultra-Orthodox schools and *yeshivas* but rather from changes in the power of the ultra-Orthodox political parties." SWIRSKI, *supra* note 50, at 3. Thus, in order to recruit a majority in the Knesset for approving the State Budget Law for 2006 the Government agreed to include in the Law special allocation for High School *Yeshivas* and Girls' Colleges affiliated with the Religious-State Education network, as well as for ultra-Orthodox *Yeshivas* and religious institutions. *See* Tzvi Zerachia, *The Cost of the Passing of the Budget: 302 Million Shekel*, HA'ARETZ, June 6, 2006; Tzvi Zerachia & Yair Ettinger, *Knesset Approved the Arrangement Law: The Torah Judaism Abstained*, HA'ARETZ, June 6, 2006.

168. *See* SWIRSKI, *supra* note 50.

dismissed the petition.[169] The Court justified the special allocation of funds for Religious-State schools since the expanded matriculation exams in Judaic subjects were compulsory on all their students.[170] The Court justified the criteria for allocation of funds to support reinforced classic Judaic studies as this was in line with the Ministry's policy to advance the teaching of these subjects.[171] The Court rejected the petitioner's argument that the criteria were tailored to suit ultra-Orthodox schools. The Court emphasized that the criteria did not provide for the content of the reinforced Judaic studies, but rather for their extension.[172] The Court also pointed out the fact that this funding was in addition to the funds allocated for the implementation of the Shinhar Report, which adopted a wider definition of Judaism and was designed exclusively for State schools.[173]

However, the most obvious discrimination is drawn between the Independent Education Network and the Centre of Fountain of Religious Education in Israel on the one hand, and all other recognized institutions on the other.[174] This is so since the Law explicitly states that the said provision does not apply to these networks. Rather, the law provides that these networks should be funded "according to uniform and equal criteria like the entire Israeli kids."[175] In interpreting this provision the Supreme Court ruled that the said networks should be funded "by the parameters according to which official education institutions are being funded."[176] This provision creates further discrimination between these networks and Religious-State schools. This is so since all of them compete, to a large extent, over the same potential student body. In this competition the

169. HCJ 11020/05 Panim for Jewish Renaissance in Israel v. Minister of Education [2006] Tak-SC 2006(3) 508.

170. *Id.* at 13-19.

171. *Id.*

172. *Id.*

173. *Id.*

174. This discrimination is a result of historical as well as political realities. The Independent Education Network is a continuation of the *Agudat Yisrael* schools that were official streams under the Compulsory Education Law but refrained from joining State education. It is perhaps worth noting that both this network, as well as and the Centre of Fountain of Religious Education in Israel belong to political parties that are represented in the Knesset and are frequent partners to the Government. *See* Compulsory Education Law, 5709-1949, 3 LSI 125, §2.6 (1948-49) (Isr.).

175. Budgetary Principles Law, 5745-1985, 39 LSI 61, § § 3A(i), 3A(j)(l) (1984-85) (Isr.).

176. HCJ 10808/04 The Movement for Quality Government in Israel v. Minister of Education [2006] Tak-SC 2006(3) 193. The Court rejected the petitioners' proposal to interpret the phrase "the entire Israeli kids" as referring to "Israeli kids who study in recognized schools." It is possible to interpret this provision as stating that in order to qualify for equal funding the said networks must also comply with the requirements imposed on State schools, namely teaching their basic curriculum. This interpretation is, however, most unlikely in view of sub-section 3A(j)(3) providing that "the nature and status of the *haredi* education in these [networks] shall be preserved." *Id.*

Religious-State schools are disadvantaged, since unlike the recognized schools, they must fully abide by the provisions and limitations imposed by State Education Law.[177] Indeed, the Supreme Court ruled that "the Budgetary Principle Law explicitly establishes the discrimination in the funding of the Torah educational networks and thereby legalizes an unequal distribution of government support."[178] This ruling has been upheld in a later opinion.[179] The Court recommended, however, that the Knesset apply this provision to all recognized schools, in order to prevent discrimination.[180]

In view of the discriminatory nature of the provision, it was ruled that it should be given strict interpretation. It should be limited to State support to the institutions within the framework of the annual budget. It does not apply to support from other authorities, such as local councils. Hence, the Court prohibited the allocation of a building, by a local council, for the use of a school affiliated with Centre of Fountain of Religious Education in a preferential manner. The Court ruled that the school does not have the same right as an official school.[181]

On December 2006, a draft bill to amend the State Education Law was submitted to the government by Minister Meshulam Nahari, from the *Shas* party. According to the bill local authorities must finance recognized non-official schools by the same ratio and conditions as the State's support. The bill follows a government decision from Nov. 20, 2006 and stems from the coalition agreement with *Shas*. If adopted the bill will put an end to the variety of municipal funding for recognized schools depending usually on the question of who runs the municipality.[182]

Just as the move from Religious State schools to ultra-Orthodox education,[183] recent years witnessed a decline of both the Independent Education Network and the Centre of Fountain of Religious Education in Israel and the strengthening of other ultra-Orthodox institutions

177. *Cf.* HCJ 306/05 The National Religious Party v. The Government of Israel [2005] Tak-SC 2005(3) 2141. *See generally* DAN GIBTON, EDUCATION ACCORDING TO LAW: LEGAL ASPECTS AND LEGAL RAMIFICATIONS OF THE TASK FORCE REPORT (Isr.) (on file with author).

178. HCJ 2828/02 Al-arfan v. Minister of Education [2004] IsrSC 2004(2) 232.

179. HCJ 10808/04 Movement for Quality Government in Israel v. Minister of Education [2006] Tak-Supreme 2006(3) 193.

180. *Id.* § 10.

181. Administrative Petition 1187/05 The Representatives of the Condominium v. The Municipality of Petach Tikva [2005] Tak-District 2005(3), 413; Appeals from the decision were withdrawn by the appellants: Administrative Petition Appeals 9150/05, 9153/05 Centre of Fountain of Religious Education & Petach Tikva Municipality v. Representatives of the Condominium [2006] Tak-SC 2006(3), 1731.

182. *Participation of the Local Authorities in Support of Recognized Education Institutes (Isr.). See Avirama Golan, Infringment of the Nationalistic Approach,* HA'ARETZ, Dec. 26, 2006; *available at*
http://www.haaretz.co.il/hasite/spages/805721.html?more=1.

183. *See supra* note 50.

. Thus, while in 1999 the said networks constituted sixty-one percent of the student body of all ultra-Orthodox student body, it dropped to 56.65 percent by 2006.[184] This phenomenon might be attributed to two factors. The first might be the fact that fragments of Israeli society turn more Orthodox. The other is Inspection of Schools Law: the fact that the state funds all recognized schools regardless of the number of students and other conditions, except for the minimal requirements under the Inspection of Schools Law,[185] encourages the establishment of small schools with minimal investments.

School funding in Israel generated heated political as well as legal controversy. Additionally, there were complaints that the State neglected its obligation to provide adequate education to students in order to prepare them for life because ultra-Orthodox institutions declined to teach "secular" subjects.[186] In this regard attention should be called to the "*status quo* agreement,"[187] which is considered as guarantying the autonomy of Orthodox Religious education. Indeed, the agreement ensured "complete autonomy for every stream in Education" and declared that "there will be no derogation by the government against the religious consciousness and the religious conscience of any section in Israel."[188] The agreement, however, explicitly declared: "Of course, the State will lay down the minimal obligatory lessons in the Hebrew language, history, sciences etc., and will supervise the implementation of this minimum."[189] Subject to this provision, the agreement stated that the State "will give full freedom to every stream to run its education in accordance with its consciousness, and will avoid any harm to the religious conscience."[190]

184. In the year 2005-2006 the total number of students enrolled in recognized non-official primary schools was 137,392. This number included 68,836 students in the Independent Education Network; 18,332 in the Centre of Fountain of Religious Education in Israel; 25,013 in other ultra-Orthodox schools; 2,379 in Jewish non-religious schools and 22,632 in Arab Christian schools. The number of students enrolled in exempt ultra-Orthodox schools was 41,664. During the budget year 1998-1999, 97,477 students were enrolled in recognized schools. They included 54,870 students in the Independent Education Network; 14,107 in the Centre of Fountain of Religious Education in Israel; some 12,532 in other ultra-Orthodox schools; less than 1,000 in Jewish non-religious schools and 15,000 in Arab recognized schools. And, 69,400 were enrolled in ultra-Orthodox exempt schools
This data is based on a comparison of the budget drafts of both years. Ministry of Education, *Budget Proposal for the Budget Year 1999 No. 11*, at 11 (Oct. 1998); Ministry of Education, *Budget Proposal for the Budget Year 2007 No. 11*, at 11 (Oct. 2006).

185. *See* Inspection of Schools Law, 5729-1969, 23 LSI 180 (1968-69) (Isr.).

186. *See* REPORT OF THE SUB-COMMISSION ON EDUCATION 237-39 (Ministry of Justice 2003) (Isr.), *available at*
http://www.justice.gov.il/NR/rdonlyres/27026F32-DBE8-424A-9FED-48DF6DCC2D5/0/DOCHHINUH.pdf.

187. *See* Fridman, *supra* note 5.

188. *Id.* (last paragraph of the letter).

189. *Id.*

190. *Id.* (last sentence of the letter).

In 1999, the founder of a secular NGO petitioned the Supreme Court arguing that the Minister of Education failed in his duty to set a basic curriculum for recognized education institutions. He argued that State Education Law was meant to ensure that every student will study core subjects in order to equip him with the necessary knowledge and tools that will enable him to become part of society. A co- petitioner, a graduate of an ultra-Orthodox education institute, claimed that he had been deprived of studying basic subjects that were necessary for his career and continuing education. In his response the Minister undertook to prepare and publish a basic curriculum as required "within 30 days." This undertaking became part of the Courts decision.[191] Following the decision the Minister of Education established a Commission for Examining the System of Budgeting, headed by Dr. Shimshon Shoshani, a former Director General of the Ministry. The Commission submitted its recommendations that were endorsed by the Minister.[192] Following, the Ministry of Education adopted a core curriculum that must be taught at all primary educational institutions in order to make them eligible for State funding. The Director General of the Ministry of Education issued a circular that implemented the decision.[193] The circular established what is known as "the Core Curriculum Scheme" for primary education in Israel (grades one though six). It stated "the common denominator, consisting of substances, skills and values that are obligatory to all the students in the Israeli education network."[194] The subjects included in the scheme have been defined as "the obligatory basis in the entire education network," on which the various schools may add complimentary subjects.[195] The Core Curriculum comprises of four compulsory and two recommended clusters of subjects. The compulsory clusters are: Heritage (including Bible and history) and social studies (including civic studies); Language and literature (Hebrew language and literature for Jewish schools; Arab language and literature for Arab schools; and English language and literature for all schools); Mathematics and Sciences; and Physical Education. The recommended

191. HCJ 2751/99 Paritzky v. Minister of Education, *available at* http://elyon1.court.gov.il/files/99/510/027/a02/99027510.a02.pdf. A similar view was presented, by Sebba and Shiffer. Referring to section 11 of the State Education Law, they state: "While this provision is drafted in discretionary language it seems to imply that financial support from the state was to be conditional upon a degree of regulation." Sebba & Shiffer, *supra* note 85, at 166.

192. *See* Ministry of Education, *Report of the Commission for Examining the System of Budgeting* (2002) (Isr.), *available at* http://cms.education.gov.il/http://cms.education.gov.il/EducationCMS/Units/Owl/Hebrew/HoraotNehalim/Mediniyut/DohShoshani.htm.

193. Ministry of Education, *Basic (Core) Program for Elementary Education in the State of Israel* (Isr.), *available at* http://www.education.gov.il/edun_doc/sf3ak3_1_25.htm.

194. *Id.* § 2.

195. *Id.*

clusters include Fine Arts and School Culture. It was stated that teaching the Core Curriculum is a prerequisite for obtaining State funding. State schools (general; religious, Arab and Druze) must teach the enitre curriculum, while recognized schools must teach seventy-five percent of the curriculum and exempt schools – only fifty-five percent.

In 2002 the Union of Teachers in High Schools, Seminaries and Colleges petitioned the Supreme Court to suspend the funding of *Haredi* high schools that do not teach the basic curriculum including "the basic pedagogical knowledge that each boy and girl in the State of Israel must obtain."[196] In a statement submitted to the Court, the Ministry of Education declared that it adopted a policy to be implemented gradually in primary schools up to the school year 2005-2006.[197] According to this policy, recognized schools that will teach the set core curriculum and, on top of that, will admit students on an integrative basis and will take part in the Growth and Effectiveness Measures for Schools [GEMS; *Meitzav*, in Hebrew acronym] including feed-back tests will obtain seventy-five percent of the budget of State schools. Recognized schools that will not admit students on an integrative basis will receive sixty-five percent and will have to teach only 65% of the curriculum. Exempt schools will not be subject to these requirements and will obtain fifty-five percent of the budget. The Independent Education Network and the *Sephardic* Centre of Fountain of Religious Education in Israel will continue to obtain full funding, provided they teach the entire core curriculum. The Ministry stated that teaching the core curriculum is a prerequisite for obtaining a permit for opening new schools and that, in some cases, permits of existing schools that do not teach it might be suspended. "As for intermediate schools and high schools," declared the Minister, "completion of the budgetary reform will need to be spread over several years." This is so since the Ministry will have to prepare a core curriculum, prepare materials, train teachers, build a proper system of inspection and implementation and obtain the necessary funding. The Minister declared, moreover, that she wishes to come to terms with the ultra-Orthodox community in view of the fact that it is being required to change its way of life in an area that is of utmost sensitivity.

The Court accepted the petition and declared that funding of institutions that do not apply the core curriculum and do not fulfill the objects of State education is illegal.[198] The Court added that the authority conferred upon the Minister to set conditions for recognizing a non-official school, are subject to the objectives of State education.[199] These, according

196. HCJ 10296/02 Union of Teachers in High Schools, Seminaries & Colleges v. Minister of Education [2004] IsrSc 59(3) 224, 228-29.

197. *Id.* at 233.

198. *Id.* at 235.

199. *Id.* at 238.

to the Court, include values of tolerance and respect for the other.[200] The Court added: "Funding of institutions that do not fulfill the conditions set by law, and do not carry out the objects of State Education Law, is done without legal authority."[201] The Court accepted, however, the Minister's argument that the implementation will have to last for several years and that immediate revoking of funding for ultra-Orthodox education will shatter the entire sector. The Court was of the opinion that in view of the long period that the present situation existed and the schools reliance on it; considerable steps must be taken in order to amend the illegal allocation of funds.[202] In conclusion, the Court accepted the petition and ordered that no funds be allocated to schools that do not fulfill the conditions and criteria set by law for the recognition of *Haredi* schools. The Court decided, however, that the order will come into effect towards the school year 2007-2008.

The adoption of a compulsory core curriculum was met with fierce criticism by the Orthodox community. Its leaders regarded the plan as an infringement on their autonomy and freedom of belief, and declared that they will never succumb to the dictate. The typical reaction of the ultra-Orthodox community to the reform is reflected in the following statement: "after generations of *mesirut nefesh* [verb., giving up one's life; Self Sacrifice] to instill children with the understanding of Torah and *yirat Shamayim* [verb., fear of the heaven; piety] as the focus of their studies, the Education Ministry cannot be allowed to convey the message that secular studies are of greater importance."[203] Not only do their spiritual leaders regard secular studies a waste of precious time that may be dedicated to religious studies; they are also concerned about exposing their children to a different culture.[204] It is interesting to note that in ultra-Orthodox girls' schools more time is being allocated to the teaching of general subjects. This is a result of two main factors. First, girls are not obliged to study *Torah* and there exist even statements in classical Judaic sources objecting

200. *Id.*

201. *Id.*

202. *Id.*

203. Yated Ne'eman Staff, *Parents Object to Meitzav Exam, in* DEI'AH VE DIBUR [Information and Insight], Nov. 30, 2005 (Isr.), *available at* http://chareidi.shemayisrael.com/archives5766/TLD66aexam.htm; M. Plaut, Betzalel Kahn & Yated Ne'eman Staff, *Education Ministry's Plan Holds Dangers for Chareidi Education, in* DEI'AH VE DIBUR, Aug. 28, 2002 (Isr.), *available at* http://www.chareidi.shemayisrael.com/archives5762/NTZ62alivnat.htm; S. Fried, *Core Curriculum: The Attempt to Reeducate the Chareidi Sector*, DEI'AH VE DIBUR, Jan. 21, 2004 (Isr.); *available at* http://chareidi.shemayisrael.com/archives5764/VRH64acore.htm.

204. *See* YOSEF SHALHAV & MENACHEM FRIDMAN, EXPANSION THROUGH SECLUSION: THE ULTRA-ORTHODOX COMMUNITY IN JERUSALEM (The Jerusalem Institute for Israel Studies 1989) (Isr.); Israel Eichler, *That's How the High Court of Justice Saved the Orthodox Viewpoint*, 8 MEIMAD 16 (1996) (Isr.).

to it. Second, since in the ultra-Orthodox community men are expected to devote their time to the study of *Torah* even at a mature age, the women support their families and need therefore to obtain a minimal general education that would enable them to acquire a profession.[205]

A further source of concern for ultra-Orthodox institutions was the implementation of the recommendations of the Shoshani Commission regarding school budgeting.[206] Generally speaking, the Commission advocated a transition from a system of budgeting schools on the basis of the number of classrooms to a system of budgeting based on the socio-economic make-up of the students. Towards this end the Commission suggested a model based on the level of neediness index of the students. This system works in opposite directions as far as the ultra-Orthodox network is concerned. On the one hand, it should benefit from the new system, since a large proportion of its student body comes from underprivileged families. On the other hand, due to the fact that their students are spread all over the country and due to the wide range of schools, their classes are small, and therefore they might loose funding. The Shoshani recommendations attempted to put an end to a range of specific allocations that they might have enjoyed.

In May 2006, the Ministry of Education stated that the Independent Education Network and the *Sephardic* Centre of Fountain of Religious Education in Israel fully apply the core curriculum.[207] Some doubt the truth of this statement and attribute it to lack of supervision. Moreover, this statement does not refer to other schools that constitute a substantial proportion of ultra-Orthodox education.

2.8 Future Developments

In 2003, the Government appointed a National Task Force for the Advancement of Education in Israel, headed by Shlomo Dovrat. The Task Force was charged with the mission of "conducting a comprehensive examination of the Israeli education system recommending an inclusive plan for change – pedagogical, structural and organizational – as well as

205. *See* TAMAR EL-OR, EDUCATED AND IGNORANT: FROM THE WORLD OF ULTRA-ORTHODOX WOMEN (Am. Oved. 1992) (Isr.).

206. Following the Ministry's decision to adopt the Shoshani Report, a special Parliamentary Committee advocated "a transition to a method of budgeting education in the spirit of the Shoshani Report recommendations." *See* Parliamentary Committee on Inquiry on the Issue of Social Gaps in Israel (M.K. Ran Cohen, Chair), *Report and Survey of the Development of the Social Gaps in Israel in the Last Twenty Years* (Knesset 2002). An English summary by Elia Heller (Susan Harris Rolef trans.) is available at http://www.knesset.gov.il/mmm/data/pdf/me00416.pdf.

207. *See* Yair Ettinger, *The Ministry of Education: 'The Core Curriculum' is Applied in All Schools of Shas and Agudat Yisrael*, HA'ARETZ, May 10, 2006.

outlining a means of implementing it."[208] After fifteen months of intensive deliberations the Task Force submitted its detailed "National Plan for Education."[209] The report calls for a comprehensive reform of the Israeli education system.[210] It stresses the State's duty,

> [to] equip all students with knowledge and tools that will enable each and every one of them to progress, succeed, and choose a future that permits self-actualization, creative and productive integration in work force, active citizenship, and a contribution to developing a successful, progressive society that respects all its members.[211]

It calls for the replacement of the State school system with a strong system of public education "of supreme importance for the strength of education and of the State of Israel."[212] The Task Force recognized "the liberal idea of pluralism in education."[213] It therefore, recommended the preservation of separate public religious education, as well as separate Arab, Druze and Circassian public education within the public education system. It recommended, moreover, the inclusion of *Haredi* education "as one possible trend in public education" because of their "distinctive, separate way of life."[214] This is so since,

> [i]n a society that suffers from numerous rifts and divisions, public education should be a comprehensive system that encompasses as many segments as possible of the Israeli education system [and] should build and reinforce what they have in common . . . and lower the walls of ignorance and mutual suspicion among the different communities.[215]

Alongside public education, the Task Force recognized the existence of independent *Haredi* schools. The Task Force endeavored to strike a balance between a strong public education system and the right of parents "to educate their children in accordance with their national, religious, and

208. The National Task Force for the Advancement of Education in Israel, *National Plan for Education*, at 10 (Ministry of Education 2005) (Isr.). An English summary is available at http://cms.education.gov.il/EducationCMS/Units/Owl/English/Figures/.

209. *Id.*

210. *Inter alia*, the Task Force recommended the reversal of a reform that took place in 1988. During that year the school system underwent a major reform. From a dual system of eight years of elementary education and four years of high school it turned into a triple system comprising of six years elementary school, 3 years of intermediate school (junior high school), and three years of high school. *See* BRITBART & TAVIVIAN-MIZRAHI, *supra* note 15. The Task Force recommended reverting to the old structure.

211. TAMAR EL-OR, *supra* note 205, at 12.

212. *Id.* at 60.

213. *Id.*

214. *Id.*

215. *Id.* at 32.

linguistic tradition."[216] It reached this balance by recognizing the State's right "to obligate parents to give their children an education in schools that it oversees and for which it sets certain minimum standards."[217] In any case, "the State must ensure students an open future, even if their parents have chosen a separate community education for them that does not prepare them for integration into society."[218]

"Public education," in the Task Force's vision, "shall strive to achieve the goals of education as set forth in the law and to foster students in line with the image of the ideal graduate that emerges from these goals."[219] "Public education," declared the Task Force,

> shall be based on a broad common denominator, including a core of values reflecting the basic consensus derived from universal human values and from Israel's being a Jewish and democratic state, and a significant academic core that enables all students to achieve their potential and prepares them to be part of an active, creative life.[220]

The Task Force recommended a national curriculum, "which reflects society's expectations of graduates of its education system." From this "complete national curriculum" a "compulsory core curriculum . . . [that] constitutes a common denominator for all students on the conceptual level and on the level of content, values, and cognitive and study skills," shall be derived. The curriculum in the schools shall be based on "the complete national curriculum."[221] However, "[s]ome non-public schools will follow only a partial version of the core curriculum."[222]

Public religious education will retain "complete autonomy with respect to subjects in the heritage and humanities cluster, including Jewish studies and modifications to the curriculum required in other subjects, and with respect to other educational activities, so as to not adversely affect the spirit of religious education."[223] Autonomy of the Arab education system "with respect to subject matter" will be retained as well. Likewise, the right of the Druze and Circassian communities to "a separate education system that reflects their unique way of life and whose subject matter is influenced by their heritage, their culture [and] their unique national identity, their religious traditions" shall be recognized.[224]

216. *Id.* at 11.
217. *Id.* at 204.
218. *Id.* at 208.
219. *Id.* at 79.
220. *Id.* at 213.
221. *Id.* at 82.
222. *Id.* at 86.
223. *Id.* at 234.
224. *Id.* at 215.

In order to ensure the education autonomy, the Council for State-Religious education shall be reinstated "to provide public leadership for State-Religious education."[225] The Council will be in charge "of shaping public State-Religious education from the spiritual, curricular, and pedagogical standpoints."[226] The Task Force recommended the preservation of the office of the Director for the Public State-Religious Education Administration that will be in charge of the "professional and pedagogical management of the public State-Religious system."[227] The Director shall serve as the professional and pedagogical authority for "everyone in the Ministry of Education who works on public State-Religious education."[228] Likewise, the Task Force recommended, in its report, to activate the Advisory Board on Arab Education "on a regular basis," and to employ Arabs "in the various administrative echelons in the Ministry of Education . . . to be responsible for the special subject matter, the activity, and the institutions of Arab public education."[229]

The Task Force made detailed recommendations regarding the funding of the various educational institutions. It recommended that public educational institutions shall receive "full public funding." On the other hand, non-public educational institutions,

> shall receive a percentage of the full funding for teaching and supplementary services commensurate with the amount of the core curriculum that they offer as the main instrument for creating the shared foundation for all Israeli students, and the extent to which they are willing to open to everyone who wants to attend.[230]

Moreover, in order to be accredited as "an educational institution entitled to public funding," the school must satisfy,

> minimum conditions that can be inspected: basic licensing conditions; activity that does not conflict with the goals of education; a policy of not screening students on the basis of ethnicity or race; a systematic program of study; a faculty that does not include anyone unfit to work with students; and nonprofit activity.[231]

225. The use of the term, "State-Religious education," as well as the institute of "the Council for State-Religious education," seems to be somewhat anachronistic. This is so since the report recommends the institution of "public education that is the State's responsibility," rather than the existing State education. Likewise, the bill the Commission drafted is entitled "Public Education Law." *Id.* at 243.

226. TAMAR EL-OR, *supra* note 205, at 208.

227. *Id.* at 209.

228. *Id.*

229. *Id.* at 34.

230. *Id.* at 205.

231. *Id.* at 204.

The Government endorsed the National Plan for Education, expressed its determination to carry out the recommended reform and regarded the implementation of its recommendations "a preferred national task." The Ministry of Education even started implementing its "first stage." However, the plan came under fire from various sectors, both on pedagogical and academic grounds and was fiercely objected to by the teachers unions. Indeed, due to widespread objections to the plan and lack of appropriate funding the implementation of the plan is tentatively on hold, and it is doubtful whether it will ever be fully implemented. This is especially so since the present Minister of Education expressed her reservations from the Report.[232] Though religious objection to the plan was not a major cause,[233] it did add to other factors that brought about the stagnation.[234] Some of the requirements set forth in the Report as a prerequisite for the recognition of a school as a public school are such that might leave out the ultra-Orthodox recognized schools thus diminishing their funding. These requirements include: the objects of public education; full application of the compulsory core curriculum; subjection to the supervision of the Ministry of Education and the District Education Administrations; and moving to five days of teaching.[235] At the time, it seemed that the National-Religious Education might be disadvantaged as a result of the Dovrat reform. There seemed to have been an intention to abolish the State-Religious Education Administration.[236] In the end though, not only was this unit preserved, it was also strengthened as was the Council for State-Religious education.[237] Nevertheless, the administrative decentralization and the establishment of regional education administrations, as well as the transfer of most pedagogical, budgetary, and personnel powers to the schools are being regarded as detrimental to religious-public education. This is so because State-religious education is scattered all over the country. Moreover, the inspectors – whose status will

232. *See* Gilad Grossman, *Social Reform Starts with Education*, NRG, May 5, 2006, *available at* http://www.nrg.co.il/online/1/ART1/420/697.html.

233. At the time the Dovrat Report was submitted to the Government the religious parties were not part of the coalition.

234. For electronic links to materials connected with the Dovrat report, see *Amnon Til, The Dovrat Report: Digital* Sources, *available at* http://stage.co.il/Stories/479818.

235. *See* Rabbi Mordechai Karelitz, *Supplement to Recommendation 7.8.5 in the Chapter on Public Education*, *in* THE ANNEX TO THE NATIONAL TASK FORCE REPORT: SUPPLEMENTS ADDITIONS AND RESERVATIONS OF MEMBERS OF THE TASK FORCE TO CHAPTER 7, *supra* note 205. *See also* Yuli Haromentchko, *Proposal: State Schools will Turn Public*, HA'ARETZ 10/10/2004 (Isr.).

236. *Id.*

237. *See Minority Opinion: Public Education and the Status of State-Religious Education*, *in* ANNEX TO THE NATIONAL TASK FORCE REPORT: SUPPLEMENTS ADDITIONS AND RESERVATIONS OF MEMBERS OF THE TASK FORCE TO CHAPTER 7 (Ministry of Education 2005) (Isr.).

be prejudiced – exercise important functions in the State-religious education, such as the instruction of teachers and principals and representing the system vis-à-vis local authorities and parent committees. Finally, the recommended reduction in the number of teachers' colleges and their reconstruction is being regarded as a blow to the widespread religious colleges and a withdrawal in the training of suitable teachers for religious schools.[238]

In the negotiations towards the formation of the new Government, both Shas & United Torah Judaism demanded to entrench the current status of their education networks. Indeed, in the coalition agreement between the *Kadima* ruling party and Shas party[239] a special chapter (sections 27-34) is dedicated to *Haredi* education. It guarantees the preservation of "the independence and unique status of the Haredi education, in all its forms, in the education system."[240] It provides, moreover, that "even in case of institutional, constructional or contextual reform of the education system, the unique status, organizational and educational independence and the budget of the *Haredi* education will not be affected."[241] The Government is supposed to initiate legislation to ensure "the equality and equivalence of the *Haredi* education in all its forms."[242] This legislation must be completed by the end of the year and should "with utmost clarity fully implement the said provisions."[243] The agreement states, that there exist "urgent problems that do not allow any postponement," which the representatives of *Shas* and the United Torah Judaism will bring before the Prime Minister who must solve them "within 60 days."[244] In failing to do so, the Government must initiate urgent legislative amendments "that will anchor the duty of equal budgeting of the Independent Education and *Mayan Ha'hinuch Ha'torani*, by the local authorities according to equal and uniform criteria as for all Israeli children.[245]

The agreement is careful not to spell out the intention that seemingly hides behind the lines; to refrain from imposing on the ultra-Orthodox education the provisions of the Dovrat Report, and possibly also of the Shoshani Report, as a condition for the continuation of the present funding

238. *See* Matityahu Dagan, *Most Conclusions of 'the Dovrat Commission' are Bad for the State-Religious Education*, HAZOFE [daily of the National Religious Party] (Isr.), *available at* http://www.hazofe.co.il/web/katava6.asp?Modul=24&id=24518&Word=&gilayon=2026&mador=.

239. http://www.knesset.gov.il/docs/heb/coal2006shas.htm (Isr.).

240. *Id.* § 27.

241. *Id.* § 28.

242. *Id.* § 29.

243. *Id.* §§ 31-32.

244. *Id.* § 33.

245. *Id.* § 34.

of their networks.[246] In doing so, the parties might have implied the experience learned from a former coalition agreement between the United Torah Judaism faction and the *Likud* faction. The agreement established a team that would endeavor "to prevent any damage to the organizational and educational independence, the exclusive status and funding of the *Haredi* education,"[247] as a result of the recommendations of the National Task Force. Both the National Religious Party and the secular *Shinui* Party petitioned the Supreme Court demanding to declare this provision illegal, as it constitutes "a commitment to abstain from applying the recommendations of the Dovrat Report on the *Haredi* educational system."[248] The Court refrained from doing so on the ground that it constitutes "a declaration of intentions only, which does not amount to a commitment to engage in operational steps."[249] The Court added, however, that "should this agreement be translated into an improper application that contradicts the basic principles of the distribution of the budget, such as infringement of the principle of equality or any other basic values, they will be examined when a concrete cause arises."[250] Another lesson from a court ruling might have been the undertaking to anchor the status of *Haredi* education in legislation rather than in an administrative undertaking. In doing so the parties might have had in mind the court ruling in the *Al-arfan* case.[251] In that decision the Court approved discrimination in the funding of the Torah educational networks since it had been "explicitly" established by law. Yet, any reliance on the *Al-arfan* decision may prove to be misleading. In order to appreciate the distinction between the two cases it should be realized that Israel lacks a comprehensive written constitution. Rather, the Knesset enacted several Basic Laws, which the Supreme Court declared as enjoying constitutional status.[252] Basic Law: Human Dignity and Liberty that was enacted in 1992 provides: "There shall be no violation of the life, body or dignity of any person as such."[253] The extent of this provision was constantly debated. Specifically there was a heated controversy over the question whether the term "human dignity" includes

246. *Id.* § 27-34.

247. § 6.11 to the coalition agreement.

248. HCJ 306/05 The National Religious Party v. The Government of Israel [2005] Tak-SC 2005(3) 2141.

249. *Id.* § 17.

250. *Id.*

251. HCJ 2828/02 Al-arfan v. Minister of Education [2004] IsrSC 2004(2) 232.

252. *See* Asher Maoz, *Constitutional Law*, *in* THE LAW OF ISRAEL: GENERAL SURVEYS 6, 6-13 (Itzhak Zamir & Sylviane Colombo eds., Harry and Michael Sacher Institute for Legislative Research and Comparative Law 1995); Asher Maoz, *The Institutional Organization of the Israeli Legal System*, *in* INTRODUCTION TO THE LAW OF ISRAEL 11, 11-14 (Amos Shapira & Keren C. DeWitt-Arar eds., Kluwer Law Int'l 1995).

253. An English translation of the Basic Law is published in the Knesset website and is available at
http://www.knesset.gov.il/laws/special/eng/basic3_eng.htm.

the principle of equality. Recently the Supreme Court ruled that the term "human dignity" includes "discrimination that does not amount to humiliation, provided it is closely connected to human dignity as an expression of the autonomy of the private will, freedom of choice, freedom of action and similar aspects of human dignity as a constitutional right."[254] Based on this qualification the Court ruled that the exemption of *yeshiva* students from compulsory military service while others are being drafted constitutes a breach of equality that amounts to the infringement of human dignity.[255] It is submitted that discrimination in school funding constitutes such a severe breach of the principle of equality as to amount to a violation of human dignity. If that is the case, section 8 of the Basic Law provides "[t]here shall be no violation of rights under this Basic Law except by a law befitting the values of the State of Israel, enacted for a proper purpose, and to an extent no greater than is required." If such violation of human dignity took place then the law must be struck down. Indeed, the Court in the *Al-arfan*, as well as in *The Movement for Quality Government* case, was aware of this possible outcome. It nevertheless approved the law since section 10 specifically provides that the Basic Law "shall not affect the validity of any law in force prior to the commencement of the Basic Law." This provision cannot shield a legislative violation that takes place after the enactment of the Basic Law.

The same goes for another possible infringement of human dignity by allowing Orthodox schools to refrain from teaching "secular" subjects.[256] This may give way for an argument, on behalf of the students enrolled in those schools, that by doing so the schools directly, and the State indirectly, infringed their human dignity and possibly also their liberty. By preventing them from acquiring proper education, their chances to acquire appropriate higher education and a desirable profession and integrate into society are being hampered.[257]

It must be noted, moreover, that although existing legislation is being shielded from repeal as a result of the Basic-Law, the courts must interpret it in light of the Basic-Law provisions.[258] Israeli legislation must furthermore be interpreted in light of International law including

254. HCJ 6427/02 The Movement for Quality Government in Israel v. The Knesset [2006] Tak-SC 2006 (2) 1559.

255. *Id.* § 41.

256. As was indeed argued in *Paritzky*, HCJ 2751/99 Paritzky v. Minister of Education, *available at* http://elyon1.court.gov.il/files/99/510/027/a02/99027510.a02.pdf.

257. Sebba and Shiffer go much beyond that. They argue that "the absence of any freedom to choose an alternative belief or life-style following a Haredi education manifestly amounts to a deprivation of personal autonomy." Sebba & Shiffer, *supra* note 85, at 173.

258. *See* CrimA 2316/95 Ganimat v. The State [1995] IsrSC 49(4) 589. *See also* Asher Maoz, *Constitutional Law*, *in* THE ANNUAL BOOK OF ISRAELI LAW 1992-1993 143 (Israel Bar- Tel-Aviv District 1994) (Isr.).

conventional law.[259] In this light, the provisions of the Convention on the rights of the Child from 1989,[260] as well as the International Covenant on Economic, Social and Cultural Rights from 1966,[261] must be considered.[262] There might, however, be some discrepancy between both documents. Thus, the Covenant on Economic, Social and Cultural Rights affords the parents the right "to choose for their children schools, other than those established by the public authorities . . . and to ensure the religious and moral education of their children in conformity with their own convictions."[263] The Convention on the rights of the Child, on the other hand, obliges to direct the education of the child "to [t]he development of the child's personality, talents and mental and physical abilities to their fullest potential" and to "[t]he preparation of the child for responsible life in a free society, in the spirit of understanding, peace, tolerance, equality of sexes, and friendship among all peoples, ethnic, national and religious groups and persons of indigenous origin."[264] The discrepancy between both conventions may be the result of the development of the doctrine of children's' rights in international law.[265] The gap between these documents might be, however, smaller than appears at first sight. Thus, the Covenant on Economic, Social and Cultural Rights subjects the parents' right to choose the education for their children, to the State's right to impose on the

259. *See* Asher Maoz, *War and Peace – An Israeli Perspective*, 14 FORUM CONSTITUTIONNE 35, 53-4 (2005).

260. Convention on the Rights of the Child, G.A. Res. 44/25, U.N. Doc. A/RES/44/49 (Nov. 20, 1989), *available at* http://www.unhchr.ch/html/menu3/b/k2crc.htm. *See* Student Rights Law, 2000, S.H. 42. *Cf.* the Supreme Court's decision in *Poriya*, HCJ 4363/00 Committee of Poriya Ilit v. Minister of Education [2004] IsrSC 56(4) 203.

261. Covenant on Economic, Social and Cultural Rights, G.A. Res. 2200A (XXI), U.N. Doc. A/6316 (Dec. 16, 1966), *available at* http://www.unhchr.ch/html/menu3/b/a_cescr.htm.

262. *See* HCJ 2599/00 Yated v. Ministry of Education [2002] IsrSC 56(5) 834, 846. An official English translation is available at http://elyon1.court.gov.il/eng/verdict/search_eng/verdict_by_case_rslt.asp?case_nbr=2599&case_year=00.

263. *See* Covenant on Economic, Social and Cultural Rights, G.A. Res. 2200A (XXI), art. 13.3, U.N. Doc. A/6316 (Dec. 16, 1966), *available at* http://www.unhchr.ch/html/menu3/b/a_cescr.htm.

264. *See* Convention on the Rights of the Child, G.A. Res. 44/25, art. 29.1(a) & (d), U.N. Doc. A/RES/44/49 (Nov. 20, 1989), *available at* http://www.unhchr.ch/html/menu3/b/k2crc.htm.

265. *See* CA 2266/93 Anonymous v. Anonymous [1995] IsrSC 49(1) 221 (Shamgar, J.). *See also* William Duncan, *Children's Rights, Cultural Diversity and Private Law*, *in* CHILDREN'S RIGHTS AND TRADITIONAL VALUES, *supra* note 2, at 15; Leora Bilsky, *Child-Parent-State: The Absence of Community in the Courts' Approach to Education*, *in* CHILDREN'S RIGHTS AND TRADITIONAL VALUES, *supra* note 2, at 134; Ze'ev Falk, *Rights and Autonomy – or the Best Interest of the Child?*, *in* CHILDREN'S RIGHTS AND TRADITIONAL VALUES, *supra* note 2, at 111. *See generally* Geraldine Van Bueren, *THE INTERNATIONAL LAW ON THE RIGHTS OF THE CHILD* chs. 6, 9 (Martinus Nijjoff 1998).

chosen school "minimum educational standards."[266] At the same time, the Convention on the rights of the Child imposes on the State a duty to supply the child with the education that will be directed "to . . . [t]he development of respect for the child's parents, his or her own cultural identity, language and values."[267] Israeli courts will have to consider these conventions in interpreting Israeli law regarding religious education.

WORD OF SUMMATION

The struggle between the melting pot policy, advocating educational uniformity, and the demand for religious autonomy in the area of education ended with a salient triumph of the latter.[268] Israel's educational system appears as a convincing example of educational autonomy, particularly religious autonomy, and as a model of multicultural education. Ultra-religious autonomous education, moreover, paved the way for other educational streams. Zionist religious circles broke out of the religious-State schools and established exclusive schools to compete with the ultra-Orthodox network. At first they were established as recognized schools. Yet, within time most of them have been included as separate networks within the religious-State stream. This reform was not confined to religious schools. At the initiative of parents and local councils, specialized schools – such as art schools, natural science schools, Democratic schools and anthroposophy schools – have been established. At the beginning, the Ministry of Education tried to resist this trend, however, in several cases the parents succeeded in overruling the Ministry's decision, whether in appellate committees or in court. Their success may be attributed to reliance on the ultra-Orthodox model. In recent years the Ministry changed its attitude and is encouraged specialty schools. This was both a result of parents' success in court and the fact that officials who were involved in developing these schools on municipal level have been elevated to senior positions in the Ministry. Moreover, the social move from socialism to liberalism encouraged this trend.[269]

Referring to this phenomenon the Supreme Court recently stated that:

> Israeli society accumulated people from various venues, from different cultures and with diversified views. During the first years of Statehood, Israeli society professed a policy of a melting pot that refines the cultural range and turns it into an entity with uniform cultural attributes. Along the years, however, Israeli

---

266. Covenant on Economic, Social and Cultural Rights, *supra* note 261.

267. *Id.*

268. *Cf.* ZAMERET, *supra* note 7, at 159.

269. For a survey, see AYELET BARAK-MEDINA, ALLOCATION OF RESOURCES IN EDUCATION, THE INTEGRATION PRINCIPLE AND EXCLUSIVE SCHOOLS IN DIFFERENT SEGMENTS: A BACKGROUND DOCUMENT (Knesset 2003) (Isr.), *available at* http://www.knesset.gov.il/mmm/data/docs/m00544.doc.

> society comprehended to recognize the uniqueness and beauty of the variety that exists within the Israeli society and started a process of acknowledging the various cultures and views and giving them space.[270]

This trend did not escape criticism, shared by the present Minister of Education, mainly on the ground that it brings about privatization of the educational system and discriminates against lower socio-economic groups. In the sphere of ultra-Orthodox education there is another basic deficiency. As one researcher put it, it is multicultural only on the "macro- level," while uni-cultural on the "micro- level." This is due to the fact that each educational sub-system is "closed, uniform and unicultural." As a result, children who are enrolled in an ultra-Orthodox sub-system are exposed to "particularistic subgroup culture and norms at the expense of the appreciation of diversity and the tolerance of other cultures and norms."[271] On top of that, the educational and cultural segregation withholds the development of a creed that would be common to all segments of Israeli society. Moreover, in granting large autonomy to these sub-systems the State fails to ensure that the youngsters are being equipped with the necessary tools to become fruitful and successful members of society. By doing so the State abstains from fulfilling its duties both under Israeli law and under international established norms.[272] As we have recently seen, Israel embarked on an arduous path to amend some of these hurdles. It still has a long way to go.

270. HCJ 1447/03 Panim for Jewish Renaissance in Israel v. Minister of Education [2004] IsrSC 59(3) 942.

271. Stephen Goldstein, *supra* note 2, at 127-28.

272. *Cf.* HCJ 4363/00 Committee of Poriya Ilit v. Minister of Education [2004] IsrSC 56(4) 203, 222 ("The preservation of educational autonomy in private education is an important value that must be honored in the framework of the persons right to self-fulfillment, subject to safeguarding the basic educational values according to State Education Law.").

ADDENDUM

Since the article was written substantial developments took place in the area of religious education in Israel. Following are short updates of the main developments:

State Schools

In 2008 the State Education Law was amended and a new category of state schools was created – the Combining State School[270]. This is a state school which "combines in its curriculum intensified Judaic studies and emphasizes Jewish identity teaching". The supplementary curriculum for such school includes comprehensive study of Judaic sources emphasizing Jewish identity and values of tolerance in Jewish inheritance and "the coexistence and common destiny and fate of all parts of the nation in Israel and in the Diaspora". An official school may be declared as a combining state school if parents of at least two thirds of the student body have so requested. A combining state school will get an extra five year budget in order to train its team and implement the special curriculum. A coordinator for Judaic studies will be appointed for the school. A Council for State Combining Education will be established consisting of fifteen members including a representative of the Council for Religious Education. The Ministry of Education expects some hundred schools to join the combining school category.

A unique state junior high school was established in the Galilee town Shlomi. The school was defined as both a religious state school and a general state school. The students of both tracks study together general subjects and study separately only when the content of the curriculum is different. The headmistress of the school is religious and the school is subject to the supervision of an inspector from the Division of Religious Education. A petition submitted to the Supreme Court challenged the power of the authority to establish a school which is both a general state school and a religious state school. The petition is pending in court.[271]

270 . State Education (Amendment no. 10) Law, 5768-2008, *Sefer HaHukim* 5768, 660, (2008).

271 . HCJ 7371/09 *Ghilon v. Minister of Education*, Tak-Supreme 2009(4) 9901.

Recognized Non-official Schools and Non-recognized Schools

The issue of autonomous education in non-official schools vis-à-vis state supervision came to sharp confrontation in the case of *"Noar Cahalach" v. Ministry of Education*[272]. Emanuel is a *Haredi* settlement, whose original residents were Ashkenazi (of European origin). Within the years the population of Emanuel changed and a significant number of Sephardic families moved in. The Ashkenazi residents complained that the Sephardic families, mainly those who were secular and turned religious, were less pious and as a result their daughters had "a negative influence" on the Hasidic students at the Beit Yaakov girl school of the Independent Education Network. In order to supposedly combat this influence the school was practically divided into two – both substantially and physically – and two separate schools were created on the same premises: to the existing school a new *Hassidic* track was added. While the Sephardic girls constitute 77% of the student body in the "general track" they comprised merely 27% of the "*Hassidic* track". An NGO petitioned the Supreme Court against what it regarded discrimination against the Sephardic girls.

The Supreme Court ruled that the right of each community to educate its children in light of its unique cultural and religious believes is recognized by Israeli law alongside the official educational institutions. Nevertheless, this privilege is not absolute and must be balanced against basic values, in this case the value of equality. A recognized school may introduce a separate track where the religious beliefs and world view of the community will be taught. It may also introduce rules of behavior in line with these beliefs. However, the school must enable each student who satisfies these requirements and is willing to abide by the rules join the said track and his or her ethnic affiliation must be disregarded. Moreover, the separation between the tracks may be introduced only when studying unique relevant subjects while other studies and school rules must be common to all students regardless of the track. The Court found that the rules introduced at Beit Yaakov were laid down not merely in order to teach *Hasidic* way of life but rather in order to separate between Ashkenazi and Sephardic students under the pretence of cultural difference. Various requirements, such as the demand that the student's parents behave according to the religious customs of the *Hasidic* school and the requirement for both students and parents to adhere by an Ashkenazi spiritual authority were introduced in order to prevent the admittance of Sephardic girls. As a result the Court ordered the removal of any indication, both formal and substantive, of the phenomenon of discrimination that existed in the school. Failing to do so should lead to the removal of the school's permit and stopping State financial assistance.

---

272 . [2009] Tak-Supreme 2009(3) 1979.

Since the Court order was not obeyed the Court imposed a daily penalty on the Independent Education Center and on the parents of the *Hasidic* track and warned that it may order their imprisonment should they continue to frustrate the order by abstaining from sending their daughters to school after the amalgamation of both tracks. The Court made this order in spite of the fact that since its ruling a girls' school of The Fountain of Religious Education was opened in Emanuel where almost all of the student body was *Sephardic* including some girls who studied previously at Beit Yaakov.

Following the refusal of the parents to abide by the Court order unless it is approved by their Rabbi, the Court convened on 15 June 2010 and ordered the imprisonment of the parents should they fail to declare within 24 hours that they will obey the Court decision.

A petition pending in the Supreme Court relates to the admittance of Falasmura children to religious schools. The Falasmura are Ethiopian Jews who converted to Christianity, mainly at the end of the 19th century, yet kept living within their community. According to a Government decision those who relate to Jewish origin on a maternal line are allowed to immigrate to Israel and get the status of permanent residents. However, due to some doubt about their Jewishness following cases of mixed marriages, after their arrival to Israel they undergo a procedure of "returning to Judaism", namely a shortened act of conversion, following which they are granted the status of *oleh* under the Law of Return[273]. During this period they must send their children to religious schools. This fact combined with the geographical concentration of Ethiopian immigrants led to the registration of Ethiopian kids to specific schools. In order to facilitate their absorption the Ministry of Education instructed the schools to accept Ethiopian kids up to 25% of the students' body. This policy was challenged and the Attorney General ordered the Ministry to stop it. Instead efforts are being made to balance the ratio of Ethiopian children in order to achieve an optimal integration. However, this is subject to the parents' approval[274]. In several cases the court ordered the Ministry and the local municipality to pay damages to parents and children following the implementation of the old policy[275].

[273] See: The Knesset Library, THE FALASMURA (2002) (Heb.), available on line: http://www. knesset.gov.il/library/heb/docs/sif015.htm; STATE COMPTROLLER, OPINION: IMPLEMENTATION OF THE GOVERNMENT DECISIONS RE IMMIGRATION OF THE FALASMURA (2008) (Heb.), available on line: http://www.mevaker.gov.il/serve/contentTree.asp ?bookid=530&id= 0&contentid=9878&parentcid= undefined &bctype=9877&sw=1920&hw=1130; Michael Corinaldi, THE ENIGMA OF JEWISH IDENTITY: THE LAW OF RETURN – THEORY AND PRACTICE (2001), pp. 161-77 (Heb.).

[274] . HCJ 9187/02 *Center for Legal assistance and Communal Assistance for Ethiopian Immigrants v. Minister of Education*, not published.

[275] . CC 5244/02 *Bugala v. Ministry of Education* [2006] Tak-Magistrate 2006 (3) 14118. Besides the Ministry of Education and the local municipality the Court ordered also the headmaster to pay compensations. In CC 2359/05 *Talalin v. The Municipality of Arad* [2010] Tak-Magistrate 2010 (1) 55385 Ethiopian children were transferred by the municipality from a religious state kindergarten to a general state kindergarten contrary to their parents wish. The municipality did so following its policy not to have more than a third non Hebrew speakers in a kindergarten in order for it to be manageable and following threats by other parents to remove their children to non-official kindergartens. The Court ruled that the municipality acted contrary to the law and ordered it to pay compensations. The Ministry of Education was ordered to pay compensations as

The issue of the abstention of private religious elementary schools – both recognized and exempt – from admitting Ethiopian students came to the fore in the petition submitted by an NGO in HCJ 7426/08 *TEBEKA - Advocacy for Equality & Justice for Ethiopian Israelis v. Minister of Education*. A committee nominated by the Director General of the Ministry found that private schools hardly admitted any Ethiopian children arguing that the degree of observing religious precepts by these kids did not satisfy the requirements of the school. This imposed on the state religious schools a high burden of admitting large numbers of Ethiopian children. Thus they found themselves with a high proportion of new Ethiopian immigrants which frustrated their optimal absorption. The petitioner asked the Supreme Court to order the Minister to issue regulations under which state budget will be denied automatically to private schools that do not practice an integrative policy in admitting students. The Ministry, on the other hand, wished to preserve the present situation under which the abolishment of state support from such school, whether in full or gradually, is discretionary. The petition is awaiting the Court's decision.

State Funding and School Curriculum

The issue of failing to implement the Court order in HCJ 10296/02 Union of Teachers in High Schools, Seminaries and Colleges v. Minister of Education[276] came before the Supreme Court in HCJ 4805/07 Israel Religious Action Center of the Israel Movement for Progressive Judaism and Union of Teachers in High Schools, Seminaries and Colleges v. Ministry of Education[277].

The case revealed a gloomy picture. Not only did the Ministry of Education fail to implement the core curriculum in small yeshivas, as ordered in HCJ 10296/02, it even did not have any concrete plans to do so. Moreover, the Ministry came up with the idea of changing the status of these institutions from recognized non-official schools to exempt schools thus avoiding the duty to teach the core curriculum.

The Court declared that although the specific order of the Court in 10296/02 refereed to recognized non-official schools, its reasoning applies to all kind of schools including exempt schools and it prohibits state funding for any school which do not implement the targets of public education by avoiding teaching the core curriculum. The Court clarified that the core curriculum creates a balance between the privilege of the parents to educate their children according to their principles and beliefs and the State's duty to provide basic common educational values to all students, prepare them for life and enable them to

well since it failed to take steps such as ordering the closure of the discriminating kindergarten or cutting its budget and submitting criminal complaints against the persons responsible for this move.

276 . Article, note 193.

277 . [2008] Tak-Supreme 2008(3) 402.

take part in society. The Court emphasized that this target is of special significance in Israeli society which consists of a mosaic of cultures and beliefs.

The Court was going to order the Ministry to implement without any delay the core curriculum in all recognized non-official high schools and withhold any financial support from both these schools as well as from exempt schools that do not teach the core curriculum. However, four days before the decision was handed down, the Knesset enacted the Unique Cultural Education Institutions Law, 5768-2008[278]. This statute created "unique cultural education institutions" defined as "an education institution where... systematic education stemming from the obligatory way of life of the unique cultural group is provided in accordance with its unique characteristics" designated for students in grades 9-12. The legislature clarified which "unique cultural group" he had in mind: This is either "the Haredi group whose students study religious studies according to Jewish Halakha in a yeshiva" or "another group which has been recognized by the Minister's order". The statute does not intervene in the curriculum taught at the unique cultural education institutions and satisfies itself with the requirement that "the curriculum and activities" of the said institutions "do not negate the values of the State of Israel as a Jewish and democratic state". It moreover provides that the Education Ordinance and the Inspection of Schools Law, 5729-1969 will not apply to these institutions. Finally, the statute provides that the said institutions will receive state budget in the amount of 60% of the budget allocated per student in state schools. This amount is higher than the amount allocated for exempt schools though lower than the financial support for recognized non-official school which teach at least 75% of the core curriculum.

In the explanatory notes to the statute bill[279] it was expressly stated that the motive for enacting the statute was to overcome the court decision in HCJ 10296/02 and enable State financial support to these institutions contrary to the said decision. It was also mentioned that the statute is needed in view of "other petitions, which are pending in the Supreme Court", which referred directly to HCJ 4805/07. Indeed, in view of the statute the Court refrained from making specific orders and mentioned that the impact of this legislation will be examined "in another legal framework".

The constitutionality of the Unique Cultural Education Institutions Law has recently been challenged. In a petition submitted to the Supreme Court[280]. The petitioners were a former minister of education and two other educational figures together with four former students of small yeshivas and other Haredi educational institutions. The petitioners argue that the statute must be struck down since it violates both Basic Laws: Human Dignity and Liberty[281] and Basic Law: Freedom of Occupation[282]. The petitioners argue that the

278 . *Sefer HaHukim* 5768, 742, (2008).
279 . *Hatzaot Hok*, 5768, 350 (2008).
280 . HCJ 3752/10 *Rubinstein v. The Knesset*.
281 Article, note 250.

statute infringes the autonomy of yeshiva students, which is part of human dignity, by preventing them from developing their self and choosing a way of life since they are being exposed only to religious studies[283]. Thus their ability to integrate into society and to develop a sense of belonging is being negated. Moreover, by being denied basic knowledge their ability to acquire higher education and prestigious professions are severely hampered[284]. As a result the statute must be struck down. Alternatively the petitioners suggest interpreting the statute as not exempting Haredi schools from teaching core curriculum. The petition is pending in court.

The Nahari initiative to impose on local authorities the duty to finance recognized non-official schools by the same ratio and conditions compared to official schools as the State's support[285] materialized in an amendment to State Education Law[286]. The amendment enables however local authorities to finance recognized school beyond the ratio set by the amendment.

In 2008 the State Education Law (Recognized Institutions) Regulations, 5714-1953[287] were amended[288]. According to the amendment recognized schools, up to grade 9, that teach the required core curriculum and on top of that carry on an integrative registration policy and whose students' socio-economic is similar to that of other schools within a local municipality will receive 75% of state budget allocated to similar official school. Recognized schools who fulfill only one of the latter requirements will receive 70% of the budget. If it fails to fulfill both requirements the school will receive 65% of the budget. In any case the school must teach the required core curriculum, which is a prerequisite for granting recognition to the school. Under the new sec. 11 of the State Education Law the school is entitled to the same budget from the local authority. The regulations do not apply to the Independent Education Network and the Sephardic Centre of Fountain of Religious Education in Israel who receive the full budget under the provision of Budgetary Principles Law[289]. No provisions were made regarding exempt institutions. While grades 9-12 of these institutions may come under the Unique Cultural Education Institutions Law, lower grades are left out and their financial assistance is left to the policy of the Minister and they keep receiving 55% of their budget in accordance with the Ministry's Director General Circular. The ironic result is that the budget of the Unique Cultural Education Institutions is the only one fortified by law while the budget of the other institutions, which are obliged to teach the core curriculum, are subject to the Minister's deci-

[282] . *Sefer HaHukim* 5754, 90 (2004); An English translation of the Basic Law is published in the Knesset website- http://www.knesset.gov.il/laws/special/eng/basic4_eng.htm.

[283] . *Cf.* Sebba and Shiffer, Article, note 254.

[284] . *Cf.* Article, pp. 537-38.

[285] . Article pp. 526-27, text to note 179.

[286] . State Education (Amendment no. 7) Law, 5767 *Sefer HaHukim* 5767, 318, (2007).

[287] . See, Article, note 84.

[288] . 5768 *Kovetz Ha'takanot* 388 (2008).

[289] . See, Article, text to notes 171-73.

sion whether by amending the regulations or by merely changing his policy as far as exempt institutions are concerned.

Word of Summation

The growth of the *Haredi* educational system continued alongside the decline of Jewish state schools and a modest growth of religious state schools. Thus, state schools which constituted 60% of the total school students in 1960 shrunk to 44% in 2009 and is expected to decrease to 40% in 2014. The population of religious state schools decreased from 24% in 1960 to 15% in 2000 and is expected to constitute 14% of the total students in 2014. At the same time the *Haredi* portion grew from 4% in 1980 to 12% in 2000 and is expected to reach 18% in 2014[290]. The number of students in state schools decreased even nominally. The percentage of Arab students grew as well from 10% in 1960 to 22% in 2000 and 25% in 2009 and is expected to reach 29% in 2014. The growth of the *Haredi* and Arab sectors is even more remarkable in kindergartens and primary schools. Thus, while the total increase in the number of kindergarten children during the last decade amounts to 22%, the growth in *Haredi* education reached 47.5% while the growth in religious state schools reached 7.6% and in state schools merely 2/4%. The growth in the Arab sector reached 54.3%. The total growth of children in primary schools during the last decade amounts to 15%, however in the *Haredi* sector it reached 51% and in the Arab sector 33%. At the same time the growth of state religious primary schools was 8% and in state schools it decreased by 3%[291]. Within the *Haredi* education the major growth was in the smaller institutions who are less supervised by the State. The total growth in the last decade was of 51%, however the growth of the Fountain of Religious Education was 64% and of the Independent Education Network merely 32%. At the same time the growth of other recognized schools was 92% and of exempt schools – 61%. The growth of private schools in the state sector and in the religious state sector is moderate – 1.1% and 3.5%. However, this may be a result of semi-private schools within the official sector especially in the state religious sector. The portion of state schools in intermediate and high schools declined during the recent decade from 60% to 52%, the state religious schools grew by 2.5%. At the same time the *Haredi* education grew by 27% and in the Arab sector by 42%[292].

290 . Nachum Balas, "The Education System – An Inner View", REPORT OF THE STATUS OF THE STATE 2009 – SOCIETY, ECONOMY AND POLICY (Taub Center, 2010, Dan Ben-David, ed.) 137, 141-42 (Heb.); *Available at: http://taubcenter.org.il/tauborgilwp/wp-content/uploads/H2009_State_ of_the_ Nation_ Report.pdf* The figures may be partially distorted since Central Bureau of Statistics did not include in the past students of *Taklmudei Torah* and of exempt schools in the statistics.

291 . *Id.*, pp. 142-44.

292 . *Id.*, at 150.

The reason for the rapid growth of the *Haredi* sector is debatable. The common belief is that it is a result of a transfer of children from state schools, mainly state religious schools, to *Haredi* schools. A research conducted at the Taub Center for Social Policy Studies in Israel revealed that such transfers are negligible and the main growth is a result of the rapid natural increase within *Haredi* society[293]. Undoubtedly, the privatization and semi-privatization of state schools and especially of state religious schools[294] was essential in keeping students within the network[295].

The threat of non-official schools to the official system may be learned from a recently amendment to section 3 of the State Education Law (Recognized Institutions) Regulations, which specifies the conditions for declaring an education institution as a recognized institution. A stipulation added to the Regulations provides that even where all the conditions for recognition are met the Minister may nevertheless decline the recognition if in his opinion "the recognition may damage the state education system". To this end the Minister may consider all relevant factors whether educational or economical. These include the possible closure of schools or classes within the state education system; decrease in the number of students and affecting the integrative make up of the students in state schools[296].

---

293 . Nachum Balas and Yigal Duchan, HORIZONTAL MOVEMENT OF STUDENTS WITHIN THE EDUCATION SYSTEM – TRANSFERS AMONG THE VARIOUS SECTORS (Taub Center, 2006) (Heb.). See also YEehuda Truan, THE NUMBER OF STUDENTS IN STATE EDUCATION AND IN HAREDII EDUCATION IN JERUSALEM IN THE RECENT DECADE (Knesset, 2007 (Heb.), *Available at www.news1.co.il/uploadFiles/540065944194794.doc*

294 . See: Article, 505-506. A study submitted to the Supreme Court in HCJ 7426/08, *supra*, revealed that in Petach Tikva, a town with substantial national religious population, there are 6 state religious schools, 2 recognized schools and 1 exempt school. The student body is divided – 60% in state religious schools and 40% in the non official schools.

295 . In an effort to improve the education in state schools the Ministry considers to increase the number of hours of additional curriculum which parents may introduce from 3 weekly hours to 12, which will constitute a third of the weekly teaching hours. The Ministry contemplates that this program may induce the strong population to keep their children in state schools. This plan invoked sharp criticism as it will increase the gap between schools in well to do neighborhoods and less privileged neighborhoods. It has been argued moreover that it will reduce the initiative to fight for the improvement of state schools; Or Kashti, "The Additional Hours in Schools Will be Multiplied 4 Times, Yet Weak Local Authorities Will Find it Hard to Finance Them", *Haaretz* 31/1/2010 (Heb.), On line: http://www.haaretz.co.il/hasite/spages/1146315.html.

296 . 5770 *Kovetz Ha'takanot* 1003 (2009).

Part III
Law, Religion and the Workplace

[12]

Protecting Religion at Work

Lucy Vickers

Clearly, the right to religious freedom is not an absolute right. For example, in Article 9 ECHR it is accepted that restrictions on the manifestation of religion can be imposed where necessary to safeguard the rights of others. Moreover, it may be that the solution to the conflict between religion and other interests in the context of the workplace will be to rely on the fact that one does not have an enforceable right to a job. Hence any conflict between rights which occurs at work can be resolved by the religious individual resigning: religious freedom persists, and indeed is arguably protected by, the right to resign.[73] However, it will be argued below that such an approach fails to provide adequate protection for religious interests, given the strength of the argument in favour of their protection set out above.

[73] See, for example, the approach of the ECHR in *Ahmad v UK* (1981) 4 EHRR 126 and *Stedman v UK* (1997) 23 EHRR CD168.

Should Religious Interests be Protected at Work?

It has been proposed above that it is legitimate for society to provide some protection for religious interests without needing to resort to religious arguments. What has not been established is why this protection should extend to the workplace, given the undeniable fact that no one is forced to enter or remain in the workplace.

The 'Right to Resign'

At its most basic, the employee's freedom of religion is protected through the employee's freedom to resign, if work and religion are incompatible. The relationship between employer and employee is voluntary, and if the employee has religious objections to complying with an employer's requirements, he or she can choose to not take up the employer's offer of employment. This freedom remains the ultimate protection for religious freedom.[74]

To take an extreme example, if a programme of 'religious instruction' were imposed upon staff who were forced to attend work, then there would clearly be a breach of religious freedom. In such circumstances, a right not to attend work would provide protection against the interference with the right to freedom of religion. The right not to work against one's will is well protected both within the interpretation of domestic labour law and in international human rights law. In domestic law it can be seen in the refusal of courts to require specific performance of employment contracts. Where employers leave their employment in breach of notice terms or other restrictive covenants, courts will not grant specific performance as a remedy to employers. Instead they opt for damages, or put employees on 'garden leave' rather than require employees to attend work unwillingly.[75]

Thus, freedom of religion at a basic level is protected by freedom to resign. Another illustration of the basic limits on religious freedom at work is that employers are never going to be required to accommodate every religious practice or belief at work: for example, a pacifist could not apply for a combatant role in the armed forces, refuse to take part in active service and then complain that she has been denied full freedom of religion. The right to religious freedom does not entail a right to be employed in the employment of the religious adherent's choice, or a right to demand that any religious practice be accommodated. Indeed, it is

[74] See A Bradney, *Religions, Rights and Laws* (Leicester, Leicester University Press, 1993), who suggests that the protection of religious interests in employment is relatively unproblematic, because the employee remains free to resign. See also R Epstein, *Equal Opportunity or More Opportunity? The good thing about discrimination* (Civitas, London, 2002) who argues that the freedom to resign is the best protector of employee interests, as the threat of resignation will cause employers to change their practices, or risk losing good staff and a good reputation. See also the counter-arguments by S Deakin in the same volume.

[75] There is no legally enforceable duty to work. The only sense in which such a duty exists is as part of the social security system, where some benefits are dependent on the recipient's willingness to try to find work, and to take suitable work that is available.

well established that religious observance does not have to be cost-free for the observer. The right to freedom of religion in Article 9 ECHR is not absolute. The freedom to practice religion, or to participate in religious observance, is only protected where it is proportionate to do so. This suggests that it is not an infringement of Article 9 to burden the practice of religion where it is proportionate to do so, for example by refusing to accommodate a religious practice which places too much of a cost on the employer.

It is clear, then, that in the final analysis protection for the religious interests of employees is provided by the right to resign. However, even though resigning may be the ultimate freedom, to limit protection to this somewhat drastic remedy may be to fail to provide adequate protection to religious interests. In order to determine the proper scope for the protection of religion in employment, it is worth considering the reasons for its protection in the context of work.

The Case for Protection in the Workplace

It was established above that the right to freedom of religion is well founded and works to help sustain individual autonomy and dignity. To fail to provide any protection for the right in the work context is to fail to protect individual autonomy and dignity in a very important sphere of life. Clearly, the purpose of most workplaces is to engage in business and generate profit, not to create space for religious observance. It is certainly not suggested that workplaces should have as a primary concern the protection of religious interests, and yet employees spend a significant part of their lives at work and it is not feasible to expect them to leave their interests in autonomy and dignity behind when they enter the workplace.

It might be tempting to suggest that an answer to the conflict between work and religion is for religion to be confined to the private sphere of the home, with work forming part of the public sphere. However, requiring the separation of work and religion in this way is not a practicable option for many workers. Some individuals' work is religious in nature, so such separation is impossible; for others, who may work at home, making any separation is impracticable. Indeed, the difficulty of separating work from other parts of life is well recognised in the case law of the ECHR:

> it is not always possible to distinguish clearly which of an individual's activities form part of his professional or business life and which do not. Thus, especially in the case of a person exercising a liberal profession, his work in that context may form part and parcel of his life to such a degree that it becomes impossible to know in what capacity he is acting at a given moment of time.[76]

Special problems arise regarding religious practices which apply to individual's whole lives and which cannot easily be separated between the home and work spheres. Religious adherents often observe special behavioural codes of conduct, such as dress codes or practices of prayer. These practices have supernatural

[76] *Niemietz v Germany* (1992) 16 EHRR 7 para 29. See discussion at pp 89–91.

significance to the believer, and often apply at all times, rather than being restricted to a religious observance at a particular time of the day or week. Of course, some practices may be accommodated outside work; observance such as a requirement to pray each day may be observed without interfering with the workplace.[77] But the same is not true of other requirements. Religious dress codes may require a woman to have her head covered at all times when in public. Such a requirement cannot simply be dropped during working hours; indeed, it may be that work is the main forum in which the requirement arises, precisely because it is not a private space. To require the individual to reserve this type of religious observance to the world outside work amounts to a denial of the option to comply with the religious requirement. Whether it is acceptable to deny this option will be considered later; at this stage, it is sufficient to note that some religious requirements apply at all times, and cannot be limited to the non-work sphere.

Even for those who do not have specialised religious duties, there are sufficient objective benefits attached to working life that mean that religious interests should be given some degree of protection.

Economic Benefits of Work

Work provides the main income stream for most people, enabling them to house, clothe and feed themselves and their dependants. For many, work also provides access to pension provision, sickness benefits, and a range of insurance services such as death-in-service payments. Paid maternity and paternity leave, tax credits for child care, and compensation for redundancy are also available for employees, with some employers providing substantial additional benefits such as subsidised housing, travel or health insurance. As well as the economic benefits provided directly by employers, there are other significant economic benefits of being in work, for example the fact that substantial sums of money can be borrowed on the promise of future earnings, providing those in work with the financial resources to buy their own homes. Those with independent financial means may also be able to achieve these economic benefits, but for the vast majority, paid work (whether as employee or self-employed) is the only way to access them. Access to such financial benefits also encourages social cohesion and helps to reduce social exclusion.[78]

Non-Financial Benefits of Employment

Apart from the obvious and extensive economic benefits of work, there is significant support for the view that work brings other non-financial benefits. Work is related to concepts of responsibility and citizenship and is the medium through which many people gain self-respect and a sense of participation and inclusion in society.[79] Engaging in the workforce can promote engagement in wider civil society for

[77] Unless prayer is required so often and for so long that it is incompatible with completing a day's work.

[78] H Collins, 'Discrimination, Equality and Social Inclusion' (2003) 66 *MLR* 16.

[79] V Schultz, 'Life's Work' [2000] 100 *Colum LR* 1881.

otherwise marginalised groups. If minority groups are not encouraged to participate in civic life, their voice within the community will be far weaker, ensuring a continuance of their marginalisation.[80]

Moreover, many people invest psychologically in their work, and, depending on the job, it can also be an important signifier of social status. What one does as a job is one of the first pieces of information that people share when meeting, suggesting that it is an important part of many people's sense of identity.[81] However, although the importance of work as part of one's identity is significant, it should not be over emphasised. It was asserted above that religious interests should be protected on the basis that religious beliefs form an essential aspect of personal identity, fundamental enough to warrant significant protection, but that the same would not be said of other less important aspects of personal identity, such as a hobby. The sense of identity granted by employment is probably of similar weight in any proportionality test as that provided by participation in other activities outside work. It may be important to the individual, but is not so strong that it should outweigh other interests based on individual autonomy.

Not only is the sense of identity provided by work a weak interest, but it is evident that a sense of identity and the social status provided by work are not experienced by all workers. A more objective work-related benefit, therefore, is the psychological benefit of active participation in the workforce,[82] including a reduced level of depression, improved sense of well-being, and higher self-esteem. These benefits are enjoyed by all types of employee, not only those doing high status work which one might expect to carry such benefits.[83] The fact that these non-financial benefits are felt by all workers, not only those who gain traditional esteem or high financial reward, suggests that being in work does provide objective non-financial benefits. Yet it also suggests that it is not necessarily being in a particular job that brings these benefits: the benefits may be derived from any job. Proper treatment for religious observers will therefore not necessarily require that a particular person should be accommodated in a particular job, or in a job of his choosing.[84] However, if a failure to accommodate religion makes it very difficult for those of a particular religion to participate at all in the workforce, it will amount to a significant failure to protect those who hold the religious views in question.

Recognition of the importance of work in non-economic terms is clear within modern employment law, which increasingly requires respect for autonomy and dignity at work. The importance of the non-financial benefits of work, and its role

[80] See A Hirschman, *Exit, Voice and Loyalty* (Cambridge Mass, Harvard University Press, 1970), for the argument that groups that are traditionally discriminated against are particularly in need of a voice, as the other method of getting heard, exit, is not effective.

[81] K Karst, 'The Coming Crisis of Work In Constitutional Perspective' [1997] *Cornell LR* 523, 533 and V Schultz, 'Life's Work' [2000] 100 *Colum LR* 1881, 1891.

[82] For references see V Schultz, 'Life's Work' [2000] 100 *Colum LR* 1881, 1890.

[83] *Ibid*, 1892

[84] On the general difficulties of upholding a right to a job, see B Hepple, 'A Right to Work?' (1981) 10 *ILJ* 65.

in upholding individual identity and dignity, has been recognised in the recent development of the content of the employment contract and the creation of specific employment rights. The new 'family friendly' employment rights[85] can be viewed as a recognition of the importance of work to individuals, as well as being economically driven. Moreover, legislatively imposed requirements on employers to consult with employees on redundancies,[86] protection for the collective rights of employees,[87] and rights to union recognition[88] arguably reflect the idea that the workplace is more than merely a means to economic benefit for staff or employer. If economics were the only driver of employment legislation, many of these employment rights would not strictly be needed. The reason for protecting job security, and the imposition of workplace democracy, must be for reasons connected to the importance of work to the individual rather than merely the pure economic benefit of the employer. After all, dismissal of staff, and their replacement by others, causes no net loss of employment; and employees who are unfairly dismissed can receive compensation even if they immediately find employment elsewhere.

Developments in the duty of trust and confidence which is implied into employment contracts also reflect the increasing recognition of the non-financial significance of work to the worker.[89] For example, the duty of trust and confidence owed by the employer goes well beyond preserving employees' economic interests, to protect them from abuse or insult from their colleagues or others.[90] It also extends beyond the treatment of employees during working hours, and provides a duty to compensate where the employer's conduct has damaged the employee's future career prospects,[91] and a general duty to safeguard the employee's economic interests.[92] In *Johnson v Unisys*, the fact that the employment relationship must involve the observance of fundamental human rights was recognised.[93] It is thus well recognised by courts that work fulfils more than just an economic role in the lives of workers. This forms part of a general trend towards recognition of a right on the part of employees to dignity, respect and autonomy both at work and beyond.

[85] See, for example, Working Time Regulations (1998) SI 1998 No 1833, Maternity and Parental Leave etc Regulations (1999) SI 1999 No 3312, and Work and Families Act 2006.

[86] TULRCA 1992 s 188.

[87] TULRCA 1992.

[88] Employment Relations Acts 1999 and 2004 amending TULRCA 1992.

[89] For example, in *Gogay v Hertfordshire County Council* [2000] IRLR 703 there was breach of the term of mutual trust and confidence even though the suspension was with pay. The loss to the employee was therefore not merely economic.

[90] For example, see *Isle of Wight Tourist Board v Coombes* [1976] IRLRL 413, and *Moores v Bude-Statton Council* [2001] ICR 271 in which it is accepted that rudeness and abuse from someone at work can give grounds for a claim of breach of the terms of the employment contract.

[91] *Malik v BCCI* [1997] 3 All ER 1 and *Spring v Guardian Assurance plc* [1994] 3 All ER 129.

[92] *Scally v Southern Health and Social Services Board* [1992] 1 AC 294.

[93] [2001] UKHL 13, Lord Hoffman, at para 37.

Protecting Religion for Equality Reasons

The reasons given above for protecting religious interests at work are based on the idea that employment is such an important aspect of life that to deny religious protection in that sphere is to create a significant infringement of religious freedom in practice. Denial of protection at work amounts to a significant reduction in religious freedom. An additional argument for protecting religion in the work context can be based on equality.

It has been argued above that work provides many benefits, both economic and psychological. The principle of equality demands that all people should have equal access to such benefits, and that life chances should not be dependent on holding a particular world view. Some people find it easy to access these benefits, because there is no incompatibility between their beliefs and employers' requirements. Such individuals will have an advantage over those whose religious beliefs make compliance difficult or impossible. The most obvious example of religious practices which may be easier or more difficult to reconcile with work is in days of rest and the requirement to attend work during the normal working week. For Christian workers in the UK, the weekly religious day of rest, together with the major religious holidays, coincide with the normal working week and working year.[94] This allows Christian workers to comply with religious observance while meeting most employers' requirements for work attendance. This is not the case for those of different faiths.

The resulting inequality in the ease with which groups can comply with employer demands in a way that is compatible with religious duties results in an inequality in access to the substantial benefits of employment, on grounds of religion. The argument from autonomy and dignity, used above to justify protecting religion, requires that religious belief should not determine access to benefits or cause differences in life chances. To argue that religious interests are protected by the right to resign is to ignore the inequalities of protection this provides.

The link between religious disadvantage and inequality is particularly stark where religious groups have suffered systematic disadvantage in the past. For these groups, access to work may represent the best way to avoid further social exclusion and economic disadvantage. Moreover, there is significant potential for religious inequality to intersect with other forms of inequality such as gender or race inequality, resulting in multiple discrimination for minority ethnic women from minority religious groups. Full equality therefore requires that access should be open to all and should not be dependent on religious affiliation.

The argument from equality suggests that it will not be possible to contend that the right to resign will provide sufficient guarantee for freedom of religion. The fact that some religious groups will need to exercise the option more often than

[94] This of course reflects the shaping of the 'normal' working calendar around the traditional Christian year, although the timing of Christmas probably reflects a much earlier accommodation by Christians of the traditions of pagan religions.

others means that the parallel right to equality is infringed, and leads to the conclusion that religious interests should be protected within the workplace.

Of course, the right to equality on grounds of religion is not absolute, and at times protection or accommodation may not be feasible. Yet the fundamental principle of equality demands that protection or accommodation be attempted, rather than leaving religious interests to be protected by the freedom to resign or withdraw from the workplace.

Contracting Out

Even if one rejects the reality of the employee's freedom to resign in practice, weight can be added to the idea that religious interests are protected by the right to resign by the argument that those who accept employment have accepted a certain restriction on their autonomy. Workers sacrifice a good deal of their personal autonomy when coming to work: their employers will control how they spend their time, where they go, and what they say, with a consequent reduction in individual autonomy, for the duration of the working day. Thus it is arguable that the notion of autonomy cannot be used to argue for protection for religious interests at work: if so much individual autonomy has been given up on entering work, it is not clear why autonomy should demand protection of religious practice.

However, this argument misinterprets what is demanded by a respect for autonomy, as the term was used above to argue in favour of granting some level of protection for religious interests. The underlying autonomy and dignity of human beings demands a core level of respect for the person, which may include respect for their religious interests. This core respect is not undermined by a person doing as he is bid and complying with his employer's instructions in order to fulfil the needs of the business, even though the individual is not a totally free agent when doing so. However, one cannot rely on the restriction on freedom inherent in being at work, rather than at leisure, to deny any protection for religious interests at work.

The reduction in autonomy that accompanies an agreement to accept an employer's instructions does not entail a consequent reduction in the extent to which an individual's core human dignity and autonomy should be respected at work.[95] It is thus not the case that entering the workplace involves an implicit acceptance that personal dignity and autonomy are limited within the workplace.

Stepping Out of the Employment Relationship

One additional way to reconcile the competing interests at stake in cases where religious interests clash with other interests is to protect religious individuals, but not within the traditional employment relationship. For example, a religious

[95] In fact, it has been suggested by Collins that much of the legal protection for employees at work can be understood to be based on the need to protect the dignity and autonomy of employees in the workplace. H Collins, *Justice in Dismissal* (Oxford, Clarendon Press, 1992) 16.

group who wished only to employ men might be refused protection: any woman who was refused employment could then claim against the employer. The resulting conflict of rights could be resolved by accommodating the needs of the religious employer and allowing such an employment policy, or by refusing to accommodate and granting the woman a remedy against the employer. An alternative might be to allow the religious group to opt out of the employment relationship altogether. That way they would not be subject to the non-discrimination rules that apply to the relationship. The difficulty here is that there may be significant consequences for other areas of employment law of widening the range of quasi-employment relationships. The definition of the term 'employee' for the purposes of the ascription of employment rights is developing very fast. As courts determine the types of contractual arrangement to which employment or worker status should be afforded, so employers seem to draft contracts in order to avoid the creation of such a status in their workers.[96] To create a sub-group of workers to whom usual workplace rights do not apply could be a dangerous option. Any alternative non-employment status could be exploited by other employers to deny protection to vulnerable workers.[97] It is thus better to seek the correct level of protection for religious interests within the employment relationship, than to achieve the same end by excluding religious organisations from the relationship altogether.

And Yet . . . The Residual Protection of the 'Right to Resign'

There are many good reasons to protect religion at work within the employment relationship. The reasons are based on the importance of religion, the importance of work, and the equality interest in distributing the benefits of employment without discrimination on religious grounds. They also reflect the failure to respect core dignity if workers are allowed to contract out of protection. Yet, despite all these reasons to protect religious interests at work, in the final analysis the right to resign does provide the ultimate protection: if the employee finds it impossible to reconcile religious practices or beliefs with her work-based obligations, she is free to leave.

The fact that religious freedom can be protected through a freedom to resign, but that other rights may also be so protected, pervades any assessment of how to resolve any conflict of rights which arises in the context of the workplace. Any assessment of the level of protection that should be afforded to religious interests must be carried out in the light of this residual protection. However, the arguments above regarding the importance of work and the importance of religion mean that resignation should remain the residual protection where accommoda-

[96] For full discussion of the development of the law on the definition of employment, and the implications of the changes, see M Freedland, *The Personal Employment Contract* (Oxford, OUP, 2003).

[97] For example, the question of whether there is mutuality of obligation between workers and employers to provide and undertake work may be determinative of the question of employment status, leading employers to draft contracts with no such mutuality, even though in practice work is offered and personal service is expected and performed.

tion of the religious interest is inappropriate, rather than the starting point for the provision of protection.

Conclusion

Religious belief has crucial significance for individual identity, linked as it is with beliefs about man's nature and place in the universe. Given the gravity of the issues involved in the lives of adherents, they should not have to relinquish their practices too lightly. However, important as they are, religious interests are not absolute. It is accepted that in some circumstances burdens may need to be placed on religious practice, and that at times the rights of others will prevail over religious interests.

However, the non-absolute nature of the rights as exercised in work cuts both ways. The rights with which religious interests may collide, if they are rights being exercised at work, are equally subject to the residual protection of resignation. If a worker is unhappy with the accommodation offered to a religious employee she also enjoys the freedom to resign. Moreover, it is well established that there is no clear right to work in a particular job.[98] In effect, the right to resign ensures that neither religious rights nor the other rights enjoy automatic precedence.

The importance of employment as a benefit to which all should have equal access means that respect for religious interests should be provided in the work context, along with respect for other rights. The importance of the benefits offered by working suggest that to deny the opportunity to some to take up those benefits because of their religious beliefs would be to significantly diminish their dignity.[99]

It is not argued here that religious interests should take priority, merely that they should not be ignored. They should take their place alongside other interests as worthy of some protection at work. Where the protection of religion gives rise to conflict with other interests, the additional and complex question arises of how much protection should be granted, and how the conflicting interests should be reconciled. As suggested at the start of the chapter, the method generally used for reconciling competing legal rights is to engage in a balancing exercise, in order to determine whether it is proportionate to uphold religious interests over other interests, or vice versa. What follows is an examination of the various interests and issues that need to be considered in order for the proportionality of any legal response to be assessed.

[98] The European Charter of Fundamental Rights Art 15 provides that everyone has a right to engage in work and to pursue a freely chosen or accepted occupation. However, this does not extend to providing a right to a particular job.

[99] D Réaume, 'Discrimination and Dignity' (2003) 63 *Louisiana LR* 645, 688.

IV The Proportionality Equation: Religion and the Workplace

The case has been made above for providing a measure of protection for religious interests at work. However, it has also been recognised that religious interests can conflict with other interests within the workplace, such as the economic freedom of the employer, and the equality and other interests of fellow employees. If both sets of interests are to be given adequate protection, then a fair balance needs to be struck between them. In some cases, the competing rights will be irreconcilable, and all that can be hoped for is for the competing interests to be held in some sort of equilibrium. The most common method of finding an equilibrium as between different interests is to restrict interests only as far as it proportionate to do so, in the light of the other competing interests.

Proportionality is a mathematical term, which implies that the correct balance can be calculated with a degree of precision. But when using it in the legal context, one is measuring incommensurable interests, and mathematical precision is impossible. Although the use of proportionality aims to introduce an element of objectivity into the analysis, it is inevitable that value judgments will be made as to the relative importance of the different interests.[100] Nonetheless, in the absence of a better analogy, the concepts of balance and proportionality are used by courts to determine conflicting interests. They enable a structured approach to be taken to balancing fundamental rights against each other, and will be adopted here.

In assessing whether it is proportionate to protect religious interests, one assesses whether the accommodation required serves a legitimate aim and whether there is a proportionate relationship between the means used and the aim one is trying realise, given the existence of competing interests. This involves considering whether the aim can be realised using alternative means which impinge less on other interests. The strength of the argument in favour of protection of religious interests at work demonstrates that their protection serves a legitimate aim. Whether or not accommodation should be required in any particular case will thus depend on whether it is proportionate to do so, bearing in mind the relative strength of the competing interests in question, and whether the aim can be realised in a way that reduces the adverse impact on those other interests.

The determination of proportionality will depend on the assessment of a complex range of factors. It is not proposed to establish with precision here what

[100] For a discussion of the theoretical difficulties inherent in any balancing exercise of this type, see L Vickers, *Freedom of Speech and Employment* (Oxford, OUP, 2002) ch 2. See also J Rivers 'Proportionality and Variable Intensity of Review' (2006) 65(1) *CLJ* 174, who argues that the values are not truly incommensurable: 'few would view with indifference a massive loss of liberty for a marginal gain in national security' (at p 201). He argues instead that the difficulty is that the balancing of rights can only be carried out in a crude manner. Further support for the use of proportionality as a method for resolving conflicts between rights can be found in D Beatty, *The Ultimate Rule of Law* (Oxford, OUP, 2004).

the outcome will be in any given case. Instead, a range of the factors that should influence the determination of whether it is proportionate to accommodate religious interests at work will be considered, on the basis that the more detailed the consideration given to the question, and the more complete the range of factors considered, the more objective the determination of the question can be. Given the incommensurable nature of the interests being considered, precision and pure objectivity are not achievable, but a reflective and detailed consideration of relevant factors may lead to outcomes which can be more readily justified to those on either side of any conflict.

The first issue in the proportionality equation is to assess the relative strength of the competing interests. The strength of the interest in protecting religious interests within the workplace was discussed earlier in the chapter. The second issue is to consider the range of interests with which such interests may compete in the workplace, such as employers' financial interests and the equality interests of other employees. These interests, considered below, will interact with each other, and may act singly or cumulatively to suggest that protection should be limited. Finally, a range of additional contextual factors will be considered which may have an effect on the determination of whether it is proportionate to require protection. Issues in this category include the type of employer, as well as background issues such as whether the workplace is viewed as a public or a private space.

Competing Rights

The Equality Rights of Others

The most obvious interests with which religion is likely to compete are the equality rights of others. For example, an employee who has religious objections to working on an equal basis with women would need to be able to show that his religious interests outweighed the interests of gender equality if he is to succeed in having his religious views protected. Similarly, a religious employer who was unhappy about employing a gay man would need to show that his religious interests should prevail against the equality interests involved.

Given that the basis for protecting religious interests in employment is the need to protect human autonomy and dignity in the practically important sphere of the workplace, it is unlikely that religious interests will often prevail over other equality interests, similarly based on dignity and autonomy. The interests in equality on grounds of gender and race are generally recognised to be the most powerful equality interests, and are granted greater legal protection than other grounds.[101] Some[102] have justified this on the ground that biological differences and ascriptive

[101] M Bell and L Waddington, 'Reflecting on inequalities in European equality law' (2003) 28 *EL Rev* 349; M Bell and L Waddingon, 'More Equal Than Others: Distinguishing European Equality Directives' (2001) 38 *CML Rev* 587.

[102] For example, D Schiek, 'A New Framework on Equal Treatment of Persons in EC Law' (2002) 8 *European LJ* 290.

differences (sex, age, ethnicity) should be granted greater protection. Others[103] point to differences in the socio-political context in which the discrimination occurs, and the differing levels of historical disadvantage, and of social exclusion. These factors suggest that, as a general rule, race and gender equality interests will take precedence over competing religious interests, and such a position would reflect the current legal and political compact.

However, the strength of the case for protecting religious interests, together with the fact that the interests are not being protected at large but in the more restricted context of the workplace, means that there may be times when religious interests should be accommodated, even when to do so involves infringing some other equality right. In effect, it may be the case that in some circumstances the factors discussed below combine in such a way that it is proportionate to accommodate religion even though to do so involves giving precedence to religious over other equality interests.

The Negative Aspect of Freedom of Religion and the Protection of Religious Interests

As noted above, tension exists in the protection of religious interests as a result of the extension of the protection to many forms of religion and belief. Those who have a particular religious belief are protected equally with those who have either a different belief or none. The double-sided nature of the protection, protecting belief and absence of belief, creates an inherent conflict. For example, to give full protection to the rights of believers to practise their religion in public places entails an infringement of the rights of non-believers to enjoy those same public places free from the influence of religion. In assessing whether it is proportionate to protect religious interests in any situation, then, it will be necessary to consider in the balance both the interests of the religious group or individual, and the interests of those who wish to remain free from the influence of religion.

Rights to Privacy, Freedom of Speech and Freedom of Association

The argument was made above that the workplace is a sufficiently important part of life for religious interests to be protected there. If this is true for religious interests, then the same must be true for other fundamental human rights such as rights to privacy, freedom of speech and freedom of association.[104] At times, the employee may enjoy a right to privacy, which will need to be balanced against an employer's need to know information regarding religious affiliation. For example, where a religious employer has a genuine occupational requirement that an employee be of a particular religion, the invasion of privacy entailed in establishing that the employee complies with the requirement is likely to be proportionate.

[103] eg, C McCrudden 'Thinking about the discrimination directives' (2005) 1 *European Anti-Discrimination Law Review* 17.

[104] Protected under Arts 8, 10 and 11 ECHR respectively.

If there is no genuine occupational requirement to be of the religion, the invasion of privacy may be viewed as disproportionate, depending on other circumstances. Clashes between religious interests and freedom of speech may also occur, particularly with regard to the protection against religious harassment at work. The freedom to debate religious doctrine may need to be balanced against the need to protect the dignity of religious workers. Again, the proportionality of any restriction will need to be considered in the light of many other factors, such as whether the harassing speech was directed at the victim.[105]

Freedom of association is another right with which religious interests interact. The interest in being free from religious discrimination may come into conflict with the rights to freedom of association of groups who need to engage employees to serve the group's needs. For example, to require that a group must employ someone who disagrees with their beliefs, in order to avoid infringing discrimination rules may, arguably, interfere with the right to freedom of association of the group. However, such an interference may be proportionate if it is viewed as necessary to uphold the religious interests of those involved.

In each case, the interaction of the competing interests must be taken into account in assessing the proportionality of any suggested protection of religious interests. Moreover, as with religious interests, the interests in privacy, freedom of expression and freedom of association are not absolute rights, and the proportionality equation will need to be assessed in the light of the freedom to resign, which remains the residual protection for all fundamental rights in the context of the workplace.

Economic Efficiency

The employer will have a number of interests to be taken into account when assessing the proportionality of any protection of religious interests, including the interest in the good management and efficient running of the enterprise. Good management and efficiency enables the employer to maximise profits, as well as serving the more general public interest. A strong economy and good levels of employment are dependent on the existence of profitable businesses, which rely on a certain level of employer freedom to manage the business free from too many external constraints.[106]

It will no doubt be the case that that protecting religious interests at work will involve the employer in financial costs in some cases. For example, allowing staff time off for religious observance increases the length of time that those staff are economically inactive. Even if time off is awarded without pay, this may still reduce the capacity for employers to use plant to maximum efficiency or generate

[105] See further discussion below at pp 145–152.

[106] For more on where the balance between employee protection and employer freedom should lie see R Epstein, 'In defense of the contract at will' (1984) 51 *U of Chicago LR* 947 and R Epstein, *Equal Opportunity or More Opportunity? The good thing about discrimination* (London, Civitas, 2002) and the reply by S Deakin in the same volume.

profit at the same rate as they are able where no time is awarded for such activity. Economic loss for the employer can also have an adverse effect on other workers, especially if it is at such a level as to risk the viability of the business. Other forms of accommodation may also be unrealistic given the need to respect the rights of other employees at work. For example, a religious employee who needed to work in a single sex environment may not be able to be accommodated without significant interference with the interests of other workers.

The need for employers to be able to run viable businesses is clearly a factor to be considered when assessing the proportionality of any protection for religious interests. It is arguable that protecting the autonomy and dignity of staff at work will lead staff to feel more valued, leading to the recruitment of better staff, higher motivation, and ultimately higher profits. However, this may not always be the case, and it is inevitable that at times protection of religious interests will lead the employer to incur costs, for example, because of the need to employ extra staff to cover religious leave; or because of a loss of custom if religious interests are accommodated.[107] Where the profitability of an enterprise would be reduced if religious interests were to be protected, this may tilt any balance against the protection. However, the employer's interest in enjoying the fruits of the business is clearly not an absolute interest. A large number of employment rights in the UK restrict the right of the employer to put profit before the rights of others, such as restrictions on working time,[108] unfair dismissal[109] and the need to safeguard health and safety.[110]

Of course, not all employers run in order to make a profit. The public sector does not operate with a primary brief to make profit. Instead, its primary purpose is the delivery of the various services it provides, although financial efficiency may be required of it in order to achieve this. As well as the public sector, there exists a large sector of not-for-profit organisations, whose aim may not be to improve economic efficiency, but to provide a service, but who are nonetheless required to use the employment relationship to regulate the relationship between the organisation and those that work for it. For example, a religious group which has as its aim the propagation of a religious message may need to utilise the employment relationship to regulate its relationship between workers and the organisation. The economic interests of such organisations are unlikely to be as significant in the analysis of the proportionality of any restriction on religion as the economic interests of for-profit organisations.

Although not an absolute interest, then, the need for an employer to run an economically viable business is a clear interest that needs to be taken into account in assessing the proportionality of any protection of religious interests.

[107] For example, an employer could argue that customers may prefer not to be served by staff wearing religious dress.

[108] Working Time Regulations 1998 (as amended).

[109] s 98 ERA 1996.

[110] The Health and Safety at Work Act 1974.

Employer Autonomy and Reputation

An additional factor to take into account in assessing proportionality is that the employer, as well as the employee, may be entitled to some respect for autonomy. Both the European and US legal systems recognise that companies as well as individuals can enjoy the right to freedom of expression.[111] In some cases, protection of employees' religious interests could clash with the right of the employer to portray the image to the public that it would wish. For example, an employer that wishes to project a secular image may not wish its employees to attend work in religious dress.

However, the need to uphold employer autonomy will not always prevail over religious interests of staff. Corporations who act as employers will not find fulfilment through self-expression, as a human right. If there are no other factors at stake, the human interest in upholding autonomy and dignity should prevail over the rights of a corporation. However, where other interests are also of relevance, such as economic interests, then the balance may be more fine.

It was argued above that the individual right to religious freedom involves a degree of protection for collective religious rights.[112] The right of a religious group to enjoy a level of autonomy is reflected in the protection for freedom of religion which extends to a right to manifest religion alone or in community with others.[113] This means that religious groups should enjoy some of the protection afforded to individual religious interests.

A respect for group autonomy should mean that religious groups are enabled to enter employment relationships, in order better to organise or facilitate religious activity. In some cases, religious groups may want to appoint someone to act as a teacher, or as a full-time religious official. In other cases, the religious group may want to appoint other staff, for example catering or administrative staff, to improve the group's ability to fulfil its manifestation or practice of religion. For example, a church which spreads its message to young people by running a youth group may wish to employ a group leader. If there are a large number of groups, it may need a leader's co-ordinator, and, of course, work with young people may be only part of the outreach work the group engages in. It is not difficult to see how a large organisation will generate its own bureaucracy and administrative systems, which will need staffing.

In other cases, religious individuals may wish to work with others of the same religious persuasion, grouping together to supply goods and services without any specific religious link. For example, a group of Christians may wish to run a café or a group of Muslims may wish to open a book shop. In these cases, the employment is not the result of the need for support for religious activity, but is a secular activity, carried out by a religious group. In these cases, the link with freedom of religion is less direct, although it is still present. In some cases the activity may

[111] *First National Bank of Boston v Bellotti* 435 US 765 (1978).

[112] See discussion at pp 42–43 above.

[113] Art 9 ECHR.

reflect a personal preference by the employer to work with co-religionists. In others, the view of the employer may be that the activity can be the forum for some type of religious outreach; it may provide opportunities for proselytism. In each case, the activity is motivated by religion, and although not directly involved in the manifestation of belief, it is the result of the outworking of religious commitment.

Full respect for autonomy involves the recognition that religious groups have an interest in being able to act as employers, as part of the respect due to group autonomy and dignity. As with the other interests discussed here, this is not absolute, and needs to be weighed against other interests. In assessing the extent of the religious employers' interest in autonomy the extent of the link between the activity engaged in and the manifestation of religion is important. Where a group acts as the employer of a religious person who officiates at religious ceremonies, the employee is playing a key role in the group's manifestation of religion and the autonomy of the religious group should be accorded great weight when set against other interests.[114] Where the activity is only motivated by religion, rather than being an outworking of religious practice, then the weight accorded to the employer's autonomy may be less.

An Interest in Being in Work

There is no legally enforceable right to work,[115] but the importance of work to the individual, for both financial and non-financial reasons, was highlighted above. The argument was made that individuals gain such benefits from work that they should not be unreasonably denied the opportunity to participate in the workplace on grounds of religion. Thus the case was made for accommodating religious interests within the workplace.

The interest in having a job is clearly not absolute. However, it can provide a significant component of individual autonomy. If an individual is excluded from employment because his religion cannot be accommodated, this will be a relevant factor to take into account when assessing where the balance should lie between clashing interests.

The extent of exclusion from work can vary: because of religion, a person may be denied access to a particular job which she would like; she may be denied access to a particular profession; or she may be denied access to the workforce altogether. Clearly total exclusion will be more serious, and more difficult to justify, than exclusion merely from the particular job for which the religious person applied.

If a religious person is unable to take up a job because she cannot meet its requirements, but remains free to take other jobs, there will only be a minor infringement of her interests, as she remains free to take up other work. For example, a Christian might be unwilling to work for a shop which requires its staff to work on Sundays. The individual remains free to work for other shops, or in

[114] See, for example, *Hasan and Chaush v Bulgaria* (2002) 34 EHRR 55 at para 62; and *Serif v Greece* (2001) 31 EHRR 20.

[115] B Hepple, 'A Right to Work?' (1981) 10 *ILJ* 65.

another occupation, and so her interest in working is not significantly reduced. Similarly, a refusal to allow staff in a café in a large town to wear headscarves would limit the choice of job for a Muslim woman who wears a headscarf, and wishes to work at that café. However, she may still be able to work in a different café. Thus her job opportunities are diminished, but only marginally so.

Of course, accommodation of particular days of work, or the wearing of headscarves, may be very simple for the employer. In such a case it may still be proportionate to require accommodation because of the ease with which the employer can achieve this, set against the infringement of freedom of the employee of any denial.

If the employer is a small employer, with no possibility of rearranging shifts, or if there are strong reasons for imposing the uniform rule, then it may not be proportionate to require accommodation: the economic or other interests of the employer may then outweigh the interests of the employee. In contrast, if all shop workers are expected to work on Sundays, then the Christian who wants to work in the retail sector may find it hard to work in the particular area of work she wishes to. This is a more serious infringement of her interest in having a job, as she is excluded from a particular sector of employment. Similarly, if a large employer such as the NHS were to ban the wearing of headscarves, this would severely limit the freedom to choose a career for many Muslim women. The interests served by such a restriction would need to be very strong if they were to counteract the interests of Muslim women in being able to choose a career as a health professional.

In some cases, a religious requirement may be very difficult to accommodate, because it may in turn involve the employer in infringing others' rights. For example, an employee might refuse to work with women on religious grounds. It is likely to be proportionate for a secular employer to refuse to accommodate such an employee, not least because to do so could amount to indirect discrimination against women. The equality rights of women in the same employment would be infringed by acceding to any such request, and these interests in dignity and respect would outweigh the rights of the individual religious employee.

However, the same might not be the case if the employer shared the religious view. Allowing a religious employer to accommodate such a request would infringe the rights of others and would amount to indirect discrimination against women.[116] However, depending on the circumstances, it is possible for this to be justified as proportionate. One factor to consider is whether the religious employee can be employed elsewhere in the absence of the accommodation. In practice, most employers would not accommodate such a request, and so if a person cannot be employed by a co-religionist, he may find it difficult to be employed at all. This amounts to a significant infringement of his interests because of the importance of work to individual dignity and autonomy. If the effect of a failure to accommodate is that an employee becomes virtually unemployable, then any

[116] The employer may not refuse to employ women, but a workplace where such requests are accommodated is likely to be a difficult place for women to work, and so they will be at a disadvantage in comparison to men.

countervailing interests will need to be extremely strong if they are to outweigh the effective denial to the employee of a chance to work at all.

Of course, the interest in working applies to both the religious employee and the female employee who will thereby be disadvantaged. If the employer is of a size or a nature that means that the woman is denied access to employment, or to a particular type of employment, then accommodation of the religious requirement is unlikely to be proportionate. For example, if a major local employer had a religious ethos, which accepted that men may wish to work separately from women, the resulting gender discrimination would be unlikely to be proportionate, because it would reduce the chances of women to work in the area. If, however, the employer were a small employer, and plenty of other job opportunities were available to women, such a practice could possibly be proportionate, if it were necessary to enable the religious minority to work at all, and depending on the interaction of the other factors that are relevant to the proportionality equation. This is not because of the size of the employer per se, but because of the effect of any denial of employment on the individual's general employment prospects.

The Right to be Free from Offence

One further competing right which should be considered when assessing the proportionality of protecting religion at work is the right to be free from offence.[117] The concept of dignity, with which autonomy and equality are so closely related, is infringed where an individual is subjected to offence or abuse. To insult or offend another on the basis of their religion, gender, sexual orientation or any other personal characteristic is to devalue the other person and treat them as of less worth. A practice cannot be said to be harmless if it involves a reduction in the dignity accorded to an individual. Even if there is no direct victim, the tolerance of such behaviour can be said to be harmful as it implies a lack of respect for individual dignity. The importance of the interests in not being offended is recognised in the inclusion of anti-harassment measures in the equality legislation: harassment on grounds of religion, gender, sexual orientation, disability and race are all prohibited on the basis that such behaviour infringes individual dignity.

However, it may be that the wrong of causing offence is one that has to be tolerated, at least to some extent, if we are to provide sufficient space to all to follow their conception of the good. Clearly, requiring an individual to tolerate being offended will only be acceptable when it is proportionate. Thus, in assessing whether it is acceptable to allow an individual to cause offence, the range of factors discussed above will also need to be assessed. The aim of this section is to assess the weight that should be given to the right not to be offended so that it can be properly taken into account in assessing the proportionality of any proposed exception to the general non-discrimination principle.

[117] See, generally, J Feinberg, *Offence to Others* (Oxford, OUP, 1985), looking at offence in the context of criminal law prohibitions on causing offence.

Offence may not only be caused by the presence of exceptions to the non-discrimination principle, but can also be caused in a variety of other ways that are of relevance here. Offence can be caused by harassment, behaviour that has the purpose or effect of violating dignity, or causing a hostile environment. In relation to the conflict between religion and other rights, harassment could occur if a religious worker were to cause offence to a co-worker by persistently telling her that her actions were sinful. Alternatively, allowing a male worker to refuse to work with women could create a hostile environment and cause offence to female workers. Where such behaviour is concerned, the interest in protecting the victim, based on her interest in maintaining dignity, is clear. The 'offender' may have some religious interests which are harmed by any restriction on his freedom of action, as the harassing behaviour may also entail the exercise of religious freedom. However, any such harm to the harasser's religious interests is likely to be proportionate given the legitimate aim of protecting the dignity interests of the 'victim'. Religious individuals may have a right to hold their beliefs, but they do not have a right to impose those views on others at work, not least because any 'victim' will find it difficult to avoid the offending behaviour, and the harasser does not have an absolute right to be in the workplace. If an employer allows an employee to treat another in a way that undermines her dignity, then the employer will have failed to provide adequate protection for the autonomy and dignity of its workers.

However, offence is not limited to that caused by direct harassment by an individual; it may be caused in other ways, and in some circumstances the interest in being free from offence may not be so strong. It may then be that the religious interests of the 'offender' can prevail over the interest of the victim in being free from offence. For example, if a religious employer is allowed to maintain an employment practice of only employing co-religionists (through use of a genuine occupational requirement) this could cause offence to those who are thereby refused a job, but would still be proportionate because of the religious interests of the group.

This becomes more problematic if individuals are denied the status of co-religionists because of their race, gender or sexuality. For example, a religious group which is intolerant of homosexuality could recruit only those of the same religion and it could be legal for such a requirement to be introduced, for example, because there is a genuine occupational requirement that the employee be of the particular religion. In such a case there may be no direct 'victim' to be offended: it is unlikely that a gay person will apply, because they are unlikely to belong to the requisite religious group. However, the denial of work to gay applicants could still cause offence in a more general sense: the dignity of gay and lesbian people is undermined by the tolerance of such behaviour within the legal system, through the acceptance of genuine occupational requirement exceptions, in such circumstances.

The question then arises of whether the fact that such practices are tolerated infringes dignity to such an extent that a genuine occupational requirement will be disproportionate in the circumstances. It is suggested below that although the harm should be recognised, it should not be accorded overriding weight in assessing proportionality. It may be that allowing such indirect harm to dignity is a price that has to be paid to enable groups with conflicting beliefs to live and work together.

The work of Feinberg in *Offence to Others*[118] may aid the analysis here. Feinberg considers a number of factors when assessing the level of harm involved in causing offence, including the seriousness of the offence balanced against the reasonableness of the offending conduct. Applied in the context of the workplace, rather than in the context of the criminal law, they suggest that the offence caused by the 'bare knowledge' of the existence of work practices which one finds offensive should not give grounds, of itself, to prohibit those practices. This is not to say that such practices should be allowed where other interests are harmed, merely that where the only harm is one of 'bare knowledge' it may not provide sufficient harm to justify prohibiting a practice.

In considering the seriousness of offence caused, Feinberg considers its magnitude in terms of its intensity, duration and extent. He also looks at questions such as whether it is possible to avoid the offence, or whether the victim has consented to be subject to it. In the work context these are difficult questions. Technically the employee who is a victim of more than single incidents of harassment may be able to resign,[119] but this freedom carries significant cost, and is not a very realistic option.[120] In the context of workplace harassment which is directed at a specific victim, the idea that a person consents to the harassment and is always free to leave will not carry much weight in assessing the seriousness of the offence. However, this may not be the case in the context of 'bare knowledge' offence. For example, a religious employer could require that staff be of the same religion, and the religion may teach that the employment of married women is wrong. In effect, requiring staff to share the religious view will mean that the employer will not employ married women. This impinges on the dignity of all married women, whether religious or not. However, the 'offence' is not directed at any particular woman, and those of the offended group are not forced to confront the offending behaviour. Thus, offence may exist, but it is less serious than that caused by direct harassment at work.

Balanced against the seriousness of the offence caused is the 'reasonableness' of the conduct which causes offence. Here Feinberg considers a number of issues[121]: the importance of the offending conduct to the actor; the social value of the behaviour; the value of freedom of expression; the presence of alternative opportunities

118 J Feinberg, *Offence to Others* (Oxford, OUP, 1985).

119 See discussion at p 45ff.

120 On the debate surrounding the freedom to resign in the context of harassment, see E Volokh 'Freedom of Speech and Workplace Harassment' (1992) 39 *UCLA LR* 1791 and D Epstein, 'Can a "Dumb Ass Woman" Achieve Equality in the Workplace? Running the Gauntlet of Hostile Work Environment Harassing Speech' (1996) 84 *Georgetown LJ* 339, and L Vickers, 'Is All Harassment Equal? The Case of Religious Harassment' (2006) 65(3) *CLJ* 579.

121 J Feinberg, *Offence to Others* (Oxford, OUP, 1985) 44.

for the conduct which might cause less offence to others; whether the conduct is motivated by malice or spite; and whether the conduct is to be expected in the locality.

Using the example of offence caused by bare knowledge that a religious employer's requirement that staff share the religion results in a failure to offer work to married women, these factors combine to suggest that offence caused should not, of itself, weigh particularly strongly in any assessment of proportionality, albeit that other factors may make the practice disproportionate. If the offending behaviour is the result of religious belief then it will be viewed as being of great importance to the actor, and the fact that religious freedom is protected within human rights law suggests that it is accorded social value: both of these factors weigh in favour of allowing the offending behaviour. The fact that the conduct is not directed at any individual and is not inspired by personal malice or spite similarly militates against the suggestion that the offence caused makes the practice disproportionate. In these circumstances, the balance between the seriousness of offence and the 'reasonableness' (in Feinberg's terms) of the offending behaviour is likely to come down in favour of allowing the offending behaviour to continue. This is because the behaviour is not directed at any particular person, relates only to 'bare knowledge' and can be avoided; and yet the behaviour is of great importance to the individual as an outworking of religious belief. Of course, there may be other factors which tip the balance against allowing the employment practice, for example, if married women are thereby significantly disadvantaged in the workplace because the employer is a major employer in the area.

The final factor suggested by Feinberg (whether the offensive behaviour can be expected and then avoided) is of more relevance in cases where an employee works for a religious employer and takes offence at some of the work practices. For example, a non-religious employee may find it offensive to be invited to pray by colleagues, or may find overtly religious conversations offensive. Here the conduct in question may be to be expected given the type of employer. If the employee has chosen to work for a religious employer, he or she cannot complain of offence when the employer acts in a religious manner.[122] The offending behaviour meets the standards of reasonableness set by Feinberg, suggesting that the balance should be struck in favour of allowing the behaviour to continue, even though the bare knowledge of the behaviour may cause offence to some. Again, if the employer is a major employer in the sector or in the area, then it is arguable that the employee has not really chosen freely to work in such an environment, and the religious practice may then be disproportionate overall.

Although it involves tolerating some level of offensive behaviour, such a compromise is essential if groups who disagree fundamentally on many issues are to co-exist in a plural democracy. It may well be that accommodating an employee

[122] Although this may also be subject to proportionality. For example, if it was not clear that religious activity would be expected at work at the start of the employment it may not be acceptable to impose such a requirement on non-religious staff.

who believes in women's inequality implicitly infringes the dignity of women. But it may correspondingly be argued by a religious employer that a refusal to allow accommodation of such views infringes the autonomy of the religious group, as it effectively prevents him from acting as an employer. Religiously motivated people should have the freedom to employ others, in order to fully exercise their freedom of religion, and their autonomy. It may therefore be proportionate to tolerate their employment policies, where there are no direct victims, even though their very existence may be offensive to some. For example, a religious group which is opposed to the employment of women could have a genuine occupational requirement to employ a co-religionist as a religious teacher. Women who share the faith will not want to work, and so there are no direct victims of the indirect discrimination involved. In contrast, where there are victims, for example, the employer is a large or monopoly employer and so the restriction on co-religionists has an impact on women's employment prospects, the level of offence caused may be one of the factors to take into account in assessing proportionality, albeit not necessarily the paramount interest.[123]

Such an approach would not create a licence to private employers simply to refuse to appoint people on religious grounds, as the right to be free from offence is only one factor in the proportionality equation. However, to return to the question of the weight to be afforded to the right not to be offended, it is suggested that 'bare knowledge' offence, caused by allowing genuine occupational requirements which may indirectly discriminate on other grounds, should not be given undue weight in the proportionality equation. It may be necessary to tolerate some level of 'bare knowledge' offence if groups who disagree fundamentally are to coexist.

Contextual Issues

The factors discussed above should all be taken into account when assessing the proportionality of any protection of religious interests at work. In addition, the contextual issues discussed below should be considered, as they may have a bearing on the final outcome of any balancing of interests that is bound to occur when assessing proportionality.

The first contextual factor to consider is the type of employer. This involves the question of whether the employer is part of the public sector or the private sector, as well as a consideration of the special status of religious employers.

[123] See also L Cariolou, 'The right not to be offended by members of the British National Party' (2006) *ILJ* 415. The net effect of these rules may be that only small religious employers will be able to restrict employment to co-religionists, but this is not because of anything inherent in being a small employer, merely because of the range of factors considered in the proportionality equation such as the impact of any restriction on the employment prospects of those outside the religious group.

The Public/Private Divide

The exact dividing line between public and private sector employers is acknowledged to be difficult to draw with any certainty.[124] The question has become increasingly complex in recent years after the privatisation of numerous public utilities, the contracting out of some parts of state-run enterprises such as cleaning and catering in hospitals to private contractors, and the move of parts of the public sector, such as individual prisons, to the private sector.[125] In the context of remedies such as judicial review, the division between the public and private sector is vital, as the status of the body determines whether the remedy is available at all. However, in the context of determining the proper scope of religious interests when in competition with other interests in the workplace, it may be best to understand the division as a continuum or spectrum rather than as a sharp dividing line.

The question of whether an employer is public or private sector could cause particular difficulties in the context of religion, as there are increasing moves to hand over the provision of public services to charitable or other private providers, some of which are religiously based.[126] Education provides a prime example of the provision of a public service by religiously based providers with a large proportion of state schools having the status of church schools. Here religious organisations provide services, funded by the state, which fulfil the fundamentally public obligations on the state to provide education for children. Other examples include charities involved in the delivery of public services, such as the provision of adaptations to the home for disabled people, of child welfare services and of health services, such as hospice care. In these cases, while the bodies themselves are not part of the public sector, they are clearly a long way along the continuum towards public status and away from purely private status.

Public Sector Employers

Where the employer can be viewed as on the public end of the continuum, to the extent that they may fairly be said to represent the state, there may be additional factors at play, which call for particular types of protection for religious interests, whilst at the same time placing limits on the scope of the protection that is appropriate.

If the employer is viewed as representing the state, protection of religious interests should only occur where it accords with the aims and interests of the state. The

[124] D Oliver, 'Common Values in Public and Private Law and the Public/Private Divide' [1997] *PL* 630; G Morris, 'The Human Rights Act and the Public/Private Divide in Employment Law' [1998] *ILJ* 293; G Morris and S Fredman, 'Public or Private? State Employees and Judicial Review' (1991) 107 *LQR* 298; G Morris, 'Employment in Public Services: The Case for Special Treatment' (2000) 20 *OJLS* 167.

[125] See G Morris, 'The Human Rights Act and the Public/Private Divide in Employment Law' [1998] *ILJ* 293.

[126] See, for example, Press Release, 11 January 2007, from The Department for Work and Pensions, referred to on p 3.

state, if it is committed to a pluralist society, may wish to accommodate a range of religious practices, so that it can encourage equal participation in the workforce for a range of religious groups.[127] The state's interests here are in reducing social exclusion to certain groups by encouraging participation in employment. This prevents detriments caused by being excluded from the economic benefits of working. Equal participation at work also encourages social cohesion by including the minorities in mainstream society, and improving integration between social groups who make up the society.[128] It is also important for the state to reflect the full range of its citizenry in some jobs to reflect the inclusive nature of the society, sending the symbolic message to the rest of society that all citizens are equal and valued. Thus, ensuring that those from minority religions can participate in the armed services, or the police force, serves a legitimate aim of public policy.[129]

Moreover, many jobs or careers can only realistically be carried out in the context of state employment. Although there is a developing role for private medicine in the UK, the overwhelming majority of health-related careers operate in the context of the National Health Service. The same can be said for careers in education, where the vast majority of primary, secondary and tertiary education comprises state provision. Those choosing careers in health or education, or indeed social work, the armed forces, professions related to the criminal justice system, and many others have little choice but to be employed within the public sector. As discussed above, there is no doubt that staff in these sectors remain free to choose other forms of employment, and the proportionality question must be determined in the light of the residual right to resign. Nonetheless, the fact that whole sectors of employment could be barred to members of particular religions if no protection is allowed, is an important contextual factor to be taken into account in assessing the proportionality of any protection.

The various interests served by the protection of religious interests by public sector employers will vary according to the circumstances, such as the extent of the protection requested, and the strength of any competing interests. It may also vary according to the exact place on the public/private continuum the particular employer holds. The importance of having a cross-section of the population in terms of gender, ethnicity and religion may be stronger in an employment sector of symbolic importance such as the police and armed services, than in the case of a religious hospice providing care to patients, some of whom are funded by the state.

[127] See J Rawls, *A Theory of Justice* (Oxford, OUP, 1999, revised edition) 196, who argues that justice as fairness requires equal participation in the state.

[128] C Estlund, *Working together: How Workplace Bonds Strengthen a Diverse Democracy* (Oxford, OUP, 2003). See also M Kelman, 'Market Discrimination and Groups' (2001) 53 *Stanford LR* 833, 885.

[129] See further, P W Edge, 'Religious rights and choice under the European Convention on Human Rights' [2000] 3 *Web JCLI*, who cites the MacPherson Report's recommendation that those responsible for staffing 'should seek to ensure that the membership of police authorities reflect so far as is possible the cultural and ethnic mix of the communities which those authorities serve' (*The Stephen Lawrence Inquiry, Report of an Inquiry by Sir William Macpherson*, London, The Stationery Office, Cm 4262-I 1999 Recommendation 7). See also the discussion of the Police (Northern Ireland) Act 2000 at p 143.

However, the fact that a public sector employer represents the state may also work to create special limits on the extent to which religious interests can be protected, because of the equal interest the state has in upholding the dignity and equality of others on grounds of gender, race, sexuality and other grounds. Thus, although public sector employers may need to provide a level of protection to religious interests in order to uphold the public policy of promoting diversity and pluralism within the state, this will not extend to protecting religious interests at the expense of other equality interests to which the state is equally committed.

The public policy imperative of protecting the dignity of all members of society means that where religious interests conflict with other equality interests those equality interests will usually prevail, especially where the employer can be identified as on the public end of the public/private continuum. The right to freedom of religion may be sufficiently strong to warrant protection in the workplace, but the case for its protection is based on the same factors as the case for protection of equality on other grounds. The need to uphold dignity and autonomy leads to a need to protect the individual on a number of grounds, and does not give reason for one ground to trump another. The protection from discrimination on religious grounds does not give rise to grounds for overriding others' equality interests. It is therefore important that the state protects equality on grounds of gender, race and sexual orientation, for all the same reasons set out above, namely the symbolic importance of public sector employment as reflecting public policy, the dominance of the public sector in certain spheres of work such as health and education, and the need to encourage employment in all social groups so as to equalise access to economic benefits and to improve social cohesion. The assessment of the proportionality of any protection of religion should therefore take into account the status of the employer, and its place on the continuum between public and private employment, along with other interests such as the need to provide a high quality of service and to achieve a degree of economic efficiency. Those engaged in employment of a public nature should have their religious needs accommodated where possible, but only to the extent that to do so does not infringe other equality rights, in order to reflect the public policy of maintaining the dignity and equality of all groups in society.

Private Sector Employers

In contrast, the private sector is not compelled to promote the state's social policy agenda, and may not have the same imperative to promote religious equality at work or to uphold other social policies within the workplace. Thus private employers may not need to provide the same level of protection for religious interests as public employers; but equally an employer which chooses to uphold religious interests may not have the same limit as public employers in terms of the extent to which they must also uphold other equality interests, at the expense of protecting those religious interests.[130]

[130] See discussion of autonomy of religious employers above at pp 59–60.

As with the public sector, the notion of private employment may also be understood as a continuum. One can draw distinctions between the levels to which enterprises engage with the public. For example, some employment relationships may resemble private family arrangements, such as employment of a nanny or domestic cleaner, or employment in a small family business. In some cases the parties might not in ordinary language understand themselves to be part of an employment relationship, but for the needs of employment law policy this classification is made.[131] Other enterprises engage to a greater degree with the public, and are more clearly within the category of employment with a more managerial relationship between employer and employee. One could go so far as to suggest that any body which provides services to the public, even though those services are not publicly funded, is somewhere along the continuum away from the purely private arrangement. An employer which wishes to engage with the general public in order to gain some benefit, such as access to the public market for the purpose of generating profits, is engaging with the public sphere to an extent, and could be required to conform to publicly accepted standards as regards the necessity to protect religion. This public level of protection is likely to involve some measure of accommodation to enable members of religious groups to achieve a degree of equality with other sections of the public, so as to reflect a basic level of protection for religious freedom. However, such employers would also be expected to limit religious accommodation where it is necessary to safeguard the equality rights of others. This argument can apply to religious ethos employers, where the religious group wishes to carry on a business, offering services to the public. They may have regard to the religious ethos in their recruitment policies, in order to respect the autonomy of the group, but this cannot be at the expense of the equality rights of others.

However, where the employment relationship is more truly private, as with the nanny or domestic cleaner, the requirements to protect religious or other interests may be lessened.[132] This may also apply to religious employers who are employing staff to serve the needs of the religious group, such as cleaning staff, or administrative staff, or employing a helper for a church toddler group. The extent to which such jobs can be viewed as religious in nature will depend on the details of the job description, and the religious beliefs of the parties involved. For example, some religious groups may require that certain services be carried out by co-religionists.[133] However, even where the work is not defined as religious in nature, the employment relationships in the case of those serving the needs of a religious employer are of a private nature, and do not involve any interaction with the pub-

[131] To interpret employment law not to apply to these essentially private arrangements would lead to different but equal difficulties in other areas of employment law. See above at pp 51–52.

[132] The point is also made by M Kelman, 'Market Discrimination and Groups' (2001) 53 *Stanford LR* 833, 849, that there may be less need for anti-discrimination rules with regard to employment relationships which are 'quasi-intimate' relationships.

[133] On the difficulty of determining the division between the religious private sphere and the secular private sphere, see R Wintemute, 'Religion vs Sexual Orientation' [2002] 1:2 *Journal of Law and Equality* 125.

lic market. Greater freedom may therefore be given to the religious group to act in accordance with their beliefs, even where to do so may indirectly interfere with other equality rights. In effect, the role of the state in requiring compliance with the socially accepted norms of behaviour is reduced where the relationship is such a private one.[134]

The treatment of religious interests within the employment relationship may therefore vary depending on where on this spectrum the employment fits, with more flexibility regarding the protection of religious interests being given to more private employment relationships. This may involve greater or lesser protection, depending on the employer's wishes, with religious ethos employers being given increased freedom to accommodate religion at the expense of other interests where the employment relationship is at the private end of the spectrum. The question of whether any particular protection or accommodation is proportionate should be assessed in the light of these contextual issues.

Work as a Public or Private Space

There is an additional dimension to the question of whether employment is public or private in nature, and this is the question of whether the workplace itself should be seen as a public or private space. Although clearly the workplace is not private in the same way that the home is, work is not entirely a public space either. For example, individuals often enjoy close social friendships with colleagues, and may well socialise with them outside work. Indeed, a remarkable number of individuals meet their life partners at work. Courts have acknowledged the cross-over between work and leisure time in sexual harassment cases where after-work socialising has come within the remit of the employer's responsibility to protect staff against harassment. Examples from this case law of the cross-over between work as a public space and the private dimension of work are after-work drinks, work parties, or works family outings.[135] The private nature of the workplace is also reflected in workplaces which encourage staff to personalise their work spaces, by decorating them with pictures or photos, for example. Such practices demonstrate the hybrid nature of the workplace, formally a public space but experienced by many in practice as having a private dimension.

This private aspect of the workplace has been recognised in the case law of the ECHR. With respect to the right to privacy, it is recognised that individuals are entitled to a degree of respect for private life at work.[136] Moreover, in *Sidabras v Lithuania*,[137] the ECHR recognised that work can play an important role in one's 'private life', with a role in developing relationships with the outside world.

[134] It is plausible to achieve the same end by excluding such relationships from the definition of employment, but to do so would create further problems for vulnerable workers, and would be counter-productive. See discussion at pp 51–52 above.

[135] *Waters v Commissioner of Police of the Metropolis* [1997] IRLR 589, *Chief Constable of Lincolnshire Police v Stubbs* [1999] IRLR 91, *Sidhu v Aerospace Composite Technology* [2000] IRLR 602.

[136] *Halford* v *UK* (1997) 24 EHRR 523.

[137] App Nos 55480/00 and 59330/00, 27 July 2004.

It was also argued above that work plays an important role in creating individual identity and providing status. These may not be interests that prevail over other interests when considering the proportionality of protecting religious interests, but the assessment of proportionality should take into account that the workplace is not solely a public arena, but can also be regarded as having a private dimension.

One aspect of the private nature of the workplace is the role it can play in educating individuals about wider society. Not only is work an important forum in which individuals live out a large proportion of their lives, it is also an important space in which individuals can meet those they might not otherwise meet in other areas of their lives. For many, particularly those who live in religiously homogenous groups in their private lives, the workplace is the main forum for meeting those with differing views, and for sharing ideas. Estlund has gone as far as to argue that the workplace is a valuable forum for religious discourse.[138] Even though the facilitation of such discourse is clearly not the primary function of the workplace, it is clear that the workplace has the potential to act as a 'melting pot', where groups that might otherwise not mix actually engage with each other. As Schultz puts it, the workplace is 'one of the few arenas in which diverse groups of citizens can come together and develop respect for each other due to shared experience'.[139] Thus, encouraging religious groups to mix within the context of work can enable religious understanding and tolerance to be developed. Clearly, employers are not responsible for providing spaces for private socialising, nor for religious debate, and it is not suggested that they should be. Nor should employees be forced to mix socially with their work colleagues. However, any assessment of the proportionality of protecting religious interests at work should take into account the hybrid public and private nature of the workplace.

The fact that the workplace can be viewed as both a private and a public space has implications for the treatment of religious issues at work, particularly by religious ethos employers. Issues that may be viewed as wholly private, and therefore irrelevant to the employer in non-religious employment, may be of relevance to religious employers, and the recognition of a private dimension to the workplace means that they cannot be dismissed as irrelevant at work. For example, from a secular point of view, matters relating to the private lives of staff, as well as matters of personal and private morality, such as marital status and sexuality, should be irrelevant to the employer. However, religious employers can be intensely interested in issues of private morality as reflecting good religious standing and loyalty to the religion. Both employer and employee may view the employment as a forum for the exercise of religion as much as any other part of their lives. It is inevitable that matters of personal morality will be relevant to a religious employer who wishes to maintain a religious ethos: part of having a religious ethos at work is that

[138] C Estlund, 'Freedom of Speech in the Workplace and the Problem of Discriminatory Harassment' (1997) 75 *Tex LR* 687, and C Estlund, *Working together: How Workplace Bonds Strengthen a Diverse Democracy* (Oxford, OUP, 2003).

[139] V Schultz, 'Life's Work' [2000] 100 *Colum LR* 1881, 1885.

matters that to outsiders would be viewed as personal and private are shared. Where the employee has chosen to work for a religious employer, it may not be inappropriate for the employer to show interest in matters that in other contexts may be viewed as private.[140]

Of course, the extent to which secular employers have regard to personal morality is not a constant. Issues of private morality, such as honesty, may be relevant to the employer: it is accepted that an employer may dismiss for theft, rather than being required to put into place mechanisms to ensure that there will be no future incidents. Thus even with regard to secular employment matters of morality may be relevant, although the range of relevant issues may be greater with regard to religious employers. In considering the proportionality of an accommodation of religious interests, the fact that it is not always simple to create clear boundaries between a public workplace and the rest of life needs to be taken into account.

Religious Manifestation or Religious Motivation

Under Article 9 ECHR a distinction is drawn between conduct which is motivated by religion and that which is a manifestation of the religion.[141] That which is merely motivated by religion is not a manifestation of religion, and so restrictions imposed by the employer on religiously motivated activity do not offend the ECHR. Although the distinction between the two can be difficult to draw at times,[142] a broad distinction may be relevant in determining the proportionality of any restriction on religious freedom. Where behaviour is mandated by the religion to which an employee adheres, any refusal to allow the behaviour will involve a greater infringement of religious interests than a refusal to accommodate religiously motivated behaviour.

To rule out employment protection for behaviours which are religiously motivated may be to provide too little protection for religious interests, not least because the distinction can be difficult to define with precision. However, taking account of the centrality of the belief to the religious individual may be of relevance for the determination of proportionality. Where a work practice prevents a religious person from observing key tenets of the religion it will be harder to justify any refusal to protect the religious interest, than where the practice interferes with a religious preference. For example, a key tenet of the religion may be a requirement to pray at certain times of day. To refuse time off for prayers will involve a more significant infringement of religious interests than either to fail to provide a comfortable space to pray (however desirable that may be), or to refuse time off for members of other religions who would like to form a prayer group, but who are not required by their religion to do so.

[140] See R Ehrenreich, 'Dignity and Discrimination: Toward a Pluralistic Understanding of Workplace Harassment' (1999) 88 *Georgetown LJ* 1, 27, who points out that the boundaries between public and private issues can be hard to draw in some harassment cases, where the judgment of whether behaviour is appropriate may be very context-specific.

[141] *Arrowsmith v UK* [1978] 3 EHRR 218.

[142] See discussion in ch 4 at pp 96–101.

Similarly, where religious interests collide with other interests, the centrality of the belief will be of relevance to the determination of proportionality. For example, where a religious group believes that religious rites can only be validly performed by men, that belief is so central to a core part of the religion that the gender equality interests of women will not prevail over the religious interests of the religious organisation. This is recognised in most human rights systems, where the freedom of religious groups to appoint their religious leaders is respected. However, where a preference for male staff applies other than in the appointment of those performing religious rites, then the equality interests of women will have more weight. In effect, the centrality of the belief to the religious belief system is of relevance to the determination of proportionality.[143]

Organic or Functional View of the Religious Workplace

One particular difficulty that can arise with respect to religious employers is that the divide between work that is viewed as religious in nature and that which is not may be difficult to draw. Where employment is religious, it would seem proportionate to allow the imposition by the employer of religious requirements, if religious freedom is to be respected, even though to do so may infringe other equality rights. For example, a requirement that an employee should be an observant Muslim may indirectly discriminate against gays and lesbians, due to Islam's intolerance of homosexuality. It would seem clear that employment as a teacher of a religion, or as an officiator at religious ceremonies, is religious employment, and that religious requirements are appropriate even though they may infringe others' rights. Refusing to accept limits on the non-discrimination principle with respect to such religious functions would be a significant restriction on religious freedom.[144]

However, once one moves from the realm of religious practitioners, matters become more difficult, as the boundaries between work within the 'religious sphere' and the 'secular sphere' are less easy to draw. Some would claim that any work for a religious ethos employer is within the 'religious sphere' and that it is acceptable to impose strict religious requirements on such workers. Others would argue that once one leaves those who officiate at religious ceremonies to one side, other staff are outside the 'religious sphere' and religious restrictions should be limited to those that do not discriminate on any other ground. The question which arises here is the extent to which we allow the idea of the religious sphere to expand.[145]

[143] See B N Bagni, 'Discrimination in the Name of the Lord: A Critical Evaluation of Discrimination by Religious Organisations' (1979) 79 *Colum LR* 1514, who suggests an analytic framework based on concentric circles of spirituality and secularity: matters relating to the core, central circle, such as appointment of clergy should be insulated from state regulation.

[144] Moreover, as discussed above at pp 51–52, the alternative response, denial of employment status, causes as many problems as it solves.

[145] See R Wintemute, 'Religion vs Sexual Orientation' [2002] 1(2) *Journal of Law and Equality* 125.

The assessment of whether it is proportionate for religious employers to impose religious requirements on staff will depend on the range of factors discussed above, such as whether either party is denied access to the workforce. It will also depend on whether an organic or functional view is taken of the workplace.[146] The functional view is that the workplace exists to fulfil various functions, and each role should be considered with regard to that function. Thus the function of an officiator at a religious ceremony is to carry out religious observance, and it is necessary to comply with the religious rules if that observance is to be valid for the religious adherents. At the other end of the scale, the function of a cleaner of a church hall is to clean the building, and the religious beliefs of the individual worker have no impact on job performance. Again, there is a spectrum between these two extremes in which the religious nature of the functions is less clear cut. For example, it could be argued that an individual whose job is to teach the religion to young people, for example a church youth leader, need only have a good understanding of religious doctrine, without actually believing the truth of what he or she is teaching. However, most religious individuals would view it as essential that those who teach the religion to young people be active believers themselves.[147]

An alternative view of the workplace is more organic in nature, and recognises that some religious workers view work as a form of worship. For example, some Christians may view working for a Christian organisation as part of their Christian witness,[148] particularly if they work in a role which involves interaction with the public. Thus, some religious workers might argue that their work entails a manifestation of their belief, even though the work does not involve direct proselytism. If one takes an organic view of the workplace, viewing it a whole, one can see that a much greater range of jobs within the workplace should be viewed as religious in nature. A religious group may view every worker, from cleaner to religious teacher, as part of a team whose role is to witness to the truth of the religion. The idea that even the lowliest of workers can be fulfilling a religious function is well established in Christian teaching, and may resonate clearly with other religions too. If such a view is recognised by courts, it would enable religious groups to argue that a wide range of employment is religious in nature, although evidence may well be needed to show that religion permeates the particular workplace in practice.

The Meaning of Equality

In assessing the proportionality of any response to religious discrimination regard should be had to the overall aim of discrimination law in promoting equality between different groups. The difficulty here is that equality has a variety of

[146] A Esau '"Islands of Exclusivity": Religious Organizations and Employment Discrimination' (1993) 33 *Univ British Columbia LR* 719.

[147] This may not be the case in relation to the teaching of theology, or the teaching of religious education in schools, where not all religious experts are necessarily active believers.

[148] This point is developed in R Fahlbeck, '*Ora et Labora* on Freedom of Religion at the Work Place: A Stakeholder *cum* Balancing Factors Model' [2004] *IJCLLIR* 1.

meanings, and determining what 'promoting equality' might require is both complex and contested. Indeed, given the wide range of understandings of the meaning of equality, McCrudden has suggested that talk should now be of *equalities* rather than equality, in recognition that no single understanding of equality is complete.[149]

The most obvious meaning for equality is formal or symmetrical equality, which requires that like cases be treated alike, with a focus on the individual rather than groups. A broader approach to equality focuses on substantive equality in which equality of outcome and equality of opportunity are the focus rather than equal treatment. Such a substantive view of equality can take into account the relative disadvantage of some groups in contrast to others. Other models focus on the link between equality and individual dignity and identity, or on the facility for equality to act as a means of addressing social exclusion, by promoting participation and engaging in redistribution.[150] A further model of equality, from Fredman, identifies the need to allow all groups an equal set of alternatives from which they can pursue their own version of a good life.[151] From this she argues for the promotion of positive measures to allow all members of society access to the particular social goods. The idea is that equality does not need to include the 'same' treatment, but may instead involve different groups being able to pursue their version of the good life. Fredman also suggests that equality law should breach the cycle of disadvantage associated with 'out-groups'; promote respect for the equal dignity of all, redressing stigma, stereotyping, humiliation and violence because of membership of an out-group; affirm community identities; and facilitate full participation in society.

The vision of equality held by any tribunal or court will be an important contextual factor which is likely to influence the determination of proportionality. For example, if formal equality is the goal, courts are unlikely to view as disproportionate neutral requirements with which religious people have difficulty complying. Where Fredman's broader concept of equality is used, with promotion of participation as part of the vision of equality, outcomes could be quite different. Tribunals may want to encourage religious groups to engage in mainstream society by limiting the extent to which they can create religiously homogenous workplaces. Or they may take account of the role of religion in shaping cultural identity, and so allow minority groups the freedom to express their cultural identity at work. Such an approach results in a very nuanced approach to equality as the facts of different cases interact with the different factors.

Assessing proportionality in order to promote 'equality' is thus a very complex process, and requires an analysis of the interaction of different factors. In addition,

[149] C McCrudden, 'Thinking about the discrimination directives' (2005) 1 *European Anti-Discrimination Law Review* 17.

[150] See: C Barnard and B Hepple, 'Substantive Equality' (2000) 59 *CLJ* 562; H Collins 'Discrimination, Equality and Social Inclusion' (2003) 66 *MLR* 16 and C McCrudden 'Thinking about the discrimination directives' (2005) 1 *European Anti-Discrimination Law Review* 17.

[151] S Fredman, *The Future of Equality In Britain*, EOC, Working Paper Series No 5 (London, Equal Opportunities Commission, 2002) 11.

broader socio-economic issues will interact with pure equality issues to influence any outcome.

Socio-Political Context

In assessing proportionality the socio-political context is also of significance where the view of equality is not purely formal. The importance of such factors as the historical disadvantage of the relevant groups, and the level of social exclusion or disadvantage currently experienced, should be taken into account in assessing whether it is proportionate to allow either religious freedom to be infringed or, indeed, whether other equality rights can be overridden in the name of religious freedom. Collins has argued[152] that discrimination law should serve the overall aim of social inclusion, and that this aim should help to determine the correct parameters of the law. Clearly this will not help resolve every contentious issue in this area, but helping increase social inclusion for groups that have suffered exclusion from society's goods in the past may help to resolve the clash between rights on a principled basis in some cases. For example, if it is acknowledged that Muslims have suffered disadvantage in access to the job market, it may be proportionate to require a greater level of protection for their religious practices than for religious groups for whom such disadvantage cannot be shown.[153] Thus the need to improve social inclusion for out-groups should be taken into account in assessing the proportionality of any religious requirement for a job.

However, factors such as historic disadvantage will not always point towards protection of religion, and what is proportionate could vary according to the religion in question: the Muslim community in Britain will have a different experience of disadvantage from the Anglican community. Where religious groups' employment practices discriminate against women, for example, historic disadvantage as a factor may cut both ways: it may favour protection of a minority religious group, as well as protection for women or lesbian and gay people who have also been subject to historic disadvantage. Where such contextual issues do not provide clear answers, the conflict will only be resolved with reference to the other factors discussed above. Thus, for example, although women have suffered disadvantage historically, this may not automatically outweigh the benefits of affirming community identities among disadvantaged communities who wish to employ only those of the same conservative religious traditions in their religious organisations.

The Role of the State

One final factor which should be taken into account in difficult cases is the extent to which it is appropriate for the state to intervene to settle disputes. Where

[152] H Collins, 'Discrimination, Equality and Social Inclusion' (2003) 66 *MLR* 16.

[153] Such groups may be Christians, who as members of the majority religion may face less systemic disadvantage.

individual human rights interests are clearly infringed, it is right for the state, through the courts, to intervene to provide protection.[154] However, where the question of whether the rights are infringed or not is finely balanced, it may be worth considering whether it is proper for the state to intervene to uphold one set of interests over another, where to do so involves intervening in the conduct of what may be viewed as a type of private relationship. It is, arguably, not appropriate to expect legislative intervention in the regulation of the religious sphere. Of course, it might be argued that the employment relationship is public in nature, and so intervention is appropriate, but it is part of the argument of this chapter that employment has a private dimension so that the employment relationship is of a hybrid public-private nature.

Moreover, one of the reasons for providing protection for religious interests is the fact that protecting religious freedom can be a useful tool in preventing or overcoming religious conflict.[155] Although it was suggested above that this reason was insufficient alone to provide a rationale for the protection of religious interests at work, it remains of significance. Despite the existence of an established church within the UK, it is still arguable that the state should remain neutral in religious disputes. Courts may well be wary of intervening where to do so amounts to state regulation of religious matters. Again, whether or not state intervention will be appropriate will be determined by considering all the proportionality factors. The decision may depend on the centrality of the religious interest to the religious group, the extent to which the job involved is religious in essence and the extent to which any restriction interferes with the individual's ability to work, as well as the other factors discussed above.

V Conclusion

It has been argued above that religious interests are sufficiently important to individual dignity and autonomy to warrant protection within the workplace. This is the product of the importance of the workplace as a forum for the exercise of fundamental rights combined with the importance of religious interests themselves. Equally important, however, are other rights based on dignity and autonomy, and rights to equality on a number of grounds such as gender, sexual orientation, race and disability. It is where these interests conflict that difficulties arise with regard to establishing the correct parameters for any protection for religion within the workplace.

It was not the aim of this chapter to reach conclusive answers on how to resolve such conflicts, as this would depend on the complex interplay of a wide range of factors. Instead, the aim was to consider the range of factors at stake in cases where

[154] *Young, James and Webster v UK* [1981] IRLR 408.

[155] See discussion above at pp 33–34.

religious matters arise at work, and to consider how those factors should be balanced in seeking proportionality in the treatment of conflicting interests. Those factors range across the personal interests of employees and colleagues, the business interests of the employer, and the religious interests of religious ethos employers, as well as wider contextual issues such as whether the employer forms part of the public or private sector, the extent to which the employer engages with public markets, whether the workplace can be viewed as a public or private space, and the socio-economic factors that are at work. Exactly how these factors interact will depend on the facts and the socio-economic context.

Within the employment context, any deliberations on proportionality must be carried out in the light of the fact that no-one has a right to a given job. This remains the basic answer when religious groups require excessive accommodation. The arguments for protection of religious interests are strong, but they do not require that an employer should have to make very costly adjustments to accommodate a religious employee. The employee's residual protection lies in his freedom to leave his job. Take the hypothetical example of an employee who wishes to work in public relations, whose core job involves 'meeting and greeting' clients, but who refuses, for religious reasons, to shake hands with women: this employee does not have a right to a job, and has no 'right' to work in this particular line of work. He remains free to exercise his freedom of religion outside work. It may therefore be acceptable for the employer to refuse to accommodate his religious practice.

However, the 'right to resign' argument will not always prevail. For example, a woman who wants to wear trousers at work for religious reasons, in a workplace where the uniform is a skirt, may need to be accommodated, unless there are very strong contra-indicators. Accommodation is unlikely to be costly to the employer, and a conclusion that her freedom of religion is protected by freedom to leave would seem inadequate, given the ease with which accommodation could be granted.

A particular problem is caused by religious ethos employers, and the question of whether it is ever proportionate to protect their religious interests at the expense of the equality interests of others. As a general rule, discrimination against others, even where motivated by religion, will not be proportionate. However, respect for autonomy may involve allowing some space for religious intolerance of others, albeit of a very limited kind. It may be that discriminatory religious groups should be allowed to retreat from mainstream society to create 'islands of exclusivity' from which they can exclude those with different views.[156] This allows adequate protection for religious freedom for individuals who hold these views, as they remain free to associate with those of the same religion. They also remain free to enter into employment relationships with others of the same faith, in order to regulate the provision of services within the group. Within this restricted sphere,

[156] A Esau, '"Islands of Exclusivity": Religious Organizations and Employment Discrimination' (1993) 33 *Univ British Columbia LR* 719.

groups can operate in an exclusive manner, without being required to provide employment for those of other religions or lifestyles. Allowing religious groups to retreat in this manner provides sufficient protection for their religious interests, without causing much harm to other interests. Other interests may be infringed, but not to a significant extent. For example, a religious group's requirement that their toddler group leader share the group's religion will not significantly reduce the job prospects of non-religious child care workers. The main detriment is the offence caused to others by allowing such practices to continue. However, in the absence of other harms, offence caused by the bare knowledge that religious practices occur should not be sufficient to determine proportionality.[157]

To the extent that the group wishes to interact with the rest of society, however, they can be expected to conform to the norms of the rest of society in terms of respect for the dignity and autonomy of others.[158] Thus if a religious group wishes to enter a contract with the state to deliver services to the public, such as medical or social services, the group should conform to the standards of respect for others that is required by the state. Thus the religious group would not be able to provide such services if the job requirements indirectly discriminate against women or against gay or lesbian workers. This requirement could be limited to cases where the religious group provides services that are paid for by the state. However, a stronger version of the argument would mean that wherever the religious group engages at all with wider society, the norms of society should be respected. Thus where a religious group offers commercial services to the public, they should be required to do so equally for all members of society. For example, a hairdressing salon staffed by religious staff would not be able to discriminate against others in its employment practices if the salon were open to the public. In contrast, a hairdresser who employs an assistant to cut the hair of others from the same religious group may be allowed to discriminate indirectly in recruitment practices, as services are only offered to members of the religious group. Thus, those who seek the advantages of access to the public market would need to respect the dignity and equality of all members of the public.[159]

Using the model of work-based religious accommodation outlined above will enable a reasonable balance to be achieved between the right to freedom of religion and other competing rights. The model is predicated on maximum respect for dignity, autonomy and equality within the public sphere, broadly defined, but retaining the right for groups, religious or not, to retreat to 'islands of exclusivity' which remain essentially private. Interpreting the relatively new UK law according to this model should result in most workplaces engaging in respect-

[157] See discussion above at pp 62–66.

[158] See S Wessels, 'The Collision of Religious Exercise and Governmental Nondiscrimination Policies' (1989) 41 *Stanford LR* 1201, who draws a distinction between the inward-looking and outward-looking activities of religious organisations, and suggests that inward-looking activities should be free from government restrictions, but that outward-looking activities, where the group has chosen to step outside its internal life, should be subject to non-discrimination rules.

[159] See the discussion of the position in the USA and Canada in ch 6, where religious requirements can only be imposed for work in the not-for-profit activities of religious organisations.

ful pluralism,[160] where religious practice can be accommodated alongside other equality and dignity rights. Where religious groups wish to dissociate from the rest of society, they should remain free to do so, out of respect for their religious freedom. However, any intolerant religious practices will be significantly burdened as they will not be able to gain any benefits from engagement with the wider society.[161]

It has been noted that religious discrimination and freedom of religion are closely linked. Later chapters consider the current law on religious discrimination at work in the UK and beyond, and assess the extent to which protection matches the model developed above. First, the human rights protection for freedom of religion under the European Convention on Human Rights will be considered, together with an assessment of the extent to which its jurisprudence can apply in the UK and in the work context.

[160] D A Hicks, *Religion and the Workplace: Pluralism Spirituality, Leadership* (Cambridge and New York, CUP, 2003).

[161] It should be noted that although some of the observations may be of use in the wider debate over how to reconcile competing rights, any conclusions suggested here are offered in the limited context of reconciling conflicting rights at work.

[13]

Class wars? Religion and (In)equality in the Workplace

AILEEN MCCOLGAN*

ABSTRACT

In this paper, I seek to demonstrate the potential for conflict inherent in the prohibition of discrimination on grounds of religion or belief with the regulation of discrimination on other grounds. I suggest that such conflict is inevitable and that it is a mistake to protect religion and/or belief in like manner to grounds such as sex, race, sexual orientation and disability. While such protection is, at present, required by EC law, I suggest that legislation along present lines is not required by the European Convention on Human Rights and that it is not justified by any special quality of religion. On the contrary, I argue that requiring the accommodation of practices or beliefs categorised as 'religious' tends to perpetuate practices and beliefs which are problematic on equality and other grounds.

1. INTRODUCTION

The prohibition on discrimination on grounds of religion or belief has given rise to a number of decisions which demonstrate the scope for conflict between this and other protected grounds. Here I want to consider two of these cases and more broadly the justification for and effects of prohibiting discrimination on grounds of religion or belief. My purpose is to expose some of the problems generated by domestic discrimination legislation and to ask whether these are (a) inevitable as a result of Article 9 of the European Convention or (b) justified by wider arguments concerning the protection of 'culture' and/or the role of religion in the constitution of identity. Having concluded that neither is the case, I go on to propose an attenuated level of protection for religious minorities which finds its rationale in the amelioration of economic and social disadvantage which flows unjustifiably from actual or ascribed religious identity or affiliation.

*King's College London, email: aileen.mccolgan@kcl.ac.uk.
This paper developed from papers delivered at the European University Institute workshop,'Religion in the European Public Sphere: A Secular Dilemma?' (May 2008, forthcoming as an EUI working paper) and at the Copenhagen Business School conference 'The Lisbon Treaty—a Step Towards Integrating Welfare Functions into EU Law?' (August 2008, forthcoming as part of a book edited by Ruth Nielsen). An earlier version of the paper was delivered at the Industrial Law Society summer conference (Oxford, 2008) and this version has benefitted from the discussion at the conference. All errors are my own.

I do not claim that this approach would be compatible with EU law (in particular, Council Directive 2000/78 and the proposed Directive on discrimination in access to goods, facilities and services), but suggest it in an attempt to challenge any assumption that discrimination on grounds of religion or belief ought to be treated in a similar fashion to discrimination on grounds such as sex, race or sexual orientation. On a more practical note, a critical approach to this ground may prevent the further extension of protection in the form, eg, of the proposed imposition of positive duties on public authorities in relation to religion or belief and might result in a retreat from the 'one size fits all' approach which appears likely to be adopted in the proposed single equality legislation. It may seem perverse at this point to suggest anything other than the legislative simplification which would accompany such an approach. But recent decisions in the areas of race and disability discrimination, also considered below, have provided powerful illustrations of the dangers of the 'one size fits all' model.

2. THE LEGISLATION

The legislation here under consideration consists in aspects of the Employment Equality (Religion or Belief) Regulations 2003 (RB Regs) and the Employment Equality (Sexual Orientation) Regulations 2003 (SO Regs), together with a number of provisions of the Sex Discrimination Act 1975 (SDA), Race Relations Act 1976 (RRA) and Disability Discrimination Act 1995 (DDA). Very briefly, all these instruments prohibit direct discrimination in the employment sphere and, except in the case of the DDA, prohibit indirect discrimination, the DDA instead imposing duties of reasonable adjustment.

Confining our attention solely to the employment sphere, direct discrimination is defined as less favourable treatment on grounds of race, sexual orientation or religion/belief or on the grounds of the complainant's sex or disability. In each case, the less favourable treatment has to be established by reference to a real or hypothetical comparator of a different race, sex, etc, whose 'relevant circumstances ... are the same [as], or not materially different' from those of the complainant or, in the case of the DDA, 'whose relevant circumstances, including his abilities, are the same as, or not materially different from, those of the disabled person'.[1] Indirect discrimination occurs where a person 'applies to [an]other a provision, criterion or practice which he applies or would apply equally to persons not of the same [group defined by reference to a protected ground], but (a) which puts

[1] Ss 1(2)(a) and 5(3) SDA, (1) and 3(4) RRA, 3A(5) DDA, and Regs 3(1)(a) and (2) of the SO Regs 2003, RB Regs 2003 and Age Regs 2006.

or would put persons of [that group] at a particular disadvantage when compared with other persons, (b) which puts that other at that disadvantage, and (c) which he cannot show to be a proportionate means of achieving a legitimate aim'.[2] Case law established under one discrimination provision is binding, where it concerns generally applicable concepts, across the board.[3]

A. Exceptions

The Equal Treatment Directive, transposed into domestic law by the SDA, provides that Member States may 'exclude from its field of application those occupational activities and, where appropriate, the training leading thereto, for which, by reason of their nature and of the context in which they are carried out, the sex of the worker constitutes a determining factor'. This SDA contains a special provision disapplying the prohibition on sex discrimination[4] in relation to (s 19) 'employment ... for purposes of an organised religion' where a requirement to be of a particular sex[5] is imposed '(i) so as to comply with the doctrines of the religion, (ii) because of the nature of the employment and the context in which it is carried out, so as to avoid conflicting with the strongly-held religious convictions of a significant number of the religion's followers'. Prior to 2005 domestic jurisprudence effectively precluded employment-related claims by ministers of religion in any event,[6] and some sex/gender discrimination by religious organisations in relation to workers other than religious ministers would be covered by a genuine occupation qualification (GOQ) or other defence. The GOQ defence permits jobs to be restricted by reference to gender where, *inter alia* (s 7(2)(e)) 'the holder of the job provides individuals with personal services promoting their welfare or education, or similar personal services, and those services can most effectively be provided by a man'. This would most likely have been accepted to extend to those working (other than

[2] Ss 1(2)(b) SDA, 1(1A) RRA and Regs 3(1)(b) of the SO Regs 2003, RB Regs 2003 and Age Regs 2006.

[3] *Hampson v Department of Education and Science* [1991] 1 AC 171; *Relaxion Group plc v Rhys-Harper* [2003] UKHL 33, [2003] ICR 867.

[4] Later also the prohibition on discrimination on grounds of civil partnership.

[5] Or requirements in connection with gender reassignment or marital or civil partnership status.

[6] See the decision of the House of Lords in *Davies v Presbyterian Church of Wales* [1986] ICR 280 and its application through a succession of cases: *Santokh Singh v Guru Nanak Gurdwara* [1990] ICR 309; *Birmingham Mosque Trust Ltd v Alavi* [1992] ICR 435 and *Khan v Oxford City Mosque Society* (unreported, 1998). See, however, *Percy v Board of National Mission of the Church of Scotland* [2005] UKHL 73, [2006] 2 AC 28 in which the House of Lords allowed a sex discrimination complaint by a woman minister. It should be noted that no doctrinal issue was pleaded in that case.

as ministers) in sex-segregated places of worship, though there is no authority to that effect.[7]

The Race Directive provides no exception for discrimination arising in connection with religion, although Article 4 does provide that 'a difference of treatment which is based on a characteristic related to racial or ethnic origin shall not constitute discrimination where, by reason of the nature of the particular occupational activities concerned or of the context in which they are carried out, such a characteristic constitutes a genuine and determining occupational requirement, provided that the objective is legitimate and the requirement is proportionate'. Article 4 of the Employment Directive provides a similar defence to discrimination on any of the regulated grounds (ie, sexual orientation, religion or belief, disability and age) and goes on to provide, in addition, (Article 4(2)) that 'churches and other public or private organisations the ethos of which is based on religion or belief', may be permitted to discriminate on grounds of religion (alone) in relation to particular occupational activities 'where, by reason of the nature of these activities or of the context in which they are carried out, a person's religion or belief constitute a genuine, legitimate and justified occupational requirement, having regard to the organisation's ethos'.

The DDA does not permit the justification of direct discrimination in the employment sphere. The RRA, SO Regs and RB Regs all contain a GOR defence based on Article 4 of the Race Directive and 4(1) of the Equality Directive,[8] which permits discrimination in relation to employment in respect of which '(a) being of a particular race or of particular ethnic or national origins [religion/belief or sexual orientation] is a genuine and determining occupational requirement; (b) it is proportionate to apply that requirement in the particular case; and (c) either (i) the person to whom that requirement is applied does not meet it, or (ii) the employer is not satisfied, and in all the circumstances it is reasonable for him not to be satisfied, that that person meets it. In addition, the SO Regs and RB Regs contain additional GOR defences directed at religious employers. These apply in relation to (SO Regs) 'employment for purposes of an organised religion' and (RB Regs) 'employer[s whose] ethos [is] based on religion or belief'. The SO Regs permit the application of a 'requirement related to sexual orientation ... so as to comply with the doctrines of the religion' or 'to avoid conflicting with the strongly held religious convictions of a significant number of the religion's follower'.[9] The RB Regs permit a requirement to be of a particular religion or belief where

[7] S 35 SDA exempts from the prohibition on discrimination the provision of services or facilities at a place restricted to men (or women) and 'occupied or used for the purposes of an organised religion, and the facilities or service are restricted to men [or women] so as to comply with the doctrines of that religion or avoid offending the religious susceptibilities of a significant number of its followers'.

[8] S.4A RRA, Regs 7 SO Regs and RB Regs.

[9] Reg 7(3) SO Regs.

such a requirement is 'a genuine occupational requirement for the job' and 'it is proportionate to apply that requirement in the particular case'.[10]

The scope of these provisions has been considered in a number of cases including *R (Amicus) v Secretary of State for Trade & Industry*, *Glasgow City Council v NcNab* and *Reaney v Hereford Diocesan Board of Finance* (the Bishop of Hereford case).[11] It is not my intention to discuss them in any detail. Suffice it to note that wider scope is provided for discrimination by religious organisations even where religion or sexual orientation is not a determining requirement for a job. I also note in passing here the claims made by some religious organisations for exemptions from the scope of, eg, prohibitions on sexual orientation discrimination outside the employment sphere. Such claims tend to be rooted in assertions about the scope of religious freedom.[12]

What I want to consider in some detail are those cases in which individuals have relied on their religious beliefs in order to seek exemption from generally applicable rules, where the exemptions sought themselves bring into play other protected grounds. The cases I want to look at are the decisions of the EAT in *Azmi v Kirklees Borough Council* and of the employment tribunal in *Ladele v London Borough of Islington*.[13] Before turning to consider these cases, however, I will mention some of the conflicts which may arise between religious freedom and protections against discrimination.

3. RELIGION, BELIEF AND DISCRIMINATION

A. The Background

Frances Raday points out that conflicts between equality rights and religion 'arise in the context of almost all religions and traditional cultures, since they rely on norms and social practices formulated or interpreted in a patriarchal context at a time when individual human rights, in general, and women's right to equality, in particular, had not yet become a global imperative'.[14] Listing among social practices which are 'defended in the name of culture' horrors such as 'a preference for sons, leading to female infanticide; ... FGM; a sale of daughters in marriage, including

[10] Reg 7(3) RB Regs.

[11] Respectively [2004] IRLR 430, [2007] IRLR 476 and case no. 1602844/2006, Cardiff Tribunal, 17 July 2006, unreported but available at http://thinkinganglicans.org.uk/uploads/herefordtribunaljudgment.html. The Respondent withdrew a notice of appeal in October 2008.

[12] See my EUI working paper, 'Religion and (in)equality in the European framework' forthcoming.

[13] Respectively [2007] IRLR 484 and case no. 2203694/2007, London Central Employment Tribunal, 3 July 2008, unreported.

[14] 'Culture, Religion, and Gender' (2002) 4 *International Journal of Constitutional Law* 663, 664–5.

giving them in forced marriage as child brides ... husband's right to obedience and power to discipline or commit acts of violence against his wife, including marital rape... honor killings ... compulsory restrictive dress codes ... and restriction of women to the roles of housewives or mothers...',[15] Raday concludes that:

> The story of 'gender' in traditionalist cultures and religions is that of the systematic domination of women by men, of women's exclusion from public power, and of their subjection to patriarchal power within the family [and] religion forms, both theoretically and empirically, the core of cultural resistance to human rights and gender equality.[16]

The patriarchal norms which are common to many religions are also hostile to the subversion of gender roles associated with homosexuality. Clashes between religious freedom and race equality are possible at least in theory, since a number of predominantly US-based 'Christian' churches including the 'Christian Knights of the Ku Klux Klan', 'Aryan Nations' and a variety of other churches within the 'Christian Identity' movement advocate white supremacism and anti-semitism. The South African Afrikaanse Protestante Kerk allows only white members and the Mormon Church reserved full membership to White men until the mid-1970s, when African American men were permitted for the first time to become elders, and its scriptures equate Blackness to the loss of grace.[17]

Less controversially, perhaps, Orthodox Judaism recognises only those whose mothers are themselves Orthodox Jews or who have undergone recognised conversion into that faith, the recent decision of the High Court in *R (E) v Governing Body of the Jews Free School*[18] highlighting the overlap between religion and something more akin to race. The *JFS* case involved a challenge to a refusal by an Orthodox Jewish school to admit a prospective pupil whose mother had converted to Judaism and who himself was an observant Jew. The school admitted only Orthodox Jews (ie, children born to women recognised as Jewish by Orthodox Judaism) but did not require that they be religiously observant. The school's admissions policy had the effect, as its Web site recorded, that, while '[m]

[15] Ibid 670, most of the practices so defended, as she remarks, being 'gender specific'.

[16] Ibid 669.

[17] Nephi 12:23 'And I beheld, after they had dwindled in unbelief they became a dark and loathsome and a filthy people, full of idleness and all manner of abominations'; Nephi 5:21 'And he had caused the cursing to come upon them, yea, even a sore cursing, because of their iniquity. For behold, they had hardened their hearts against him, that they had become like unto a flint; wherefore, as they were white, and exceedingly fair and delightsome, that they might not be enticing unto my people the Lord God did cause a skin of blackness to come upon them'. Brigham Young, the second President of the Church, wrote in his *Journal of Discourses* (10:110) 'Shall I tell you the law of God in regard to the African race? If the white man who belongs to the chosen seed mixes his blood with the seed of Cain, the penalty, under the law of God, is death on the spot. This will always be so'.

[18] [2008] EWHC 1535 & 1536 (Admin), [2008] All ER (D) 54 (Jul).

any [of its intake] come from families who are totally committed to Judaism and Israel; others are unaware of Jewish belief and practice'. And a history of the school published in 1998 recorded that:

> There is no requirement that the Jewish mother must be a practising Jewess or member of an orthodox synagogue. Anomalies abound. The accepted 'Jewish' mother whose child is eligible to go to JFS might now be a member of the Reform synagogue or of no synagogue, be an agnostic or an atheist—that would not debar her child from entrance. An observant mother, who regularly attends synagogue and keeps a kosher home cannot enter her child at JFS if she, the mother, is Jewish by conversion under Reform or Liberal auspices.[19]

The High Court in *JFS* decided that the race discrimination there at issue was indirect and justified on the facts, a judgment which is under appeal. The case serves to illustrate that real potential conflicts between religion and other protected grounds are not confined to gender and sexual orientation. It is also possible that conflicts may arise between religion and disability. In 1999 the-then England football coach Glen Hoddle was sacked after suggesting that people were disabled because of sins committed in a past life. His remarks appear to have been based on a muddle of evangelical Christianity and a (non-Christian) belief in reincarnation, but many disabled commentators suggested that they were reflective of more widely held opinions. The concepts of karma and reincarnation, which are common to Hinduism, Buddhism, Sikhism, Jainism and other Vedic belief systems, are centred around the movement of an eternal soul from life to life until it achieves ultimate liberation and the idea that all actions will produce a reaction. The principle appears to be that suffering is rooted in mistakes made in the present or a former life and it is not difficult to (mis)read this to the effect that the disabled are being punished for their past misdeeds.

B. 'Belief' and the RB Regs

The scope for conflict between the RB Regs and other prohibitions on discrimination is open-ended, as the Regs prohibit discrimination on grounds of 'belief' as well as

[19] Dr Gerry Black *JFS—A history of the Jews' Free School, London since 1732* (Tymsder Publishers: London, 1998). The decision records that one of the other prospective pupils whose application was rejected had been born to a mother who converted in Israel and was married by an Orthodox Rabbi in an Orthodox synagogue, but whose son was subsequently refused ritual circumcision by the London Beth Din (Jewish court) because his father, the man whom the converted mother had married, was a cohen (a member of a Jewish tribe by descent) who was prohibited by Jewish law from marrying converts. The very basis upon which the Beth Din rejected her conversion was that she had contracted a forbidden marriage so soon after it, such that her conversion was not accepted as having manifested full commitment to the tenets of the orthodox faith. She (the mother) herself taught at JFS but her daughter's application to JFS was rejected on the basis that she (the daughter) was not a Jew.

'religion". While it appears, as Lucy Vickers points out, that 'a devotion to football" is outside the scope of the Regulations' protections,[20] it is at least arguable that adherence to a belief in white supremacy may fall within their protection.[21] Barry Fitzpatrick's 2007 report for the Trades Union Congress on the early case law under the SO Regs and RB Regs[22] refers to one tribunal case in which it was ruled that British National Party membership did not fall within the RB Regs as the British National Party did not 'require members to belong to a particular religion or hold particular religious or similar philosophical beliefs. It has no proven links with religion or religious beliefs'.[23] But the RB Regs have subsequently been amended to remove the requirement that 'beliefs' be of a 'similar philosophical' nature to religious beliefs to qualify for protection. By virtue of amendment by the Equality Act 2006, the Regulations now protect (Reg 2(1)) 'any religion ... any religious or philosophical belief ... lack of religion, and ... lack of belief'. In any event, as Fitzpatrick goes on to report, even under the pre-amendment Regulations another tribunal 'refused to dismiss another BNP member's claim at a preliminary stage and granted a full hearing', the chair commenting that 'his views are the result of an ideology relating to the preservation of a British ethnic group which has some prospect of meeting the test in the 2003 Regulations'.[24] And although Fitzpatrick suggests that 'Court of Appeal case law on the Race Relations Act has established that such opinions should not be protected by anti-discrimination legislation',[25] the decision in *Redfearn v Serco Ltd*,[26] on which he appears to found that view, deals with the very different question whether discrimination against a racist is discrimination on racial grounds.

C. Challenging 'Religious' Beliefs

Further difficulties arise, in relation to religion, because of impossibilities of classification. It may be possible to determine, on the balance of probabilities, whether an individual adheres, at least outwardly, to a certain set of religious or other beliefs (where, eg, he or she regularly attends a particular religious

[20] *Religious Freedom, Religious Discrimination and the Workplace* (Hart, 2007), 23.

[21] Such a belief would not be analogous to the belief which the EAT ruled in *McClintock v Department of Constitutional Affairs* [2008] IRLR 29 was not covered by the Regs (and would not be post-amendment): ie, the belief that placement of children with same-sex couples had not been shown to be in the children's best interests. According to the EAT, to constitute a belief there must be a religious or philosophical viewpoint in which one actually believes, rather than merely an opinion based on some real or perceived logic or based on information or lack of information available.

[22] *Sexual Orientation and Religion or Belief Cases*, available from the TUC Web site at http://www.tuc.org.uk/extras/SORBreport.pdf (accessed 11 November 2008).

[23] Ibid 24, discussing *Baggs v Fudge*, Case No 140011/05, March 2005.

[24] *Finnon v Asda Stores Ltd*, Case No 2402142/05, August 2005, unreported.

[25] Ibid 9.

[26] [2006] EWCA Civ 659, [2006] ICR 1367.

service, or outwardly manifests over time a commitment to pacifism, veganism or Communism). But even the model of attendance as an indicator of religious affiliation is, as was pointed out by the Administrative Court in the *JFS* case,[27] of no application to a religion such as Orthodox Judaism in which 'attendance at the services of a synagogue has no bearing on a person's Jewish status as a matter of Jewish religious law', Judaism being exclusively a question of status.

More generally, while enquiry could be made as to whether an exemption sought by an individual from a generally applicable rule rationally relates to his or her commitment to an identifiable set of non-religious beliefs such as pacifism, veganism or Communism, the same is not true of an exemption sought on the basis of an asserted religious belief given the inability of secular courts to adjudicate doctrinal disputes within a religious collective as to what the religion requires, much less to determine the contents of an individual's religious belief. Thus, eg, in *R (Williamson) v Secretary of State for Education and Employment and Others*,[28] the House of Lords accepted that a belief in the mandatory nature of corporal punishment in the educational setting was a religious belief for the purposes of Article 9 of the European Convention. Lord Nicholls, with whom Lord Bingham agreed, stated that the court could consider, if it was at issue, whether a belief was genuinely held. But:

> This is a limited inquiry. The court is concerned to ensure an assertion of religious belief is made in good faith, 'neither fictitious, nor capricious, and that it is not an artifice' [[29]]. But, emphatically, it is not for the court to embark on an inquiry into the asserted belief and judge its 'validity' by some objective standard such as the source material upon which the claimant founds his belief or the orthodox teaching of the religion in question or the extent to which the claimant's belief conforms to or differs from the views of others professing the same religion. Freedom of religion protects the subjective belief of an individual ..."[30]

Lord Walker, who pointed out that '[s]ome sects claiming to be Christian' regarded polygamy as mandatory,[31] that others regarded blood transfusions

[27] n 18 above.

[28] Domestic law has always been inclined to deal with accommodation cases in this way—see *Ahmed v* ILEA [1978] QB 31 in which the Court of Appeal, by contrast with the commission (in *Ahmed v UK*), accepted that there had been an interference, though the Court ruled that it was justified.

[29] Citing Iacobucci J in the decision of the Supreme Court of Canada in *Syndicat Northcrest v Amselem* (2004) 241 DLR (4th) 1, 27 (para 52).

[30] Para 22, also citing *Metropolitan Church of Bessarabia v Moldova* (2002) 35 EHRR 306, 335 (para 117): 'in principle, the right to freedom of religion as understood in the convention rules out any appreciation by the state of the legitimacy of religious beliefs or of the manner in which these are expressed'.

[31] Para 56, citing *Reynolds v United States* (1879) 98 US 145; *Late Corp of the Church of Jesus Christ of Latter-Day Saints v United States, Romney v United States* (1890) 136 US 1.

as prohibited 'even if it is the only means of saving life'[32] and that '[c]ountless thousands' had been tortured and killed in the name of Christianity as 'apostates, heretics and witches' (characterising 'a belief in a scriptural basis for smacking children' as 'fairly small beer' by comparison with these 'horrors'), expressed his disapproval of the suggestion made by Arden LJ in the Court of Appeal that 'to be protected by art 9, a religious belief, like a philosophical belief, must be consistent with the ideals of a democratic society, and that it must be compatible with human dignity, serious, important, and (to the extent that a religious belief can reasonably be required so to be) cogent and coherent'.[33] He did not accept that 'it is right for the court (except in extreme cases ...[34]) to impose an evaluative filter [in determining the existence of a belief], especially when religious beliefs are involved. For the court to adjudicate on the seriousness, cogency and coherence of theological beliefs is to take the court beyond its legitimate role'.[35]

In *R (Begum) v Head Teacher and Governors of Denbeigh School*,[36] similarly, the House of Lords accepted that the claimant's view that, as a Muslim, she was obliged to wear a full length jilbab was a religious belief notwithstanding the proliferation of different views on this issue among Muslims, although a majority did not accept on the facts that her freedom to manifest this belief had been interfered with by the imposition upon her of a school uniform policy when she was free to attend another school.[37]

It would of course be absurd to excuse an individual from a prohibition on race, sexual orientation or sex discrimination on the basis that he or she was racist, homophobic or sexist. The question posed by the lack of common ground between religion and law, ie, by the law's powerlessness in the face of assertions

[32] Ibid, citing *Re O (a minor) (medical treatment)* [1993] 1 FCR 925; *Re R (a minor) (medical treatment)* [1993] 2 FCR 544.

[33] [2003] 1 All ER 385, para 258.

[34] *X v UK* (1977) 11 DR 55, which he regarded as exceptional, concerned an Article 9 complaint by a prisoner as to a Governor's failure to register his asserted religious affiliation which was dismissed as manifestly ill-founded on the basis that the facilities for manifestation of his religion to which registration entitled a prisoner were 'only conceivable if the religion to which the prisoner allegedly adheres is identifiable [whereas] ... in the present case the applicant has not mentioned any facts making it possible to establish the existence of the Wicca religion'. The applicant in *X* did not complain of any interference with his right to manifest his religion, or any failure on the part of the prison authorities to facilitate that manifestation in any specific way.

[35] Citing Richards J in *R (on the application of Amicus—MSF section) v Secretary of State for Trade and Industry* [2004] EWHC 860 (Admin), [2004] IRLR 430, para 36, and decisions of the High Court of Australia, the Supreme Court of Canada and the US Supreme Court in the *Church of the New Faith* case (1983) 154 CLR 120 especially 129–30, 174; *Syndicat Northcrest v Amselem* (2004) 241 DLR (4th) and *Employment Division, Department of Human Resources of Oregon v Smith* (1990) 494 US 872, respectively.

[36] [2006] UKHL 15, [2007] 1 AC 100.

[37] Paras 21 (per Lord Bingham) and 50 (per Lord Hoffmann), Lord Nicholls and Baroness Hale concurring on the basis that any interference was justified on the facts.

about religion, is whether allowing religious exemptions to prohibitions on discrimination does not serve irreparably to undermine those prohibitions. In *Williamson* the House of Lords avoided a fatal holing of the prohibition on corporal punishment in schools by balancing the acceptance that the parents' views as to the necessity for such punishment were 'religious' with the finding that any interference with those views was justified under Article 9(2). In *Begum* the case was decided by various members of the House of Lords on the basis that the claimant's beliefs had not been interfered with and/or that any interference was justified on the facts. But where religious individuals assert that the imposition of a general obligation upon them amounts to discrimination against them on grounds of their religion or belief, the danger is raised that religion will trump because there is no general justification defence available (in respect of direct discrimination) under the statutory scheme.

4. THE DECISIONS IN *AZMI* AND *LADELE*

A. The Decisions

Azmi v Kirklees Metropolitan Borough Council[38] concerned a challenge under the RB Regs by a Muslim woman who wished to wear a niqab (full-face covering) while acting as a classroom assistant concerned primarily with language support for students for whom English was not a first language. The school refused her request because the evidence showed that language support could be carried out more effectively where the teacher's face was visible. The decision was based both on general research and on observation of Ms Azmi teaching veiled and unveiled. Ms Azmi was permitted to wear the niqab outside the classroom, but not while she was teaching. The school also declined her suggestion that she be isolated from male teachers while engaged in classroom duties, this because, as a classroom assistant, she was assigned to a particular group of children who were taught by both men and women. Ms Azmi's claim that the school's actions amounted to direct discrimination against her failed, an employment tribunal and the EAT agreeing that the discrimination at issue was of the indirect form and that it was justifiable on the facts.

The claimant in *Ladele v London Borough of Islington* was a Christian registrar (responsible for conducting civil marriages and, with the recognition in the UK of same-sex civil partnerships, such partnerships). She took the view that participation in same-sex civil partnerships was inconsistent with her disapproval, as a Christian, of homosexuality.[39] Her employers had allowed her to avoid a requirement, of general application, that all registrars officiate at civil partnerships, but did require

[38] n 13 above.

[39] n 13 above, overturned by the EAT (UKEAT/0453/08/RN, 10 December, 2008).

that (in common with all other registrars) she perform administrative (as distinct from ceremonial) functions in relation to such partnerships if required to do so. Ms Ladele's refusal to comply with the attenuated job requirements exposed her to the threat of disciplinary action and she was refused promotion and subjected to a number of other detriments.

A tribunal accepted Ms Ladele's claim that she had been the victim of direct discrimination on grounds of her religion. The tribunal stated that '[a]pplying a rule to all Registrars does not mean that the Respondent has demonstrated that it did not commit an act of discrimination'. It went on to hold that the fact that Ms Ladele had been subject to detriments including disciplinary proceedings, refusal of promotion, being required to carry out civil partnership duties and being described as homophobic breached the prohibitions on direct and indirect discrimination on grounds of religion. Nothing in the tribunal judgement indicates that the causation for the acts and omissions of which she complained was anything other than her refusal to comply with a rule of general application or, accordingly, that more favourable treatment would have been accorded a registrar whose refusal to comply with the requirements of the job was related to a factor other than his or her adherence to Ms Ladele's particular religious beliefs or to any other religious or belief. Thus, the fact that she had suffered detriment for a reason related to her religious views, whatever the nature of those views and however justifiable the actions of the employer, appears to have been accepted by the tribunal as breaching the prohibition on religious discrimination. This conclusion was not accepted by the EAT on appeal (see below), but the Tribunal judgment is interesting nevertheless in highlighting some of the difficulties which may arise from regulating discrimination on grounds of religion or belief.

B. The Analysis

Barry Fitzpatrick, in his 2007 report for the TUC on sexual orientation and religion or belief cases, was critical of what he saw as an over-narrow approach on the part of the tribunals to religion or belief cases, instancing *Azmi* as giving rise to 'concern [over] the neutrality of tribunals', this because of the difficulty in establishing direct discrimination.[40] That report pre-dated the *Ladele* decision. Fitzpatrick complains that 'By treating many examples of religious adherence as indirect discrimination, respondent employers are given the opportunity to objectively justify their treatment of the individuals concerned'.[41] It may be, as he suggests, that 'Drawing comparisons with a person wearing a balaclava helmet [as the tribunal did in *Azmi*] is a rather embarrassing means of reaching a conclusion on the direct discrimination

[40] n 22 above, 10.
[41] Ibid.

issue'.[42] It is, however, quite clear that the employers in that case would not have been prepared to accommodate a classroom assistant having his or her face covered for any reason given the impact on the ability to fulfil the job function.

Had the employers in *Azmi* allowed the claimant to teach in a niqab they would knowingly have been delivering sub-standard educational provision to educationally disadvantaged, minority ethnic pupils the advancement of whose language skills was the raison d'être for the claimant's presence in the school. Had they complied with her alternative suggestion, by 'protecting' her from the adult male gaze while she was teaching her pupils, they would have discriminated against male staff on grounds of their sex. The 'Catch 22' which may be created by a broad approach to direct discrimination is also illustrated by *Ladele*, in which the employers were under threat of sexual orientation discrimination claims by members of staff who had been made aware (by Ms Ladele) of the claimant's views on same-sex relationships and who took the view that her refusal to be involved in civil partnerships was indicative of homophobia and breached the employer's dignity at work policy.

I do not suggest that pressure from employees, or indeed customers, should provide a defence to a discrimination claim. And it is possible to debate whether or not it was reasonable for individual colleagues of Ms Ladele to feel personally affronted by their knowledge of her views (which she had not discussed with them). But whatever the precise effect of Ms Ladele's stance on her colleagues, it is quite clear that potentially intractable conflicts may be caused by the statutory regime, at least if a broad approach is adopted to the scope of direct discrimination on grounds of religion or belief.

Ladele was overturned on appeal, the EAT adopting a narrower approach to the concept of direct discrimination. Suffice it to say here that there are also difficulties with the narrower approach to the RB Regs adopted by the EAT and the tribunal in *Azmi*. It could be argued that, because only Muslim women are in practice likely to wish to cover their faces, the prohibition of such a practice should be regarded as direct discrimination. On the face of it this might be regarded as analogous to the approach to pregnancy discrimination prior to the legislative amendment of the SDA expressly to prohibit such discrimination. The difficulty which would arise is that, whereas recognising pregnancy discrimination as a form of direct sex discrimination does not threaten any interests other than the economic interests of the employer, the application of this approach to religion or belief discrimination would threaten the conclusion that penalising race discrimination by a person whose religious or other beliefs prohibit, eg, 'miscegenation' or sex discrimination by a person whose religious or other beliefs

[42] Ibid 47.

are that married women should not work outside the home, would itself amount to direct discrimination contrary to the RB Regs.

Above I outlined the added problem that the test for determining a person's religious or other beliefs is entirely subjective. Even leaving this aside, penalising a white supremacist because she acts as a white supremacist would, on the approach of the tribunal in *Ladele*, be an act of direct discrimination on grounds of belief. The adoption of such an approach in this context would, even taking into account the possibility that an employer might be able to plead the GOR defence, place employers between the rock of a religious discrimination claim and the hard place of a claim on other protected grounds. Further, the GOR defence would not apply to an employer whose objection to employing acknowledged white supremacists, or dyed-in-the-wool sexists, or homophobes was a matter of principle unrelated to the jobs for which they are employed. The defence allows an employer to require that someone be 'of a particular religion or belief' where 'having regard to the nature of the employment or the context in which it is carried out', being of that 'particular religion or belief is a genuine and determining occupational requirement'. It is clear that 'being of a particular religion or belief' can here include *not* being of a particular religion or belief. But without robbing the GOR defence of any limitations, it is not possible to interpret it so as to permit an employer to refuse to employ an acknowledged white supremacist, sexist or homophobe, on the basis that such a person is (eg) likely to trigger harassment complaints from other members of staff or (in a decision-making role) to act in a prejudicial way or at least be suspected of so doing.

C. The Dangers of Legislative 'Overstretch'

Any attempt to manage the conflict produced by the regulation of discrimination on grounds of religion or belief by adopting a narrow approach to general concepts such as direct discrimination, eg, or a broad approach to justification or the GOR defence, threatens to infect the whole statutory discrimination regime. Examples of the tension generated by the extension of anti-discrimination provisions to previously unregulated territory, and the ensuing potential for damaging interpretations of previously settled concepts, are provided by the decisions in the *Roma Rights* case[43] (prior to that of the House of Lords) and that of the House of Lords in *R (Gillan) v Commissioner of Police of the Metropolis*.[44] In these cases (though in the latter only *obiter*), the long-established approach to direct discrimination (ie, the 'but for' test established by the House of Lords in *James*

[43] *R (European Roma Rights Centre) v Immigration Officer, Prague Airport* [2005] 2 AC 1 (HL), [2004] QB 811 (CA), [2002] EWHC 1989 (Admin) (QBD).

[44] [2006] 2 AC 307.

v Eastleigh Borough Council[45]) was abandoned in favour of one which took into account the justifiability or otherwise of treatment differentiated on racial lines. This happened in cases in which immigration and security (rather than the more familiar territory of employment or the provision of goods and services) were, respectively, at issue. What drove the decisions was the understanding of judges not intimately acquainted with the statutory discrimination provisions of what 'common sense' required in these contexts.[46]

The *Roma Rights* and *Gillan* cases illustrate the enormous strain imposed on the RRA by its extension to cover the actions of public authorities *qua* public authorities. This is not to say that such extension is to be regretted. On the contrary, the prohibition of discrimination by public authorities is to be welcomed, in my view. But such extension carries costs. Prohibitions on discrimination do not inevitably accord with common sense. Indeed, it is the very common sensical nature of much discrimination which has resulted in its pervasiveness and tenacity. This is partly why irrationality review at common law has been of very limited utility in challenging discrimination: cases such as *R (Smith) v Secretary of State for Defence* (the 'gays in the military case') make the point well.[47] Where anti-discrimination provisions are well established, as in the context of employment, legal rules which may appear antithetical to common sense are normalised to the extent that 'common sense' shifts, as arguably in the case of pregnancy discrimination (economically rational but now legally understood to amount to unjustifiable sex discrimination). Applying those rules in a new context, however, opens the door once again to common sense as a trump card. The additional danger is that the re-interpretations which result may feed back into the previously established order, thus overturning victories won in the employment context (in the case of *Roma Rights* and *Gillan*)[48] or in relation to other protected grounds (where religion or belief cases involving conflicts are at issue).

The apparently intractable conflicts posed by the regulation of discrimination on grounds of religion or belief provoke the question whether broad protection of religious belief is required as a matter of European Convention law.

[45] [1990] 2 AC 751.

[46] See, eg, the remarks of Simon Brown LJ (with whom Mantell LJ agreed) in the Court of Appeal in the *Roma Rights* case, n 43 above, paras 66, 69, and (now elevated to the House of Lords) in the *Gillan* decision, n 44 above, paras 88–91.

[47] [1996] QB 517. See also *Short v Poole* [1926] Ch 66 (discrimination against red-heads would be irrational and therefore unlawful, but dismissing a woman teacher because she was married was not).

[48] See also, on a different issue, the House of Lords' decision in *Malcolm v Lewisham* [2008] 3 WLR 194 in which, confronted with a limited statutory justification to disability-related discrimination in the context of premises, the House chose to gut the concept of disability-related discrimination of all meaning in a move which involved, *inter alia*, ignoring clear Parliamentary guidance as to the intended meaning, as well as the unambiguous words of the statute.

5. ARTICLE 9

A. Direct Interferences

Article 9 of the European Convention on Human Rights, which guarantees freedom of religion, provides that:

> 1. Everyone has the right to freedom of thought, conscience and religion; this right includes freedom to change his religion or belief, and freedom, either alone or in community with others and in public or private, to manifest his religion or belief, in worship, teaching, practice and observance.
> 2. Freedom to manifest one's religion or beliefs shall be subject only to such limitations as are prescribed by law and are necessary in a democratic society in the interests of public safety, for the protection of public order, health or morals, or the protection of the rights and freedoms of others.

There is nothing unusual about the limited nature of the right to manifest religious belief, Articles 8, 10 and 11 of the Convention adopting a similar approach in respect of rights to privacy, to freedom of expression and to freedom of association and assembly.

Freedom of religion is accorded a high level of protection by most human rights instruments. The 'right to freedom of thought, conscience and religion ... includ[ing] freedom to change [one's] religion or belief' is one of the very few unqualified rights recognised by the European Convention. Any interference with this 'psychic' or 'internal' individual freedom will breach Article 9 regardless of its aims and without consideration of any competing interests or rights: religious freedom trumps. *Indirect* interferences with the 'psychic' freedom do not, however, necessarily breach Article 9.

The European Commission and Court of Human Rights have in fact shown scant hesitation in accepting constraints imposed upon religious individuals in their engagement with the wider world, even where those constraints have prevented them from reconciling their religious convictions with their occupational or educational ambitions. The tone was set by the early decision of the Commission in *Ahmad v UK*[49] in which the applicant, a teacher who sought accommodation of his obligation to attend religious worship on a Friday afternoon by his employers, found his claim dismissed as 'manifestly ill-founded' on the basis that he 'remained free to resign if and when he found that his teaching obligations conflicted with his religious duties'. This decision, reached in 1982, was reiterated in 1997 in *Stedman v UK*,[50] in which the Christian applicant had been subject to

[49] (1982) 4 EHRR 126.
[50] (1997) 23 EHRR CD.

the unilateral imposition of an obligation to work on Sundays. The Commission ruled that she 'was dismissed for failing to agree to work certain hours rather than for her religious belief as such and was free to resign and did in effect resign from her employment'.

In *Stedman* and *Ahmad*, the Commission refused even to acknowledge that the applicants' rights had been interfered with. In *Karaduman v Turkey*, the Commission reached the same conclusion in respect of a woman refused permission to graduate from her university studies unless she was prepared to be photographed without her headscarf: 'by choosing to pursue her higher education in a secular university a student submits to those university rules, which may make the freedom of students to manifest their religion subject to restrictions as to place and manner intended to ensure harmonious coexistence between students of different beliefs'.[51] And even in those cases in which, more recently, the European Court of Human Rights has appeared willing to accept that restrictions with which members of particular religious groups find it difficult in practice to comply with amount to 'interference' with the religious beliefs of individual applicants, it is ready to find that the restrictions are justified for the purposes of Article 9(2). Thus, in *Dahlab v Sweden* the Court rejected as manifestly unfounded an Article 9 challenge to a headscarf ban imposed on a Muslim primary school teacher. The Court thought it 'very difficult to assess the impact that a powerful external symbol such as the wearing of a headscarf may have on the freedom of conscience and religion of very young children', expressed concern that 'the wearing of a headscarf might have some kind of proselytising effect, seeing that it appears to be imposed on women by a precept which is laid down in the Koran and which ... is hard to square with the principle of gender equality' and concluded that it was 'difficult to reconcile the wearing of an Islamic headscarf with the message of tolerance, respect for others and, above all, equality and non-discrimination that all teachers in a democratic society must convey to their pupils'.

The justification in *Dahlab* rested significantly on the fact that the applicant was a teacher of young children. In the more recent decision of *Şahin v Turkey*,[52] however, the Grand Chamber upheld a complete headscarf ban imposed by a Turkish university, agreeing with the fourth section[53] that the principles of secularism and gender equality, on which it is accepted that the ban was based, justified the interference with the applicant's Article 9 rights. The fourth section had expressed concern about the impact of the headscarf, 'presented or perceived

[51] (1993) 74 DR 93, 108. See also the majority view in *Copsey v WWB Devon Clays Ltd* [2005] EWCA Civ 932, [2005] ICR 1789 and the views of Lords Scott, Hoffmann and Bingham in *R (Begum) v Headteacher and Governors of Denbigh High School*, n 36 above.

[52] (2007) 44 EHRR 5.

[53] (2005) 41 EHRR 8[53].

as a compulsory religious duty ... on those who choose not to wear it' in Turkey: 'a country in which the majority of the population, while professing a strong attachment to the rights of women and a secular way of life, adhere to the Islamic faith'.[54] That Court had adverted to the perceived politicisation of the headscarf in Turkey in recent years and to 'the fact that there are extremist political movements in Turkey which seek to impose on society as a whole their religious symbols and conception of a society founded on religious precepts'.[55] The Grand Chamber agreed, stating that 'the principle of secularism ... is the paramount consideration underlying the ban on the wearing of religious insignia in universities':

> In such a context, where the values of pluralism, respect for the rights of others and, in particular, equality before the law of men and women are being taught and applied in practice, it is understandable that the relevant authorities should wish to preserve the secular nature of the institution concerned and so consider it contrary to such values to allow religious attire, including, as in the present case, the Islamic headscarf, to be worn.[56]

The Grand Chamber went so far as to suggest that, given the diversity of approaches across Europe on the issue, the extent and form of regulations concerning the wearing of religious symbols in educational institutions 'must inevitably be left up to a point to the state concerned, as it will depend on the domestic context concerned',[57] though 'this margin of appreciation goes hand in hand with a European supervision embracing both the law and the decisions applying it'.[58] It further suggested that '[a] n attitude which fails to respect th[e] principle [of secularism] will not necessarily be accepted as being covered by the freedom to manifest one's religion and will not enjoy the protection of art 9 of the convention'.[59]

I note in passing that the problematic nature of *Karaduman*, *Dahlab* and *Şahin* from a gender equality perspective. Despite somewhat glib assertions in *Şahin* that the headscarf ban was justified in part by considerations of gender equality, the impact of any restriction on the visible manifestation of religious belief is felt disproportionately by women who are forced to choose between adherence to religious obligation and the pursuit of education or economic empowerment through work. Further, the approach taken in *Şahin* to the perceived manifestation of '[a]n attitude which fails to respect th[e] principle [of secularism]' involves

[54] n 502 above, para 108.
[55] Ibid, para 109.
[56] Ibid, para 116.
[57] n 52 above, para 109, citing, *Gorzelik v Poland* (2004) 38 EHRR 4, para 67, and *Murphy v Ireland* (2004) 38 EHRR 13, para 73.
[58] Ibid, para 110.
[59] Ibid para 114, citing *Refah Partisi v Turkey* (2002) 35 EHRR 3, para 93. For a critical discussion of *Şahin*, see, eg, Manisuli Ssenyonjo, 'The Islamic Veil and Freedom of Religion, the Rights to Education and Work: a Survey of Recent International and National Cases' (2007) 6 *Chinese Journal of International Law* 653.

'determin[ing] in a general and abstract way the signification of wearing the headscarf [and] impos[ing] its viewpoint on the applicant', a move characterised by Judge Tulkens, dissenting, as going beyond as the proper role of the Court.[60] Finally, the decision in *Şahin* stands in stark contrast to the decision in *Gündüz v Turkey*,[61] to take just one example, in which Article 10 provided protection in respect of explicit and extreme Islamic denouncements of the secular state. It may be, of course, that the difference in approach can be explained by the fact that, in Article 10 cases, challenge is typically brought to punitive action directed by the state to the person or organisation whose freedom of expression is claimed, whereas in the Article 9 cases considered above the religious individual is seeking accommodation of his or her religious beliefs or practices, as distinct from bare freedom of expression in the sense that that expression is not criminalised. But the limited nature of the Article 9's protection is such that the provision does not necessarily protect even those individuals whose religious beliefs bring them into direct conflict with the criminal law.

B. Problematising the Boundaries: Conflicts of Conscience

Below I will return to Article 9 and questions of gender equality. Here I want to consider further the distinction drawn by Article 9 of the Convention between the *holding* and the *manifestation* of religious beliefs. Individual accommodation cases can in practice involve interferences with former, as well as the latter,[62] as where a person's beliefs demand action which is not regarded as a matter of personal choice in circumstances in which conflict with the state cannot be avoided. Examples might include the practice, as a religious obligation, of female genital mutilation,[63] the avoidance of blood products or adherence to pacifism or a particular mode of dress. Where such practices are legally prohibited the believer may have to choose between obedience to the state and obedience to his or her religious obligations. The prohibition by the state of female genital mutilation or of a particular dress code in schools attendance at which is compulsory, or the imposition of a state override on parental refusal of blood transfusions for

[60] n 52 above, O-II12.

[61] (2005) 41 EHRR 5.

[62] This has been recognised by the US Supreme Court, eg, in *Wisconsin v Yoder* [1972] 406 US 205, though only to the extent of recognising that interference with *action* as distinct from *belief* could require justification from the state under the first Amendment: see Gabriel Moens, 'The Action-Belief Dichotomy and Freedom of Religion' (1989–90) 12 *Sydney Law Review* 195, 207–10 and, for discussion of the case generally, William Galston, 'Two Concepts of Liberalism' (1995) 105 *Ethics* 59.

[63] Neither the Koran nor the Sunnah (the two main sources of Islamic law) mention FGM and most Islamic scholars agree that it is not required of Muslim women but the UN estimate that over 130 million (mainly Muslim) women, including 98% of women in Somalia, have been subject to the practice which is seen to guarantee female sexual purity.

children or an obligation to perform military service, does not on its face interfere with the *holding* of religious beliefs: the relevant *beliefs* are not itself proscribed. But those *beliefs* are manifestly interfered with when the individual is prevented from acting in accordance with them, at least where there is not the opportunity to avoid the conflict even at cost.[64]

Just as the European Court of Human Rights has proven unsympathetic to Article 9 challenges to dress codes, so it has to date rejected Article 9-based challenges to compulsory military service without the option of alternative service.[65] The extent and duration of such punishment are controlled by decisions such as those in *Thlimmenos v Greece* and *Ülke v Turkey*, in which the Court found breaches of Articles 14 and 3, respectively, arising from arbitrary and manifestly excessive punishment of refusal to serve.[66] But to date no direct challenge has succeeded.[67]

Another example of intractable conflict might arise in relation to proselytism (more neutrally, evangelism) which is considered by many Christians to be an obligatory aspect of their Christianity.[68] Proselytism is prohibited in Greece as a criminal offence, a position which was found to be inconsistent with Article 9 of the Convention in *Kokkinakis v Greece*[69] (the first Article 9 case to be heard by the Court) only to the extent that the ban applied to what the Court regarded as 'bearing Christian witness'[70] as well as to 'improper proselytism' ('a corruption or deformation of' 'true evangelism' which 'may … take the form of activities

[64] Another example of potentially irresolvable conflict is found in the *Wisconsin v Yoder* case, n 62 above, where Amish parents were eventually permitted to withdraw their children from schooling at 14 years (education generally being compulsory to age 16) because of the Amish that view being that state education beyond this age would (Moens, n 62 above, 207) 'threaten their way of life and violate their religious beliefs'.

[65] Note that Article 4, which prohibits 'forced or compulsory labour' exempts military service from this prohibition.

[66] Respectively (2001) 31 EHRR 15 and appl. no. 39437/98.

[67] In *Peters v the Netherlands*, *Heudens v Belgium* and *Valsamis v Greece* (appl. no. 22793/93, Commission decision of 30 November 1994, not published; appl. no. 24630/94, Commission decision of 22 May 1995, not published and (1997) 24 EHRR 294, respectively), the European Commission rejected Article 9 challenges to mandatory military service itself. Note, however, that in *Bayatyan v Armenia* (appl. no. 23459/03), the Court ruled admissible a challenge to mandatory military service. The decision in *Bayatyan* was reached in December 2006 and the matter has yet to receive full consideration by the Court.

[68] Matthew's last verses report Jesus' command to 'Go to all the nations and make disciples. Baptize them and teach them my commands'.

[69] (1994) 17 EHRR 397.

[70] Ibid, para 48. The latter is, according to the 1956 World Council of Churches' report, 'an essential mission and a responsibility of every Christian and every Church' ('Christian Witness, Proselytism and Religious Liberty in the Setting of the World Council of Churches', revised by the Central Committee in 1956 and 1960 and received by the WCC Third Assembly (New Delhi, 1961)).

offering material or social advantages with a view to gaining new members for a Church or exerting improper pressure on people in distress or in need [and] may even entail the use of violence or brainwashing'[71]). The European Court took the view that 'improper proselytism' was 'not compatible with respect for the freedom of thought, conscience and religion of others' but found, in the instant case, an unjustifiable interference with Mr Kokkinakis' Article 9 rights because he had been criminalised without reference to how it was alleged that he 'had attempted to convince his neighbour by improper means'.

Had Mr Kokkinakis' missionary activities strayed beyond that which the World Council of Churches had deemed acceptable in 1956, his conviction would have been regarded as consistent with Article 9 whether or not those activities were the result of his religious obligations. That an individual may, consistent with Article 9, be prohibited from acting in a manner required by his or her religious beliefs is inherent in the approach taken until recently by the European Convention organs of not accepting even that an *interference* had been established with Article 9 rights if the individual was left with a choice to comply with his or her religious obligations by (eg) finding alternative work (in the cases of *Ahmed* and *Stedman*), attending a different university (*Karaduman*), etc. This being the case, the inability to comply with a matter of religious obligation appeared to be taken as an ingredient of (potentially justifiable) interference with the manifestation of religious belief, there bring no suggestion that such interference would be *per se* illegitimate. There would appear to be no reason to suggest that Article 9 requires more favourable treatment of religious collectives, ie, that it prohibits the subjection of religious collectives to rules of general application which in fact are in conflict with the collective's religious doctrine.

6. VALUING RELIGION?

The question which then arises is whether there is reason to depart from the Article 9 jurisprudence and to provide a broader scope for accommodation of individual religious or other belief. Communitarians will argue that individual identity is shaped by cultural communities which ought therefore to be protected.[72]

[71] Defined in accordance with the World Council of Churches' 1956 report, ibid.

[72] See, eg, Charles Taylor, *"Atomism" in Philosophy and the Human Sciences: Philosophical Papers 2* (Cambridge University Press, 1985), Michael Sandel, *Liberalism and the Limits of Justice* (Cambridge University Press, 1981), A Margalit and J Raz, "National Self-Determination", in Will Kymlicka (ed), *The Rights of Minority Cultures* (Oxford University Press, 1995), 79. These arguments are frequently made in relation to 'ethnic' communities but could equally well apply to 'communities' identified by reference to religious belief, as Margalit and Raz recognise at 85.

Will Kymlicka's modified liberalism also assumes the importance of 'culture' in determining 'the context of choice':[73] creating cultural narratives by reference to which 'we decide how to lead our lives by situating ourselves within [these] narratives, by adopting roles that have struck us as worthwhile, as ones worth living'.[74]

Recognition of the importance of community and culture is not problematic from an equality perspective; it has long been a feminist complaint that the characterisation of persons as autonomous individuals is one which is particularly problematic for women given their disproportionate share of caring tasks.[75] But this recognition does not require the reification of static 'cultures',[76] whether those cultures are defined by reference to religion or otherwise. A similar point is made by Jeremy Waldron, who criticises Kymlicka's assumption that the cultural embeddedness of choice requires 'one cultural framework in which each available option is assigned a meaning' as distinct from 'items or fragments from a variety of cultural sources', 'cultural materials ... not ... "a rich and secure cultural structure"', 'access to a variety of stories and roles' but not 'something called *membership* in a culture'.[77]

Waldron likens 'immersion in the traditions of a particular community in the modern world' to 'living in Disneyland and thinking that one's surroundings epitomize what it is for a culture really to exist. Worse ... demanding the funds to live in Disneyland and the protection of modern society for the boundaries of Disneyland while still managing to convince oneself that what is happening inside Disneyland is all there is to an adequate fulfilling life'. [78] Even if he is wrong, and community or cultural membership is important in a stronger sense than he allows, Sonu Bedi points out a tension between the increasing tendency to view religion and religious belief as mutable and demands for the provision of 'religious exemptions'. Unless, she argues, religion is unchosen, an 'immutable and fixed belief system', [79] there is no basis to differentiate 'the Jew from the

[73] *Liberalism, Community, and Culture* (Oxford University Press, 1989), 178.

[74] Ibid 165.

[75] See, eg, Susan Okin, 'Equal Citizenship: Gender/ Justice and Gender: An Unfinished Debate' (2004) 72 *Fordham Law Review* 1537, Anne Phillips 'Defending Equality of Outcome' (2004) 12 *The Journal of Political Philosophy* 1.

[76] See generally Madhavi Sunder, 'Cultural Dissent' (2001–2) 54 *Stanford Law Review* 495.

[77] 'Minority Cultures and the Cosmopolitan Alternative' (1991–2) 25 *University of Michigan Journal of Law Reform* 751, 783–4.

[78] Ibid 763.

[79] Sonu Bedi, 'Debate: What is so Special about Religion? The Dilemma of the Religious Exemption' (2007) 15 *The Journal of Political Philosophy* 235, 237.

Rotarian ... the Sikh from the mere hat-wearer',[80] and no overriding reason to provide religious exemptions to rules of general application.

Religion is clearly not immutable, given the shifts in doctrine which occur over time.[81] The creation of legal exceptions designed to accommodate religious demands risks, in the words of Yael Tamir, 'strengthen[ing] dominant subgroups within each culture and privilege[ing] conservative interpretations of culture over reformative and innovative ones'.[82] Further, the grant of exemptions on religious grounds creates pressure to characterise as 'religious' cultural practices which may serve to disadvantage the less powerful within groups. A benign example is the turban which, Bedi suggests, is not mandatory as a matter of Sikh doctrine.[83] It is clear from the discussion above, however, that a secular court cannot determine what is or is not required as a matter of religious doctrine and that (in any event) the existence of such an obligation as regards dress, etc, is a subjective question for the believer (*Begum*). Wearing a turban is not a practice which carries any overtones of gender inequality or subordination, or which imposes on its adherents any physical harm.[84] But practices such as FGM, coerced and polygamous marriage and compulsory restrictive dress codes are more or less damaging for those (generally or exclusively women) subject to them. The identification of many of these practices as 'religious' as distinct from 'cultural' is strongly contested, and privileging those accepted as 'religious', as distinct from merely 'cultural', increases the incentive to categorise them as 'religious' and

[80] Ibid 234. Cf Lucy Vickers who argues (n 20 above, 40) that religious beliefs can be distinguished from others and their protection demanded on grounds of dignity because 'it is only those ... which feed into an individual's ability to make sense of the world, and through which they develop a sense of the good, that require protection'. Vickers concludes, on the basis of this assertion, that 'religious freedom is an important aspect of the individual autonomy and self-respect due to all people as a result of their humanity. If we accept that all humans are equal, we need to give equal concern and respect to the world views they develop'.

[81] Within Anglicanism, eg, as to women priests, within Catholicism as to correct punishment for heresy and the existence of 'limbo'.

[82] 'Siding with the Underdogs', in Susan Moller Okin, Joshua Cohen, Matthew Howard and Martha Nussbaum (eds), *Is Multiculturalism Bad for Women?* (Princeton University Press, 1999), 47. This argument is discussed in more detail in my EUI working paper, 'Religion and (in)equality in the European framework' forthcoming.

[83] See also Bhikhu Parekh, *Rethinking Multiculturalism: Cultural Diversity and Political Theory* (Macmillan, 2000), 198; Brian Barry (on the Jewish *yarmulke*), *Culture and Equality* (Polity Press, 2001), 33. Contrast the letter written to Jacques Chirac arguing that the turban was cultural and not religious, this in order to seek its exemption from the French ban on 'ostentatious' religious dress in schools ('French Sikhs threaten to leave country' *Guardian* 23 January 2004) with the forthcoming Article 9 challenge to that ban by Sikhs expelled in December 2004 from the Louise-Michel High School of Bobigny.

[84] Similarly the kara (Sikh bangle) which was the issue of dispute in *R (on the application of Watkins-Singh) v Governing Body of Aberdare Girls' High School* [2008] EWHC 1865 (Admin), [2008] 3 FCR 203, [2008] All ER (D) 376 (Jul) (a case in which the RRA was successfully relied upon).

thereby helps to perpetuate them.[85] The provision of religious exemptions may result in the expansion of 'religious' obligation and the reinforcement of religious hierarchies.[86]

7. CONCLUSION: WHAT ROOM FOR PROTECTION OF RELIGIOUS BELIEF?

I stated in the introduction to this paper that I would suggest an attenuated form of protection against discrimination on grounds of religion, this *in addition to* the freedoms guaranteed religious individuals by Article 9 of the European Convention. The additional protection which may be justified notwithstanding the concerns expressed above recognises both the similarities between some forms of religious hostility and racism, and the non-neutral state, and acknowledges the shortcomings of Article 9 as a shield to disadvantage suffered by persons of disadvantaged minority groups because of their religious affiliation (real or perceived).

Dealing first with the issue of direct discrimination, one issue that springs to mind is the fact that in Northern Ireland the terms 'Catholic' and 'Protestant', in the context of arguments about justice and equality, have very little to do with nuances of doctrine or even individual belief, and everything to do with ethnic identification (actual or perceived). The overlap between race and religion has been recognised by the RRA, which accommodates claims concerning discrimination against Sikhs and Jews as a result of the House of Lords' recognition in *Mandla v Dowell Lee*[87] of Sikhs as an ethnic group. This understanding did not, however, stretch as far as Muslims, many of whom who are among the most disadvantaged in Britain at present. But it captures something of the essence of the hostility directed against Muslims in recent years. The vilification of Muslims today, Catholics in previous years and Roma across much of Europe is indistinguishable in its effects from racism.

'Race' is not a biological construct, racial categories being instead 'fundamentally social in nature'.[88] At the beginning of the twentieth century, the USA was absorbed

[85] As Madhavi Sunder points out ("Piercing the Veil" (2003) 112 *Yale Law Journal* 1399, 1441, discussing the experience of the network Women Living Under Muslim Laws) 'religious claims are particularly hard to challenge, and therefore [WLUML] expends effort to deconstruct religious claims as, in part, contingent and political'.

[86] See generally Sunder ibid and n 76 above.

[87] [1983] 2 AC 548.

[88] Lucius Outlaw, 'Towards a Critical Theory of Race' in David Goldberg (ed), *Anatomy of Racism* (University of Minnesota Press 1990) 58, 68. See also Angela Harris, 'Equality Trouble: Sameness and Difference in Twentieth-Century Race Law' (2000) 88 *California Law Review* 1923. At 1923 Harris highlights the role of law in the USA in regulating the 'formation, recognition, and maintenance of racial groups, as well as ... the relationships among these groups'.

with the question whether the Poles, Irish, Jews and Armenians who were finding their way in large quantities to that country's shores were 'white enough' to be worthy of citizenship.[89] It is the case that the demands for recognition made by many Muslims are focused on their identity as Muslims and not on questions of 'race' understood in terms of colour. This is not inconsistent, however, with a legal response which focuses on the racialised aspects of Muslim disadvantage while attempting to avoid the conflicts which arise out of the extension of protection against discrimination to religion or belief more generally. Direct discrimination of this sort should be recognised as breaching Article 9 itself or in conjunction with Article 14 of the Convention but the limited horizontal application of those provisions in my view justifies a domestic legal response.

Turning to the non-neutral nature of the state, working life remains organised to some extent around a Christian calendar such that working time is, for many, constructed in such a way as to permit religious observance by Christians while rendering observance by Muslims and Jews (among others) problematic. Similar observations can be made about what is regarded as 'normal' in terms of dress and practices around food and eating. To the extent that society is not neutral, it is at least arguable[90] that accommodation should be made of those religious obligations the equivalent of which are facilitated for those of the 'favoured' faiths, to the extent that such accommodation is reasonable. Some such accommodation may be required under Article 9 of the Convention. But the case law of the ECtHR set out above makes it clear that decisions to this effect are unlikely in practice, even where (as in *Ahmad*) Article 14 is explicitly relied upon.

Suggesting this kind of accommodation does not entail granting to religion the same status as race, sex or other protected grounds, with all the difficulties created by such a step. It is, rather, a pragmatic response to the fact that religious belief is an important organising feature of many people's lives and that present arrangements are not even-handed in the extent to which they enable people to manage the competing demands upon them. By 'reasonable' here I mean that the accommodation is such as would be required in a case of (say) *prima facie* indirect race discrimination, ie, where the disparate impact is disproportionate to any legitimate need appropriately and necessarily served by the disparately impacting measures, those measures should not be applied to those disproportionately disadvantaged by them. Examples of such cases might include the existing exemptions for Sikh turbans on building sites and on motorcycles, particularly in the absence of statistical evidence of disproportionate rates of serious injuries

[89] Adrienne Wing, 'Brief Reflections Toward a Multiplicative Theory and Praxis of Being' (1990–1) 6 *Berkley Women's Law Journal* 181.

[90] Though see the decision of the European Commission on Human Rights in *Choudhury v United Kingdom*, appl no. 17439/90.

resulting therefrom;[91] the provision of Halal and Kosher food by prisons and by schools where, eg, Muslim or Jewish pupils are entitled to free school meals or attend the school in significant numbers; flexibility as regards appearance rules and early finish times for observant Jewish workers on Friday evenings where necessary to permit compliance with Sabbath restrictions and accommodation of other religious requirements for Sabbaths and religious festivals. Such observation is not, for the most part, problematic for majority Christians given the organisation of the calendar around Christian Sabbaths and holidays but can create real difficulties for others.

It is the case that accommodating such religious requirements may create a degree of inconvenience for others, but no more so than the inconvenience of accommodating colleagues on maternity or parental leave or 'family friendly' working hours, or those with other commitments which impinge on their working time.[92] This inconvenience is quite a different cost from that associated with permitting religious individuals or collectives themselves to discriminate on grounds of sex, race, etc, at least in the public sphere, involving as it does no assault on individuals' equality rights or dignity. Further, it does not require the understanding of religion or culture as immutable or homogeneous.

This approach is a modified version of that espoused by Brian Barry.[93] Barry himself is fairly dismissive of equality arguments in this context, suggesting that the rule-and-exemption approach adopted in the UK in relation (eg) to humane slaughter and the requirement that motorcyclists wear helmets is neither necessary nor justifiable. His general approach is that (1) no rules should exist as to, eg, clothing and appearance or safety requirements unless they are justifiable in the general public interest, in which case (2) exceptions should generally not be made to such rules. Thus, if stunning has been collectively agreed to be desirable in the case of animals about to be slaughtered, then providing an exception to those whose religious beliefs forbid pre-slaughter is analogous to allowing only those 'who could show it was part of their culture' to hunt.[94]

The shortcomings of Barry's position lie in his unwillingness to countenance that perceptions of religious obligation might be weighed in the balance at all,

[91] For an analysis of the increased marginal risks associated with non-use of helmets by Sikhs in British Columbia, see *Dhillon v British Columbia (Ministry of Transportation and Highways, Motor Vehicle Branch)* [1999] BCHRTD No. 25, British Columbia Human Rights Tribunal, 11 May 1999.

[92] This could include those who sit as magistrates, local councillors, etc. Barry objects that employers should not 'be licensed to carry out intrusive investigations into their employees' religious affiliations simply in order to be able to deny permission to "rogue" headscarf-wearers' (n 83 above, 59) and there is no dispute that the same general rule should apply to all where that rule can be made to be neutral as between religions. The issue is, however, more difficult when, as in relation to working hours, neutrality may not be possible (though it is equally possible that general flexibility around working time will accommodate many employers' as well as workers' needs).

[93] *Culture and Inequality*, n 83 above.

[94] Ibid 43.

and in his elision of religious adherence with the 'expensive tastes' on which so much recent equality jurisprudence has been focussed.[95] Thus, eg, in his response to complaints of disparate impact: 'The essence of law is the protection of some interests at the expense of others when they come into conflict ... The point is a completely general one'.[96] His response to the Sikh who (absent an exception from the obligation to wear a helmet) would be prevented from riding a motorbike is that he has suffered no interference with his Article 9 rights: 'the inability to ride a motorcycle does not prevent a Sikh from observing any demands of his religion'. And to the question of kosher/halal meat: if the law condones ritual slaughter and the additional animal suffering involved in it is 'accommodating the tastes of a subset of carnivores, not observing the demands of religious freedom'.[97]

Barry does accept that ban imposed, in the context of employment, on the wearing of a headscarf is objectionable, this on the basis that 'there is no non-trivial reason in support of a ban on headscarves' so because 'to abandon a long-established custom that enjoins women not to appear in public with uncovered heads is no trivial matter ... the ban is rightly to be regarded as a denial of equal opportunity, or at the very least an unreasonable infringement of a right to make a living without having to make a gratuitous sacrifice'.[98] Where, however, the sacrifice is other than gratuitous, because the aim served by the disparately impacting rule is a legitimate and weighty one, Barry would brook no exceptions except, it appears, where there are strong pragmatic grounds for so doing.[99]

Barry's statement that 'special treatment for members of disadvantaged groups is justified only for so long as the inequality persists'[100] is, I think, correct. But his statement that 'the object of special treatment for members of disadvantaged groups is to make the need for that special treatment to disappear as rapidly

[95] See, eg, Ronald Dworkin, 'What is Equality? Part 2: Equality of Resources' (1981) 10 *Philosophy and Public Affairs* 283, Phillipe Van Parijs, 'Why Surfers should be Fed' (1999) 20 *Philosophy and Public Affairs* 101, Richard Arneson, 'Equality and Equality of Opportunity for Welfare', in Louis Pojman and Robert Westmoreland (eds), *Equality: Selected Readings* (Oxford University Press, 1997), 231; G. A. Cohen, 'On the Currency of Egalitarian Justice' (1980) 99 *Ethics* 906. For a critique of this literature, see Elizabeth Anderson, 'What is the Point of Equality?' (1999) 109 *Ethics* 287. At 288, eg, she complains that the excessive focus on 'divisible, privately appropriated goods, such as income and resources, or privately enjoyed goods, such as welfare ... neglects the much broader agendas of actual egalitarian political movements'.

[96] n 80 above, 34.

[97] Ibid 46.

[98] Ibid 59.

[99] In the case of Sikh construction workers because their number and geographical concentration would mean that the absence of an exemption to the hard hat rule would have a very high social cost (ibid 49–50) and in the case of school uniform which Barry sees as serving 'no interest that was worthy of protection' (at least in the case of *Mandla v Dowell Lee* [1983] 2 AC 548).

[100] n 83 above, 13.

as possible'[101] is, although apt in relation to measures designed to lift people out of poverty or ameliorate historical disadvantage, less so in this context: the accommodation of religious needs will not itself make the need for such accommodation disappear. It is at least arguable that neither will the achievement of a formally neutral state.

Remaining exceptions to formal state neutrality consist predominantly in the arrangement of conventional working hours and schooling arrangements around the Christian calendar, the role of Anglican bishops in the House of Lords and (likely of minority concern) restrictions on accession to the throne of Catholics. (Blasphemy laws, which applied to Christianity (possibly Anglicanism) alone were abolished in May 2008.[102]) The focus of those who favour religious equality should be in ridding the state of these exceptions and, in the meantime, negotiating appropriate accommodations with them for individuals who adhere to the non-'favoured' faith, rather than in ensuring to religious individuals rights to discriminate on other grounds.

Likely to persist even in the event of formal neutrality are the difficulties thrown up by different rules or norms concerning clothing, appearance and food. It has already been suggested that these can be dealt with, by and large, by pragmatic accommodations. In many cases, the result of these accommodations would not differ greatly from those which would flow from the prohibition of indirect discrimination on grounds of religion (as at present). Where the difference would be felt, however, is in those cases in which accommodation is sought by those whose religious beliefs do not place them in a disadvantaged minority group, or where it conflicts with the legally protected rights of others.

In the former case, there would simply be no right of accommodation over and above that provided by Article 9 and the other Convention provisions: absent a prohibition on religious discrimination *per se* no additional claim to protection arises. As to the latter type of case, an example arises from the facts of cases such as *Azmi*, where the claimant's wishes could be met only at cost to her educationally already disadvantaged pupils, or to male staff members whose freedom of movement around their workplace would have to have been curtailed to protect Ms Azmi, when she was unveiled, from their gaze. In such a case, and given the absence of a right to accommodation of religious belief *qua religious belief*, the claim fails. This is the same outcome as was actually achieved in *Azmi*, but it does not depend upon the characterisation of the discrimination at issue as indirect rather than direct, rather on the fact that *reasonable* accommodation could not require an employer to override a prohibition on direct sex discrimination or (I would argue) the obligation owed to already disadvantaged students.

[101] Ibid.

[102] The Criminal Justice and Immigration Act 2008 abolishes the offence of blasphemy.

Other interesting questions arise where that of which accommodation is sought is questionable in and of itself, irrespective of immediate conflicts with the rights of others. In *Şahin* the ECtHR accepted that a prohibition on the wearing of the headscarf pursued gender equality, a legitimate aim. It did not appear to take into account the difficulties posed by the ban for real, individual Turkish women confronted with the choice between education and religion, and unable to utilise the avoidance mechanism open to the daughters of then-Prime Minister Erdogan who were able to study in the USA.[103] In *Begum* Baroness Hale was explicit in confining her finding that the school's refusal to allow the claimant to wear the jilbab was justified to a case, such as that one, involving a non-adult, citing Yasmin Alibhai-Brown to the effect that 'What critics of Islam fail to understand is that when they see a young woman in a hijab she may have chosen the garment as a mark of her defiant political identity and also as a way of regaining control over her body'.[104] As against this, as Baroness Hale noted,[105] is the fact that control over women is:

> central to the project of fundamentalism, which attempts to impose its own unitary religious definition on the grouping and its symbolic order. The "proper" behaviour of women is used to signify the difference between those who belong and those who do not; women are also seen as the "cultural carriers" of the grouping, who transmit group culture to the future generation; and proper control in terms of marriage and divorce ensures that children who are born to those women are within the boundaries of the collectivity, not only biologically but also symbolically.[106]

Difficult questions as to the limits of accommodation may well be better managed by an approach which focuses on disadvantage, exclusion and alienation from 'mainstream' society, and asks how best equality might be furthered, than on one where outcomes differ according to sometimes hair-splitting distinctions between 'indirect' and 'direct' discrimination in the context of religion, and/or a wide approach to the GOR defence, particularly where such tactics threaten to reverberate across the spectrum of discrimination law.

[103] BBC News, 25 February 2004.

[104] *Who do we think we are?* (Penguin, 2000), 246. See also Judge Tulkens, dissenting, in *Şahin*, para 95.

[105] Citing Gita Saghal and Nira Yuval-Davis, *Refusing Holy Orders, Women and Fundamentalism in Britain* (Women Living under Muslim Laws, 2000), 14.

[106] For further discussion, see, eg, Nicholas Gibson, 'Faith in the Courts: Religious Dress and Human Rights' (2007) 66 *Cambridge Law Journal* 657; Anastasia Vakulenko, 'Islamic Dress in Human Rights Jurisprudence: A Critique of Current Trends' (2007) 7 *Human Rights Law Review* 717.

[14]

GOD AT WORK: RELIGION IN THE WORKPLACE AND THE LIMITS OF PLURALISM IN CANADA

Lorne Sossin†

INTRODUCTION

Religious freedom includes both the freedom to express religious beliefs and the freedom from having the beliefs of others imposed. The workplace has become the testing ground for religious freedom in Canada. The protection of religious freedom in the workplace, however, also sheds light on a broader struggle for political norms. In Canada, two normative aspirations are reflected in the protection of religious freedom: the narrative of pluralism and the narrative of exceptionalism.

There are two competing narratives that have come to define Canada, both to itself and the world. The first narrative is of a vibrant, pluralist, immigrant society. This narrative begins with the founding of the Canadian state in 1867 as a compromise federation between the English Protestant and French Catholic communities that resided in what was then British North America. From the outset, the Canadian Constitution was a vehicle for the expression and protection of minority rights. Postwar civil liberties in Canada in the 1950s were forged not on the crucible of racial equality, but on religious equality, and specifically the protection of the Jehovah Witness community in Quebec.[1] With the advent of the Canadian Charter of Rights and Freedoms in 1982, the protection of religious freedom once again drove the rights discourse—this time protecting employees and customers from having a "Sabbath" imposed on them through the Lords Day Act.

---

† Faculty of Law, University of Toronto. This paper was first presented at the Conference on Religious Expression in the Workplace, sponsored by the University of Illinois College of Law and the Nantes Institute for Advanced Studie, held in Nantes, France, in May, 2008. A later version was presented as part of the Religion in the Public Sphere series at the University of Toronto's Jackman Institute for the Humanities, on February 5, 2009. I am grateful to the participants of both events for the constructive comments and suggestions I received. I am also grateful to Anver Emon, Fay Faraday, and Kerry Rittich for reading and commenting on earlier versions of this paper.

1. *See* Saumur v. City of Quebec, [1953] 2 S.C.R. 299 (Can.).

In *R.* v. *Big M. Drug Mart Ltd.*,[2] the first significant case to be decided by the Supreme Court of Canada, the Lords Day Act was struck down. In the course of the majority's reasons, Dickson C.J. observed,

> A truly free society is one which can accommodate a wide variety of beliefs, diversity of tastes and pursuits, customs and codes of conduct. A free society is one which aims at equality with respect to the employment of fundamental freedoms and I say this without any reliance upon s. 15 of the Charter. Freedom must surely be founded in respect for the inherent dignity and the inviolable rights of the human person. The essence of the concept of freedom of religion is the right to entertain such religious beliefs as a person chooses, the right to declare religious beliefs openly and without fear of hindrance or reprisal, and the right to manifest religious belief by worship and practice or by teaching and dissemination. But the concept means more than that.
>
> Freedom can primarily be characterized by the absence of coercion or constraint. If a person is compelled by the state or the will of another to a course of action or inaction which he would not otherwise have chosen, he is not acting of his own volition and he cannot be said to be truly free. One of the major purposes of the Charter is to protect, within reason, from compulsion or restraint. Coercion includes not only such blatant forms of compulsion as direct commands to act or refrain from acting on pain of sanction, coercion includes indirect forms of control which determine or limit alternative courses of conduct available to others. Freedom in a broad sense embraces both the absence of coercion and constraint, and the right to manifest beliefs and practices. Freedom means that, subject to such limitations as are necessary to protect public safety, order, health, or morals or the fundamental rights and freedoms of others, no one is to be forced to act in any way contrary to his beliefs or his conscience.[3]

This narrative has culminated in the celebration of religious, ethnic, and cultural pluralism in Canada. As Michael Adams argues in his 2007 study, *Unlikely Utopia: The Surprising Triumph of Canadian Pluralism*, Canada is an experiment in pluralism that has flourished.[4]

The second narrative is that of exceptionalism. According to this narrative, Canada began as and has remained a conservative English Protestant society that tolerated, but never considered as equal, all other minority religious communities. This narrative highlights the fact that the French Catholic community was given second class status in Quebec (until the Quiet Revolution of the 1960s and the rise of Quebec separatism in the 1970s), and that aboriginal communities were systematically

2. [1985] 1 S.C.R. 295 (Can.).
3. The Queen v. Big M Drug Mart Ltd., [1984] 2 S.C.R. 145, ¶¶ 94–95 (Can.).
4. MICHAEL ADAMS, UNLIKELY UTOPIA: THE SURPRISING TRIUMPH OF CANADIAN PLURALISM (2007). *See also* Michael Adams, *Surprise, Canadian Pluralism is Working*, TORONTO STAR, Nov. 10, 2007, *available at* http://www.thestar.com/article/274900.

disenfranchised. As religious communities become established, the Jewish, Muslim, Hindu, Buddhist, and other "outsider" communities are accommodated, but only within a paradigm that accepts English Prostestants (or, post-1970s, French Catholics in Quebec) as the "norm" and other religious communities as "minorities." For example, Christmas Day and Easter remain publicly enforced "statutory holidays" in Canada despite the obvious religious connotation of both holidays, and the large (and growing) segment of the population that does not observe these holidays. Under this narrative, it goes without saying that no other religious community's holy days are accorded state recognition.

These narratives collide in workplace settings in a variety of ways. Should all exployees receive a secular day off from work each week, or should employees who observe several different Sabbath days have their preferences accommodated? Should employers be able to select the day that corresponds with the preference of the majority? What if the issue of religious preference is not a day off but relates to workplace safety, such as where religious head coverings preclude wearing a helmet?

These narratives also shape the intersection of three related but distinct legal regimes governing the Canadian workplace. The first is the Constitutional regime, under which "freedom of religion" is expressly protected. The second is the anti-discrimination regime, which is the jurisdiction of Canada's ten provinces and three territories, and varies somewhat according to the particular language of those jurisdictions' human rights legislation. The third is the labor law regime, also a matter of provincial and territorial jurisdiction, which sets out the procedural and substantive relationship between employers and employees.

Ultimately, I conclude these narratives each capture an important and legitimate aspect of religion in the workplace in Canada. The challenge, going forward, is how these narratives may be reconciled, both as a matter of political and social discourse, and as a matter of legal doctrine.

This study is divided into two sections. The first section examines the present approach to religious accommodation in the workplace under Canadian constitutional law, human rights law, and labor law. The second section links the ambivalence of the Canadian legal system's response to religion in the workplace to broader social and political narratives of reasonable accommodation.

I. THE DILEMMA OF RELIGIOUS ACCOMMODATION IN A MULTICULTURAL SOCIETY

Canadian Constitutional law, anti-discrimination law, and labor and employment law each suggest a commitment to religious pluralism and yet also appear to reinforce the paradigm of a religious majority that is the norm and minority communities that must be accommodated. I refer above to this approach as exceptionalism. Below, I explore the tension between pluralism and exceptionalism within each of these legal regimes.

A. The Charter

The Canadian Constitution, known as the Canadian Charter of Rights and Freedoms, or simply the Charter, was introduced in 1982 and represented a limitation upon the principle of parliamentary sovereignty previously unknown to Canadian constitutional law.

The Charter applies to all laws and to all government action in Canada, and empowers the courts to strike down laws or invalidate any government decision that is inconsistent with the Charter's protections. The Charter, unlike the U.S. Constitution, does not expressly protect "free exercise,"[5] however, sections 2(a) and 15(1) provide for religious freedom. Section 2(a) provides:

> 2. Everyone has the following fundamental freedoms:
>
> (a) freedom of conscience and religion
>
> Section 15(1) states that every individual is equal before and under the law and has the right to the equal protection and equal benefit of the law without discrimination . . . based on . . . religion.[6]

Both sections 2(a) and 15(1), however, are subject to section 1 of the Charter under which infringements of Charter rights may be justified by Government. That section provides:

> The *Canadian Charter of Rights and Freedoms* guarantees the rights and freedoms set out in it subject only to such reasonable limits prescribed by law as can be demonstrably justified in a free and democratic society.

Finally, section 33 of the Constitution Act, 1982, provides a mechanism for Parliament to override certain sections of the Charter, including both the guarantee of freedom of religion and the guarantee of equality, for renewable, five year periods. On paper, at least, the

5. For a comparative perspective on freedom of religion in the United States and Canada, see Andrew M. Zeitlin, *A Test of Faith: Accommodating Religious Employees' "Work-Related Misconduct" in the United States and Canada*, 15 COMP. LAB. L.J. 250 (1994). *See also* Iain T. Benson, *The Freedom of Conscience and Religion in Canada: Challenges and Opportunities*, 21 EMORY INT'L L. REV. 111 (2007).

6. *Constitution Act, 1982*, being Schedule B to the *Canada Act 1982*, (U.K.), 1982, c.11, *available at* http://www.canlii.org/en/ca/const/const1982.html.

constitutional guarantees of religious freedom in Canada appear contingent and potentially fragile. In practice, however, the Charter has proven more robust in the area of religious freedom.

In Canada, the separation of religion and state has historically not constituted governmental or legislative policy. On the contrary, section 93 of the Constitution Act, 1867, which guarantees religious education rights, suggests an institutionalized (and constitutionalized) accommodation of majority religions.[7] For example, the Preamble to the Charter refers explicitly to the "supremacy of God," alongside the rule of law. While I have argued elsewhere that this reference to the "supremacy of God" does not necessarily imply the predominance of particular religious denomination,[8] it is certainly widely cited as a statement of fidelity to Judeo-Christian ideals.

The religious references in the Canadian Constitution have led some to assert that Canada has a constitutional guarantee of free exercise of religion, without a corresponding guarantee against establishment.[9] Notwithstanding the absence of an express provision, however, the Canadian Supreme Court has interpreted the freedom of religion in Canada under the Charter to include both the freedom to express religious belief *and* the freedom from having religious observance imposed through state action.[10]

The freedom of religion has been the subject of relatively frequent litigation in the Supreme Court of Canada. In *Syndicat Northcrest v. Amselem*,[11] the Supreme Court held that, in order to establish that his or her freedom of religion has been infringed, a claimant must demonstrate (1) that he or she sincerely believes in a practice or belief that has a nexus with religion, and (2) that the impugned conduct of the state interferes, in a manner that is non-trivial or not insubstantial, with his or her ability to act in accordance with that practice or belief.

To be protected under the Charter, the religious belief must be asserted in good faith and must not be "fictitious, capricious or an artifice"[12] As the Court explained in *Amselem*, freedom of religion consists:

---

7. For discussion, see RELIGION AND PUBLIC LIFE IN CANADA: HISTORICAL AND COMPARATIVE PERSPECTIVES (Marguerite Van Die ed., 2001).

8. Lorne Sossin, *The "Supremacy of God", Human Dignity and the* Charter of Rights and Freedoms, 52 U. NEW BRUNSWICK L.J. 227 (2003); see also Jonathon W. Penney & Robert Danay, *The Embarrassing Preamble? Understanding the "Supremacy of God" and the Charter*, 39 U.B.C. L. REV. 287 (2006).

9. Zeitlin, *supra* note 5.

10. In The Queen v. Big M Drug Mart Ltd., [1984] 2 S.C.R. 145 (Can.), the Canadian Supreme Court agreed, interpreting section 2(a) of the *Charter* to include the notion of the centrality of individual conscience and the inappropriateness of governmental intervention to compel or to constrain its manifestation.

11. [2004] 2 S.C.R. 551 (Can.).

12. *Id.* ¶ 52.

of the freedom to undertake practices and harbour beliefs, having a nexus with religion, in which an individual demonstrates he or she sincerely believes or is sincerely undertaking in order to connect with the divine or as a function of his or her spiritual faith, irrespective of whether a particular practice or belief is required by official religious dogma or is in conformity with the position of religious officials.[13]

So, for example, if a Sikh public servant argues that religious freedom should entitle him to wear a kirpan (ceremonial dagger) to the workplace, he must prove that the kirpan is central to observing Sikh traditions and that it is necessary that the kirpan be worn in the particular way adopted by the employee. As the Court observed in *Multani*, a case dealing with the right of a student to wear a kirpan in a school, the threshold to establish a breach of the freedom of religion under the Charter is a low one: "In order to demonstrate an infringement of his freedom of religion, Gurbaj Singh does not have to establish that the kirpan is not a weapon. He need only show that his personal and subjective belief in the religious significance of the kirpan is sincere."[14]

The constitutional regulation of religion in the workplace involves not simply interpreting the scope of the freedom of religion and conscience under section 2(a) and the equality guarantee under section 15(1) of the Charter but also the interaction between those sections and the "reasonable limits" saving provision under section 1, as noted above. Given the broad reading the Court has given to the freedom of religion under the Charter, the important balancing work of the Court takes place under section 1 of the Charter.

For example, in *B. (R.) v. Children's Aid Society of Metropolitan Toronto*,[15] the claimants, who were Jehovah's Witnesses, contested an order that authorized the administration of a blood transfusion to their daughter. While acknowledging that freedom of religion could be limited in the best interests of the child, La Forest J., writing for the majority of the Court, stated the following:

This Court has consistently refrained from formulating internal limits to the scope of freedom of religion in cases where the constitutionality of a legislative scheme was raised; it rather opted to balance the competing rights under s. 1 of the *Charter* . . .

In my view, it appears sounder to leave to the state the burden of justifying the restrictions it has chosen. Any ambiguity or hesitation should be resolved in favour of individual rights. Not only is this consistent with the broad and liberal interpretation of rights favoured by

13. *Id.* ¶ 46 (emphasis in original).
14. Multani v. Commission scolaire Marguerite-Bourgeoys, [2006] 1 S.C.R. 256 ¶ 37 (Can.).
15. [1995] 1 S.C.R. 315 (Can.).

this Court, but s. 1 is a much more flexible tool with which to balance competing rights than s. 2(*a*).[16]

The Court has developed a proportionality framework for its section 1 analysis. This framework consists of two parts. The onus is on the person challenging state action to prove that, on a balance of probabilities, the infringement is reasonable and can be demonstrably justified in a free and democratic society. To this end, two requirements must be met. First, the legislative objective being pursued must be sufficiently important to warrant limiting a constitutional right. Next, the means chosen by the state authority must be proportional to the objective in question, including that the means be rationally connected to the objective, that the right in question be infringed no more than necessary, and that the effects are not disproportionate.[17]

The heart of the section 1 proportionality analysis is the requirement that the law or state activity infringe the right of the claimant no more than necessary. The Supreme Court has referred to this standard, at least in the context of justifying an infringement of the freedom of religion, as one of reasonable accommodation to the point of undue hardship.[18] In other words, to impair the freedom of religion no more than necessary amounts to a requirement on the state to accommodate religious differences to the point of undue hardship. To return to the example of the kirpan, it would be difficult to say that an outright ban on kirpans could meet the burden of demonstrating that an employee had been provided with a reasonable accommodation. However, where the workplace setting involves some legitimate safety issues (say, in the context of an airport where all weapons are banned), accommodating a traveler who wishes to wear a ceremonial dagger may well constitute an undue hardship. In such circumstances, the Court would look to see if a reasonable accommodation was possible, and if so, whether it was pursued. For example, could the employee be asked to wear a kirpan made out of fabric or plastic, rather than metal, so that it would not pose a safety risk, or could the employee perform his duties outside secure areas of the airport where the risk would be reduced.

As discussed below, the Court has adopted as part of its section 1 Charter analysis a framework first developed in the context of statutory human rights protections against discrimination on the basis of religion in the workplace.

16. *Id.* ¶¶ 109–10.

17. *See* R. v. Oakes, [1986] 1 S.C.R. 103 (Can.).

18. *See* J. Woehrling, *L'obligation d'accommodement raisonnable et l'adaptation de la société à la diversité religieuse*,, 43 MCGILL L.J. 325 (1998); see also *Multani*, *supra* note 14, ¶ 53.

B. Human Rights Law

In addition to the Constitutional regime discussed above, human rights statutes have been enacted at the federal, provincial, and territorial jurisdictions. These statutes protect human rights, including freedom from discrimination in the workplace on grounds of religious identity or expression. While the Charter applies solely to state action, these human rights statutes protect against discrimination in both public and private settings, including the workplace. These human rights statutes also provide for specialized administrative mechanisms for investigating and prosecuting cases of discrimination (human rights commissions) and for adjudicating complaints of discrimination (human rights tribunals, etc).

In terms of how the protection against discrimination is framed, each human rights statute may define the scope of protection differently, but the Ontario Human Rights Code provides a representative example:

> Employment
>
> 5. (1) Every person has a right to equal treatment with respect to employment without discrimination because of race, ancestry, place of origin, colour, ethnic origin, citizenship, creed, sex, sexual orientation, age, record of offences, marital status, family status or disability.
>
> Harassment in employment
>
> (2) Every person who is an employee has a right to freedom from harassment in the workplace by the employer or agent of the employer or by another employee because of race, ancestry, place of origin, colour, ethnic origin, citizenship, creed, age, record of offences, marital status, family status or disability.
>
> Vocational associations
>
> 6. Every person has a right to equal treatment with respect to membership in any trade union, trade or occupational association or self-governing profession without discrimination because of race, ancestry, place of origin, colour, ethnic origin, citizenship, creed, sex, sexual orientation, age, marital status, family status or disability.[19]

This provision is qualified by the following general provision dealing with discrimination:

> Constructive discrimination
>
> 11. (1) A right of a person under Part I is infringed where a requirement, qualification or factor exists that is not discrimination on a prohibited ground but that results in the exclusion, restriction or preference of a group of persons who are identified by a prohibited ground of discrimination and of whom the person is a member, except where,

19. R.S.O. ch. H.19 (1990).

(a) the requirement, qualification or factor is reasonable and bona fide in the circumstances; or

(b) it is declared in this Act, other than in section 17, that to discriminate because of such ground is not an infringement of a right.

Idem

(2) *The Commission, the Tribunal or a court shall not find that a requirement, qualification or factor is reasonable and bona fide in the circumstances unless it is satisfied that the needs of the group of which the person is a member cannot be accommodated without undue hardship on the person responsible for accommodating those needs, considering the cost, outside sources of funding, if any, and health and safety requirements, if any.*[20] (Emphasis added.)

The effect of these human rights provisions is to establish a duty to accommodate on employers, which means taking steps to eliminate disadvantages to employees (and prospective employees) resulting from a rule, practice, or barrier that has an adverse impact on an individual or group protected under the statute. These accommodations will be required unless and to the extent they give rise to "undue hardship" on the point of the employer.

The duty to accommodate in the workplace in contexts of religious belief has arisen in at least three distinct settings: Sabbath observance, dress codes, and religious observance during working hours. These are each discussed below.

1. Sabbath Observance

One setting of frequent human rights litigation in workplace settings is where an employee wishes to observe a holiday or Sabbath of their religion on a day that the employer otherwise would expect the person to be at work.[21] Variations on this setting will be where employees require certain break times for prayer or have flexible scheduling needs to accommodate religious practice or observance.[22] Another setting is where a workplace dress code conflicts with religious dress or custom.[23] Finally, decorations in an office or other conditions of work may conflict with religious practice or religious values.[24]

20. *Id.*

21. *See O'Malley*, discussed below.

22. *See Dairy Pool*, discussed below.

23. *See Bhinder*, discussed below.

24. In Jones v. C.H.E. Pharmacy Inc. et al., [2001] B.C.H.R.T. 1 (Can.), for example, the practice of requiring employees to participate in hanging Christmas decorations was held to be discriminatory where an employee belonged to the Jehovah's Witness community. A human rights tribunal found that the employee was constructively dismissed for refusing to participate in the seasonal practice.

The wide variety of circumstances in which freedom of religion claims have been asserted in the employment context in Canada has been well documented. Conflicts have arisen when religious employees request days off to observe their Sabbaths, when they wear religious headgear or other apparel, or when they request permission to attend religious assemblies. Additional cases concern employment rules governing facial hair and leaves of absence. Freedom of religion cases in the employment context have reached the Canadian Supreme Court in three significant cases: *Ontario Human Rights Commission v. Simpsons-Sears Ltd. (O'Malley)*;[25] *Bhinder v. Canadian National Railway Co. (Bhinder)*;[26] and *Alberta Human Rights Commission v. Central Alberta Dairy Pool (Dairy Pool)*.[27]

O'Malley, decided in 1985, involved a plaintiff who became a member of the Seventh-Day Adventist Church during her employment with a department store. Her religion required her to miss work on Friday evenings and Saturdays in order to observe her Sabbath. O'Malley alleged discrimination when her employer refused to accommodate these needs. The Canadian Supreme Court found the employer guilty of violating the Ontario Human Rights Code, which prohibits discrimination against employees with regard to any term or condition of employment, because of "creed." In reviewing the Ontario Human Rights Code, the Court noted that legislation of this type is of a special nature, not quite constitutional but certainly more than the ordinary—and it is for the courts to seek out its purpose and give it effect. Writing for a unanimous Court, Justice McIntyre held that intent is not a necessary prerequisite to establish a violation of the Ontario Human Rights Code; absent undue hardship, the employer has a duty to accommodate observant employees and bears the burden of showing that undue hardship will result by accommodating the employee.

2. Dress Codes

A second, frequent setting for human rights conflict has been where an employer has a dress code or uniform that conflicts with an employee's religious observance. For example, *Bhinder*, handed down on the same day as *O'Malley*, involved a Sikh maintenance electrician employed by Canadian National Railways (CN). During Bhinder's employment, CN initiated a policy requiring employees to wear hard hats, a rule directly contrary to the Sikh religious policy mandating the wearing of turbans. Bhinder's employment ended when he refused to wear the hard hat, and he subsequently filed a complaint against CN alleging a violation of the

25. [1985] 2 S.C.R. 536 (Can.).
26. [1985] 2 S.C.R. 561 (Can.).
27. [1990] 2 S.C.R. 489 (Can.).

Canadian Human Rights Act. The Federal Court of Appeal reversed a ruling in favor of Bhinder by a human rights tribunal on the basis that CN's policy constituted a "bona fide occupational requirement" (BFOR) and thus complied with the Canadian Human Rights Act.

In a 5-2 decision—and over a strong dissent by Chief Justice Dickson—the Supreme Court affirmed. The Court recognized that the risk borne by Bhinder by wearing a turban instead of a hard hat was only increased by a small amount. Consequently, providing an exception to Bhinder would be unlikely to impose a hardship on CN. Again writing for the majority, Justice McIntyre held that the Canadian Human Rights Act, unlike the Ontario Human Rights Code, does not require an employer to accommodate a religious employee when the employee's religious practice conflicts with a BFOR. The majority held that, in considering the validity of a BFOR, courts are required to examine the employer's reasons for adopting the work rule. If the employer did so for genuine business reasons, with no malicious intent, the employer is not guilty of discrimination. According to the majority, the BFOR could not be considered on an individual basis. The words of the statute speak of an "occupational requirement." This must refer to a requirement for the occupation, not a requirement limited to an individual. It is, by its nature, not susceptible to individual application. As one commentator has noted, the effect of the *Bhinder* decision was that a law with a BFOR allowance would permit employers to prevail over the religious requirements of an individual employee.

An illustration of how the approach in *Bhinder* has had ripple effects throughout workplaces in Canada is provided by the case study of the Royal Canadian Mounted Police (RCMP).[28] In 1987, the RCMP adopted affirmative action policies within the force to remove barriers to minority groups, including religious and visible minorities. In particular, the RCMP clarified that Sikh Muslims could wear beards and turbans instead of the traditional felt hat required of RCMP officers. However, in situations where the officer is performing duties that require special headdress or safety equipment, the officer would have to remove the turban. The RCMP, in part, was simply reacting to the evolving jurisprudence from Canadian courts interpreting religious accommodation requirements in the workplace. Canadian courts have required a "beard exemption" policy to extend equally to religious and non-religious employees.

28. For a more detailed consideration of this setting, see L. Grunloh, *Religious Accommodations for Police Officers: A Comparative Analysis of Religious Accommodation Law in the United States, Canada and the United Kingdom*, 16 IND. INT'L & COMP. L. REV. 183 (2005).

The Waterloo Regional Police Services (WRPS) implemented a policy allowing officers to only wear beards for religious, medical, or investigative purposes.[29] Once the beard policy was challenged, the court found it to be an irrational rule because WRPS lacked a legitimate reason for such a broad prohibition. The court found that a beard policy taking into account health and safety or a policy merely regulating appearance and maintenance of a beard would be legitimate. Therefore, the accommodation of appearances cannot unduly affect other police officers in the force.

The RCMP created an application for Sikhs that were exempted from the traditional uniform policy. It required them to agree to the following language: "Notwithstanding that I may be granted the exemption requested . . . I hereby undertake to perform all duties assigned to me by the RCMP and to wear any special headdress or safety equipment that is necessary for bona fide operational reasons or is required by law."[30] As Lynn Grunloh has observed of this requirement, "Therefore, although religious employees are allowed exemptions for appearance when appearance is not a BFOQ, they appear to be mostly excluded from accommodations regarding work schedules and job reassignment by signing the application form."[31] Once again, there is an ambivalence detectable in such compromises. Employers may be willing to accommodate and remove barriers, but only to a point, and this point falls far short of genuine pluralism.

It is also worth emphasizing that the RCMP's acceptance of religious minorities was met with a fair degree of societal resistance. In *Grant v. Canada,*[32] concerned members of society brought suit against the RCMP challenging the enacted policy of allowing turbans and beards. The plaintiffs claimed pride and attachment in the traditional appearance of the RCMP, and that the religious neutrality of the uniform, in particular, had significant value to society generally and to them specifically. The court held that there was no evidence that officers wearing turbans deprived any person of liberty or security as a matter of Constitutional law, and furthermore, the plaintiffs assertion that a "visible manifestation of a Sikh officer's religious faith, as part of his uniform, will create a reasonable apprehension of bias"[33] was not based upon any concrete evidence.

29. *Id.* at 204.
30. *Id.* at 205.
31. *Id.* at 205.
32. [1995] 1 F.C. 598 (T.D.), appeal dismissed at [1995] 125 D.L.R. (4th) 556 (F.C.A.).
33. *Id.* ¶ 93.

3. Religious Observance during Working Hours

The third area of human rights scrutiny in the context of religion in the workplace is where religious holidays occur during working hours. The most important dispute in this area was the *Dairy Pool* case.

Dairy Pool involved Jim Christie ("Christie"), an observer of the Worldwide Church of God. Christie's religion required him to refrain from working from Friday evening until Saturday evening and on ten religious holidays. His employer, the Central Alberta Dairy Pool, denied Christie's request to be excused from work on a religious holiday which fell on a Monday, since that day of the week was particularly busy. The Dairy Pool subsequently fired Christie. Pursuant to Alberta's Individual's Rights Protection Act, Christie brought a discrimination complaint. His claim was initially upheld by an Alberta Board of Inquiry, but was later denied on appeal by both the Alberta Court of Queen's Bench and the Alberta Court of Appeal on the basis of the Supreme Court's decision in *Bhinder*.

On appeal, however, the Canadian Supreme Court reversed its decision in *Bhinder*, concluding that the Court should have considered whether the employer could have accommodated the individual religious employee without experiencing undue hardship.[34] The Court held that, once again, even under jurisdictions permitting a bona fide occupational qualification (BFOQ) exception, an employer has a duty to accommodate individual religious employees unless such accommodation would impose an undue hardship on the employer.

Thus, in the wake of the *Dairy Pool* approach, the duty to accommodate in Canadian human rights jurisprudence appears to hover somewhere between the narrative of pluralism and the narrative of exceptionalism. As discussed below, this standard has also come to permeate the adjudication of disputes between employers and employees before labor boards and arbitrators.

C. Labor and Employment Law

In addition to the Constitutional protection of freedom of religion and the protection contained within provincial human rights statutes against discrimination on religious grounds, a third important legal regime governing religion in the workplace is labor and employment law. Like human rights law, labor and employment law differs in the various provinces and territories (in addition to a federal labor scheme for employees in national enterprises), but these various statutes share a

---

34. *See supra* note 26.

number of common features. Employment statutes set out minimum standards that all workplaces must met. Labor legislation governs rights of collective bargaining, establishing unions, grievance procedures, and the forum in which disputes between employers and employees will be resolved—usually an arm's length labor board.

Protections relevant to religion in the workplace may arise expressly in collective agreements or contracts of employment or may be incorporated by reference, such as where a collective agreement incorporates provisions of the human rights code.[35]

An example of how labor law interacts with issues of religion in the workplace in Canada is the *Commission scolaire régionale de Chambly v. Bergevin* case.[36] The case involved three Jewish teachers employed by the a Quebec School Board, who took a day off to celebrate Yom Kippur. The School Board had granted them leave of absence but without pay and the teachers' union brought a grievance seeking reimbursement for the day's pay. The school calendar, which is part of the collective agreement, fixed the teachers' work schedule. The majority of the arbitration board found that the school calendar requiring Jewish teachers to work on Yom Kippur had the effect of being discriminatory and that the School Board had failed to take reasonable steps to accommodate the Jewish teachers in the observance of their religious holy day. The case reached the Supreme Court of Canada, which unanimously upheld the arbitration board's interpretation of the collective agreement.

One preliminary issue for the Court in *Bergevin* is that of deference to the arbitration board. The provincial labor statutes, including the Quebec Labour Code at issue in *Bergevin*, contain privative clauses that attempt to insulate the determinations of labor boards and arbitrators from judicial review. As a result, Courts generally will show deference to those determinations, and only interfere where they find the board or arbitration decision "unreasonable"; this stands in contrast to the Court's approach to human rights tribunals, which is to review their decisions on a standard of correctness.[37] The result is that where religion in the workplace issues arise as human rights issues interpreting a human rights statute, courts are more likely to intervene than where those same issues arise as interpretations of a collective agreement by a labor board or arbitration panel.

In *Bergevin*, beyond affirming deference to the arbitration board's interpretation of the collective agreement, the Supreme Court confirmed that the school calendar, although neutral on its face, had the effect of

35. For discussion, see Fay Faraday, *The Expanding Scope of Labour Arbitration: Mainstreaming Human Rights Values and Remedies*, 12 CAN. LAB. & EMP. L.J. 355 (2006).

36. Commission scolaire régionale de Chambly v. Bergevin, [1994] 2 S.C.R. 525 (Can.).

37. Canada (Attorney General) v. Mossop, [1993] 1 S.C.R. 554 (Can.).

adversely discriminating against Jewish teachers. As a result of their religious beliefs, they must take a day off work and, in the absence of some accommodation by their employer, must lose a day's pay to observe their holy day while the majority of their colleagues have their religious holy days recognized as holidays from work. It follows that the effect of the calendar is to discriminate against members of an identifiable group because of their religious beliefs and that the employer must take reasonable steps to accommodate the individual or group of employees adversely affected. The Court confirmed that a *de minimis* test should not apply to the evaluation of either the existence or the extent of the duty to accommodate.

Adopting the same approach to reasonable accommodation discussed above, the Court held that, in permitting the Jewish teachers to take a day off work without pay in order to celebrate Yom Kippur, the School Board did not, however, meet the burden resting upon it to demonstrate that it took reasonable steps to accommodate these teachers, short of undue hardship. The Court concluded that the provisions of the collective agreement could reasonably be interpreted to provide for such an accommodation. The agreement specifically provided for the payment of teachers who were absent for what the parties considered to be a good or valid reason and for a number of days for a variety of reasons. On a reasonable, indeed a correct, interpretation of the collective agreement, the observance of a holy day by teachers belonging to the Jewish faith should constitute a "good reason" for their absence and should qualify them for payment of a day's wages. Finally, by incorporating the provisions of the Quebec Charter of Human Rights and Freedoms, the collective agreement provided further support for this position by stressing that principles of equality and freedom from religious discrimination would guide the parties in their relations. Thus, while issues of religion in the workplace may arise as a matter of constitutional law, human rights law, or labor law, the approach of "reasonable accommodation" provides a unifying thread for the legal regulation of religion in the workplace.

Reasonable accommodation reflects the ambivalence of the Canadian legal system toward religious difference, especially in employment settings. This dynamic is discussed further in relation to the social and political debate surrounding reasonable accommodation in Canada below.

II. Reconciling Pluralism and Exceptionalism in the Workplace

The issue of religious accommodation in the workplace, and the place of multiculturalism in a constitutional democracy such as Canada's, has spawned a vibrant and voluminous literature.[38] Canada and Canadian scholars (such as Charles Taylor,[39] Will Kymlicka,[40] and James Tully,[41] among others) have been at the forefront of these diversity/difference debates, in part because Canada was founded on a compromise federation to respect cultural autonomy, and in part because Canada today is an immigrant society with an increasingly high concentration of religious and visible minorities.

In Toronto, Canada's largest city, for example, over 2.3 million residents (of a total population of just over five million) were born outside Canada, with over a million of those immigrants coming from Asia and the Middle East.[42] For obvious reasons, disputes involving accommodation and difference have come to dominate constitutional jurisprudence and political debate in Canada.[43]

Since at least the late 1960s, it has been generally uncontested in Canada that accommodation of minority cultures is desirable (as opposed to policies of assimilation), and further that the state must actively pursue accommodation policies and not simply allow majority communities to marginalize minority communities in the marketplace for social goods (education, employment, etc.).

In passing the Canadian Multiculturalism Act,[44] Canada formally chose to recognize cultural difference and a model of differentiated citizenship. That *Act* provides:

> **3.** (1) It is hereby declared to be the policy of the Government of Canada to
>
> (*a*) recognize and promote the understanding that multiculturalism reflects the cultural and racial diversity of Canadian society and acknowledges the freedom of all members of Canadian society to preserve, enhance and share their cultural heritage;

---

38. Some of the more influential works include: JANICE GROSS STEIN ET AL., UNEASY PARTNERS: MULTICULTURALISM AND RIGHTS IN CANADA (2007); MULTICULTURAL QUESTIONS (Christian Joppke & Steven Lukes eds., 1999); JOSEPH H. CARENS, CULTURE, CITIZENSHIP, AND COMMUNITY: A CONTEXTUAL EXPLORATION OF JUSTICE AS EVENHANDEDNESS (2000); BHIKHU C. PAREKH, RETHINKING MULTICULTURALISM: CULTURAL DIVERSITY AND POLITICAL THEORY (2000); AYELET SHACHAR, MULTICULTURAL JURISDICTIONS: CULTURAL DIFFERENCES AND WOMEN'S RIGHTS (2001).

39. Charles Taylor, *The Politics of Recognition*, *in* MULTICULTURALISM AND THE POLITICS OF RECOGNITION (Amy Gutman ed., 1992).

40. CITIZENSHIP IN DIVERSE SOCIETIES (Will Kymlicka & Wayne Norman eds., 2000).

41. JAMES TULLY, STRANGE MULTIPLICITY: CONSTITUTIONALISM IN AN AGE OF DIVERSITY (1995).

42. *See* Statistics Canada, http://www40.statcan.ca/l01/cst01/demo35c.htm (last visited Apr. 10, 2008).

43. *See* C. Sheppard, *Constitutional Recognition of Diversity in Canada*, 30 VT. L. REV. 463 (2006).

44. R.S.C. C.24 (1985).

(*b*) recognize and promote the understanding that multiculturalism is a fundamental characteristic of the Canadian heritage and identity and that it provides an invaluable resource in the shaping of Canada's future;

(*c*) promote the full and equitable participation of individuals and communities of all origins in the continuing evolution and shaping of all aspects of Canadian society and assist them in the elimination of any barrier to that participation;

(*d*) recognize the existence of communities whose members share a common origin and their historic contribution to Canadian society, and enhance their development;

(*e*) ensure that all individuals receive equal treatment and equal protection under the law, while respecting and valuing their diversity;

(*f*) encourage and assist the social, cultural, economic and political institutions of Canada to be both respectful and inclusive of Canada's multicultural character;

(*g*) promote the understanding and creativity that arise from the interaction between individuals and communities of different origins;

(*h*) foster the recognition and appreciation of the diverse cultures of Canadian society and promote the reflection and the evolving expressions of those cultures;

(*i*) preserve and enhance the use of languages other than English and French, while strengthening the status and use of the official languages of Canada; and

(*j*) advance multiculturalism throughout Canada in harmony with the national commitment to the official languages of Canada.

Canada's embrace of multiculturalism and the ideal of a national "mosaic" in contrast to the American "melting pot," however, are not the only dynamics influencing issues of religion in the workplace.

In Quebec, the embrace of multiculturalism is complicated and exacerbated by linguistic politics and the province's role in protection Francophone culture and society. The Taylor-Bouchard Commission was established by the Quebec Government in 2007 following a number of high-profile conflicts to investigate the Quebec experience with accommodating religious, cultural, ethnic and racial minorities.

A number of high profile incidents of religious tension in 2007, mostly arising in Quebec, prompted both the panel and intense public interest in the topic in Canada more generally.[45] These incidents included pressure by the Federal Government on Elections Canada, the independent regulator of elections, to require Muslim women to remove their veil for identification

45. These events are chronicled in the final report of the Taylor-Bouchard Commission, *Building the Future: A Time for Reconciliation*, *at* http://www.accommodements.qc.ca/documentation/rapports/rapport-final-integral-en.pdf, at 53–60.

purposes in order to vote,[46] a girl removed from a soccer team for refusing to remove her hijab;[47] the owner of a sugar shack in Quebec received threats of violence for removing pork from his pea soup in an attempt to attract Muslim customers;[48] the Quebec's Human Rights Commission awarded a man $10,000 after he was asked to leave a kosher dining hall at Montreal's Jewish General Hospital because he had been eating a lunch of spaghetti with non-kosher sauce;[49] and a downtown Montreal YMCA being asked to cover its windows by an orthodox Jewish school across the street so that students at the school would not see women exercising.[50]

Hearings were held across the province of Quebec in the Fall of 2007 exploring topics of Islamophobia, Anti-Semitism, and the limits of reasonable accommodation for religious minorities in a secular society. The Panel issued its final Report in May of 2008.[51] Most controversial among its findings was the Commission's recommendation (following the French Republican approach) that judges, police officers, and prison guards be prohibited from wearing religious symbols, although, permitting other employees of public systems, such as teachers in public schools, to wear such symbols.[52]

Another catalyst for the intense scrutiny of religious accommodation was the decision by the Ontario Government in 2005 not to allow Courts to recognize the decisions of a Shari'a tribunal in family law matters, after an outcry of protest, particularly from women's groups to the Government's initial acquiescence to the tribunal's decisions being recognized.

The notion of a public backlash against policies of promoting pluralism and accommodation in Canada is not without foundation, and is not isolated to formal state recognition of religious law, as in the Ontario Shari'a tribunal case.

---

46. *See Harper Slams Elections Canada Ruling on Veils*, http://www.cbc.ca/canada/story/2007/09/09/harper-veil.html.

47. *See Muslim Girl Ejected from Tournament for Wearing Hijab*, *at* http://www.cbc.ca/news/yourview/2007/02/muslim_girl_ejected_from_tourn.html.

48. Philip Authier, *Boisclair Talks Tough on Pea Soup*, MONTREAL GAZETTE, Mar. 20, 2007, *available at* http://www2.canada.com/montrealgazette/features/quebecvotes2007/story.html?id=c35d1e53-4b41-4c01-bdfe-7ce163b72f49&k=19677.

49. Martin Patriquan, *Canada's Renown for Tolerance is Breaking Down*, MACLEANS MAGAZINE Oct. 22, 2007, *available at* http://www.thecanadianencyclopedia.com/index.cfm?PgNm=TCE&Params=M1ARTM0013162.

50. See the discussion of these events Linda Deibel, *Uneasy Mosiac: When Rights Collide with Freedoms*, TORONTO STAR, May 28, 2007, *available at* http://www.thestar.com/News/article/218355 (last visited Apr. 15, 2008).

51. The Commission's Report, *Building the Future: A Time for Reconciliation*, and its thirty-seven recommendations, are available at http://www.accommodements.qc.ca. These recommendations include that employers adopt policies of paid leave for employees to observe religious holidays and practices, and that government owned corporations take a leadership role in designing and implementing such policies (at p. 267).

52. *Id.*

The results of a poll conducted for the Institute for Research on Public Policy in the Fall of 2007 reflect the rising tensions in Canada.[53] When asked if they agreed with the following statement—"it is reasonable to accommodate religious and cultural minorities"—a mere 18% said yes. Over 50% thought immigrants should "adapt fully to culture in Canada." When it came to accommodating religious and cultural minorities in public places, such as schools, hospitals, and government buildings, 37% thought there should be no accommodation at all, with smaller portions accepting some accommodation but only 6% advocating full accommodation.

The polling results were even more striking for accommodation in the workplace, with 45% saying there should be none, and just 4% agreeing with full accommodation. The poll indicated that by significant majorities in Canada as a whole, and by overwhelming majorities in Quebec, the emphasis in the public discourse is on limiting accommodation, not extending it.

While some regional disparities were evident (with those areas of the country with the smallest multicultural populations supporting accommodation in the highest numbers), education, income, and age appear better predictors of support for accommodation. Those with less education, as well as older Canadians, tended to be less accommodating. For example, only 17% of Canadians aged 55 to 64 thought it was reasonable to accommodate, compared with 24% of those aged 25 to 34. And as for education, just 24% of those with a university education saw accommodation as reasonable as against 9.6% of those with just a high-school education. Another countrywide survey suggested Canadians believe conflict between Christians and Muslims will eventually overshadow the country's long-standing quarrel between the English and French.[54]

Yet, as Michael Adams work shows, there are also survey data showing that the Canadian approach to promoting pluralism has been successful, especially when compared with the violent encounters witnessed in recent years in France and elsewhere in Europe. Adams included in his study survey information from Canada's fast-growing Muslim population. While he noted that people generally express two fears about Muslims in Canada: they are unwilling to integrate into secular society and they are sympathetic to terrorism, Adams found Canadian Muslims to express views similar to other immigrant groups in Canada (Canada's Muslims are 90% foreign-born): 9 in 10 are proud to be Canadian, 8 in 10 think the country is headed in the right direction and reasons cited for national pride are the

53. See the discussion of these polling results in Patriquin, *supra* note 49.

54. *Id.*

same as in the population at large: freedom and democracy, peacefulness, and the friendliness they perceive among their fellow Canadians (although 3 in 10 Canadian Muslims say they have experienced discrimination). Muslim Canadians condemn acts of global terrorism in similar numbers to the rest of Canadian society.[55]

Recognition of Canada's aboriginal community as a founding people (or First Nations) is another dynamic that characterizes Canadian legal and political institutions. The aboriginal community is not viewed as simply a religious, cultural, or linguistic minority to be accommodated but as a people whose relationship with Canada must be reconciled. Some aboriginal communities entered into treaties with Canada governing land use and rights, while others were simply dispossessed.

Religious accommodation also cannot be disentangled from other social, economic, and political realities. Socioeconomic stratification in Canadian society, regionalism, the urban/rural divide, the impact of globalization, and the war on terror, all shape in different ways the Canadian response to issues of religious tensions in the workplace.

CONCLUSION

The Canadian approach, discussed above, of reasonable accommodation as a burden owed by employers to employees who express their religious beliefs or observances in workplace settings, is based on two premises.

The first premise is that Canada, as a matter of state policy, is a secular society. This is a rejection of the idea to true pluralism. As Premier Dalton McGuinty asserted when announcing that Ontario would abandon the recognition of Shari'a Tribunal decisions in family law, "There will be no Shariah law in Ontario. There will be no religious arbitration in Ontario. There will be one law for all Ontarians."[56]

The second premise is based on mutual recognition and the promotion of multiculturalism. The Canadian government and employers have embraced the view that they must accommodate a variety of religious expression, so long as this embrace is contingent, limited both by the first premise (that Canada as a matter of state policy is secular), and by the notion of "undue hardship," which allows employers to bracket accommodation within a set of commercial and cultural bounds.

55. *See* ADAMS, *supra* note 4; Adams, *supra* note 4.

56. *See McGuinty Rules out Use of Sharia Law in Ontario*, http://www.ctv.ca/servlet/ArticleNews/story/CTVNews/1126472943217_26/?hub=TopStories (last visited Apr. 15, 2008).

The challenge for the future will be how to reconcile these competing narratives. To this end, Canadian labor boards, human rights commissions and tribunals, and the courts have advanced the discourse of reasonable accommodation as a reconciliatory approach. For example, as noted above, in *Multani v. Commission scolaire Marguerite-Bourgeoys*,[57] the Supreme Court found that a Sikh boy should be permitted to wear a ceremonial kirpan to school, so long as it was sewn into his clothes in a manner that would not allow him to access it. The Court was quick to point out, however, that such accommodation might not also be permitted if that same boy were flying in an airplane or attempting to enter the courtroom. As Abella J. notes in her concurring judgment in *Multani*, "The process required by the duty of reasonable accommodation takes into account the specific details of the circumstances of the parties and allows for dialogue between them. This dialogue enables them to reconcile their positions and find common ground tailored to their own needs."[58]

Ultimately, a deeper form of intercultural engagement may be needed before this project of reconciliation can be realized—an approach based on building bridges between cultural communities rather than the premise of multiculturalism, which is to recognize and provide rights to cultural communities within their boundaries.[59] The goal of this project, in my view, should be to move beyond the narrative of the "other" that permeates the discourse of multiculturalism, and at the same time to promote the dignity enhancing framework of protecting religious expression under the Charter, human rights, and labor/employment law.

While pluralism and exceptionalism may be mutually exclusive frameworks for governing the workplace, they have been pursued for the most part in an uneasy but stable balance in Canada. Reconciliation, in this sense, is a journey rather than a destination. Whether Canadians are prepared to undertake this journey together in the long run remains unclear. If there is one national trait that unifies Canada, however, it is the ability to sustain compromise, and if necessary, to live peaceably with contradiction.

57. Multani v. Commission scolaire Marguerite-Bourgeoys, [2006] 1 S.C.R. 256 (Can.).

58. *Id.* ¶ 133.

59. *See* STEIN ET AL., *supra* note 38, at 19.

Part IV
Religion and Family Law

[15]

STATE, LAW AND FAMILY

Mary Ann Glendon

> [W]hat did you want meddling with the like of us,
> when it's a long time we are going our own ways...?
> J. M. Synge, *The Tinker's Wedding*[1]

I. Marriage as a Social Institution

"Factual custom everywhere has begotten a feeling of oughtness", said Max Weber in discussing the transition from custom to law.[2] So it is that we in the late 20th century take State regulation of marriage and divorce for granted. But so it is also that, upon reflection, we may be led to wonder how it came about that custom, in a matter so basic as marriage, became what it is today. We know that, let us say, Cro-Magnon men and women did not go before a Registrar to be joined together, nor did they go before a judge to be separated. With the help of ethologists, anthropologists and sociologists we are gaining increased understanding of how different mating customs and rituals may have evolved in different cultures, and over the course of time in each. But coming back to Weber, we may still wonder how it is that, in the West, the innovations of *law*, ecclesiastical or secular, could themselves have become, to a great extent, our marriage customs. How, for instance, did marriage in the West become indissoluble in principle, or dissoluble only for serious cause? How did the Church and the State succeed in gaining social acceptance of rules that persons had to pass before an official in order to be married or unmarried? To what extent did they succeed?

The answers are to be sought first in a long story of struggles by and among various worldly institutions, kinship groups, property owners, the Christian Church (later churches), emperors, kings and nation states. The chief episodes of that story are recounted here in order to account for the state of the law as it stood on the eve of the current process of legal change that has been described in this work, and to bring out the significance of the present series of changes.

We cannot start the story at its very beginning, for the beginnings of actual regularity and usage in human conduct are shrouded in darkness. No one knows when the evolutionary shift from biological to cultural patterns of mating occurred. Nor, for that matter, does anyone yet know much about what is innate and what is cultural in man. We do know that it is useful to distinguish between marriage and the family, since the importance of marriage in various societies is quite variable, while the same cannot be said of the family.[3] In some societies marriage, as distinct from other sexual relationships, is said to be barely visible, and in some societies marriage is viewed as irrelevant to family formation.[4]

Concerning the Germanic and Roman antecedents of those modern systems which we have examined here, we do know something about how community or kinship group interest in who mated whom manifested itself and about the early forms of rank and status derived from marriage and birth. Marriage existed in the sense of being a definite social status. But the wedding, or marriage rite, itself seems to have been important only under special circumstances, in particular where property was exchanged. The two earliest forms of Roman marriage rites of which we know were a religious rite, used by the patrician class, and a symbolic purchase. Although there are traces of marriage initiated by capture in earliest Germanic laws, the usual form was a purchase marriage.[5] While purchase marriage certainly did not exclude the possibility of turning a profit on the occasion, Pollock and Maitland think its essential function among the Anglo-Saxons was the bargaining by the bride's kinfolk for her honorable treatment as a wife and widow. Among the early Germans, marriage was different from other sexual unions only in that the wife and children of the marriage enjoyed a more secure position in relation to the husband and his kinship group than other women with whom he cohabited and their offspring.[6] The distinction between "legitimate" marriage and other unions which though not disapproved are of lower status appears not only in primitive systems, but also in Roman law and in pre-Tridentine canon law, and in the civil law of France until the 16th century. Only the legitimate wife shared the social rank and status of her husband.

In the widespread custom of high status families to give away their daughters only on assurances of preferred status for the daughter and her children, Max Weber saw the origin of the earliest *legal* characteristics of the legitimate marriage: dowry, the agreement to support the wife and to pay her compensation upon abandonment, and the successoral position of her children.[7] From a sociological point of view, the significance of the legitimate marriage is that it enables the family to function as a status-conferring institution.[8] We shall return to this point after we consider how legitimacy, expressed in social norms, became, through a long and tortuous process, "legality", expressed in rules of positive law.

In cultures where marriage is simply the decision of the partners to live together and raise common children, and involves no exchange of property, it tends to be dissolved simply by desertion and separation.[9] But as marriage formation becomes more complex, the procedure for dissolving it does too. The emphasis on procedures for formation and dissolution seems to vary with the importance of rank and property. Where these are important, there is a need to clearly distinguish which sexual relationships will give rise to rights. The need to justify the dissolution of marriage and to furnish reasons to neutralize the objections of relatives appears.[10]

This was already beginning to be the case in the earliest periods of Roman and Germanic customary law of which we have knowledge. It is said that the early Germanic folk were relatively monogamous, although plurality of wives was permissible among them; and that for the first 500 years Rome had a tradition of marital stability, although marriages were dissoluble there. In the morally strict society of early Republican Rome, a man would incur disapproval if he repudiated his wife without some cause such as barrenness or infidelity.[11] Old Germanic law recognized marriage dissolution by agreement between the husband and the wife's relatives. The husband, and eventually the wife, could unilaterally end the marriage for certain causes.[12]

The first point to observe, if we wish to understand the process of juridification of marriage, is that in Roman times, and among the Germanic peoples by whom the Roman empire eventually was overrun, marriage was not regulated as such by norms of law but rather by social norms. A second significant point to keep in mind is that lack of *legal* regulation did not mean that marriage was unregulated. Nor, in Rome, did lack of legal regulation of marriage as such mean that the law was indifferent to marriage. The existence or not of a marriage was indirectly significant for the Roman law when it had to deal with problems involving membership of the "houses" of which the body politic was composed, with succession on death, or with allocation of responsibility for civil wrongs.[13] But in making these determinations, Roman law contented itself with referring to the mores and accepting as a marriage whatever was recognized by the mores as such. Roman law also imposed a kind of political taboo upon marriages between Romans and most non-citizens, between free persons and slaves and, at one time, between Senators or other upper-class men with women of lower rank.

But social norms governing marriage varied considerably in the long period of Roman history of which we have knowledge.[14] In early times, marriage among the leading class of patricians was initiated by a religious ceremony, *confarreatio*. Two other forms of marriage also existed: *coemptio*, initiated by a form which is thought by some to be a symbolic purchase; and *usus*, which began with no particular form but existed when a couple had lived as husband and wife for a year. The forms that existed for initiating marriage were, according to Corbett, "in great part legally indifferent" (except to a limited degree in *confarreatio*), in the sense that the validity of the marriage did not depend on their observance. Originally, it seems these three forms of marriage involved the wife coming under the legal control, *manus*, of her husband.

By late Republican times these three kinds of marriage became obsolete. They gave way to the so-called free marriage, marriage without *manus*, in which the man and woman married simply by starting life in common, provided they had *affectio maritalis*, that is, that they regarded each other as husband and wife. Free marriage had been recognized as early as the time of the earliest Roman code of laws, the XII Tables (451–450 B.C.). It became a common practice in the third and second centuries B.C., and was the customary mode of marriage in late Republican times. There was nothing but *affectio maritalis* to distinguish free marriage from any other type of sexual union. If this intention ceased, the marriage was at an end in principle. The free marriage was treated by the law as dissolved when the parties separated, or when one spouse left the marriage and notified the other of his or her intention to terminate the relationship. It may have been that originally only the husband could unilaterally terminate the marriage. But the parties were on an equal footing by the end of the third century B.C., and perhaps from the beginning. The use by both husband *and* wife of this power to terminate a marriage is said to have been common in the first century B.C., almost the only deterrent being rules governing the return of dowry. Thus, in Rome, marriage had become a formless transaction dissoluble at the will of either party, and remained so at the time of the first Christian Emperor, Constantine (285–337 A.D.).

Little that the Christian emperors did changed this situation. From Constantine until Justinian (c. 482–565 A.D.), the Christian emperors confined themselves to punishing unjustified repudiations. If a spouse repudiated the other without some good reason, he might have to give back the marriage portion or lose other property rights; or eventually, he could even be deported, confined within a monastery, or subjected to restrictions on remarriage. But these laws did permit repudiation for cause and did not affect divorce by mutual agreement. Thus, Professor Noonan seems correct in saying that the legislation of the Christian emperors assumes the dissolubility of marriage, with remarriage as the normal sequel to dissolution; and that, at least so long as the sanctions were only property-related, the law's concern was limited to the upper classes.[15] Noonan concludes that it was "...a good question...whether the prohibitions of divorce from Constantine to Anastasius had any teeth to them", if someone was able to pay the price or work out a settlement.[16]

Even the strongly religious Emperor Justinian at first did not disturb the effectiveness of marital dissolution by mutual agreement, declaring in 535 A.D. that "all that has been joined together by man can be separated by man".[17] Later, Justinian broke with Roman tradition and established penalties for mutual consent divorce as well as for unjustified repudiation.[18] According to Corbett, the reason Justinian sought to restrict this kind of divorce was that children had been using divorce or the threat of divorce to defraud parents of their contingent rights in dowries or to hasten the payment of dowries.[19] In any event, Justinian's law was neither well-received nor well-observed, and was repealed in 566 by Justinian's successor, Justin II, in one of his first acts after ascension to the throne.[20]

At the close of the Roman period, then, it can be said that the law took little notice of the social institution of marriage. Marriage itself was formless so far as the law was concerned; the idea of legal regulation of marriage formation or the conduct of married life was unknown; legal regulation of marriage dissolution had been attempted only to a very limited degree by the legislation of the Christian emperors which implicitly accepted the premise of the essential dissolubility of marriage.

Hence in Rome and among the Germanic peoples, marriage was not a legal institution. To find the answers to the questions how marriage became formal, indissoluble and subject to far-reaching state regulation, we must turn to another legal system which, at the time of Christian Roman legislation, was not a legal system at all but only an evolving body of doctrine: the system of Roman Catholic canon law.

II. The Rise of Ecclesiastical Jurisdiction over Marriage Formation and Dissolution

A. The Struggle for Jurisdiction

After the Roman Empire in the West broke down in the course of the 5th century A.D., the Christian Church not only remained intact but became stronger than ever. The new kingdoms had not yet developed those political organizations on the Roman pattern that were later to grow into the new pattern of feudalism. The Church was able to exercise great influence over, and was closely associated with the secular power of, the new Visigothic kings, and the later Merovingian and Carolingian dynasties.[21] Even so, the establishment of the doctrine of indissolubility of marriage and of ecclesiastical jurisdiction over matrimonial matters took centuries.

The Church's claim to exclusive jurisdiction over marital causes and the novel idea that marriage was indissoluble were both closely connected to the new Christian idea that marriage was a sacrament. But the sacramental nature of marriage and the ideal of indissolubility were not settled all at once as matters of firm doctrine. Both ideas had powerful proponents: St. Ambrose (c. 339–397) for indissolubility; and his convert, St. Augustine (354–430), for the sacrament. St. Augustine went on record for indissolubility too, by opposing "adulterous marriages" (remarriage by one who has put aside a spouse even for a grave reason such as adultery). But at the end of his life he returned to the problem dissatisfied. In his *Retractations*, he says "I think that I did not reach a perfect solution of this question."[22] He calls it a "very difficult question" (*difficillimam quaestionem*), and speaks of its "obscurities". All during the period of the development of Roman Law under the Christian emperors described in the preceding section, it has been said that "Christians in good faith could believe that marriage was dissoluble or indissoluble...".[23]

The greatest obstacle to the direct enforcement by the Church of the new Christian ideas about the ethics of sex and marriage arose from the fact that marriage was regarded everywhere in Europe in the first half of the Middle Ages as a personal and purely secular matter, almost entirely outside the scope of law. Conversion to Christianity in the Roman empire and in the lands inhabited by the Germanic tribes did not automatically result in immediate acceptance of Christian sex ethics: of the notions that marriage was strictly monogamous and that all sexual relations outside marriage were prohibited.[24] Nor did the Church insist on this. Marriage matters continued to be governed by social taboos including rules about marriage age, choice of partners, and legitimacy. Sometimes these social rules were grounded in custom and convention, sometimes in ancient pagan religious practices. The story of the rise of ecclesiastical jurisdiction over marriage is in large part one of compromise with, adaptation to and even incorporation of indigenous practices. In the early centuries the Church hardly tried to exercise jurisdiction in its own name.[25] Its mingling in these matters began slowly, as a matter of custom, as with the priestly blessing of marriages of the early Christians. Gradually it was recognized as a matter of right.

The idea of the indissolubility of marriage did not easily gain a foothold in the ancient world, where marriages were dissoluble, (without the intervention of any judge) by mutual consent or by unilateral repudiation, perhaps with payment of a penalty.[26] The indissolubility doctrine, as elaborated by the Church fathers, was based on several sayings of Jesus as reported in the Gospels. If his sayings were correctly interpreted, the doctrine was a novelty. Even within the Church, especially in ancient times, some held the opinion that the sayings of Jesus in the Gospels did not absolutely prohibit divorce, at least in the case of adultery.[27] As ecclesiastical doctrine became more or less fixed, the Church still had to compromise with the firmly established secular customs. The Anglo-Saxons, the Franks, the other Germanic tribes and the Romans, all had permitted divorce. For centuries, when all the Church had to work with was its disciplinary power over Christians, it had to exercise a great deal of tolerance. To some extent, it even accepted divorce and remarriage.[28]

As for the idea that a couple must pass before a priest in order to be validly married, that would have to wait until the Tridentine Decree *Tametsi* in 1563 when the authority of the Church had already begun to wane. The variety of marriage rituals among the Christian nations was great and the Church from the beginning had adapted its own rituals to them. In the view of the Church, marriage was and is formed simply by the exchange of consents between the spouses.[29] No particular form was or is imposed for the exchange, it being permitted even today to exchange consents in any form "sanctioned by praiseworthy custom", as well as in the forms to be found in ritual books of the Church. The custom for Christians to seek a blessing for their marriages seems to have begun as early as the first century, but the Church constantly stressed that the blessing was not the essential factor. Consent sufficed to constitute a valid marriage without the participation of a priest. Even today the parties, not the priest, are the ministers of the sacrament, though his presence as a witness is now obligatory. During the Middle Ages the custom of exchanging vows at the church door developed. Then the Church began to prescribe this public religious ceremony. But where the prescribed form was not followed, no doubt was cast on the validity of the marriage.[30] Thus, until Trent, there were two equally valid sorts of marriage, one public and formal, the other private and informal. For a long time the only type of informal cohabitation among the laity to receive specific condemnation was adulterous or incestuous cohabitation.[31] Only with the Council of Trent was informal marriage made invalid, and even then, as we shall see, the Church compromised with reality.

The Church's long tolerance of and adjustment to secular and pagan customs even when they were at variance with its own evolving doctrine, is thought by some to reflect its concern not to "multiply sins".[32] But in reality we cannot separate the Church's policy of adaptation from the gradual and eventually successful assertion of its total control over regulation of marriage. No wiser course than accommodation could have been chosen. Adaptation to, and blending in of indigenous customs must have contributed significantly to the ultimate success of the Church in establishing and extending its jurisdiction. When the Pope told the first Irish missionaries to England not to be too severe with their new converts so far as incest and marriage prohibitions were concerned, he was helping to assure the success of their missions, just as later Popes made similar concessions to local customs in dealing with other primitive civilizations.[33]

B. The Canon Law Prior to the Council of Trent

Full legislative and judicial authority over matrimonial causes and the rudiments of a canon law system were established in what is now France and the Germanies by the end of the 10th century,[34] and in England by the middle of the 12th century.[35] In its long competition with the State for temporal authority, the Church had made its bid for exclusive control of other matters as well, such as succession on death, jurisdiction over all matters pertaining to Church land, and civil and criminal authority over the clergy.[36] But it was only with respect to marital causes that its path was clear and its success was eventually complete. Any exercise of jurisdiction in those times was desirable as a source of "tax" revenue in the form of fees and fines. However, with respect to marriage, it was taken for granted either that this was a matter people could regulate themselves, or that it was an essentially religious matter. The development of the doctrine of sacramental marriage was therefore important as furnishing the theoretical basis for regulation by the Church of matters which previously had not been subject to any kind of systematic official control. The idea that regulation of marriage or adjudication of disputes concerning marriage could or should be conducted by the secular political community was not seriously considered before the 16th century and the Protestant Reformation.

The exercise of jurisdiction by ecclesiastical courts and the application by these courts of the ecclesiastical doctrine which had become a body of canon law was in a sense a remarkable innovation in human history. It was an innovation which had long been impending, yet at the same time one which did not gain immediate acceptance in social life. But while the norm system of the canon law, formulated and systematically organized after the manner of the law of the late Roman empire, may have had little immediate effect on the mores, it had far-reaching and long-lasting effects on all Western marriage law down to the present day.

As Max Weber has demonstrated, canon law grew naturally out of what had gone before. After the Church itself developed a bureaucratic and hierarchical structure, it was not surprising that it also developed a system of courts and procedures and a body of law of the type that has come to be known as "formally rational", radically different from the law of other religious legal systems.[37] Gratian is credited with beginning the application of scholastic methodology to the study of the sources of canon law. His Decretum of 1140 together with the Decretals of Pope Gregory IX of 1292 formed the core of the *Corpus Juris Canonici* which was for centuries the official source of the positive law of the Church.[38]

We now begin to get the answers to some of our questions: how marriage came under any official regulation at all, how it became the subject of legal norms, and how it came to be indissoluble. But we are only beginning, for there is abundant evidence that marriage continued to be considered as basically a private matter even after ecclesiastical jurisdiction was established and canon law had fixed the norm of indissolubility. In other words, even when the Church's authority was successfully established *vis-à-vis* the *political* authority (which had never regulated marriage as such anyway), its norms had not yet fully penetrated the *mores*. The Church bided its time, winning social acceptance of its norms in much the same way as it had gained jurisdiction, through a long patient process of action and interaction with social life. Meanwhile, canon law took the form which was to be of crucial importance for the future, even where and when the authority of the Church much later had been eroded.

Once the rule of indissolubility had been established, an important consequence followed. It had to be spelled out in minute detail exactly which unions were of the type that now could not be dissolved, and outside of which all sexual intercourse was unlawful. "Marriage" had to be defined with more precision than ever before. Out of this need came the whole complex canon law system of marriage impediments and prohibitions. The multiplication of causes of nullity in turn led to the need to investigate whether impediments in fact existed, and thus to the origin of the publication of the banns, the Church's increasing insistence on public marriage, as well as to the elaboration of procedures for declaring marriages invalid. In addition, since marriage between persons not under any impediment was based uniquely on consent, it became relevant to determine whether their consent had been real and free. The result was, of course, that the principle of indissolubility was considerably mitigated by the rules on consent and by the existence of impediments based on blood or marital relationship, spiritual relationship (as between godparents and children), impotence, insanity and nonage. The proliferation of grounds for annulment has been variously interpreted as: following from the necessities of intrinsic logic; related to money and power in the sense that annulments gave the Church a source of revenue and a certain amount of control over families; a humane response to the need of some individuals to escape from intolerable situations and to remarry; and a "safety valve", substituting for the necessary but missing institution of divorce. No doubt all these factors played a role.

The Church's own records, according to recent English and French studies, show the continuation of the habit of contracting marriages informally, and the stubborn persistence of older notions of marriage as a private matter. Helmholtz concludes, on the basis of his study of 13th through 15th century marriage litigation in Church courts in England, that it took a long time for the idea to disappear that people could regulate marriage for themselves.[39] At the same time, he was able to trace a process, equally gradual, of social assimilation of the Church's standards, and to demonstrate considerable room for variety and growth within the canon law itself.

The Church mitigated the harshness of its indissolubility rule in other ways besides through the many causes for annulment. It provided for judicial separation in situations where one spouse had committed adultery, apostasy or heresy, or had deserted or seriously mistreated the other. But unlike annulment, judicial separation did not give rise to permission to remarry. Thus, apart from the avoidance of sin, the main interest in judicial separation must have been in connection with the assignment of support rights to a blameless spouse and denial of them to a blameworthy one. But it is of interest to us in answering one of our questions about the origin of that divorce law which we have come in Western societies to take for granted. Foreshadowed itself by the grounds of justifiable repudiation in the imperial Roman decrees, the canon law of judicial separation prefigures that doctrine of divorce as a sanction for marital misconduct which reappeared in the ideas of the Protestant reformers and which came to dominate Western divorce law until the recent events described in Chapter 5 of this work.

C. The Tridentine Marriage Law

So far we have not found the answer to the question of how the formation of marriage has come to require, in nearly all Western legal systems, the presence of an official. Up to the Council of Trent, the Church had shown its interest in this subject only by making the blessing in church a religious duty sanctioned by penance or censure. To find out why the Roman church suddenly insisted on public formal marriage as a condition for the *validity* of marriage in the Trentine Decree *Tametsi*, we must look, not to ecclesiastical doctrine, but to the pressures and events of the secular world.

The Anglican Church, which had taken over the exclusive jurisdiction of matrimonial causes from the Roman Church in England in 1534, continued to recognize informal marriages as valid until 1753. But in continental Reformation Europe, the stress under which the Church found itself, combined with social and economic changes which in certain levels of society pressed for family control over the shifts of wealth and power which marriages could produce, prepared the way for a modification of the time-honored doctrine that Christians formed their marriages by consent alone. This doctrine, it should be noted, had had the beneficial side effect of liberating the individual from constraints which parents, kinship groups or political authority might try to impose on the choice of spouses. But it was this very liberating effect which began to be troublesome in 16th century Europe, especially in France and Spain, in those circles where increasing amounts of money were changing hands upon marriage.

It had undoubtedly always been true that so long as informal marriages were valid, the difficulty of either proving or disproving them would permit some persons to depart from valid marriages, and others to profit by inheritance or otherwise from invalid marriages. But this longstanding potential for abuse does not seem to have been the precipitating cause of reform. Prominent among the proponents of compulsory ceremonial marriage at the Council of Trent were the French and Spanish delegates who (contrary to the Christian idea of marriage as a voluntary union) were also pressing to make parental consent an ecclesiastical marriage requirement.[40] The parental consent proposal found little support, and the question of compulsory ceremonies was a controversial one at the Council. The validity of informal marriage was defended by theological purists who said it was morally neutral in itself.[41] They also pointed out that it had the virtue of protecting the spiritual liberty of the individual to marry or not to marry from interference by others, particularly parents. The advocates of change claimed that informal marriages threatened inheritance rights, preservation of families, social peace and private morality.[42] They won, 133–59.[43] The Decree *Tametsi* provided that henceforth no marriage was valid which had not been celebrated in the presence of a priest and witnesses. This Decree, which also prescribed the publication of banns of marriage and the keeping of official records of marriages, aided families at least to keep up with the marriage plans of their children, and thereby perhaps to exercise some control over marriages. But it did not go so far as the French and Spanish prelates would have liked.

Other contemporary developments are evidence of the strength of the pressures of the times for preventing secret marriages and for supporting parental control of the marriage decision. A French royal edict of 1556 had empowered parents to disinherit children who married without parental consent and it provided punishments for anyone assisting such a marriage.[44] Martin Luther himself had criticized "secret" marriages as enabling strangers to marry into wealthy families without prior parental approval and to obtain a share of estates.[45] Pressures for making couples marry in public resulted in the requirement of a minister's presence in the Reformation ordinances of Geneva (1561); the protestant principality of Württemberg (1553); and the Palatinate of the Rhine (1563).[46] These ordinances all made parental consent a requirement for marriage.

The requirement of parental consent, which had not found acceptance at Trent, was made part of French civil law by the Ordinance of Blois of 1579. In various forms, as we saw in Chapter 2, it came to penetrate Western marriage law generally. England, however, long remained an exception to the parental consent requirement as well as to the ceremonial marriage requirement. In the end, *Tametsi* as such was not promulgated in France. But there the monarchy enacted the Tridentine reforms as civil legislation in the Ordinance of Blois. Through the 17th century French law continued in various ways to try to discourage secret marriages.[47]

As with the Christian Roman marriage legislation it is questionable whether these changes were evidence of anything more than a concern with the marriage practices of the upper class, whose property interests are reflected in the laws they alone were in a position to influence. Even in these circles, and in spite of the pressures operating in favor of parental authority and the maintenance of class lines, Professor Hunt found a persistent

> ...conflict between public legislation on the one hand and generally accepted popular custom and usage on the other. The edicts and ordinances clearly show that legists recognized the strength of the tradition they were trying to uproot: the continuing belief that cohabitation, simple mutual consent, made a marriage.[48]

So far as the Church was concerned, *Tametsi* itself, by its terms, was not effective where it was not promulgated. Thus informal marriages continued to be valid under canon law in many parts of the world until a decree of Leo XIII in 1892, followed by the decree *Ne Temere*, which went into effect in 1908 and was consolidated in the present Code of Canon law which went into effect in 1918.[49] But the code still preserves the validity of informal marriages in certain circumstances.[50] Also, in the Decree *Tametsi* the church was careful to provide specifically that "if...any laudable customs and ceremonies are in use" besides those prescribed by the decree, "the holy Council of Trent desires that they should be retained".[51]

III. The Protestant Reformation and Secularization of Jurisdiction over Marriage Formation and Dissolution

The history of Canon Law up to the Council of Trent begins to answer the questions posed at the outset of this chapter by showing how marriage became subject to a kind of official and legal regulation, namely, that of the Church courts, applying canon law. It also shows the origin of the idea of legal indissolubility and the beginning of compulsory ceremonial marriage. But how did these matters become concerns of the secular State which previously had been largely indifferent to them? As Rheinstein has pointed out, in the medieval world the State, in in the sense of the omnipresent legal sovereign, did not even exist.[52] Law in those times was not the equivalent of the norm system sanctioned by the State, because the State was not yet the exclusive political organization. Rather, the political organizations of emperor, kings, barons, boroughs, guilds and the Church were all constantly vying with one another for supremacy in various areas of social life.[53]

From the 16th to the 18th century, in great parts of Western Europe, the Catholic Church lost its jurisdiction over marriage: in Protestant regions as a consequence of the Reformation, and in France in connection with Gallicanism and the progress of the monarchy. But in what Esmein calls "a remarkable phenomenon", the law which the Church had created still continued to govern marriage, although it received a new interpretation on certain points.[54] In France from the mid-16th century the State was competing with the Church for jurisdiction of matrimonial causes, and by the 18th century most marital cases were before royal courts. Nevertheless, these courts continued to apply the law developed by the Church.[55]

In Protestant areas, when the Roman Church lost its monopoly over matrimonial causes, the State acquired jurisdiction more or less by default. But to a great extent it simply took over the ready-made set of rules of the canon law, the prior law on judicial separation and maintenance becoming the model for the new secular divorce law.[56] Although Luther and others had claimed that marriage was a proper subject for the civil courts and not subject to exclusive ecclesiastical control, they little dreamed that marriage would one day be regulated by the State according to other than Christian principles. While the reformers held that marriage was not a sacrament, they thought that secular regulations should conform to Christian teaching.[57] Christian teaching was of course reinterpreted by them to permit divorce as a punishment for grave violation of marital duties, for adultery in particular, but gradually for other causes as well. This well-known instance of departure from Roman Catholic doctrine should not, however, obscure the fact that Catholic canon law was still widely applied. Nor should the importance of the introduction of divorce itself be exaggerated, for it was accompanied by a tightening up of nullity which the Church had at times offered rather freely.[58] Protestantism did not return divorce to the private order by any means: no divorce by mutual consent was recognized and divorce for cause had to be granted by an official. Only in the Enlightenment did a true antithesis to the Roman Catholic attitude appear.

IV. The "Enlightened" Absolutist State and Statization of Family Law

The effects of the Protestant Reformation take us further toward understanding how marriage formation and dissolution came under the jurisdiction of the secular State, and thus how some of the law described in Chapters 2 and 5 of this book (marriage formation and dissolution) took shape. However, we have yet to learn how the State came to apply its own secular, as opposed to ecclesiastical, norms of law.

In addition, we still have no answer to the question of how the secular law came to regulate or at least to purport to regulate a matter from which canon and Roman law had abstained, namely, the organization and conduct of married life, the subject considered in Chapter 4. To understand the evolution of this branch of law, account has to be taken of two developments for which the Protestant reformers cannot be held responsible, although in a sense they helped pave the way. These developments are the appearance of the humanistic and individualistic thought of the Enlightenment and the rise of the absolutist State, the *Polizeistaat*.

The developments occurred in different fashion in France and the various regions of Germany, but resulted eventually in unprecedented comprehensive regulation of family relationships there. England, on the other hand, remained in many ways a special case, and so, in consequence, did the United States.

Rulers like Frederick II of Prussia, Joseph II of Austria, Napoleon, and their legal scholars and bureaucratic administrators felt the need for a clear and complete codification of all private law.[59] Further, these rulers were in a position to impose their own ideas as rules of positive law in their Codes.

The new secular law of the Codes drew substantially on the former law, just as the reformed Protestant church had drawn heavily on canon law. But marriage law, cut loose from its Catholic and Protestant religious moorings in the established medieval order, increasingly began to be affected by the trends of the times, by humanism and individualism, as well as by the practical concerns and interests of the secular state and the dominant groups within it.[60] Thus, as Müller-Freienfels has pointed out, the idea of marriage as a civil contract took a new turn. Consent had been the essence of marriage in the Church's law. The State, however, shifted its concern to the rights and duties of the spouses, constructing a network of legal relationships on the basis of which each spouse had a full set of claims against the other that could be made the basis of legal action before a judge.[61] In the great codifications, as we have already seen in Chapter 4, the law intervened in the smallest details of the most intimate relationships in a way unknown to the Roman and Canon law. Sometimes these extremes of juridification seem to be in the furtherance of some interest of the State (as with population-related provisions), or of dominant groups in society (as with the paternal authority over children). Sometimes they seem to be merely the result of that urge for completeness so evident in other aspects of, say, the Prussian General Code of 1794.[62]

In the endeavor not to leave any gap whatever in the codification, the Prussian Code concerned itself with such matters as when marital intercourse may be declined, when the absence of a spouse from home is excused, and how often and how long a baby can be taken into bed and nursed. Professor Carbonnier describes this legal atmosphere as "panjurism", the idea that everything is law, or "...at least that law has a vocation to be everywhere, to envelop everything, and, like a god, to hold up the entire inhabited world".[63]

The development of two important modern marriage institutions dates from this period: the compulsory civil marriage ceremony in France and Germany, and the development of comprehensive registration systems of civil status. Both spread from France to the world.

The compulsory civil marriage is the child of the French Revolution (which made a great point, as everyone knows, of refusing to distinguish between legitimate and illegitimate children). The civil marriage ceremony had been made available in the Calvinist Netherlands and in New England but was made compulsory by the French revolutionary decree of 20 September 1792. This decree marked the shift in France from secularization to statization. By the time of the Revolution the royal courts had already quietly assumed control of marriage cases from the Church without any outright confrontation, so that by 1789 the jurisdiction of the Church courts was purely theoretical.[64] All that remained for the Revolution was to substitute, for the ecclesiastical doctrine still applied by the royal courts, the starting point that marriage was a civil contract organized by the State. Even so, later events down to the present time in France show the persistence of canon law ideas. As we saw in Chapter 5, the Napoleonic Code of 1804 rejected some of the revolutionary ideas about marriage. What clearly remained of the revolutionary marriage legislation of 1792 was the civil ceremony which spread all over the world, as at least an optional method of marrying, and that system of secular registration of civil status which is now also in world-wide use. Compulsory civil marriage was retained by the Napoleonic Civil Code and was later adopted in various regions of Germany, finally becoming the law of the whole German empire by the Personal Status Law of 6 February 1875, and finding its place in the German Civil Code of 1896. Registration of civil status had been preceded in France and elsewhere first by ecclesiastical record-keeping, then by governmental regulation of church registrations.[65]

Another child of the French Revolution and of the Code of Frederick the Great, unilateral divorce, seems to have been born too soon. But we have seen its rebirth in Chapter 5, as well as the full maturity of mutual consent divorce which had been recognized by the revolutionary law and the Codes of Frederick the Great and Napoleon.

As has already been mentioned, England remained a case apart. Ecclesiastical jurisdiction over marriage survived the Reformation without real disruption until 1857. Briefly under Cromwell, it seems, civil marriage was available and divorce may have been permitted. But civil marriage did not reappear in England until 1836 and then only as an optional system. Informal marriages were valid in England until Lord Hardwicke's Act in 1753 which like the Decree *Tametsi* made an ecclesiastical ceremony compulsory and required publication of the banns.[66] Divorce was available after 1660 but only by special parliamentary act, and then only for adultery. It was expensive, complicated and rarely used. Divorce as such became available only by the Matrimonial Causes Act of 1857, effective in 1858.

In the United States,[67] those areas settled by Protestants had divorce laws from early times, while those with a strong Anglican influence initially had no divorce at all. Legislative divorce survived in many colonies and states into the 19th century. The Western frontier states were more liberal, so that by 1860 migratory divorce had already appeared. With the English background, and in the Southwest[68] with the indulgence of the canon law prior to *Ne Temere,* informal marriage became an established legal institution in some places. "Common law" marriages are still recognized in some 13 states and the District of Columbia. Sweden, interestingly enough, did not finally implement a secular version of the Tridentine requirement of formal marriage until 1915.[69] Thus, the recent rise in informal marriage in Sweden must be viewed against the background of a very late legal acceptance of the compulsory formal marriage.

The processes of secularization and eventual statization of marriage law just described coincided with certain trends in legal thought which were to reach their high point in the 19th century. So far as legislation is concerned, panjurism is probably most fully reflected in the Prussian General Code of 1794. But in 19th century case law and doctrine legal norms and concepts were formalized and expressed in that conceptualistic way which had been typical of revived Roman law and the canon law.[70] Legal rules which often were but the expression of moral value judgments or the resolution of conflicting interests, came to appear to have life of their own, producing "logical" and "necessary" consequences. At the same time, as Max Weber noted, the notion of legitimacy had come to be identified with that of "legality", understood as the quality of enactments which are formally correct and made in the accustomed manner.[71]

In view of all we have seen of the evolution of marriage regulation, this is a rather curious notion. It reminds one of the attachment which infant monkeys in captivity can be induced to have for a rag on a stick. Conduct among primitive people is oriented to ideas of legitimacy expressed in customs, convention and religion. As we have seen, the legal method of regulation appeared rather late in human history. Yet, once it appeared, it interacted with the mores and eventually acquired the force of tradition. Enactments which are formally correct and which have been made in the accustomed manner became themselves the matrimonial customs of the West.

However, much of what has been related in Chapters 2 through 5 of this book can be seen as evidence that we are now experiencing a period of dissociation between legality and legitimacy. Much of the law of formation, organization and dissolution of marriage, which has its origins in social and political conditions different from those of modern society, has long been irrelevant to vast areas of human conduct. Now it seems that behavior and ideology are pulling away from the law. Behavior and ideology can of course be *oriented* to an idea of legitimacy expressed in the law even when the legal norms are not *obeyed*.[72] In the recent past with respect to divorce, for example, it seems to have been necessary for society to go through a period of maintaining strict divorce law on the books, even though divorce in practice was freely available.[73] Presently, as Chapter 5 shows, in many places conduct is no longer even oriented to the ideals of the law, and the legal forms are being repealed or simply ignored.

V. Dejuridification: Marriage as a Social Institution?

It has been one of the purposes of the historical survey presented in this

Chapter to show how the law of marriage came to assume the form it had when the developments described in Chapters 2 through 6 began. We have seen that struggles among Church, State and politically powerful groups; popular customs and practices; and sheer historical accident have all had their part. This last factor in particular seems to account for the fact that in the United States divorces are heard in the same kind of proceedings as are disputes arising out of personal injuries or commercial contracts.[74]

More important from the point of view of this work, however, is the fact that against this background of the gradual establishment and eventual triumph of juridification and official regulation of the social institution of marriage, the present period of change can only be seen as a downward curve of *dejuridification* and *deregulation*, a return to forms of social control other than legal rules concerning the formation, dissolution and organization of married life. As the title of this book indicates, it is my belief that a close look at the discrete elements of the current period of legal evolution reveals a shift in the posture of the State with respect to the family, a shift which is approached in magnitude only by that which occurred in connection with the Reformation in most European countries, when the State acquired jurisdiction over matrimonial causes from the ecclesiastical authorities. Neither that process of juridification of family matters nor the present process of change is characterized by suddenness. In fact, both processes have involved long periods of discontinuity between social and legal phenomena, or as Professor Carbonnier puts it, between law and non-law. In what way has the posture of the State with respect to the family changed? Precisely in redefining what is law and what is non-law.

In the area of marriage formation and especially marriage dissolution, social conduct has for a long time gradually been pulling away from the law, treating the law as irrelevant. Now the law is pulling away from the social conduct, leaving questions of who marries whom and how, what rights and duties the spouses have toward each other, as well as how such unions are terminated, increasingly in the private order.

If we now recall the description of current developments in the formation of legal marriage and the legal treatment of informal marriages described in Chapters 2 and 3, we can see that the modern State has retreated considerably from the role it had assumed by the beginning of the 20th century. The ideas of freedom to marry, of privacy, and of neutrality with respect to different customs and life styles, have been the accompanying strains to which the corporate welfare state has drifted away from interfering with the choice of spouse, the eligibility to marry and the insistence on formalities. Like its predecessor the *Polizeistaat*, however, the State continues to pursue its own interests in population control and record keeping.

With respect to the law of the on-going marriage, it will be recalled from Chapter 4 that these largely symbolic rules had their origin for the most part in the excesses of the codification movements. Now we have seen that the law has either withdrawn completely, in the name of tolerance, or it has replaced the portraits on the wall. Where the hierarchical family headed by husband and father was once depicted, there now hangs a photo of the family composed of equals, all of whom are closely bound together in community but each of whom is a separate independent individual. There is some reason to doubt, as we saw, whether either version was a good likeness. But in the area of Chapter 4, the on-going marriage, perhaps realism is neither necessary nor even of particular virtue.

Finally, in Chapter 5 on divorce, dejuridification was most dramatically apparent. Free divorce has widely appeared in the legal norms, and official regulation through the courts has become perfunctory, often amounting to little more than registration.

Chapters 2 through 5 of this book show in varying degrees in the different countries: marriage by registration, with optional *de facto* marriage on the increase; divorce by registration; and deregulation of the on-going marriage. But, the wheel has not come full circle and we have not returned to Rome. For as the discussion of the effects of marriage dissolution in Chapter 6 showed, the modern State has not ceased to interest itself in the family. Yet since the family law of Chapter 6 is by and large marriage-neutral and unconcerned with legitimacy or illegitimacy of children, we can say that marriage itself seems once more to be becoming a purely social rather than a legally regulated institution.

If this is so, we may well wonder whether and how marriage will be regulated by social norms as it was before legitimacy came to be so strongly identified with legality. Anthropologists and sociologists have insisted on the importance of marriage as a determinant of status, and on its role in distinguishing those persons entitled to derive rank and property through the family.[75] But a survey of the recent law indicates that marriage law seems to be withering away precisely because rank and status, wealth and power, in society are decreasingly determined by family relationships. It would of course be naive to think that family relationships are unimportant with respect to these matters, but certainly they are less important than before.[76]

The significance of marriage was once comprehensive, when society was organized in clans and sibs in which membership depended, wherever the organization was patrilineal, upon descent from the man with whom an individual's mother was married. Marriage then constituted the basic relationship upon which an individual's position in society was determined and upon which the organization of society was based. For centuries a person's entering upon marriage has been regarded as the assumption of a status by which his position in society was fixed in aspects of basic importance. Today, under the impact of the postulate of equality the concept of status is being abandoned; and with the increasing importance of jobs and pensions rather than inherited wealth, the significance of the legitimate family in property matters is reduced. This trend is at once symbolized and advanced by the recent reforms assimilating the legal status of children born outside marriage with that of "legitimate" children. In addition, as the groups to which we belong become more and more heterogeneous, it becomes impossible to define, much less punish, the deviant. Marriage becomes primarily a concern of the individuals involved and is governed by their individual sense of ethics or utility, as the case may be.

From another point of view, however, we might say that the change is not so great as it first seems. Most family law, like most family history of which we have knowledge, has been concerned only or mainly with the upper and, later, the middle classes. In the twentieth century, the law began to take increasing notice of groups which it had previously neglected and they began to take notice of it.[77] There is reason to believe, for example, that in France and Germany the entry into formal as opposed to informal marriages was a way in which the members of the working class gave expression to their aspirations to rise in social status.[78] There is a hint of this kind of motivation in Sarah's character in *The Tinker's Wedding*. As more and more groups were included, and included themselves, under the umbrella of laws devised mainly for propertied groups, the discrepancy between law and mores widened. From this perspective then, we may only be seeing how narrow the application of "law" really was all the time. Like the tinkers Michael and Sarah, most of the travellers through this world have been ignored by the State and its laws made for fine ladies and gentlemen. The Church has usually generously excused them from strict compliance with its more formalistic rules. But when it didn't, then like Michael and Sarah, sure, they must have excused themselves.

VI. Statization and the Family in the Modern Welfare State

It must be admitted here that the theory of delegalization of marriage just sketched glosses over two extremely troublesome problems. If we accept the argument of Chapters 2 through 5 that society, once again, is leaving the formation, conduct, and dissolution of family relationships to social regulation, is there any reason to think that leaving these matters to regulation by the norms of custom, ethics, convention and religion means that they will be subject to any norms at all? Second, the trend just described does not mean that the theories of those philosophical proponents of the minimal state who would say marriage and family matters are of no legitimate concern to the State have suddenly found their terrestrial home. In fact the State is more heavily involved in such matters than ever before, but in a different way. Adjusting to the increasing tendency of people to look to the State rather than the family or any other groups to solve their problems, governmental agencies have become deeply involved with the economic consequences of marriage dissolution and with the welfare of children produced by cohabitation of a formal or informal kind. Bringing the State into ever more intimate contact with legal and *de facto* families is the strange and unwieldy edifice of national and municipal dispensaries of money, food, medicine, advice, comfort, recreation, nursing care and education with their army of bureaucrats. It seems clear that social conditions are such that this State intervention is often required. But here is the second problem: how can we tell what kind of State involvement will shore up and strengthen family life, and what kind will undermine and weaken it?

These questions are in a sense outside the scope of this book. Certainly no one has yet furnished their answers. But a few observations with respect to them may not be out of place, especially since law reform efforts must proceed on the basis of assumptions, however imperfect, about the probable effect of law on behavior. Let us first consider the modern statization of family law. Then, in the concluding section we will turn to those legal changes which have blurred the distinctions between marriage and non-marriage, and between legal and informal family relationships.

In considering the posture of the State toward the family as expressed through its laws, we must peel back and peer behind the slogan of privacy. Philippe Ariès and others have described how in the 18th century the family began to hold society at a distance, and to push it back beyond a steadily expanding zone of private life.[79] The evolution of private life spread from nobles to the middle class to other social strata until it has come finally to embrace nearly the whole of society. But, at the same time, the family was losing many of its functions to a series of impersonal institutions. Thus the progress of privacy can also be seen as Lawrence Stone sees it:

> Its [the family's] legal, political and economic functions declined before the ever-encroaching march of the institutions of the modern state....

Furthermore, the power of the state undermined the influence of the kin, and thus increased the isolation and privacy of the nuclear family....[80]

The care which the State and its laws once lavished on the protection of private property has now been extended to maintaining the machinery of the social welfare state. Every country with which we have been here concerned, to a greater or lesser extent, has taken over the economic and educational tasks which were once primarily the responsibility of the family. All these countries have systems, varying in detail from each other, for distributing the risks of unemployment, sickness, death of a provider, and for providing security in old age. State concern is currently shifting from providing protection against the worst aspects of insecurity to attempting to provide each individual in society with the minimum wherewithal for a decent level of existence.

By removing the threat of total misery these trends should theoretically provide the conditions for a full and happy family life. But the situation is immensely complicated. Relieved of many of its economic and educational functions, the family seems indeed to have become organized around new ideals. It is supposed to be a private place where satisfying personal relationships between husbands and wives, and parents and children, can flourish. It is supposed to be a refuge from the psychic assaults of society and the disappointments of the world of work. But the refuge seems more and more to be itself the place of disillusion. Partly this may be because too much is expected of marriage and the small modern family. But one also has to consider the influence which society and the family have upon each other. The family shapes the individuals who compose society, but society in turn limits what families can do in forming its members. One might mention, among those aspects of twentieth century life which seem to have an effect on family life, as well as on other areas of human behavior: changes in the nature of work; the increasing number of choices open to individuals in many areas of life; and the tendency for one's activities, such as work, recreation, home life, education and so on, to be divided into different and separate areas, rather than to take place in one area with the same companions.

Testifying in 1973 before the U.S. Senate Subcommittee on Children and Youth, Urie Bronfenbrenner said that the forces of family disorganization

...arise primarily not from within the family itself, but from the circumstances in which the family finds itself and the way of life which these circumstances, in turn, impose. Specifically, when...there is no support or recognition from the outside world for one's role as a parent, and when time spent with one's family means frustration of career, personal fulfillment, and peace of mind – it is then that the development of the child becomes adversely affected.[81]

Pressures originating in social life, together with exaggerated expectations of what the family can provide in the way of compensating for deprivations elsewhere, may have made the ideals of family intimacy and cohesion harder to obtain. At the same time, as families under stress disintegrate, they may be producing the sort of individuals who are ready-made to take their place in Robert Heilbroner's dreadful vision of the authoritarian states of the future.[82] Thus, the banner of privacy may be flying over a wasteland of psychic, and ultimately social, devastation. The ideology of privacy may be in fact nothing more than what we have already seen as tolerance and neutrality sloganized to cover up a constant undermining of conditions that could make privacy meaningful.[83]

Philippe Ariès in France and Kenneth Keniston in the United States are now saying that the attention and importance given to childhood in society since the beginning of the 18th century are beginning to wane; that once again indifference to children, at best, is becoming the norm.[84] More illustrative perhaps than intellectual theorizing about the possible anti-family tendencies inherent in the organization of modern social life is the following letter which appeared in the correspondence section of *Le Nouvel Observateur* of 19 January 1976:

> I have read the article by François-Henri de Virieu concerning the birth rate.
>
> Bernadette and I do not want to have children.... She works at the Post-Telephone-Telegraph Service and I am a delivery man. We live in a studio apartment (630 F per month) in a nearby suburb.
>
> Although the majority of people we run into do not understand us, we do not plan to pass the rest of our life like this; that is, with each of us carrying out every day a monotonous task, which is repetitive, without initiative, without responsibility, without real social meaning, and, furthermore, on the physical level, exhausting and numbing.
>
> If we had had one or two children, we would have had to put them in a nursery, then in day care, then in school, which means spending even more time in transportation, and seeing one's children "on the fly" in the evening, with even more work to do around the house. Our salaries do not permit either one of us to stop working. I think that children brought up under present-day conditions will be even more unhappy and disoriented than we are if our mode of living is not changed by reducing the number of working hours. A real family is a family where a common task is carried out every day with the sole aim of making those who survive us happier than we are.

Some optimistic observers suggest that marriage and the family are now merely undergoing a difficult transitional stage, and that better adaptations and accommodations than ever before will eventually be worked out.[85] Thus, a view of the future can be constructed in which the State furnishes individuals and families with minimum economic security, and the society as a whole facilitates participation by men in family life and by women in work life.

But in the long run we have to consider that, with the decline of affluence, the State may not be able to fulfill the task it has set itself and that the family will continue to be the major institution through which society deals with dependence. It is possible too that tolerance of diversity and liberty of the individual will one day be seen as phenomena of affluence. Some may see the trends described in this book as themselves signs of social disintegration. The question becomes more pressing whether and how the State can assist and strengthen the family. As we adjust to a world of diminishing resources and expanding population, we may come to search in family law as elsewhere for mechanisms and models through which we can learn to live in community.

At present, the law, mirroring society and individual families, is filled with tensions and contradictions. With respect to these contradictions, I think it is important to cultivate what John Keats in another context called negative capability – that is, the ability to hold opposed interpretations of the present and visions of the future in our minds without flinching or turning away. We should, in the spirit with which we approach these problems, avoid both the naive optimism according to which family relationships need only to be cleansed of their economic sediment, and the currently fashionable neo-Manichaeism which sees the disintegration of the family and society as imminent. If we are able to do this, we may hope that these same tensions which have the potential to tear a society, an individual or a family apart, can also perhaps generate in legal and social policy that enormous creative human energy that they have been known to generate in art.

VII. Afterword

> "Sit down, the two of you, there before me", said Neary, "and do not despair. Remember there is no triangle, however obtuse, but the circumference of some circle passes through its wretched vertices. Remember also one thief was saved."
>
> "Our medians," said Wylie, "or whatever the hell they are, meet in Murphy".
>
> "Outside us," said Neary. "Outside us."
>
> "In the outer light," said Miss Counihan.
>
> Samuel Beckett, *Murphy* (1938).[86]

The puzzles of law, behavior and ideology with which we are now left are knotted together, each strand is turned in on itself. No one can foresee how they will be resolved. Yet as they unfold, future developments will be seen to follow naturally from what has been set forth here. This is because, as the political theorist Raymond Aron has put it, complex events are always the simultaneous result of a large number of circumstances, but minute facts can determine the course an important movement will take.[87] Thus, says Aron, we all, in a sense rightly, believe that the past was determined but the future is not.

It is perhaps appropriate to acknowledge here that the theories advanced in this book have a certain hypothetical character. It is necessary to construct and employ concepts and theories in the effort to understand the relationships among law, behavior and ideology. But human reality is not stylized and rationalized. It is complex, obscure and, ultimately, mysterious.

If, however, it is correct to see the present period as one of delegalization, perhaps there is much to be said for leaving the social institution of the family to social regulation. If one adopted without question the slogans of freedom to marry, individual liberty, and tolerance of diverse life styles, one could anticipate with some pleasure the day when all of the encrusted layers of law will finally be peeled away, and the social institution of the family is once again subject to none but social regulation, "free by the laws and restrained by manners", in Montesquieu's phrase. This position is not without difficulty, however. One difficulty is that in modern Western societies we cannot say that a change from what has been rather extensive legal regulation of marriage and family matters to "delegalization", is completely neutral. This is because, in an indefinable but nonetheless real way, much of our law performs educational and hortatory functions. In a society where there are few sources of common inspiration, the law can take on in some instances a sacred character: it can become what the American sociologist Robert Bellah calls a "civil religion".[88] This is particularly true, for example, of the pronouncements of the Supreme Court of the United States or of what is written in the French Civil Code. To the extent that legitimacy is still identified with legality, laws permitting unilateral divorce on demand for example must have a certain, though impossible to quantify, moral significance. Thus, we cannot say in our societies that the law is completely unimportant in comparison with other factors. In fact, it interacts with and reacts back upon social change.

While not dismissing this point, I believe that the effect which changes in marriage and divorce law may have on marriage behavior, under present conditions, is minimal. When the law is in tune with other social forces, when they are all running in the same direction, it is possible that they will enter into a synergistic relationship and that the law will produce a greater effect in combination with other forces than it could on its own. But when the law runs counter to what is happening in society, and legitimacy is decreasingly identified with legality, the effect of law must be small. Rheinstein has shown once and for all the lack of correlation between strict or easy divorce laws and marriage stability or instability.

Thus, I conclude that the possible effect of changes in laws governing marriage formation, dissolution and the conduct of married life is not a reason to struggle against what in any event is probably an inevitable process of deregulation. However, matters are otherwise when we turn from marriage formation, organization and dissolution, to the economic and child-related consequences of marriage dissolution, and when we consider the problems of dependency generally. There the question is not whether the State should intervene, but how and how much.

Another theoretical difficulty which some might have with delegalization is that in modern societies no one can be really sure that leaving marriage and family matters to the norms of convention, ethics, and religion, means that they will be subject to any norms at all. In other words, thinking about delegalization brings us back to the problem that the social institution itself is facing serious challenges. Our wise men tell us that the extent of family disorganization is serious, that we have a disease called alienation, and that our only common value is hedonism.

But, if all this is true (it may be permitted to wonder, since wise men these days often live in such places as California, New York or Paris), it is hard to imagine that enacted norms would succeed where all others have failed. Perhaps there is some comfort in Koñig's observation that while the family changes slowly, new forms of the family are constantly emerging. Perhaps the social institution will adapt to yet another set of challenges.[89]

Finally, although I have here emphasized the diminishing importance of the legal aspects of the family, there is every reason to believe that its other aspects, however frail and faltering they may be, are as important as ever. For most of us, the family remains the theater in which we each realize our full capacity for good or evil. Relationships between husband and wife, parents and children, give rise to crises and tensions, conflicts between love and duty, reason and passion. They also provide the framework for resolving them. For most of us, the family furnishes our one opportunity to aspire to heroism, greatness or even sainthood. On the other hand, as Dostoevsky well knew, it provides most of us with our principal occasions to really do or suffer evil. Even though, after the loosening of legal ties that has been described in this book, the only bonds which remain to unite the family may be the ties of human affection, we can perhaps – if we are hopeful – recognize in those fragile connections analogies for that Love which is the Law that binds all of us together in the Family of Man and the City of God. A note sounded by a player on one instrument may call forth a corresponding note from another; a child, hearing an accordion outside the window, may begin to sing and dance.

Notes

[1] J. M. Synge, *The Tinker's Wedding*, in The Complete Plays of John M. Synge 180, 207 (1960; orig. publ. 1907).
[2] *Weber* 3.
[3] *König* par. 96.
[4] *Winch* 1.
[5] *Hübner* 593; *II Pollock and Maitland* 364.
[6] *Hübner* 588.
[7] *Weber* 134.
[8] *Winch* 2.
[9] *König* par. 96–97.
[10] *Ibid.*
[11] *Jolowicz* 117–118.
[12] *Brissaud* 142; *Hübner* 613.
[13] *Rheinstein, M.S.D.L.* 15.
[14] In the following discussion of the Roman marriage, I rely on *Corbett* 68–105; 218–248.
[15] *Noonan* 44–46.
[16] *Id.* at 53.
[17] Novel 22.
[18] Novel 117 of 542 A.D.
[19] *Corbett* 242–243.
[20] *Rheinstein, M.S.D.L.* 16.
[21] *I Esmein* 14.
[22] St. Augustine, The Retractations, in LX The Fathers of the Church 247 (1968).
[23] *Noonan* 87.
[24] *Rheinstein, M.S.D.L.* 13–14.
[25] *Bassett* 129.
[26] *II Esmein* 49.
[27] *Id.* 50–51.
[28] *Id.* at 49–50; *Brissaud* 143–144; *Hübner* 614; *II Pollock and Maitland* 392–393.
[29] Canon 1100.
[30] de Reeper, The History and Application of Canon 1098, 14 Jurist 148, 152 (1954).
[31] Buckley, "Concubinage", in IV New Catholic Encyclopedia 120 (1967).

[32] *II Pollock and Maitland* 370.
[33] *Id.* at 366.
[34] *Bassett* 129–130; *Brissaud* 88–89; *Hübner* 614.
[35] *II Pollock and Maitland* 367.
[36] *Rheinstein, M.S.D.L.* 18.
[37] See generally, *Weber* Ch. 8, esp. 250–255.
[38] *Bassett* 130.
[39] *Helmholtz* 5.
[40] *Brissaud* 115; *Gottlieb* 35–37; *Kidd* 104.
[41] *Gottlieb* 59–60; 62–63.
[42] *Gottlieb* 38–39.
[43] *Kidd* 104.
[44] *Hunt* 60.
[45] *Gottlieb* 16.
[46] *Id.* 124–135.
[47] *Hunt* 62.
[48] *Id.* at 63.
[49] *Bouscaren and Ellis* 581–583.
[50] Canon 1098, see Chapter 1 of this book at n. 23.
[51] Thurston, "Marriage, Ritual of", in IX The Catholic Encyclopedia 703, 704 (1910).
[52] *Rheinstein, Int. Encyc.* par. 7.
[53] *Ibid.*
[54] *I Esmein* 34.
[55] *Ibid.*
[56] *Ibid.*
[57] *Rheinstein, M.S.D.L.* 22.
[58] *Id.* at 23.
[59] *Id.* at 25–26.
[60] Müller-Freienfels, Ehe und Recht 18–25.
[61] *Id.* at 20–21.
[62] *Id.* at 22–23.
[63] *Carbonnier, Flexible Droit* 20.
[64] *Brissaud* 91–92.
[65] *Rheinstein, M.S.D.L.* 198; see also Chapter 2 of this book *supra* at 58.
[66] *II Pollock and Maitland* Chapter 7.
[67] See *Clark CB* 7–11.
[68] See generally Baade, The Form of Marriage in Spanish North America, 61 Corn. L. Rev. 1 (1975).
[69] *Schmidt (1970)* 203–204.
[70] *Rheinstein, M.S.D.L.* 19.
[71] *Weber* 9.
[72] *Id.* at 45: "Very frequently the order is violated only in one or another partial respect, or its violation is sought to be passed off as legitimate, with a varying measure of good faith. Or several different interpretations of the order coexist alongside each other. In that case the sociologist will regard each one as valid in exactly so far as it is actually determinative of conduct. It is, indeed, in no way difficult for the sociologist to recognize that several, possibly mutually contradictory, orders are valid within the same group. Even one and the same individual may orient his conduct toward mutually contradictory orders. He can do so successively; such cases can, indeed, be observed all the time; but...[this] can [also] occur with respect to one and the same conduct.... Where, however, evasion or violation of the order (i.e., of the meaning generally ascribed to it) has become the rule, the order has come to be valid in but a limited sense or has ceased to be valid altogether.... Fluid transitions exist between validity and nonvalidity, and mutually contradictory orders can be valid alongside each other. Each one is valid simply in proportion to the probability that conduct will actually be oriented toward it."

[73] *Rheinstein, M.S.D.L.* 247–260.

[74] *Id.* at 20.

[75] See especially, B. Malinowski, Sex, Culture and Myth 63–65, 139–140 (1962), and *Goode* 19–30.

[76] The fact that the family, in a broader sense, contributes to inequality in the sense of providing different life prospects for individuals who may be equally endowed, has troubled John Rawls in his Theory of Justice, 301, 511–512 (1971).

[77] *Rheinstein, Int. Encyc.* par. 14.

[78] *Carbonnier, 2 Droit Civil* 194; *Rheinstein, M.S.D.L.* 301.

[79] *Ariès* 398–404; see also *Braudel* 223–224.

[80] Stone, The Massacre of the Innocents, The New York Review of Books, Nov. 14, 1974, 25, 27.

[81] Hearings on American Families: Trends and Pressures, Subcomm. on Children and Youth, Senate Comm. on Labor and Public Welfare, 93 Cong., 1st Sess. (1973), reproduced at 119 Cong. Rec. S 18,011 (daily ed. Sept. 28, 1973).

[82] R. Heilbroner, An Inquiry into the Human Prospect (1975).

[83] Christopher Lasch points for example to what he calls the "flight from feeling...rooted in developments that have undermined intimacy and privacy in the family: most obviously, the absence of the father", in What the Doctor Ordered, The New York Review of Books, Dec. 11, 1975, 50, 54. In March 1975, in the United States one out of seven children was living in a family without a father, as compared to one out of ten in March 1970, according to Beverly McEaddy of the Bureau of Labor Statistics: Women who Head Families: A Socioeconomic Analysis, Monthly Labor Review, June 1976, at 3, 6.

[84] Ariès, L'enfant: la fin d'un règne, Autrement No. 3, 169, 171 (1975); Keniston, The Emptying Family, The New York Times, Feb. 18, 1976, p. 33 cols. 2–4.

[85] Giele. Changing Sex Roles and the Future of Marriage, Feb. 13, 1973 (lecture delivered at Wellesley College).

[86] S. Beckett, *Murphy* 213–214 (Grove Press ed. 1957; orig. publ. 1938).

[87] II Main Currents in Sociological Thought 237, 241 (1967).

[88] Beyond Belief, Ch. 9 (1970).

[89] *König* thinks that the fact that the family may be an inheritance from the higher animal species and the family's endurance capacity as demonstrated through the chaos of history permit "a well-grounded statement of doubt as to all the schools of thought that from time to time predict an imminent dissolution of marriage and the family, or believe they can point to a period of decline in our day and age". par. 29. See also par. 55.

[16]

THE PLACE OF RELIGION IN FAMILY LAW: A COMPARATIVE SEARCH

Jane Mair

1. WHY SEARCH FOR RELIGION IN FAMILY LAW?

At times of uncertainty, change and crisis, it is common for individuals to turn to religion for guidance, insight and comfort. It might be suggested that similar motivations lie behind the current notable and rapid growth in academic interest in religion and law. Within the last few years there has emerged a significant body of debate and writing on the interaction of law and religion which, although wide ranging in terms of specific religions, particular legal issues and theoretical frameworks, nonetheless converges in its shared analysis of how law and religion intersect. This shared focus is hardly a coincidence and can be linked to various common trends and developments and to a number of specific key events. Within a UK context, the now notorious speech of the Archbishop of Canterbury, Rowan Williams,[1] was a significant catalyst, sparking controversial debate specifically with regards to the relationship between Shari'a law and civil law. The range and level of debate which has ensued is,

> "due not only to disparate views about the nature and attractiveness of Shari'a, but [has] also exposed subterranean unease about the identity of the West itself, especially given its mixed inheritance of humanistic, religious, and post-modern elements."[2]

The repercussions of this speech have spread to many other European countries and have helped to open up discussion on a wider range of issues surrounding

---

1 The Archbishop of Canterbury The Rt Rev Dr Rowan Williams, *Civil and Religious Law in England: a Religious Perspective*: text of the Foundation Lecture at the Royal Courts of Justice delivered on 7 February 2008. The full text of the speech is available at www.archbishopofcanterbury.org/1575.

2 AHDAR, R. and ARONEY, N., "The Topography of Shari'a in the Western Political Landscape" in AHDAR, R. and ARONEY, N. (eds.), *Shari'a in the West* (Oxford University

law and religion, whether Islam, Christianity or Judaism, contributing to the current situation where it can be said that:

> "Everyone today agrees on the new prominent role religions have acquired in politics, law and economics, not to mention other fields of public life. Nevertheless we still miss the necessary instruments to decipher and understand the causes and effects of this re-enchantment of the world."[3]

It is as part of that process of deciphering and understanding, within the specific context of religion and family law, and with a view to exploring some of that "subterranean unease", that this book was conceived.

The current interest in religion and law is inspired by a range of concerns and reflects the convergence of various distinct trends. Migration and the consequent establishment of ethnic minority communities within predominantly Christian societies have led to growing awareness of, and demands for recognition of, cultural and religious differences. Human rights, and in particular protection against discrimination on the grounds of religion and belief, have given rise to debate over the complexities of ensuring religious freedom and religious tolerance.[4] Increasing secularisation of many liberal Western legal systems has highlighted those who have strong religious beliefs which do not always fit with the majority view. Concern about a lack of meaning in postmodern law and society have encouraged renewed interest among some to search for meaning within religious or other belief systems. There are many explanations for the current shared interest in religion and there is a range of different legal issues arising specifically in respect of particular religions.

Although, traditionally, family law has not been a key area for comparative study, that has changed significantly in recent years.[5] The belief that family law is embedded in cultural specificity, previously hindered comparative[6] analysis but much recent work has begun to challenge that perception.[7] In conjunction with religion, family law is a highly appropriate area for consideration. The personal nature of the family and the close ties between emotions, individual

---

3 FERRARI, S. and CRISTOFORI, R. (eds.), *Law and Religion in the 21st Century: Relations between States and Religious Communities* (Ashgate, 2010), Preface, p. xvii.

4 See e.g. RIVERS, J., "Law, Religion and Gender Equality", (2009) 9 *Ecc LJ* 24.

5 Similarly, until recently, there has been relatively little comparative analysis of the interaction of law and religion: see, e.g., BERMAN, H.J., "Comparative Law and Religion" in REIMANN, M. and ZIMMERMANN, R., *The Oxford Handbook of Comparative Law* (Oxford University Press, 2006), 739, at p. 740.

6 For discussion of this argument see ANTOKOLSKAIA, M., *Harmonisation of Family Law in Europe: A Historical Perspective* (Intersentia, 2006), pp. 3–47.

7 See e.g. BOELE-WOELKI, K., "What Comparative Family Law Should Entail?", (2008) *Utrecht Law Review* 1.

personality, affective relationships and religious beliefs make it an ideal aspect of law in which to trace the influence of religion. Family and religion may each be classified as private and yet are frequently the subject of debate in terms of the interaction of public and private. Love, which is often cited as being at the heart of modern familial relationships, is also a key element of religious teaching and faith. Our aim in this book was not to focus on any particular religion, or to adopt in advance a specific theoretical or thematic approach, but instead to embark on a search for incidents of the place which religion has or might have within family law.

2. RELIGION AND FAMILY LAW: VIEWS FROM THE PAST

The primary focus of our search is family law within Europe and therefore, historically, the key religious influence is Christianity, as mediated through the principles and institutions of canon law. It has been argued that "[t[he medieval uniform canon family law of the Roman Catholic Church was the common cradle from which all Western European countries started their evolution."[8] The extent to which this universal source was similarly implemented in different countries and regions is debated[9] but nonetheless it is widely acknowledged that, throughout Europe, there was a certain level of commonality based on canon law, as it related to the family. There are significant shared elements: the origins of Western legal systems in canon law, the liberalisation and individualisation of family law which followed from the Reformation and the more recent trends towards secularisation and declining levels of personal religious belief and conformity. Although the speed and timing of change may be different in each of the systems considered, there is nonetheless considerable common ground. There is no straightforward graph to be drawn, showing a clear trend from a time when canon law was largely synonymous with family law to a time when it has little remaining influence. Instead there is a much more nuanced picture of the complex relations between the two. In this comparative assessment, our aim is to highlight juxtapositions and intersections rather than to identify disappearances or to discover complete and conclusive patterns.

2.1. CHURCH AND STATE

One of the key issues to emerge from historical analysis of family law and religion, within a western European context, is the interaction between church

8 ANTOKOLSKAIA, *supra* note 4, p. 154.

9 See, e.g,. discussion by FINLAY, in this volume, *supra* at p. 276.

and state; the relative importance of canon law being to a great extent a reflection of the shifting relationship of power between church and state. The Reformation was obviously a significant moment of change in this power struggle but there were other relevant factors and influences. The Catholic Church exercised power, not only by influencing the principles and rules of family law, but also through education of the lawmakers and judges. The simple enactment of a legal and political separation between church and state was unlikely to result in a strict divide between matters religious and secular. The recognition of certain churches, as established churches or as state churches, provided for ongoing links and ensured a special place for those religious bodies within the society. In the absence of a radical change, such as, for example, that which occurred with the coming into being of the Soviet Union, there was unlikely to be a clean break with religious law of the past and therefore its influence continued long after the formal separation of religious establishments and the state.

Although formal, legal reform indicates a break from religion at various points in history, the accounts in several of the essays in this volume highlight the resilience of religion and the ingenuity of legislators and judiciary in maintaining and adapting religious principles, particularly where they have strong support from society. Where a break has been made in one respect between religion and family, its connection may later be detected in a new and surprising context. Speaking of the Reformation in England, Lawrence Stone observed that,

> "the household was the inheritor of many of the responsibilities of the parish and the Church; the family head was the inheritor of much of the authority and many of the powers of the priest. Thus the Word of God was to some degree removed from the parish church and transferred to the private home: the Holy Spirit was partly domesticated."[10]

The interaction between canon law and state was in itself complex and therefore the Reformation, while signalling a significant change in the church's relationship with the secular state and its legal rules, did not amount to the removal of religion from the equation. In tracing the developing impact of religion in family law, we should not restrict our vision to a single church or religious body and its formal relationship with the state.

---

10 STONE, L., *The Family, Sex and Marriage in England 1500–1800* (abridged) (Penguin, 1979), pp. 104–105.

2.2. SCRIPTURE AS LAW

Religion was influential in family law not only through institutional structure but also in terms of the creation and formation of rules; recognising the fact that the "canonists ... were expert in developing legal principles from scripture".[11] Canon law was particularly influential in the development of a modern legal model of marriage: the domesticated, nuclear marriage which was to form the basis for family life. It is argued that this was not a given, a direct consequence of scripture, but instead a carefully developed model of the medieval Roman Catholic Church. There are examples, in some systems of family law, of the express incorporation of passages from scripture but, often, the reliance was more subtle:

> "The Bible itself was rarely quoted directly in Scots statutes ... But parliament certainly felt free to legislate on the basis of religious fiat in the realm of the family, and in statute the Bible, in particular Mosaic law, often either lies silent in the background or was subsumed under the general phrase 'the laws of God'."[12]

The skill of jurists and judges is evident in Harding's discussion, for example, of the Irish law on nullity, where, guided by pragmatism, they attempted to preserve the tenets of canon law but in ways which would not unduly alienate the non-Catholic sections of the society.

Throughout the various historical accounts in this volume, and in discussion of current issues,[13] the flexibility of scripture and its openness to interpretation is clear. Not only within Christianity, but also in terms of Judaism and Islam, there is evidence that, despite what may at times be taught, there is considerable room for difference of opinion and interpretation. This has undoubtedly assisted religion in remaining relatively resilient and adaptable throughout historical change. It also lies behind some of the key differences between the substance and development of different European family law systems. The treatment of marriage as a sacrament by some legal systems but not by others, and the schism between those Christian systems which adopted a consensual approach to marriage formation and those which did not, requiring either consummation or priestly declaration in addition to individual exchange of consent, are examples of how the same passages of scripture can lead to quite distinct legal rules. This scope to interpret and mould the same words into different models should offer some

---

11 FINLAY, in this volume, *supra* at p. 276.

12 *Ibid.* at p. 288.

13 See in particular the essays of DE BLOIS and NORRIE, in this volume, *supra* at pp. 232 and 304, where they highlight the different interpretations of liberal and traditional, or orthodox, religious groups.

hope to those who seek to reconcile what may seem to be intractable clashes of dogma.

2.3. THE CHURCH IN THE COMMUNITY

Following the Reformation in Scotland, the direct link between the Roman Catholic Church and family law was broken but, in other ways, the church continued to play an important role. As the church's role as lawmaker and lawgiver declined, there was evidence of its considerable power as law enforcer. In Scotland,

> "[t]he kirk regarded itself, in the service of a godly community, as having an interest not only in preserving individual souls but also having a licence to interfere directly in household life in the name of protecting the wider interests of the parish."[14]

This support, and consequent interference, could be seen, for example, in the context of the provision of parish support for the poor. Kirk sessions operated a far reaching network of local policing, not only controlling and enforcing but supporting too, "much like a combination of modern social welfare agency, marriage counselling service and police domestic violence unit."[15] The blurring of boundaries between, on the one hand, religious doctrine and faith and, on the other, religious community as a source of social support or control can also be seen, for example, in the ongoing influence of the Swedish church in social life and the breadth of social services provided by the Roman Catholic Church in Malta.

Just as there may be a perception of a declining role for religion in society and in the individual lives of many people, so there is a perception that there has been a shift from a time when religion played a central and defining role in family law to the present situation where religion may be relevant in specific aspects of family law or for particular groups and communities but of much less impact on family law in general. This decline reflects the changing relationship between state and religion, a diminishing legal reliance on a particular religious family model and a weakening in individual religious belief and observance. Tracing the changing relations between religion and state, individuals and religious authority and religious belief and law highlights the complex and fragmented channels by means of which the church, or other religious body, governed, instructed, inspired, infiltrated and enforced. Both historically, and in terms of

14 FINLAY, in this volume, *supra* at pp. 279-280.

15 *Ibid.*, at p. 281.

current analysis, greater enlightenment may come from awareness of new intersections rather than disappearing links.

3. RELIGION AND FAMILY LAW: CURRENT DILEMMAS

Our search for the place of religion in family law does not aim or pretend to be comprehensive but instead seeks to highlight current instances of the interaction of religion and family law. Some of these reflect ways in which family law and religion are linked because of the functions and forms of each. Others highlight specific issues which arise because of clashing or competing values, in particular legal systems, between state and religion. We have grouped individual contributions to our search into four themes, to assist in identifying shared concerns and contrasting approaches. Clearly, however, there is considerable overlap between these themes, and consideration of individual contributions should not be confined within a single classification.

The first focuses on Accommodating a Place for Religion: dealing specifically with issues which arise in respect of the treatment of a particular religious group within a larger society, which does not share its religious values or laws. The concept of "accommodation" is also considered, however, in many of the other papers, in a variety of ways: the accommodation of tradition and culture within laicism;[16] an "accommodationist approach" to the right to freedom of thought, conscience and religion within the context of the provision of education;[17] the accommodation not only of law to religion but also of religion to law, as evidenced by the accommodation of "religious groups and individuals" to "social and legal developments" in respect of same-sex relationships.[18] The second theme focuses on Denying a Place for Religion; considering states which have specifically adopted a principle of secularism and, by so doing, may be said to "deny" a place for religion within the legal system. While secularism does not ignore the existence of religion, it does deny it a formal place within state policy and law. The third looks at instances in which the legal system may be seen to be Supporting a Place for Religion, either on a wide scale basis or in respect of a particular issue. Finally, we explore the extent to which legal systems, and particular aspects of family law, may be viewed as Reflecting a Place for Religion, by analysing the roles which religion and religious beliefs or values may play.

16 ÖRÜCÜ, in this volume.
17 McCARTHY, in this volume.
18 NORRIE, in this volume, *supra* at p. 304.

3.1. ACCOMMODATING A PLACE FOR RELIGION

Much of the current interest in religion and law stems specifically from the treatment of religious minorities within jurisdictions which do not share their particular faith or belief system. This is the challenge, identified by the Archbishop of Canterbury within the UK context, which is posed by "the presence of communities which, while no less 'law-abiding' than the rest of the population, relate to something other than the British legal system alone."[19] This is not an entirely new challenge to the extent that, in many countries where there has been a dominant, or established church or religious body, migration and social trends have from time to time raised the issue of how to accommodate non-conformists or non-believers. To a large extent, however, issues previously faced by European countries related to the accommodation of other churches or sects but still within a broadly Christian framework: the accommodation of different views but within an essentially common frame of reference.[20] The most obvious challenge which is now emerging is how to deal with a Muslim community, which wishes to live and be regulated according to Shari'a, within a civil legal system which is either loosely based on Christianity or which is secular.

Various approaches as to how to deal with minority communities have been considered and may be summarised as ranging from assimilation to accommodation. Within these choices, there is further flexibility, with accommodation in particular being described as "an elastic term".[21] Two contributions in this volume directly address the extent to which minority religious laws and practices are, or should be, "accommodated".[22] Crawford and Carruthers trace the development of rules of international private law, and their judicial application, and in so doing demonstrate a well-established and accepted means by which to "accommodate and resolve issues of cross-cultural diversity".[23] The rules of international private law, and their application within the UK, clearly fit within a model of accommodation,

> "seen as a gracious *concession* conferred by the framers of the single overarching law for all citizens and decidedly not the acknowledgement of a rival legal order that some citizens, by virtue of their faith, can avail themselves of."[24]

---

19 *Supra* note 1.

20 For further discussion, see BHANDAR, B., "The Ties That Bind: Multiculturalism and Secularism Reconsidered", (2009) 36(3) *Journal of Law and Society* 301.

21 AHDAR *et al.*, *supra* note 2, p. 24; BUDZISZEWSKI, J. in AHDAR *et al.* (eds.), *supra* note 2, pp. 181–206.

22 MENSKI, and CRAWFORD and CARRUTHERS, in this volume.

23 CRAWFORD and CARRUTHERS, in this volume, *supra* at p. 37.

24 AHDAR *et al. supra* note 2, p. 24.

The approach supported by Menski comes much closer to "acknowledgement of a rival order." He firmly rejects the assimilationist approach as overly simplistic and as failing to take account of the two way process on which it is based: "Simplistic assumptions about assimilation of migrants like 'salt into water' are manifestly wishful thinking, because simple common sense suggests that the water itself changes quality when the salt dissolves."[25]

Both of these contributions share substantial focus on Muslim communities and Shari'a,[26] and issues are specifically raised in that context. One aspect of current debate is substantive, in that it relates to the content of particular rules and practices within Shari'a, and it is recognised that some of the hostile reaction to the suggestions made in the Archbishop of Canterbury's speech, and much of the debate which has followed, focuses on the substance or alleged substance of specific rules.[27] Our focus here is more on the structural possibilities for accommodation rather than on critique of the substance of Shari'a in respect of family law. Menski argues that the current attitude of most lawyers, judges and academics towards "new ethnically and ethically pluralising developments in our midst"[28] is to ignore them or to pretend to have no knowledge of them. In so doing they fail to take account of "others", risk creating unfair and discriminatory outcomes and cling to an unjustified belief in the existence of or need for a fixed and settled legal code. This narrow perspective is being sustained in the face of "emerging scenarios of 'superdiversity' and even of 'plutopia,' an emerging condition where no single community has absolute control."[29] The reluctance to acknowledge or to engage with the religious, and often informal, laws of minorities within our society may spring partly from hostility towards those religious or ethnic groups and perceptions of their rules and practices but also from a fear of unfamiliar, alien and complex procedures, systems and frameworks.

The open and fluid approach advocated by Menski contrasts sharply with the more traditional and clearly defined application of the rules of international private law as a way of dealing "with diversity, principally legal diversity, and subsidiarily cultural and religious diversity" and of accommodating "that diversity as the forum from time to time sees fit".[30] The distinctions and divisions in the latter approach are much more clearly drawn and the relevant place of the

---

25 MENSKI, in this volume, *supra* at p. 16.

26 Although Crawford and Carruthers deal with a wider range of religions and Menski acknowledges that the issues he discusses do not arise only in the context of Islamic law.

27 See e.g. SHACHAR, A., "State, Religion and the Family: The New Dilemmas of Multicultural Accommodation" in AHDAR *et al.* (eds.), *supra* note 2, pp. 115–133.

28 MENSKI, in this volume, *supra* at p. 16.

29 *Ibid.*, at p. 17.

30 CRAWFORD and CARRUTHERS, in this volume, *supra* at p. 68.

domestic and secular legal system and the role of "secular judge" within it are firmly established. The way in which UK courts have developed over time, and adapted to accommodate aspects of the personal laws of individuals, reflects a clear legal structure although at the same time a growing awareness and understanding of the foreign law.

A key issue which Crawford and Carruthers highlight, although do not further explore, in their essay is the fact that, "[i]n international private law, religious law typically has been encountered under the banner of 'foreign law'. This assumes that foreign law starts at the border."[31] It is here that the difference is evident between the treatment of an individual who acts in compliance with the rules of foreign law when outside the UK and an individual who complies with these same rules but when territorially within the UK.[32] For those legal systems which have previously accommodated ethnic, cultural and religious diversity primarily through recognition, in appropriate cases, of the foreign law, the establishment and settlement of substantial ethnic minority communities within their own territory increasingly highlights the difference in treatment based on location. The sharp contrast between these two contributions may begin to alight on some common ground in their shared acknowledgement that there can be resulting unfairness from the recognition of personal law where it is foreign law but not in the situation where the foreign territorial element is missing.

3.2. DENYING A PLACE FOR RELIGION

Several of the legal systems considered in this book have adopted an expressly secular system of family law and the principle of secularism features to some extent in most of the contributions. Three examples in particular are explored, each of which has an apparently secular system of family law. Sweden is well known for being the ultimate secular state; a system which developed gradually over a period of time. Turkey has a principle of laicism which it imported to replace, and modernise, a previously pluralist system. Russia has experienced both religious and secular systems of family law, with sudden shifts between them as a result of political change. In each analysis, there is an opportunity to consider the nature of secularism while at the same time exploring the fit between that express principle and the role of religious establishments, private religious belief and behaviour within the particular society.

The term "secular" is used widely to describe a legal system which is quite separate from organised religion and religious principles, and it is often posited

31 *Ibid.*

32 See for a recent example their discussion at p. 52 of *Sulaiman v Juffali* [2002] 2 FCR 427.

as the opposite of religious. This distinction is increasingly questioned and the nature and effect of "truly" secular laws challenged.[33] The very notion of secularism, and its claim of separateness from religion, is argued to be "itself derived historically from Western Christian religious beliefs."[34] In the examples considered in this volume, a range of meanings and effects of secularism can be seen.

For Sweden, "by reputation ... one of the most secularised countries in the world",[35] secular family law is a legal framework which reflects "exclusively secular values" and which has evolved largely in line with its other Nordic neighbours.[36] Swedish secularism has become associated with modern, liberal family laws which emphasise equality and neutrality and the principle has been presented confidently as fitting well with Swedish society. Turkish laicism, by contrast, appears far out of line with the views and expectations of a large part of Turkish society, and its adoption, as part of the borrowed Swiss legal code, marked an abrupt split with the previously pluralist system. During the Ottoman Empire, "there was no one language, no single distinct culture, no one religion and therefore no one law."[37] Pluralism was firmly entrenched within the previous legal system "both as to substantive law to be applied and the courts which had jurisdiction to apply the law"[38] and family matters were governed by the personal, and in many cases religious, laws of individuals.

These two secular systems outwardly have little in common but both Jänterä-Jareborg and Örücü refer to structural imbalances in the operation of the secular principle. In Sweden, there is a state recognised church, the Church of Sweden, which continues to have a relatively high level of membership, whilst in Turkey, laicism is described as being "one-sided" due to the fact that, although "the interference of religion into state affairs and politics is not permitted, the interference of the state into religious affairs is."[39] In both countries, what is clear is that, while there should be no direct influence of religion in law that does not mean the absence of a role for religion.

In Russia, there have been sharp swings from religion to secularism; from a position where "Russia had no family laws other than religious ones" to a period,

---

33 See e.g. BHANDAR, *supra* note 20.

34 BERMAN, *supra* note 5, at p. 742.

35 JÄNTERÄ-JAREBORG, in this volume, *supra* at p. 73.

36 For discussion of the Church of Sweden and those of the other Nordic countries, see CHRISTOFFERSEN, L., "Not Even Believing in Belonging: States and Churches in Five North-European (Post-) Lutheran Countries" in FERRARI *et al.*, *supra* note 3, pp. 187–197.

37 ÖRÜCÜ, in this volume, *supra* at p. 118.

38 *Ibid.*

39 *Ibid.*, at p. 122.

following the Bolshevik Revolution, of "militant atheism".[40] Russia, as with Sweden and Turkey, has a population, a high proportion of which, adheres to one single religion or church and therefore, until recently at least, the issues have not been further complicated by pluralist claims. In Russia, although there has been a strong revival in the Russian Orthodox Church and in individual religious belief post-independence, the legal principle of secularism remains. For the time being, Antokolskaia comments that church and state exist in relative harmony, although it may be questioned to what extent this is a reflection of their recently troubled past and the current period of re-emergence and tolerance.

In Sweden, there is a sense that secularism as a legal principle has developed largely in line with the views of the population, although with relatively little impact on the role of the Swedish Church in the life of the population; in Turkey, laicism represented a political "aspiration",[41] adopted almost without regard for the views of Turkish society and in Russia, the secularism of the Soviet Union was a much more extreme attempt not only to remove the church from society but to change the beliefs of individuals: "to roll back the influence of religion – the Bolsheviks' greatest ideological rival."[42] These three different examples offer some insight into the different meanings of secularism and its differing implications for state religion, cultural religion and individual faith. While for the time being, religion and religious belief appear to be providing relatively little difficulty for secular Russia, in Sweden and in Turkey, the secular state is to some extent being challenged by issues of multiculturalism, strong personal Islamic belief and by the difficulties inherent in distinguishing religion from culture.

3.3. SUPPORTING A PLACE FOR RELIGION

In contrast to legal systems which have adopted an expressly secular attitude, there are others which support religion, either by giving a particular religion or church special protection within the Constitution or by recognising or incorporating specific religious concepts, rules or procedures within aspects of the family law framework. We have included papers considering Ireland and Malta, in both of which the Roman Catholic Church has had a privileged role or privileged status. We have also included consideration of the Jewish *get* and various ways in which this form of religious divorce has been recognised or "supported" in different legal systems. Provision for, or accommodation of Jewish law in respect of the *get*, although apparently a relatively minor aspect of a family law system, constitutes a significant instance of legal support for religious law.

---

40 ANTOKOLSKAIA, in this volume, *supra* at p. 97.

41 ÖRÜCÜ, in this volume, *supra* at p. 121.

42 ANTOKOLSKAIA, in this volume, *supra* at p. 105.

The treatment and protection of faith schools, particularly within the UK context, is another example of an otherwise secular legal system supporting religion, by making special provision for religious education.

Malta offers the most overt and wide-ranging support for religion, by means of its Constitution which "proclaims the Roman Catholic Apostolic Religion as the religion of Malta".[43] Despite some historical changes in the relationship between the church and the state, Roman Catholicism has a long, and relatively unchallenged, position within Malta, and its teachings, laws and traditions not surprisingly have been highly influential in the "ethos" of family law.[44] What is notable, however, is the way in which the Maltese courts have attempted to accommodate the demands of European human rights within the confines of the domestic, religious family law; albeit with the significant exceptions of same-sex relationships and divorce. The latter are instances of challenge to the dominant Catholic model of marriage-based family which, to date, have been beyond the stretch of what has otherwise been shown to be a relatively flexible model.

Flexibility and responsiveness to change and to diversity are similarly evident through the judicial decisions of the Irish courts, which demonstrated that, by means of a "'catholic' approach to Church doctrines", they have been able in the past to "find a way to reflect a prevailing liberal morality even if they must use the tools of an inherently conservative framework."[45] Ireland's support of a specific family model, which is clearly, if not always expressly, moulded on Roman Catholicism, has been moderated through awareness of the need to accommodate a range of religious and other social views. There is no direct line between canon law and Constitutional provision, but an astute pattern of interpretation, with a clear objective in mind but also with awareness of the need for accommodation. Harding suggests that it is the lack of such a clear objective, now evident "in the absence of homogenous religious values", that is resulting in the more recent inconsistency of "the constitutional protection of marriage".[46] The success of constitutional protection of religion or a religious model is to a large extent dependent on the strength of the majority belief and the careful accommodation of other influences, whether religious, moral, cultural or social.

Jewish family law, and in particular the *get*, has been considered by several jurisdictions in recent years. While Jewish law is expressly supported in Israel, with at least part of Israel's family law being based on religious law, other secular jurisdictions have also provided support for the *get* by recognising or

43 FARRUGIA, in this volume, *supra* at p. 187.

44 *Ibid.*

45 HARDING, in this volume, *supra* at p. 161.

46 *Ibid.*, at p. 184.

incorporating it in various ways into their secular divorce laws. Whereas there is considerable diversity in the individual approaches of legal systems towards accommodating this clash between civil and religious requirements, and there are other jurisdictions which have chosen not to recognise the *get*, this stands out as an area of religious law which has attracted a relatively supportive reaction from several legal systems. This recognition of extra-judicial divorce by some secular states stands in contrast to the more widespread resistance to recognition of Shari'a divorce provisions and raises questions as to the level and consistency of support for any or some religious family laws.

The continued support within the UK for religious education may be simply a reflection of a relatively high level of support for faith-based education but it may also, to some extent, be due to the fact that it has not always been identified as an issue of central importance in the religious/secular debate. From one view, education is at the outskirts of family law, but teaching and guidance is central to the relationship between parent and child and, as McCarthy points out, "religion is built into British schools from the foundations." Support for religion in education can therefore be seen as central both to the development and continuation of family relationships and to the place of religion within the state. There are obvious tensions between secular state, parental responsibilities and wishes and children's rights; tensions which are underlined if a further distinction is made between "education" and "religious education".[47]

3.4. REFLECTING A PLACE FOR RELIGION

In the final section, we have included discussion of ways in which religion, and religious values or beliefs, may influence and be reflected in family law, regardless of the particular commitment of the overall legal system to either a religious or secular principle. Just as it might be argued that the decline in public stature of religion and church within many societies has been balanced to some extent by the internalisation of religious based beliefs and models, so there is evidence of the continuing reflection of religion in outwardly secular laws.

Historical analysis tends to indicate that, although for most of Europe, the Reformation signalled a split between church and state, there was not necessarily such a clear shift in direction within family law. Although canon law ceased to be directly enforceable and the system of enforcement itself changed from church based to civil courts, the tenets of canon law in many areas continued to exercise strong influence. This is particularly evident in respect of marriage and adult

[47] As seen, e.g., in Turkey where the parents have the sole right to decide on the religious education of their children: discussed by ÖRÜCÜ, in this volume, *supra* at pp. 138–139.

relationships, where the Christian model of marriage has continued to exert control. Where the debate is between "formal" marriage and "marriage-like" relationships, the barriers to change have been relatively weak; not surprisingly perhaps, as, for many European jurisdictions, the canon law consensual model had already accepted that it was the consent of the parties rather than any third party intervention or declaration which created the bond. Of all of the reflections of religious law and teaching in family law, those relating to the inherently heterosexual nature of Christian marriage have been most obvious. Only in Russia, during the Soviet period of atheism, was there evidence at a relatively early stage in the twentieth century of some legal acceptance of non-marital and same-sex relationships. In some states that legal acceptance has not yet been secured and in many countries, even where same-sex partnerships have been legally recognised and treated as being equal to marriage, gender neutral marriage has remained out of reach. Unlike in other areas, where more progressive and obviously secular developments in European human rights provided an impetus for domestic change, the slowness of the European Court of Human Rights to accept a same-sex family model has allowed domestic legal systems to remain relatively unchallenged.

While the influence of religion has remained strong within the context of adult intimate relationships, in other areas of family law its grip is much weaker. In the historical account of religion and family law within Scotland, Finlay highlighted the relatively modern nature of "family law" and the lack of universal applicability of canon law to all aspects of what we might now conceive of as family law. In particular, there was a split between issues of status and family relationships, centred on marriage, and regulation of matrimonial property. In the empirical analysis of recent social attitudes in Scotland, a similar split can to some extent be detected with regard to questions relating to relationships, where the apparent reflection of religiosity was strongest, and those relating to familial obligations, where there was much less evidence of a divide.

In looking for reflections of religion in law, there is a risk of misinterpretation. Finlay argues that,

> "[i]solating religion as a causal force is ... potentially to misunderstand the fact that there were many causal forces, social, economic and psychological, which influenced the development of the idea of the family and also the law which regulated its place in the social structure of the community."[48]

It is a risk also highlighted in Rosie and Wasoff's interpretation of current Scottish attitudes but, even taking account of other influential factors such as

---

48 FINLAY, in this volume, *supra* at pp. 270–273.

age, social class and education, they conclude that, "[a]ll measures of *religion* point the same way: there is a sharp division between the religious and the non-religious."[49]

Whereas much of the focus in the individual contributions in this volume, and more widely in the current debate on religion and law, is on diversity and pluralism, analysis of Scottish social attitudes towards family values and family law indicates a different divide: "a religiosity divide".[50] In many aspects, there is more that unites those with some form of religious belief or connection than divides them in terms of specific affiliation or practice. Although,

> "there is a hierarchy between those who state they have both a religious affiliation and regularly attend religious services, those with an affiliation but who are infrequent or non-attenders and those who state they have no religious affiliation,"[51]

the authors nonetheless conclude that "religiosity matters" even where that takes the form of a religious affiliation without accompanying religious practice; a conclusion which lends weight to the paradoxes highlighted in the context of Sweden. Whether it is a case of "believing without belonging" or "belonging without believing",[52] the message is clear; religion continues to be reflected in family law and, in searching for the place of religion in family law, we should cast our net wide.

4. SHOULD THERE BE A PLACE FOR RELIGION IN FAMILY LAW: CONTINUING DEBATES?

Current debates surrounding religion and law reflect changes in population, human rights, family law and religious beliefs and practices, but while the immediate motivation behind the interest is "change", the issues that emerge show consistency with long-established concerns. Previous struggles between church and state, religious and secular, private and public, function and form, unity and diversity re-emerge in new guises. An "eternal conflict of interests and values, with victory swaying back and forth between the various contestants for priority"[53] has the consequence that, while the details of current issues are new, there is resonance with existing debates within family law and in particular with the Western enlightenment tendency towards dichotomies.

---

49 ROSIE and WASOFF, in this volume, *supra* at p. 342.

50 *Ibid.*, at p. 353.

51 *Ibid.*, at p. 351.

52 For further discussion of these different approaches to religious belief and religious affiliation, see e.g., CHRISTOFFERSEN, *supra* note 35 and DAVIE, G., *Religion in Britain since 1945: Believing Without Belonging* (Blackwell, 1994).

53 STONE, *supra* note 10, p. 425.

4.1. RELIGION AND FAMILY LAW: A PUBLIC/PRIVATE DICHOTOMY?

A classic academic debate, within family law, concerns the position of families and their legal regulation in the context of a public/private dualism.[54] Family life and familial relationships are often presented as part of the private sphere, governed by values of individualism, freedom, emotion and love, whereas the regulation of families and the effectiveness of services provided by and within them are clearly identified as being of considerable public importance. Religion too occupies a difficult and unsteady place within this dichotomy: at times identified with the state, at others relegated to the private sphere. Love, which is often presented as central to both family relationships and to religious belief, is viewed as a concept to be kept in private.[55] Lacking in the rationalism necessary for the public sphere, it is contained and nurtured within the private. Many aspects of the discussion of family law and religion resonate with this well-established framework of public and private.

4.1.1. Public space for religion

There is an initial split between those legal systems which retain a space for religion within the public state and those which have adopted, in public, a policy of secularism. Questioning of this split, however, quickly demonstrates inconsistencies: those states which are publicly secular may nonetheless recognise, and to some extent support, an established church or religious body.[56] By so doing they give public status to that organisation which may in turn result in unequal treatment of other religious bodies which do not share its recognised position. Even in a system which appears strongly secular, such as Sweden, a continued role for the church, in the public celebration of family relationships, gives it a legal and social status which is to some extent paradoxical.[57] A number of European countries operate a dual system of marriage celebration, giving equal legal status to religious and civil marriage. Aside from issues of diversity and equality, which may stem from state control of those religious bodies which are permitted to solemnise marriage, questions may also be raised as to the dividing line between "religious" celebrants and "others":

---

54 See e.g., O'DONOVAN, K., *Sexual Divisions in Law* (Weidenfeld and Nicolson, 1995); OLSEN, F., "The Family and the Market: A Study of Ideology and Legal Reform", (1983) 96 *Harvard Law Review* 1497.

55 For some thoughts on love, both romantic and Christian, and its unsuitability to the public sphere, see ARENDT, H., *The Human Condition* (University of Chicago Press, 1958) and discussion of this in CHIBA, S., "Hannah Arendt on Love and the Political: Love, Friendship and Citizenship", (1995) *The Review of Politics* 505, especially pp. 524–531.

56 In the case of Turkey, the *Diyanet*. For discussion, see ÖRÜCÜ, in this volume, *supra* at p. 123.

57 See JÄNTERÄ-JAREBORG's discussion of the "Swedish paradoxes", *supra* at pp. 77–80.

what of those who hold strong beliefs but which do not fit within a traditional theist model, as in the case of humanists?[58] In Sweden, the continued strength in practice of the public celebration of marriage within a church may also challenge the neutral, inclusive legal provisions for same-sex and opposite-sex relationships which are enshrined in the secular legal framework. Control of access to the church or religious building, as a public space, to some extent questions the secular nature of the state.[59]

In other systems, although religious belief appears firmly relegated to the private sphere, it might be argued to have remained or re-emerged under the guise of "public" culture. In Turkey, the courts have shown adaptability towards religious belief by transforming it into culture and in that way gaining flexibility to accommodate it within the strict framework of laicism. In similar ways, the Irish courts are described as having incorporated elements of canon law in the form of culture. In Sweden, the folk and cultural significance of the Swedish Church has resulted in it retaining a surprisingly public significance. The place of religion and religious bodies is to some extent dependent on what we view as religion and how we distinguish it from broader notions of cultural identity. Declining levels of personal religious adherence mask the continuing and strong public presence of religion in the form of public buildings and cultural space.[60]

4.1.2. The private nature of belief

One view of religion identifies it in terms of personal faith; religious belief. A principle of freedom of religion and religious tolerance may provide a negative right to individuals to private belief and to personal adherence to that belief but may not fully address the interaction of that private belief with civil law and state.[61] Many western legal systems adopt a position similar to that set out in *Sulaiman v Juffali*, to the effect that "[r]eligion ... is no doubt something to be

58 For some discussion of these issues within a Scottish context, see MAIR, J., "Public Ceremony and Private Belief: the Role of Religion in the Scots law of Marriage", (2007) *Juridical Review* 280.

59 Further evidence of these tensions can be seen in the attempts to reform the UK's Civil Partnership Act 2004 which originally prohibited civil partnerships from being registered within religious premises. For discussion, see NORRIE, in this volume, *supra* at pp. 314–315.

60 There are, of course, also examples of the removal of religious signs and symbols from public space. See, e.g., BIRNBAUM, P., "On the Secularization of the Public Square: Jews in France and in the United States", (2008–2009) 30 *Cardozo L Rev* 2431; RORIVE, I., "Religious Symbols in the Public Space: In Search of a European Answer", (2008–2009) 30 *Cardozo L Rev* 2669.

61 Issues arising from the interaction, within a European context, of freedom of religion, tolerance and non-discrimination are explored in TULKENS, F., "European Convention on Human Rights and Church-State Relations: Pluralism vs. Pluralism", (2008–2009) 30 *Cardozo L Rev* 2575; EVANS, M.D., "The Freedom of Religion or Belief and the Freedom of Expression", (2009) 4 *Religion and Human Rights* 197.

encouraged but it is not the business of government or of the secular courts".[62] Secular legal systems choose to contain religious beliefs within the context of the private sphere but that division, it is argued, is itself the product of a specifically Christian perspective.[63] Speaking particularly of Judaism, de Blois observes that "in religious law, there is no 'public' and 'private' distinction"[64] and this holistic approach is also firmly grounded in Islam. To construct a place for religion within the context of a public/private divide is in itself to deny recognition of some religions and religious law. Speaking specifically of Islam, it has been commented that "religious identity tends to blur the border between what is political and what is not political, as well as what is 'private' and what is 'public'"[65] and rejection of this classic dichotomy is particularly appropriate within the context of family law, where attempts to divide public from private and personal from political have often been criticised.

4.1.3. Personal meaning of public relationships

Regardless of the secular nature of a state, private religious belief may be tolerated, or even welcomed, particularly if it reinforces publicly agreed values and contributes to a sense of shared and sharing community. The individual nature of family relationships has been acknowledged as precluding a necessarily shared understanding of the shape of the personal interaction[66] but, arguably, this lack of common purpose has been exacerbated by changing legal regulation of marriage, with greater emphasis being placed on personal affect and emotional satisfaction than on a single, state imposed model of spousal relations. This opening up of legal marriage has allowed for inclusion of unmarried cohabitants within the legal framework and, to some extent, of same-sex couples, but it has consequently shaken whatever certainty there might previously have been as to the legal nature of marriage and, more broadly, as to why family law chooses to regulate certain types of relationship. As de Blois comments, "[i]t is remarkable that the whole idea of marriage as a legal concern is, in general, not questioned in even the most liberal of states."[67] The interaction of personal meaning with publicly recognised and regulated family relationships is most evident in the context of marriage which has, "long been regarded as both a legal and a spiritual

62 [2002] 2 FCR 427, *per* Munby J. at p. 439, as quoted and discussed by CRAWFORD and CARRUTHERS, in this volume, *supra* at p. 38.

63 Although this is not always fully acknowledged: BERMAN, *supra* note 5, at p. 740.

64 DE BLOIS, in this volume, *supra* at p. 209.

65 GAUDREAULT-DESBIENS, J.-F., "Religious Courts' Recognition Claims: Two Qualitatively Distinct Narratives" in AHDAR *et al.* (eds.), *supra* note 2, at p. 68.

66 For an interesting discussion of the "subjective" nature of intimate relationships in contrast to commercial contracts, see WIGHTMAN, J., "Intimate Relationships, Relational Contract Theory and the reach of Contract", (2000) 8(1) *Feminist Legal Studies* 93, particularly pp. 105–107.

67 DE BLOIS, in this volume, *supra* at p. 227.

institution – subject at once to special state laws of contract and property and to special religious canons and ceremonies."[68] With the declining certainty of a public legal conception of intimate relationships, space is being opened up for greater attention to focus on the "spiritual institution". Strong private belief may gain greater influence over the public framework, where the public model lacks clear and agreed foundations.[69] Much focus in the law and religion debate has been on the challenges posed to legal systems by religious beliefs of "others" but these challenges also provide opportunities to reconsider and redefine the nature of family relationships and family law.

4.2. RELIGION AND FAMILY LAW: FORM OR FUNCTION?

Another familiar framework employed in analysis of families and family law is that which seeks to distinguish between form and function. All European jurisdictions have seen similar trends during the twentieth century, and into the twenty first, away from emphasis on the form of relationships, dictated by compliance with legal rules and religious models, towards increasing recognition of the similar functions of a variety of differently constituted relationships.[70] This has been particularly evident within the context of the regulation and recognition of adult relationships: demonstrated by a move away from heterosexual marriage towards inclusion of informal relationships of cohabitation and of same-sex partnerships, both formal and informal. There is, however, no clear consensus in terms of the legal and political preference for either form or function and their interaction is complex. So too, it appears, when a similar analytical model is applied to religion.

4.2.1. Form of family relationships

In discussion of religion and family law, it is clear that the area which has attracted most attention is marriage. The Christian model of the family, based on a monogamous, opposite sex, permanent union, has exerted strong and lasting influence throughout the European jurisdictions considered. Several of the particular issues discussed in individual essays in this collection relate to this

68 WITTE, J., "The Future of Muslim Family Law in Western Democracies" in AHDAR *et al.* (eds.), *supra* note 2, at p. 281.

69 See e.g. the contrasting approach to the formation of marriage in the Scottish Outer and Inner House decisions in *SH v KH* 2006 SC 129. Is marriage a civil status entered into by compliance with the statutory provisions for formation or does it require personal consent to an underlying model of commitment to act as husband and wife? For further discussion of this issue in a Scottish context, see MAIR, J., "Marriage: Legal Status or Personal Relationship", (2007) *Edin LRev* 117.

70 See e.g. McCLAIN, L., "Love, Marriage and the Baby Carriage: Revisiting the Channelling Function of Family Law", (2006) 28 *Cardozo L Rev* 2133.

model: recognition of unmarried cohabitation; grounds for nullity; acceptance of divorce and, most recently, legal recognition of same-sex partnerships. Even where the biblical origins of modern family law are not openly acknowledged, the continuing force of their influence is clear, as can be seen, for example, in the Swedish reaction to a proposal, "to transform the legal institution of marriage into a gender-neutral concept, thus permitting also same-sex marriages", a reaction which "clearly demonstrated how deeply intertwined marriage is with religion."[71]

Religion has impacted on the form of family relationships, not only within the context of Christianity, but also when broadly Christian, albeit formally secular, legal systems come into contact with family forms of other religions. In the case studies presented by Menski, differing rules and understandings of family form clash. Particularly within the context of Ahmadi marriages in Pakistan, the variety of form and formation, according to the personal law of the individuals, further exacerbates "legal insecurities"[72] and the resulting reluctance of lawyers and officials to engage with the legal validity of various types of relationship.

4.2.2. Function of family relationships

In discussion of international private law developments, there is evidence, particularly within the context of polygamous marriages, of the UK courts developing a greater openness towards recognition of such marriages, not "in general or in the abstract", but in the context of a particular purpose and with focus on the incidents of marriage, rather than the status of marriage itself.[73] Although subsequent developments led to a much more widespread recognition of polygamous marriage, it is noteworthy that recognition was easier in the early stages where it could be linked to the function and consequences of marriage rather than to its inherent form. It might similarly be argued that when the focus is on function rather than form, it becomes more acceptable to acknowledge the Jewish *get* despite a legal system's requirement otherwise of judicial divorce. The unfairness to the "chained wife" of *get* refusal has clearly been of considerable influence in persuading legislators or courts to recognise the particular function, within religious family law, of this form of divorce. Evidently, however, focus on function is maintained at best inconsistently in most legal systems, as the accommodation of the Jewish *get* is a relatively isolated incident of willingness to take into account "religious" divorce.

---

71 JÄNTERÄ-JAREBORG, in this volume, *supra* at p. 74.
72 MENSKI, in this volume, *supra* at pp. 29–34.
73 CRAWFORD and CARRUTHERS, in this volume, *supra* at p. 39.

The function of family relationships is of concern not only to the state but to religious organisations and communities. The symbiotic nature of interaction between families and faith is highlighted particularly in the issue of religious education, where the function of parents as guardians and guides for their children overlaps with their duty as individual members of a faith community to broadcast and promote their religious beliefs. Commitment, support and obligation are values at the heart of both family and faith and the interaction of both can be seen as central to their respective maintenance.

4.2.3. Form of religion

It has not been a principal aim of this work to consider in detail, or to criticise, the differing form of individual religions or religious beliefs but some distinctions clearly emerge between religious beliefs which are more, or less, acceptable within broadly secular legal systems. Partly that might be explained within the context of a human rights analysis although, as de Blois, for example, has highlighted, in discussion of many aspects of religion and family law there are arguments on both sides.[74] It is clear that some forms of religion appear to be less threatening and more easily accommodated than others and this has had an inevitable impact on the extent to which they are resisted or incorporated.

The form which religion takes within a particular society has emerged as a point of some interest. Is it religion as a source of rules, as a form of culture, as individual belief, or as a way of life? A high level of religious belief amongst individual citizens does not necessarily correlate with legal protection for that religion or reflection of the religious rules and concepts within the provisions of family law. In fact, in some systems it is quite the opposite.[75] In other systems, a very low level of individual religious adherence or faith is ironically situated within a society in which the church has a central cultural role. This is most obviously evidenced in Sweden where,

> "Scandinavians belong to the State Churches without even believing in belonging, since faith is only partly the function of the Churches, alongside ensuring arrangements for the central institutions of life, the family, national heritage and nation building."[76]

The form, or formulation, of religion or certain religious practices or beliefs as culture or tradition can be seen either to mask the apparent secularism of a

[74] DE BLOIS, in this volume, *supra* at pp. 228–233.

[75] Most obviously Turkey.

[76] CHRISTOFFERSEN, *supra* note 35.

society or to assist in the accommodation of personal religious faith into a system which otherwise allows no place for religion.[77]

Attempts to step away from individual beliefs and differences and to look for some common ground may help to highlight what is shared and may facilitate better and more productive communication. The concept of "civil religion" emphasises common ground and casts light not only on what is shared between different religions but also between religion and law.[78]

4.2.4. *Functions of religion*

Differing forms of religion and religious belief within various societies raise questions as to the function of religion. Historical accounts give some indication of a range of functions which religion and church may fulfil: a source of rules; a system of moral principles and beliefs; a structure of courts and judges; a framework for regulation and registration of relationships; a method of social control. In modern comparative analysis too, it is clear that religion can fulfil a variety of functions. In practical terms, the role of the Roman Catholic Church within Malta can be seen not only as providing much of the substance of family law rules but also as upholding principles of the Christian family model and providing practical support in the community. The social benefits, it might be argued, to some extent help to balance what some at least will view as the conservative restrictions which continue to apply. The relatively high levels of church membership within Sweden's strongly secular society, may reflect strong cultural and national ties rather than any "religious" affiliation. As Jänterä-Jareborg comments, "to *renounce* one's membership in the Church to which one was born and which continues to be well-established in society, requires taking a position on what religion is about."[79] Just as family lawyers are aware of the need to challenge an assumption of a universal understanding of "family" so we need to question our understanding of religion.

While civil courts are much happier with "arguments drawn from secular rationalism than from divine revelation"[80] and religion, perceived as strong, or even extreme, individual faith, may struggle for accommodation within secular law, the support which religion and religious thought can provide to family relations should not be overlooked.[81] The functions of religion are not necessarily

77 See in particular, in this volume, ÖRÜCÜ and HARDING.

78 See in particular BERMAN who discusses the concept of "civil religion" as identified by Jean-Jacques Rousseau: BERMAN, *supra* note 5, particularly at pp. 744–746.

79 JÄNTERÄ-JAREBORG, in this volume, *supra* at p. 78.

80 NORRIE, in this volume, *supra* at p. 306.

81 See e.g., BROWNING, D.S., "Modern Law and Christian Jurisprudence on Marriage and Family", (2008) 51 *Emory LJ* 31.

far removed from the functions of law, both of which communicate their values through "ritual", "tradition", "authority" and "universality".[82] While secular legal systems are likely to fear or mistrust strong expressions of faith or belief, preferring more "rational" behaviour and scientific motivation, the common ground inhabited by faith in religious belief and belief in affective relationships should not be overlooked.

4.3. RELIGION AND FAMILY LAW: CERTAINTY OR CHAOS?

The aim of much modern family law is to design and implement a clear and consistent set of principles and rules which foster certainty and limit discretion. Against that stated aim, however, is posited the pragmatic view that families and relationships are by their very nature chaotic and that we should expect nothing different of family law.[83] For modern, secular systems of family law, which have attained a relatively certain framework of legal rules, the prospect of recognising religious pluralism is a disturbing thought, whether in terms of particular religions or of tolerance of personal religious meaning in the context of legally established relationship models. Ironically, however, the clear, modern rules of secular family law may mask a lack of certainty and shared understanding of meaning; a certainty which is, in turn, associated closely with religious faith.

4.3.1. Clear laws but chaotic meaning

A driving force behind much family law reform in recent decades has been to clarify and simplify the legal framework. Replacement of discretion with clear rules or principles and the development of consistency and certainty are key objectives of modern family law. Civil rules for marriage and registration of relationships have replaced earlier systems allowing for informal constitution of marriage; restriction of the availability of declarators of nullity in favour of simplified divorce and detailed provisions for establishing parentage can all be seen as driven by a desire for clarity and coherence.

As legal rules have moved towards definition and administrative certainty, however, there has been a simultaneous fragmentation of meaning. What does it mean to say that a couple live together as husband and wife, except that they have the outward evidence of marriage in the form of an extract from a legal register; what does it mean to be the legal "parent" child when there is no necessary connection between those who appear on the legal birth certificate and those who "parent" the child? Emphasis on personal freedom and individual

---

82 BERMAN, *supra* note 5, at p. 746.

83 DEWAR, J., "The Normal Chaos of Family Law", (1998) *Modern Law Review* 467.

satisfaction within relationships has contributed to the demise of any shared notion of what it means to be "husband and wife". As soon as we accept the possibility that marriage need not be between a man and a woman, then the potential for diversity and fragmentation is clear. Modern family law may be set out in clear, formal terms but what it means in any deeper sense is increasingly chaotic. Legal rules have developed to define in detail the wide range of scientific or social paths to becoming a parent, but these clear legal rules overlay an underlying chaos as to what it means to be a parent. Simply seeking to protect the clarity which has been achieved in the formal provisions of modern, secular family statutes, against the messy invasion of diverse and complex religious beliefs, overlooks the chaos of meaning which lurks beneath these formal rules. Increasingly it is clear that some reconsideration of underlying concepts is needed and here again it is the interaction between apparent opposites, rather than their separation, which provides an opportunity "to explore ... conceptual deserts ... more thoughtfully."[84]

4.3.2. *Clear belief but chaotic laws*

When Menski says that many lawyers may not want to know about diverse personal laws, at least part of the explanation lies in a reluctance to open up an outwardly clear, secular legal framework to the operation and influence of a myriad of personal laws. He recognises that "we often instinctively desire more uniformity and certainty"[85] and, measured against that desire, the complex and, to our eyes, chaotic web of formal and informal practices, subject to regional variation and multiple interpretation, of shari'a appears entirely contradictory. To permit the operation of personal religious law, within a system of universal, civil rules, gives rise to an image of chaos. The extent to which many secular, family law systems currently operate, however, according to clear rules of general application, is questioned when we examine the place within these systems of private ordering. Increasingly legal systems offer a pick and mix approach to family regulation, with opportunity for, and state encouragement of, privately negotiated modification and settlement. Public systems of matrimonial property, from which individuals can choose to opt out through private contract, and principles of child welfare, which may evade public scrutiny as a result of private parental agreement, result in limited application in practice of the general rules. Alternative dispute resolution, family mediation and private ordering play an increasingly significant role in the day-to-day regulation of family relationships and operate beside or beneath the outwardly universal system of family law. While such private ordering takes place to a greater or lesser extent within the

84 BERRY, P., "Postmodernism and post-religion" in CONNOR, S. (ed.), *The Cambridge Companion to Postmodernism* (Cambridge University Press, 2004), 168, at p. 179.

85 MENSKI, in this volume *supra* at p. 17.

shadow of the law, it significantly undermines an image of modern family law as a coherent system of defined principles and provisions.

That is not to challenge such private agreements in themselves but simply to highlight that family law is already well accustomed to the incorporation or substitution of private rules into a public system. "[W]e have long known that many aspects of human life import dynamic and inherently messy legal dimensions"[86] and increasingly, secular family law systems leave those aspects to private regulation by means of personal agreement. As with each of the dualisms considered here, the interaction of religion and family law can shed light on both sides. Legal acceptance of civil private ordering, but not of religious based alternative dispute resolution, highlights an inconsistent approach. While there is considerable concern expressed in current debate about potential unfairness and inequality, particularly towards women, which may result from settlements mediated through faith, there is much less voiced concern about the implications of civil, negotiated settlements; although there is significant underlying unease as to their gendered impact.

5. THE RESULTS OF OUR SEARCH

Our search for the place of religion in family law was not undertaken with any real hope or expectation of "finding" but it was instead an attempt to explore, to highlight and to encourage discussion. The very mention of religion and the suggestion that it might have a place in secular family law, or that conflicts between different religious beliefs might require to be addressed within the context of monolithic legal systems, are uncomfortable thoughts for those who feel secure within the framework of a clear, modern, secular system. Part of our purpose was to consider possibilities as to how religion does, or could, infiltrate or integrate with family law: to begin to open up connecting channels between religious and secular. By doing so we were only following two well-known principles of good relationships: fostering open communication, in which we seek to "speak with one another" and not "merely about one another",[87] and accepting the possibility of compromise.

There have been many insights into particular issues involving religion and family law and into specific impact within the context of individual legal systems. Perhaps the strongest lesson is that strict distinctions, between church and state, between private belief and public policy, and between faith and rationalism, are

86 *Ibid.*, at p. 19.

87 HABERMAS, J., "An Awareness of What is Missing" in HABERMAS *et al.*, *An Awareness of What is Missing: Faith and Reason in a Post-secular Age* (Polity Press, 2010), at p. 16.

unhelpful and far from clear. We should learn from previous misconceptions which have resulted from false dichotomies and challenge the notion that religious and secular are, or should be, in opposition. Doing so is not simply an academic exercise in finding out more about other legal and religious systems of family law. Nor should it be viewed negatively in terms of necessity: an enforced accommodation of differing values. While competing requirements of plural belief and belief-based systems pose challenges for legal frameworks, they also offer opportunities. The aim of this volume was to search for the place of religion: a search embarked upon with confidence from within the citadel of family law, with religion quite clearly placed in the position of challenger. Admitting the possibility of another, however, inevitably demands self-reflection. Searching for the place of religion may in turn lead to questioning the role of family law.

[17]

The Overlooked Costs of Religious Deference

Robin Fretwell Wilson*

Abstract

Citing the Qur'an, a German divorce court judge this year denied a fast-track divorce to a Muslim woman who had been the victim of domestic violence and death threats from her husband. The judge rejected her application because the husband's exercise of his "right to castigate does not fulfill the hardship criteria" for an expedited divorce. The decision, which sparked a firestorm of controversy, comes at an important time in the movement to embrace pluralistic understandings of family relationships. Scholars and policymakers around the world are advancing various schemes for sharing state control over domestic disputes with religious groups—ranging from proposals to share jurisdiction over family disputes with religious bodies to enforcing religious understandings, like any other prenuptial agreement.

This Article asks how women and children will fare in a system of religious deference. It maintains that the state has an important protective function to play for these traditionally vulnerable groups. Enforcing certain religious understandings of marital relationships will likely undermine a woman's ability to exit the relationship and, consequently, prevent her from policing the conduct in her own relationship and with respect to her children. Policymakers should proceed cautiously with any proposal to hand over authority for marital disputes since family violence occurs in religious communities, as it does throughout society, but is tolerated by some religious leaders and adherents. Drawing on our experience with faith-based exemptions to the duty to provide medical care for children, this Article concludes that the costs of giving greater deference to religious understandings

* Professor of Law, Washington and Lee University School of Law; J.D., 1995, University of Virginia; B.A., 1989, University of Virginia. I would like to thank the participants in this Symposium, the panel on The Interface of Family Law and Religion at the International Society of Family Law's North American Regional Conference in Vancouver, British Columbia, and the conference on multi-tiered marriage at Pepperdine University School of Law for their thoughtful comments. I am indebted to Erin Willoughby, Francis McWilliams, and Garrett Ledgerwood for their painstaking research assistance.

of family relationships must seriously be considered before we are willing to rob women and children of the state's protections.

Table of Contents

I. Introduction

In March of 2007, *Der Spiegel* reported that a German divorce court judge denied a fast-track divorce based on hardship to a German citizen of Moroccan origin who had been the victim of domestic violence and death threats from her spurned husband.[1] In rejecting the application, the judge relied on a passage in the Qur'an that she read as permitting a man to castigate his wife.[2] The judge explained that the husband's exercise of his "right to castigate does not fulfill the hardship criteria," one of the grounds for an expedited divorce in Germany.[3]

1. Veit Medick & Anna Reimann, *A German Judge Cites Koran in Divorce Case*, DER SPIEGEL, Mar. 21, 2007, *available at* http://www.spiegel.de/international/germany/0,1518,473 017,00.html (last visited Feb. 22, 2008) (on file with the Washington and Lee Law Review).

2. *Id.*

3. *Id.* Ironically, if the plaintiff had been a Moroccan citizen, the judge would have applied Moroccan law. *See* MARION BOYD, DISPUTE RESOLUTION IN FAMILY LAW: PROTECTING CHOICE, PROMOTING INCLUSION 83 (2004) (on file with the Washington and Lee Law Review). In Germany,

> the citizenship of the party to a dispute determines what family law will apply if that party is not a German citizen, although "this general principle is, of course, subject to German public order and to any international conventions to which Germany is a party." . . . [A]s a result, German courts have had to deal with the interpretation and application of foreign laws, including Sharia.

A firestorm of controversy erupted in response to the ruling.[4] Feminists read it as giving the husband the right to beat his wife.[5] Muslim scholars disputed whether the Qur'an authorized physical violence against a spouse.[6]

When challenged on the ruling and asked to recuse herself, the judge again cited the Qur'an—this time citing a passage that says that a man's honor is injured when his wife acts in an unchaste manner.[7] Legislators across the spectrum then weighed in.[8] One called the ruling "an extreme violation of the rule of law," while another labeled it a "sad example of how the conception of law from another legal and cultural environment is taken as the basis of our own notion of law."[9]

As this case unfolds, a vibrant movement is taking hold—both in the United States and outside it—to give greater deference to religious understandings of family relations.[10] In the last year, numerous academics in the United States have proposed various schemes for sharing state control over domestic disputes with religious groups.[11] This Article argues that the effect of these proposals would be to pull the state out of marriage. While the proposals focus largely on the theoretical desirability of pluralistic understandings of marriage, they overlook pragmatic concerns that arise: What happens to women and children in a system of religious deference?

This Article maintains that the state has an important protective function to play for traditionally vulnerable groups, a function that should not be lightly set aside. Binding women who want to exit a marriage to a religious community's norms—whether by enforcing religious contracts or ceding jurisdiction over

Id. (quoting PASCALE FOURNIER, APPLICABILITY OF SHARIA/MUSLIM LAW IN WESTERN LIBERAL STATES (2004)). Under Moroccan law, the woman would have been entitled to a divorce, thanks to a series of family law reforms in 2004 that specifically allow divorce for harm, including intimate violence. FAMILY CODE pmbl., § 7 (2004) (Morocco), *translated in* Global Rights, *The Moroccan Family Code (Moudawana) of February 5, 2004*, at 5 (2005), http://www.globalrights. org/site/DocServer/Moudawana-English_Translation.pdf (last visited Jan. 29, 2008) (defining harm to include "lack of financial support, abandonment, violence, and other harm, in view of endorsing the general legal principle: 'neither harm nor be harmed,' [in order] to promote equality and equity between the two spouses") (on file with the Washington and Lee Law Review).

4. *See* Medrick & Reimann, *supra* note 1 (reporting that numerous politicians "voiced their horror at the verdict" and "demanded disciplinary action against the judge").

5. *See id.* (noting the opinions of members of *Terre des Femmes* and the Network for Muslim Women).

6. *Id.*; *see also infra* note 73 and accompanying text (discussing disputed interpretations of religious texts).

7. Medick & Reimann, *supra* note 1.

8. *Id.*

9. *Id.*

10. *See infra* Part II.

11. *Id.*

marriage to religious authorities—will raise the costs of exiting, undermine a woman's ability to exit, and prevent her from privately regulating the conduct in her own relationship and with respect to her children.

Part II surveys three proposals that would give greater deference to religious understandings of marriage and family relations, ranging from proposals to share jurisdiction over family disputes with religious bodies to enforcing religious understandings like any other prenuptial agreement. Part III then marshals empirical evidence showing that domestic violence occurs in religious communities, like it does in other parts of society. This Part shows not only that violence will occur, but that religious leaders and community members frequently tolerate "wife-abuse" and other forms of domestic violence.[12] This tolerance stems in part from the belief that "the marriage [must] be maintained"[13] at all costs.

Part IV maps out important breaks between some religious understandings of marriage and the rules society would otherwise apply, and argues that religious deference will have the effect of trapping some women in abusive relationships. Although the proposals outlined in Part II would not enforce religious understandings about the care of children, this Part argues that enforcing religious understandings about the adult relationship and financial matters cannot so neatly be divorced from the child's well-being. Part V concludes with cautionary lessons from another context in which society gives great religious deference—faith-based denials of medical treatment—and urges that the human costs of deference are far greater than these proposals blithely assume.

II. *Proposals for Religious Deference*

Several proposals have emerged over the last year advocating greater deference to religious understandings of marriage and family relationships. In one proposal, the state would cede some of its jurisdiction over family disputes to religious groups, while other proposals advocate the total abolition of state-sponsored marriage and a move to a purely contractarian form of domestic relationships. While different in many key respects, each proposal shares a common,

12. *See* S. Douki et al., *Violence Against Women in Arab and Islamic Countries*, 6 ARCHIVES WOMEN'S MENTAL HEALTH 165, 168 (2003) (discussing the "conspiracy of silence" in which various community members fail to adequately report or persecute instances of domestic violence).

13. Ruksana Ayyub, *Domestic Violence in the South Asian Muslim Immigrant Population in the United States*, 9 J. SOC. DISTRESS & HOMELESS 237, 243 (2000).

dangerous assumption: that protections for women and children can be preserved in a system of greater religious autonomy *without* substantial state oversight of marriage.

One such proposal comes from Professor Joel Nichols.[14] Nichols advocates that the government should cede some of its jurisdictional authority over marriage and divorce to religious communities, which, in turn, would allow for multiple understandings of family relations.[15] Nichols draws on New York's get statute and the covenant marriage statutes in three states to argue for greater accommodation of Muslim, Jewish, Christian, and other religious understandings of marriage.[16] Under a "multi-tiered" system of marriage, couples could choose a civil marriage with "minimal formalities" and hurdles to exit, but "capable and competent parties" would also be able to "enter more binding unions under the auspices of their religious traditions" if they so desire.[17] Religious communities could then "draw upon their own theological and legal resources to aid in governing their adherents."[18] Crucially, Nichols would accommodate multiple understandings of family relations *only so long as* "we are careful to balance that pluralism with protections for women and children."[19]

Taking the idea of removing state authority over marriage even further, Professor Edward Zelinsky sets forth a "pro-marriage case for abolishing civil marriage," largely in response to the debate about gay marriage and the future of marriage.[20] Under his proposal, marriage would be a religious and cultural institution with no legal definition or status.[21] For Zelinsky, abolishing civil marriage would depoliticize and

14. *See* Joel A. Nichols, *Multi-Tiered Marriage: Ideas and Influences from New York and Louisiana to the International Community*, 40 VAND. J. TRANSNAT'L L. 135, 140–41 (2007) ("This Article posits that . . . religious groups have an appropriate role to play in assisting the state to define the metes and bounds of the marital relationship.").

15. *See id.* at 195–96 ("[I]t is unnecessary for the state to retain sole jurisdictional control over a unitary, least-common-denominator system of marriage and divorce law.").

16. *See id.* at 148–54 (discussing the background and theory behind covenant marriage law in Louisiana, Arkansas, and Arizona and the get statute in New York).

17. *Id.* at 138, 196.

18. *Id.* at 196.

19. *Id.* at 140.

20. Edward A. Zelinsky, *Deregulating Marriage: The Pro-Marriage Case for Abolishing Civil Marriage*, 27 CARDOZO L. REV. 1161, 1165 (2006).

21. *See id.* at 1220 ("Whatever the arguments for civil marriage might have been in the past, today perpetuating the monopoly that is civil marriage is a mistake. The time has come to rectify that mistake by

"strengthen marriage by encouraging competition among alternative versions of marriage."[22] Zelinsky sees the "law following the deregulation of marriage [as] both contractual and pluralistic."[23] He envisions a "regime [that] would be heavily contractual in nature as the secular and sectarian sponsors of marriage develop their own agreements for couples," which the courts would then enforce, as they would any other contract.[24] The one specific exception to enforcement for Zelinsky would be when it would impair the state's ability to protect the interests of minor children.[25]

In a third proposal, Professor Daniel Crane also argues that states should separate religious marriage from civil unions.[26] He envisions a system in which "the state would no longer attempt to define the parameters of marriage or to specify mandatory rules other than those necessary to preserve the minimum values of a liberal state."[27] Thus, the state's role as to marriage would be limited "to enforcing contracts between private parties."[28] The functional result of this arrangement, Crane states, is that a couple voluntarily could delegate jurisdiction over their marriage to a specified religious institution which would apply religious law.[29] Like Nichols and Zelinsky, Crane would hold the parties to this religious understanding so long as it conforms to the "minimal norms of [a] liberal democratic society."[30]

Despite their different formulations, Nichols, Zelinsky, and Crane each share the idea that society can embrace pluralism without sacrificing protections for women and children.[31] This is a dangerous assumption. Two concerns immediately arise: first, whether family violence is likely

abolishing civil marriage.").

22. *Id.* at 1173.

23. *Id.* at 1182.

24. *Id.* at 1219.

25. *See id.* at 1184 ("[C]ourts (and legislatures) in a world without civil marriage should not invalidate voluntary arrangements except upon very compelling grounds, e.g., to protect minor children.").

26. *See* Daniel A. Crane, *A "Judeo-Christian" Argument for Privatizing Marriage*, 27 CARDOZO L. REV. 1221, 1222 (2006) (contending that marriage is the province of the religion and not the state and arguing "against the secular legalization of marriage and in favor of the secular privatization of marriage").

27. *Id.* at 1250.

28. *Id.* at 1252.

29. *See id.* (examining the scenario in which a couple could sign a prenuptial agreement agreeing that a religious tribunal would arbitrate any dispute concerning their marriage).

30. *Id.* at 1253.

31. *See supra* notes 14, 20, and 26.

to occur in religious communities; and second, if violence is likely to occur, what effect would these proposals have on the state's ability to police that violence. As the next Part explains in detail, family violence does occur in religious communities, and the victims of violence often receive little or no support from the religious community itself for exiting the marriage.[32]

III. Family Violence in Religious Communities

Deference to religious understandings would not be troubling if society could predict with confidence that the safety and welfare of traditionally vulnerable groups—women and children—would not be impaired.[33] Yet the triumvirate of family violence (domestic violence, child physical abuse, and child sexual abuse) is more likely to occur in insular, patriarchal communities in which women have little power or influence[34]—raising questions about how women and children will fare if society hands over greater authority to religious groups.[35]

Despite the presence of these classic risk factors, researchers have found it surprisingly difficult to measure the incidence of family violence within religious groups.[36] The empirical studies that have been

32. *See infra* Part III.

33. Other scholars have also argued that giving greater autonomy to cultural groups puts the less powerful in those groups, often women and children, at a further disadvantage. *See, e.g.*, Natasha Bakht, *Family Arbitration Using Sharia Law: Examining Ontario's Arbitration Act and Its Impact on Women*, 1 MUSLIM WORLD J. HUM. RTS. 1, 18 (2004) (arguing that a "regressive interpretation of *Sharia* will be used to seriously undermine the rights of women").

34. *See* EMERSON DOBASH & RUSSELL DOBASH, VIOLENCE AGAINST WIVES: A CASE AGAINST THE PATRIARCHY 33 (1983) ("The seeds of wife beating lie in the subordination of females and their subjection to male authority and control."); David Finkelhor, *Risk Factors in the Sexual Victimization of Children*, 4 CHILD ABUSE & NEGLECT 265, 269 (1980) (finding in a study of 796 college undergraduates that "[w]hen a father has particularly conservative family values, for example, believing strongly in children's obedience and in the subordination of women, a daughter is more at risk for sexual abuse").

35. *See* VIRGINIA RAMEY MOLLENKOTT, WOMEN, MEN, AND THE BIBLE 23–24 (1989) (acknowledging that, while the Bible promotes mutual submission, both Roman Catholicism and many Protestant churches lend their support to patriarchal dominance and repressive authoritarianism); Muhammad M. Haj-Yahia, *Wife Abuse and Battering in the Sociocultural Context of Arab Society*, 39 FAM. PROCESS 237, 252 (2000) [hereinafter Haj-Yahia, *Battering in Arab Society*] ("In Arab societies, power in marital relations is based on patriarchal principles, and equality is not considered a central value.").

36. *See* Anahid Dervartanian Kulwicki & June Miller, *Domestic Violence in the Arab American Population: Transforming Environmental Conditions Through Community Education*, 20 ISSUES IN MENTAL HEALTH NURSING 199, 204 (1999) (explaining that studies on

undertaken reveal a complex pattern of intimate partner abuse and child abuse in religious communities.[37] As this Part documents, religious observance is, on the one hand, weakly protective of both adults and children from family violence. On the other hand, these studies show that abuse nonetheless occurs in religious communities.

A. The Influence of Religious Participation

Studies of family violence reveal that religion is sometimes weakly protective against the risk of domestic violence. For example, a study by Ellison and colleagues in 1999 found that men and women who attend religious services regularly are less likely to commit acts of domestic violence than persons who attend rarely or not at all.[38] A second study of Protestant male believers found a similar phenomenon: "[A]ctive conservative Protestant husbands are significantly less likely to commit domestic violence compared to active mainline Protestant husbands as well as nominal conservative Protestant husbands."[39]

Although religious participation confers some protection, these same studies show that domestic violence and child abuse will occur in religious communities, like they do in any other.[40] Moreover, when they occur, the victims of the violence receive little support for exiting the relationship from community members and religious leaders.[41]

domestic violence among Arab American immigrants had to be conducted with home interviews "[b]ecause of the high percentage of illiteracy in both Arabic and English, and because of the cultural norm related to the reluctance of Arab Americans to discuss sensitive questions outside their homes").

37. *See* W. BRADFORD WILCOX, SOFT PATRIARCHS, NEW MEN: HOW CHRISTIANITY SHAPES FATHERS AND HUSBANDS 181–82 (2004) ("Nominal conservative Protestant husbands . . . are significantly more abusive than unaffiliated husbands, active conservative Protestant husbands, and nominal mainline Protestant husbands."); Christopher W. Dyslin & Cynthia J. Thomsen, *Religiosity and Risk of Perpetrating Child Physical Abuse: An Empirical Investigation*, 33 J. PSYCHOL. & THEOLOGY 291, 296 (2005) (finding that conservative Protestant religious affiliation is not related to physical child abuse, but that extrinsic religiosity among conservative Protestants is linked to child abuse risk).

38. *See* Christopher G. Ellison et al., *Are There Religious Variations in Domestic Violence?*, 20 J. FAM. ISSUES 87, 104 (1999) ("[T]he frequency of attending religious services bears an inverse relationship to the likelihood of perpetrating abuse for both men and women.").

39. WILCOX, *supra* note 37, at 182.

40. *See* Ellison et al., *supra* note 38, at 87 ("[I]ntimate violence is the most prevalent form of interpersonal violence in the United States.").

41. *See infra* Part III.B.

There are countless anecdotes that domestic abuse is on the rise in Muslim communities[42] or prevalent among Conservative Protestants.[43] An empirical literature is also emerging. A study of 291 married Arab women in Israel by Dr. Muhammad Haj-Yahia demonstrates the prevalence of domestic violence in Arab religious communities, albeit abroad.[44] In that study, "[81%] of the participants knew of women who had experienced verbal and psychological abuse by their husbands; [while] 78% knew of Arab women who had experienced 'moderate physical violence' (slapping, pulling hair or clothes, pushing)."[45] Nearly two-thirds, 64%, knew Arab women who had experienced "severe physical violence," defined as "hard pushing at frequent intervals, attacking the wife and throwing her body against the wall, or attacking the wife with a hard object such as a chair, belt, or stick."[46]

Studies of domestic violence among conservative Protestant husbands also show that domestic violence is a reality for many families.[47] Using the second National Survey of Families and Households ("NSFH2"), Professor Brad Wilcox found that "4.8 percent of conservative Protestant married men with children committed domestic violence in the year prior to NSFH2, compared to 4.3 percent of mainline Protestant married men with children and 3.2 percent of unaffiliated married men with children."[48] Although the differences for these groups were not statistically significant, when Wilcox took church attendance into account, the "differences between religious groups [became] statistically significant."[49] Wilcox

---

42. *See* Fatima Agha Al-Hayani, *Arabs and the American Legal System: Cultural and Political Ramifications*, *in* ARABS IN AMERICA: BUILDING A NEW FUTURE 74, 80 (Michael W. Suleiman ed., 1999). Al-Hayani states:

> Almost all lawyers have admitted that cases of domestic violence among Arabs are on the rise. . . . Domestic violence seems to be on the rise for various reasons, such as availability of economic independence for the wife through public assistance, a situation that diminishes the husband's control over his wife and family and creates friction and discord within the family.

Id.

43. *See* Ellison et al., *supra* note 38, at 89 ("[I]f some popular images are accurate, Conservative Protestant (i.e., fundamentalist and evangelical) affiliation and belief may be linked with an elevated risk of domestic violence, particularly by men.").

44. *See* Haj-Yahia, *Battering in Arab Society*, *supra* note 35, at 242, 244 (reporting results of a survey of 291 women in Israel, 72% of whom were Muslim, 18% Christian, and 10% Druze).

45. *Id.* at 244.

46. *Id.*

47. Wilcox classified any denomination that "adhere[s] to a theologically conservative worldview as conservative," including Pentecostal, Baptists, Anabaptists, Southern Baptists, Church of God in Christ, and Reformed Churches. WILCOX, *supra* note 37, at 15.

48. *Id.* at 181.

49. *Id.*

found that "[n]ominal conservative Protestant husbands have a domestic violence rate of 7.2 percent and are significantly more abusive than unaffiliated husbands, active conservative Protestant husbands, and nominal mainline Protestant husbands."[50]

Like domestic violence, child physical abuse also occurs in religious communities. Here the studies have focused less on Arab religious communities than on conservative Christian communities. One study by Professors Christopher Dyslin and Cynthia Thomsen is particularly instructive. Motivated largely by the popular belief that "Conservative Protestants"[51] engage in more corporal punishment than the rest of society, Dyslin and Thomsen explored whether religious affiliation or mere religiosity was related to child physical abuse risk.[52] Because many states specifically authorize corporal punishment of children, the researchers distinguished mere spanking from child physical abuse, which they defined to "entail[] more extreme forms of physical aggression," such as being hit with a fist, burned, or choked.[53]

Although the results showed that conservative Protestant religious affiliation was *not* related to child physical abuse risk, the researchers found that "[i]ndividuals with high levels of *extrinsic religiosity* had higher [child abuse proneness]" than those individuals with lower extrinsic religiosity.[54] Extrinsic religiosity is akin to wearing one's religion on one's sleeve; it places an emphasis on religion as membership in a "powerful in-group,"[55] providing protection, consolation, and social status.[56]

Just as domestic violence and child physical abuse occur in religious communities, so does child sexual abuse. Studies of sexual abuse have found that while religious affiliation mutes a child's risk of sexual abuse in early childhood,

50. *Id.* at 181–82.

51. Dyslin & Thomsen, *supra* note 37, at 33 (classifying the following as conservative Protestants: Adventists, Assemblies of God, Baptists, Church of God in Christ, Evangelical Free Foursquare Gospel, Full Gospel, Holiness, Missouri or Wisconsin Synod Lutheran, Nazarene, Non-denominational (Evangelical), Pentecostal, and Wesleyan).

52. *See id.* at 292–93 (employing the Child Abuse Potential Inventory to measure participants' attitudes towards abuse, as opposed to self-reports of behavior).

53. *Id.* at 292 ("[D]espite a general tendency to conflate the two, corporal punishment and [child physical abuse] are not isomorphic.").

54. *Id.* at 296.

55. Vicky Genia & Dale G. Shaw, *Religion, Intrinsic-Extrinsic Orientation, and Depression*, 32 REV. REL. RES. 274, 274 (1991).

56. *See generally* Gordon W. Allport & J. Michael Ross, *Personal Religious Orientation and Prejudice*, 5 J. PERSONALITY & SOC. PSYCHOL. 432 (1967); *see also* Wilcox, *supra* note 37, at 129 (finding that "conservative Protestant fathers are more likely to report using corporal punishment," but also "are more likely to praise and hug their children and less likely to yell at them than are mainline Protestant and unaffiliated fathers").

there are nonetheless pockets of elevated risk among some religious groups in adolescence.[57]

Together, these studies show not that being a member of a religious community makes one more likely to be a victim of domestic violence or child abuse, but instead that family violence will occur in religious communities like it does elsewhere. For this reason, it is important to examine the views of religious communities and their leaders toward family violence before embracing any proposal to give greater deference to religious groups.

B. Tolerance by Religious Communities of Family Violence

Studies across multiple faiths reveal that victims of family violence often find cold comfort in their religious communities, whether from religious leaders or other members. Religious groups often acquiesce in or, worse, condone family violence within the community.

Because this Symposium focuses on Gender-Relevant Legislative Change in Muslim and Non-Muslim Countries, this Part principally examines studies of family violence among adherents to the Islamic Faith.[58] A 1999 study by Professors Anahid Kulwicki and June Miller evidences the tacit acceptance of domestic violence by some Muslim communities in the United States.[59] In that survey of Arab American immigrants, nearly all of whom were Muslim,[60] the

---

57. *See* Rebecca M. Bolen, *Predicting Risk to Be Sexually Abused: A Comparison of Logistic Regression to Event History Analysis*, 3 CHILD MALTREATMENT 157, 167, 168 tbl.2 (1998) (finding that Protestant and Catholic children had odds ratios of less than one for experiencing child sexual abuse when compared to children with no religious affiliation, meaning that they were much less likely to be sexually abused, but also reporting that Protestant children, although "significantly less likely to be abused in early childhood . . . were more likely to be abused during adolescence"; this increase in their relative risk was on par with other risk factors that intuitively impact a child's risk of sexual abuse, such as living with a male in the household); Ruth Stout-Miller et al., *Religiosity and Child Sexual Abuse: A Risk Factor Assessment*, 6 J. CHILD SEXUAL ABUSE 15, 23, 30–31 (1997) (finding in a survey of 397 freshmen students at a southern university that among individuals who had been sexually abused as a child, persons who came from "fundamental Protestant" religious family backgrounds—defined as Baptist, Southern Baptist, Church of Christ, Church of God, Pentecostal, and Holiness—were more at risk of being sexually abused by a relative, and concluding that "the type of religious affiliation and involvement in religious activities (measured as frequency of church attendance and practice of religious beliefs at home) affect the nature and extent of child sexual abuse").

58. For a more in-depth look at patterns of family violence in other faiths, see Robin Fretwell Wilson, *The Perils of Privatized Marriage*, *in* MULTI-TIERED MARRIAGE (Joel Nichols ed., 2008).

59. *See* Kulwicki & Miller, *supra* note 36, at 207 tbl.1.

60. *See id.* (reporting that 97.5% of the survey respondents were Muslim).

researchers asked women and men "when it would be appropriate for husbands to slap their wives."[61] Women were more accepting of this practice than men in a number of different circumstances, ranging from when a wife disrespects her husband in the home when no one else is around[62] to when the husband discovers that his wife is cheating.[63] Perhaps most shocking, 18.2% of women in the study said they would "approve" of a husband killing his wife if he discovered adultery.[64]

Other studies mirror Kulwicki and Miller's findings. A study conducted by Haj-Yahia of 356 Jordanian women, 92% of whom were Muslim, found that "Jordanian women have a strong tendency to justify wife-beating."[65] Haj-Yahia found that 33.4% "agreed or strongly agreed that a husband ha[d] the right to beat his wife if she challenged [his] manhood" and 46.6% agreed or strongly agreed if a wife "constantly disobey[ed] her husband."[66] Moreover, 68.5% "agreed or strongly agreed that a husband ha[d] the right to beat his wife . . . if she [didn't] respect her husband's parents or siblings."[67] Indeed, Jordanian women often blamed the wife for violence against her. Almost half agreed that in most cases "a husband beats his wife due to her mistaken behavior, such as squandering money or neglecting the house and children," or that "the wife's behavior toward her husband or children is the cause of violence against her."[68]

---

61. *Id.* at 209 tbl.3.

62. *See id.* (showing that 34.8% of female respondents would approve of a man slapping his wife if she insults him when they are at home alone, compared to 33.3% of male respondents).

63. *See id.* (showing that 48.4% of female respondents approve of a man slapping his wife if he learns that she has been having an affair, compared to 22.5 % of men). The researchers also asked when it would be appropriate for a man to slap his wife in other circumstances and received these responses:

Would you approve of a man slapping his wife if:	% Females Who Responded Yes	% Males Who Responded Yes
She won't do what he tells her to do	20.4	5.1
She insults him in public	17.2	43.6
She comes home drunk	56.3	51.4
She hits him first when they have an argument	58.7	59.0

64. *Id.* The researchers did not have a large enough sample to present parallel statistics for men on this question.

65. Muhammad M. Haj-Yahia, *Beliefs of Jordanian Women About Wife-Beating*, 26 PSYCHOL. WOMEN Q. 282, 284–85 (2002) [hereinafter Haj-Yahia, *Jordanian Beliefs*].

66. *Id.* at 286.

67. *Id.*

68. *See id.* (reporting that 41.8% and 47.5% of the participants strongly agreed or agreed

Muslim men share these views, as well. In 1998, Haj-Yahia surveyed Palestinian men from the West Bank and Gaza Strip, the majority of whom were Muslim.[69] Nearly a quarter, and sometimes more than two-thirds of the respondents, justified wife beating when a wife engaged in sexual infidelity, insulted the husband in front of his friends, challenged the husband's manhood, disobeyed the husband, failed to meet the husband's expectations, refused to have sex with the husband, disrespected the husband's parents and relatives, or reminded the husband of his weak points.[70]

It is not only community members who accept violence; religious leaders often tolerate domestic violence as well. A study by Ruksana Ayyub examining domestic violence among South Asian Muslims in the United States observed that "[v]iolence in marriage is generally condemned but when it does happen the religious community gives no clear consequences for the violent behavior."[71] Acquiescence among South Asian Muslims is so pervasive that "Islamic Centers themselves fail to impart any information on domestic violence protection and prevention programs available in the community, seeing them as too radical."[72]

This tolerance of family violence stems both from sharply-contested readings of religious texts[73] and from the belief that "the marriage [must] be

with the statements presented in the text, and concluding that "[t]he results revealed a strong tendency among Jordanian women to blame the wife for violence against her"). *Compare* Haj-Yahia, *Battering in Arab Society*, *supra* note 35, at 245 (finding that among 291 married Arab women living in Israel, 82% did not believe that husbands have a right to beat their wives in certain situations, but of the 8% who did agree, 73% felt that beating would be justified in the event of the wife's sexual infidelity; 64% said beating would be justified if the wife fails to conform with the husband's demands, requests, and expectations; and 49% believed beating would be justified if the wife talks back to the husband at home).

69. *See* Muhammad M. Haj-Yahia, *Beliefs About Wife Beating Among Arab Men From Israel: The Influence of Their Patriarchal Ideology*, 18 J. FAM. VIOLENCE 193, 196 (2003) [hereinafter Haj-Yahia, *Battering Beliefs in Israel*] ("Eighty two percent of the respondents were Muslim . . . , 13% were Christian . . . , and 5% were Druze . . . .").

70. *See id.* at 199. Although most respondents were Muslim, men from multiple religious backgrounds justified domestic violence. *See id.* ("[A] substantial proportion of the [male] respondents justified wife beating. Fifty-eight percent strongly agreed or agreed that 'there is no excuse for a man to beat his wife' . . . whereas about 28% strongly agreed or agreed that 'sometimes it is OK for a man to beat his wife' . . . . Moreover, between 15 and 62% strongly agreed or agreed that wife beating is justified on certain occasions.").

71. Ayyub, *supra* note 13, at 242.

72. *Id.*

73. Some scholars note that portions of the Qur'an "clearly imply that obedience and respect for husbands is the Muslim wife's duty and that in some situations wife-beating is justified." Haj-Yahia, *Jordanian Beliefs*, *supra* note 65, at 283. They rely on *Sura* 4:34, which provides:

Men are the maintainers of women because Allah has made some of them to excel maintained."[74] The emphasis on family privacy, family reputation, and family solidarity makes maintenance of the marriage and family unit of paramount importance, as a result of which "abusiveness almost becomes invisible."[75]

Beyond tacit acceptance, some religious groups actually discourage women from seeking outside help.[76] Professor Ayyub explains that the Muslim community "condemns any woman who seeks legal protection from an abusive spouse."[77] Dr. Haj-Yahia notes that an Arab woman who seeks to have her husband removed from the home "may be ostracized by [her] community and blamed for undermining family stability and unity."[78] Preserving the marriage is of such great importance that physical violence is seen by some members as "preferable to divorce."[79]

Tolerance of family violence is not limited to members of the Islamic faith. Similar studies of religious leaders from Christian traditions confirm that they also frequently acquiesce in physical violence between husbands and wives. A 2000 study of 158 Christian religious leaders found that many

---

> others and because they spend out of their property; the good women are therefore obedient, guarding the unseen as Allah has guarded; and (as to) those on whose part you fear desertion, admonish them, and leave them alone in the sleeping-places and beat them . . . .

Under this reading of Islamic law, "a refractory wife has no legal right to object to her husband's exercising his disciplinary authority." Douki et al., *supra* note 12, at 168. Such verses are not uniformly interpreted; some scholars argue that the Qur'an allows only a "symbolic beating of a wife if she disobeys," while others "cling to a more literal meaning." Ayyub, *supra* note 13, at 242. A "selective preference of one verse from the Qur'an over many other verses that talk about kindness and justice toward women has created an atmosphere that tolerates and allows violence toward women." *Id.* Similar disputes arise about Biblical passages. *See, e.g.*, Dyslin & Thomsen, *supra* note 37, at 295.

74. Ayyub, *supra* note 13, at 243.

75. *Id.* at 243; *see also* Douki et al., *supra* note 12, at 166 ("Arab families tend to emphasize mutual support, and individual members are expected to sacrifice their own needs, well-being and welfare for the benefit of the family as a unit.").

76. *See* Ayyub, *supra* note 13, at 239 ("Muslim women in America look for and find limited help in government-sponsored programs like shelters for battered women, support groups, and legal and social services. However, they face strong opposition from their religious and cultural institutions in utilizing these services.").

77. *Id.* at 242.

78. Haj-Yahia, *Battering in Arab Society*, *supra* note 35, at 238, 239–40 (attributing this response to "the prevailing belief that the children's best interests, the woman's personal reputation, and the reputation of her family of origin take precedence over her own well-being and safety").

79. Douki et al., *supra* note 12, at 169 ("[E]ven texts which imply that violence is permissible do not mean that it is desirable. Such a measure should always be seen as an extreme, preferable to divorce, a 'lesser of two evils' which may be used to save a marriage threatened by a wife's misconduct.").

believed "marriage must be saved at all costs"—even when domestic violence occurs—and that a realistic solution was "forgiving and forgetting the abuse."[80] Older studies of female victims show that they overwhelmingly received this type of advice from clergy. A 1981 study of abused women found that of the 28% who asked clergy for advice, 80% were told either to go back home since it's a wife's duty, to forgive their husbands, or to go to a marriage counselor; or received only religious advice.[81] A 1988 survey of conservative Protestant pastors found that 92% of respondents would "never advise a woman to divorce an abuser."[82] These same religious leaders felt that "the victim's lack of submissive behavior was in part responsible for the violence."[83]

Clearly, no religious group is immune from violence. States should weigh carefully the risks to women and children before ceding jurisdiction over family disputes to bodies that may be unwilling or unable to vindicate their rights. The next Part demonstrates that giving deference to religious understandings of marriage will materially change the calculus a woman makes in deciding to leave, or not leave, an abusive relationship.

IV. The Practical Effects of Religious Deference

Society polices and regulates family relations in a number of different ways: through the criminal law; through the child abuse and neglect system; through civil domestic violence statutes; and through the law of marriage and divorce.[84] Admittedly, none of the proposals in Part II is intended to remove the existing protections of criminal law or the child abuse and neglect or domestic violence statutes. But those systems are reactive, and they have a

---

80. Colleen Shannon-Lewy & Valerie T. Dull, *The Response of Christian Clergy to Domestic Violence: Help or Hindrance?*, 10 AGGRESSION & VIOLENT BEHAV. 647, 649 (2005) (citing AL MILES, DOMESTIC VIOLENCE: WHAT EVERY PASTOR NEEDS TO KNOW 149–50 (2000)).

81. Mildred Daley Pagelow, *Secondary Battering and Alternatives of Female Victims to Spouse Abuse*, *in* WOMEN AND CRIME IN AMERICA 277, 287–88 (Lee H. Bowker ed., 1981).

82. Shannon-Lewy & Dull, *supra* note 80, at 651 (citing J. M. Alsdurf & P. Alsdurf, *A Pastoral Response*, *in* WHEN PRAYING ISN'T ENOUGH 165, 168 (Anne L. Horton & J. A. Williamson eds., 1990)).

83. *Id.* at 167; *see also* Heidi M. Levitt & Kimberly N. Ware, *Religious Leaders' Perspectives on Marriage, Divorce and Intimate Partner Violence*, 30 PSYCHOL. WOMEN Q. 212 (2006) (concluding from a study of 22 religious leaders in Memphis, Tennessee, across many different religious traditions, that "[a]lthough there was diversity in beliefs, most of the leaders expressed concerns related to balancing the sacredness of marriage with the urgency of divorce in cases of [interpersonal violence]. Many suggested that divorce be considered as a 'last resort' and would urge reconciliation if possible").

84. *See generally* HOMER H. CLARK, JR. & ANN LAQUER ESTIN, DOMESTIC RELATIONS: CASES AND PROBLEMS (7th ed. 2005).

woeful track record of preventing abuse before it occurs.[85] The law of marriage and divorce empowers spouses to exit relationships on equitable terms without harsh sanctions that some religious norms would impose. As a result, the state must empower women to exit abusive relationships when they are victims of violence themselves or believe their children are being victimized.

By giving deference to religious understandings that are not now held by both adults, society increases the cost to women who want to exit for their own safety or the safety of their children. To make the collision between religious norms and safety more concrete, consider Muslim practices about custody.[86] Under Islamic law, male children over the age of seven are placed in the custody of their fathers upon divorce, as are female children after the onset of puberty.[87] In some Muslim communities in the world, like Western Thrace, a geographic region of Greece, a woman must waive "her right to the custody of the children" before she can receive a divorce.[88] Presently in the United States, the best interests of the child would control this decision in nearly every jurisdiction, which may or may not result in paternal custody.[89] Imagine the catch-22 that some women may find themselves in if we enforce Muslim understandings about custody. If a father is harshly disciplining his son—discipline that outside the community might be seen as child abuse—and we enforce the religious norms about custody against the woman, she then is in a classic bind. If she stays, her child continues to be beaten. Yet if she exits, her child stays with the husband and continues to be beaten.

To avoid precisely this catch-22, the proposals for giving greater deference attempt to cherry pick—that is, they propose to give deference to some religious norms about the adult relationship but to leave decisions about children to the state.[90] Yet, the adult relationship cannot be so neatly divorced from what

85. *See generally* Robin Fretwell Wilson, *Sexually Predatory Parents and the Children in Their Care: Remove the Threat, Not the Child*, *in* HANDBOOK OF CHILDREN, CULTURE AND VIOLENCE 39 (Nancy E. Dowd, Dorothy G. Singer & Robin Fretwell Wilson eds., 2006).

86. *See* O. Spies, *Hadana*, *in* ENCYCLOPEDIA OF ISLAM (P. Bearman, Th. Bianquis, C.E. Bosworth, E. van Donzel & W.P. Heinrichs eds., 2007) (describing the different schools of Islamic law pertaining to child custody).

87. M. Hashim Kamali, *Islamic Law: Personal Law*, *in* ENCYCLOPEDIA OF RELIGION 4705, 4711 (Lindsay Jones ed., 2d ed. 2005). While the mother maintains custody over young children in the event of divorce, she loses this right if she remarries. *Id.* at 4711.

88. Aspasia Tsaoussi & Eleni Zervogianni, *Multiculturalism and Family Law: The Case of Greek Muslims*, *in* COMMISSION ON EUROPEAN FAMILY LAW 1, 8 (*forthcoming* 2007).

89. *See* Patrick Parkinson, *The Past Caretaking Standard in Comparative Perspective*, *in* RECONCEIVING THE FAMILY: CRITIQUE ON THE AMERICAN LAW INSTITUTE'S PRINCIPLES OF THE LAW OF FAMILY DISSOLUTION 446 (Robin Fretwell Wilson ed., 2006) [hereinafter RECONCEIVING THE FAMILY].

90. *See supra* Part II.

happens with the children. What happens between the adults affects a woman's ability to protect her children. For example, if the adult understanding would result in certain poverty for the woman and her children upon divorce, then she may not leave the relationship.

In many instances, enforcing the religious understanding about the adults' relationship would hasten just such a result. Consider property distribution under Islamic religious law. Islamic marriage contracts often include a deferred *mahr* that is to be paid upon the husband's death or a divorce.[91] In some instances, payment of a *mahr* upon divorce would facilitate exit from the relationship—for example, if a *mahr* provided for half of the man's property upon divorce and he was wealthy.[92] But some religious authorities preclude payment of the *mahr* to a wife if she initiates the divorce.[93] Other authorities go further, requiring a wife to "waive[] her right to alimony" before they will grant a divorce.[94] Now, if society defers to religious authorities, divorce on these terms could impoverish the wife and her child. Threatened with the prospect of certain poverty, some women will surely be forced to stay in an abusive relationship.

Not only should policymakers worry about concrete outcomes in specific cases,[95] but they should also worry about the expressive effect of giving deference to religious understandings about the adult relationship. The mere

91. *See* Spies, *supra* note 86 (describing *mahr* as "the gift which the bridegroom has to give the bride when the contract of marriage is made and which becomes property of the wife"). The *mahr* may be paid at the time of the contract, or alternatively, the parties may agree to defer it. Kamali, *supra* note 87, at 4707 ("A deferred dower remains a debt on the part of the husband and is payable upon the dissolution of the marriage by death or divorce.").

92. *See* Ann L. Estin, *Embracing Tradition: Pluralism in American Family Law*, 63 MD. L. REV. 540, 571 (2004) (describing a California case where a court would not enforce a *mahr* because it encouraged "profiteering by divorce").

93. *See* Mosa Sayed, *The Muslim Dower (mahr) in Europe—with Special Reference to Sweden*, *in* EUROPEAN CHALLENGES IN CONTEMPORARY FAMILY LAW: THIRD CONFERENCE ORGANIZED BY THE COMMISSION ON EUROPEAN FAMILY LAW AND THE DEPARTMENT OF PRIVATE LAW, UNIVERSITY OF OSLO: CONFERENCE BOOKLET 23 (2007) (citing an Egyptian law that allows a woman to bypass the husband's unilateral right of divorce by initiating divorce herself but requires that she give up all her *sharia* rights and return the *mahr*); *see also* Kamali, *supra* note 87, at 4708 (describing a type of divorce, *khul*, that the wife initiates and in which the "wife secures her release from the marital tie by offering the husband financial consideration, commonly return of the dower").

94. Tsaoussi & Zervogianni, *supra* note 88, at 8.

95. There are other areas where religious and societal norms will diverge, including how to treat the marriage of minors, arranged marriages, and polygamous marriages. *See id.* at 11 (discussing departures between *Sharia* family law and Greek civil law). Zelinsky acknowledges in his proposal that a system of deference would have to include specific rules about such marriages. Zelinsky, *supra* note 20, at 1184.

fact that *some* religious understandings about property and other matters will be enforced may lead a woman to believe that *all* such understandings will be enforced, including those about custody. At the very least, a scheme of deference is going to require extensive public education about what receives deference and what does not.

Indeed, any scheme of deference will require numerous safeguards to ensure that the parties have knowingly bound themselves to a specific, shared understanding in advance—although the nature of the safeguards may differ depending on the particular scheme. Zelinsky argues, for example, for the enforcement of standard-form religious contracts.[96] Yet ordinary prenuptial agreements are subjected to exacting review for voluntariness, complete disclosure, representation by separate counsel, and other procedural protections before they are enforced against the parties.[97] Moreover, all the ordinary concerns that courts have over the ability of prospective spouses to bargain at arm's length and appreciate the consequences are exacerbated when a religious body, which can exert considerable influence on its members,[98] supplies the standard form contract. It is not clear from the proposals described in Part II that such protections would be in place.[99]

Sharing jurisdiction with religious bodies over family matters is fraught with risk for vulnerable parties as well. Given the routine acceptance of family violence by some religious communities,[100] it seems unlikely that these communities will relax the application of harsh financial understandings in instances of domestic violence, as courts routinely do when there is a material change of circumstances after the execution of a prenuptial agreement.[101]

Neither is it clear that the determination of a religious body will track the parties' understanding of their duties going into the relationship, or that like cases

96. Zelinsky, *supra* note 20, at 1182–84.

97. Brian H. Bix, *The ALI Principles and Agreements: Seeking a Balance Between Status and Contract*, *in* RECONCEIVING THE FAMILY, *supra* note 89, at 372, 373–74 (2006). Importantly, covenant marriages, on which Professor Nichols relies heavily as an example of multi-tiered marriage, include numerous protections for the parties. *See, e.g.*, Katherine Shaw Spaht, *Postmodern Marriage as Seen Through the Lens of the ALI's 'Compensatory Payments,'* *in* RECONCEIVING THE FAMILY, *supra* note 89, at 249, 265 (requiring premarital counseling and a Declaration of Intent).

98. *See supra* notes 72–73 and accompanying text.

99. As Professor Crane acknowledges, "leaving marriage up to families or mediating institutions [c]ould render marriage a more oppressive institution to women," as critics charge. Crane, *supra* note 26, at 1223. Crane, however, does not address these issues, finding them "outside the purview of [his] essay." *Id.*

100. *See supra* Part III.B.

101. Bix, *supra* note 97, at 373–74.

will be treated alike. A live example of shared jurisdiction operates today in Western Thrace.[102] Muslims in Western Thrace are the "only official minority recognized by the Greek government"[103] and enjoy unique independence as a result of the Treaty of Lausanne, signed by Turkey and Greece in 1923 to accommodate Turks living in Greece and Greeks living in Turkey.[104] Muslims in Western Thrace maintain their own religious and legal institutions, headed by three religious leaders, or *Muftis*.[105] Under *Sharia* law, the *Muftis* "conduct all matters related to civil law."[106] The decisions of the *Mufti* are not final judgments unless declared enforceable by the Greek courts, but review of those judgments is "restricted: it may only be examined, whether the *Mufti* remained within his field of competence and whether the law applied contravenes the Constitution."[107] The judgments of the *Mufti* are routinely declared enforceable; in one study, Greek civil courts "denied enforceability in only eleven cases out of 2,679."[108] This was so even though *Sharia* family law departs significantly from Greek civil law in four important areas: polygamy, namely polygyny; the marriage of minors; divorce proceedings, especially the repudiation of the wife by her husband (*talaq*); and post-divorce child custody awards.[109] Importantly, because there is no system of appellate review for decisions under *Sharia* law as there is with other judicial systems, there is no guarantee of consistent decisions between jurisdictions.[110] The social pressure among Muslims in Western Thrace is so strong that, even when likely facing an unfavorable outcome, "the vast majority of cases are brought before the *Mufti*, even when the plaintiff is the weaker party."[111] None of the proposals in Part II address such potential inequities.

---

102. A Muslim minority of about 110,000 lives in Western Thrace. Irini Lagani, *Greece's Muslim Minority in Western Thrace*, *in* 3 BRIEFING NOTES ON ISLAM, SOCIETY, AND POLITICS 8, 8 (2000). These Muslims of Turkish origin are Greek citizens.

103. *Id.* at 9.

104. *Id.* at 8. The treaty "was based on the principle of reciprocal obligations on the part of the two countries toward each of these minority groups," and "contains specific obligations relating to the cultural and religious rights of these communities." *Id.*

105. *Id.* at 9.

106. *Id.*

107. Tsaoussi & Zervogianni, *supra* note 88, at 5.

108. *Id.* at 11.

109. *Id.* at 7–10.

110. *See* David S. Powers, *On Judicial Review in Islamic Law*, 26 LAW & SOC'Y REV. 315, 315 (1992) ("The prevailing wisdom among Islamicists for over a half-century has asserted that there are no appellate structures in Islamic law, that the decision of a judge is final and irrevocable, and that a judgment may not be reversed under any circumstances.").

111. *Id.* at 12.

V. A Cautionary Tale of Deference

In the United States, deference to religious understandings of the need for medical treatment has had tragic effects. Generally, parents have a duty to provide their children all necessary medical treatment.[112] Two mechanisms exist to discourage and punish parental failures to treat: civil child abuse and neglect laws and criminal charges, such as manslaughter. In many states, however, parents are shielded from both civil and criminal liability by religious exemptions that "allow religious parents . . . to refuse medical care for their sick children."[113] Thirty-nine states give religious exemptions to civil charges, and thirty-three states allow religious defenses to criminal charges.[114] The costs of this deference are heart-breaking.

A 1998 study by Asser and Swan reviewed 172 child deaths across the country from 1975 to 1995 in which the children were denied medical care as a result of parental beliefs in faith healing.[115] The results are chilling. Of the 172 children studied, 140 would have had a 90% chance of survival with medical intervention.[116]

---

112. *See generally* 2 ANN M. HARALAMBIE, HANDLING CHILD CUSTODY, ABUSE AND ADOPTION CASES § 18.03 (1993).

113. Richard A. Hughes, *The Death of Children by Faith-Based Medical Neglect*, 20 J.L. & RELIGION 247, 248 (2004–2005). The federal Child Abuse Prevention and Treatment Act originally required states to exempt faith-based denials from the child abuse statutes as a condition of receiving child abuse funds. The statute was later amended to permit states, but not require them, to have such exemptions.

114. *Id.* Only five states (Hawaii, North Carolina, Nebraska, Maryland, and Massachusetts) do not exempt faith-based denials from civil or criminal charges. *Id.*

In theory, even when there is an exemption, the state may intervene in the family to authorize the treatment on the child's behalf. *See* Joan H. Krause, Freedom or Responsibility: When Spiritual Healing Fails, 32 (Summer 1991) (unpublished paper, on file with author) (noting that while a spiritual exemption "shields the parents from liability, it does not prevent the state from aiding the children"). But in practice, the state rarely knows about the denial until after the child's death because the family does not seek any medical treatment, making civil and criminal charges essential to changing treatment practices in insular communities. *See* Hughes, *supra* note 113, at 247 (noting that in response to the deaths of seventy-eight children in Oregon within the Followers of Christ Church, the Oregon legislature amended Oregon's laws in 1999 to permit prosecution of parents who failed to seek medical care for their injured or sick children, and that between the time of the amendment in 1999 and 2003, there were no deaths of children whose parents belonged to the Followers of Christ Church).

Further, when there are faith-based exemptions, child protective service caseworkers and other officials often believe they cannot intervene to protect the child even when they know about the denial. *See, e.g.*, Seth M. Asser & Rita Swan, *Child Fatalities from Religion-Motivated Medical Neglect*, 101 PEDIATRICS 625, 628 (1998) ("Believing they were powerless in the face of the parents' wishes, some teachers ignored obvious symptoms and sent lessons home to bedridden children. Some social workers and law enforcement officers allowed parents to decline examinations of children reported to be ill.").

115. Asser & Swan, *supra* note 114, at 625.

116. *Id.*

Eighteen more would have had better than a 50/50 chance.[117] Thus, 158 of the children, or 92%, would more probably than not have survived if they had received medical treatment.[118]

Significantly, the researchers also separated cancer deaths from non-cancer deaths because the prognosis for cancer is especially hard to predict.[119] The results for children without cancer are equally sobering. Out of 98 children who died as a result of non-cancer deaths, 92 would have had "an excellent prognosis with commonly available medical and surgical care," four would likely have had a good outcome, and only two "would not have clearly benefited from [commonly available medical and surgical] care."[120]

Asser and Swan's study did not include 78 child deaths in Oregon between 1955 and 1998 or 12 child deaths in Idaho between 1980 and 1998.[121] The deaths in those two states resulted from "faith healing practices that occurred within the Oregon-based Followers of Christ Church."[122] Of the Oregon children who died, it is likely that 21 "could have lived if they had received medical treatment."[123]

So, in just this handful of reports, more than 150 children are dead because states prized deference over the child's welfare. Clearly, children in families that practice faith healing are not more disease riddled than other children. Rather these tragic, preventable deaths arose because we removed the state's protection from some of our most vulnerable members. Given our experience with faith-based exemptions, there would seem to be no compelling reason to stand back and watch the predictable repercussions of deference unfold again.

VI. Conclusion

Religious communities are not hot spots for family violence, but they do experience family violence just like the rest of society does. The costs of giving greater deference to religious understandings of family relationships must seriously be considered before we are willing to leave the decisions about marriage and divorce to religious communities—robbing women and children of the state's protections.

---

117. *Id.*

118. *Id.*

119. *See id.* at 626.

120. *Id.*

121. Hughes, *supra* note 113, at 247.

122. *Id.*

123. *Id.*

Part V
Religious Symbols in the Public Space

[18]

Ancient and Modern Boundary Crossings Between Personal Laws and Civil Law in Composite India

Werner Menski

I. INTRODUCTION: THE REALITIES OF PLURALISM

The starting point of this chapter is somewhat different from that of most contributors to this volume, in part because of my late-comer status to the project, as well as my outsider perspective. Some European legal systems, but also Canada and the United States, have over time developed highly regulated state-centric methods of family law management that seemed to leave little or no room for religious and other authorities to make any input. Today's agonized debates over the emergence of some eighty-five Sharia Councils and Muslim Arbitration Tribunals in Britain thus reflect surprise, to put it mildly, that supposedly strong states are in fact not fully in control of family law regulation.

Such debates (if one can call them that) show that it is not sufficiently well known in a global context that European and North American models of regulatory framework are not universally replicated all over the globe. Colonialism never fully achieved its ambitious civilizing missions. In particular, it did not wipe out most preexisting sociocultural (and thus legal) traditions, but it did influence them. Today there is certainly no single, global method of managing family relations through state intervention. Rather, there are many ways of handling family law. Individual states have gradually developed patterns that suit their country-specific needs and national identities. In many cases, however, colonial intervention and other interferences imposed certain patterns that are not even close to what one may call "indigenous." Hybridity of legal regulation is thus a global fact everywhere; pluralism of methods, specifically in the management of family relations, is a global reality.

For many scholars, this raises the question (in my view quite misguided) of whether it is possible to conceive of and develop an ideal model suitable for all. In this respect, it seems that the grass is always greener on the other side of the fence. Hence many countries with state-centric regulation mechanisms, including the United States and Canada, are now debating whether there should be less state control or a more sophisticated method of state-driven intervention such as a revised multi-tiered system of legal regulation.[1] At the same time, many legal systems that have retained less state control have been engaged in equally tortuous discussions over increasing state involvement.

In the world as a whole, I see today three types of legal systems[2]: (1) those that claim to have state-centric regulation through all-encompassing general laws for all citizens or residents, with France being a somewhat extreme example; (2) countries like the United States, Canada, Australia, New Zealand, and many others that maintain a fairly centralized system but allow a unique legal position for one particular group of people, often the original inhabitants of the land; and (3) countries and legal systems that incorporate an explicitly pluralistic combination of "general law" and various country-specific "personal laws" for different groups of people, not necessarily on the basis of religion. The third category is much larger than Eurocentric scholars seem to be aware. It certainly includes countries like South Africa[3] and actually comprises most countries of Asia and Africa. For example, the Indian legal system has had to manage religious and legal pluralism for thousands of years. It has coped with the presence of Muslim personal law for centuries and today covers more than 150 million Muslims within an officially secular legal framework.[4]

Various personal law methods of legal regulation apply to the majority of the world's population today and are not historical remnants from Roman or Ottoman times. These powerful legal realities deserve respect for their capacity to operate intricate regulatory frameworks for billions of people. Assuming that one's own system, or any one particular system for that matter, is somehow the norm is a fatal methodological error. We must acknowledge that no legal system in the world has managed to maintain perfect justice at all times before we pass judgment on distant "others."

On the one hand, it is evident from this volume that state-centric types of legal systems in the first and second categories currently face debates about pluralization;

[1] On governability, see Katherine Osterlund, "Love, Freedom and Governance: Same-Sex Marriage in Canada," *Social & Legal Studies* 18:1 (March 2009): 93–109. See also Joel A. Nichols, "Multi-Tiered Marriage: Ideas and Influences from New York and Louisiana to the International Community," *Vanderbilt Journal of Transnational Law* 40 (January 2007): 135–196; and Joel A. Nichols, "Multi-Tiered Marriage: Reconsidering the Boundaries of Civil Law and Religion" (in this volume).

[2] Werner Menski, "Law, Religion and South Asians in Diaspora," in *Religious Reconstruction in the South Asian Diasporas: From One Generation to Another*, ed. John R. Hinnells (Basingstoke: Palgrave Macmillan, 2007), 243–264, 252–257.

[3] See Johan D. van der Vyver, "Multi-Tiered Marriages in South Africa" (in this volume).

[4] In India, "secular" means equidistance of the state from all religions, which is not quite the same as the U.S. system, although there are remarkable overlaps. See Gerald James Larson, ed., *Religion and Personal Law in Secular India: A Call to Judgment* (Bloomington, IN: Indiana University Press, 2001).

relaxation of state control; less rigid formality regarding marriage, aspects of divorce, and related matters; and post-divorce maintenance law.[5] They face pressure to adopt pluralization and more explicit recognition of various interactive boundary crossings between state regulation and other normative orderings. On the other hand, states in the third category have found themselves under various pressures to modernize, impose uniform rules, and effect more centralized state control, specifically to reform and control "religious" personal law systems. Often explicitly portrayed as an urgent matter of justice, these pressures aim for what in India is called a "Uniform Civil Code." Found in Article 44 of the Indian Constitution of 1950 and framed as a program for the future, it envisages a new civil law structure that would apply to all people.[6]

Although pulling the state out of marriage and family law altogether is rightly considered risky and is probably not really sustainable, de facto pluralization, particularly as a result of new sociocultural developments and recent migrations from other parts of the world,[7] has become a part of social reality in the Western world.[8] Such developments – nothing new in countries outside the Western hemisphere – have given rise to whole new sets of literature that largely agonize over fears of state-centric mechanisms losing control to religious authorities and other forces right in our midst. This loss of control is perceived as undermining various forms of human rights protections and is portrayed as particularly negative for women and children.[9] Somehow, it is never questioned in depth whether state regulation does not also pose risks of certain kinds of violence and infringements of basic rights. In South

5 See, e.g., Brian H. Bix, "Pluralism and Decentralization in Marriage Regulation" (in this volume); Daniel Cere, "Canadian Conjugal Mosaic: From Multiculturalism to Multi-Conjugalism?" (in this volume); Ann Laquer Estin, "Unofficial Family Law" (in this volume); Nichols, "Reconsidering the Boundaries" (in this volume).

6 As shown in this chapter, this anticipated development did not materialize. An astute early critic of excessive positivism quite rightly called this "no more than a distant mirage." Antony Allott, *The Limits of Law* (London: Butterworth, 1980), 216.

7 Rather than treating this as a form of legal transplant, I speak about reverse colonization and call this private importation of ethnic minority legal concepts "ethnic implants." See Werner Menski, *Comparative Law in a Global Context: The Legal Systems of Asia and Africa* (Cambridge: Cambridge University Press, 2d ed. 2006), 58–65.

8 For Britain, much before the Archbishop of Canterbury made his comments and caused a storm, I devised the concept of British Muslim law (*angrezi shariat*) as a hybrid entity to indicate that state control over family law can never be absolute. Various communities and individuals in their daily lives, rather than states, face the challenges of navigating the boundaries of official and unofficial laws. For details, see David Pearl and Werner Menski, *Muslim Family Law* (London: Sweet & Maxwell, 3d ed. 1998). On the U.S. scenario, see Saminaz Zaman, "*Amrikan Shari'a*: The Reconstruction of Islamic Family Law in the United States," *South Asia Research* 28:2 (July 2008): 185–202.

9 See, e.g., Linda C. McClain, "Marriage Pluralism in the United States: On Civil and Religious Jurisdiction and the Demands of Equal Citizenship" (in this volume) and Robin Fretwell Wilson, "The Perils of Privatized Marriage" (in this volume).

Asia, at any rate, states are well known as the worst violators of the law. Moreover, secular civil law regulation is certainly not value-neutral, but scholars often seem to "know" what is good and bad, prejudging the entire field through preconceived notions. Scholars thereby exhibit various forms of amnesia and myopia, specifically when it comes to assessing developments in non-European legal contexts. As someone with one foot in the East and one in the West, I find myself having to write one article after the other about such issues.[10]

The present volume seeks to take the debate about management of family law further than the existing literature. The main question appears to be whether delegating authority to religious authorities would be a feasible method of meeting the challenges of increased sociocultural pluralization and of new forms of family arrangement. New patterns often go well beyond the standard norm of marriage as a lifelong bond between one man and one woman to the exclusion of all others; they comprise both the retraditionalizing effects of global non-Western migration in all directions and also the recent manifestations of modern Western sociocultural changes. I find the focus of analysis a little too narrowly put on the competition of state law and religion, when in fact the field is much more complex and plural than mere binary pairings of these elements – of East and West, or North and South, or of tradition and modernity. Reality almost everywhere is increasingly marked by super-diversity.[11] Whereas the focus in this volume is largely on U.S. law and whether a multi-tiered marriage system would be a suitable form of legal regulation, my contribution to this debate aims to show that a sophisticated pluralistic regulatory system has already existed in India for thousands of years, only more recently supplemented by stronger and more explicitly targeted state control. This indicates that abandoning the state altogether does not seem feasible, but ignoring the other inputs and players is not a feasible solution either. So perhaps we must be active, conscious pluralists, whether we like it or not.

Starting from ancient pluralistic roots of legal self-regulation, Indian law offers a model that has always respected various competing religious and cultural normative patterns while gradually developing increasingly fine-tuned overall state control, albeit with notable limits to positivist intervention. This Indian method of managing "good governance" has turned into a specific form of a social welfare state. However, in this system of partial regulation, the state is neither willing nor able to devote sufficient resources to rescue disadvantaged citizens; it mainly aims to create supportive conditions for self-controlled ordering of human actions. This is also true when

[10] See, e.g., Werner Menski, "Beyond Europe," in *Comparative Law: A Handbook*, eds. David Nelken and Esin Őrűcű (Oxford: Hart Publishing, 2007), 189–216.

[11] On Britain still overlooking the legal dimensions of such super-diversity, see Steven Vertovec, "Super-Diversity and its Implications," *Ethnic and Racial Studies* 30:6 (November 2007): 1024–1054.

it comes to social welfare arrangements.[12] With many more than a billion citizens today, the flip side of state respect for religious and social self-control in India is now increasingly manifesting itself as explicit reliance on family and communal support mechanisms, especially among women, children, and the elderly.[13] As a result, the state calls on men and other persons who have control over resources to operationalize enhanced obligations rather than enjoy superior rights. This responsibility arises from the basic foundations of traditional value systems in Indic cultures, which are built on presumptions of interconnectedness and duties toward others rather than on individual rights.

Managing this particular method of family law regulation has never been easy or uncontroversial. The Indian state today largely continues to sit back and let people decide the details of how to lead their lives. The state offers merely a symbolic safety net through somewhat symbolic fundamental rights guarantees, and little more. However, these minimal guarantees undergird Indian state interventions if there are unsustainable or blatantly unjust or imbalanced developments within various societies and religious normative orders. For example, the definition of "wife" in Indian law has since 1973 included "divorced wife."[14] It took decades for this deliberate manipulation of social relations to occur, yet this subtle move has proven powerful in the long run. These seemingly symbolic state interventions probably now also influence private interactions between individuals in their homes. (Laborious fieldwork would be necessary to ascertain that.) Formal interventions may take the form of such symbolic legislation or significant judicial pronouncements, reflecting the fact that India is not just a traditional common law system but an extremely hybrid jurisdiction. This intricate interplay of various judicial and legislative elements creates powerful legal dynamisms with remarkable outcomes.

It should surprise no one that the traditional Indian method of relying on self-controlled ordering in society was never fully effective on its own. However, it is a mistake to dismiss it as too problematic rather than seeing its intrinsic ameliorative potential. Before jumping to conclusions about certain perceived crises of the state or significant alleged maldevelopments,[15] one first needs to understand what has

[12] Recent evidence of bureaucratic abuses of India's meager welfare program strengthens doubts over the feasibility of state-centric welfare mechanisms. See Subhash Mishra, "Ghosts in the Darkness," *India Today*, August 20, 2009, available at http://indiatoday.intoday.in/site/Story/57748/States/Ghosts+in+the+darkness.html (detailing how women connive with officials under a new Widow Pension Scheme to declare their husbands dead).

[13] See Werner F. Menski, *Modern Indian Family Law* (Richmond, UK: Curzon, 2001).

[14] India Code of Criminal Procedure § 125 (1973).

[15] Attractive-looking books such as Rajeshwari Sunder Rajan, *The Scandal of the State: Women, Law and Citizenship in Postcolonial India* (Durham, NC: Duke University Press, 2003) are political manifestos rather than factually reliable legal analyses. Such writing must be treated with caution, because even basic legal facts are misrepresented.

actually been going on in Indian law "on the ground" and how such intricate pluralistic regulatory methods, grounded in thousands of years of experience handling legal conflicts, pan out today.[16]

Remarkably, this complex story is hardly ever told because too few legal scholars are also trained as Indologists, historians, or social scientists. Indian textbook writers are mostly sterile "black letter" lawyers who typically list one judgment after another and fail to analyze what they report. Most damaging, much writing on Indian law these days comes from scholars, often Indian scholars based abroad, who are highly politicized commentators and self-appointed social reformers. Ideological blinders and often personal agendas prevent them from giving global readership a comprehensive account of Indian legal developments. As a result, selective and highly partisan reporting on Indian family law (and many other non-Western legal systems in the world, especially neighboring Pakistan and Bangladesh) has not allowed us to gain a full picture of the various methods of legal management that exist in the interplay between so-called religious laws and civil laws in various jurisdictions around the globe and specifically in South Asia.

In this chapter, I seek to show that India's long-tested method of handling family law intricately combines overall state control with ongoing deep respect for – and explicit recognition of – social and religious authorities. In such explicitly pluralist scenarios, no one form of authority is ever beyond criticism. No entity is allowed to control the entire field autonomously. Legal monism is restrained and every component, as Sally Falk Moore suggested decades ago, is "semi-autonomous."[17] Hence, all players in South Asian legal scenarios have had to be somewhat altruistic in their interactions with other legal actors to maintain stability and continuity. Legal pluralism has long been a fact in South Asia, and such complex management is not easy to achieve; it may become unbalanced or uprooted, as can be seen from the unfortunate developments in Afghanistan and Pakistan, and to a lesser extent in Bangladesh and Sri Lanka. India appears to have reached reasonably stable democratic standards in pursuing sustainable methods of family law regulation. Recent

A prominent example is the persistent global misrepresentation of the *Shah Bano* saga in Indian law. The story of how an old Muslim lady was thrown out of marriage, deprived of her legal entitlements by an unscrupulous lawyer-husband, and then let down by a gender-insensitive legal system is brilliant scholarly fiction. This fiction has been used to support familiar allegations that "religious law" is bad for women and that modern secular state intervention in India has been totally ineffective. The real story will be discussed further in its wider context later in this chapter.

[16] For a sample of excellent fieldwork-based study, see Sylvia Vatuk, "Divorce at the Wife's Initiative in Muslim Personal Law: What are the Options and What are Their Implications for Women's Welfare?" in *Redefining Family Law in India*, eds. Archana Parashar and Amita Dhanda (London: Routledge, 2008), 200–235.

[17] Sally Falk Moore, *Law as Process: An Anthropological Approach* (London: Routledge & Kegan Paul, 1978).

historical scholarship suggests, however, that this may have been achieved at a cost: allowing the Pakistanis to have their own neighboring state only to find that Muslim law remains a critical component in India's legal scenario.

My coverage of recent Indian developments in marriage law and post-divorce maintenance arrangements is prefaced by a brief historical overview to inform readers on the remarkable cultural and conceptual continuities in South Asian legal systems. These continuities are embedded with ancient concepts of self-controlled ordering and accountability for one's own actions, ideas originally developed outside state-centric legal regulation in various Hindu, Buddhist, Jain, and Muslim religio-cultural contexts. These multicultural building blocks are now subtly incorporated into – and ultimately supervised by – officially "secular" and religiously equidistant formal legal structures. A clear reflection of such "soft" duty-based approaches is embodied in the new Article 51A of the Indian Constitution, which comprises a set of Fundamental Duties. These include the duty "to promote harmony and the spirit of common brotherhood amongst all the people of India transcending religious, linguistic and regional or sectional diversities; to renounce practices derogatory to the dignity of women";[18] and "to value and preserve the rich heritage of our composite culture."[19]

Although modern Indian law thus looks at first sight like a Western legal system and even seems to resemble U.S. law,[20] the trajectory of Indian legal developments and outcomes is in fact very different from what we find in Europe or North America. Lessons from the Indian experience are therefore not directly transposable to our contexts. However, by showing how the Indian law of marriage and post-divorce maintenance has developed in recent times, I seek to illustrate that an intricate pluralist combination of state control and socioreligious management can and does work. This model offers sustainable solutions, even though it remains subject to never-ending manipulations and fine-tuning. Law, after all, is a culture-specific, dynamic process and not merely a set of rules.

II. ANCIENT ROOTS OF PLURALISM AND BOUNDARY CROSSING

India's so-called composite culture has manifestly ancient roots.[21] Diversity management has been an integral element of South Asian social and legal systems for centuries. Examples include the much-maligned and heavily abused caste system,

18 *Constitution of India*, Article 51A(e) (1950).
19 Ibid., Article 51A(f).
20 Larson, *Religion and Personal Law in Secular India*.
21 It seems the word "multiculturalism" – which perhaps suggests polluting mélanges – has become disfavored.

which evinces the basic recognition that humans have different functions in life, and also the enormously important ancient ethnic encounters that specialist scholars are still struggling to unravel.[22] Very few lawyers, Western or Indian, are able to perceive these basically cultural Indic roots as potent and intrinsically plural growth stimulants for an amazingly versatile system of gradually developing legal regulation.[23] "Hinduism" may well be a more recent term and a constructed entity, but Indic culture itself has unquestionably ancient pedigree and is manifestly more than a religious tradition.[24]

Indic cultural traditions include ancient textual evidence, dating to circa 1000 BCE, that explicitly and intimately connects human marriage rituals to macrocosmic phenomena.[25] These texts laid conceptual foundations that have receded into the past and tend to be forgotten and ignored today. They are deliberately omitted by many scholars today because of their allegedly suspect religious provenance. However, such deep-rooted concepts within the subconscious of Indic people of all kinds, including now many South Asian Muslims and Christians, continue to exert much invisible and indeed some visible influence. Many legal systems in Asia have been influenced by the migration of such early Indic concepts, especially throughout Southeast Asia and into the Far East, extending from Japan west past Afghanistan and Iran.[26] Excavating these ancient pluralisms helps to explain why India is so different from other jurisdictions today regarding management of family law regulations.

Given such ancient Indic foundational concepts, it is not surprising that modern Indian family law struggles with implementing state control of marriage. Marriage was, first of all, a new relationship of a man and a woman, linked to family, clan, and community and ritually connected through the solemnization of increasingly elaborate rituals directed toward the Universe. It was not primarily a matter for the state.[27] Interconnectedness was the key element of early Indic thought, conceptually embedded in dynamic terms like *karma* (action and its consequences) and *dharma* (the duty of everyone to do the right thing at any moment of one's life). This concept

22 A key issue here is whether Indic cultures were significantly influenced by early European or Central Asian models ("the Aryan question") as a result of migrations. A related issue is the relative input of non-Aryan cultures, specifically Dravidian and various tribal models. The latter would bring Indians closer to Africans, which is widely resented.

23 For details, see Werner F. Menski, *Hindu Law: Beyond Tradition and Modernity* (New Delhi: Oxford University Press, 2003).

24 Werner Menski, "Hindu Law as a 'Religious' System," in *Religion, Law and Tradition: Comparative Studies in Religious Law*, ed. Andrew Huxley (London: Routledge Curzon, 2002), 108–126.

25 Menski, *Hindu Law*, 86–93.

26 Ibid.

27 See Stephen B. Presser, "Marriage and the Law: Time for a Divorce?" (in this volume) (concerning the nature of marriage and its connection to the state in the Western common law tradition).

was manifested in the expectation that microcosmic entities and processes should perennially be harmonized with visions of macrocosmic Order.[28]

The failed imperial and colonial efforts – by Muslims and especially by the British – to restructure Indian personal laws and to privilege state control are simplistically characterized by many post-colonial scholars as mischievous actions that afforded unwarranted prominence to religion. As a result, even the most recent studies on Indian family law are content to presume that Indian personal laws are just religious constructs. This intellectually impoverished approach completely ignores the intense interaction and constant border crossing between various forms of law within Hindu and Indian law and precludes even analyzing interactions between secular "general laws" and allegedly religious "personal laws."[29]

Ignorance of Indic cultural traditions and unwillingness to accept and interrogate the complex subsequent developments within India's deeply plurality-conscious family law are also reflected when surprised legal observers note and/or are forced to admit that in India today a Hindu (or indeed Muslim) marriage still becomes legally valid not through an act of state-ordained registration but through performance of requisite religious and social ceremonies. It is worth emphasizing that both religious *and* social aspects exist, underscoring the fact that manifestations of legal pluralism are not restricted to struggles between law and religion; they comprise every aspect of human existence. Marriage registration documents are not unknown, but they are normally not the appropriate final proof that a legally valid marriage exists, especially because documents can be purchased and forged.[30] Scholars, including many South Asian lawyers, became brainwashed by legal positivism and focus solely on "the law" and therefore struggle to understand what is really going on in the complex field of South Asian laws.

Moreover, many scholars, as this volume confirms, have deep-seated ideological problems with legal pluralism and thus tend to advise that state-centric control mechanisms promote good governance and rule of law better than allegedly limitless pluralism.[31] This shows that we still live in the age of positivism, which

[28] Ibid., 71–130; Menski, *Comparative Law in a Global Context*, 196–234.

[29] See Parashar and Dhanda, *Redefining Family Law in India*. Notably, the very first sentence of the editors' introduction decrees conceptual blindness and tolerates no dissent: "Family law is synonymous with religious personal laws in India." Ibid., ix.

[30] This was illustrated in the Workshop on Informal Marriages and Dutch Law, held in Amsterdam on March 13, 2003, under the guidance of Dr. Leila Jordens-Cotran. Although the proceedings from that Workshop are unpublished, unfortunately, they include papers explaining why Dutch immigration officials had wrongly assumed for some time, simply on the basis of marriage documents, that many marriages between foreign Muslim men and Dutch women were legally valid.

[31] See, e.g., McClain, "Marriage Pluralism in the United States" (in this volume); Katherine Shaw Spaht, "Covenant Marriage Laws: A Model for Compromise" (in this volume); Wilson, "The Perils of Privatized Marriage" (in this volume).

proudly claims to have developed out of earlier stages of legal theorizing that were focused on more or less religio-centric natural law. Such misguided evolutionary thinking among lawyers and other observers is simply not maintainable in the long run. Revision is reflected in the currently growing attention at last given to legal pluralism as an ever-present phenomenon,[32] expressed in various ways as the ubiquitous nature of law[33] (which is a simple word with many meanings).

This trend toward more open-minded acceptance of the law as internally plural, and thus always as its own other, was reflected in my earlier studies of legal pluralism as a global phenomenon.[34] My analysis has recently further considered the current expectation that international human rights norms are new forms of natural law that need to be built into global pictures of law. The result of such plurality-conscious theorizing has been the emergence of new, complex models of envisaging law and pluralism.[35] The messy realities of legal pluralism do not comport neatly with popular obsessions with legal certainty and will therefore irritate "black letter lawyers."

Whereas strong Indian legal pluralism, in the sense that John Griffiths uses the term,[36] is partly a postmodern phenomenon, recent research has uncovered important lessons about the ubiquity of legal pluralism in time and space. It appears that Indic laws always operated beyond the boundaries of tradition and modernity. For example, evidence of acute consciousness of patterns of legal pluralism existed already in Vedic times (circa 1500 to 1000 BCE). This consciousness was characterized by heavily contested and competing truth claims in relation to law (in the wider sense of cosmic Truth – that is, natural law rather than state law) along patterns quite akin to today's struggles over the "war on terror."[37] State law was certainly not absent, but it also was clearly not dominant. Emerging concepts of the state (particularly of rulers as sponsors of certain elaborate ritual performances) remained subservient to higher forms of order, particularly macrocosmic Order. But in this heavily contested

[32] Brian Z. Tamanaha, "Understanding Legal Pluralism: Past to Present, Local to Global," *Sydney Law Review* 30 (September 2008): 375–411.

[33] Emmanuel Melissaris, *Ubiquitous Law. Legal Theory and the Space for Legal Pluralism* (Farnham and Burlington, VT: Ashgate, 2009).

[34] Menski, *Comparative Law in a Global Context*, 82–192.

[35] *See* Masaji Chiba, ed., *Asian Indigenous Law in Interaction with Received Law* (London and New York: KPI, 1986), excerpted in Menski, *Comparative Law in a Global Context*, 119–128; Werner Menski, "Flying Kites: *Banglar Ghuri – Iccher Ghuri*. Managing Family Laws and Gender Issues in Bangladesh," *Stamford Journal of Law* 2:1 (2009): 23; Werner Menski, "From the Amoeba to the Octopus. Socio-Legal Analysis of Plural Perspectives," Osaka Symposium Paper, 2009 (to be published in Japanese) (forthcoming).

[36] See John Griffiths, "What is Legal Pluralism?" *Journal of Legal Pluralism and Unofficial Law* 24 (1986): 1–56.

[37] Werner Menski, "Sanskrit Law: Excavating Vedic Legal Pluralism," paper for the 14th International Sanskrit Conference in Kyoto, September 2009 (to be published in the Conference Proceedings) (forthcoming).

field, "religion" was also clearly not the sole or unquestionably dominant force. There were many religions and competing philosophies and visions, including atheism and agnosticism. Everything was contested among the people that lived at that time, just as we see today.

Because fine conceptual distinctions of invisible religious truth and macrocosmic Order (*rita*) are recorded as coexisting with secular visible truth (*satya*) in such early textual sources, I can now firmly deduce that struggles over law and religion are actually much older than previously imagined. However the later concept of *dharma* developed – both as a central Hindu law term and as an idea of microcosmic ordering – it is evident that Indian law today remains influenced by such early key concepts,[38] which we see in the Indian Constitution of 1950 and in many current laws.

The most recent legal developments in Indian family law, with which this chapter is mainly concerned, are also invisibly but deeply influenced by ancient cultural notions that link religion, society, law, and everything else into a giant web of normative elements that humans have at their disposal to arrange their day-to-day affairs. That this inevitably introduces "religion" into "secular" patterns of law making and management is a lesson that Americans should find relatively easy to understand and accept. Many South Asian scholars and others who are deeply influenced by the post-Enlightenment ideal of strict separation of law and religion sometimes find it difficult to grasp the basic meaning of "secularism" in Indian law and misunderstand it to be French-style separation of law and religion. This creates a huge obstacle for a plurality-conscious analysis of how today's Indian family law handles competing claims among more than a billion citizens.

In such a complex field as family law, aiming for state-centric legal regulation would never lead to realistic and just outcomes and would run diametrically counter to ancient Indic principles of self-controlled ordering. These include, among others, *dharma* – the expectation to do the right thing at the right time at any point of your life.[39] Some fifteen years ago, the self-appointed social reformer Madhu Kishwar rightly highlighted that modern Indian legislators, conscious of such powerful ancient legal history and concepts, did not completely abolish "tradition" but rather presented ancient customs and normative patterns in a new, statutory form.[40] Even the flavor of this old wine in new bottles irritates many modernity-focused

[38] There are ongoing debates about whether the term *dharma* has more Buddhist rather than Hindu antecedents. See Patrick Olivelle, "Hindu Law: The Formative Period, 400 B.C.E. – 400 C.E.," in *The Oxford International Encyclopedia of Legal History*, vol. 3, ed. Stanley N. Katz (New York: Oxford University Press, 2009), 151–155.

[39] For details see Menski, *Hindu Law*, 198–237.

[40] See Madhu Kishwar, "Codified Hindu Law: Myth and Reality," *Economic and Political Weekly* 29:33 (August 13, 1994): 2145–2161.

scholars who are still desperately arguing for the abolition of tradition and seeking to segregate law and culture. They constantly attempt to hide from public view what is actually going on in Indian family law in this impossible endeavor. Seeking to redefine the whole field on their own terms, they claim to search for justice,[41] but they fail to remember Derrida's famous message of legal dynamism and innate plurality – namely, that justice is always *à venir*.[42] In reality, such efforts are merely attempts to inject certain value judgments into ongoing global debates and to deliberately silence other voices. Such scholars disregard the voices of hundreds of millions of Indians who continue to live by what I call "slumdog law," a law aware that its people live in atrocious conditions, are desperately poor, and face rights deprivation every second of their lives.[43]

A legal system that knows most citizens struggle to feed themselves and their children can nevertheless endeavor to promise people fundamental rights that may then be claimed in situations of dire emergency. For most Indian legal scenarios, however, informal regulations and self-controlled ordering are much more effective remedies than formal litigation, resulting in what has now become known as "law-related outcomes."[44] These outcomes are not based on strict adherence to the letter of state law, which is often too contemptuous of the average citizen to be able to offer just and acceptable solutions. To analyze such multilayered phenomena, multiple lenses are required and even open-minded analysts must be prepared for surprises. If formal laws do not always mean what they seem to say, open-eyed observation is only a first step.[45] Many preconceived notions of what "law" is really about are challenged by evidence of strong and deep Indian forms of legal pluralism.

In such a hotly contested and ideologically poisoned field as family law, how does one analyze the significant boundary crossings and ongoing interactions between India's personal law systems and the country's general laws? This is the major challenge for the remainder of this chapter. The next section will first outline what the legal system appears to look like, and then following sections detail various examples of plurality-conscious interaction and purposeful boundary crossings.

41 Parashar and Dhanda, *Redefining Family Law in India*.

42 See Melissaris, *Ubiquitous Law*, 20, 93.

43 Werner Menski, "Slumdog Law, Colonial Tummy Aches and the Redefinition of Family Law in India," *South Asia Research* 30:1 (February 2010): 67–80.

44 This term surfaced in conversation with Professor Mohan Gopal, former Director of the Bangalore National Law School of India and Head of the National Judicial Academy in Bhopal.

45 An important recent example is the Prohibition of Child Marriage Act of 2006, which makes child marriages in India voidable but not outright void. Additional reform proposals by the Indian Law Commission in 2008 seem to have been stalled by the realization that invalidating all child marriages would cause havoc among the very people the law seeks to protect. Such considerations did not arise from blind respect for any one religion, but owe to broader social concerns. The same goes for reform efforts to introduce compulsory registration of all Indian marriages.

III. HINDU FAMILY LAW WITHIN COMPOSITE INDIA

India inherited an extremely complex legal system characterized by a remarkable plurality of laws when the country gained independence in 1947. Even though Pakistan was carved out at the same time as a separate state for Muslims, India (as the major successor state of the colonial Empire) knew it would need to cater to an extremely diverse population, including many Muslims. In the short-term, this meant that the traditional personal law system would need to be retained. However, India employed a common tool of nation building – also a hallmark of modern legal reform in South Asian states – to tackle personal law reforms first, beginning with the respective majority personal law. Hindu law was thus subjected to vigorous reform efforts in India, whereas Pakistan was introducing legal reforms to Muslim family law. Both countries initially ignored the minority laws altogether.

The trend of modernizing and unifying Hindu family law was first promoted by the British during the nineteenth century, and it was then carried forward by some sections of the Indian elite. These elites were instrumental in securing further legislative reforms, particularly the Hindu Women's Right to Property Act of 1937, which gave Hindu widows a "limited estate" in the share of the deceased husband to help ensure their dignified maintenance. Heated debates about various aspects of Hindu law reforms continued during the 1950s.[46] They were closely linked to tortuous ongoing discussions about the position and future of India's various personal laws.[47] The official Anglo-Hindu law at that time was mainly based on case law and precedent, whereas the major source of post-colonial Hindu law has been prominent legislative interventions.[48] Modern India clearly went much further than the colonial rulers in seeking to modernize and secularize Hindu law.[49]

Immediately after independence, vigorous debates about the future of Hindu law in India resulted in the preparation of what is often misleadingly called the "Hindu Code." This ambitious project of comprehensive codification, which also involved much proclaimed secularization and Westernization, was driven by a reform-focused

[46] They are well documented in J. D. M. Derrett, *Hindu Law Past and Present* (Calcutta: A. Mukherjee & Co., 1957). See also J. D. M. Derrett, *A Critique of Modern Hindu Law* (Bombay: N. M. Tripathi, 1970).

[47] See Tahir Mahmood, *Personal Laws in Crisis* (New Delhi: Metropolitan, 1986); Archana Parashar, *Women and Family Law Reform in India: Uniform Civil Code and Gender Equality* (New Delhi: Sage, 1992); Flavia Agnes, *Law and Gender Inequality: The Politics of Women's Rights in India* (New Delhi: Oxford University Press, 2000).

[48] For details, see Marc Galanter, *Law and Society in Modern India* (New Delhi: Oxford University Press, 1989).

[49] However, modernist reformers still did not attempt to abolish the traditional joint Hindu family altogether. This happened, formally, only in the southern Indian state of Kerala through the Kerala Joint Hindu Family System (Abolition) Act of 1975.

London-trained barrister, Dr. B. R. Ambedkar, who became a Buddhist to signal his disgust with Hindu caste discrimination. He was ultimately defeated, however, because his agendas were too radical. Instead, Indian lawmakers constructed an uneasy compromise between tradition and modernity: a typical pluralist assemblage in the form of four separate acts of Parliament regulating most aspects of modern Hindu family law.[50]

At first blush, especially to outside observers, the result appears modern, reform-focused, and uniform. However, this fragmented, state-made family law system often merely codified customary law.[51] On paper, polygamy was banned for Hindus,[52] but this reform has never been vigorously implemented. Polygamy among Hindus continues to exist and quite appropriately gives rise to rights for any affected women and children.[53] Numerous fault grounds for divorce were introduced in the Hindu Marriage Act.[54] However, the reformers not only retained the traditional law on Hindu marriage solemnization in Section 7 of the Hindu Marriage Act (discussed later in this chapter) but also allowed traditional Hindu customary patterns of divorce to continue.[55] This shows that India's lawmakers in the 1950s still knew the old Hindu law fairly well and were acutely aware that it would continue to apply even after the formal statutory reforms. This underscores that effective law reform clearly does not – and cannot – happen overnight or at the stroke of a pen – a fact that Indian legislators know well.

Today, most Hindu divorces do not have to go through formal proceedings in state courts, contradicting the widespread presumption that earlier supposedly religious Hindu law did not accept or even know divorces.[56] In socio-legal reality, divorce was always possible. Yet because it was thought to be a serious deviation from the ideal of everlasting sacramental marriage, it was downplayed and hidden. Although reformist euphoria ruled the roost for some time during the 1960 and 1970s,[57] and in

[50] These are the Hindu Marriage Act (1955), the Hindu Succession Act (1956), the Hindu Adoptions and Maintenance Act (1956), and the Hindu Minority and Guardianship Act (1956).

[51] Kishwar, "Codified Hindu Law."

[52] For details, see Menski, *Modern Indian Family Law*, ch. 3; Menski, *Hindu Law*, ch. 10.

[53] This means that if husbands wish to engage in polygamous arrangements, they now have to pay for the privilege, as the extremely brief but powerful Supreme Court verdict in *Sumitra Devi v. Bhikhan Choudhary*, AIR 1985 SC 765, establishes.

[54] Specifically in Section 13. For details, see Menski, *Modern Indian Family Law*, ch. 2; Menski, *Hindu Law*, ch. 11.

[55] Hindu Marriage Act § 29(2).

[56] Today, the picture "on the ground" remains extremely pluralistic, and Indian courts appear to give increasing recognition to customary divorces. Excellent fieldwork-based evidence on this, including reference to an instructive documentary film, is found in Livia Holden, *Hindu Divorce: A Legal Anthropology* (Aldershot and Burlington, VT: Ashgate, 2008).

[57] J. D. M. Derrett, *The Death of a Marriage Law* (New Delhi: Vikas, 1978), makes reference to earlier field studies about the impact of state-driven relaxations in divorce law for middle-class Hindu

1976 divorce by mutual consent was introduced, there have been no major statutory reforms to Hindu matrimonial law since then.[58]

Post-colonial Indian lawmakers were unable to enact fully codified, state-centric Hindu law reforms. Postmodern Indian lawmakers, including many far-sighted judges and a silently active class of bureaucrats, seem to have covertly cultivated a new "slumdog law."[59] Middle-class Indians detest such a term, but my students readily adopt it as an analytical tool to cut through myopic middle-class rhetoric. Cheap, simple, and efficient self-controlled ordering processes that utilize informal methods of settling disputes remain an important component of India's family law regime. Strong evidence is found in several significant facts and developments analyzed in this chapter: (1) Indian marriage laws largely do not require formal state registration to establish the legal validity of a marriage, but they rely on evidence of customary solemnization rituals; (2) Indian divorces do not always have to go through formal court proceedings, and Indian divorced wives, in such a potentially perilous and hostile climate, came to benefit from special protective measures in the mid-1980s onward; and (3) the overall picture is not one of total state control through official laws, but rather a pluralistic scenario in which the constant navigation of boundaries between state law and non-state law is a central systemic factor. Because Indian matrimonial law has been multi-tiered for a very long time, its analysis might indicate some significant perils and potential benefits of plurality-conscious navigation for other jurisdictions.

IV. THE TORTUOUS AGENDA OF LEGAL UNIFORMITY IN INDIAN LAW

Before turning to substantive family law, it is important to examine the more general issue of India's continued refusal to develop Western-style state-centric legislation in the form of the projected Uniform Civil Code. As discussed previously, the four acts on Hindu family law are not a comprehensive code and do not purport to abolish or completely supersede the old Hindu law. Rather, they serve as a tool for further sociocultural, religious, and legal negotiations. Beyond Hindu law, the gradually restructured plurality of family law regulation for India has maintained much space for the concurrent system of traditional personal laws. This worked well even for some small minorities – including the Parsis, who lobbied successfully

women, raising doubts about the usefulness of modern matrimonial reforms. See Rama Mehta, *Divorced Hindu Woman* (Delhi: Vikas, 1975).

[58] Indian judges, among others, have voiced the sentiment that legislative intervention has had deeply dangerous side effects, that divorce has become too easy, and that "we are not America."

[59] By "slumdog law" I mean to describe the actual ordering structures that are applied by and govern, apparently with official sanction, the numerous millions of people in India that live far below the poverty line.

during the mid-1980s for modernizing reforms to retain their ethnic identity.[60] Just as Hindu law (the majority personal law system) was continuously subjected to reforms, we also find separate Muslim, Christian, Parsi, and Jewish laws. The much-overlooked optional secular family law, critically important as an exit route from religious restrictions and as an alternative for foreigners, was also further reformed.[61] Buddhists, Jainas, and Sikhs have also been governed by the modern codified Hindu law since the 1950s, officially to reduce communal diversities. Because of the large space granted to customary traditions within the codified Hindu law, however, the inclusion of these communities has actually in practice increased the internal plurality within modern Hindu law regulation.

Although it retained the personal law system and granted much space for non-state law, India also put the agenda of state-centric national unification of laws into the Constitution. Article 44 of the Indian Constitution is an uncomfortable compromise between traditional self-controlled ordering within a personal law structure and reform-focused, state-centric legal regulation. The wording of Article 44, namely that "[t]he state shall endeavour to secure for the citizens a uniform civil code throughout the territory of India," indicated a long-term program for development of the nation, through a Directive Principle of State Policy rather than a guaranteed and justiciable Fundamental Right. This article, however, has remained an empty declaration despite constant rhetoric from scholars and many judges about the supposed advantages of legal uniformity and the desirability of a Uniform Civil Code.

The diverse Hindu foundations of modern Indian law, as well as the massive demographic presence and considerable conceptual input of Muslim law, preclude an easy path for formal, uniform legal development in accordance with Western models. Modern Indian law thus remains and will remain a culture-specific Asian legal system in its own right rather than an imperfect copy of some Western model. Legal plurality in Indian law will never disappear because it makes sense to retain it in a vast country that is conscious of its composite legal culture. From this perspective, too, pluralism is definitely an asset rather than a liability. Yet much agitated scholarly writing remains in favor of legal uniformity.[62]

60 The result is the Parsi Marriage and Divorce (Amendment) Act of 1988, which contains provisions that are harmonized with the rules of the Hindu Marriage Act of 1955, as amended in 1976, and the similarly amended Special Marriage Act of 1954.

61 The main provisions of this are found in the Special Marriage Act (1954), which remains an optional secular law for most spouses. Under this act, a marriage becomes legally valid when the official registration documents are signed. Significantly, this act is not used by many couples, and its provisions and cumbersome procedures are now increasingly criticized as outdated.

62 See Narmada Khodie, ed., *Readings in Uniform Civil Code* (Bombay: Thacker, 1975); Vasudha Dhagamwar, *Towards the Uniform Civil Code* (Bombay: Tripathi, 1989); Madhu Deolekar, *India Needs a Common Civil Code* (Mumbai: Vivek Vyaspeeth, 1995); Kiran Deshta, *Uniform Civil Code:*

India's concept of secularism also strengthens strategies to use law as a tool for creating a more cohesive composite nation. In modern Indian law, secularism does not have the same meaning as the Western concept of separation between law and religion or between church and state.[63] Rather, Indian law guarantees the state's equidistance from all religions (and is somewhat akin to U.S. law in that respect)[64] and clearly seeks to prevent India from ever declaring itself a majoritarian Hindu Republic. This notion of equidistance proved important when Indians, some years ago, elected a Hindu nationalist government of the Bharatiya Janata Party. More people then began to understand that calls for a Uniform Civil Code would actually mean advancement of Hinduization and vigorously maligned culture-specific *hindutva* tendencies.

The nuanced Indian concept of secularism arose from historical awareness of internal pluralities among and within religions and of their ancient coexistence in the sociopolitical and legal fields. Hence, the new leaders of independent India (initially even of Pakistan) used this concept to promise religious minorities that they would not be treated as second-class citizens. In India, "secularism" posits equidistance – that is, the state's equal respect for all religions – as a *Grundnorm* of the Indian Constitution; it protects "others" against undemocratic majoritarian excesses and annihilation. Many are still haunted by the lived experience and memory of the massive ethnic cleansing conducted on the basis of religion that followed the achievement of independence in August of 1947. History demonstrates that the multiethnic, multireligious nature of the Indian polity needs vigilant protection because allegedly nonviolent Indic people can and often do use violent means of self-preservation. Even today, we hear of communal riots and virtual pogroms against certain groups of people in parts of India: the destruction of the Babri Masjid mosque in Ayodhya in 1993; the 2002 riots in Gujarat that left a disproportionate number of Muslims dead; and more recent killings of Christians in Orissa, to name a few. Managing a plural nation remains a major challenge. Simply blaming either pluralism or religion for such problems is not a sensible

In Retrospect and Prospect (New Delhi: Deep & Deep, 1995); Dina Nath Raina, *Uniform Civil Code and Gender Justice* (New Delhi: Reliance, 1996); Madhukar S. Ratnaparkhi, *Uniform Civil Code: An Ignored Constitutional Imperative* (New Delhi: Atlantic, 1997); Virendra Kumar, "Uniform Civil Code Revisited: A Juridical Analysis of *John Vallamattom*," *Journal of the Indian Law Institute* 45:3–4 (July–December 2003): 315–334.

63 See T. N. Madan, "Secularism in its Place," *Journal of Asian Studies* 46:4 (November 1987): 747–759; T. N. Madan, ed., *Religion in India* (Oxford: Oxford University Press, 2d ed. 1994); Robert D. Baird, ed., *Religion and Law in Independent India* (New Delhi: Manohar, 1993); Arun Shourie, *A Secular Agenda* (New Delhi: ASA, 1993).

64 For U.S. law, see John Witte Jr. and Joel A. Nichols, *Religion and the American Constitutional Experiment* (Boulder, CO: Westview Press, 3d ed. 2011); see also John Witte Jr. and Joel A. Nichols, "The Frontiers of Marital Pluralism: An Afterword" (in this volume).

academic approach, and secular fundamentalism is not a useful guiding principle in such culture-conscious surroundings.

While awaiting the implementation of a Uniform Civil Code, modernists pushed for the gradual creation of a more secularized, modernized Hindu law regarding families. Currently, there is pressure to bring about certain further reforms as evidence of modern secularity, specifically requiring compulsory registration of all marriages and making divorces available on the basis of irretrievable breakdown. Such reformist approaches, initially pursued in a spirit of post-colonial euphoria, are today pressed with seemingly desperate and stubborn determination despite evidence that they would be bad for many "slumdog citizens." Such culture-blind prescriptions ignore the enormous tension between uniformity and diversity, failing to appreciate that any new legal regulation would influence the nature of the interaction between official laws and unofficial laws, between state law and the various forms of people's law. To understand this legal labyrinth from a plurality-conscious perspective, one must look well beyond official law reports and statutes. The lived differences between the converged personal laws are currently rather small, but politicized sloganeering continues to exaggerate them by employing simplistic models and concepts of law to gain adherents to an allegedly progressive cause.

This leads to a depressing picture, and it seems remarkable how easily scholars get away with such games. The most prominent examples cited are that Muslims in India may have up to four wives (and thus, of course, many children) and their men can pronounce instant *talaq*. Few writers admit that far too many Hindu families continue also to have large numbers of offspring and that Hindu men are not exactly restrained from metaphorically throwing their wives to the wolves. Hindu polygamists openly benefit from the persistent nonimplementation of laws that would send Hindu polygamous males to jail for up to seven years. (And, of course, it seems unfair that Muslim polygamists would not face such penalties.) Indian courts have thus continued to administer the consequences of Hindu polygamy rather than enforce its abolition.[65] In reality, because Hindu men have found it much easier over the years to procure divorces,[66] and because South Asian Muslim women can – and increasingly do – abandon and divorce their husbands,[67] there are no significant legal differences between codified Hindu law and uncodified Muslim law. Even the extremely outdated Christian divorce law of India was quietly harmonized two weeks after 9/11 in the Indian Divorce (Amendment) Act of 2001, which introduced ten different grounds for divorce virtually overnight. Scholars thus use purported

[65] Menski, *Modern Indian Family Law*, ch. 3.
[66] Derrett, *The Death of a Marriage Law*.
[67] Vatuk, "Divorce at the Wife's Initiative."

legal contrasts between personal laws as political footballs without taking account of the application of the law itself.

The secular framework of the Indian Constitution, in its disavowal of religiously colored legal discourse, creates additional areas of underexplanation.[68] The extensive reform of modern Hindu law during the 1950s, for example, was, in reality, partly designed to make it acceptable to all Indians. This hidden uniformizing agenda, later reinforced by the Hindu Marriage (Amendment) Act of 1964 and particularly the Marriage Laws (Amendment) Act of 1976, created further convergence with the formal provisions of the secular Special Marriage Act of 1954. This strategy of artificial uniformization soon turned out to be hostile to women and children in practice, however. Merely assuming gender equality within a patriarchal setting actually advantaged men, creating new legal problems for women and other disempowered individuals.[69] Finally, as indicated earlier, the modernist ideology of legal uniformization collapsed as soon as the Hindu nationalist party rose to prominence in the 1990s and more people realized that insisting on a Uniform Civil Code might mean imposing Hindu law on all Indians. Since then, the Indian debates over the unification of family law have died down and scholars now openly refuse to discuss this issue.[70]

The desired uniformization strategy was bound to fail for other reasons as well. One of these is directly relevant to the present analysis. Postmodern Indians somehow began to remember fragments from their ancient legal past and realized the impossibility of total legal uniformity within Hindu law itself, let alone between the various personal laws and their partly religious identity markers. Recent recourse to old Hindu concepts suggests that legal reformers have at least partly overcome modernist myopia and have become more aware that modern statutory law could never completely replace the historically rooted, multi-tiered regulation mechanisms. Ridding this region of ancient cultural practices and its rich range of customs by ignoring the socio-legal and religious aspects of such mechanisms would mean depriving India's own people of their legal identity. Perhaps Indian lawmakers have also wisely realized the unsustainability of promoting laws tending toward extreme individualism, especially for a massive "slumdog" population. Postmodern legal positivism in India therefore now often explicitly accounts for socioreligious norms and local values within legislative provisions and in case law, even from the highest courts. The policy of harmonization or convergence, as some scholars

[68] See S. P. Sathe and Sathya Narayan, eds., *Liberty, Equality and Justice: Struggles for a New Social Order* (Lucknow: EBC Publishing (P) Ltd., 2003).

[69] Derrett's 1978 study, *Death of a Marriage Law*, marks the beginning of the end of specialist scholars' belief in following English legal developments through modernizing reforms in Indian family law.

[70] E.g., Parashar and Dhanda, *Redefining Family Law in India*, ix.

prefer to call it,[71] of India's personal laws is not a meek surrender to outdated concepts of non-state authority. Rather, it is a deliberate, plurality-conscious and highly sophisticated postmodern construct; it is a new attempt to make sense of the never-ending challenges of legal pluralism. This policy is virtually impossible to appreciate through applying only a state-centric lens and a superficial positivist analysis. It is increasingly evident that only pluralistic methodologies and techniques can open our eyes to what is really going on in Indian family law and can help the country fine-tune a sustainable system of family law regulation that straddles state and non-state laws.

V. POSTMODERN INDIAN AND HINDU MARRIAGE LAW

Although major Indian legal scholars seem bored with the perennial prominence of Hindu law, it constantly brings new surprises. The existing Hindu marriage law in India is a good example of a recycling of old substantive rules in the shape of modern statutory regulation. For example, at first sight modern Hindu law on marriage solemnization, codified and written in English, looks Westernized. However, the statutory law almost completely preserves the diversity-conscious, situation-specific methods of traditional Hindu law. Section 7 of the Hindu Marriage Act of 1955 provides for the solemnization of Hindu marriages:

> 7. Ceremonies for a Hindu marriage. –
>
> (1) A Hindu marriage may be solemnized in accordance with the customary rites and ceremonies of either party thereto.
>
> (2) Where such rites and ceremonies include the *saptapadi* (that is, taking of seven steps by the bridegroom and the bride jointly before the sacred fire), the marriage becomes complete and binding when the seventh step is taken.

Subsection 1 confirms unambiguously that the legal validity of a Hindu marriage in India is not determined primarily through state-controlled procedures such as formal registration, but rather the relevant criterion remains performance of customary marriage rituals. The modern state has thus chosen to put the old shastric law into statutory form without even attempting to change the law's substance or challenge its universal validity (provided that both parties to the marriage are Hindus). In cases of doubt, such as interreligious marriages solemnized according to Hindu rituals, Hindu litigants must simply prove that they followed the respective customary norms of marriage solemnization of either family. Although the statute seems to

[71] See Narendra Subramanian, "Legal Change and Gender Inequality: Changes in Muslim Family Law in India," *Law & Social Inquiry* 33:3 (Summer 2008): 631–672.

presume that customs are fixed and certain, observation in practice shows that every marriage solemnization can be treated as a uniquely constructed sequence of rites and rituals whose totality is then simply perceived and treated as customary. This is legal pluralism "on the ground," with enormous and often highly meaningful variations in ritual patterns from case to case. Nobody, it seems, knows enough about these practices today to make final judgments about details.[72] Helpfully, the role of custom as a source of Hindu marriage law has been explicitly respected in general terms by statutory Hindu matrimonial law, as the statute defines custom as a usage "followed for a long time."[73] How this squares with the perception of every ritual as an ad hoc construct eludes precise analysis. The most relevant issue here, however, is that a legally valid custom under the newly codified Hindu law need no longer be a custom observed "since time immemorial" (as was required under the earlier strict and hostile Anglo-Hindu law), but merely "for a long time." This leads to some instructive cases addressing how long is "long."

Two lines of judicial decisions address this question. The first reflects a type of patriarchal interference with basic gender justice through positivism, and it condones deliberate misuse of state law, in most cases to let polygamous husbands "off the hook." *Bhaurao Shankar Lokhande v. State of Maharashtra*, in my view a misguided precedent, is still misused more than forty years later.[74] In that case, a Hindu husband successfully claimed that he was not validly married to his wife. The whole ceremony was held to be legally invalid merely because some element of the rituals was allegedly not "customary." Few people realize that this case was about the emergence of new Buddhist customs, and many authors and cases blindly rely on this gender-insensitive decision.

The second line of cases better accounts for customary plurality and displays sensitivity to sociocultural factors, gender justice, and situation specificity. In *Sumitra Devi v. Bhikhan Choudhary*, a polygamous Hindu husband tried to claim that he was not validly married.[75] The court held for the wife by applying a presumption of

[72] On the problems of determining prohibited degrees of marriage among Hindus and the issue of custom, see Patricia Uberoi, "Saving Custom or Promoting Incest? Post-Independence Marriage Law and Dravidian Marriage Practices," in Parashar and Dhanda, *Redefining Family Law in India*, 54–85.

[73] This, too, recycles tradition. Section 3 of the Hindu Marriage Act of 1955 provides:

> 3. Definitions
>
> In this Act unless the context otherwise requires,
>
> (a) the expressions "custom" and "usage" signify any rule which, having been continuously and uniformly observed for a long time, has obtained the force of law among Hindus in any local area, tribe, community, group or family: Provided that the rule is certain and not unreasonable or opposed to public policy; and provided further that in the case of a rule applicable only to a family it has not been discontinued by the family...

[74] AIR 1965 SC 1564.

[75] AIR 1985 SC 765.

Hindu marriage, in part because there had been a Hindu marriage ritual and there was also a child. Where local practice can be proved to exist over a few decades, especially among a large number of people, those new rituals are entitled to official legal recognition per this line of cases.[76]

Feminist, modernist observers argue that people should register their marriages, and then women would simply not have such problems. However, this state-centric remedy does not work in the "slumdog" conditions of India (a fact recognized by the statutory law).[77] The key issue thus is not whether judicial interpretations will privilege state law over social norms or religion, but whether there will be a fair hearing for both parties. More specifically, the question is whether judges will be gender-sensitive enough to resist the temptation to privilege men and their perspectives by relying exclusively on positive law. In a patriarchal setting, with very few senior women judges, there is no assurance that gender justice will be achieved. However, to abolish the existing law as a result of such problems seems an inadequate and rather excessive form of state intervention.

The potential conflict, moreover, is not actually between "law" and "religion," because the modern Hindu law on marriage solemnization measures the legal validity of a Hindu marriage by recourse to traditional sociocultural norms rather than "religion" as a superior entity. I highlight this to emphasize that a multi-tiered system of family law regulation does not necessarily pit formal state law against religious authority. In the Indian case, formal state law is normally primarily opposed to countervailing social norms, not to religion as such. So the critical criterion for achieving better gender justice is how flexibly decision makers interpret socio-legal facts, and not whether they give in to religious authority.

This argument can be further strengthened. A more apparently religious element does exist and has caused some havoc, but only because gender-insensitive, tradition-focused judges have allowed it to dominate. Subsection 7(2) of the Hindu Marriage Act, cited previously, states that "[w]here such rites and ceremonies include the *saptapadi* ... the marriage becomes complete and binding when the seventh step is taken." The statute itself thus indicates that this ritual may not always be performed. The ritual of *saptapadī* – the taking of seven steps by bride and bridegroom together, which in its pristine ancient form is a wonderfully dramatized friendship

[76] See the neo-Buddhist case of *Baby v. Jayant*, AIR 1981 Bombay 283, which is instructive even though only a High Court case.

[77] Section 8(5) of the Hindu Marriage Act of 1955 provides that "[n]otwithstanding anything contained in this section, the validity of any Hindu marriage shall in no way be affected by the omission to make the entry." This means that the modern Indian state (like many states in Asia and Africa) accepts that the ultimate legal criterion of legal validity of a Hindu marriage remains a matter for society and depends on societal norms and facts rather than religious doctrine or bureaucratic criteria provided by state law, such as registration formalities.

ritual near the end of the ceremony as the spouses walk away from the fire – is not performed in most Hindu marriages. The assumption of the modern statutory wording clearly reflects that the Hindu ritual of *saptapadī* may be executed in many different ways – or not at all, depending on custom. The rest of the section indicates that its completion on the seventh step shall be the precise point at which the ritualized solemn contract of Hindu marriage becomes legally valid and binding.[78] This rule was copied directly from the ancient text of *Manusmriti* 8.227, where it had the obvious function of determining the precise point at which a Hindu marriage was legally binding.[79] The sacramental Hindu contract of marriage, according to the *Manusmriti* as well as Section 7(2) of the Hindu Marriage Act, may thus be completed on the seventh step of this particular ritual, but the *saptapadī* may be omitted entirely and the marriage will nonetheless still be treated as legally valid. However, some judges have failed to read the statute accurately and thus quite unfairly hand down adverse decisions to women.

Significantly, allegations by some Hindu husbands (or after their death by their male relatives) that a woman was not validly married mainly arise in disputes over property or maintenance or when husbands are faced with criminal prosecution for polygamy. In such cases, devious lawyers and tradition-fixated judges facilitate legal mischief of depriving women of property entitlements and status, regrettably even in the Supreme Court.[80] The battle over this issue continues in India today.

Plurality-conscious legal positivism, informed by culture-sensitive modern statutory Hindu law, has the capacity to take account of specific sociocultural factors to achieve situation-specific justice. This is done in Indian law by increasingly liberal use of powerful presumptions of marriage, as authoritatively stated in a leading handbook for practitioners:

> Where it is proved that a marriage was performed in fact, the court will presume that it is valid in law, and that the necessary ceremonies have been performed. …

[78] Contrary to almost exclusive emphasis on the sacramental nature of Hindu marriage in almost every textbook, a Hindu marriage is both a solemn contract and a sacrament.

[79] The verse suggests that the performance of certain rituals and use of *mantras* are an indication that Hindu marriage rituals are being performed, but the decisive ritual element shall be the seventh step of the *saptapadī*. One can envisage distressing situations where it might be crucial to know when precisely during the lengthy marriage rituals the parties were actually husband and wife: What if the groom died during the extended rituals? Was the bride to be treated as a widow, or could she undergo a further marriage to another man?

[80] *Bhaurao Shankar Lokhande v. State of Maharashtra*, AIR 1965 SC 1564, asserted that every Hindu marriage must involve a *saptapadī* and invocation of the fire to be legally recognized. Injustice was also done in *Surjit Kaur v. Garja Singh*, AIR 1994 SC 135, where apparent male chauvinist contempt for a remarried Sikh woman – specifically, slandering her to grab her deceased husband's property – did not strike the judges as a blatant abuse of the modern law. For excellent examples of judicial alertness, see *M. Govindaraju v. K. Munisami Gounder*, AIR 1997 SC 10 and *P. Mariammal v. Padmanabhan*, AIR 2001 Madras 350.

> There is an extremely strong presumption in favour of the validity of a marriage and the legitimacy of its offspring, if from the time of the alleged marriage, the parties are recognised by all persons concerned as man and wife and are so described in important documents and on important occasions. The like presumption applies to the question whether the formal requisites of a valid marriage ceremony were satisfied.[81]

This legal position reinforces another important observation about multi-tiered Hindu matrimonial litigation. Modern Hindu law, like the old system, relies ultimately on judicial alertness – the skill of judges in dispute processing (described as "extracting the thorn" [*vyavahāra*]). The primary function of India's modern judges continues to involve the removal of particular social hurts, including gender injustices, and not simply the slavish application of statutory law. Application of the *dharmic Grundnorm* on a case-by-case, situation-specific basis remains pertinent in Hindu law today. Reading modern Hindu family law through the pluri-focal lenses of the old law thus offers important lessons for global comparative lawyers and serves the ultimate aim of justice. Regrettably, most modernist observers cannot perceive Hindu law in this way because they too quickly presume that anything "Hindu" is necessarily (and unhelpfully) "religious."

In India today, then, even in the absence of formal registration documents, a married woman's legal status is protected by law if she can show through other evidence that she was in fact married. Indian state law has carefully crafted mechanisms to account for such claims and clearly remains conscious of "living law." Given the public nature of Hindu marriage rituals, there will likely always be some witness to a marriage ritual who could speak in support of an individual faced with denial of her marriage. Applying presumptions of marriage offers a socially meaningful and effective remedy.[82] Significantly, some recent Indian reports suggest that unmarried cohabitation should now be recognized as equivalent to marriage. This modernist turn seeks to rename unregistered marriage as "unmarried cohabitation." However, that renaming effort, seeking to copy Western models and apparently anticipating eventual recognition of same-sex relationships in Indian law, does significant cultural violence to many millions of Indians by treating traditional cultural patterns and legal practices with typical modernist contempt by failing to accord them the definition of marriage.

Modern Hindu and Indian law itself, however, quietly admits that there are limits to state-centric positivism, and it does not fuss about strictly preserving and following, let alone obeying, religious tradition. The question arises whether to interpret this

[81] Satyajeet A. Desai, ed., *Mulla's Principles of Hindu Law* (New Delhi: Butterworths, 2004), 770–771.

[82] Presumptions of marriage are now also applied in some cases among Asians in Britain. See *Chief Adjudication Officer v. Kirpal Kaur Bath*, [2000] 1 Family Law Reports 8 [CA].

as giving in to *hindutva*, that is, a blanket recognition of Hindu tradition as evidence of continued self-controlled ordering or instead more as a consequence of resource limitations in "slumdog territory." Probably all these factors (and others) play some role. The continuing legal recognition of unregistered marriages in Indian law is not an oversight or a slippage, however; it is a systemic necessity. Although modern Indian state law could dream of developing comprehensive socio-legal control, reliable records of how several hundred millions of people marry in their homes will never be produced.[83] India's post-colonial positivists employed the ancient model of customary self-regulated order as a useful ingredient for reconstructing modern Hindu law. The real challenge today is to navigate gender-sensitivity and justice across the boundaries of state law and non-state law when contested cases come up before courts. Another challenge, and probably a more difficult one, is to persuade scholars that this multi-tiered system can be trusted to deliver justice to the people who need it most – women and children.[84]

Legal scholars today tend to argue that if individuals have a legal problem, they should turn to state law for help. They should not access traditional sources and certainly should not use religious authorities. However, evidence from Britain's eighty-five Sharia Councils and Muslim Arbitration Tribunals confirms that such centralist claims overlook social reality and do not match with what is happening around the world. The Indian evidence clearly shows that most people do not turn straight to lawyers or courts; they first negotiate within their respective sociocultural spheres. Even if warring parties eventually turn to modern Hindu law mechanisms, the official law itself refers Hindus swiftly back to custom and lower-level processes for dispute settlement and ascertainment of what is appropriate. Superior Indian courts are far too busy, and seriously plagued by arrears, to become involved in airing "dirty laundry" in public, especially in divorce law.[85] The ancient Sanskrit term of *vyavahāra*, inadequately and too narrowly translated for centuries as "court proceedings," in fact comprises all these various forms of dispute settlement, both

[83] Formal marriage registration remains an option for the elite and for those who require official documentation (e.g., to facilitate travel abroad). It is important to be aware that registered Hindu marriages are not automatically treated as legally valid in India. Indian law still requires proof that the requisite customary rituals were followed, a fact that causes much surprise in European embassies and courtrooms. See *Joyita Saha v. Rajesh Kumar Pandey*, AIR 2000 Calcutta 109, and the interesting case studies of Perveez Mody, "Love and the Law: Love-Marriage in Delhi," *Modern Asian Studies* 36:1 (February 2002): 223–256.

[84] See McClain, "Marriage Pluralism in the United States" (in this volume) and Wilson, "The Perils of Privatized Marriage" (in this volume).

[85] Disgust over such warmongering is elaborately expressed in *V. Bhagat v. D. Bhagat*, AIR 1994 SC 710. This decision modified the Indian judicial approach to irretrievable breakdown of Hindu marriages as a ground for divorce, allowing it in exceptional circumstances, but without opening the floodgates because the case is not taken as a precedent. Significantly, the husband was a senior lawyer.

formal and informal, and is in itself a multi-tiered entity.[86] It is striking that such realizations are only evident to us now, in the postmodern age of reinventing the wheels of Indian justice.

VI. POST-DIVORCE MAINTENANCE LAWS, THE INDIAN CONSTITUTION, AND HINDU LEGAL CONCEPTS

Although postmodern Indian state law happily allows self-ordering in matrimonial matters, it has purposefully intervened to protect basic social welfare frameworks that continue to rely on traditional family structures for delivery. Rather misleadingly, this has been portrayed in most writing as a battle between state law and religion, and specifically between the secular Indian state and Islamic authorities (as epitomized in the world-famous *Shah Bano* affair and its aftermath). But this complex saga, too, is actually a contest between state-centric legal regulation and sociocultural delegation of important aspects of India's matrimonial law rather than simply a battle over "law" and "religion." Middle-class analysts conveniently forget that the Indian state actually seeks to avoid recourse to its formal support mechanisms as a critically important aspect of its "slumdog law" strategy, particularly when that would implicate state financial resources.[87] It is thus important to review how informal support mechanisms in Indian matrimonial law have evolved in the recent past and how they continue to contribute a vital element to India's multi-tiered marriage regulation by working to subjugate so-called religious dogma to the sophisticated social welfare agenda of the Indian state.

India's radically activist post-divorce maintenance law apparently seeks to protect "pre-existing rights" of divorced or widowed women.[88] As in earlier traditional patriarchal contexts, married women are entitled to receive support from their husbands during marriage, and they remain entitled to maintenance after the marriage ends, whether by death or otherwise. As indicated earlier, this neatly matches the redefinition of "wife" under Indian law after 1973, which explicitly includes "divorced wife" and presumes the inclusion of widows.[89] In brief: Postmodern Indian state law is clearly not afraid to confront, tackle, and co-opt other forms of law, including religious law, to construct a revised, gender-sensitive legal framework that protects and

86 See Werner Menski, "On Vyavahāra," *Indologica Taurinensia* 33 (Turin: CESMEO, 2007), 123–147 (proceedings of the "Law and Society" Section of the 13th World Sanskrit Conference in Edinburgh, July 10th–14th, 2006).

87 See Menski, *Modern Indian Family Law*.

88 This concept is found hidden in fierce litigation during the 1970s over the succession rights of Hindu widows under Section 14 of the Hindu Succession Act of 1956. See *V. Tulasamma v. V. Sesha Reddi*, AIR 1977 SC 1944, and *Bai Vajia v. Thakobhai Chelabhai*, AIR 1979 SC 993.

89 Code of Criminal Procedure § 125 (1973).

helps impoverished individuals, especially women, to "keep body and soul together" (as a famous judicial phrase goes).[90]

This remains an under-analyzed phenomenon in legal circles, even though I have written about it in some detail.[91] Significant Indian legal developments can be closely linked to 9/11, and Indian legal developments today are significantly influenced by the presence of a large Muslim minority that seeks to assert "religion" as an alternative legal authority. My analysis of politically sensitive issues along these lines has resulted in blacklisting by several Indian legal publishers, for it seemingly upsets the presuppositions of many scholars and lawyers about gender and law, law and religion, and especially about the political football of legal uniformity in India. I have nonetheless continued such writing and analysis because it comports with what actually goes on in Indian law today, even if it is not politically popular because it addresses the reality of "slumdog law."

As a legal realist who conducts his own fieldwork, I observe that the Indian state today does not shy away from employing sociocultural and religious concepts to navigate and redefine, where necessary, the boundaries of state law and non-state law. Because such skillful navigation takes place on several levels at the same time, and because much other literature wrongly claims that the Indian state has surrendered power to religious dogma, a few extra words are needed here.

In essence, the Indian state employs two methods (often conceptually contradictory) to improve the financial position of potentially vulnerable individuals. First, since colonial times there have been efforts to strengthen the legal rights of women regarding property entitlements. These have given rise to some notable but piecemeal reforms. The Hindu Succession Act of 1956 went much beyond the earlier Hindu Women's Right to Property Act of 1937 and its provision of a "limited estate" to Hindu widows. It secured, on paper at least, greater rights for Hindu women as

[90] *Bai Tahira v. Ali Hussain Fissalli Chothia*, AIR 1979 SC 362 (Mr. Justice V. R. Krishna Iyer (as he then was). *Bai Tahira* was an important case before the more famous *Shah Bano* case, *Mohd. Ahmed Khan v. Shah Bano Begum*, AIR 1985 SC 945.

[91] See Werner Menski, "Asking for the Moon: Legal Uniformity in India from a Kerala Perspective," *Kerala Law Times* 2006(2), Journal Section: 52–78; Werner Menski, "Double Benefits and Muslim Women's Postnuptial Rights," *Kerala Law Times* 2007(2), Journal Section: 21–34; Werner Menski, "Literate Kerala, Bribes and a New Case of *Mata*: On the Limits of Judicial Patience and Legal Realism," *Kerala Law Times* 2008(4), Journal Section: 21–31; Werner Menski, "The Uniform Civil Code Debate in Indian Law: New Developments and Changing Agenda," *German Law Journal* 9:3 (March 2008), available at http://www.germanlawjournal.com; Werner Menski, "Indian Secular Pluralism and its Relevance for Europe," in *Legal Practice and Cultural Diversity*, eds. Ralph Grillo et al. (Aldershot: Ashgate, 2009), 31–48; Werner Menski, "Law, State and Culture: How Countries Accommodate Religious, Cultural and Ethnic Diversity: The British and Indian Experiences," in *Cultural Diversity and the Law: State Responses From Around the World*, eds. Marie-Claire Foblets, Jean-François Gaudreault-DesBiens, and Alison Dundes Renteln (Brussels: Bruylant, 2010), 403–446.

absolute owners of property that earlier used to be joint family property. Section 14 of the 1956 act immediately made such Hindu widows the absolute owners of any share they previously held as a "limited estate," leading to thousands of cases filed by enraged males, including many Sikhs.[92] The transition from joint family ownership to individual property rights was, however, never fully completed. Postmodern Indian law has gradually begun to rediscover the role and value of the family, particularly the joint family, as a most basic element of social welfare.

At the same time, Indian law has tenaciously pursued modernist tendencies and seeks to strengthen women's property rights at the individual level. Most evidently for Hindus, this was finally achieved by amending the Hindu Succession Act in 2005 to grant equal birthrights in joint family property to Hindu sons and daughters throughout India. Such reform had gradually been implemented earlier in several southern states, which often – although not always – tend to be a little more enlightened when it comes to gender sensitivity. Concurrently, however, and to the chagrin of modernists and feminists, Indian law has also continued to make vulnerable individuals dependent on various welfare duties toward them delivered by those (mostly male) individuals who hold the purse strings and control property rights. This means not only that all parents have to pay for their children's upbringing and welfare, but also that children have a legal duty to maintain their parents, when necessary, in accordance with the Maintenance and Welfare of Parents and Senior Citizens Act of 2007.

Further, in a move that upset some feminists, either Hindu husbands or wives may officially have to pay maintenance to their indigent spouse under Sections 24 and 25 of the Hindu Marriage Act of 1955. Whereas a Hindu husband who seeks to live off his wife in this way is publicly ridiculed in several reported cases, women who go to court claiming maintenance can today increasingly count on the state's support for such gendered claims. The results have been truly amazing. Recent legal changes are now beginning to create new gender imbalances. A highly significant movement in the navigation of India's multi-tiered maintenance laws occurred two weeks after 9/11 when the Code of Criminal Procedure (Amendment) Act of 2001 (Act No. 50 of 2001) removed the maximum allowable monthly maintenance payment (500 Rupees) that had been in place under Section 125 of the Criminal Procedure Code of 1973. The new law now permits all Indian wives (and ex-wives, by definition) to claim appropriate post-divorce maintenance. The principle is by now firmly entrenched in case law.

However, some recent cases suggest risks of new transgressions of gender balance when women attempt to misuse such rightly protective provisions.[93] The relative

92 See *Partap Singh v. Union of India*, AIR 1985 SC 1695.

93 See Menski, "Double Benefits and Muslim Women's Postnuptial Rights" and Menski, "Literate Kerala, Bribes and a New Case of *Mata*." Both articles concern cases in which divorced Muslim

scholarly silence about such emerging imbalances evinces either ignorance of case law developments at the High Court level (a familiar problem for Indian legal scholarship) or disgust that many Indian women ask for handouts from men rather than making claims in their own right. Either way, gender relations and marital expectations rather than matters of religious authority still occupy the center stage of Indian marriage dramas.

Silence about such significant recent legal developments also hides the fact that under current Indian law women can abuse the system in the precise manner that a leading Muslim scholar, Tahir Mahmood, warned of in 1986.[94] The strategy is simple. Marry a prosperous man, then divorce him or bring about a divorce (it does not really matter how), and then proceed to demand the considerable legal entitlements to post-divorce maintenance that Indian state law quietly introduced two weeks after 9/11. Such developments illustrate the concurrent contradictory moves of strengthening individual property rights for women, particularly through succession laws, on the one hand and reconnecting women to male authority through maintenance arrangements on the other. It is possible that this bifurcated, multi-tiered approach is actually designed to cater to elite women through one strategy while providing for India's millions of "slumdog women" through the other route. Nobody talks about this; legal developments just seem to happen. Here again, sophisticated official policies disclose lawmakers' plurality consciousness and acute awareness about an enormously different range of expectations among Indians when it comes to social welfare mechanisms.

Ultimately, the underlying agenda can be linked to protection of the constitutionally guaranteed right to life under Article 21 of the Indian Constitution as well as several other constitutional provisions. India's method of implementing such guarantees is to hold social actors accountable and restrain religious authority, where necessary, to ensure the survival of vulnerable individuals. This is, in my analysis, a solution based primarily on the ancient Indian concept of limited state regulation of the private sphere. The development of India's radical post-divorce maintenance law thus confirms that Hindu law has remained a much more important ingredient of Indian constitutional law than modernist writers would wish to know. The realities of such "soft legal positivism" in Indian family law influence the entire legal system as a whole and thus offer a blueprint for more sophisticated and culture-specific legal development in this internally pluralistic jurisdiction.

The focus of scholarly agitation, however, has distractingly been on Muslim law. Such agitation depicts a gender war between the supposedly secular post-colonial

women were able to rely on pro-women approaches. Another way to phrase this analysis, however, is that men have been unsuccessful in their attempts to avoid responsibilities.

94 Tahir Mahmood, *Personal Laws in Crisis* (New Delhi: Metropolitan, 1986), 127–130.

Indian state and the medieval-rooted Muslim authorities who seek to deny Muslim wives basic entitlements from an ex-husband after divorce. Verse 2.241 of the Quran itself, typically vague, merely suggests that a divorcing husband should be kind to the woman he divorces. Early Islamic scholar-jurists interpreted this verse to impose responsibility on the husband for maintenance of an ex-wife until it was clear that any child she might bear was the child of the ex-husband. Then she could, and should, move on. This means that a Muslim woman who has just given birth cannot even rely on the traditional *iddat* rule for one day;[95] she is instantly without support, even though the father has an obligation to maintain the child. There is strong evidence that Muslim men everywhere manipulate such rules to their advantage, and it is clear that Muslim jurists agreed over time to limit the *iddat* payments to roughly three months. This is also unjust.

Under Indian law, however, a guiding principle has been established since 1979 that maintenance arrangements must be sufficient to "keep the woman's body and soul together."[96] In the infamous *Shah Bano* case of 1985, this development was dramatically challenged by a senior Muslim lawyer through reliance on Islamic religious authority.[97] Terminating his marriage to Shah Bano after some forty years, he had offered her some small amounts of payment that technically complied with Muslim law but violated the emerging principles of Indian general law. On appeal before the Supreme Court, Shah Bano won a crucial victory and secured maintenance for life. Five Hindu judges interpreted the relevant Quranic verses and held that there was no conflict between the Quran and India's secular Criminal Procedure Code of 1973 (which overrode the religious personal law in any event). Because the Indian Supreme Court further needled Muslims by suggesting that India should introduce a Uniform Civil Code, widespread public unrest followed almost instantly.

The rest is much-misunderstood recent legal history. The Indian government quickly promulgated an act that seemed to take away the right of divorced Muslim wives to post-divorce maintenance beyond the three-month *iddat* period.[98] However, despite the assertions of irate scholars and many others, the Indian government did not let Muslim women down. It cleverly hid within the 1986 act a wording that became, in due course, a silver bullet for all Indian ex-wives. Section 3(1)(a) states that a divorced Muslim wife shall be entitled to "a reasonable and fair provision and

[95] The *iddat* period is basically a woman's menstrual cycle of three months, or about ninety days.

[96] *Bai Tahira v. Ali Hussain Fissalli Chothia*, AIR 1979 SC 362.

[97] *Mohd. Ahmed Khan v. Shah Bano Begum*, AIR 1985 SC 945. See also Bix, "Pluralism and Decentralization" (in this volume) and Nichols, "Reconsidering the Boundaries" (in this volume).

[98] The Muslim Women (Protection of Rights on Divorce) Act (1986) actually does what its name suggests, however: It protects the rights of divorced Muslim wives. This was authoritatively confirmed by the Indian Supreme Court in *Danial Latifi v. Union of India*, 2001 (7) SCC 740.

maintenance to be made and paid to her within the *iddat* period by her former husband." Since 1988, this provision has been authoritatively interpreted to mean that divorced Muslim wives are entitled to two types of support: maintenance during the *iddat* period and reasonable provision for her life after that. Both types of support must be made during the *iddat* period, so that a wife who finds herself virtually on the pavement in "slumdog land" has instant access to the courts. The Supreme Court, in *Danial Latifi*, calmly confirmed that position, albeit after fifteen years of studied silence – and no riots ensued at that particularly well-chosen moment, two weeks after 9/11.

Worldwide scholarship, however, continues to misguidedly assert that Indian law gave in to religious fundamentalism from 1986 onward. Nothing could be further from the truth. India's multi-tiered post-marriage law has clearly subjugated allegedly religious doctrine, and it works assiduously for better gender justice by remembering and actively co-opting religious and social normative orders. Navigation of the boundaries of general laws and personal laws has been a remarkable success. Now the challenge is to protect such achievements and to avoid turning gendered rebalancing into gender war.

VII. CONCLUSION

The conceptually mature nature of postmodern Indian family law as a harmonized personal law system is beginning to become more apparent today. There is solid evidence that the Indian state has managed to regulate the majoritarian Hindu family law in a uniquely hybrid manner, navigating the boundaries of past and present, tradition and modernity, state law and non-state laws. Additionally, by overriding traditional and "religious" dogma when necessary, postmodern Indian family law has created an increasingly strong social welfare net through combining old principles of socioeconomic responsibility with newly worded and socialism-inspired constitutional principles.[99] Indian state law's strategically wise and financially prudent reliance on traditional self-control mechanisms within society illustrates the extent of navigation between the multiple tiers of general law and personal laws. It also makes sophisticated use of internal tiers of pluralism within the various personal laws.

This analysis confirms that today's modern-looking Indian family law system is not just "modern," but consciously postmodern. It is definitely no longer built on a primary assumption that total legal control of society can be exercised by state-made laws. New methods of "soft legal centralism" or "soft positivism" illustrate that India's state law has again learned to delegate much legal authority to society, but not – I must reiterate here – to religious authority. Linking concepts

[99] See Menski, *Modern Indian Family Law*.

like *hindutva* (Hinduness) with theocracy is merely ideological scaremongering. Crucially, the "soft positivism" of Indian law today is able to trust the social sphere, while co-opting it ever more closely. After all, both have been sharing the same social space and awareness of ancient legal tradition and are deeply sensitized to each other's presence. The mutually beneficial collaboration between old and new in Indian matrimonial laws is clearly a plurality-conscious reconstruction, a multi-tiered arrangement that works with increasing efficiency for more than a billion people. It is protected by an umbrella of powerful constitutional guarantees, some of which have acquired increasingly direct relevance. The inevitable result of this strategic alliance is that state law thereby delegates a considerable amount of legal authority to the social sphere and to non-state laws. This is, at least for me, not only a good and sustainable form of managing positive law, but it also evidences the living reality of legal pluralism as a superior technique in today's multi-tiered world for handling the immense, never-ending challenges in the search for justice.

My pluralistic analysis also supports the argument that the so-called religious personal laws of Asian and African countries today are themselves multilevel mechanisms of governance that are crucial to the maintenance of appropriate standards. They are largely secular, not just "religious," and they not only show remarkable resilience but are also essential for good governance and maintenance of the nation's identity. These "traditional" laws and their sociocultural norms are now clawing back territory that seemed lost earlier. Meanwhile, to many skeptical observers, they seem to have infiltrated, undermined, and subverted modern state laws in Asia and Africa, causing consternation and surprise among modernists and positivists. However, these "traditional" forces are not coming back to rule absolutely; they never did so in the first place. Rather, they are actually making their customary contributions as support mechanisms for governance within postmodern systems that we can observe and study as intrinsically multi-tiered and internally pluralistic.

In India, state-centric positivism of the colonial and early post-colonial type has clearly lost credibility and stands on increasingly questionable moral authority. Similarly, insistence on simple universal "rule of law" arguments or on globally uniform standards of human rights sounds increasingly absurd for a legal system that fails to provide direct welfare remedies for hundreds of millions of people living below the poverty line. Speaking and writing about "slumdog law" seems to irritate some of my colleagues as well as Indian lawyers, but how does one protect the rights of those people who have no means to assert them? India knows many ancient answers to such burning questions and has been experimenting with various methods. When a leading Indian scholar argues that human rights are not gifts of the West and highlights instead that the local, and not the global, "remains the crucial site for the enunciation, implementation, enjoyment, and exercise of human rights,"[100] we should realize that India still needs a sensible state – but it has to be a soft and yet strong central state, prepared to listen to other voices than its own.

This retraditionalization of post-colonial Indian laws and their transformation into postmodern laws is partly built on vague memories and sketchy knowledge of ancient legal concepts. It has gone hand in hand, however, with a conscious and gradually more vocal rejection of state-centric Western models and legal rules. This development was foretold in the 1970s when Derrett observed that prominent Supreme Court judges like V. R. Krishna Iyer were turning their backs on the "Anglophilic bias in Bharat's justice, equity and good conscience," arguing that "free India has to find its conscience in our rugged realities and no more in alien legal thought."[101]

Indira Gandhi must have thought about *dharma* rather than positive law when she engineered the Indian Emergency during the 1970s, partly to remind Indians that legal developments were not going in the right direction. Of course her self-serving actions overshadow much of the analysis. However, her most famous electoral slogan, *garībī hatāo* (banish poverty), anticipates concern for "slumdog law." It contains a manifesto of development that cannot be implemented unless the ancient concepts of inevitable interconnectedness and responsibility for "the other" are remembered and practiced. This restructuring, based on ancient Hindu concepts of *rājadharma*, includes the ruler's duty to maintain a sustainable balance in a deeply heterogeneous society. Recent Indian phenomena like public interest litigation show that recycling ancient concepts can promote badly needed forms of justice today.

Using such borrowings from the legal past, it has become possible for secular Indian constitutional law to develop a new culture-specific style of plurality-focused legal positivism that remains closely related to Hindu principles and elements of other personal laws, including Muslim law. Rather than constituting evidence of the state giving in to religious claims, as some modernists suggest, this sophisticated strategy of reconnection makes society and religion work for the overarching agenda of the state. Relying on ancient holistic concepts of duty, it seems that Indian public and private law can actually make somewhat larger claims on individual citizens than can Western-style laws. Politician-lawmakers of modern India, as well as many judges, are now appealing more openly to such duty consciousness, asking for greater moral integrity and even *dharma* sensitivity.

My observations suggest that Indian law has been moving toward further indigenization in two other major ways. First, through increased awareness of the continued relevance of traditional sociocultural concepts, Indian state law is acutely sensitive to legal pluralism and its manipulative and dynamizing potential. Second, there

[100] Upendra Baxi, *The Future of Human Rights* (New Delhi: Oxford University Press, 2002), vi and 89.

[101] J. Duncan M. Derrett, *Essays in Classical and Modern Hindu Law: Anglo-Hindu Legal Problems*, vol. 3 (Leiden: E. J. Brill, 1977), xxi.

is stronger realization that the application of foreign-style laws and Western legal concepts like individualism and privileged treatment of contract law and private property do not suit Indian socioeconomic and legal "slumdog" conditions; instead, readjustment by strengthening duty-based normative systems is necessary.

It is prudent (and realistic) to be constantly alert to the never-ending expectations of justice to face the existing enormous challenges. The lessons learned by post-colonial India in this respect point to serious dissatisfaction with positivistic modernity. There is nothing religious or fundamentalist about this, as the search for appropriateness and justice within the composite pluralistic structure of Indian legal systems is not a doctrinal matter of religious belief or social dictate. It is instead an endeavor to establish a somewhat idealistic approach in which religion and ethics, society and state (and really all aspects of life) are intimately interconnected.

Indian legal realism, today no longer in its embryonic stage, has managed to cultivate the customary plurality of traditional Hindu family law. It has not abandoned reformist agendas and human rights ideals by listening to such tradition. But neither is it blinded by intellectual dogmatisms. Rather, Indian law is desperately searching for sustainable practical justice and appropriateness, not for an ideal Hindu ideology as opponents of the personal law system constantly insinuate. Taking a holistic, plurality-conscious approach to the development of Indian personal laws, one can therefore see that the postmodern Indian state values substantive reforms more than ideology and rhetorical uniformity, especially when financial implications are involved.

This exceptionally sophisticated legal rearrangement, outwardly engineered by swift positivist lawmaking but inspired by deeply considered socio-legal and ethical concerns, may eventually be understood as a key example of postmodern legal reconstruction. It demonstrates a spirit of plurality consciousness, helps us to understand plurality of law as a global phenomenon, and suggests that all legal systems are culture-specific constructs that need to match their respective populations. Because the population of the United States, as an immigrant country, is composed of so many different elements and entities, it is hardly surprising that multi-tiered methods of regulating family law have been developing over time.[102] It is thus necessary, it seems to me, to acknowledge that exclusive state control of the wide domain of family law is not a realistic possibility in our postmodern times. That message, an ancient and almost forgotten truth, is evidently being remembered and now applied in Indian family law. It is a globally valid message that countries need to translate into suitable legal arrangements to fit the culture-specific needs of their respective populations. Trying to exile religion from this pluralistic scenario appears to be, in light of the Indian experience, an entirely futile endeavor.

[102] See Estin, "Unofficial Family Law" (in this volume) and Nichols, "Reconsidering the Boundaries" (in this volume).

[19]

Unveiling the limits of tolerance: comparing the treatment of majority and minority religious symbols in the public sphere

SUSANNA MANCINI AND MICHEL ROSENFELD

1 The constitutional treatment of religion: the challenge of strong religion and fundamentalisms

Globalization poses two daunting challenges to traditional approaches to reconciling constitutionalism and religion. First, large-scale migration makes constitutional democracies much more religiously diverse, leading to confrontations between newly arrived religions that are at significant odds with prevailing mores and well-entrenched religions established in the country of immigration. Moreover, intensification of religious fanaticism and fundamentalism – including that behind global terrorism – are presumed a direct reaction to dislocations and inequities associated with globalization[1].

Second, the concurrent process of globalization and privatization has led to a blurring of the line between the public sphere and the private sphere. Religion has become "deprivatized," in a trend started in the 1980s in countries as different as Iran, Poland, Brazil and the United States,[2] thus not only seeking a much increased role in the public sphere but also in the political arena. Consequently, reconciliation of constitutionalism and religion through adherence to secularism in the public place becomes increasingly difficult and contested.

The revival of religion in pluralist and multicultural settings steeped in identity politics seriously challenges the legitimacy of the dominant conception of constitutionalism anchored in the principle of secularism. Theoretically, there is a radical challenge to the essential tenets

[1] G. Borradori, *Philosophy in a Time of Terror: Dialogues with Jürgen Habermas and Jacques Derrida* (Chicago University Press, 2003).

[2] J. Casanova, *Public Religions in the Modern World* (Chicago University Press, 1994).

that animate the project of the Enlightenment: a clear-cut distinction between faith and reason; commitment to entrusting the public sphere to the rule of reason; and promotion of equal liberty for all. Moreover, certain practices associated with the Enlightenment project may have often been inconsistent, but its theoretical foundations have been steadfast throughout. For example, a political actor can be motivated by his religious faith and yet his political actions would remain consistent with secularism so long as he sought to influence and persuade other political actors through arguments deriving from public reason.[3] Indeed, certain contemporary religions are compatible with such use of public reason, but others are not. Fundamentalist religions often seem incompatible with the rule of public reason, and in the context of the revival of religion, even certain non-fundamentalist religions may find it unduly constraining.

Concurrently, a radical postmodern philosophical attack has been launched against a key Enlightenment tenet, namely the cleavage between the realm of reason and that of faith.[4] The postmodern challenge builds on the "disenchantment of reason" associated with the perception that reason as the means to the implantation of a universally justified rational order gives way to purely instrumental reason – that is a use of reason for purposes of advancing the narrow interests of the powerful, fostering colonialism and neo-colonialism, exacerbating disparities in wealth, and so on.[5] The reduction of reason to instrumental reason turns the means of the Enlightenment against its ends, and particularly against the pursuit of liberty and equality for all.

As instrumental reason spreads, alienated social actors tend to retreat to individualist isolation in futile opposition to an increasingly oppressive and meaningless social reality.[6] This produces a fragmentation of competing postmodern visions fueled by subjectivism stemming from disenchanted individualist isolation.[7] In this postmodern setting, all

[3] See J. Rawls, *Political Liberalism* (New York: Columbia University Press, 1993).

[4] M. Rosenfeld, "A Pluralist Critique of the Constitutional Treatment of Religion" in András Sajó and Sholomo Avineri (eds.), *The Law of Religious Identity: Models for Post-Communism* (The Hague: Kluwer Law International, 1999) pp. 39–40.

[5] J. Habermas, "Conceptions of Modernity: A Look Back at Two Traditions" in J. Habermas, *The Postnational Constellation: Political Essays* (Cambridge: Polity Press, 2001), pp. 130, 138–40.

[6] *Ibid.*, p. 140.

[7] See J. Habermas, "The Postnational Constellation and the Future of Democracy" in J. Habermas, *The Postnational Constellation: Political Essays* (Cambridge: Polity Press, 2001), pp. 58, 88.

competing discourses and conceptions of the good emerge as ultimately purely subjective and equivalent, thus negating any priority to secularism, modernism, reason or Enlightenment values.[8] Accordingly, the Enlightenment project is full of contradictions and irrationalism, and passion and subjectivism are frequently prone to overcome the rule of reason. As the line between reason and the irrational blurs and the private and public spheres collapse into one another, the foundations that lend support to the nexus between constitutionalism and secularism seem increasingly precarious.

These developments have huge theoretical and practical implications that are closely linked to one another. For those both religious and secular who wish to avert the implantation of religious hegemonies or of war among religions, it is imperative to rethink how a new viable nexus between constitutionalism and religious pluralism may be theoretically grounded and practically implemented. Under current constitutional practice, there are essentially five different models for managing the relationship between the state and religion. These are:

1. the militant secularist model bent on keeping religion completely out of the public sphere (e.g., French and Turkish *laïcité*);
2. the agnostic secularist model which seeks to maintain a neutral stance among religions but does not shy away from favoring religion over atheism and other non-religious perspectives (this is close to current American constitutional jurisprudence);
3. the confessional secular model, which incorporates elements of the polity's mainstream majority religion, primarily for identitarian purposes, and projects them as part of the polity's constitutional secularism rather than as inextricably linked to the country's main religion (e.g., Italy's or Bavaria's adoption of the crucifix as a secular symbol of national identity);
4. the official religion with institutionalized tolerance for minority religions model (e.g. the United Kingdom, Scandinavian countries, Greece);
5. and the *millet*-based model in which high priority is given to collective self-government by each religious community within the polity (e.g., Israel).

[8] For a discussion of the contrast between Derrida's and Habermas' understanding of the historical deployment of the Enlightenment project, see M. Rosenfeld, "Derrida's Ethical Turn and America: Looking Back from the Crossroads of Global Terrorism and the Enlightenment," *Cardozo Law Review* (2005), 815, 826–31, 836–7.

All of these models have serious shortcomings. The militant secularist model, purportedly neutral toward religion, often seems downright hostile to it and, particularly, to minority denominations. Think of the French law of March 17, 2004, which prohibits "the wearing of symbols or clothing by which students conspicuously manifest a religious appearance" in all state schools.[9] This law is neutrally worded and therefore theoretically applicable to all symbols, including Christian ones. Controversies, however, have arisen exclusively in relation to the right of pupils belonging to religious minorities to wear symbols such as the veil, the *kippah*, and the turban, which, unlike the small crucifixes usually worn by Christians, are by nature conspicuous. The agnostic secular model, though arguably open to all religions, puts those who do not embrace a religious conception of the good at a disadvantage. In the confessional secularism model the state privileges the "national religious inheritance" as a key element of civic cohesion, thus granting preferential treatment to the "historical national religion" and mere tolerance to all others. This is potentially doubly problematic: on the one hand, it excludes minority religions and non-religious ideologies from the mainstream in such a way as to cut off or diminish the role of the latter in the building of national identity; on the other hand, if adherents to the majority religion are divided among the culturally attached and the deeply religiously committed to it, the latter may object to attempts to "secularize" sacred symbols. The Italian and German controversies over the display of the crucifix in public schools are good examples of this phenomenon. The official national religion model is explicit about privileging the country's majority religion, but seems prone to insufficient tolerance of minority religions and of non-practicing members of the official religion. Thus, Greece, which operates under this model, is the only European Union country to ban proselytism in its constitution.[10] Finally, the *millet* system is unsatisfactory too in that it tends unduly to disadvantage non-conformists or dissidents within recognized religious communities, and to thwart secular initiatives such as the polity-wide pursuit of gender-based equality.

This chapter focuses on key current questions through a comparative analysis of the treatment of displays of religious symbols in public places. These questions include: whether, assuming commitment to pluralism, multiculturalism and religious and non-religious comprehensive

[9] Law No. 2004-228 of March 15, 2004, Journal Officiel de la République Française [JO][Official Gazette of France], March 17, 2004, p. 5190.

[10] See Art. 13, para. 2, Greek Constitution, 1975

views, there may be ways to improve on existing models or to replace them with better suited ones given the new religious and political realities; and whether tolerance can be redeployed to boost pluralism while avoiding irreconcilable conflicts between religious fundamentalism and secularism.

The place of religious symbols in public spaces provides a particularly good case study in as much as conflicts over such symbols constitute a direct challenge to the legitimacy of the dominant conception of constitutionalism as inextricably linked to secularism. In a pluralistic society, religious symbols play a key role in identity-related dynamics. Moreover, globalization, large-scale migration and the aftermath of September 11, 2001 have dramatically increased the quest for social cohesion and strong collective identities. Religious symbols figure prominently in this quest because they evoke absolute, and therefore reassuring, truths, although they can easily turn into catalyzers of aggression, to the extent that they generate blind fixations and unquestioned adherences.[11] Religious symbols at once unite and divide, thus setting barriers between self and other. Majorities and minorities seek shelter in religious symbols, as a reflex against the increasing difficulty they experience in finding a common core of shared civic values. Moreover, a comparative analysis of the reactions of courts and legislators confronted with such conflicts reveals a tendency to counter or minimize pluralism, rather than to seek a reasonable accommodation of the different religions within the polity.

Furthermore, conflicts over religious symbols lead to blurring of the line between secularism and religion. Whether in conflicts over majority (e.g. the crucifix) or over minority (e.g. the Islamic veil) symbols, courts and legislators often secularize the meaning of religious symbols and interpret it consistent with the sensibilities, prejudices and identitarian claims of the majority. On the one hand, the religious significance of majority (Christian) symbols is watered down and presented in "cultural" terms as indicia of the historical and cultural dimensions of national identity only incidentally linked to a particular religion. On the other hand, minority, and, particularly Islamic, symbols are cast as expressions of cultural and political values and practices at odds with liberal and democratic ones. As a practical consequence of this trend, crucifixes may be displayed in public schools because secularized Christianity becomes a structural element

[11] L. L. Vallauri, "Simboli e Realizzazione" in E. Dieni, A. Ferrari and V. Pacillo (eds.), *Symbolon/Diabolon: Simboli, Religioni, diritti nell'Europa multiculturale* (Bologna: Il Mulino, 2005), p. 14.

of Western constitutional identity, while the wearing of Islamic symbols is banned or restricted because they are portrayed as portents of illiberal and undemocratic values.

2 Religious tolerance and cultural Christianity

From a constitutional standpoint, the modern state steeped in the normative order issuing from the Enlightenment should at once be neutral regarding religion, by neither favoring it nor disfavoring it within its public sphere, and be equally protective of its citizens' freedom *of* and *from* religion within the private sphere. Many constitutions reflect this dual constitutional prescription. Thus, the US Constitution's "Establishment Clause" prohibits the state from adopting, preferring or endorsing a religion whereas its "Free Exercise Clause" enjoins the state from interfering with the religious freedom of its citizens.[12] Article 1 of the French Constitution specifies the secular character of the Republic and the duty of the state to respect all beliefs.[13] Other constitutions only contain a free exercise clause, but implicitly embed the principle of separation in the founding principles of the system. This is the case in Italy where in the absence of any explicit constitutional provision, the Constitutional Court's jurisprudence[14] has instituted secularism (*laicità*) as a fundamental principle of the Italian legal system, prescribing state "equidistance and impartiality with respect to different faiths ... in order to protect freedom of religion in a context of religious and cultural pluralism."[15] The United Kingdom, in contrast, has an official church, but also a high degree of accommodation for minority religions yielding a model of "inclusive multiculturalism." In Germany there is no strict separation between church and state and the constitution of the each *Land* regulates the role of religion in the public sphere according to its dominant religious tradition. All *Länder* constitutions, however, protect religious freedom and prohibit discrimination on the ground of religion.

[12] US Constitution Amend. I, 1791.

[13] Art. 1, French Constitution, 1958.

[14] Corte cost., April 11, 1989, n.203, available at www.giurcost.org/decisioni/1989/0203s-89.html (last accessed September 5, 2011).

[15] Corte cost., July 1, 2002, n.327; Corte cost., November 13, 2000, n.508; Corte cost., October 11, 1997, n.329; Corte cost., September 30, 1996, n.334; Corte cost., November 29, 1993, n.421; Corte cost., April 19, 1993, n.195; Corte cost., January 11, 1989, n.13; Corte cost., May 23, 1990, n.259; Corte cost., April 11, 1989, n.203. All of these cases are available at the Constitutional Court's website www.cortecostituzionale.it/actionGiurisprudenza.do (last accessed September 5, 2011).

In all the above cases the constitutional handling of the relationship between religion and the state draws on the Enlightenment but remains far short of its ideals. This is hardly surprising given the wide gap between Enlightenment ideals and how they have actually fared since they were launched in the eighteenth century. A telling example of this is provided by contemporary constitutional jurisprudence regarding the relationship between religion and the state. Secularization and the transition to liberalism resulted in a state model no longer endorsing a conception of the good related to a particular religion, but that put in question the powers of integration of a secularized society. The nation state with its emphasis on a distinct national identity anchored in a common history, language, tradition and culture displaced religious belief as the source of integration of the polity, but that did not preclude religion's persistent survival as an implicit mainstay engrained in the secular nation's tradition and culture. And because of Europe's overwhelmingly Christian heritage, repression of the latter quite naturally prompted its return as (Christian) culture and tradition.[16]

Conflicts over religious symbols provide a particularly salient example of how the entanglement between national identity and the polity's Christian heritage actually shapes the understanding of religious tolerance and informs the interpretation of religious rights. To illustrate this, we will first analyze the type of conflict that arises when a religious symbol deriving from the majority religion is used as a component of the "public language" of identity by state authorities. We will then turn to the kind of conflict that arises when the individual right to wear religious symbols and clothing is sought to be limited in the name of other rights and principles that bear equal constitutional value. In principle, this second type of conflict may arise equally in relation to the majority religion and to minority ones. Comparative analysis will demonstrate, however, that controversies have almost exclusively concerned minority symbols, chief among them the Islamic headscarf.

3 The putative neutrality of Christianity and the desecration of majority symbols

The display of Christian symbols in state schools has been challenged in many countries, including the United States, Switzerland, Germany and

[16] See D. Augenstein, *A European Culture of Religious Tolerance*, European University Institute Working Paper LAW 2008/04, p. 7.

Italy. The Italian and Bavarian judgments on the display of the crucifix are particularly clear examples of the blurring of the line between religion and secularism.

In 2005 Italian administrative courts ruled on the legitimacy of the display of the crucifix in state schools,[17] and concluded that "[t]he crucifix ... may be legitimately displayed in the public schools because it does not clash with the principle of secularism, but, on the contrary, it actually affirms it."[18] Much to the disbelief of most constitutional law scholars stands the assertion that secularism has been achieved in Italy thanks to the founding Christian values. Accordingly, it would be paradoxical to exclude a Christian symbol from the public domain because of the principle of secularism, which is supposed to be actually rooted in Christianity.

According to these courts, the crucifix does not have a univocal religious significance, but several that are context dependent. In a church it has a religious significance, but in a school it also embodies social and cultural values widely shared even among non-believers. In the public schools the crucifix is a religious symbol for believers, but it also evokes the fundamental state values that constitute the basis of the Italian legal order for all citizens. The crucifix, therefore, has an important educative function regardless of the religion of the schoolchildren.

Earlier, in 1991, the Bavarian Supreme Court had similarly reasoned:

> [w]ith the representation of the cross as the icon of the suffering and Lordship of Jesus Christ ... the plaintiffs who reject such a representation are confronted with a religious worldview in which the formative power of Christian beliefs is affirmed. However, they are not thereby brought into a constitutionally unacceptable religious-philosophical conflict. Representations of the cross confronted in this fashion ... are ... not the expression of a conviction of a belief bound to a specific confession. They are an essential object of the general Christian-occidental tradition and common property of the Christian-occidental cultural circle.[19]

[17] The crucifix is listed in the "furnishing of all classrooms" of public schools in two royal decrees that date back to the 1920s (Art. 19 of the royal decree n. 1297 of April 26, 1928 and Art. 118 of the royal decree n. 965 of April 30, 1924). The two royal decrees had been enacted by the fascist government before the 1948 Constitution came into force. These decrees are administrative law sources, and thus the Constitutional Court cannot review them, as it may only review primary sources originating in the legislature.

[18] TAR Veneto, Mar. 17, 2005, n.1110, para. 16.1.

[19] Bayerischer Verwaltungsgerichtshof [BayVGH] [Bavarian Higher Administrative Court] June 3, 1991, p. 122; Bayerische Verwaltungsblatter [BayVBl] pp. 751–4, (FRG), reprinted in *Neue Zeitschrift fuer Verwaltungsrechts [New Journal of Administrative Law]*, Issue 11, 1991, p. 1099.

It follows that the placing of a crucifix in classrooms of state schools does not injure the basic rights (to negative freedom) of pupils and parents who, on religious or philosophical grounds, reject such representation.

A liberal democracy cannot plausibly impose an *obligation* to display the crucifix in public schools, without weakening or neutralizing its religious significance. The Italian and Bavarian courts accordingly had to proceed to disarticulate the semantic significance of the crucifix.[20] Thus, the crucifix loses its specific (religious) value and becomes a general symbol of civilization and culture, available for free use by the state to meet the needs of the political community. Such an instrumental use of religion is not only inappropriate from a secular political and ethical point of view, but it also prompts government interference in church matters contrary to the principle of state neutrality or equidistance. This was actually stressed in the German Federal Constitutional Court's 1995 judgment prohibiting the display of the cross in Bavarian state schools on the ground that the pressure to learn "under the cross" is in conflict with the neutrality of the state in religious matters.[21] Moreover, according to the Court,[22] not considering the crucifix as a religious symbol connected with a specific religion violates the religious autonomy of Christians and actually produces a desecration of the crucifix itself. A similar argument is found in Justice Brennan's dissenting opinion in the US Supreme Court decision in *Lynch* v. *Donnelly*[23] where the Court's majority concluded that the city of Pawtucket, RI, had not violated the Establishment Clause by including a crèche in its annual Christmas display. However, in Brennan's view:

> The crèche has been relegated to the role of a neutral harbinger of the holiday season, useful for commercial purposes, but devoid of any inherent meaning and incapable of enhancing the religious tenor of a display of which it is an integral part. The import of the Court's decision is to encourage use of the crèche in a … setting where Christians feel constrained in acknowledging its symbolic meaning and non-Christians feel alienated by its presence. Surely, this is a misuse of a sacred symbol.[24]

[20] A. Morelli, "Simboli, religioni e valori negli ordinamenti democratici" in E. Dieni, *I simboli religiosi tra diritto e culture* (Milan: A. Giuffrè, 2006) [hereinafter *I simboli religiosi*), p. 85.

[21] Bundesverfassungsgericht [BVerfG] [Federal Constitutional Court] May 16, 1995 (*Kruzifix-Urteil*), 93 Entscheidungen des Bundesverfassungsgerichts [BVerfGE] 1 (FRG), available at www.kirchen.net/upload/1232_Kreuz.pdf (last accessed September 5, 2011).

[22] *Kruzifix-Urteil*, 93 BVerfGE 1.

[23] *Lynch* v. *Donnelly*, 465 U.S. 668 (1984).

[24] *Lynch* v. *Donnelly* [465 U.S. 668, 728].

Another recurrent element in the "crucifix cases" is the supposed universal character of Christianity *as opposed* to the parochial nature of other denominations. Although neither the Italian nor the Bavarian challenges to the display of the crucifix were brought by Muslims, the two judgments rely explicitly on a comparison between Christianity and Islam, concluding that whereas the former is rooted in the state's democratic values, the latter is incompatible with them. Thus Christianity, *unlike other religions*, is presumed inherently inclusive of the tolerance and freedom that are pillars of the secular state. According to the Italian court, there is "a perceptible affinity ... between the essential core of Christianity" and that "of the Italian Constitution." The Court does admit that "during history, many incrustations were settled on the two cores, and especially on Christianity,"[25] but nonetheless, harmony between the two endures because "despite the Inquisition, anti-Semitism and the Crusades" it is "easy" (!) to recognize the most profound core of Christianity in the "principles of dignity, tolerance and religious freedom and therefore in the very foundation of a secular state."[26] Moreover, the display of the crucifix does not discriminate between Christians and non-Christians, because "exclusion of infidels is common to all religions except Christianity, which considers faith in the omniscient secondary to charity, that is to say respect for the others." It follows that "the rejection by a Christian of those who do not believe implies the radical denial of Christianity itself, a substantial abjuration, which is not the case in other religions."[27] Which "other religions" the judge refers to is no mystery as the judgment refers to "the problematic relationship between certain states and the *Islamic* religion."[28] The Court also refers explicitly to the two principal preoccupations that cause Westerners sleeplessness after 9/11: the clash of civilizations and the threat of Islamic fundamentalism. According to the Court, globalization and large-scale migration make it "indispensable to reaffirm, even symbolically, our identity (through the display of the crucifix), in order to avoid a clash of civilizations." Consistent with this, the Court emphasizes that the crucifix – which embodies the value of tolerance – must be displayed in public schools, in order to teach "*non European* pupils ... to reject all forms of *fundamentalism*."[29]

In the Bavarian case the Court draws the contrast even more starkly. Its judgment explicitly differentiates between the approved display of the crucifix and "cases in which the teacher ... through the wearing of

[25] TAR Veneto, Mar. 17, 2005, n.1110, para. 11.7.

[26] *Ibid.*, para. 11.6. [27] *Ibid.*, para. 13.3.

[28] *Ibid.*, para. 10.1, emphasis added. [29] *Ibid.*, emphasis added.

attention-drawing clothing (Baghwan) ... which unambiguously indicates a specific religious or philosophical conviction, impermissibly impairs the basic right to negative religious freedom of pupil and parent."[30]

A similar belief in the universal nature of Christianity, but not of other religions, was recently expressed by US Supreme Court Justice Antonin Scalia, during the oral argument in the case of *Salazar* v. *Buono*,[31] a case dealing with the constitutionality of the display in a military cemetery of an eight-foot-high Christian cross, originally erected as a memorial to soldiers killed in war. Justice Scalia defined as an "outrageous conclusion" the observation made by the plaintiff's attorney, that "the only war dead that that cross honours are the Christian war dead." Stating that "the cross is the most common symbol of the resting place of the dead," Scalia asked "What would you have them erect? – A cross – some conglomerate of a cross, a Star of David, and you know a Moslem half moon and star?"[32]

The attorney's reaction ("I have been in Jewish cemeteries. There is never a cross on a tombstone of a Jew"[33]) apparently provoked a burst of laughter in the Courtroom,[34] but Scalia's comment remains troubling.

In many constitutional democracies, the notion of secularism as equidistance by the state in relation to the different faiths is increasingly under attack. It Italy, for example, not only the Vatican, but also leading political players suggest that a "new" understanding of secularism is needed, a "positive" or "healthy" one to counter the relativistic wave that Western democracies are supposedly currently experiencing. "Positive" secularism does not place all denominations on an equal footing: it calls for the state to recognize that the "national religious inheritance" is not just one among several denominations, but rather a key component of civic cohesion.[35] This seeks to justify preferential treatment for the "historical national religion" and mere tolerance for the rest.[36]

This "positive" understanding of secularism is by no means "new." Gustavo Zagrebelsky defines it as a "pale reincarnation of the past, a sort of 'semi-secularism' that represents what remains of the old dream of the 'Christian Republic', and is based on the opposite of the Westphalian principle: *cuius religio, eius et regio*."[37] The result is a "new form of alliance between religion and public power, where the ethical force of the first one upholds the political force of the latter and vice versa."[38]

[30] *Neue Juristiche Wochenschrift*, 38 (1995), p. 1101.

[31] *Ken L. Salazar et al.* v. *Frank Buono*, No. 08–472, October 7, 2009, oral argument.

[32] *Ibid.*, p. 39. [33] *Ibid.* [34] *Ibid.*

[35] G. Zagrebelsky, *Stato e Chiesa. Cittadini e cattolici, Passato e Presente*, Issue 73, 2008, p. 16.

[36] *Ibid.*, p. 17. [37] *Ibid.*, p. 18. [38] *Ibid.*, p. 19.

The crucifix cases mesh with this "new" understanding of secularism, which can be characterized as "post-secular"[39] or "confessional" secularism. Judges do not contest the viability of secularism, but they interpret it in a way that makes it compatible with granting privileges to Christianity, thus denying any clear-cut distinction between the realm of faith and that of reason, and refusing to confine the public sphere to the latter realm.

4 Unveiling the limits of tolerance: Islam as the irreconcilable "other"

There is a striking contrast between the treatment of Christian symbols and those belonging to religious minorities, particularly in the context of public schools. Surprisingly, in spite of significant variations in their country's management of the relationship between religion and the state, German, British and French cases all subject Islamic symbols to a process of semantic disarticulation resulting in interpretation according to majoritarian cultural parameters. The mechanism is analogous to the one applied by the Italian and Bavarian judges in the crucifix cases analyzed above. Unlike in the latter, however, the conclusion in cases involving Islamic symbols is that these (or certain variants of them) cannot be legitimately displayed because they are associated with beliefs and behavior that contradict the essential values that state schools must promote. Among such values, gender equality, characterized as a singularly Western value, plays a key role.

The same pattern emerges in the European Court of Human Rights' "veil jurisprudence." In adjudicating the legitimacy of bans on wearing the veil, the ECtHR, while formally relying on the doctrine of the margin of appreciation, consistently interprets the *hijab* as a religious symbol which cannot be reconciled with Western values. Thus, the Court not only grants wide deference to national authorities in determining the significance of the veil, but it also makes the value judgment, concluding that wearing the *hijab* can be legitimately prohibited because it objectively endangers democratic values.

A Germany

Five German *Länder* have adopted laws that prohibit Islamic symbols but specifically permit Christian ones in public schools

[39] *Ibid.*

(Baden-Württemberg,[40] Saarland,[41] Hesse,[42] Bavaria[43] and North Rhine-Westphalia[44]). These laws constitute a direct reaction to a Constitutional Court judgment concerning the wearing of the veil by a teacher.[45] That teacher was refused a permanent civil servant post in a primary school in the conservative *Land* of Baden-Württemberg because she insisted on wearing the veil, which prompted the conclusion that she had a "lack of personal aptitude." The Constitutional Court ruled that German *Länder* had the right to ban teachers from wearing the veil as long as they passed specific laws on the matter, which prompted the *Länder* with the strongest Catholic traditions to adopt specific laws on the issue. The law enacted in Baden-Württemberg in 2004 prohibits teachers from "exercis[ing] political, religious, ideological or similar manifestations," particularly if they constitute "a demonstration against human dignity, non discrimination." However, the "exhibition of Christian and occidental educational and cultural values and traditions does not contradict" such prohibition. Human Rights Watch interviewed officials from the Baden-Württemberg Ministry of Education, Youth and Sport, who confirmed that Christian clothing and display were deliberately exempted by the legislature and that nuns' habits, the cross, and the *kippah* are permitted.[46] The law adopted in Saarland affirms that the "[s]chool has to teach and educate pupils on the basis of Christian educational and cultural values." The Hessian law bans all civil servants including public school teachers, from wearing religious clothing and symbols that may jeopardize the "neutrality of the administration and state" or endanger the "political and religious peace" in the state. To determine what is banned under this law, the "humanist- and Christian-influenced Western tradition of the Land of Hesse has to be taken into due account."

[40] Gesetz zur Änderung des Schulgesetzes, April 1, 2004, and Gesetz zur Änderung des Kindergartengesetzes, February 14, 2006.

[41] Gesetz Nr. 1555 zur Änderung des Gesetzes zur Ordnung des Schulwesens im Saarland (Schulordnungsgesetz), June 23, 2004. In the explanation to the draft law, it is stated that the regulation is not limited to headscarves; however, the wearing of Christian and Jewish symbols remains possible.

[42] Gesetz zur Sicherung der staatlichen Neutralität, October 18, 2004.

[43] Gesetz zur Änderung des Bayerischen Gesetzes über das Erziehungs- und Unterrichtswesen, November 23, 2004.

[44] Erstes Gesetz zur Änderung des Schulgesetzes für das Land Nordrhein-Westfalen, June 13, 2006.

[45] Ludin, Bundesverfassungericht, September 24, 2003, 2BvR, 1436/02.

[46] Human Rights Watch, "Discrimination in the Name of Neutrality. Headscarf Bans for Teachers and Civil Servants in Germany," p. 26, available at www.hrw.org/reports/2009/02/26/discrimination-name-neutrality-0 (last accessed August 11, 2011).

In Bavaria nuns' habits are allowed[47] because, as a ministry official stated, a nun's habit is not a political symbol, while a headscarf can also be a political symbol conflicting with the equality of women.[48]

The governing parties introducing the draft laws in the North Rhine-Westphalia parliament emphasized the importance of the "Christian Western and European tradition," arguing that it is "not a breach of the neutrality requirement if a teacher commits to this tradition."[49] It follows that "the nun's habit and Jewish *kippah* remain permissible."[50]

B The United Kingdom

The United Kingdom has not adopted any general regulation concerning the wearing of religious symbols and clothing by teachers and pupils. Schools have different rules and the Islamic headscarf is commonly worn in British state schools. One particularly thorny case, however, directly questioned the basis of religious tolerance and revealed a number of ambiguities regarding the British inclusive multicultural model. The case decided by the House of Lords in 2005 concerned the uniform policy of a maintained secondary community school. With about 79% of its pupils being Muslim, the school offered three uniform options. The dress code was decided after consultation with parents, students, staff and the imams of the three local mosques. All agreed that one of the options, the *shalwar kameez*, satisfied Islamic requirements of modest dress for Muslim girls. However, Shabina Begum, a Bengali pupil who had worn the *shalwar kameez* without complaint for two years, claimed the right to wear a long coat-like garment (*jilbab*), which alone met her religious requirements of concealing the contours of the female body, as was required for maturing girls, more than the *shalwar kameez* was able to do. Her claim was rejected and she never returned to school. The House of Lords upheld the school's uniform policy.[51]

"The substance of its majority position – It has been argued – may be summarized as follows: the head teacher is clearly a good and sensible head teacher, the dress code was drawn up in a reasonable way after wide consultation, schools are entitled to have dress codes, and therefore we

[47] Human Rights Watch, "Discrimination in the Name of Neutrality," p. 26.
[48] *Ibid.* [49] *Ibid.* p. 28. [50] *Ibid.*
[51] *Regina (Shabina Begum)* v. *Governors of Denbigh High Sch.* [2006] UKHL 15, [2007] 1 AC 100 (H.L.) (appeal taken from Eng.).

feel no inclination to interfere." Added by Baroness Hale is the proposition (paraphrased here) "and she is a child, whose religious views may be taken less seriously than those of an adult, and for whom schools should provide a place of protection from undue religious pressure from family and community."[52]

Many children are likely to encounter similar pressure within a number of religious communities, including fundamentalist Christians and orthodox Jews. Moreover, pressuring children to comply with religious duties is regarded as normal in mainstream religion. No judge has ever ruled that it is illegitimate for a Catholic family to impose on its children attendance at Sunday Mass, even if they would prefer to spend the day differently. When it comes to Islam, however, judges and legislators seem to feel a greater necessity to protect children's rights. There is a final disturbing element in the *Begum* case, which is expressed in the concern that allowing the *jilbab* would create two categories of Muslims within the school, which might lead to conflict, threatening the harmony and good functioning of the school as a whole. Their Lordship are certainly aware that in the many-sided Islamic world, there exist more than two categories of Muslims and that the idea that a head teacher, three local imams and a group of parents from Luton are entitled to vouch for the preferences and the needs of *all* Muslims is rather absurd. However, the Court seems to embrace this reductive version of Islam, where there is no room for diversity or for minorities within minorities: in short a watered-down version of Islam that seems less foreboding.

C *France*

In July 2003, after the French courts had struggled for over a decade over the right of Muslim schoolgirls to wear the veil, President Chirac set up an investigative committee, with the task to reflect on the application of the principle of secularism. The commission, chaired by Bernard Stasi, the French state's ombudsman, interviewed representatives from different groups: political and religious leaders, school principals, social and civil

[52] G. Davies, "(Not Yet) Taking Rights Seriously: The House of Lords in *Begum* v. *Headteacher and Governors of Denbigh High School*," Human Rights & Human Welfare, Working Paper No. 37, 2006, available at www.ssrn.com/abstract=945319 (last accessed August 11, 2011).

rights groups. In December 2003 it issued a report,[53] which eventually led to the introduction of the law of 2004 which prohibits the display of religious symbols in state schools. Moreover, in order to clear the field of all ambiguities concerning what symbols the law was meant to target, after the law's enactment the Minister of Education issued a decree according to which "[t]he prohibited signs and dress are those by which the wearer is immediately recognizable in terms of his or her religion, such as the *Islamic veil*, whatever its name, the *kippah* or a crucifix of *manifestly exaggerated dimensions*."[54]

It had been estimated that less than one percent of the Muslim students in France had actually worn the veil. In particular, a total of 1,256 *foulards* were reported in France's public schools at the start of the 2003–04 school year. Only twenty of these cases were judged "difficult" by school officials.[55]

Five years after the enactment of the "veil law," after suffering a heavy electoral defeat in the regional elections, French President Sarkozy launched a campaign against the *burqa/niqab* type of veil. In September 2010 the French parliament adopted a new law making it illegal to wear full-face veils in public.[56] The statistics of the Interior Ministry indicate that the number of women who wear the *burqa* in France is no more than 1,900.[57]

In preparation of the enactment of the "burqa law," the French National Assembly drafted a report,[58] which is in many ways analogous to that released by the Stasi Commission. In the view of the latter, the ban of religious symbols was necessary to maintain public order, as "wearing an ostensibly religious symbol … suffices to disrupt the tranquillity of the life of the school."[59] The relationship between the presence of the symbols

[53] Commission de reflexion sur l'application du principe de laïcité dans la republique, "Rapport au president de la republique," available at www.lesrapports.ladocumentation-francaise.fr/BRP/034000725/0000.pdf (last accessed August 11, 2011).

[54] Circulaire Nr. 2004–084 of May 18, 2004, Journal Officiel de la Republique Française [JO] [Official Gazette of France], May 22, 2004, emphasis added.

[55] Elaine R. Thomas, "Keeping Identity at a Distance: Explaining France's New Legal Restrictions on the Islamic Headscarf," *Ethnic & Racial Studies* 29 (2006), 237, 239.

[56] Law n. 2010–1192 of October 11, 2010 (Journal Officiel, October 12, 2010). The Conseil Constitutionnel upheld the constitutionality of this law, stipulating only that the ban should not apply to public places of worship; judgement n. 613 DC of October 7, 2010.

[57] Assemblée nationale, "Rapport d'information n. 2262, au nom de la mission d'information sur la pratique du port du voile intégral sur le territoire national," January 26, 2010, p. 28. [hereinafter Rapport 2262], available at: www.assemblee-nationale.fr/13/rap-info/i2262.asp (last accessed September 5, 2011).

[58] Rapport 2262.

[59] Commission de reflexion sur l'application du principe de laïcité dans la republique, "Rapport au president de la republique," p. 41.

and the disruption of school studies, however, is far from clear. The Stasi Commission referred to a number of practices (all associated with Islam), such as "course and examination interruptions to pray or fast," the refusal by schoolgirls to engage in sporting activities and the objections by pupils to "entire sections of courses in history or earth science,"[60] which certainly have a disruptive potential, but are neither caused nor aggravated by the use of the veil. The Commission also viewed Islamic headscarves as a threat to public order because they are associated with communitarianism.[61] The report mentions the difficult socio-economic situations of the *banlieue* inhabited by "many nationalities" (unemployment, poor school attendance etc.) and the risk that "communitarian groups with politics based on religion exploit this actual social unrest in order to mobilize activists."[62]

A similar pattern used by the drafters of the new proposed resolution on the *burqa* heavily relies on unproven assumptions and on the dialectic of the clash of civilizations. According to it, "The evidence we have gathered during our hearings show also the difficulties and the deep unease felt by people who every day are in contact with the public ... Barbarity is growing. Violence and threats are frequent ... This is not acceptable, and each time such an attack takes place, it is our living together based on the Spirit of Enlightenment that is violated."[63] The language of this passage – and in particular the juxtaposition of "barbarity" and the "Enlightenment" – is a clear assertion of the incommensurability of "Occident" and "Orient." Moreover, the only nexus between these "barbarities" and the full veil is the assumption that the latter is worn by subjugated women, whose husbands recur to violence in order to maintain control over them – an assumption contradicted by all available data.[64] The proposed resolution, however, heavily relies on the said assumption: "We know that this degrading garment goes hand in hand with the submission of women to their spouses, to the men in their family, with the denial of their citizenship."[65] Again, the nexus between poverty, segregation, communitarianism and the use of the veil is not clear. All the two reports suggest is that the use of the veil is imposed on women who live in the *banlieue* by communitarian groups without producing any hard data as support. Hence, just like in

[60] *Ibid.* [61] *Ibid.*, pp. 45–6. [62] *Ibid.*

[63] Rapport 2262, p. 14.

[64] See the research done by anthropologist John Bowen, a world authority in comparative social studies of Islam at: *Student Life*, www.studlife.com/news/2009/09/25/france-asks-anthropologist-to-testify-on-burqa-debate/ (last accessed August 11, 2011).

[65] *Ibid.*

the German, British and the European Court of Human Rights cases, the argument that Muslim women are often not autonomous agents within their culture, and that they must therefore be protected by state authorities in order to advance gender equality, remains a totally unproven, and a heavily paternalistic, assumption.

D *The European Court of Human Rights*

The ECtHR has also dealt with the "Islamic veil issue." In all cases, it has held the ban on the veil to be consistent with the Convention. The main argument throughout has been that states are best placed for determining when interference with religious freedom becomes necessary in a democratic society, thus justifying the grant of a wide margin of appreciation.

In the past, the ECtHR had often legitimized the interference by states with certain rights, and in particular free speech, in order to protect the cultural/religious sensitiveness of the (Christian) majority. In several cases, the Court upheld measures against dissemination of ideas in order to protect morals as defined by the majority culture.[66] Thus, for example, in *Otto-Preminger Institut* v. *Austria*[67] the Court stated that those who exercise freedom of expression relating to religious beliefs and opinions may have an obligation "to avoid as far as possible expressions that are gratuitously offensive to others, and thus an infringement of their rights, and which therefore do not contribute to any form of public debate capable of furthering progress in human affairs."[68]

The ECtHR further specified:

> [The Austrian courts found the film objected to] to be an abusive attack on the Roman Catholic religion according to the conception of the Tyrolean public ... The Court cannot disregard the fact that the Roman Catholic religion is the religion of the overwhelming majority on Tyroleans. In seizing the film, the Austrian authorities acted to ensure religious peace in the region ... [and did not] overstep[] their margin of appreciation.[69]

In all the cases involved, the application of the doctrine of the margin of appreciation resulted in the protection of the collective religious and cultural freedom of the majority. Just as in the "Bavarian Crucifix Order," the

[66] Eur. Ct. H. R., *Müller and Others* v. *Switzerland*, April 28, 1988, *Serie* A 212; Eur. Ct. H. R., *Wingrove* v. *United Kingdom*, November 25, 1996.

[67] Eur. Ct. H. R., *Otto-Preminger-Institut* v. *Austria*, September 20, 1994, *Serie* A 295.

[68] *Ibid.*, para. 49.

[69] *Ibid.*, para. 36. But see *ibid.*, p. 60 (Palm, Pekkanen, and Makarczyk, JJ, dissenting).

ECtHR balancing approach resulted in an extra guarantee of protection to cultural homogeneity and in a denial of rights to individuals belonging to ideological minorities.

The Court also relied on the doctrine of the margin of appreciation in *Dahlab* v. *Switzerland*,[70] but in that case did not end up on the side of religion as it decided that prohibiting women from wearing a headscarf in the capacity of teacher at state schools did not amount to interference with their right to freedom of religion. According to the Court, "in displaying a powerful religious attribute on the school premises ... the appellant may have interfered with the religious beliefs of her pupils."[71] In addition, the Court emphasized:

> It must also be acknowledged that it is difficult to reconcile the wearing of a headscarf with the principle of gender equality, which is a fundamental value of our society enshrined in a specific provision of the Federal Constitution and must be taken into account by schools.[72]

Moreover, the Court feared that the appellant's attitude could provoke reactions and conflicts:

> [A]llowing headscarves to be worn would result in the acceptance of garments that are powerful symbols of other faiths, such as soutanes or kippas.[73]

With this, the Court sanctioned a clear double standard, as it did not question the fact that "the principle of proportionality has led the cantonal government to allow teachers to wear discreet religious symbols at school, such as small pieces of jewellery."[74] In short, it is now compatible with the Convention for teachers to wear "discreet" crucifixes, but not "conspicuous" veils.

In two cases decided on December 4, 2008 – *Dogru* v. *France*[75] and *Kervanci* v. *France*[76] – the ECtHR decided that the expulsion of two veiled pupils from state schools did not violate the Convention. The Court noted that in France the principle of secularism is fundamental and that states must be granted a wide margin of appreciation regarding the relationship

[70] Eur. Ct. H. R. (2nd section), *Dahlab .v Switzerland*, February 15, 2001.
[71] *Ibid.* (quoting the Federal Court of Switzerland).
[72] *Ibid.* (quoting the Federal Court of Switzerland) (internal citations omitted).
[73] *Ibid.* (quoting the Federal Court of Switzerland).
[74] *Ibid.* (quoting the Federal Court of Switzerland).
[75] Eur. Ct. H. R., *Dogru* v. *France*, December 4, 2008.
[76] Eur. Ct. H. R., *Kervanci* v. *France*, App. No. 31645/04 (Eur. Ct. H. R. 2008) (no English translation available).

between the state and religious denominations. The Court went on to stress that in France, as in Turkey or Switzerland, secularism is a constitutional principle, and a founding principle of the Republic, to which the entire population adheres and the *protection* of which appears to be of prime importance, in particular in schools. Accordingly, "an attitude which fails to respect that principle will not necessarily be accepted as being covered by the freedom to manifest one's religion and will not enjoy the protection of Article 9 of the Convention." Said differently, the Court legitimated France's adoption of preventive measures in order to protect a fundamental constitutional value (secularism) from mere *attitudes* that fail to respect it. It is worth noting that the *attitude* in question in *Dogru* is the refusal of an 11-year-old to remove her headscarf during sports class.

In contrast to the trend established in Western European cases, the margin of appreciation has been applied by the Court in the Turkish veil case, *Şahin* v. *Turkey*,[77] in order to legitimize the interference with the religious freedom of the majority. The Court considered the Turkish notion of secularism – which is shaped as a militant democracy clause and meant to protect the Kemalist regime *from Islam* – to be consistent with the values underpinning the Convention.[78] Thus, the Court accepted that, in protecting the principle of secularism, the state may impose certain limitations on individual rights. The Court observed that "the principle of secularism … is the paramount consideration underlying the ban on the wearing of religious symbols in universities,"[79] and accordingly:

> when examining the question of the Islamic scarf in the Turkish context, there must be borne in mind the impact which wearing such a symbol, which is presented or perceived as a compulsory religious duty, may have on those who choose not to wear it … Imposing limitations on freedom in this sphere may, therefore, be regarded as meeting a pressing social need … especially since … this religious symbol has taken on political significance in Turkey in recent years.[80]

The Court went on to stress that "democracy does not simply mean that the views of the majority must always prevail: a balance must be achieved which ensures the fair and proper treatment of people from minorities and avoids any abuse of a dominant position. Pluralism and democracy must be based on dialogue."[81] And this led the Court to the conclusion that Turkey, in imposing the scarf ban, did not overstep its margin of appreciation.[82]

[77] Eur. Ct. H. R., (Grand Chamber), *Leyla Şahin* v. *Turkey*, November 10, 2005.
[78] *Ibid.*, para. 114. [79] *Ibid.*, para. 116. [80] *Ibid.*, para. 115. [81] *Ibid.*, para. 108.
[82] *Ibid.*, para. 122. But see *ibid.*, p. 99 (Tulkens, J., dissenting).

It is curious that the Court used the margin of appreciation doctrine to protect *minorities* when the majority religion happens to be Islam. If we read this together with the legitimization of Turkey's militant anti-Islamic notion of secularism and with the statement in *Dahlab* that the veil cannot be reconciled with certain fundamental principles, the Court seems to imply a certain degree of incompatibility between Islam and liberal democracy (something that is explicitly stated in the case of *Refah Partisi*).[83] In contrast, all the cases, such as *Otto-Preminger*, in which the Court protected the sensibilities of mainstream Christianity, suggest that the latter is fully compatible with democracy and with the values that underlie the Convention. In sum, Christianity and Christian values can be defended even at the expense of trampling on fundamental individual freedoms, because the ECtHR does not perceive them as conflicting with the core values of the Convention system. Islam, on the other hand, even when it is the religion of the vast majority, can be restrictively regulated on the ground that it threatens the democratic basis of the state.

This trend was confirmed by the decision in *Lautsi* v. *Italy*,[84] which settled the Italian crucifix controversy discussed above. Using the margin of appreciation, the Court concluded that the mandatory display of crucifixes in Italian state school does not violate religious freedom and the parents' right to educate children according to their beliefs. This decision is particularly incoherent on several grounds; chief among them is that it stands the margin of appreciation doctrine on its head. The margin of appreciation presumes deference to a country's authoritative determination that a particular practice is consistent with the Convention. However, as the ECtHR acknowledges, Italian courts are divided over the legitimacy of the display of the crucifix. Hence, the Court took sides in a domestic dispute among courts, embracing the Catholic position. Second, the Court purports to distinguish the crucifix from the headscarf, on account that the first is an "essentially passive symbol" and the latter a "powerful" one. Indeed, Christ did suffer passively on the cross, but to imply that representing his suffering is much less likely to have an

[83] Eur. Ct. H. R. (Grand Chamber), *Refah Partisi (The Welfare Party) and others* v. *Turkey*, February 13, 2003.

[84] Eur. Ct. H. R. (GC) Application no. 30814/06, March 18, 2011. The Chamber had previously held Italy in violation of the Convention: Eur. Ct. H. R. (2nd section), *Lautsi* v. *Italy*, November 3, 2009. On this decision see S. Mancini, "The Crucifix Rage: Supranational Constitutionalism Bumps against the Counter-Majoritarian Difficulty," *European Constitutional Law Review* 6 (2010), 6–27.

impact on children than the wearing of a mere piece of cloth on a teacher's head defies all logic.

5 The lesson of religious symbols: the religious as secular and the secular as religious

Given the "disenchantment of reason" and the consequent retreat from modernism, postmodern subjectivism and the revival of religion, including the spread of religious fundamentalism,[85] loom as two sides of the same coin as they seek to fill the void left by the retreat of reason. Religion, accordingly, becomes "de-relativized" at the same time that it becomes "deprivatized," and as a corollary, secularism falls off its modernist pedestal and becomes akin to one more religion. Or more precisely, religion (gauged from within) finds more room to project its truth as absolute, while secularism viewed from the outside can be more readily cast as yet one more (false) religion. This, moreover, transforms the conflict between faith and reason into one among competing faiths. For example, in the 1980s Protestant fundamentalist parents brought cases before the US federal courts, in which they sought condemnation of the curriculum of the public schools attended by their children as unconstitutionally imposing the "religion" of "secular humanism" in violation of the Establishment Clause.[86] The courts rejected these claims, but in so doing did little to debunk the logic of the complaining parents.

Since fundamentalists regard their religion as the absolute truth that accounts for everything to the last detail, any utterance at odds with their religious truth strikes them as issuing from another (false) religion. A mere statement in a literary text read during English class to the effect that "nature is powerful and beautiful in its mysterious ways," which would strike an average contemporary reader as innocuous and devoid of significant religious connotation, would hence be doubly offensive to fundamentalist parents like those who brought suit. First, the statement in question is contrary to these parents' religion, which asserts that nature

[85] A distinction must be drawn between religious fundamentalism as a religious matter and as a politico-constitutional matter. From a purely religious standpoint, a "fundamentalist" is someone who takes holy texts literally; from a politico-constitutional standpoint, in contrast, a "religious fundamentalist" is one who considers his or her religion as the exclusive and absolute truth and who insists that the state be ruled pursuant to the dictates of the true religion.

[86] See *Smith* v. *Bd. of Sch. Comm'rs*, 827 F.2d 684 (11th Cir. 1987); *Grove* v. *Mead Sch. Dist. No. 354*, 753 F.2d 1528 (9th Cir. 1985).

can in no way be considered as being independent from the will of God. And second, in requiring these parents' children to read such statements, the school is spreading a false religion that denies the existence of God or at least his omnipresence and omnipotence.

This conflict between the visions of fundamentalist Protestants and US federal judges in the 1980s may seem arcane and no more than an isolated instance, pitting a handful of religious fanatics against the secular establishment committed to reason, constitutionalism and religious freedom for all. Upon closer scrutiny, and particularly as set against the case on religious symbols discussed above, however, the conflict in question looms as emblematic of the current predicament.

The comparative analysis of religious symbols-related conflicts has revealed that these are often characterized in terms of a sharp antagonism between Islam and the Christian "West." As emphasized above, majority symbols are legitimized as representing cultural values that are universally shared by the citizenry, in spite of the presence of minorities, and particularly Muslims who are cast as "the other."

In relation to minority symbols, when the contest is over the Islamic headscarf, judges and legislators restrict or ban its display either as incompatible with certain core principles of a democratic system (frequently gender equality) or with democracy *tout court*. The relevant cases openly rely on this dichotomy between Islam and Christianity to prescribe restrictive regulation of manifestations of Islamic religion and culture in the public sphere.

The French case seems different at first, but ultimately falls within the same pattern. In France it is not secularized Christianity, but militant secularism that is used to incorporate the forcibly shared, dominant values. Indeed, French secularism assumes the characteristics of a majority religion. The French State does not confine itself to ensuring the peaceful co-existence of all religions and non-religious perspectives, but becomes a party in the conflicts among them. The State identifies itself with one (the secular, majoritarian) conception and forcibly extends it to all groups and individuals. The secular republic requires a secular attitude from its citizens.[87]

The ideological use of secularism suggests the existence of a community of destiny, unified not by a common ethnic origin, but rather by the will of the French *philosophes*, which finds its natural expression in a secular

[87] J. W. Scott, "Veiled Politics," *The Chronicle Review*, November 23, 2007, at B10, available at www.chronicle.com/ (last accessed August 11, 2011).

state culture. Secularism, however, goes hand in hand with a Christian outlook, being the product of the historical process of separation between European states and Christian churches. Even in its French militant version, therefore, it ends up preferring the (secularized) Christian majority. In sum, both "militant secularism" and "secularized religion" are used by public authorities in order to protect cultural and religious homogeneity. While in the other cases secularism is watered down, in France the admission of Christian symbols in spite of secularism has the effect of diluting religion while preserving homogeneity. Both the compulsion to learn "under the cross" and that to learn bareheaded testify to the existence of a homogeneous collective identity and of outsiders who either accept to share, even symbolically, the values of the majority, or face exclusion from the public sphere.

6 The ideal conditions

As our analysis of religious symbols-related conflicts has demonstrated, none of the types of constitutional treatment of religion actually in force in contemporary democratic polities fully conforms to the dictates of the Enlightenment. Given the number and variety of experiences involved, it seems most unlikely that any entirely successful alternative is looming over the horizon. It seems useful, accordingly, to inquire into the ideal conditions that would be best suited to allow for the optimal relationship between secularism and religion, consistent with full realization of the objects set by the Enlightenment project. These ideal conditions could provide a workable counterfactual[88] yielding a baseline against which to assess existing arrangements and furnishing adequate criteria for determining whether existing models of constitutional regulation might be perfectible, or whether the Enlightenment project is ultimately doomed to failure (at least as it pertains to the handling of religion).

Establishing the ideal conditions in question would depend above all on achieving the following essentials: first, setting a clear and workable divide between faith and reason; second, elaborating a conception of secularism that is truly *areligious* in that it neither favors nor disadvantages any religion or the non-religious; third, instituting a public

[88] A counterfactual is a constructed model that is contrary to fact but bears sufficient connections to relevant factual orderings to furnish workable criteria of perfectibility or appropriate standards for purposes of critique. See M. Rosenfeld, *Just Interpretations: Law Between Ethics and Politics* (Berkeley: University of California Press,1998), p. 124.

sphere clearly and firmly delimited from the private sphere and entirely amenable to the rule of areligious secularism; and fourth, populating the private sphere with religions and non-religious ideologies susceptible of being veritably treated equally – that is of benefiting from *substantive* as opposed to merely formal equal treatment[89] – and amenable to confining their expression and activities within the precincts of the private sphere.

The first of the four essentials clearly seems the easiest to achieve in theory and to set in motion as a fruitful counterfactual. This can be done by drawing the line between what is amenable to the methods of scientific inquiry or of empirical verification, on the one hand, and that which is not, such as religious beliefs or metaphysical convictions, on the other. At a counterfactual level at least, this line can be consistently and systematically maintained, but not so under actual historical circumstances. Moreover, strict adherence to this divide would not only exclude religion from the public sphere, but also morals and even arguably certain political claims. Take, for instance, Kant's famous moral claim that we ought to treat all fellow humans as ends and not as means. This claim is certainly not susceptible to empirical or scientific validation or falsification.

One may object that Kantian morality (and Kant himself) appeal to public reason, that is to "reasons accessible to all, irrespective of their religious belief,"[90] and Kantian morality is therefore clearly within the realm of reason as conceived by the foremost philosopher of the Enlightenment. This is an undeniable historical fact, but one can still defend the narrower conception of reason carved out to be consistent with our counterfactual as being better suited for purposes of constructing ideal conditions. As a matter of fact, one can plausibly accuse Kantian morality of being ultimately an expression merely of the "religion" of "secular humanism." Not only are the claims made by Kantian morality beyond any factual verification, but also, unlike the propositions of logic, they need not be accepted as valid by anyone who makes proper use of her rational capabilities. By drawing the line narrowly, the counterfactual would exclude some claims that would be acceptable under a Kantian or Rawlsian conception of public reason, but would also protect against endless discussion and blurring

[89] For example, in a polity comprised of Christians, Jews and Muslims, a legal prohibition of male circumcision would treat all three religions equally from a formal, but not from a substantive, standpoint. This is because whereas Judaism and Islam prescribe male circumcision, Christianity does not.

[90] See A. Sajó, "Constitutionalism and Secularism: The Need for Public Reason," *Cardozo Law Review* 30 (2009), 2401.

and against the constant danger of unleashing interminable slippery slopes.[91]

The second among four essentials, namely a version of secularism that is areligious and that neither favors nor disfavors any religion or the non-religious looms as impossible to achieve. This is because one cannot rely on the epistemological distinction between what falls within the purview of science and what does not to craft a secularism that could qualify as areligious. Indeed, acting in conformity with science may readily qualify as anti-religious from the standpoint of at least some religions. For example, state-mandated vaccination of the entire population to prevent a deadly epidemic would be justified pursuant to universally accepted standards of contemporary medical science and yet at the same time counter a particular religion's prescription of any medical intervention as being against the will of God. The latter religion need not question the effectiveness of the vaccine, as that may be irrelevant in terms of the belief in the divine proscription to which it feels compelled to adhere.

In view of the preceding observations, no plausible conception of secularism emerges as *inherently* areligious, even as a purely counterfactual matter. This does not mean that the second essential must be dropped, but it does require that it be coordinated in a relational manner with the third and fourth essentials. Indeed, for secularism to be able to count as being areligious, it need not avoid conflict with all religions, but only with those with a presence within the relevant polity.

The characteristics of the third essential, a public sphere clearly distinguishable from the private sphere and amenable to exclusive rule under the precepts of areligious secularism, readily emerge in light of the previous discussion. From a counterfactual perspective, the divide between the public and the private sphere should track the counterfactual divide between reason and faith that informs the first essential. The public sphere should be exclusively confined to the realm of reason; the private sphere, on the other hand, would be equally amenable to the realm of faith and to that of reason. However, since even under the best of circumstances there would seem to be relatively little chance that adherents to all

[91] This counterfactual achievement does not imply, of course, anything similar at the factual level. There is a crucial difference between the realm of science and that of morals. What *counts* as science – as opposed to its relevance, utility or desirability – can be systematically determined in accordance with a set of established standards open to all. Because of this, to determine whether an assertion does belong to the realm of science (or empirical observation or logic) does not involve any act of faith in the sense that any assertion to validity in morals does.

different ideologies within a given polity would agree to characterize its public sphere as areligious, the ideal public sphere should be as reduced in scope as possible.

The fourth essential is that religions and non-religious ideologies being relegated to the private sphere be susceptible of substantive equal treatment within the confines of that sphere. For this to be possible, even counterfactually, it is necessary that no religion involved claim an entitlement in accordance with its own religious norms to priority or exclusivity with respect to other religions or non-religious ideologies within the polity, or to a stake in that polity's public sphere. Fundamentalist religions would obviously squarely negate any possibility of coming close to achieving the counterfactual requirements in question, as would any religion that requires intervention into the public sphere.

Before shifting from the counterfactual to the actual historical record concerning the relationship between secularism and religion, two further points warrant brief mention. The first of these is that certain political ideologies are better suited than others for purposes of approximating the counterfactual; the second, as already alluded to above, that some religions and some types of religion are more suited than others with the same purposes in mind.

The three principal political ideologies that are consistent with contemporary constitutional democracy and the ideals of the Enlightenment are liberalism, republicanism and communitarianism.[92] Some of these – and even some versions of the same one[93] – carve out a larger and more intrusive role in the public sphere than others. Moreover, some allow for greater autonomy of religious communities than others.

Concerning the second point mentioned above, it is obvious that some religions seem more inherently compatible with areligious secularism than others. Thus, a merely contemplative religion is obviously compatible with areligious secularism whereas an aggressively proselytizing one is definitely not. Moreover, beyond these extremes, certain combinations of religions within a polity may be more amenable to approximation to areligious secularism than others. Furthermore, of the three major Western religions, as indicated by the jurisprudence on religious symbols, Christianity seems much better suited to secularism than Islam or Judaism. This is due, in important part, to Christianity's commitment to

[92] For a comparison of these three ideologies from a pluralist perspective, see Rosenfeld, *Just Interpretations*, pp. 217–24.

[93] For example, libertarian liberalism calls for a more limited public sphere than its egalitarian counterpart.

the separation between the realm of God and that of Cesar as opposed to Islam's and Judaism's all-encompassing approaches requiring that religious rule extend over both the public and the political sphere. Because of this key difference, the counterfactual construct pointing to ideal conditions would be better off embracing Christianity rather than its two major Western counterparts in order to yield the best possible approximation of areligious secularism. But that would create a paradox. If the pursuit of areligious secularism leads to a preference for Christianity, would that not undermine the whole project by lifting Christianity above Islam and Judaism?

Based on the preceding analysis, the counterfactual elaborated above does not provide a pristine model that many would be eager to emulate. On the one hand, this counterfactual contains features that are undesirable or impossible to approximate. It provides a sharp and sustainable divide between reason and faith, but the idea that Kantian morals should be barred from the public sphere for the same reason as fundamentalist religion seems highly unattractive. On the other hand, even at the counterfactual level, the model in question is remarkably tenuous as it provides a conception of areligious secularism that cannot stand on its own. Finally, even if the counterfactual does not automatically favor Christianity – and there is a good argument that it does not, but that it is rather only open to certain liberal versions of many religions, such as liberal Protestantism, Reform Judaism, and so on – it would require suppression of a large number of religious ideologies with large followings in most contemporary constitutional democracies.

7 Beyond the present predicament: can and should the Enlightenment project be salvaged?

The preceding discussion suggests that it would be unproductive to seek ever greater approximation of the above elaborated ideal counterfactual. Does that mean that the Enlightenment project must be completely abandoned when it comes to the constitutional treatment of religion? And even assuming that it need not, should it be abandoned?

The Enlightenment project has not become futile, but it ought to be transformed and reoriented. The divide between reason and faith need not be abandoned, but it must be conceived as much more fluid and uncertain, and it must be redeployed to address current threats to core Enlightenment values as opposed to those of the past. In the eighteenth century it was organized religion that was the Enlightenment's fiercest adversary; today, it is fundamentalist and strong religions, with more moderate and more liberal religions often barely, if at all, at odds with scientific reason. One possibility, therefore, is to switch to a situational and relational approach.

The distinction between the public and the private sphere may no longer be useful for present purposes, but it might be fruitfully replaced by reliance on the contrast between *intra*-communal and *inter*-communal relationships. Broadly speaking, all those who share the same religious ideology[94] can be said to belong to a single religious community. Consistent with this, moreover, dealings within a single religious community are "intra-communal," whereas those involving two or more religious communities, or a religious and a secular community, or those that purport to transcend the bounds of all relevant religious communities, are "inter-communal."

The attractiveness of framing relationships in terms of the distinction between the intra-communal and the inter-communal is enhanced given that the citizen of a typical contemporary constitutional democracy is bound to become immersed in a number of different communities at once and to have to negotiate conflicts and tensions that arise as a result. A German-speaking Swiss Catholic feminist woman, for example, belongs to the Swiss nation, to one of its four main linguistic groups, to one of its two dominant religions, and to one socio-political group with particular aims and views regarding women's equality and gender-based relationships. Depending on the circumstances, the woman in question may focus more on her national identity than her linguistic group identity, or vice versa. On some occasions, her Catholicism may be in tension or conflict with her feminism. Because of that, she may decide to live with a certain amount of dissonance and inconsistency unless her various commitments become so incompatible that she must withdraw from some of the communities to which she belongs.

What is crucial for our purposes is that this single individual must constantly shift from intra-communal to inter-communal perspectives in the management of her multiple allegiances. Moreover, the kinds of operations that take place at the individual level can also be carried out at the collective level by various groups within the polity and the polity itself as the group of the whole. Except in cases of clear incompatibility, the dynamic between intra-communal and inter-communal dealings should

[94] We emphasize "religious ideology" rather than "religion" in order to allow for the characterization of different sects or denominations to be treated as different communities.

afford numerous possibilities for peaceful coexistence within a constitutional order among proponents of numerous and diverse religious and secular ideologies.

The dynamic between intra-communal and inter-communal dealings can also be helpful in reconfiguring secularism in light of the futility of pursuing a neutral areligious ideal and of the seemingly inevitable links between secularism and religion revealed in the course of retracing the history of the various actual incarnations of the concept. Functionally, secularism should promote peaceful and productive inter-communal relationships within the polity combined with guaranteeing maximum room for intra-communal autonomy consistent with preserving the integrity of the space needed for inter-communal exchanges. Substantively, on the other hand, secularism would draw on two distinct sources of identity. In part, secularism would draw on that which makes possible and facilitates inter-communal coordination and cooperation among religious ideologies, and among the latter and non-religious ones. What would be encompassed within this rubric would vary from one setting to the next, depending on the religions, history and cultures involved. In any case, incorporation of elements drawn from religion or religious culture would be entirely permissible. The criterion of validity for such elements derived from religion would not depend on how close or removed they may be from religion itself, but on whether they advance or hinder the smooth functioning of the requisite channels of inter-communal exchange.

In part also, secularism would draw on another source of identity, rooted in the traditional Enlightenment conception of the term. In contrast to the first source of identity, which could be characterized as secularism's inter-communal identity, this second source could be regarded as secularism's intra-communal identity, or in other words, as secularism's conception of itself as a separate and distinct ideology. Indeed, in all contemporary constitutional democracies, there are certain citizens who are secular rather than religious, who put science ahead of faith, and who believe that the pursuit of liberal liberty and equality for all should trump any divine prescription to the contrary. These "intra-communal" secularists have as much a right to have a place at the inter-communal table as do the proponents of the various religious ideologies.

Secularism's inter-communal identity is contextually dependent on the actual ideologies involved, whereas its intra-communal identity is self-contained, as one can easily imagine a well-functioning, self-enclosed, homogeneous, secular society cut off from all religion. In actuality, however, the gap between these two identities is likely to prove far less stark for three principal reasons. First, intra-communal secularism must figure in the elaboration of its inter-communal counterpart to the extent that the secularist ideology is present in the relevant polity. Second, given the tendency to develop plural identities and multi-group memberships, elements of the secularist ideology are bound to slip into intra-communal precincts of competing ideologies. Thus, some liberal religions are quite compatible with commitment to liberal liberty and equality for all. Moreover, some adherents of non-liberal religions may nonetheless embrace certain secular values and cope with the tensions involved through compartmentalization. And, third, by the same token, proponents of intra-communal secularism need not shut the door to religion, and may in fact embrace religion without contradiction so long as they adhere to the primacy of the secular outlook.

From the standpoint of traditional Enlightenment values, secularism occupied a privileged place and the acceptance of religion was conditioned on compatibility with deployment of the secular project. In the context of the present reconfiguration of secularism, however, no such clear answers readily emerge. Secularism and the constitutional order it fosters are inherently tolerant of diversity, but why prefer secularism's tolerance over other kinds of tolerance or even over intolerant ideologies once one concedes that secularism as such is but one intra-communal ideology among many?

This last query forces one to focus on the larger question of whether the Enlightenment project is worth preserving at this point in time, or whether it would be preferable to abandon it in favor of a more suitable alternative. And, given the recent inroads of postmodernism and derelativized religion as well as the continuing progression of the disenchantment of reason, no readily available or obvious all-encompassing answer could be offered with confidence.

One can advance, however, two more modest answers. The first one is somewhat circular, but may nonetheless carry significant weight among proponents of constitutional democracy. Constitutionalism requires secularism (in some form) and they both go hand in hand with certain core Enlightenment values. Constitutionalism may thrive with a reconfigured on redeployed Enlightenment project, but it cannot survive the complete abandonment of the latter. Therefore, if for no other reason, the Enlightenment project ought to be preserved for the sake of constitutionalism.

The second answer is that contemporary polities are typically multiethnic, multicultural and religiously diverse, and that secularism, at least in its inter-communal dimension, provides the best means to preserve the peace and to maintain the good functioning of such pluralistic societies. This second answer may be buttressed by either a lesser evil prudential argument or a more positive normative argument deriving from a pluralistic conception of the good. The former argument is predicated on the conviction that unless a stand-off among competing ideologies is maintained, a serious threat to the public order would ensue. The latter more positive argument relies, for its part, on the premise that pluralism is good and worthy of pursuit because it multiplies and enhances every person's opportunities for self-realization and self-fulfillment.

The preceding discussion leaves one with a vexing lingering question. The version of the Enlightenment project needed for the legitimation and operation of contemporary reconfigured secularism is dramatically more modest, less assertive, and less encompassing than that which emerged in the Age of the Enlightenment. Is that due to the ravages of postmodernism and derelativized religion? Or, is it rather due to the fact that much of the Enlightenment project has met with success and has become quietly internalized and subconsciously stored in the public psyche of contemporary constitutional democracies?

Both the preceding theoretical discussion and the prior analysis of the constitutional jurisprudence regarding religious symbols point to one distinct conclusion. The reconceived principle of secularism and the Enlightenment values it relies upon loom as indispensable to peaceful coexistence within our increasingly multi-ethnic, multicultural and multi-religious polities. This reconceived secularism is above all pluralist, and although it may not be able to set itself fully apart from religion – and even from some religions more than others – or from seeping into the inner walls of discrete religious communities, it is the best hope for harmonizing (as best as possible) intra-communal and inter-communal dealings. Pluralist secularism's principal creed is that no intra-communal truth is entitled to command inter-communal acceptance. This, in turn, commands a broad and generous conception of tolerance and of acceptance of the other. In terms of religious symbols, this translates into refraining from official imposition of majority ones and greater acceptance of minority ones as long as they are not proven to pose a threat to the survival of pluralist secularism itself – a very high threshold indeed.

[20]

Crosses and Culture: State-Sponsored Religious Displays in the US and Europe

MARK L. MOVSESIAN*

This article compares the recent jurisprudence of the US Supreme Court and the European Court of Human Rights on the question of state-sponsored religious displays. Both tribunals insist that states have a duty of religious 'neutrality', but each defines that term differently. For the Supreme Court, neutrality means that government may not proselytize, even indirectly, or appear to favour a particular church; neutrality may even mean that government must not endorse religion generally. For the ECtHR, in contrast, neutrality means only that government must avoid active religious indoctrination; the ECtHR allows government to give 'preponderant visibility' to the symbols of traditionally dominant churches. The different conceptions of neutrality reflect institutional and cultural realities. In particular, the differences reflect what sociologists of religion describe as the 'American' and 'European' religious models.

1. *Introduction*

It is, in Joseph Weiler's words, '[t]he debate that won't go away'.[1] In both the United States and Europe, controversies continue to erupt over the legality of state-sponsored religious displays. In April 2010, a fractured US Supreme Court decided *Salazar v Buono*,[2] a case discussing the constitutionality of a Latin cross on public land, the latest in a long line of decisions addressing government's ability to display religious symbols.[3] Across the Atlantic, less than a year after *Salazar* in March 2011, the Grand Chamber of the European Court of Human Rights (ECtHR) decided *Lautsi v Italy*,[4] a case concerning the legality, under the European Convention on Human Rights (European Convention), of Italy's practice of placing crucifixes in public school classrooms. National courts in Europe had been struggling with similar issues for close to two decades, and judging from the public and media attention

*Frederick A. Whitney Professor and Director, Center for Law and Religion, St John's University School of Law (New York). I thank Robin Charlow, Marc DeGirolami, Larry Joseph, John McGinnis, Peggy McGuinness, and Adam Zimmerman for careful readings of earlier drafts, and William Manz and Arundhati Satkalmi of the Rittenberg Law Library at St John's for helpful research assistance.

1 Joseph HH Weiler, 'State and Nation; Church, Mosque and Synagogue—the trailer' (2010) 8 ICON 157, 157.

2 [2010] 130 SCt 1803.

3 In addition to *Salazar*, the cases are *McCreary County v ACLU* [2005] 545 US 844; *Van Orden v Perry* [2005] 545 US 677; *Capitol Square Rev and Advisory Bd v Pinette* [1995] 515 US 753; *Allegheny County v ACLU* [1989] 492 US 573; *Lynch v Donnelly* [1984] 465 US 668; *Stone v Graham* [1980] 449 US 39.

4 *Lautsi v Italy* No 30814/06 (Judgment of 18 March 2011) (Grand Chamber).

Lautsi drew throughout Europe—not just in Italy, where opinion widely supported the crucifix—people cared deeply about the outcome.

The fact that cases like *Salazar* and *Lautsi* continue to arise reveals something important about the state of religion at the start of the 21st century. Long past the point when it was supposed to have disappeared as a public concern, religion remains a vital, even growing force. Governments continue to place religious symbols in courtrooms, classrooms, city halls and parks. And citizens continue to consider such symbols worth a fight. Even in Western Europe, perhaps the most secular place on the planet, millions of people object to removing religious symbols from public places. Other millions consider such symbols an affront to pluralism and a throwback to an unenlightened time. The key point is this: both in the US and Europe, religion's continuing influence means that cases like *Salazar* and *Lautsi* will recur. Indeed, because of religious symbols' peculiar power to elicit emotional responses—alternately to inspire, comfort or offend—we should expect such controversies to be passionate, prolonged and persistent.

In this article, I compare the jurisprudence of the Supreme Court and the ECtHR on state-sponsored religious displays and explain how, and why, they differ. For both tribunals, the law on religious displays is a matter of themes, not rules. The main theme is neutrality. Both the Supreme Court and the ECtHR emphasize that government must remain religiously neutral in order to promote social harmony. Yet 'neutrality' has different meanings for the two tribunals. For the Supreme Court, neutrality means, at a minimum, that government may not proselytize, in the sense of pressuring people to join a religion. Neutrality goes beyond that narrow conception, however. The Justices have also indicated that government may not display symbols in a way that suggests preference for a particular sect. Indeed, the Court sometimes says that government may not endorse religion even generally, though the Court's decisions do not consistently support that view. For the ECtHR, in contrast, neutrality means only that the state must avoid proselytism, understood as active religious indoctrination—classroom catechism or prayers, for example. Giving 'preponderant visibility'[5] to the symbols of a particular sect does not qualify, to say nothing of endorsing religion generally.

The different conceptions of neutrality reflect institutional and cultural realities. Institutionally, the Supreme Court's status as a constitutional court allows it to adopt a stricter version of neutrality than the ECtHR, which must accommodate a variety of national church-state arrangements, including establishments. Culturally, the Supreme Court's conception of neutrality reflects what sociologists of religion refer to as the American model, which sees churches as voluntary associations that must compete in a free religious market.[6] The American model rejects government expressions of support for particular churches as inappropriate market distortions. In contrast, the ECtHR's thinner conception of neutrality comports with what sociologists refer to as the European model. National religious cultures in Europe vary, of

[5] *Lautsi* (n 4) [71].

[6] Roger Finke and Rodney Stark, *The Churching of America, 1776-2005* (Rutgers 2005); John Micklethwait and Adrian Wooldridge, *God Is Back* (Penguin 2009).

course, but important similarities exist that allow one to speak in terms of a common model, including the tendency to see churches, not as 'competing firms', but as 'public utilities' that provide a kind of religious infrastructure for the nation as a whole.[7] Although the European model rejects outright state indoctrination, it accepts what the American model would forbid as impermissible symbolic endorsements of the dominant local church.

I develop these arguments in detail below. In Part 2, I use *Salazar* as a vehicle for exploring the three visions of neutrality that appear in the Supreme Court's jurisprudence: non-proselytism, non-sectarianism and absolute neutrality. In Part 3, I show how *Lautsi* reflects the ECtHR's thinner conception of neutrality as a non-indoctrination principle. In Part 4, I demonstrate how the different visions of neutrality adopted by these tribunals reflect underlying institutional and cultural factors, particularly the competing 'American' and 'European' religious models. In Part 5, I offer some brief reflections on the value of comparative studies like the one I undertake here.

2. *The Supreme Court and Religious Displays*

A. *Salazar v Buono*

For a case that has drawn so much attention, *Salazar*'s holding is actually rather narrow. The district court had determined that an eight-foot Latin cross erected as a war memorial on federal land in the Mojave Desert violated the Establishment Clause[8] and issued an injunction forbidding its display. In response, the government conveyed the land to a private organization, which continued to display the cross. When the district court ruled that the conveyance violated the terms of its injunction by allowing the cross to remain, the government appealed. The proper interpretation of the injunction, therefore, not the underlying constitutional issue, was the precise question before the Supreme Court, which reversed and remanded on a 5-4 vote. In the course of considering the terms of the injunction, however, both the plurality opinion and the principal dissent extensively discussed the legality of the cross itself. They disagreed both about the cross's constitutionality and the proper test for deciding the question.

Justice Kennedy's plurality opinion, which he wrote for himself and two other Justices, strongly suggested that the cross was constitutional.[9] 'Although' the cross was 'certainly a Christian symbol', the government had not been trying to 'proselytize'.[10] Nor did display of the cross in this context indicate official approval of a specific sect.[11] The government had simply attempted to honour America's war dead in a culturally familiar way:

> [A] Latin cross is not merely a reaffirmation of Christian beliefs. It is a symbol often used to honor... those whose heroic acts, noble contributions, and patient striving

[7] Grace Davie, *The Sociology of Religion* (Sage 2007) 86.
[8] US Const Amend 1 ('Congress shall make no law respecting an establishment of religion').
[9] Two other Justices believed that plaintiff lacked standing and voted to reverse on that basis.
[10] *Salazar* (n 2) 1816.
[11] ibid 1818.

help secure an honored place in history for this Nation and its people. Here, one Latin cross in the desert evokes far more than religion. It evokes thousands of small crosses in foreign fields marking the graves of Americans who fell in battles... whose tragedies are compounded if the fallen are forgotten.[12]

In a concurring opinion, Justice Alito argued that removing the cross, as the district court had ordered, would have sent the message that government was not 'neutral' with respect to religion, but actually 'hostile... and bent on eliminating... any trace of our country's religious heritage'.[13]

The principal dissent in *Salazar*, written by Justice Stevens for himself and two other Justices, scoffed at the idea that the cross was constitutional.[14] The proper test was not whether government was proselytizing or even expressing a sectarian preference—although in this case, Stevens wrote, government surely had done the latter. Rather, the test was whether government had 'endorsed' religion in any way.[15] Here, 'any reasonable observer' would understand that the display expressed favouritism not only for religion, but for Christianity in particular.[16] 'Making a plain, unadorned Latin cross a war memorial does not make the cross secular', Stevens wrote. 'It makes the war memorial sectarian'.[17]

B. *Neutrality: Three Conceptions*

Salazar reflects the unsettled quality of the Supreme Court's religious display jurisprudence.[18] The Justices have never committed to a single test in this area. Although some scholars treat the endorsement test that Justice Stevens mentioned in *Salazar* as the operative standard,[19] the Court has not always applied that test, or applied it consistently. Cases turn on broad principles and specific facts;[20] the jurisprudence is one of themes, not rules. One important theme is neutrality.[21] '[O]fficial religious neutrality', the Court has said, is a 'central Establishment Clause value' that promotes 'tolerance', 'liberty and social stability'.[22] The Justices have not always agreed on what neutrality requires, however. Three conceptions appear in their decisions.

The first is neutrality as non-proselytism: government may not display symbols in a manner that pressures citizens to convert or to join a particular religion. Justice Kennedy once famously remarked that a city could not erect 'a large Latin cross on the roof of city hall', since that action would represent

[12] ibid 1820.

[13] ibid 1823 (Alito J, concurring in part and concurring in the judgment).

[14] Breyer J dissented separately, arguing it was not necessary to discuss the constitutional issue.

[15] ibid 1832 (Stevens J, dissenting).

[16] ibid.

[17] ibid 1835.

[18] For a helpful discussion, see Kent Greenawalt, 2 *Religion and the Constitution* (Princeton 2008) 74–90.

[19] Noah Feldman, *Divided by God* (Farrar, Straus and Giroux 2005) 212. Douglas Laycock writes that, notwithstanding inconsistencies and exceptions, the endorsement test embodies the Court's 'formal doctrine'. Douglas Laycock, 'Substantive Neutrality Revisited' (2007) 110 W Va L Rev 51, 69.

[20] Marc O DeGirolami, *Tragedy and History: The Quality of Religious Liberty* (Harvard University Press forthcoming 2013).

[21] For an interesting discussion of the different possible meanings of state neutrality respecting religion, see W C Durham Jr and Brett G Scharffs, *Law and Religion: National, International, and Comparative Perspectives* (Wolters Kluwer 2010) 121.

[22] *McCreary County* (n 3) 860.

'an obvious effort to proselytize on behalf of a particular religion',[23] but essentially all the Justices accept this conception of neutrality.[24] One might think of the non-proselytism principle as a variation on the psychological coercion test the Court has applied in a different Establishment Clause context. In *Lee v Weisman*, the Court held that the 'subtle and indirect' pressure to remain respectfully silent during a school-sponsored prayer could have a coercive effect on a listener 'as real as any overt compulsion'.[25] The psychological pressure to remain respectfully silent in the face of a symbol one finds objectionable might also have a subtle coercive effect. To use Justice Kennedy's example, a cross on city hall would not directly force viewers to do anything, but its permanent, prominent display might indirectly pressure citizens to conform.

The non-proselytism principle appears in *Salazar*'s plurality opinion, which asserted that the government had not been attempting to proselytize when it erected the cross as a war memorial. The principle also appears in *Stone v Graham*,[26] the Court's first religious display case, decided more than 30 years ago. In *Stone*, the Court struck down a Kentucky statute requiring public schools to post copies of the Ten Commandments in every classroom, along with small-print disclaimers referring to the Commandment's 'secular' function 'as the fundamental legal code of Western Civilization and the Common Law of the United States'.[27] Notwithstanding the disclaimers, the Court worried about the effect the displays would have on impressionable children. The displays, it believed, would 'induce the schoolchildren to read, meditate upon, perhaps to venerate and obey, the Commandments'.[28] To be sure, children could simply ignore the displays, but subtle pressure would remain, since students would be 'confronted ... every day', in every classroom, by an officially sponsored religious text.[29]

The second conception of neutrality to appear in the Court's decisions is neutrality as non-sectarianism.[30] This conception bars displays that favour or appear to favour a particular sect, even if the displays avoid proselytism as such. Here, too, the Justices have been essentially unanimous, at least as a matter of principle. Justice Scalia has written that the American 'constitutional tradition' forbids 'sectarian' endorsements, that is, those that 'specify[] details upon which men and women who believe in a benevolent, omnipotent Creator and Ruler of the world are known to differ (for example, the divinity of Christ)'.[31] Of course, 'sectarian' is a contestable term, and the Justices have disagreed whether particular displays fall within the category. Justice Scalia has argued that generally monotheistic references qualify as non-sectarian—the

[23] *Allegheny County* (n 3) 661.
[24] Adam M Samaha, 'Endorsement Retires: From Religious Symbols to Anti-Sorting Principles' [2005] Sup Ct Rev 135, 149.
[25] *Lee v Weisman* [1992] 505 US 577, 593.
[26] *Stone* (n 3).
[27] ibid 41.
[28] ibid 42.
[29] *Van Orden* (n 3) 691 (plurality).
[30] For arguments in favour of the non-sectarianism principle, see Michael W McConnell, 'Religious Freedom at a Crossroads' (1992) 59 U Chi L Rev 115, 156; Steven D Smith, 'Nonestablishment "Under God"? The Nonsectarian Principle' (2005) 50 Villanova L Rev 1.
[31] *Lee* (n 25) 641.

Ten Commandments, for example, which Christians, Jews and Muslims all accept.[32] Other Justices, in contrast, maintain that even generally monotheistic displays like the Ten Commandments are 'sectarian' in that they implicitly reject polytheistic and non-theistic traditions.[33]

The cases suggest that context can give an otherwise sectarian display a neutral, cultural meaning. The *Salazar* plurality, recall, asserted that, as a war memorial, a Latin cross was not a sectarian symbol but an acceptable cultural reference evoking the memory of America's fallen soldiers. The two crèche cases, *Lynch v Donnelly*,[34] and *Allegheny County v ACLU*,[35] provide further examples. In *Lynch*, the Court upheld the constitutionality of a crèche in a city's annual Christmas display. Notwithstanding the crèche's depiction of 'an event that lies at the heart of Christian faith',[36] the Court maintained that the display was essentially cultural. The city was commemorating a national holiday with its traditional symbols; any sectarian meaning was 'indirect, remote, and incidental'.[37] Justice O'Connor's concurrence echoed this point. Christmas had its 'religious aspects', she conceded, but was also a 'public holiday' with 'cultural significance'.[38] The city had displayed the crèche alongside secular holiday symbols like reindeer and candy-striped poles,[39] thus ensuring that observers would understand that the city had commemorated Christmas's cultural, rather than sectarian, importance.

Allegheny County involved two public displays, a crèche with a banner reading 'Gloria in Excelsis Deo!' and a composite display containing a Christmas tree, a Chanukah menorah and a sign saluting liberty. The Court held that the first display violated the Establishment Clause but not the second. Unlike the crèche in *Lynch*, the Court explained, the crèche in *Allegheny County* stood alone; no secular images 'detract[ed] from [its] religious message'.[40] The display thus went beyond 'acknowledg[ing] Christmas as a cultural phenomenon' and endorsed the holiday's religious content.[41] With respect to the composite display, no single analysis commanded a majority of the Court. For the two swing votes, the fact that the display contained the holiday symbols of two religions, as well as a secular salute-to-liberty sign, helped lead to the conclusion that the display was cultural rather than sectarian.[42]

The third conception of neutrality is what one might call an 'absolutist' position.[43] Not only must government avoid proselytizing or expressing preference for a particular sect, but government must also refrain from displays that promote or appear to promote religion generally. As between

[32] *McCreary* (n 3) 894.
[33] *Van Orden* (n 3) 719.
[34] *Lynch* (n 3).
[35] *Allegheny County* (n 3).
[36] *Lynch* (n 3) 711 (Brennan J, dissenting)
[37] ibid 683.
[38] ibid 691 (O'Connor J, concurring).
[39] ibid 671.
[40] *Allegheny County* (n 3) 598.
[41] ibid 601.
[42] Ira C Lupu and Robert W Tuttle, 'The Cross at College: Accommodation and Acknowledgement of Religion at Public Universities' (2008) 16 William & Mary Bill Rts J 939, 991. On the importance of the multiple symbols, see *Allegheny County* (n 3) 614–16 (Blackmun J), 626 (O'Connor J, concurring in part and concurring in the judgment).
[43] *Lynch* (n 3), 678.

religion and non-religion, government cannot appear to 'take sides'.[44] The endorsement test embodies this version of neutrality. Unlike the first two conceptions, on which the Justices agree in principle, the absolutist position remains controversial on the Court and in the academy,[45] and the endorsement test faces uncertain prospects now that its chief proponent, Justice O'Connor, has retired.[46] Notably, in *Salazar*, only the dissent relied on the endorsement test;[47] the Justices in the plurality referred to it only in passing, for the sake of argument.[48] The controversy arises from the fact that the test casts doubt on many traditional and widespread American practices. Public expressions of a generally religious nature abound in American life and always have. To give just two examples, the National Motto, inscribed on all US currency, is 'In God We Trust', and the Great Seal of the United States includes the eye of Providence and the words 'Annuit Cœptis', or, in the official translation, 'He (God) has favored our undertakings'.[49] If one took seriously the admonition against generic religious displays, the Motto, the Seal and other similar expressions would have to go, unless one were willing to 'grandfather[]' them as a kind of ceremonial deism.[50]

In sum, for the Supreme Court, neutrality means that government may not display religious symbols in a manner that proselytizes, even indirectly, or that demonstrates approval for particular sects; some cases suggest that displays may not suggest approval for religion generally, but that is more controversial. In contrast, as I explain below, the ECtHR has a much narrower conception of neutrality. For that tribunal, neutrality means that only the state may not proselytize, in the sense of engaging in active religious indoctrination. Displays of sectarian symbols, even displays that give 'preponderant visibility' to the symbols of the dominant local church, are permissible.

3. *The ECtHR and Religious Displays*

A. *Lautsi v Italy*

Lautsi's facts are well known, so I will only sketch them here.[51] Italian regulations, often characterized as fascist-era decrees but actually originating earlier, from the time of the Risorgimento, require public elementary school classrooms to display crucifixes. Soile Lautsi, the mother of two schoolchildren, challenged the regulations in the Italian administrative courts, arguing that the

[44] *McCreary* (n 3) 860.

[45] For a summary of criticisms of the endorsement test, see Jay D Wexler, 'The Endorsement Court' (2006) 21 Wash U JL & Pol'y 263, 271–77. Wexler thinks many of the criticisms are 'overstated'. ibid. 305.

[46] Samaha (n 24) 137.

[47] *Salazar* (n 2) 1832 (Stevens J, dissenting).

[48] ibid 1819 (plurality), 1824 (Alito J).

[49] US Department of State, *The Great Seal of the United States* (US Department of State 2003) 15.

[50] Andrew Koppelman, 'The New American Civil Religion: Lessons for Italy' (2010) 41 Geo Wash Intl L Rev 861, 864. Breyer J took a similar approach in one of the Ten Commandments cases. The fact that a Ten Commandments monument had stood on the Texas state capitol grounds for decades without apparent objection, he wrote, argued against its removal at this late date. *Van Orden* (n 3) 702–03 (Breyer J, concurring in the judgment).

[51] For an interesting recent discussion of *Lautsi*, see Javier Martínez-Torrón, 'The (Un)Protection of Individual Religious Identity in the Strasbourg Case Law' [2012] OJLR 21–22 (http://ojlr.oxfordjournals.org/content/early/2012/01/12/ojlr.rwr021.full.pdf+html) (accessed 24 May 2012).

crucifixes violated the constitutional doctrine of *laicità* or secularism.[52] The administrative courts rejected her challenge on the somewhat dubious ground that the crucifix represented not Christianity but secularism. The lower administrative court maintained that Christianity, understood correctly, contained within itself 'those ideas of tolerance, equality and liberty which form the basis of the modern secular State, and ... the Italian State in particular'.[53] The crucifix thus stood for Italian constitutional values, including *laicità*. On appeal, the Consiglio di Stato affirmed. Although it avoided the lower court's more questionable forays into theology, it agreed that the crucifix represented civic values, such as tolerance and freedom of conscience, which happened to have a Christian origin.[54]

Lautsi then sued Italy in the ECtHR, arguing that the crucifixes violated article 2 of the First Protocol to the European Convention, which provides that '[i]n the exercise of any functions which it assumes in relation to education and to teaching, the State shall respect the right of parents to ensure such education and teaching in conformity with their own religious and philosophical convictions',[55] and article 9 of the Convention, which confers the right 'to freedom of thought, conscience, and religion'.[56] In a brief opinion, a chamber of the court agreed. Together, the chamber held, articles 2 and 9 imposed on states a duty of religious 'neutrality and impartiality' that prohibited proselytism.[57] Public schools must not be places of 'missionary activities';[58] government must 'refrain from imposing beliefs, even indirectly', on impressionable schoolchildren.[59] Here, the chamber reasoned, the presence of the crucifix could indeed create pressure for students; even though students need not take any action in response, the crucifix was a powerful, permanent symbol they could not ignore. The chamber dismissed Italy's argument that the crucifix represented 'neutral', secular values: whatever other meanings might exist, the sectarian message was obviously 'predominant'.[60]

The chamber's reasoning thus closely tracked the Supreme Court's analysis in *Stone*, the classroom Ten Commandments case, which also focused on the potential of passive displays to proselytize schoolchildren.[61] The chamber's decision also comported with the most famous European religious display case before *Lautsi*, the *Classroom Crucifix II Case*,[62] in which the German Federal Constitutional Court held that a similar classroom crucifix requirement violated the duty of neutrality under the German Basic Law, also because of

[52] The Italian Constitutional Court declined jurisdiction, as the challenge involved administrative regulations rather than statutory provisions. Susanna Mancini, 'Taking Secularism (not too) Seriously: the Italian "Crucifix" Case' (2006) 1 Religion and Hum. Rts. 179, 183.

[53] *Lautsi* (n 4) [15].

[54] ibid [16].

[55] *Lautsi v Italy* [2009], No 30814/06 (Judgment of 3 November 2009) [27].

[56] ibid.

[57] ibid [47]. The ECtHR's jurisprudence refers to the duty as one of 'neutrality and impartiality', but I refer to it in the text as a duty of 'neutrality', for consistency's sake.

[58] ibid.

[59] ibid [48].

[60] ibid [51].

[61] *Stone* (n 3).

[62] [1995] 93 BVerfGe 1. For a translation, see Donald P Kommers, *The Constitutional Jurisprudence of the Federal Republic of Germany* (2nd edn, Duke University Press 1997) 472.

the danger of indirect proselytism.[63] When Italy referred the chamber's decision in *Lautsi* to the Grand Chamber, then, most observers expected that the GC, too, would hold that displaying the crucifix violated the state's duty of neutrality.

In the end, however, the GC rejected the chamber's analysis and held that displaying the crucifix did not violate Italy's duty of neutrality. The GC began by noting the 'diversity of...practice[]' in the Council of Europe regarding religious symbols in public schools:[64] a few states prohibited such symbols; a few, like Italy, expressly required them; and several allowed them without specific authorization.[65] National courts that had considered the legality of such symbols under domestic law had reached inconsistent results.[66] Given the diversity of practice, the GC argued, states must have a wide 'margin of appreciation' in determining, with respect to public religious displays, how best to apply the duty of neutrality in light of local circumstances and traditions.[67] Italy, the GC believed, had not exceeded that margin.

Like the chamber, the GC understood neutrality as a non-proselytism principle. It conceived of proselytism more narrowly, however. The GC conceded that display of the crucifix gave 'preponderant visibility' to the symbol of Italy's 'majority religion'. But 'indoctrination', not 'preponderant visibility', was the test, and indoctrination meant something more than placing an 'essentially passive symbol' on a wall.[68] The GC emphasized that teachers had no obligation to incorporate the crucifix into their class instruction; indeed, as far as the record revealed, no teacher had ever referred to the crucifix in a proselytizing manner.[69] Moreover, other circumstances minimized the danger of indoctrination. Italian schools allowed minority students to wear their religious attire to class and often celebrated minority religious holidays like Ramadan; schools also provided optional religious instruction for students from minority religions.[70] Finally, the GC said, Ms Lautsi always could guide her children outside school in conformity with her own convictions.[71]

The GC demurred with respect to Italy's argument that the crucifix represented neutral, cultural values as well as sectarian ones—that Italy's history gave the crucifix an 'identity-linked' meaning that justified its display.[72] Although the administrative courts had endorsed that argument in *Lautsi*,

[63] For a helpful discussion of this case, see Gerhard Robbers, *Religion and Law in Germany* (Wolters Kluwer 2010) [637]–[638].

[64] *Lautsi* (n 4) [61].

[65] ibid [27].

[66] ibid [28]. Swiss, German, and Spanish courts had ruled against such displays, but Polish and Romanian courts had allowed them.

[67] ibid [61], [70]–[76]. For criticisms of the role the 'margin of appreciation' doctrine played in the GC's decision, see Paolo Ronchi, 'Crucifixes, Margin of Appreciation and Consensus: The Grand Chamber Ruling in *Lautsi v. Italy*' (2011) 13 Ecc LJ 287; Lorenzo Zucca, '*Lautsi* – A Commentary of the Grand Chamber decision' (2011) 11 (manuscript on SSRN <http://papers.ssrn.com/sol3/papers.cfm?abstract_id=1809577>) (accessed 24 May 2012).

[68] *Lautsi* (n 4) [72].

[69] ibid [74].

[70] ibid. For criticism of this section of the GC's opinion, see Claudia E Haupt, 'Transnational Nonestablishment' 80 Geo Wash L Rev (forthcoming 2011) (manuscript at 33-34) (http://papers.ssrn.com/sol3/papers.cfm?abstract_id=1912842) (accessed 24 May 2012).

[71] *Lautsi* (n 4) [75].

[72] ibid [67].

Italian courts were in fact somewhat divided, and the GC did not wish to interpose itself.[73] In other words, even assuming the crucifix was a sectarian symbol, the GC believed that Italy was acting within its margin of appreciation in continuing its traditional, pervasive classroom display—always provided Italy did not cross the line of indoctrination.[74]

B. *Neutrality as Non-Indoctrination*

In defining neutrality in terms of a duty to avoid religious indoctrination, *Lautsi* follows a line of ECtHR cases, dating back to 1976, on the duty of religious neutrality in public education.[75] The GC relied on two in particular, *Folgerø v Norway* and *Zengin v Turkey*.[76] *Folgerø* concerned a mandatory class, 'Christianity, Religion, and Philosophy', that Norway offered in its public schools.[77] Among other things, the class attempted to impart to students 'thorough knowledge of the Bible and Christianity in the form of cultural heritage and the Evangelical Lutheran Faith'; to educate students about other religions; and to 'promote ... respect for Christian and humanist values'.[78] The class description implied that teachers could lead students in 'religious activities' like prayers, scripture readings and religious plays,[79] although parents could ask that the school excuse their children from activities the parents believed to be 'the practice of another religion or adherence to another philosophy of life'.[80]

The ECtHR held that the class violated the duty of neutrality. In principle, schools could offer a class in comparative religion, and the emphasis on Lutheran Christianity did not pose a difficulty, given the place of that religion in Norway's 'history and tradition'.[81] The problem arose from the requirement that the class 'promote respect' for Christian values, and, especially, the possibility that teachers would conduct Christian exercises in class. These exercises could affect impressionable schoolchildren in a manner that Article 2 prohibited—that is, they could amount to indoctrination by the school.[82] Although parents could request that their children be excused from religious exercises, parents might well decline to do so, since requesting an exemption might reveal 'intimate aspects of [the parents'] own religious and philosophical convictions'.[83] Moreover, the opt-out provisions were so complicated as to be

[73] ibid [68].

[74] As Malcolm Evans writes, under the GC's approach, '[t]he State can be "neutral and impartial" whilst "perpetuating" the traditional place of religions in the public life of the country.' Malcolm D Evans, '*Lautsi v. Italy*: An Initial Appraisal' (2011) 6 Religion and Hum Rts 237, 243.

[75] The first case was *Kjeldsen v Denmark* [1976]. For a helpful discussion of the duty of religious neutrality in the ECtHR, see Malcolm D Evans, 'From Cartoons to Crucifixes: Current Controversies Concerning the Freedom of Religion and the Freedom of Expression before the European Court of Human Rights' (2010–2011) 26 JLR 345.

[76] *Lautsi* (n 4) [71]–[74].

[77] *Folgerø v Norway* No 15472/02 (Judgment of 29 June 2007) (Grand Chamber) [3]. For a recent discussion of *Folgerø*, see John Witte Jr and Nina-Louisa Arold, 'Lift High the Cross? Contrasting the New European and American Cases on Religious Symbols on Government Property' (2011) 25 Emory Intl L Rev 5, 19–20.

[78] *Folgerø* (n 77) [23].

[79] ibid [94].

[80] ibid [96].

[81] ibid [89]

[82] ibid [94].

[83] ibid [98].

unworkable, effectively requiring parents to monitor classrooms and identify objectionable exercises on a continual basis.[84]

Zengin also concerned instruction in comparative religion. Turkey required public school students to take classes in 'religious culture and ethics'.[85] The classes were supposed to comply with 'principles of secularism and freedom of thought, religion and conscience' and 'transmit knowledge concerning all of the major religions' in a spirit of tolerance.[86] In fact, however, they actively inculcated the doctrines of Sunni Islam. For example, teachers were required to demonstrate that, 'far from being a myth, Islam [was] a rational and universal religion' and to impress upon students the value of worship that showed 'love, respect and gratitude towards Allah'.[87] Students received instruction in Sunni rites, prayers and holidays and had to memorize chapters from the Koran.[88]

A parent belonging to the Alevi faith, a branch of Islam that differs from the Sunni form, sued Turkey, arguing that the class violated his article 2 rights. The ECtHR agreed. As in *Folgerø*, the difficulty was not that public schools offered comparative religion classes or that the syllabus emphasized Sunni Islam, which was, after all, Turkey's majority religion.[89] The problem was that schools were not teaching the classes in an objective and pluralistic way.[90] Once again, there existed a real threat of indoctrination. Teaching students that Islam is 'a rational and universal religion', and requiring them to study Islamic prayers and memorize chapters from the Koran, obviously lent itself to active proselytism. Moreover, even though Alevis made up a 'very large' proportion of the Turkish population,[91] the classes conveyed little information about Alevism; this inattention showed disrespect for the religious convictions of Alevi parents like plaintiff.[92] Finally, unlike Christian and Jewish students, whose parents could request they be exempted from the classes, Alevi students were required to attend. Even with respect to Christians and Jews, the court noted, the opt-out was problematic, since, as in *Folgerø*, parents might well be reluctant to reveal their religions publicly.[93]

Cases like *Folgerø*, *Zengin* and of course *Lautsi* itself do not even hint at the non-sectarian or absolutist versions of neutrality that appear in the Supreme Court's jurisprudence. For the ECtHR, neutrality means the absence of active religious indoctrination, understood as classroom religious exercises, assignments that require students to memorize religious texts, and lessons that endorse the truth of religious doctrine or fail to account properly for religious diversity in the student body. As long as public schools refrain from such activities, they avoid engaging in proselytism and comply with the duty of neutrality. Once one understands this rather narrow conception of neutrality,

[84] ibid [97].
[85] *Zengin v Turkey* No 1448/04 (Judgment of 9 October 2007) [58].
[86] ibid.
[87] ibid [60].
[88] ibid [61]–[62].
[89] ibid [63].
[90] ibid [70].
[91] ibid [67].
[92] ibid [70].
[93] ibid [71]–[75]. There was some debate whether Alevi students might also be exempted from the classes. ibid [75].

Lautsi's holding about the 'essentially passive' display of crucifixes in public school classrooms—a pervasive, sectarian display if ever there was one—is completely comprehensible. The interesting question is why the ECtHR's conception of neutrality is so thin in comparison with the Supreme Court's. I turn to that question next.

4. *Institutional and Cultural Realities*

A. *Institutional Factors*

To explain the different conceptions of neutrality, one must look to institutional and cultural factors. Institutionally, the Supreme Court's position differs dramatically from the ECtHR's. The Supreme Court has formal appellate jurisdiction in a unified constitutional system. Its judgments bind lower courts, state and federal, as a matter of law. Moreover, the American Constitution contains an anti-establishment clause that applies to the states as well as the federal government.[94] Thus, the Supreme Court can plausibly seek to fashion a uniform, comparatively rigorous national standard regarding public religious displays. This does not mean that the Court's efforts are completely consistent or successful. The fact that so many similar cases about religious displays appear on the Court's docket year after year, and the fact that the Court has had such difficulty reaching consensus about them, indicate the complexity of the task.

The Supreme Court is much better positioned to attempt such a task than the ECtHR, however. The ECtHR is not a constitutional court,[95] but a supranational tribunal without formal appellate authority over domestic courts. Over time, in a process international-law scholars have studied extensively, domestic courts in Europe have come to accept the ECtHR's judgments and conform their jurisprudence to its interpretations of the European Convention.[96] Notwithstanding the powerful incentives to comply, however, if the ECtHR were to 'move[] too far out of line with a prevailing domestic democratic consensus', domestic authorities, including courts, might decline to 'follow'.[97] Moreover, the Convention does not have an anti-establishment provision, nor could it, given the variety of church-state arrangements in the Council of Europe. With regard to state-sponsored religious displays, in particular, a consensus does not exist.

An attempt to fashion a uniform, rigorous neutrality requirement thus would be neither legitimate nor feasible for the ECtHR. Given the diversity of state practice, the ECtHR can only announce a minimum standard and leave the rest to countries' 'margin of appreciation'. Consider the likely result if the ECtHR had adopted the approach of the chamber in *Lautsi*—the same

[94] US Const Amend 1. In *Everson v Board of Education* [1947] 330 US 1, the Supreme Court held that the Fourteenth Amendment to the Constitution incorporates the Establishment Clause as against the states.

[95] Dominic McGoldrick, 'Religion in the European Public Square and in European Public Life—Crucifixes in the Classroom?' (2011) 11 Hum Rts L Rev 451, 500.

[96] Mark L Movsesian, 'Judging International Judgments' (2007) 48 Virginia J Intl L 65, 105.

[97] Anne-Marie Slaughter, *A New World Order* (Princeton 2004) 82.

approach, recall, as the American Supreme Court in *Stone* and the German Federal Constitutional Court in *Classroom Crucifix II*—and announced a more rigorous neutrality requirement forbidding display of the crucifix. The crucifix had overwhelming support in Italy; according to some polls, 84% of Italians favoured its presence in public schools.[98] Political leaders 'from the President of the Republic to the Prime Minister' had vied with each other to defend it.[99] Twenty European countries, almost half the membership of the Council of Europe, had expressed public support for Italy;[100] ten had intervened at the GC in favour of Italy's position.[101] In these circumstances, Italians would likely have seen a ruling against the crucifix as illegitimate and found a way to subvert it, whatever the GC held.[102]

B. *The American Religious Model*

Institutional explanations only go so far, however. To account fully for the divergent meanings of neutrality, one must look to differences in underlying religious culture. Recent literature in the sociology of religion addresses these differences. America and Europe are complex societies, of course, and one must avoid over-simplification. Nonetheless, sociologists speak in terms of American and European religious models, and some generalizations are possible.[103] The American model treats religion as a market. It sees churches as voluntary, private associations that compete for members, much in the way businesses compete for customers. Success depends on satisfying consumer demand; churches rise or fall based upon their ability to attract and retain adherents. As with any market, government provides public goods that make 'commerce' possible, for example, infrastructure, security and the rule of law. In fact, in the American model, government can promote religion generally as a public good, much as governments everywhere try to foster favourable business environments. But government cannot promote or protect particular churches.[104] Favouritism would create perverse incentives, making beneficiaries lazy and unresponsive to the wishes of the faithful. Preferential treatment for particular churches, in other words, would distort the religious market in a way that would ultimately injure religious consumers.

The American model reflects historical and intellectual origins, what Tocqueville would have called America's 'point of departure'.[105] Most British

[98] Andrea Pin, 'Public Schools, the Italian Crucifix, and the European Court of Human Rights: The Italian Separation of Church and State' (2011) 25 Emory Intl L Rev 95, 98.

[99] Silvio Ferrari, 'Civil Religions: Models and Perspectives' (2010) 41 Geo Wash Intl L Rev 749, 755.

[100] European Centre for Law and Justice Press Release, ECHR Crucifix Case: 20 European countries support the Crucifix (21 July 2010) <http://www.eclj.org/Releases/Read.aspx?GUID=983c3dd3-9c17-4b70-a016-37851446ec0e>.

[101] Eight countries—Armenia, Bulgaria, Cyprus, the Russian Federation, Greece, Lithuania, Malta and San Marino—made a joint submission. Monaco and Romania submitted their views separately. *Lautsi* (n 4) [47]–[49].

[102] When the German Federal Constitutional Court invalidated the Bavarian ordinance in *Classroom Crucifix II*, the Bavarian legislature soon enacted a new ordinance reinstating the crucifix requirement but providing a mechanism for parents to object if they had 'serious and understandable reasons'. Robbers (n 63) [637]. This 'Bavarian solution' may 'actually accentuate[] the pressure' on followers of minority faiths, since they now have 'the burden to contest the display of the majority group symbol'. Mancini (n 52) 193.

[103] Peter Berger, Grace Davie and Effie Fokas, *Religious America, Secular Europe?* (Ashgate 2008).

[104] Robert D Putnam and David E Campbell, *American Grace* (Simon & Schuster 2010) 519.

[105] Alexis de Tocqueville, *Democracy in America* 27 (Harvey C Mansfield and Delba Winthrop trs) (U Chicago Press 2000).

colonies in North America had established churches, defined by law and supported by tax assessments. For example, the Church of England was established in Virginia and the other Southern colonies, as well as New York; the Congregational Church was established in New England.[106] But conditions made establishments difficult to maintain.[107] In a frontier society with a deracinated and transient population, people found it relatively easy to evade ecclesiastical discipline. One could simply relocate, as Roger Williams famously did when he ran into trouble with church authorities in Massachusetts.[108] The religious movements that succeeded were those that adapted to the new conditions and offered less institutionalized, more egalitarian forms of religion that depended not on ties to established bodies but voluntary commitment from the faithful. Itinerant preachers like George Whitefield, for example, whose tours of America in the 1740s drew huge crowds and sparked the First Great Awakening, succeeded precisely because they appealed to a mobile, hardscrabble population that valued straightforward, emotional preaching over intellectual sermons and church formality.[109]

After independence, although some states continued to have established churches for a time, an opposite trend formed. The Establishment Clause prohibited establishments at the federal level, of course. Even for states that wished to maintain establishments, the task became increasingly difficult as the population spread beyond the eastern seaboard. Once again, the churches that succeeded were those that adapted to the egalitarianism of the frontier, like the Baptist and Methodist Churches, whose polities were 'surprisingly democratic', even compared with Congregationalists.[110] These churches drew clergy principally from the local populations they served, not from eastern seminaries, an important factor in attracting and retaining members. In Finke and Stark's phrase, 'Baptist and Methodist preachers looked like ordinary people because they were, and their sermons could convert and convince ordinary people because the message was direct and clear and the words were not read from notes'.[111] Revival meetings, for which Methodists, in particular, became famous, combined church services with huge picnics that 'provided the ideal religious and social solution to the isolated circumstances of American farmers'.[112] In short, Baptists and Methodists succeeded because they identified a new market and devised ways to attract and retain enthusiastic followings.

The American model did not result simply from geography, however. Ideology played a major role as well. As George Marsden writes, a 'peculiar ... alliance' between evangelical Protestantism and Enlightenment rationalism has informed American religious culture from the start.[113] Evangelical Protestantism stressed the importance of personal conversion and individual conscience. Salvation, it

[106] Finke and Stark (n 6) 43.
[107] ibid 35.
[108] John M Barry, *Roger Williams and the Creation of the American Soul* (Viking 2012).
[109] Finke and Stark (n 6) 49–53.
[110] ibid 74.
[111] ibid 86.
[112] ibid 96.
[113] George M Marsden, *Religion and American Culture* (Harcourt Brace Jovanovich 1990) 56.

argued, required a genuine commitment from the believer, a voluntary, unreserved response to God's gift. Evangelicals understood the church as an association of people who had made this commitment—the saved—not as an institution that civil authority maintained.[114] Indeed, they argued, civil authority inevitably corrupted the church by offering worldly inducements and encouraging people to believe they could achieve salvation through formal membership in an official body. State churches, with elaborate rituals and hierarchies, tended to substitute human tradition for the Bible, which, to the evangelical mind, was humanity's only reliable authority. 'The common person who stood by the plain, common sense meaning of the Bible', they believed, 'could confidently disregard the authority of educated clergy or prestigious churches'.[115]

Evangelicalism thus opposed establishment. Opposition also came from Enlightenment rationalism. Many of the founding generation—Jefferson and Franklin, for example—were Deists who had 'abandoned those parts of the Christian heritage that they thought were not based on reason'.[116] Like evangelicals, they rejected restraints on individual conscience. They did so not because they thought an unrestricted conscience would lead inevitably to Christ, but because they believed that conscience, left to itself, would inevitably conform to reason. By prescribing forms of worship and belief, and, even worse, by preserving irrational superstitions, established churches interfered with conscience and prevented reason's ultimate triumph. Moreover, rationalists associated establishments with political repression. Established churches, like the Anglican Church during the American Revolution, inevitably supported traditional authority and opposed liberty.[117]

Evangelical Protestantism and Enlightenment rationalism thus made common cause in the battle against establishment in the early Republic.[118] Jefferson sent his famous letter extolling the separation of church and state to Baptists in Connecticut.[119] Madison's Memorial and Remonstrance against Religious Assessments in Virginia provides another example.[120] In 1784, Patrick Henry introduced a bill in the Virginia legislature that would have assessed a tax to supplement the salaries of Christian ministers.[121] Opposing the bill, Madison blended evangelical and Enlightenment rhetoric. He argued on theological grounds that religion 'must be left to the conviction and conscience of every man' and that Christianity did not need establishment to succeed. In fact, establishment historically had corrupted Christianity, resulting in 'pride and indolence in the Clergy, ignorance and servility in the laity; in both, superstition, bigotry and persecution'.[122] Madison also made a political argument: establishment corrupted civil government. '[I]n many instances', established churches 'have been seen upholding the thrones of political tyranny; in no instance have they been seen the guardians of the liberties of the

114 ibid 20.
115 ibid 59.
116 ibid 32.
117 ibid 39.
118 Finke and Stark (n 6) 60.
119 Letter to a Committee of the Danbury Baptist Association (1 January 1802).
120 Memorial and Remonstrance against Religious Assessments (1785).
121 A Bill Establishing a Provision for Teachers of the Christian Religion (1784).
122 Memorial (n 120).

people'.[123] Establishments inevitably opposed civil equality and 'just government'.[124]

By the 1830s, establishments had ended in America.[125] In addition, a consensus formed that government could not act in ways that suggested preference for particular sects. As Michael McConnell explains, the idea that government must not favour one sect over another appears 'repeatedly in both statements and constitutional enactments of the founding period'.[126] The non-sectarianism principle came up mainly in the context of government's provision of material benefits to religion, but the principle covered public religious expressions as well.[127] Indeed, public religious expressions in the early Republic—Thanksgiving proclamations, congressional statements, presidential addresses—almost invariably spoke of God or Providence rather than Christ.[128] This reticence comports with the broader non-sectarianism that Tocqueville found so remarkable in American politics. Americans, he observed, believed that religion was 'necessary to the maintenance of republican institutions', but denominational differences did not overly concern them.[129] 'In the United States', he wrote, 'when a political man attacks a sect, it is not a reason for the partisans even of that sect not to support him; but if he attacks all sects together, each flees him and he remains alone'.[130]

To be sure, in an overwhelmingly Protestant society, listeners could easily interpret vague expressions about 'God' and 'Providence' as Christian references, and most Americans surely did. Most simply assumed that 'nonsectarian' meant generically Protestant, which explains how so many could oppose 'sectarian' influence in public education but nonetheless support classroom Bible readings that inculcated a Protestant understanding of scripture,[131] and why politicians 'informally continued to speak of the nation as though it were a Christian nation, or at least a biblical nation'.[132] People rarely perceive their own ironies, and Protestantism so pervaded 19th-century America that few apparently noticed the inconsistencies.[133] Some thought non-sectarianism did not go far enough; Jefferson, for example, declined to issue Thanksgiving proclamations as president because he thought government should avoid all implication of religious belief and practice, even purely hortatory statements.[134] But the frequent public, non-sectarian expressions in

[123] ibid.

[124] ibid.

[125] Massachusetts was the last state to end establishment, in 1833.

[126] Michael W McConnell, 'Free Exercise Revisionism and the Smith Decision' (1990) 57 U Chi L Rev 1109, 1130.

[127] McConnell (n 30) 157.

[128] McCreary (n 3) 897–98 (Scalia J, dissenting); Laura Underkuffler-Freund, 'The Separation of the Religious and the Secular: A Foundational Challenge to First Amendment Theory' (1995) 36 William & Mary L Rev 837, 954.

[129] *Democracy in America* (n 105) 280.

[130] ibid.

[131] For an excellent discussion, see Philip Hamburger, *Separation of Church and State* (Harvard 2002) 219–29.

[132] Marsden (n 113) 43.

[133] Douglas Laycock, '"Nonpreferential" Aid to Religion: A False Claim about Original Intent' (1986) 27 William & Mary L Rev 875, 918–19.

[134] Underkuffler-Freund (n 128) 951–52.

the early Republic suggest that most Americans thought government could promote religion generally.

I lack space to detail how the early Republic's understanding of church-state relations has ramified through history. The market model certainly captures the situation in America today. In Micklethwait and Wooldridge's phrase, '[t]he American religious marketplace is almost a study in perfect competition: there are no real barriers to entry, the domestic market is big enough to support a mind-boggling variety of religious producers, and new religious entrepreneurs are always rising up to challenge incumbents'.[135] On the 'demand side', Americans increasingly see religion as a matter of personal choice.[136] Although most have 'the same religious identity as their parents',[137] political scientists Putnam and Campbell estimate that 'at least one third' of contemporary Americans have chosen 'their religion rather than simply inheriting it', and that the percentage is increasing.[138] About 25% have 'shopped around' for a new place of worship at least once, not counting those who have looked because of a move.[139] Religious 'brand loyalty' is 'surprisingly low'.[140]

Similarly, Americans tend to see churches not as traditional institutions into which one is born but as voluntary associations of like-minded persons.[141] Thus the congregation, 'an all-purpose association with members who choose it, belong to it, and make contributions to it' is the 'most prevalent form' of religious association in America today.[142] This is not surprising with respect to Protestants, since the congregation is the quintessential Protestant polity. But non-Protestant and even non-Christian groups also adopt the form. For example, Alan Wolfe observes that American mosques operate as Protestant-style congregations. They have members who support them through voluntary contributions and who elect committees and officers to run them.[143] They sponsor Sunday schools and social activities.[144] Members expect imams to act as 'professional clergy' and handle day-to-day management responsibilities.[145] None of this is typical in predominately Muslim societies, where mosques are 'convenient places' to pray rather than religious organizations.[146] American Hindus and Buddhists similarly adopt the congregational form.[147]

On the supply side, religious bodies compete fiercely to attract and retain adherents.[148] Just as Baptists and Methodists shaped their messages to appeal to the egalitarianism of the American frontier, today's 'pastorpreneurs' focus on the 'total service excellence' that American consumers expect.[149] One of the most important phenomena in contemporary American religion is the

[135] Micklethwait and Wooldridge (n 6) 174.
[136] Putnam and Campbell (n 104) 148.
[137] ibid 136.
[138] ibid 148.
[139] ibid 168–69.
[140] ibid 148.
[141] Berger and others (n 103) 29–30.
[142] Putnam and Campbell (n 104) 30.
[143] Alan Wolfe, *The Transformation of American Religion* (Free Press 2003) 228.
[144] ibid.
[145] ibid 229.
[146] ibid 227–28.
[147] Putnam and Campbell (n 104) 31.
[148] Finke and Stark (n 6) 202.
[149] Micklethwait and Wooldridge (n 6) 185.

megachurch—defined as a church with at least 3000 weekly attendees—which offers multiple worship services and opportunities for charity work, as well as amenities like banks, basketball courts, child care, coffee shops, pharmacies, even martial arts classes.[150] Thousands of such churches exist.[151] Adaptability, innovation and niche marketing are crucial; megachurches often have services directed at specific affinity groups.[152] Indeed, whole denominations have sprung up to appeal to particular demographics.[153] The variety is staggering. The *Yearbook of American and Canadian Churches* for 2011 lists roughly 200 Christian bodies alone in the United States, from the Catholic Church, with roughly 70 million members, to the Pentecostal Fire-Baptized Holiness Church, with roughly 200.[154]

Finally, although Americans continue to oppose state favouritism for particular sects, they remain very comfortable with public support for religion in general. As Putnam and Campbell observe, 'rather than a wedge pushing Americans apart, public expressions of religion often serve to pull them together'.[155] Two hundred years after the founding, public 'appeals to God at times of national unity are still de rigueur'.[156] Only recently, for example, the House of Representatives voted, by a margin of 396 to 9, to reaffirm 'In God We Trust' as the National Motto.[157] Americans support such expressions because they believe, overwhelmingly, that religion plays a positive role in society. In recent surveys, large majorities even of secular Americans agreed that religion has had a good influence in American life.[158] Only a small segment of the most secular Americans expressed discomfort with religion's role.[159] Moreover, a large majority of Americans, about 80%, say they value religious diversity and think it has benefitted the country,[160] and almost 90% believe that followers of other religions can go to Heaven.[161] Given these broadly ecumenical attitudes, it is not surprising that Americans overwhelmingly support what they conceive as inclusive, non-sectarian public expressions.

The Supreme Court's religious-display jurisprudence comports with the market model. Forbidding state-sponsored displays that proselytize or suggest preference for particular sects ensures that government does not interfere with the market by attempting to identify winners and losers. Non-sectarian displays that promote religion generally as a public good do not pose the same threat of market distortion, in contrast, and the Court allows them. To be sure, the endorsement test's prohibition of non-sectarian displays goes further than the market model would require. Perhaps, as others have written, this aspect of

150 ibid 184–86.
151 ibid 186.
152 ibid 184–85.
153 ibid 185.
154 *Yearbook of American & Canadian Churches 2011* (Eileen W Lindner ed, Abingdon Press 2011) 363–73.
155 Putnam and Campbell (n 104) 494.
156 ibid 518.
157 David A Farenthold, '"In God We Trust": House reaffirms national motto – yet again' (Washington Post, 2 November 2011) <http://www.washingtonpost.com/politics/in-god-we-trust-house-re-affirms-national-motto--yet-again/2011/11/02/gIQAiZRWfM_story.html>
158 Putnam and Campbell (n 104) 497.
159 ibid 497, 515.
160 ibid 520.
161 ibid 534.

the Court's jurisprudence reflects the fact that Justices and their clerks tend to come from the more secular elements of American society and fail, in this respect, to reflect consensus American values.[162] In any event, as I have explained, the Justices do not rigorously or consistently apply the endorsement test and indeed may be poised to abandon it.

C. *The European Religious Model*

The European situation differs substantially. As in America, religion in Europe is a complicated phenomenon. Variations exist among and within nations; one must avoid accepting surface realities. Even in secular France, for example, government has more ties to religion than simplistic accounts of *laïcité* would suggest.[163] Nonetheless, one can make some generalizations and speak meaningfully of a European religious model. That model assumes a 'dominant' territorial church as 'the "normal" form of religious organization'.[164] Where the American model treats churches (plural) as voluntary associations that compete for members, the European perceives the church (singular) as a traditional, state-supported institution whose membership comprises society as a whole.[165] One does not join a church, as in the American model; one is born into the dominant local church and remains there unless one takes steps to leave.[166] The church performs social functions like weddings and funerals and hosts significant national and community events. Most people will require its services at some point in their lives and simply assume it will be there for them when they need it, whether or not they are active supporters; indeed, whether or not they are practicing Christians.[167] As Grace Davie writes, in European societies, churches—particular churches, not religion in general, as in the American model—are 'public utilities' that maintain a kind of religious infrastructure for the nation as a whole.[168]

Like the American, the European model reflects historical origins. European history has ensured that national and sectarian identities intertwine in a way Americans find difficult to grasp.[169] For many European states, especially those that formed during the second great wave of Christianization at the start of the last millennium, conversion served as 'the founding event of [the] nation'.[170] For example, the late French historian René Rémond writes, national consciousness in Denmark and Norway began with the baptism of Scandinavian monarchs around 1000 years ago; Hungary, Poland and Russia similarly trace their origins as nations to royal conversions around the same time.[171] European nations traditionally do not identify with 'Christianity in

[162] McConnell (n 30) 126.
[163] 'Laïcité in Comparative Perspective' (2010) 49 J Cath Legal Stud 1.
[164] Berger and others (n 103) 24; ibid 98.
[165] ibid 25.
[166] ibid 24.
[167] Davie (n 7) 86–87.
[168] ibid 86.
[169] ibid 40.
[170] René Rémond, *Religion and Society in Modern Europe* (Antonia Nevill trs, Blackwell 1999) 18.
[171] ibid; ibid 109.

general', however. As a consequence of centuries of inter-Christian conflict, different churches predominate in different countries.

For example, the Great Schism of 1054 split Europe into a Catholic West and an Orthodox East, a division that remains salient today, especially on the borders. In the West during the Reformation, national identities formed around Catholicism or Protestantism, and, within Protestantism, around particular forms. So, for example, Austrian and Spanish identity crystallized around loyalty to Catholicism and resistance to Protestant rebels like the Czechs, Dutch and northern Germans; the same could be said, in reverse, for the rebels themselves.[172] British identity became strongly Protestant under the Tudors; within Britain, Calvinist Scotland distanced itself from Anglican England. This is not to say religious differences created national identities, only that religious differences had a very important role in the formation of national self-images across Europe. The Westphalian settlement, and, in particular, the principle of *cuius regio, eius religio*, strengthened the link between national identity and religion.[173] By allowing rulers to determine the religion of their territories and excluding outside interference, the principle solidified national religious identities as of the mid-17th century.

Westphalia also strengthened official ties between church and state. The state church, an official monopoly that suppressed competitors and coerced conformity by law, became the norm both in Catholic countries, like France and Spain and Protestant countries, like Britain, the Netherlands and Sweden.[174] Indeed, state and church formed particularly strong links in Protestant polities—the Lutheran principalities of Germany, for example—where the state appointed clergy, abolished independent church courts and generally assumed responsibility for church government.[175] In short, in Europe, the traditional form of religion was that which America rejected from the start.

Over the last two centuries, in a process too complicated to describe here, European nations have departed from the historical pattern of the confessional state, even if some, like Britain, have maintained mild establishments. The historical experience continues to resonate, however. To be sure, no European country today enforces religious conformity by law. Nowhere do civil rights depend on religious affiliation; legal equality exists everywhere and people are free to worship or not as they choose. In these important ways, religious neutrality indeed obtains in Europe. As Grace Davie observes, however, the legacy of national religious identities and state churches means that equality for faith traditions, as a cultural matter, cannot exist.[176] Throughout Europe, historically dominant churches, even those churches that have been officially disestablished, continue to exert disproportionate social influence.

[172] ibid 112–13.

[173] ibid.

[174] Berger and others (n 103) 16. See also Steven G Calabresi, '"A Shining City on a Hill": American Exceptionalism and the Supreme Court's Practice of Relying on Foreign Law' (2006) 86 BU L Rev 1335, 1407.

[175] Harold J Berman, *Law and Revolution, II* (Harvard 2003).

[176] Grace Davie, *Religion in Modern Europe* (Oxford 2000) 177.

Italy itself provides a good example. As I have explained, the doctrine of *laicità* renders Italy a 'non-confessional secular State'.[177] The Italian Constitution provides that '[t]he State and the Catholic Church are independent and sovereign, each within its own sphere',[178] and that 'religious denominations are equally free before the law'.[179] Yet the Catholic Church has privileges other sects lack. In Italy, bilateral agreements govern relations between the state and religious organizations, including the Catholic Church. The Concordat with the Catholic Church, however, has a higher status in Italian law than the analogous agreements, called *intese*, which the state has with non-Catholic organizations.[180] Many religious bodies have not been able to secure *intese* at all, making their situation even less advantageous.[181] Moreover, the Concordat gives the Catholic Church preferential treatment. For example, Italian public schools must offer classes in Catholicism at public expense; local bishops select the instructors.[182] Non-Catholic groups with *intese* can offer religious education in public schools, if students or parents request it, but these groups must pay the teachers themselves.[183] Catholic marriages (and annulments) have essentially automatic civil effect; non-Catholic religious marriages do not.[184] Other examples exist as well.[185]

One could hardly argue for the neutrality of these preferences in an abstract sense. Given the dominant role of Catholicism in Italian society, however, one can explain them. As a state, Italy is fairly young, having come into existence only in the mid-19th century. Attempts to promote a republican consciousness have not greatly succeeded. Catholicism has served as the integrating force in society, from the founding to the present. During the Risorgimento, Alessandro Ferrari writes, Catholicism 'was the only cement binding the new country together: a country without a common language and without a widespread culture capable of founding civic engagement'.[186] Catholicism continues to provide a sense of cohesion in contemporary Italy, where the vast majority of the population identifies as Catholic.[187] In fact, Catholicism provides a kind of background norm that gives content to legal doctrines like *laicità*.[188] In Silvio

[177] Marco Ventura, 'The Permissible Scope of Legal Limitations on the Freedom of Religion or Belief in Italy' (2005) 19 Emory Intl L Rev 913, 918.

[178] Italian Const art 7.

[179] Italian Const art 8.

[180] Ventura (n 177) 919.

[181] ibid 920. Parliament has approved *intese* for only six non-Catholic bodies. Alessandro Ferrari and Silvio Ferrari, 'Religion and the Secular State: The Italian Case' in Javier Martínez-Torrón and W C Durham Jr (eds), *Religion and the Secular State: National Reports* (ICLRS 2010) 431, 438. On the legal status of groups without *intese*, see ibid 440–42.

[182] Ferrari and Ferrari (n 181) 446. Classes are taught in a non-proselytizing way and students may opt out. ibid.

[183] ibid 446–47; Ferrari (n 99) 754–55.

[184] Ferrari and Ferrari (n 181) 444–45. There are complications unnecessary to discuss here.

[185] Ventura (n 177) 921, 925. Recent chamber decisions have indicated that multi-tier recognition regimes like Italy's are subject to art 14's non-discrimination requirement: any differences in treatment must have 'objective and reasonable justification[s]'. *Religionsgemeinschaft der Zeugen Jehovas and Others v Austria* No 40825/98 (Judgment of 31 July 2008) (First Section) [87]. For more on this subject, see Durham and Scharffs (n 21) 484–89.

[186] Alessandro Ferrari, 'Civil Religion in Italy: A "Mission Impossible"?' (2010) 41 Geo Wash Intl L Rev 839, 842.

[187] For example, '[a]bout ninety percent of the pupils at State schools take part in Catholic religious education classes.' Ferrari and Ferrari (n 181) 431.

[188] Ferrari (n 186) 850–51.

Ferrari's phrase, Catholicism provides Italy's 'civil religion', the set of overarching cultural values to which everyone implicitly assents.[189]

The fact that Catholicism has a dominant place in Italian culture does not mean that Italians are markedly pious on a personal level. In fact, only about 30% of Italians attend Mass regularly.[190] And Italians are among the more observant people in Europe. By comparison, only 5% of French attend religious services on a weekly basis;[191] in Sweden, the number is more like 2%.[192] Taken as a whole, the percentage of Europeans who say that religion is important to them is low. 'Overall, only 21 percent of Europeans say that God plays an important role in their lives, compared with 60 percent of Americans (and 90 percent in many Muslim countries)'.[193] In terms of personal commitment, Europe is indeed a rather secular place.

Paradoxically, though, this secularism at the personal level is consistent with the dominant influence of traditional churches at the collective level. Two concepts from the sociology of religion, 'belonging without believing' and 'vicarious religion', help explain why.[194] Even if they do not practice their religion, large numbers of Europeans continue to maintain formal affiliation with traditional churches. For example, despite the fact that Scandinavians attend church very rarely and report very low levels of personal belief, an 'extraordinarily high' number have their children baptized.[195] In Germany, to give another example, the state collects a 'church tax', equal to about 8% of the taxpayer's income tax liability, which the state directs to the church the taxpayer designates.[196] All the taxpayer must do to avoid the tax, which might amount to a significant sum, is to declare that he is 'religiously unaffiliated'.[197] Notwithstanding the low rate of religious observance in Germany—less than 10% attend religious services weekly[198]—relatively few people, particularly in the west, have formally renounced church membership in order to avoid the tax.[199] Most opt to belong, even if they do not believe.

Why would people who do not believe continue to maintain an affiliation with the traditional church? Some might believe the church has an important role in educating children[200] or value the moral cohesion the church promotes.[201] Some might see the church as a vehicle for preserving continuity

189 Ferrari (n 99) 753.

190 This percentage comes from recent Gallup surveys. Robert Manchin, 'Religion in Europe: Trust Not Filling the Pews' (21 Sept. 2004), <http://www.gallup.com/poll/13117/Religion-Europe-Trust-Filling-Pews.aspx?utm_source=email-a friend&utm_medium=email&utm_campaign=sharing&utm_content=titlelink> (accessed 24 May 2012). Ferrari and Ferrari say the number is less than 25%. Ferrari and Ferrari (n 181) 431.

191 Micklethwait and Wooldridge (n 6) 134.

192 Maarit Jänterä-Jareborg, 'Religion and the Secular State in Sweden' in *Religion and the Secular State* (n 181), 669, 669.

193 Micklethwait and Wooldridge (n 6) 134.

194 Berger and others (n 103) 15, 39.

195 ibid 115.

196 Durham and Scharffs (n 21) 126.

197 Berger and others (n 103) 15.

198 Manchin (n 190).

199 Berger and others (n 103) 15.

200 ibid.

201 ibid.

with the nation's past.[202] Some might retain their affiliation out of inertia or as a Pascalian Wager. And some, particularly political leaders, might worry about the dislocations that would follow if long-standing social equilibria among religious groups, established after centuries of conflict, were disrupted. The important point is this: belonging is the default position that apparently few people wish to alter, even if they no longer have a personal commitment, or only a very weak one. For a great many people, formal affiliation with the traditional church is simply part of what it means to be a member of the national community.

The second concept, 'vicarious religion', is associated principally with Grace Davie.[203] The term describes a situation in which the majority of society expects that 'an active minority' will maintain the traditional church in its behalf—perform liturgies, celebrate marriages, repair sanctuaries and so on.[204] The majority is not indifferent; indeed, it believes the church has an important social role.[205] The majority simply expects other people, presumably at state expense, to maintain the church so that it will be available when the majority needs it. For example, Davie notes, even though Europeans do not attend church regularly, they often protest when church buildings in their communities close.[206] The buildings make up an important part of the local landscape to which people feel they have a right. Similarly, Europeans often resent being asked for entry fees at church buildings 'on the grounds that such buildings, particularly those that belong to the historic churches, are ... public rather than private space, to which everyone (believer or not) should have the right of access'.[207] The church buildings, in other words, belong to society as a whole, not 'exclusively to those who use them regularly'.[208]

Funerals provide perhaps the best illustration of both 'belonging without believing' and 'vicarious religion'. Notwithstanding the widespread availability of secular funerals, not many Europeans choose to have them.[209] Most Europeans would not think of anything other than a religious funeral, and they expect the church to perform this service for them when they die, whether or not they have been believers while alive. For example, when British foreign minister Robin Cook died in 2005, his funeral took place in the Church of Scotland, even though he was an avowed atheist. This was appropriate, the officiating minister explained, apparently without irony, because Cook had been a 'Presbyterian atheist'.[210] When François Mitterand, the very *laïc* French President, died in 1996, the Catholic Church gave him not one funeral Mass,

[202] Danièle Hervieu-Léger, *Religion as a Chain of Memory* (Simon Lee trs, Rutgers University Press 2000) 162.
[203] Davie (n 7) 127.
[204] ibid.; Berger and others (n 103) 39–40.
[205] Davie (n 176) 179.
[206] Davie (n 7) 141.
[207] ibid 142.
[208] ibid. Lisbet Christoffersen writes of a similar concept in Denmark, the 'Folkekirke' or 'People's Church', which belongs, not to believers or clergy, but to the Danish people as a whole. Lisbet Christoffersen, 'State, Church and Religion in Denmark At the Beginning of the 21st Century' in Lisbet Christoffersen and others (eds), *Law and Religion in the 21st Century – Nordic Perspectives* (Djøf 2010) 145.
[209] Grace Davie, 'Law, Sociology and Religion: An Awkward Threesome' [2012] 1 OJLR 235, 245-46.
[210] Dan Barker, *The Good Atheist* 154 (Ulysses Press 2011).

but two.[211] When a gunman massacred 93 people at a youth camp in Norway in 2011, a national memorial service took place in Oslo's Lutheran Cathedral, attended by the royal family, the prime minister and large numbers of Norwegians from around the country.[212]

The ECtHR's conception of neutrality is broadly consistent with the European religious model. Acts of state indoctrination, such as holding religious exercises in public school classrooms and requiring students to memorize scriptural passages, obviously create pressure for individuals to conform to official religious orthodoxy, and the ECtHR forbids them. On the other hand, the ECtHR allows government to display symbols of the dominant local church in a manner that one can only see as an endorsement—to give such symbols 'preponderant visibility', in the ECtHR's words—even where impressionable schoolchildren are involved. In a model that assumes the existence of historically rooted, state-supported churches with which national populations continue to identify, if principally as a cultural matter, and that encompasses a variety of domestic religious arrangements which the ECtHR cannot realistically superintend, a more rigorous, uniform definition of neutrality would be incongruous. American-style non-sectarianism would not fit, to say nothing of the endorsement test's prohibition of even generic religious references.

To be sure, some observers argue that the European model is changing. Increasingly, they say, Europe is becoming an American-style religious marketplace in which membership in a dominant local church is no longer a given.[213] Unsurprisingly, the churches that do best in the 'new' religious 'economy' are those that adopt American ways.[214] For example, Pentecostalism, a Protestant movement born in America in the last century, has experienced remarkable growth in Europe in the last generation.[215] American megachurches see Europe as mission territory; their European church 'plants' evangelize in a very American fashion. For French scholar Olivier Roy, the emergence of the new religious market in Europe reflects the 'deculturation' of religion that is occurring around the world.[216] '[T]he good old days', he writes, 'when religion was embedded in culture and culture imbued with religion', are gone.[217] '[C]ulturally religious non-believers' in the European style 'are vanishing';[218] around the world today, religion is a function of personal seeking and self-definition, not national or cultural identity.

If European religion really is moving towards the American market model, the ECtHR may ultimately shift towards a more American understanding of neutrality as well. Reasons exist, however, to think that the historical link between religion and culture in European society will only grow stronger in coming years. As increasing numbers of Muslims immigrate to Europe, they seem to be causing resurgence in Christian identity among their neighbours. For

[211] Davie (n 176) 78.
[212] Steven Erlanger, 'Amid Tears, Flickering Candles and Flowers, a Shaken Norway Mourns', *NY Times* (24 July 2011) <http://www.nytimes.com/2011/07/25/world/europe/25oslo.html?pagewanted=all> (accessed 24 May 2012).
[213] Micklethwait and Wooldridge (n 6) 25.
[214] ibid 136.
[215] In France, Pentecostalism is 'the fastest-growing religion', even ahead of Islam. ibid.
[216] Olivier Roy, *Holy Ignorance* (Columbia University Press 2010) 8.
[217] ibid 135.
[218] ibid 8.

example, in surveys, 'the percentage of white Britons who call themselves "Christian" (rather than "no religion") is considerably higher' in 'neighborhoods with high Muslim populations' than in 'similar, less mixed neighborhoods, even after one reckons in income and other complicating factors'.[219] The rise in Christian identification probably does not reflect an increase in personal piety, however. Sociologist Martin Riesbrodt notes that Europeans who reengage with Christianity seek principally to revive the 'dominant Christian culture'.[220] 'If this "dominant" culture then wanted to tell them how they should spend their Sundays or how they should behave in the bedroom', he says, they 'would quickly lose their enthusiasm'.[221] Most likely, these re-Christianized Europeans are 'simply professing a tribal allegiance to Team Christianity', [222] rather than choosing religion in an individualized, American way.

5. *Conclusion*

My purpose in this article has been comparative and critical: I have attempted to explain different legal regimes in terms of fundamental institutional and cultural commitments. Comparative work, particularly interdisciplinary comparative work, is still a bit new in law and religion scholarship. As Grace Davie recently has written, law and sociology ask different questions and rely on different methods; 'conversations' between lawyers and sociologists can therefore be 'difficult'.[223] Nonetheless, such conversations are essential.[224] For law both reflects and influences underlying social conditions. In Mary Ann Glendon's phrase, 'law, in addition to all the other things it does, tells stories about the culture that helped to shape it and which it in turn helps to shape: stories about who we are, where we came from, and where we are going'.[225] The law on state-sponsored religious displays reveals very different understandings about the place of religion in American and European society. This article is an effort to illuminate those understandings and contribute to an emerging path in law and religion scholarship.

[219] Christopher Caldwell, *Reflections on the Revolution in Europe: Immigration, Islam, and the West* (Doubleday 2009) 184.
[220] Martin Riesbrodt, *The Promise of Salvation* (Steven Rendall trs, U Chicago Press 2010) 176.
[221] ibid.
[222] Caldwell (n 219) 184.
[223] Davie (n 209) 235.
[224] ibid 247.
[225] Mary Ann Glendon, *Abortion and Divorce in Western Law* (Harvard 1987) 8.

Name Index